The Radical Middle Class

POLITICS AND SOCIETY IN TWENTIETH-CENTURY AMERICA

Series Editors
WILLIAM CHAFE, GARY GERSTLE, LINDA GORDON, AND JULIAN ZELIZER

THE RADICAL MIDDLE CLASS

Populist Democracy and the Question of
Capitalism in Progressive Era Portland, Oregon

Robert D. Johnston

PRINCETON UNIVERSITY PRESS

PRINCETON AND OXFORD

Second printing, and first paperback printing, 2006
Paperback ISBN-13: 978-0-691-12600-5
Paperback ISBN-10: 0-691-12600-3

The Library of Congress has cataloged the cloth edition of this book as follows

Johnston, Robert D.
    The radical middle class : populist democracy and the question of capitalism in
progressive era Portland, Oregon / Robert D. Johnston.
        p.   cm. — (Politics and society in twentieth-century America)
    Includes bibliographical references and index.
    ISBN 0-691-09668-6 (alk. paper)
        1. Middle class—Oregon—Portland—History—20th century.   2. Small business—
Oregon—Portland—History—20th century.   3. Middle class—United States—History.
    4. Progressivism (United States politics)   I. Title.

HN80.P8 J65 2003
305.244'0975'49—dc21   2002074997

British Library Cataloging-in-Publication Data is available

Published with the assistance of the Frederick W.
Hilles Publication Fund of Yale University

This book has been composed in Berkeley Book

Printed on acid-free paper. ∞

pup.princeton.edu

Printed in the United States of America

10   9   8   7   6   5   4   3   2

FOR ANNE

I want to sleep beneath peaceful skies
in my lover's bed
with a wide open country in my eyes
and these romantic dreams in my head.

CONTENTS

ILLUSTRATIONS AND MAPS

Illustrations

Maps

PREFACE

A state aims at being, as far as it can be, a society composed of
equals and peers; and the middle class, more than any other has
this sort of composition. . . . It is clear from our argument, first,
that the best form of political society is one where power is vested
in the middle class, and, secondly, that good government is
attainable in those states where there is a large middle class. . . . It
is therefore the greatest of blessings for a state that its members
should possess a moderate and adequate property.
—ARISTOTLE, *The Politics*

If a modern writer wishes to win an imperishable name as a
historian, he has only to write an exhaustive monograph on the life
of such a town.
—RANDOLPH BOURNE, 1913

This book has a large ambition—to reorient our thinking about the American middle class. Indeed, I argue that there is no such entity as *the* American middle class. Scholars' belief in such a creature has been unwise and inaccurate at best—and, at its worst, part of most intellectuals' often unconscious, although too often conscious, antidemocratic dogma.

Ordinary middling folks, however, have generally been much more acute in their use of and reflections upon the category of "the middle class" than have academics. Their insights are the ones upon which I seek to build my interpretation of middle-class politics and culture. Beginning with such a grassroots sensibility, I go further to contend that people in the middle have created one of America's most democratic political traditions, a populism that has often represented a radical challenge to the authority of economic, political, and cultural elites and that has called into question many of the fundamental assumptions of a capitalist society.

Although we must recognize, then, that middle-class people have a tradition of generating some of the most significant political ideas and ideals in American history, most middling folks have grounded themselves in local concerns. Therefore my study, too, has a firm attachment to a particular locale. Few American historians know much about Portland, Oregon, during the Progressive Era. During this period, however, the Rose City was one of the most fertile grounds for the construction of our national civic life, as ordinary citizens vigorously thought through how the United States might come to grips with social changes such as the rise of big business, the role of popular sovereignty as politics moved away from partisan spectacle, and the increasing ability of experts to define appropriate behavior for the masses.

While grappling with these changes, Portlanders generated a number of rather unconventional—and from the perspective of the twenty-first century unpopular—ideas. Yet I take seriously those people who wished to experiment in visionary forms of democracy such as direct legislation, unicameralism, and proportional representation; who believed that housewives should constitute the dominant portion of the legislature; and who wanted to prevent all immoral wealth creation while preserving private property. Perhaps most curiously, I seek to rehabilitate the great mass of Portlanders who opposed compulsory vaccination. Perhaps, then, I should be upfront about my own commitments. I not only wish to take these folks seriously and rehabilitate them; I hope to vindicate them as well. For along with my central protagonists, I too am (within limits) a radical direct democrat, a unicameralist, a proportional representationist, a single taxer, a petit bourgeois anticapitalist, and even . . . an antivaccinationist.[1]

In many ways these populist projects represented dead ends—some might whisper that they bespoke an inability to come to grips with the "modern" world. Still, their defeat was only partial. The culture that generated such discontent with the status quo, and in response such democratic visions, has bequeathed a much broader legacy than intellectuals have recognized. We must, then, work not only to uncover the noble defeats of the past but also to reckon with the subtle victories won by history's far-too-often invisible middling people.

I am disturbed about how my story turns out—in the brief victory of the Ku Klux Klan in 1920s Portland—and much of what I write testifies to the grip of undemocratic institutions and ideas. Still, this book stands fundamentally as a testament of hope. I am confident that I have my history straight, but I also cannot deny that I am writing out of a passion for rediscovering what I find most attractive about our history. In telling about the radical middle class in Portland, I seek to reinvigorate our memory of just where a crucial part of the promise of American life once lay. We might even continue to find it there today.[2]

I do not expect mine to be a fashionable argument within the academy, where the too-often intolerant populism of our day has encouraged intellectuals to reawaken their easily accessible dread of the masses. Yet if the discussions—and most of all disagreements—that this book provokes provide something of a model for the kind of dialogue we need as citizens in order to reconstruct our decaying democracy, then all the better.

A note on style. One of the distinctive contributions I hope to make in this book is a reinvigoration of substantive historiographical debate within a profession that seems to have abandoned the promise of such intellectual engagement. After a generation that too eagerly chased after the abstractions of social science, historians from across the political spectrum have begun to implore us to offer new narratives that might captivate the general public.

Now I have nothing against a well-told story, nor attempts to reach out to lay readers. Still, such an emphasis on smooth and flowing narrative potentially suffers from two conceits. First, it implies that citizen-readers should not have access to scholarly debates, so many of which are of critical civic importance and do not need to be dumbed down, or locked away in secret vaults. Second, rushing quickly through an often unreflective discussion of the work of other historians in one's introductory chapter strikes me as an extraordinarily ungenerous—even anti-intellectual—way of treating the sages who have come before us. The scholarship upon which ours rests required many years and many careers to come to fruition. Whether I agree or disagree with various works of scholarship, my respect for their intelligence requires that I attempt to engage them thoroughly, in order to continue a dialogue that I hope will endure for many generations. After all, the questions involved here are truly ancient, dating back to Aristotle. We can only answer them together.[3]

So please regard my book an example of what James Goodman has recently imagined: one of many possible "experiments with *interpretive* forms." I do, though, share with many new narrative histories the deeply personal roots of my study. Consider the geography. You might say I grew up almost in, but certainly not of, Portland. I spent most of my formative years in "East County," a physical space just ten miles from downtown Portland but of a distinctively different cultural and political universe. East County's most famous residents have, I suppose, been Gary Gilmore and Tonya Harding— hardly icons of radical democracy. Still, in revealing the populism of East Portland during the Progressive Era, I hope in a small way to rescue the semiredneck/semirespectable culture of my origins from the cosmopolitan condescension of both the past and the present.[4]

Consider, as well, my ancestral roots. One of my maternal great-grandfathers was a jitney driver—the significance of which will become clear about one-third of the way through the book. On my father's side, my great-great-grandfather James Clark was one of John D. Rockefeller's first business partners. Rockefeller characterized Clark as "a big, noisy, vulgar Englishman of bad habits" and "an immoral man." The tycoon later reflected, "I ever point to the day when I separated myself from them [James Clark and his two brothers] . . . as the beginning of the success I have made in my life." Ever since I discovered that the achievements of the ruthless titan depended on squeezing my ancestors out of business, I realized that coming to the rescue of the benighted petite bourgeoisie had truly become my destiny.[5]

Michel Foucault wrote: "Historians take unusual pains to erase the elements in their work which reveal their grounding in a particular time and place,

their preferences in a controversy—the unavoidable obstacles of their passion."
I am not one of those historians. What, though, do I want from this book,
other than some measure of justice (or is it revenge?) for my ancestors and
my fellow East County citizens? Besides offering a general political and moral
redemption of middling folks, *The Radical Middle Class* contains a number of
analytical claims I would like to toss into academic, as well as public, debate.
Summed up quickly: from the time of the Anti-Federalists until the 2000
election, Americans have promulgated a long tradition of middle-class radicalism. This tradition has been hidden by a pervasive intellectual scorn toward the middle class, as well as by a need to see "the middle class" as a
unitary and ahistorical category or entity instead of a product of constant
political and cultural struggle. Through a focus on, and humanization of, one
particular part of the middle class—its independent small business sector, or
petite bourgeoisie—*The Radical Middle Class* seeks to reveal the democratic
populist, and even anticapitalist, legacy of the middle class. Despite the
death knells pronounced by *Fortune* magazine and postmodernists alike,
class still matters in America. But only if we dramatically reconceive the
politics and culture of the leading player in class matters in America,
the middle class, particularly focusing on the relation of the middle and the
working classes. We can do such reenvisioning particularly effectively by
humanizing the middle class, and therefore I feature the biographies of four
remarkable middle-class radicals: Harry Lane, Will Daly, William U'Ren, and
Lora Little. In the end, rehabilitating the American middle class provides us
not only with better scholarship, but firmer grounds for an expansive democratic hope.[6]

Why Portland? Precisely because of its cozy, "bourgeois" reputation, which
makes the Rose City an ideal place to explore the politics and social life of
the middle class. The city's citizens have long accepted a kind of paradise
mythology, seeing Portland—set amidst tremendous natural beauty—as a
haven from violence, radicalism, and the extremes of wealth and poverty.
Journalists have noted for nearly a century how much the supposedly middle-class characteristics of stability, complacency, and moderation tending toward conservatism have dominated the city's culture. Wilbur Hall, for example, personified Portland for the readers of *Collier's* in 1917 as "a middle-class
New England country spinster," an "ultraconservative, exclusive, maidenly
minded, and acquisitive" sister to wild Seattle and San Francisco. As the
Nation asked in 1914, "If a community so composed is not fairly conservative, where should we look for one?"[7]

The existence of this myth is not surprising; all viable communities live off
such fictions. What is significant about the legend is its acceptance by so
many scholars. The moral of Portland, according to historians, is the resolutely middle-class nature of both the city's values and its social structure. As
Dorothy Johansen, for many years dean of Pacific Northwest historians, put

it a generation ago, "Portland's citizens were 'proper Oregonians.' Their virtues and their vices were suspended in a narrow middle range." A popular history of the city sums up, "Portland seemed to have been born middle-aged and middle-class respectable."[8]

Much of Portland's history during the late nineteenth and early twentieth centuries supports such a consensual viewpoint. Unlike most cities in the industrial belt, Portland did not suffer much from the period's intense class struggles. Even in comparison to other urban areas on the West Coast, Progressive Era Portland appears as a haven of conservatism in light of the sway labor held in San Francisco, the 1919 general strike in Seattle, and the *Times* bombing and strong socialist movement in Los Angeles. Nor was Portland's racial and ethnic composition particularly cosmopolitan. The overwhelming majority of residents came from northern Europe. If any city exemplified "bourgeois" virtues during the period of American industrialization, it was Portland. Perhaps for that reason, historians have overlooked the city—when not simply neglecting it, sharing the scorn of the age's most prominent native son, John Reed.[9]

Yet despite its surface calmness, Portland witnessed intense political and social struggles during the early twentieth century. Largely because of those conflicts, the Rose City played a significant role in the construction of the era's public culture. Most importantly, as the primary social base of the "Oregon System" of direct legislation, Portland during this period became the center of the national movement for direct democracy. Prominent reformer Frederic Howe even enthusiastically (and, I think, in many ways accurately) called Oregon "the most complete democracy in the world." The eyes of a politicized nation gazed often upon the Rose City.[10]

All this raises the question of whether Portland was or was not typical, was or was not exceptional. This is a fair question, but in the end an uninteresting one. To take one telling example: I will show that Portland had an extremely strong small business backbone through the 1920s. Surely that should make us suspicious, because historians tell us that the Progressive Era was an age when great corporations completely remade the nation's economy. Yet the average size of enterprises in Portland was almost exactly the same as in the great metropolises of New York and Los Angeles. Now we could take this finding and calculate what we might call a typicality equation (the economies of Portland and Los Angeles were 62 percent similar, but their cultures were only 23 percent the same). What, though, would that tell us? It ultimately proves much more interesting not to worry about the issue of exceptionalism and instead concentrate on the suggestiveness of the questions I pose. If my answers seem to click for Portland, then it is worth pondering them for Akron, Atlanta, and Albuquerque.

In the end, I realize that there can be only one place with a proper claim to being "the most complete democracy in the world." Progressive Era Portland was a special place, and largely for that reason it holds an attraction for me. If, however, we wish in our own day to complete our own imperfect democracy, we can do little better than to ask searching questions that reflect off Portland's roses, rain, and rivers, shining light on all our nation's past.

ACKNOWLEDGMENTS

The cardinal rule of the petite bourgeoisie is exploitation of the family economy, and I have unfortunately taken far too much advantage of this strategy during the production of this book. Not only is it my pleasure, but it is my obligation, to thank Anne, Sandy, and Isaac Johnston for the huge amount of kindness and sustenance that they have given me, as well to acknowledge the many hardships that they have endured in the service of this project.

First and foremost is my beloved Anne. She has not wanted to read every word, but every word still reflects her passion for wisdom and justice, as well as her impatience for the pathologies of academic life. I made a promise, I swear I'll always remember.

The life of this project has, alas, coincided with that of our brilliant and beautiful bar mitzvah, Sandy Perry Sequoya Johnston. Sandy has provided me with the kind of loving support that I will always treasure. He has been willing to tolerate my boring kind of history, while using his unparalleled knowledge of the past to convince me that Little Round Top might possibly have been more important in American history than my heroine Lora C. Little. Sandy has also at least tried to tolerate his rambunctious brother Isaac Theodore Ravi, now six years old and persistently typing his "manuscript" when not spreading peace, love, and kindergarten joy throughout the world. Isaac started imbibing his lessons in direct democracy at the age of three, when one of his favorite books was Virginia Lee Burton's populist tale *Maybelle: The Cable Car*.

Isaac was, in part, named after my own father, Theodore Homer Johnston, of blessed memory. When I came up with the great collegiate-age certainty that our family could be classified as "lower middle class," my father made sure I knew that *he* was not "lower anything." I'll forever value his impatience with administrators, bureaucrats, Republicans, and scholars, as well as his pungent wit. I miss him still; he was the dearest dual unionist (American Federation of Teachers and American Federation of Musicians) I'll ever know. But my dad's love continues to shine through in my mother, Beth Perry Johnston, who besides being my forever foundation has assisted the book in all kinds of ways, especially with genealogical research. She remained confident that I could pull this off, even if everyone else was beginning to wonder. My sister, Karen Johnston, confirmed that I was on the right track when she too realized that the label *lower middle class* had something to do with our fate, but that is only the beginning of her infinite wisdom and compassion. My thanks too to Karen's partners, Sue Phillips and Ricky Greenwald. I also wish to thank my aunt, Barbara Perry, and my uncles, Bob Perry, the late

Doug Perry, and Bob Weiss, for helping me to understand—in very different ways—some of the more problematic parts of the petit bourgeois personality. My great-aunt Ruth Feldman has literally opened up whole new, as well as old, worlds for me. Anne's family—Harry, Margaret, Jill, and Gail Johnson, as well as my in-laws Linda Young and Kevin Macmillan—have also provided me with unstinting love and material support.

This manuscript has gone through the ringer many times over, benefiting immeasurably from those willing to keep up my flagging spirits, and even more from those willing to tell me how wrongheaded I was. Those who have read the entire manuscript in one form or another and offered extremely helpful and detailed comments include Sven Beckert, Michael Cassity, David Delmar, John Demos, Michael Kazin, Elaine Tyler May, Michael Mullins, Aaron Sachs, Cathy Stock, my fellow curlicue Nick Salvatore, and an extraordinarily conscientious anonymous reader for the University of Pennsylvania Press. Sven and Elaine proved crucial midwives to the book's long-delayed and somewhat troubled birth, and I will be forever grateful. Michael Kazin has been a consistent cheerleader, even while offering a more chastened perspective on the populist past. Cathy Stock has been a fast friend, despite my causing her at least one nightmare about compulsory vaccination. John Demos has been the best kind of mentor—unappointed and unassuming, but with unfathomable depths of concern, as well as a gentle way of bringing his reflections on writing to one of the untutored masses. When he cared about my characters, I knew I had done something right. In turn, Aaron Sachs has been the best writing teacher I have ever had. Whatever fluidity of prose the reader encounters here owes so much to Aaron, who also helped me think through some of the toughest intellectual and political issues I faced. Besides, Aaron is just one of the greatest people in the world. And Glenda Gilmore is one of the greatest historians, and friends, I know. We often do not see eye to eye on a number of issues, but our disagreements have been productive of considerable creativity, and they have never outweighed our shared passion for rediscovering what is best in our past. Glenda has been my professional bedrock. And when the profession just gets to be too much, I can always turn to my other bedrock, Brendan McConville, for classical wisdom—alongside tough love.

Worthy of special mention are the students who were exposed to unwieldy versions of the manuscript in my graduate Introduction to U.S. Historiography class, as well as in the junior seminar on the American middle class that I had the privilege of teaching with Kate Dudley. These scholars-in-training from The 700 Club include Barry Braeken, Kat Charron, Ariela Dubler, Christopher Geissler, Blake Gilpin, Will Inboden, Gretchen Krueger, Carrie Lane, Christian McMillen, Ted Melillo, Michael Mullins, Hang Nguyen, Rebecca Rix, Adriane Smith, Josh Tyrangiel, Catherine Whalen, Mark Williams, Owen Williams, and Sandy Zipp, and for extremely close and conscientious editing Lila Corwin, Melissa Ganz, Brian Herrera, Elaine Lewinnek, Michael Jo, Bethany Moreton, Tony Light, and Aaron Sachs. Those who were particularly insightful from the undergraduate seminar include Sarah Crews, Scott McNab, and Brian Wallach. Overall, the discussions in these classes were models for how scholarly criticism should work, full of friendship but also extremely serious criticism that at times shook the project to its foundations.

Others who have read portions of the manuscript include those who have helped me to meditate on capitalism: Joyce Appleby, Robert Brenner, Sven Beckert, Andrew Wender Cohen, David Igler, Bruce Laurie, David Monod, Philip Scranton, Frank Couvares, Joyce Berkman, Jennifer Klein, and Ben Sasse; those who have done much to help me figure out the strange world of antivaccination: Logie Barrow, Kat Charron, Henrique Cukierman, Nadav Davidovitch, Kevin Dew, Nadja Durbach, David Hecht, Greg Field, James Hanley, my great friend and populist basketball foe Ben Johnson, George Joseph, Lil Fenn, Sue Lederer, Judy Leavitt, Elaine Lewinnek, Maisie Maisie, Jim Mohr, Scott Nelson, Marty Pernick, Rahul Rajkumar, Naomi Rogers, Jim Scott, Annette Timm, Brett Walker, John Warner, and Eberhard Wolff; scholars of the Ku Klux Klan: David A. Horowitz, Nancy MacLean, Leonard Moore, Chris Rhomberg, and Eckard Toy; those who have aided me in my quest for Harry Lane: Kathryn Abbott, Steven Dow Beckham, Brett Flehinger, Paul Holbo, Fred Hoxie, Peter Iverson, Matt Jacobson, Ben Johnson, Christian McMillen, Jeff Ostler, and Nancy Unger; and my fellow direct democracy aficionados Thomas Goebel, Sarah Henry, and Kevin Mattson. Indeed, the collaboration I have had with Sarah has convinced me that scholars can share material and ideas at least as avidly as the most enthusiastic kindergartners, and I am grateful for her generosity as well as her questioning of the religion of democracy. Nancy Woloch has been similarly enthusiastic and generous as we have tried to uncover the complex world of Curt Muller. Readers who can't be so easily classified include Ira Berlin, Cindy Cumfer, Jackie Dirks, Rebecca Edwards, Tom Edwards, Ron Formisano, David Frisk, Herbert Gans, Mike Green, Marjorie Harrison, Daniel Walker Howe, David Koistinen, Shafali Lal, Christopher Lasch, Jesse Lemisch, Ted Liazos, Mike Magliari, Lary May, Karen Merrill, Sylvie Murray, my excellent friend Jeff Ostler, Steven J. Peitzman, Lis Pimentel, Mark Pry, Matthew Roth, Adolph Reed, Bill Robbins, Ron Schatz, Carlos Schwantes, William Toll, Eckard Toy, Steve Wasby, Robert Woodward, and Ron Yanosky.

My most long-term scholarly support network has been my colleagues in and of Portland. Carl Abbott, Gordon Dodds, Margaret DeLacy, Megan Holden, David Horowitz, Julie Lay, Bob Liebman, Jane Malarkey, Gloria Myers, Lee Nash, Terry O'Donnell, Peter Sleeth, Janice St. Laurent, Susan Wladaver-Morgan, and Craig Wollner never hesitated to supply documents and insight. It is the Rose City's great fortune to have a historian like Kimbark MacColl. Kim was personally generous to me, and without his writings I literally may not have been able to pen mine. Peter Boag and I tried to track down the queer obscurities of the direct democracy underworld while ruminating on our shared class origins. David Del Mar eloquently told me how important it was to recognize the importance of both local and larger stories. David Johnson made sure that even as a lowly graduate student I always had a scholarly home in the Rose City, and that that the doors remain open. Rick Harmon provided me with an ongoing example of middle-class radicalism, a stern and challenging perspective on what history was all about, and the first opportunity to publish my findings. And Harry Stein has been there all the way, helping me to rein in my verbosity, finding last-minute photos, and in general simply being a wonderful buddy. In terms of Greater Oregon, Richard Maxwell Brown stands alone in his encouraging and generous spirit. I also wish to recognize Dee Brown for good fellowship as well as insights into the strength of antivaccination sentiment.

My intellectual home will in some ways always be Rutgers University, where this project was born under the guidance of Richard L. McCormick, James Livingston, Jackson Lears, Suzanne Lebsock, and David Oshinsky, and where my friends Jennifer Jones, Lynn Mahoney, Lisa Norling, Jonathan Nashel, Charlie Ponce de Leon, Chris Rasmussen, and John Spurlock provided such fruitful comradeship. I have now taught at Buena Vista College, in Storm Lake, Iowa, and Yale University, in New Haven, Connecticut. Both places greatly sharpened my sense of class, as well as my general intellectual orientation. I want to thank my many colleagues who have read all or parts of the manuscript or who proved crucial to my figuring out the puzzle of the American middle class: in Storm Lake, the tragically late Laura Inglis, Angie Jameson, Jeff Perrill, Lemiel Pierre, Oddalys Serpa-Pierre, Peter Steinfeld, Traci Scheuermann, and Dan Toft; in New Haven, Jean-Christophe Agnew, Jennifer Baszile, David Bell, Dick Brodhead, Jon Butler, Alicia Schmidt Camacho, Hazel Carby, Nancy Cott, David Davis, Michael Denning, Johnny Faragher, Paul Freedman, John Lewis Gaddis, Valerie Hansen, Jim Heinzen, Larry Holmes, Jonathan Holloway, Paula Hyman, Matt Jacobson, Gil Joseph, Don Kagan, Ben Kiernan, Sue Lederer, Mary Lui, Michael Mahoney, John Merriman, David Montgomery, Steve Pitti, Kevin Repp, Naomi Rogers, Cynthia Russett, Jim Scott, Fred Shapiro, Rogers Smith, Steven Stoll, Bill Summers, Mary Summers, David Waldstreicher, John Warner, Robin Winks, and Keith Wrightson. Jean Cherniavsky, Gerri Cummings, Lynn Fitzgerald, Liza Joyner, Florence Thomas, Valerie Van Etten, and—above all—Essie Lucky-Barros have provided crucial support. The best part of teaching at Yale has been witnessing the growth of a courageous and inspirational institution of middle-class radicalism, the Graduate Student Employees' Organization. GESOniks are my heroes. And, in the end, Avihu Zakai and the American Studies program at the Hebrew University in Jerusalem offered me a stimulating institutional home and many kindnesses; Laura Kalman made sure, in many humorous and interesting ways, that my professional life did not atrophy amid the spiritual fervor of the Holy Land; and Rani Jaeger as well as Danny Porat convinced me that hope remains possible even amidst tragedy.

I've been shielded from some of the pathologies of Yale by our loving community in New Haven. Above all, our synagogue, Beth El–Keser Israel, is one of the finest flowerings of middle-class culture around. My love, along with huge doses of appreciation, go out to Carole and Paul Bass, Miriam Benson and Jon-Jay Tilsen, Ruthie Greenblatt, Brian Karsif and Terri Stern, April and Matt Lieberman, Mary Ellen Mack, Amy and Stephen Pincus, Kathy Rosenbluh and Michael Stern, and Sascha van Creveld for providing us with a grounding that allowed me to understand what the writing was all about.

I have presented portions of the book before the American Historical Association, David Johnson's seminar on Oregon History at Portland State University, the Northwest Independent Scholars Association, the Organization of American Historians, the Pacific Coast Branch of the American Historical Association, the Pacific Northwest History Association, the conference "Plural Medicine: Orthodox and Heterodox Medicine in Western and Colonial Countries during the 19th and 20th Centuries," the Second International Public Conference on Vaccination, the Western History Association, the Five College History Seminar, the Department of History at Portland State University, and Yale's American Studies and History of Science/History of Medicine colloquia. I want to thank all those who attended these stimulating sessions, in particular commentators Paula Baker, Thomas Bender, Richard Maxwell Brown, Robert Cherny, Barbara Ehrenreich, Rick Harmon, Michael Kazin, Bill Lang, Earl Pomeroy, Jack Pressman, Cathy Stock, Ronald Walters, and Olivier Zunz.

When starting a project of this sort, it is impossible to understand what kind of debt of gratitude a scholar will end up owing to the unselfish acts of librarians and archivists. I have been the beneficiary of countless kind acts, above all from Jodie Morin and Cori Melohn at Buena Vista's Ballou Library and Nancy Godleski of Yale's Sterling Memorial Library. I also greatly appreciate the help of the following institutions and individuals: the Archives of the American Medical Association (in particular, Roberta Ghidara); the Battle Creek, Michigan, public library; the Bancroft Library; the Boston Medical Library of the Francis A. Countway Library of Medicine (in particular, Jack Eckert); the Chicago Historical Society (in particular, Lesley Martin); Columbia University's Rare Book and Manuscript Library (in particular, Jean Ashton and Bernard Crystal); the Cook County Office of Vital Statistics; Harvard University's Baker and Houghton libraries; the Huntington Library (in particular, Jennifer Martinez); the John Pitcairn Archives and Carriage House (in particular, Jerome Sellner); the Library of Congress; the Minneapolis Public Library; the Minnesota Historical Society; the National Library of Medicine;

the New York Public Library; New York University's Tamiment Library; the Church of Jesus Christ of Latter-day Saints Family History Center in Newport, Oregon; Princeton's Seeley G. Mudd Manuscript Library; Radcliffe's Schlesinger Library; the Springfield, Missouri, public library (in particular, Inabell Williams); the State Historical Society of North Dakota (in particular, James A. Davis); the Swedenborg Library (in particular, Carroll Odhner); and Yale's Beinecke, Cross-Campus, Epidemiology and Public Health, Law, Medical, Mudd, Social Science, and Sterling libraries, as well as Sterling's Interlibrary-Loan service. Most important were the libraries on my own Oregon turf: the Multnomah Public Library, one of the state's glories; the library of the *Oregonian* (in particular, Sandy Macomber); the Oregon State Archives; the Oregon State Library; Portland State University; my beloved alma mater Reed College; the Stanley Parr Archives and Records Center of the City of Portland; the University of Oregon's Special Collections (in particular, Duffy Knaus); the University of Portland; and, above all, my home away from home, the Oregon Historical Society, where Loretta Burnett, Peggy Haines, Lou Flannery, Steve Hallberg, Sharon Howe, Jack Levine, Ken Lomax, Susan Seyl, Sieglinde Smith, Fran Wagner, Todd Welch, Kris White, Elizabeth Winroth always accommodated me, whatever my hair length.

Those who unselfishly uncovered or provided documents and photos, along with the wisdom to interpret them, include Shannon Applegate, Gretchen Boger, Nadav Davidovitch, Nadja Durbach (who made it possible to complete the life of Lora Little), Lil Fenn, Thomas Goebel, Ben Johnson, Sue Lederer, Maisie May, Sharon Nesbit, Peter Sleeth, W. Thomas White, and Ron Yanosky. Hildred Powers provided photos as well as a living link with her grandfather, Will Daly. Similarly, Barbara Whisnant enthusiastically passed along photos and crucial material about her relative, Hans Curt Muller. Joe Poracsky introduced me to the issues involved in making the electoral maps, and Paul Fyfield magnificently carried through on the very hard research and imagination necessary to their execution.

In the course of this project I also became a small employer, having the chance to benefit from the most amazing team of research assistants that I could imagine. Craig Clark, Sara Cole, Anamaría De La Cruz, Mark Dinner, David Del Mar, Christine Evans, Tammy Fladebo, Robert Hodgson, Karene Grad, Brian Knott, Sharon Leon, Elaine Lewinnek, Ted Melillo, Dreama Jean Preston, Ashley Riley, Todd Russell, Eran Shalev, Mike Tuttle, and Liza Zamd never seemed to tire of photocopying or library runs, although I am sure that they more than once got exasperated at my middle-of-the-night email requests for more material. Above and beyond the call of duty were Greg Earhart, a wizard with electoral statistics and so much more; Michael Jo, a master of the literature on Nazism; Trudi Kastner, who combed through old microfilms with great skill; Aaron Sachs, who discovered obscure Harry Lane material and boiled census data with equal dedication; and Michael Mullins, without whose extraordinary patience and dedication I would not have reached the finish line.

At Princeton University Press, Thomas LeBien embraced this project even though the labor it required was much greater than usual, and for that I will be forever grateful. Thomas conscientiously tutored me in the intricacies of the publishing world, all the while urging me to break the mold of the regular scholarly monograph. His civic and intellectual vision stand as a great artisanal rebuke to university press publishing in the age of capitalist enterprise and overspecialization. Maura Roessner took up where Thomas left off, gracefully reassuring an anxious author and skillfully shepherding the manuscript. Richard Isomaki did a superb job copyediting. Bill Laznovsky, Lauren Lepow, and Neil Litt supervised the production process, while Brigitta van Rheinberg, Jonathan Hall, and Hugh Lippincott cheerfully took care of details. Dimitri Karetnikov made sure that the maps were in fine order.

For financial assistance, I wish to gratefully acknowledge the Rutgers Graduate School; the Buena Vista College Faculty Development Fund, under the direction of deans Jim Zabel and Rick Lampe; the Buena Vista College Financial Aid office, for its policy of providing research assistants to faculty; Yale's Morse Faculty Fellowship and Senior Faculty Fellowship funds; Yale's provost's office; the Frederick W. Hilles Publication Fund and the A. Whitney Griswold research fund of Yale's Whitney Humanities Center; and the American Historical Association's Littleton-Griswold Legal History research fund.

I cannot discount the power of Bruce Springsteen in keeping me going, and I thank Paul Owen May and Blake Gilpin for supplying me with the bootlegs that many times saw me through to the light of day. Above all, my historical heroes provided me with excellent examples of staying tough in the face of hardship. If it is appropriate, I would like to conclude by thanking William Simon U'Ren, Lora C. Little, Will Daly, and Harry Lane for their utopian democratic visions, which have been such a personal inspiration and could still be such a powerful part of the reconstruction of American civic life.

July 2002
New Haven, Connecticut
Jerusalem, Israel

PART I

REHABILITATING THE AMERICAN MIDDLE CLASS

> Either you are born a bourgeois or you are not. It must be in the blood; it is a natural inclination. We all feel that. Everybody knows the middle-class nature; it has a sort of aroma of its own.
> —WERNER SOMBART, *The Quintessence of Capitalism*

> What we need, then, are riskier histories that more explicitly implicate the categories that inform our own historical questioning.
> —DAVID D. ROBERTS, *Nothing but History*

The myth that most sustains our increasingly tenuous common identity as Americans is the conception of ourselves as "middle class." For example, one of the most important searches in recent years for a shared national moral heritage, *Habits of the Heart*, proclaims that even when it is inappropriate, "everyone in the United States thinks largely in middle-class categories." We all believe we are part of an "Imperial Middle." That is why, according to Benjamin DeMott, "Americans can't think straight about class."[1]

Empirically, these claims are highly suspect. Still, most of us think we do understand what being "middle class" is all about. In our everyday lives as citizens as much as in our reflective lives as intellectuals, we seem to have an almost preconscious intuition that we know who is in the middle class—and even more, what such membership means. After all, *we* are the middle class.

But do we really grasp the meaning of *the* American middle class?

CHAPTER ONE

RETHINKING THE MIDDLE CLASS
Politics, History, and Theory

From Yeoman to Yuppie: The Demonization of the American Middle Class

Arguably no class in human history has received so much comment, but so little systematic study, as the American middle class. And although the great multitude of ordinary Americans have been favorably disposed toward the solid and upstanding middle class, intellectuals have by and large held a different view. In scholarly circles, the middle class has, to put it mildly, an image problem. We cannot, therefore, even begin to think straight about—much less systematically to rethink—the middle class without first considering the one-dimensional vision that has served as the faulty tradition of American intellectuals.

Radicals have been the prime shapers of mainstream intellectual perspectives on the American middle class. Left-wing social theorists have characterized the middle class as politically retrograde, morally inert, and economically marginal for more than a century. Prominent socialist Robert Rives La Monte set the tone in 1908 when, casting about for an appropriate metaphor for the American middle class, he found what he desired in the writings of Maxim Gorky. *Sycophants* and *vampires*, Rives La Monte announced, were the proper labels, for "in the middle stand the people who lick the hands of those who beat you in the face and suck the blood of those whose faces are beaten. That's the middle!"[1]

Unfortunately, Rives la Monte's nightmarish imagery would reign supreme across the political spectrum among the high thinkers of the twentieth century. Max Weber denounced the hypocrisy and "highly grotesque" characteristics of the American middle class. The entire middle class of the interwar era, David J. Saposs argued, suffered from a profound "inferiority psychosis" and general "inner feeling of defeat and helplessness in the clutches of capitalism." Even a self-proclaimed defender of the "intermediate millions," Charles Henry Melzer, could not keep himself from unleashing a torrent of (self?) abuse, calling the middle class "futile, shiftless, feeble." And, of course, Sinclair Lewis's *Babbitt* remains a common symbol of the philistinism at the core of middle-class life.[2]

As one might expect, though, it is Marxists who—having learned to denounce all that is not proletarian—have formulated the most exhaustive case against the middle class. Here Lewis Corey's 1935 *The Crisis of the Middle Class* stands out for its uncompromising censure. Corey did happily grant "the middle class," particularly its lower segment of independent small property holders, its due in modern history as the primary carrier of democracy and enlightenment, despite its general dread of the masses. Yet with the development of capitalism and "the progressive slaughter of small capitalists," a complete sea-change of reaction had set in. Traditional American middle-class political struggles such as antimonopoly had become, according to Corey, "desperate," "hopeless," and the work of "a handful of bewildered and disunited malcontents." Corey succinctly appraised the future: "the middle class is doomed." Before it died, however, it would issue forth "the monster of fascism."[3]

In the postwar period, when the prototypical middle-class figure of the era became the lonely, trapped, and desperate Willy Loman, non-Marxist radicals and liberals gladly joined their few Marxist comrades in middle-class bashing. C. Wright Mills crystallized and codified this demonization of the American middle class in his 1951 masterpiece *White Collar*, still after half a century the most important book we have about the American middle classes. *White Collar* quickly turned from balanced—if passionate—social analysis to a jeremiad that became what Cornel West calls a "brazen condemnation of the middle classes": a "total damnation," Mills admitted in private correspondence, "of everything in this setup." Mills's middle-class subjects were essentially hopeless: alienated, confused, dependent, full of illusions and misery; in the best light, they were "cheerful robots."[4]

An equally astute book, E. Franklin Frazier's 1955 *Black Bourgeoisie*, fits neatly into the trashing genre. Analytically, Frazier emphasized oppression, but he nonetheless remained pitiless toward his subjects. Frazier's white-collar workers had no values higher than money, adultery, and poker. The black middle class lived in a "world of make believe," identifying totally with white middle-class values and serving as pawns for the "white propertied classes." Its religion was an artifice, its "contempt for the Negro masses" boundless. Overall, Frazier wrote—in the grand year of the Montgomery bus boycott—that the black middle class was "in the process of becoming NO-BODY."[5] As Deborah White notes, Frazier's "attack" was "malicious" and "singularly vicious."

Even those postwar social scientists who rejected radicalism in order to celebrate American liberalism shared the animus of Mills and Frazier. Although according to these scholars the American working class was uniquely immune to socialism, the American middle class shared its European counterpart's penchant for irrational, right-wing pseudofascist politics. Seymour Martin Lipset, for example, noted in 1960 that segments of the middle class had historically been participants in effective, egalitarian anticapitalist movements. Yet far from taking such crusades seriously, Lipset theorized that the impulses behind them were increasingly becoming channeled into destructive, ignorant, psychologically impoverished attempts to fight against the bigness of the modern world.[6]

The perspective of these 1950s scholars has shown a remarkable tenacity. A troika of prominent recent works provides evidence of the continuing one-dimensional portrait of the American middle class. In defense of a communitarian left-liberalism, Robert Bellah and his collaborators in *Habits of the Heart* show sympathy for older middle-class traditions of religious and political republicanism. Yet they depict the contemporary middle class as relentlessly success-driven, lacking in familial or communal roots, dedicated to the preservation of private cultural enclaves, and so enmeshed in "the monoculture of technical and bureaucratic rationality" that it chooses all larger social goals in a completely arbitrary manner. Bellah and his colleagues thus give us every reason to simply abandon the middle class, rather than try to locate any political hope in its midst.[7]

Mike Davis presents an even harsher and more pessimistic vision in his *Prisoners of the American Dream*. According to this provocative revolutionary, during the Reagan years the middle class turned toward a "home-grown fascism." As part of "the mass ruling class of the American world system," the middle class maintains its "boutique lifestyles" within "sumptuary suburbs." From inside "the *laager* of Yuppie comfort," the American middle class is poised to undertake military offensives against third-world liberation forces as well as, eventually, its own ghetto inhabitants.[8]

Between Davis's Marxism and Bellah's liberalism lies the caustic treatment of the American middle in Barbara Ehrenreich's acclaimed *Fear of Falling: The Inner Life of the Middle Class*. Ehrenreich optimistically envisions a revival of social concern on the part of the middle class, hoping that antielite sentiments and a desire to uphold the dignity of labor will lead to an alliance with workers and minorities. Once again, though, Ehrenreich's analysis leaves little reason for such hope. The story she tells is one of "prejudice, delusion, and even, at a deeper level, self-loathing." Her middle class became in the 1980s—although it was never much better—mean, selfish, and "indifferent to the nonelite majority." Operating under a general moral anesthetic, perpetually anxious about its ability to consume the right kind of commodities, the middle class has become a defensive and self-conscious *elite*, tending further and further toward the political right.[9]

Overall, then, twentieth-century intellectuals—whether because of guilt over their privileged backgrounds, or because of their lack of democratic faith—have transformed an entire category comprising millions and millions of people into some sort of demon intended to embody many, if not most, of the sins of American society. We therefore live in an age that has recast the typical member of the middle class from yeoman to yuppie: from the democratic representative of an all-inclusive American culture to a self-absorbed, and dangerous, excrescence on the country's social landscape. We must, and can, do better.[10]

The Countertradition

To reorient our thinking about the middle class, we must break free from the demonization paradigm, moving away from its unsatisfactory moral and political sensibility and toward an engaged, critically respectful vision of middle-class Americans. Fortunately, a neglected intellectual countertradition has also come down to us, one that acknowledges the complex nature of the history of middling Americans at the same time that it denies that "the" American middle class has any timeless political or cultural essence.[11]

The countertradition itself has grown out of an oppositional vernacular heritage, dating back to our national origins. For example, many Anti-Federalists considered themselves representatives of a democratic middling sort whose fate was politically linked with those below them. Voicing his opposition to the Constitution, Patrick Henry proclaimed: "I dread the operation of it on the middling and lower class of people," and Luther Martin warned that taxation under the new regime would crush "the middle and common class of citizens." A century later the supposedly working-class Knights of Labor thought of themselves, Leon Fink writes, as a grand producerist "middle social stratum, balanced between the very rich and very poor." In a like manner the Populists saw themselves in the Omaha Platform as being squeezed between "tramps and millionaires."[12]

A handful of latter-day scholars have also been articulate voices of the countertradition, arguing that American middling folks have been quite diverse in their culture and politics, with that diversity including a radical democratic heritage. The outstanding challenge to the "restraining myths" about the middle class came with the 1972 publication of sociologist Richard Hamilton's *Class and Politics in the United States*. By means of an intensive quantitative study of national voting patterns in the 1950s and 1960s, Hamilton argued that the middle class was not at all monolithic in composition or political attitudes. The fundamental division in American society, he contended, lay not between bourgeoisie and proletariat, nor middle class and working class, but between a lower middle class and an upper middle class. Unlike the civil libertarian upper middle class of the consensus sociologists, Hamilton's high-level white-collar professionals and managers felt most comfortable in the conservative "party of order." In contrast to the intellectuals' intolerant and antiradical lower middle class, Hamilton's clerks and small businessmen held political attitudes consonant with social democracy. Thus Hamilton's lower middle class was fully capable of forming social and political alliances with the blue-collar working class, and Hamilton maintained—

correctly, we can see three decades later—that the fate of those alliances would be one of the chief determinants of future American politics.[13]

The recognition and rehabilitation of the *lower middle class* was Hamilton's major purpose and accomplishment. Unfortunately, his insight nearly disappeared in the ensuing decades. On the other hand, the upper or professional middle class—far too often the surrogate among the cultural Establishment for the entire middle class—has received significantly more scholarly attention. Here the major achievement of the countertradition has been to recognize not just the complexities, but also the potential *radicalism* of this well-to-do segment of the middling population.

Ironically, the most compelling argument for the possibilities of middle-class radicalism came in Barbara and John Ehrenreich's 1977 "enormously influential" treatise "The Professional-Managerial Class." Although placing themselves within a traditional leftist framework and eschewing the use of the term *middle class*, the Ehrenreichs sought to counter orthodox Marxists' refusal to countenance the development of a third class within capitalist society. They delineated the development of a high-level white-collar class both crucial to the successful functioning of corporate capitalism *and* capable of radical opposition to its would-be masters within the bourgeois ruling class.[14]

In his imaginative *Middle Class Radicalism in Santa Monica*, political scientist Mark Kann picked up on the Ehrenreichs' core analysis to argue that "middle class" and "radical" are far from categories of binary opposition. Kann writes that in Santa Monica during the late 1970s and 1980s a powerful radicalism grew out of—not in antagonism to—traditional middle-class American visions and desires. This strain of radicalism, deeply rooted in the American tradition, nurtured dreams of independence, decency, self-respect, and community at least as subversive of the relentless market orientation of modern corporate society as any socialist vision. In Kann's work the past and the present thus compellingly come together so that we might recognize what intellectual blinders have for too long prevented us from seeing—*the radical middle class*.[15]

Historians and the Middle Class

American historians have no more been able to transcend the demonization of the middle class than have other intellectuals, nor have they chosen to recognize the radicalism that has periodically flowed out of middle-class life. In the post–World War II heyday of consensus history, most took for granted the middle-class character of American society. Intellectuals as talented as Louis Hartz recognized such a complete hegemony to middle-class values that they felt it unnecessary to examine the middle class itself. As Hartz put it, "A triumphant middle class . . . can take itself for granted."[16]

Despite the reorientation of historical studies after the 1960s to matters of race, class, and gender, power and diversity, at least one significant constituent of American life remained trapped in the 1950s: the middle class. Historians wielded a yardstick of condescension when measuring the impact of middling folks on America's past. In two influential studies of white-collar families in late-nineteenth-century Chicago published in 1969 and 1970, for example, Richard Sennett exposed the attitude of many of his generation when he castigated the "slavery," "emotional poverty," "disaster," "counterfeit-nurturance" and "self-instituted defeat" of his subjects. Burton Bledstein's pioneering *The Culture of Professionalism* (1976) likewise concluded that "social idealism in middle-class America has existed only at the edge of personal cynicism and duplicity."[17]

Furthermore, the three most significant books that then marked a genuine renaissance of the study of the American middle class consistently retreated back to the old pieties after making significant attempts to move away from them. The first, Paul Johnson's *A Shopkeeper's Millennium*, skillfully analyzed the social context of the Second Great Awakening in Rochester, New York. Johnson's discussion of the middle class is brief and unsystematic, perhaps because his analysis fits so well into the larger intellectual tradition. "To put it simply," pronounced Johnson, "the middle class became resolutely bourgeois between 1825 and 1835." The implication: since then, it has never been anything but. The sensitivity of Johnson's analysis to matters of religion correspondingly fades as being "bourgeois" means, unproblematically, an interest above all in the social control of the proletarian workforce.[18]

Mary Ryan, on the other hand, set out self-consciously to avoid the one-dimensional equation of middle class and social control in her pathbreaking *Cradle of the Middle Class*. Ryan explicitly directed her attention to the "problem" of the middle class, and to the family in particular. In Ryan's hands Utica's middle class is publicly active, full of energetic reform activity, creative in its cultural uses of evangelical religion, and nearly self-conscious at its creation. Ryan succeeded above all in treating her middle class with respect, realizing its complexity, and understanding that we cannot neatly assimilate middle-class hopes and desires into entrepreneurial ambitions. That is, her analysis proceeds in this manner until she reaches the mid-1800s. By the 1850s a stereotypical middle class comes to the fore, having abruptly realized the fulfillment of its historical mission and cozied up to the quiet, intensely privatized existence that Mills ranted about—there to slumber until the 1960s. Ryan's post–Civil War middle class unproblematically packed up and moved to a "darkened corner of history."[19]

The other work crucial to renewed historiographical interest in the American middle class, Karen Halttunen's *Confidence Men and Painted Women*, also sought to capture a nearly timeless *essence* of the American middle class. Halttunen's depiction of the creation of middle-class canons of sincerity, theatricality, and domestic parlor rituals did sensitively demonstrate how such private performances could serve to subvert as well as to reinforce the entrepreneurial orientation of the middle class. In the end, though, the familiar refrain returned as the complexities of nineteenth-century middle-class culture disappeared. By the late 1800s, according to Halttunen, middle-class sincerity became little more than anxious deception of self and manipulation of others.[20]

The works of Johnson, Ryan, and Halttunen launched a new era in the historical study of the American middle class, bringing to bear intriguing and complex theoretical considerations in matters of work, religion, family, and culture. Yet just as these historians launched their subject off the ground of condescension, their trial balloons fell back down to earth. The middle class common in these histories remains fixated on its own status, greatly fears outsiders, and lives a privatized existence with an increasingly tenuous relationship to the larger community or world.[21]

We can therefore tell that as the New Left generation has ascended to power in the historical profession, it looks back upon its roots in (professional) middle-class culture largely with fear and self-loathing. Few historians would today be so naive as Kevin Mattson and argue, "I believe middle-class people can be committed to democratic activity and leadership. Privilege need not lead to domination." And only exceptional scholars have the self-conscious willingness to "celebrate" their middle-class subjects, as Glenda Gilmore does in her eloquent portrayal of the democratic politics of middle-class African Americans in North Carolina during the early years of Jim Crow, much less speak of their "most amazing grace," as James Goodman does in *Stories of Scottsboro*.[22]

Two books, though, have attempted to reopen most of the old questions about the middle class, the process of its creation, and its social and political roles. Stuart Blumin's *The Emergence of the Middle Class* in many ways attempts to do for the middle class what the new labor history of the 1970s and 1980s sought to do for "the" working class—simply establish its discrete existence. Blumin's theoretical claims in the book are, however, much grander. He promises to be the first historian to locate the middle class within a coherently examined three-class structure. Tracing the fall of the eighteenth-century artisanal middling orders and the rise of a self-conscious class of white collars, Blumin takes good advantage of recent scholarship in working-class history to make his contrasting empirical arguments about everyday middle-class social life. Yet beyond that, Blumin falls, if not directly into the demonization trap, at least smack dab into an embrace of the suburbanization trope. His middle class is, culturally, little different from the 1950s garden variety. Blumin's middling folks remain above all intensely private, with the men worried most about getting ahead at work and the women with keeping order in the home. Totally cut off from those below them, they look only up in admiration of capitalist elites. No complex contests over politics, morality, or the social order intrude into Blumin's middle class. It is comfortably "individualistic"—an insight that he derives *not* from contemporary evidence but from a modern social theorist, Anthony Giddens, as well as from the very problematic social theory of the 1950s.[23]

Olivier Zunz's *Making America Corporate, 1870–1920* represents the fullest break by a historian from prevailing conceptualizations of the middle class. What makes *Making America Corporate* refreshing is Zunz's insistence on the relative autonomy of white-collar people, not their passivity and degradation. Through an imaginative use of a range of corporate archives, Zunz examines the role of a new class of white-collar executives, managers, and clerks in the creation of large corporations. According to Zunz, members of this middle class independently helped to build the new corporations. Unfortunately, Zunz also fails to break away from old stereotypes. His analysis turns out to be a fairly deterministic reduction of social to economic experience. Zunz's corporate executives almost heroically respond to the market imperatives driving them to build, with great self-confidence, the new continental corporate economy. With few exceptions, "they bypassed larger ideological debates"; all segments of the middle class unproblematically "continued to take their cues from business values." In the end, Zunz's middle class is just as intensely privatized as those of Ryan and Blumin—or Bellah and Ehrenreich.[24]

Toward a Political History of the Middle Class

We can sum up the crucial missing element in the works of Zunz, Blumin, and almost all other historians, in one word—*politics*. In fact, we need to go back more than forty years for the most sustained historical exploration of middle-class politics. Although correctly located in the consensus camp, and a firm believer that members of an unproblematically defined middle class above all sought conservative respectability, Richard Hofstadter did understand the complexity of the relationship between the middle class and capitalist democracy. Historians still use *The Age of Reform* as evidence of the futile politics of a declining middle class desperately trying to maintain its status. Yet Hofstadter actually presented significantly more complicated insights. Foremost, he showed that the middle class lived in an intensely public and politicized world during the Progressive Era. Middle-class politics derived from moral conceptions of character and justice in a manner substantively different from—and Hofstadter strongly implies better than—the technocratic politics that came to the fore in the New Deal. In the end, Hofstadter's Progressives passed "one of the primary tests of the mood of a society," "whether its comfortable people tend to identify, psychologically, with the power and achievements of the very successful or with the needs and sufferings of the underprivileged. In a large and striking measure the

Progressive agitations turned the human sympathies of the people downward rather than upward in the social scale."[25]

A handful of books have revealed the fine intellectual fruits that we can harvest by extending Hofstadter's insights. Most ambitious in its theorizing is Jurgen Kocka's *White Collar Workers in America.* Kocka conducts a systematic comparison between German white-collar workers, with their alleged predisposition to Nazism, and the new class of American salaried workers. Kocka convincingly places middling Americans in the leftward portion of the political spectrum. He establishes that white-collar workers in the United States, even at the height of the Great Depression, were not susceptible to fascist appeals and did not substantially differ from blue-collar workers in political ideology or behavior. Alan Brinkley has, in turn, explored the worlds of the two middle-class insurgencies that might most easily qualify as quasi-fascist, the movements of Huey Long and Father Coughlin. Brinkley finds that while Long and Coughlin's populist ideology represented a futile protest against centralization, the two movements were fundamentally democratic. They directed their anger at genuine economic problems while eschewing xenophobia and intolerance.[26]

If Brinkley presents a last honest, even valiant—but ultimately ineffectual—stand by those in the middle, Catherine Stock shows how the same kind of middling folks actually were able to come to grips with "modern" life. In *Main Street in Crisis,* Stock demonstrates how an "old middle class" in the Dakotas neither disappeared under the weight of the twentieth century nor acted out of panic and anxiety as corporations and big government threatened its traditional way of life. Her small business owners, family farmers, independent professionals, and skilled workers instead survived the economic and political crisis by balancing "fundamentally contradictory, but equally heartfelt, impulses: loyalties to individualism and community, to profit and cooperation, to progress and tradition." Perhaps most critically, the "moral economy" that these old middle-class Americans had constructed from roots in producerism endured the depression, emerging battered and transformed but still powerful. Through their encounter with the modernizing New Deal, middle-class Dakotans built a society that celebrated both the striving for individual success and "a cooperative vision of community life." Profit, competition, and growth were good, but only within limits that prevented the communal honoring of excessive wealth.[27]

Through a focus on politics and political economy, Kocka, Brinkley, and Stock have reinvigorated fundamental questions about the relationship between "the" American middle class, capitalism, and democracy. The historian who most forcefully extended this line of argument was the late Christopher Lasch. In *The True and Only Heaven* Lasch brilliantly analyzed intellectual, religious, and labor history to argue that "lower middle class populism" has been the most distinctive form of opposition to American capitalism. Lasch contended that a political ideology based on petit bourgeois small property—not on supposed proletarian virtues—has represented the most expansive of democratic hopes in American history. Within this rich tradition, based above all on respect for the masses, Lasch insists that Americans might still discover a solution to our cultural and political crises. Most fundamentally, the populist impulse insists on cultural, economic, and environmental limits in the face of a corporate consumer juggernaut. Despite the book's one-dimensional valorization of middling folk, *The True and Only Heaven* should help to insure that a new, and fully politicized, reconceptualization of the middle class will become a part of the debates of both historians and cultural critics. And, also, that we will take seriously the idea of a lower middle class.[28]

What *Is* the Middle Class? Toward an Antidefinition

Significantly, the historians who have done the most important work in undercutting the demonization tradition, such as Kocka, Brinkley, Stock, and Lasch, have not attempted to analyze "the" middle class. Instead, they have pointed to critical *divisions* within that beast—above all, considering its "lower" segment as something of an autonomous actor. In other words, they have taken a decisive step away from considering the middle class as one monolithic entity. In order to take the next step, we must confront the problem of definition. For when all is said and done, don't we still need to be able to answer the question: "what *is* the American middle class"?

I will argue that the simple answer to this question is *no*. In fact, we cannot formulate a satisfactory a priori theoretical definition that a scholar can use to examine the middle class with any chronological depth—if at all. "The" middle class has always stood within history. To examine middling folks as they have constituted (or not constituted) a class *over time* requires giving up the illusion that sociological abstraction can aid us much beyond providing interesting ideas to reflect upon and use in a highly flexible manner. We must therefore blend together an eclectic mix of occupation and ideology, gender and culture, property and politics, in order to bring out a middle class—really, middle class*es*—with any significant complexity and historical meaning.

The book as a whole provides evidence for this argument—and for why, at the same time, class itself remains a valuable analytical tool in an age where so many intellectuals announce its death. Here, though, it is worth providing a brief theoretical defense of what I call an "antidefinition" of the middle class through an extension of the insights of E. P. Thompson. Thompson's 1963 preface to *The Making of the English Working Class* deservedly endures as the most influential treatise for the dwindling band of historians who persist in their loyalty to the concept of class.[29]

Scholars, however, have been unwilling to follow through on the full implications of Thompson's ideas. For example, Thompson decisively rejects the idea that class is a thing, an abstract theoretical or sociological category. Rather, class is a process—a historical relationship—that patterns conflictual human experience arising primarily out of the sphere of production. In applying Thompson's formulation, labor historians have produced invaluable studies of working people that have, generally, made the concept of class much more flexible. Collectively, however, these works have implicitly rejected Thompson's theoretical wisdom, for they have—at the very least, by the end of the time period they consider—almost always found roughly the same "working class" anywhere and everywhere they have looked. Certainly if we use a Thompsonian approach, it is inconsistent to argue that classes have the agency to actually make themselves—and then always end up with the same classes.[30]

Instead, let us take Thompson to his logical conclusion. We need to see that if people are genuinely making their own history, they are making *their own classes* as well. And if they are doing this, then we need to be open to the possibility that people very well might construct "classes" that do not fit into standard academic or political conceptions and categories. As Thompson himself put it, "Class is defined by men [people] as they live their own history, and, in the end *this is its only definition*."[31]

Therefore, a true Thompsonian, when asked, "What is the working class?" must logically answer that "the" working class does not exist. Instead, different working classes make and unmake themselves over various periods. At times one kind of "working class" exists; two generations later a fundamentally different kind of "working class" has likely come into being—or perhaps none has at all. And sometimes curious, unexpected kinds of classes—perhaps like the hybrid grouping that I discuss most extensively in this book—will play a critical social role.[32]

The same insight applies just as forcefully to the American middle class. As J. H. Hexter waxed metaphorical half a century ago, "the middle class is as fluid as water. A concept that at a distance seems solid gold turns out on closer inspection to be mere melted butter." We must, therefore, finally abandon one of our favorite grand, timeless, universal, and monolithic analytical categories, a classification that historians have used in almost as changeless a fashion as social scientists. In the place of "the middle class," we will find a much more complex and interesting way of looking at middling people.[33]

Class should help tell us, most fundamentally, how society organizes power and inequality in the economic sphere, but with spillover effects to other areas of life. Class therefore affects—often structurally—educational opportunity as well as taste in music, the neighborhoods in which people dwell, as well as the way they raise their children. All human beings, however, react to power and inequality in ways that are ultimately contingent and patterned only in the loosest sense. Therefore *politics*—the mediation of struggles over power and inequality—is central to the way people in any society construct their classes.[34]

Adam Przeworski has most forcefully explained the primacy of politics for the analysis of class relations. This prominent political theorist insists that "Social cleavages, the experience of social differentiation, are never given directly to our consciousness. Social differences acquire the status of cleavages as an outcome of ideological and political struggles." Like others intensely critical of the Marxist tradition of polar and objective class categorization, Przeworski notes that the issue of the middle class "forces us to rethink the entire problematic of class formation." Przeworski's most striking insight is his declaration that "struggle *about* class precedes eventual struggle between classes." Scholars must therefore understand the dangers in approaching the past with static categories of class, because we risk missing the critical contests that all societies have over whether, how, and to what extent class will actually be an operating principle. Because of these conflicts, "the process of class formation is a perpetual one: classes are continually organized, disorganized, and reorganized."[35]

As historians, then, we need to understand that when we are looking for "the" middle class, we cannot know beforehand what we will find. Or at the very least, even if we have a good idea of what prize we are searching for, we need to be ready to find big surprises. Only through the use of an antidefinition of class—and of the middle class—will we get closest to uncovering historical reality. The sociologist Löic Wacquant writes eloquently, "The epistemic ambition of defining, once and for all, the correct classification, of discovering the 'real' boundaries of the middle class, is doomed to failure because it rests on a fundamentally mistaken conception of the ontological status of classes: The middle class, like any other social group, does not exist ready-made in reality. . . . The indeterminacy, wooliness, and contention that exist and partly define it should not be destroyed but preserved in sociological models of this reality." Or, as Franklin Palm wisely declared in 1936, "Anomalous, mutable, with tenuous fringes, the middle classes never have been and are not now a fixed entity, to be encompassed by a simple, rigid definition. . . . Thus, the meaning of middle classes is likely to remain with good cause in a state, so to speak, of suspended definition."[36]

Fortunately, a small band of historians has finally begun to accept the challenge of moving away from the boxlike categories that have constricted previous investigations of the middle class. Most challengingly, Dror Wahrman has written about British representations of class in the period from the French Revolution to the Reform Bill of 1832. He argues compellingly that the middle class has always been first and foremost an "imagined constituency." The correspondence between social "reality" and linguistic conceptions of the middle class has never been straightforward; instead, politics always makes class concepts meaningful in society. Wahrman reminds us that those who employ the category "middle class"—whether pamphleteers, novelists, or historians—are always using "a purposeful construction, politically defined, conditional and malleable, and forwarded to bolster a particular agenda." Other historians have extended this insight. D. S. Parker, for example, takes seriously the ideological and political construction of the middle class in Peru during the first half of the twentieth century. Likewise Sanjay Joshi recognizes that "the middle classes in colonial north India were constituted not by their social and economic standing, but through public-sphere politics," and thus were "constantly in the making."[37]

Bruce Laurie, in an innovative analysis of antebellum politics, provides a bold example of how powerfully a historian of the United States can revise our ideas of a period when freed from orthodoxies of class. In an article setting out the agenda for a book on what he labels the "popular bloc" in antebellum America, Laurie argues that we need to distinguish between our usual "middle class"—with its core of well-to-do business owners and professionals—and "the *middling* class" (a term that is a hybrid of contemporary and scholarly categorization). These middling folks included, above all, small employers who because of their tenuous economic condition, low levels of property ownership, and limited aspirations cannot be considered capitalists. Middling people, used to dealing with their employees in a fairly mutualistic manner, easily allied with workers. According to Laurie, it was this bloc that, primarily due to its hostility to the rich but also to immigrants, provided the backbone for the multitude of third-party movements before the Civil War.[38]

A "middling class" *versus* a "middle class"? Such strangeness surely means it has finally come time to rethink completely what we will find when we all come to look for the middle of America. Indeed, Laurie's argument should help us realize that it has become absolutely necessary for historians to fully deconstruct our current ideas about the middle class. The binary oppositions that structure our instinctive comprehension of class, in particular the stark polarity of "middle class" and "working class," have become untenable.[39] Much important scholarship has recently demonstrated how race and gender are inherently unstable categories, socially and politically constructed in historically contingent ways. Yet as often as historians talk the talk about the social construction of *class*, residual materialist and political loyalties lead almost all scholars to fall back into a reified and essentialist conception of a monolithic American middle class. We must therefore transform how we talk about the people in the middle, focusing on previously neglected cracks and fissures, while intensively investigating the way that actual middling folks came to grips with their own constructions of being middle class.[40]

Does this then mean that we must also rule out of order the very term *middle class*? That we must constantly use those dreaded quotation marks to destabilize the category? Certainly, I want to radically problematize historians' rhetoric of "the middle class." Yet for analytical—as well as stylistic—reasons, I will generally no longer use quotation marks when speaking of the middle class. For the label represents a reality, even if a highly ideological one. That means that the battle for control over the *category* has historically been an intensely political struggle, both inside and outside the academy. And by calling my subjects middle class—as well as, inconsistently, *middling, petit bourgeois, lower middle class*, and similar terms that help us capture their character, even if in an imperfect fashion—I validate their political and cultural claims to being not just part of the middle class, but "the middle class" itself.

For *the middle class* matters, if only because millions of people believe it matters. We need to start following the intellectual lead of those millions—who of course disagree vigorously among themselves—and not worry nearly so much about the theoretical winds blowing in from lecterns across the Atlantic or from sociology departments across campus.

Rehabilitating the Middle Class

My goal, of course, is to do far more than deconstruct the middle class. Rehabilitation also requires positive reconstruction. Here I take the lead not from scholars, but from my protagonists. Whether relatively known and influential, or points of light in a statistical table, the middling-class people in Progressive Era Portland used their ideas about being middle class to fight for a fully democratic world. People like Senator Harry Lane, who voted against American entry into World War I; Will Daly, who went from a milieu that straddled organized labor and small business to nearly become mayor of Portland in 1917; William U'Ren, who gained national prominence as the era's chief architect of direct legislation; and Lora Little, Portland's most influential antivaccinationist, actively worked—along with their fellow citizens—to create a middle-class utopia that would, through a vigorous expansion of populist democracy, abolish most class distinctions, eliminate capitalist exploitation, bring women to full political power, allow ordinary families to make decisions about their lives in an age of expert control, overturn American imperialism, and even (although this was the most provisional) subvert racial privilege.

The issues that these middling folks latched onto were classic middle-class issues, with deep resonance in mainstream middle-class, and especially "petit bourgeois," American culture: small business, home ownership, family life, taxes, education, and fundamental fairness for all people. Yet those among the Portland middling sorts stretched well beyond the boundaries we usually imagine for them when they imagined a middle-class democracy. For example, those we usually consider "workers" were at the center of their construction of "the middle class." Indeed, this book, unusually, has as one of its fundamental sources the *Portland Labor Press*, precisely because in a middle-class utopia the working class and the middle class would meld into "the people." Such a vision of the ideal society did not arise from deluded ideas of classlessness; rather, modern notions of justice inspired this fully twentieth-century version of populism. By retelling these stories, we can reclaim lost heroes as well as restore a lost thread in American political history.

Members of the radical middle class had many successes in Progressive Era Portland. They brought about a fundamental democratic renewal of Oregon politics; they preserved their culture of small business through at least the 1920s; they stymied the efforts of unelected public health officials to control basic medical decisions; and they ensured that unions would have an increasingly strong and effective political role in municipal affairs. That they more often failed, and at times even faltered in their democratic vision, is not surprising. The purpose of utopians is not to rule society. It is to provide the ideas, and the political passion, that can energize their fellow citizens to work toward the world to come.

Like a rainbow, the world to come will forever fade from view. Yet, in crucial ways, that world is already here, and in good part because of the hard work of middle-class radicals who have carried a middling populism continuously through American history, from the eighteenth century to the present. In our new millennium, populism tends to be cramped and constrained, often succumbing to exclusionary impulses. Too many intellectuals therefore simply want to abandon its political ideals. Yet the democratic radicalism of middling folks is far from dead. A study of the past can, first and foremost, help historicize middle-class radicalism, showing its complexities and how it survived and changed, as well as what used to be politically possible. Once we understand, we can also cultivate, for middle-class populism could provide a foundation for a new and more meaningful—perhaps even redemptive—politics in the United States. As we throw ourselves into the very different historical world of early-twentieth-century Portland, Oregon, we should, then, see the radical middle class not just as a product of our Progressive Era past, but potentially even as a harbinger of our democratic future.

CHAPTER TWO

CURT MULLER AND THE CAPITALIST MIDDLE CLASS

Social Misconstructions of Reality

"The Middle Class" and *Muller v. Oregon*

The heart of this book is an exploration of some of the most significant ways that ordinary Portlanders sought, primarily through politics, to create different kinds of middle classes. Indeed, Portland politics during the Progressive Era revolved around struggles over the very meaning of the category. Who would be part of the middle class? What role would white-collar workers have in the middle class? Blue-collar workers? Unionists? Professionals? In what ways would middling people be allied, and in what ways would they be divided? How rich could one be and still consider oneself part of the middle class? How poor? When one invoked the category middle class, what social visions accompanied the term? And most crucially in this era of utopian politics, what dreams of capitalism and democracy did use of the phrase *middle class* imply?

Many of these controversies among Portlanders gained considerable national attention. The U.S. Supreme Court decided a considerable number of cases from Progressive Era Portland, several of the utmost national significance. Most prominent—both then and later—was the pioneering case of *Muller v. Oregon*, in which the Court upheld a 1903 Oregon statute preventing women from working more than ten-hour days in a "mechanical establishment, or factory, or laundry," thus providing for the first time constitutional legitimacy to women's protective labor legislation. We know a great deal about *Muller* from a national perspective. Yet the case began in Portland, in crucial ways as an internal squabble over gender and political economy among the Rose City's middle class. These origins have considerable historical significance as a means of helping us unravel the complex and unpredictable struggles over the meaning of being "middle class" in American history.[1]

Historians will likely never cease offering a wide variety of alternative explanations of the reform impulse at the turn of the last century. Yet insofar as scholars have focused on one main foundation for Progressivism, they have targeted the middle class. Robert Wiebe's 1967 *The Search for Order* remains the leading interpretation, contending that "the heart of progressivism was the ambition of the new middle class to fulfill its destiny through bureaucratic means." Like so many historians, however, Wiebe sweeps into one mono-lithic middle class lawyers, doctors, chamber of commerce executives, settle-ment house workers, architects, schoolteachers, and labor officials, giving them a "common language" and an uncanny ability to work happily together on reform campaigns. Rather than trying to unify a contentious set of occu-pations and their accompanying moral visions, Wiebe might have fruitfully pushed the idea that, in his own words, "the new middle class was a class only by courtesy of the historian's afterthought." We, however, have the op-portunity to move beyond Wiebe and focus on the divisions, the conflicts, the multiplicities, and the strange confusions that make up the history of the American middle class.[2]

What do such conceptual concerns have to do with the local roots of *Muller v. Oregon*? After all, the story of *Muller* supposedly belongs to Louis Brandeis and Florence Kelley, Josephine Goldmark and Justice David Brewer. The case, however, also needed—well, *Muller*.

That we have lost Curt Muller speaks tellingly to the scholarly instinct to expunge the petite bourgeoisie from the historical record. Muller would seem all too easy to characterize as a prototypical small business owner, upholding a dying laissez-faire social vision in his struggle against a caring, enlightened group of reformers seeking to bring a semblance of ethics to the industrial workplace. Yet recent feminist scholarship has greatly problematized the *Muller* case. As a result we have the opportunity to rethink Muller himself. Since we do not actually possess the evidence to determine if Curt Muller was a cruel and desperate employer, and thus the clear villain in the telling of the tale, we can use him in a much more interesting way to help us to discern decisive differences within the middle class—and the crucial political consequences of such divisions.

Who was Curt Muller? He is difficult to discover in the historical record. From the public historical record, it is tough even to tell his real name. The Curt Muller around whom great national political battles swirled also ap-pears in city directories as Hans Muller and Hans Mueller. (His actual name was Hans Curt Muller.) Born in 1877, in Johanngeorgenstadt, Saxony, Muller has strong roots in the petite bourgeoisie, as his father owned a bookstore and bookbindery. Muller served in the German army before coming to the United States in 1903. The next year he controlled the concession for the provision of linen at the 1904 St. Louis World's Fair, later declaring, "I made a fortune out of this." He moved on to Portland in 1905, in order to take advantage of the Lewis and Clark exposition. That spring Muller and Alex-ander Orth bought the Columbia Laundry, which had begun as a union cooperative located at Seventeenth and Quimby in northwest Portland. Mul-ler and Orth renamed their operation the Grand Laundry. According to the *Portland Labor Press* the partners were "patronized very largely by our best people, for the reasons that here they have the best treatment given to their

Curt Muller, with workers, in front of the Lace House Laundry. Muller is the man with folded arms. (Courtesy Barbara Whisnant.)

clothing, as well as because it is operated by union labor workmanship and living wages to American workingmen."[3]

Yet by September Orth had disappeared from view, and Muller went out of his way to have his foreman Joe Haselbock force ardent unionist Emma Gotcher to work, on Labor Day, beyond the ten hours provided for by the state's maximum-hours statute. After his day in the constitutional limelight, Muller returned to the arduous grind of the laundry business. In 1906 he sold the Grand and bought the Lace House Laundry in North Portland. He resided above the laundry—perhaps the result of a hardscrabble existence—until 1914. In 1908 Muller married Marie Snyder; they went on to have two daughters. He and Marie lived next door to the laundry for several years before putting down roots in northwest Portland. Muller relocated his laundry twice more before selling it to Fred Rosumny in 1940. He died ten years later.[4]

Curt Muller faded into anonymity during his later years, but the case he inspired certainly did not. This obscure small business owner set off one of the most important legal conflicts in all of American history. As Melvin Urofsky recognizes, "on *Muller*, as on few other cases of this era, a great decision hung in the balance." Coming soon after the infamous *Lochner* decision outlawing any government regulation of workers' freedom of contract, the Supreme Court's decision in *Muller* to uphold protective legislation for women seemed to herald a generous new constitutional order. And as Nancy Woloch notes, through the early seventies, the case "enjoyed (and in many ways still enjoys) an overwhelmingly positive press." For example, contemporary local reactions to the case, while surprisingly rare, praised this "epoch in American civilization" for removing "woman from the category of beasts of burden whose labor may be exploited by her industrial masters without restraint." At a national level, the *Outlook* similarly noted that the decision "may put heart in those who believe that ultimately we shall make industry for the sake of humanity and not regard humanity as existing for the sake of industry." Mainstream legal analysis still largely hews to this heroic view of *Muller*, holding that Louis Brandeis and his allies were above all advocates for "socially responsive law."[5]

Some feminist historians also honor the genuine altruism that provided much of the motivation behind *Muller*. Yet, on the whole, women's historians have in the last quarter century turned against *Muller* with a vengeance. To many feminists, the decision now represents a "repository of retrograde ideas" and "a colossal mistake" that "impeded the arrival of sexual equality." This interpretation has considerable power. Take the language of the decision itself, suffused as it is with antifeminist assumptions. Justice Brewer went out of his way to note that "history discloses the fact that woman has always been dependent on man" and "is so constituted that she will rest upon and look to him for protection." The *Oregon Journal* thus understandably came to the conclusion, in reporting on the handing down of *Muller*, that "the supreme court evidently takes the view that women are not citizens in the fullest sense of the term."[6]

In the scholarly realm, Alice Kessler-Harris—the foremost and most balanced student of such laws—rightly complains of the "vicious and clearly ideological attack on women as workers" embedded in the fight for gendered labor laws. Kessler-Harris recognizes the admirable motives of the period's advocates of protective labor legislation, but she points out that their good intentions "provided justification not merely for regulating, but for prohibiting altogether, the work of women in certain occupations." Deborah Rhode likewise indicts the highly undemocratic nature of the decision, which effectively silenced working women's own wishes. Summing up "the long-term deleterious impact of *Muller*," Joan Hoff notes that the case "bolstered a highly traditional and restrictive definition of woman's role in society generally as well as in the workplace. Beyond any doubt *Muller* opened the door to gender bias in protective legislation."[7]

Now the argument might be made that all this is an anachronistic projection on the past, that, as Melvin Urofsky wrote in 1971, it is "inane" to condemn these "men of good will" for their "chauvinistic paternalism." This assumes that no one at the time voiced the same kind of concerns. Yet as Nancy Erickson has shown, a small number of feminists *were* quite troubled by *Muller* at the time of its passage. We have, in fact evidence of—at the very least—feminist ambivalence from Portland itself. Two years before the national decision, when *Muller* and related cases were still working their way through state courts in Oregon, Washington, and New York, suffragist Clara Colby, editor of the Rose City's *Woman's Tribune*, offered a prescient commentary: "the whole subject is very difficult and it had better be left to woman's own judgment as to what is necessary and desirable. The State has no right to lay any disability upon woman as an individual and if it does as a mother, it should give her a maternity pension which would tend to even up conditions and be better for the family."[8]

The strongest voice of legal equality for women in this debate over protective labor legislation, however, came from none other than Curt Muller. Surely feminism was not his sole motivation. Yet in their briefs before the Oregon and U.S. Supreme Courts, Curt Muller and his attorneys offered a compelling and eloquent defense of women's equality. Muller emphatically insisted that women were full "citizens, and as such entitled to all the privileges and immunities" provided under constitutional law. He decried the "paternalism" inherent in legislative acts that did not place the same restrictions on men, asking, "upon what theory can the state become her guardian"? Women would in fact become "wards of the state" under protective legislation. Anticipating Alice Kessler-Harris, Muller acknowledged the growth of women's wage labor, remarking that "social customs narrow the field of her endeavor. Shall her hands be further tied by a statute ostensibly framed in her interests, but intended perhaps to limit and restrict her employment, and whether intended so or not, enlarging the field and opportunity of her competitors among men?" Overall, Muller firmly rejected the social welfare argument, "based as it is on the assumption of the inferiority of women." He proclaimed simply that "it is time we had ceased to classify women, in general, with children, criminals and idiots." Perhaps Muller's most eloquent peroration was his antiracist call for the end of political "chivalry":

> If any limitation is sought to be imposed, it must rest upon the inherent dangers of the particular service, independent of the nationality, race or sex of the employees. . . . The health of men is no less entitled to protection than that of women. For reasons of chivalry, we may regret that all women may not be sheltered in happy homes, free from the exacting demands upon them in pursuit of a living, but their right to pursue any honorable vocation, any business not forbidden as immoral, or contrary to public policy, is just as sacred and just as inviolate as the same right enjoyed by men. In many vocations women far excel, in proficiency, ability and efficiency, the most proficient men.[9]

We generally grant lawyers intellectual property rights over their briefs. Yet there is no reason to strip Muller of ownership of these ideas, since they were

presented to the courts in his name and because he did have formal authority over his attorneys. How genuine, though, were Muller's feminist reflections? As Nancy Erickson notes, "the argument sounds a bit strained, coming
as it did from the employer, not the woman." Indeed, it does seem as if
Muller's main motivation was a fairly straightforward laissez-faire economic
vision. Before the Oregon Supreme Court he contended that the protective
labor law represented "a species of paternalism and class legislation so much
in vogue nowadays, which, if not restrained, may go to any limits, and we
shall find ourselves sooner or later instructed as to what color of clothes we
shall wear, and what kind and amounts of food we shall eat." He was even
more emphatic before the U.S. Supreme Court, insisting that if "the Court
holds that all property is held subject to rules regulating the common good
and the general welfare of the people," the result of such "reasoning would
lead to ultimate state socialism." Still, as Nancy Woloch has pointed out,
Muller's feminism could have been both a "cynical ploy" *and* a "prescient
insight into the logic of sexual equality," since "arguments for freedom of
contract and sexual equality were natural allies; they were branches of the
same tree, individualism."[10]

If only because of his feminist wisdom, we should bring Curt Muller fully
into the historical picture for the first time, recognizing that this benighted
petit bourgeois is worth listening to as the discussion continues in our own
day over issues of equality versus difference. By paying Muller closer and
more respectful attention, we can also use him as a window into the confusion and complexity of the politics of the Portland middle class. A solid
small enterpriser for more than three decades, Muller had, after all, as good a
claim on membership in the middle class as anyone. Indeed his fame comes
precisely because of his role in a conflict *within* the Portland middle class, or
perhaps we should say *between* middle classes. Curt Muller can therefore
help us banish the myth that middle-class politics in American history has
ever been easy to unearth or facile to fathom.

Insofar as scholars have turned any attention to Curt Muller, they have
been tempted to see him as a minor adjunct to his attorney, William Fenton.
"One of the foremost corporation lawyers of the Pacific northwest," Fenton
sat at the very top of the Portland power structure. A proud member of the
prestigious Arlington Club, he served as president of the Oregon Historical
Society at the same time that he was representing Muller. Fenton's most
important client was the Southern Pacific Railroad, and he also served as the
local lawyer for Standard Oil and American Steel and Wire. Fenton abandoned the Democratic Party in 1896 over free silver and, in the ensuing
decades, stayed safely on the conservative side of Rose City politics. Predictably, Fenton found little use for unions. In one unpublished speech Fenton
griped that "there never was a more unfeeling heel planted upon the bowed
neck of honest toil than that of the labor unionist." Unions struck not for

freedom but "in reality that they may have more time to drink drinks, smoke tobacco and talk socialism, and devise methods to more effectually corner all lucrative employment and to terrorize their employers."[11]

Curt Muller surely understood the reactionary politics of his talented lawyer when he, and the Laundrymen's Association that funded his legal battle, hired Fenton. Yet even while allying with the corporate behemoth, Muller and his petit bourgeois allies might have had more autonomy than we first assume. For example, the laundrymen who guaranteed Muller's bond for appeal were not members of the city's elite, but rather L. T. Gilliland and John Tait, two otherwise anonymous East Side laundry owners. And the lawyer who did the most important legwork for Muller early on in the case was not Fenton, but rather E.S.J. McAllister, a suffragist, single taxer, and avid direct democrat who served as a prounion thorn in the side of the Rose City's Establishment until his downfall during a 1912 homosexuality scandal. Surely the radical McAllister was a strange choice for a lawyer if all Curt Muller wanted was to exploit women in the name of corporate capitalism.[12]

Besides, we can now see that small business owners like Curt Muller had a legitimate beef with the discriminatory effects of protective legislation on small enterprisers, for such laws did effectively target Portland's petty commerce. Father Edwin O'Hara, the chief spokesperson for protective labor legislation, declared the conflict as one of "unscrupulous employers" versus "more decent competitors." Yet this morality play obscures how those Portlanders arrested—like Curt Muller—for violation of the maximum-hours law came substantially from immigrant backgrounds and thus likely held precarious footholds in the business world. As an illustration, in 1910 only seven of the thirteen entrepreneurs given citations were born in the United States. The others came from China, Hungary, Japan, and Norway—with two, including a woman—claiming German nativity. We have even better evidence in relation to the pioneering Oregon minimum wage law for women, passed in 1912 and upheld by the U.S. Supreme Court in the 1917 case of *Stettler v. O'Hara*. After the U.S. Supreme Court reversed itself and overturned the constitutionality of minimum wage legislation in 1923, big business organs such as the Portland Chamber of Commerce, the Portland Commercial Club, and the Manufacturers and Merchants Association of Oregon pledged to uphold the wages and hours rulings of the Oregon Industrial Welfare Commission (OIWC), which the state had empowered to set wage rates. Corporate enthusiasm for protective legislation made considerable economic sense. As the *Oregon Voter*, the keenest observer of the Portland business community, noted, "most of the big department stores are reconciled to operating under the rulings of the Oregon minimum wage commission. They find the law has hurt their small competitors. . . . The big fellows keep on growing bigger, helped by the very regulations intended for their embarrassment. The higher the cost of doing business, the greater the burden upon the small storekeeper, who cannot pass all the high costs along to his customers as easily as can the big stores."[13]

In turn, supporters of protective labor law in Portland articulated an ideology that, perhaps inadvertently, ended up quite compatible with the legislation's procorporate consequences. In contrast to the petit bourgeois radicals who provided the foundation of the direct democracy movement in the Rose City, these reformers expressed no hostility to corporate capitalism itself, instead hoping simply to reform the worst excesses of the economic system. For example, Edwin O'Hara, a social justice Catholic priest and popular head of the OIWC, denounced "the radicalism of unregulated greed, with its contemptible and picayunish policies, especially toward employees who are unorganized; greed, with its cry for dividends and its contempt for humanity." The radical potential in O'Hara's thinking, however, remained unrealized as he lent his support to the nascent regulatory state. In seeking to ameliorate its most extreme pathologies, O'Hara ended up accepting the basic economic order. As he remarked, "if any business is so necessary to the community that it must be maintained by a subsidy, in the name of decency and humanity let the subsidy come from the public treasury and not from the earnings of working women and the homes of the poor." Subsidizing business in this manner, though, would not have involved overturning the general structure of inequality but would have, instead, effectively reinforced prevailing social relations.[14]

O'Hara's allies even more forthrightly defended a paternalistic brand of corporate capitalism. When, for example, attorneys for the State of Oregon and the OIWC first prepared to defend the minimum wage law in the *Stettler* case, they argued both that "women, like minors, are to be considered wards of the state," and that "this law is not only to protect the health of women, but to deal with the system of employment that has grown up. That combinations control every branch of industry is a matter of common knowledge. . . . It then becomes necessary for the state, or some controlling force, with authority to act, to see that proper laws are enacted for the protection of the weaker members of society." Sister Miriam Theresa, who as Caroline Gleason had served as O'Hara's primary assistant on the Welfare Commission, later articulated the goal of harmony underlying this basic acceptance of the corporate order: "The belief is prevalent that labor and capital are opposed to each other, that what is to the advantage of one is to the disadvantage of the other. . . . A statute such as the Oregon act thus becomes the means of industrial conciliation."[15]

Industrial conciliation. Here is a middle-class vision just as compelling as Curt Muller's, spoken by a reformer with just as good a claim on the "middle class" label as the contentious laundry owner. Indeed, the Oregon Consumers' League—Caroline Gleason and Edwin O'Hara's primary organizational base—served as a prototypical vehicle for Robert Wiebe's new middle class. The OCL was a voluntary organization of professionals with close ties to Portland's ruling elite, searching for order amidst the upheavals of industrialization by means of bureaucratic governmental solutions. Indeed, we could see the conflict over protective legislation—reaching its apotheosis in *Muller*—as a simple triumph of the new over the old, with the petite bourgeoisie desperately scurrying to stay on board the ship of history as the corporate liberal future of the new middle class rolled over the laissez-faire small business past.[16]

Yet keeping in mind Curt Muller's keen feminist analysis, perhaps we can recognize that the history of the middle class is not nearly so neat and tidy. Yes, middling folks were central in the struggle to fulfill the destiny of Progressivism, but they were just as likely to be in conflict with one another as to present a united front. And as different members of the middle class (or, effectively, different middle classes) sought to figure out, and act on, what being middle class was all about, they all brought ideas and visions to the political table still very much worthy of reflection and, almost always, respect. In recognizing the promising as well as problematic qualities of both sides of the protective legislative debate, we are better able to proceed to the larger task of deconstructing "the middle class." Then, once we move beyond dichotomy and declension in the grand middle-class narrative, we can begin to reconstruct our own theories—and ideals—of class, capitalism, and democracy.

Capitalism and the Middle Class:
A Social Misconstruction of Reality

Curt Muller helps us immensely in our attempt to understand the complexity of middle-class politics. Yet, in the end, his economic perspective is that of the classic libertarian petit bourgeois, albeit a feminist one. By supporting the freest and most unfettered of markets, Muller effectively gave his assent to the capitalism that served as the foundation for so many of the era's social struggles. This should not be surprising, for what else would we expect from a small enterpriser? Ultimately, Curt Muller gives us no reason to doubt Karl Polanyi's dictum: "The middle classes fulfilled their function by developing an all but sacramental belief in the universal beneficence of profits."[17]

What *is* a surprise, however, is how little Muller's advocacy of capitalism typified the entire spectrum of small business politics. For throughout the Progressive Era many members of the Portland petite bourgeoisie expressed a strong strain of anticapitalism, in distinct contrast to the economic visions of both Curt Muller and his social reformer antagonists. To come to grips with this opposition to the liberal tradition in America, we must dramatically rethink the received wisdom about the relationship between capitalism and the middle class.

Too often in the study of capitalism, that seemingly most solid and basic of bedrocks in our society, we unconsciously labor under a double sense of cultural irreality. On the one hand, a great many—perhaps the majority—of American historians have long had a reflexive anticapitalist bias. The predominantly left-of-center academy assumes the dominance of capitalism but often celebrates the vigorous anticapitalist ideas and practices at the margins of the American past—among, for example, pirates and Wobblies. On the other hand, the major Establishment cultural organs of our country constantly inform us, in this post–Cold War era, of the triumph, indeed the inevitability, of The Market, globalization, and the companion elements of the architecture of capitalism. Those few citizens who deign to fight against this destiny are resisting History itself—or, rather, are refusing to come to terms with the End of History.[18]

Yet, upon further examination, these two apparently incommensurate ways of looking at capitalism in the United States turn out to have much in common. For intellectuals from across the political spectrum assume that one group of Americans has always offered its almost undivided support for capitalism—the middle class. As Alexis de Tocqueville commented:

> If we attentively consider each of the classes of which society is composed, it is easy to see that the passions created by property are keenest and most tenacious among the middle classes. . . . [T]he men who have a competency, alike removed from opulence and from penury, attach an enormous value to their possessions. As they are still almost within the reach of poverty, they see its privations near at hand and dread them; between poverty and themselves there is nothing but a scanty fortune, upon which they immediately fix their apprehensions and their hopes. Every day increases the interest they take in it, by the constant cares which it occasions; and they are the more attached to it by their continual exertions to increase the amount. The notion of surrendering the smallest part of it is insupportable to them, and they consider its total loss as the worst of misfortunes

And after all, if Tocqueville recognized this, it must be an eternal verity.[19]

What, happens, however, if we find that the idea of the middle class's support for capitalism is one of Richard Hamilton's daringly titled academic "social misconstructions of reality"? After all, no historian has *ever* conducted a systematic study of the ideas about or relationship to "capitalism" of either "the American middle class" or actual middling folks. Thus, this hegemonic thesis has much eloquence behind it but no substantive supporting evidence.[20]

Indeed, when we look at the small business owners who form such an important part of this study's middle class, the intellectuals' consensus is even firmer. These are the marginal property holders who, we are told, would kick, scratch, bite, and gouge to prevent any threat to their precious holdings. Yet Hamilton, again the most intelligent commentator on these matters, urges us to look carefully at the one sociological study that has substantively examined such issues. Alfred Winslow Jones wrote *Life, Liberty, and Property* in 1941, but its lessons remain critical for us decades later.[21]

Jones examined the different attitudes toward property among depression-era Akron residents. Those nearest to the city's norm were the "little business men," who—counterintuitively to us—were *much* closer in their perspectives on property to Akron's industrial workers than they were to the city's leading industrialists. To be sure, Akron citizens on the whole upheld property rights. So on this, the scholarly consensus is correct—Americans have believed, and continue to believe overwhelmingly, that private property is a key part of the good life, and even of civilization itself.[22]

Does this, however, make middling folks upholders of capitalism? Only in a most idiosyncratic way. For as Jones argued, small business owners, like Akronites as a whole, were convinced that the property rights of the rich, and of corporations, must be "very seriously impaired by human considerations." The majority believed that unemployed miners should steal coal to keep warm, that the Flint sit-down strike was proper, and that neighbors should prevent farm auctions and the eviction of renters. They consistently sought a "middle ground" between collectivism and absolute property rights—a stance of (often subversive) moderation that, as we shall later see, many contemporary middle-class Americans maintain.[23]

There's something going on here, and . . . Mr. Jones *does* know what it is. Middle-class Americans have had a much more complex relationship with capitalism than we have previously recognized. Another example, from the era of the Reagan Revolution: when the Marxist sociologist Erik Olin Wright asked members of different classes to respond to the question, "Is it possible for a modern society to run effectively without the profit motive," the highest percentage to answer yes—a full 35 percent—came from the petite bourgeoisie.[24]

One of the primary burdens of this book is to take seriously these sociological revelations. A close examination of middling-class economic life and politics, with its powerful small business foundation that culminated in the movement for the single tax at the height of Portland's Progressive Era, reveals a strong strain of what is—at the very least—radical ambivalence toward capitalism. We should in all likelihood designate this politics as *anti-capitalism*. And in our current public dialogue about the future of The Market, we should reach out to the past and reconsider this tradition of a middle-class moral economy. What previously we have looked for only on the margins can, instead, become what we see in the mainstream. We must reopen the Question of Capitalism.

CHAPTER THREE

HARRY LANE AND THE RADICALISM OF MIDDLE-CLASS REFORM

Middle-class opposition to capitalism in Portland was no mere impersonal force. Rather, it became embodied in the lives of particular individuals. We must resist the ways in which the American middle class has become, in the hands of scholars, not just a demon, but even more an abstraction. Look through almost every history book about the middle class—from C. Wright Mills to those of the present day—and you will not see any faces. Theory and scholarly argumentation play large roles in this book. Of equal intellectual significance, however, is my desire to humanize the middle class.[1]

Therefore, in the midst of wrestling with big issues such as the Question of Capitalism, I also pay sustained attention to four *individuals*. This quartet of middle-class radicals—Harry Lane, William U'Ren, Will Daly, and Lora Little—rarely turns up in history books. None of the four left any collection of papers. Two of the four have no record in the scholarly literature longer than a paragraph. Even U'Ren, the most well known at the time as a friend and advisor of presidents and intellectual partner of prominent thinkers such as Charles Beard and Herbert Croly, is literally a "lost man in American history" who more often than not is incorrectly identified in current histories when he appears at all. Perhaps one of the reasons for this obscurity: they were all independent proprietors, and scholars have long denied the intellectual creativity and political originality of small business owners.[2]

By recovering these individuals from obscurity, and providing them with the extended treatment they deserve, we learn not only about their remarkable lives and politics. We literally can gain a new vision: a different way to see the middle class in American history, not just as a *category*, but as a collection of complex and often surprising human beings who stand apart from the Lonely Crowd. So, when small business owners appear as irrelevant and/or reactionary bumps on the landscape of American politics, think of Will Daly. When your faith in democracy needs refreshing, turn to William U'Ren. When you just can't understand the crazy (even dangerous?) extremists running loose in our political culture, try to come to grips with Lora Little. And when you need political inspiration in an age of cynicism, then reflect on the courage and heroism of middling folks in Portland politics by reflecting on the life, and death, of the most powerful middle-class radical in Progressive Era Portland, Harry Lane.

Legend has it that Harry Lane named Portland the Rose City. Lane, Portland's reform mayor and most colorful Progressive Era politician, certainly deserved at least some of the credit for this apt titling. Instrumental in bringing what eventually became a relatively raucous Rose Festival to Portland each June, Lane supposedly also "proposed that every other residential street be vacated and planted with shade trees and roses." This after all was a perfectly natural idea for a cozy middle-class City of Homes.[3]

Harry Lane, however, also developed much less cozy and much more radical ideas than planting roses during his political career, which eventually brought him to the U.S. Senate and a world historic moment of decision in the late winter and early spring of 1917. Lane's career is a remarkable demonstration of the complexity and porousness of middle-class politics in Portland, and Progressive Era America more generally. Lane's eccentricities often made him a lonely dissenting voice—and, in the end, his conscience made him a martyr—but the democratic populism that he articulated flowed naturally from his own distinctive middling roots and constituency.

Harry Lane represented Portland's middle-class radicalism on its most prominent contemporary national stage. He also continues to show us some of its greatest promise.

Harry Lane became mayor of his beloved City of Roses in 1905, was re-elected two years later, and was elected by popular vote to the United States Senate in 1912. There his career was so uncommon that historian Thomas Ryley has written: "Regardless of how much of the legend of Harry Lane one wishes to believe, there is more than enough to substantiate the view that he was one of the most unusual individuals ever to sit in the United States Senate." But can we legitimately call this member of the Millionaire's Club a representative of the middle class? His status as the descendant of prominent and powerful pioneers actually qualified him as a junior member of the Portland elite. Yet for much of his life Lane had been an independent professional—and, at that, really only a semiprosperous member of the petite bourgeoisie. Although Lane demonstrates the futility of forcing many, if not most, people into class category boxes, both his personal background and his ideological appeal clearly drew from the broad and powerful middling world of Portland politics. Lane's personal experiences as a self-governing business owner as well as a populist politician played a fundamental role in determining his radically democratic convictions.[4]

Harry Lane's grandfather was Joseph Lane, first territorial governor of Oregon and recipient of seventy-two electoral votes for vice president on the ill-fated 1860 Southern Democratic ticket. Harry's father Nathaniel lived a classic frontier life, prospering in the California Gold Rush before returning to Oregon to build a mill; his uncle Lafayette served the state in the U.S. House of Representatives. Harry Lane himself was born in Corvallis, Oregon, in 1855, four years before statehood. The family mill burned down, and Harry

Harry Lane, mayor of Portland, 1905 to 1909, U.S. senator, 1913 to 1917. (Courtesy Oregon Historical Society, # CN011924.)

began his working life at the Lane's Corvallis general store at the age of thirteen. While a senator, he recalled how toiling behind a retail counter was not what his soul demanded. As a child he had learned how to make bows and arrows from those who remained among the indigenous population that his grandfather had so actively worked to dispossess. Since "Clerking—repeat the word slowly—was tame business," Harry longed to be an Indian. Lane's encounter with the Other would profoundly shape not only his fantasies but his later political vision.[5]

Lane began his career as a physician upon his 1876 graduation from Willamette University's medical school. After postgraduate study in San Francisco, New York, and Europe, he became one of the earliest members of the Portland Medical Society. He later served as president of the city, county, and state medical societies. Lane had an active political life as well. A good Democrat by family lineage, he received an appointment from Governor Pennoyer as superintendent of the State Hospital for the Insane in 1887. Yet Lane showed—as he would throughout his career—unseemly party irregularity in the post, particularly during his vigorous investigations of corruption. As a result, Pennoyer pressured him to resign, an experience that, according to one of his allies, left Lane "embittered and suspicious of—even to despise—most politicians with whom he came into contact." The next Democrat to serve as governor, George Chamberlain, selected him for the Oregon State Board of Health in 1903. By then, Portland's working-class residents considered Lane a "poor people's doctor" who usually collected no fees from those in need. As his wife Lola commented wistfully well after his death, "my husband was a better hand at making friends than at making money." A story, perhaps apocryphal, has Lane throwing his account books into the fire as he neared death so that his executors would not hound insolvent debtors.[6]

Lane ran unsuccessfully for the state senate in 1902 on an independent reform ticket. Three years later, a veto of a meat inspection ordinance by Mayor George Williams convinced him to seek the office of mayor. Not particularly effective in office, Lane wielded a routinely powerless veto against saloon, prostitution, and corporate utility interests. Nevertheless, one historian has noted that Lane was "as spectacular a municipal reformer as any of the colorful city officials of the progressive era." One example: Lane, disgusted with municipal inspectors on the take, regularly toured neighborhoods to check up on the work of shoddy and corrupt contractors. Tapping all sidewalks and curbs, he smashed the hollow ones open with a hammer, and he encouraged local children to help him in his lonely mission.[7]

More substantively, Lane led a mild revolt of East Side business and professionals against the downtown Establishment–backed chamber of commerce. His reelection in 1907 amply demonstrated one of Portland's basic political divisions. All six West Side wards of a malapportioned city gave their votes to Lane's opponents; all four East Side wards went to the mayor. With his authority severely constrained, Lane encouraged Portland voters to use their newfound power under direct democracy to battle the "interests." Lane had lost an earlier referendum fight on municipal ownership of electric power. But in 1909, thirty-two measures went before city voters, with Lane winning favorable returns on a proposal to subject all new franchises to popular vote and on several other regulatory measures. Middling voters provided the core of support for Lane's crusade against the interests.[8]

While mayor, Lane gradually began to articulate a distinctive ideology that ultimately blended the high hopes of Oregon's direct democracy, the populism of the petite bourgeoisie, a powerful racial egalitarianism, and his own idiosyncratic class background and personal experiences. In his first run for mayor he proclaimed, "We'll have to go up against moneyed interests," a theme that came to dominate his political thinking. In a 1906 address honoring Portland rabbi Stephen Wise, Lane decried "the devilish ingenuity of a system, the competitive system, which unerringly results in 95 failures out of every 100 business undertakings." Lane praised Jesus as a Jew who preached "socialistic and communistic propaganda." And in a foreshadowing of one of his most important concerns in Congress, Lane proclaimed, upon the unveiling of a statue of Sacajawea in 1905, that all wars between the two races "resulted from the white people ill-treating the Indians who had befriended them."[9]

Lane's radicalism deepened as his political career ascended. A split in Republican ranks allowed Lane to enter the U.S. Senate in 1913, even though he spent only seventy-five dollars plus travel expenses while campaigning as one "of the plain people of this State." The Democratic *Portland Journal* praised Lane's promise to work for a radically reduced tariff, which would help block the attempt by the "money trust" to make citizens into "serfs." Lane was most angry about monopolists' takeover of the country's natural resources, a development that threatened the nation's very future. Lane also displayed a genuine hatred of the rich on the campaign trail. The poor doctor asked voters: "In the name of God. . . . will we ever stop the Morgans and the Rockefellers and the Carnegies from putting their hands down in their pockets and taking bread from the mouths of little Americans?"[10]

Lane extended his critique of the current exploitative class order when he warned that capitalism must reform itself or die. Criticizing the police terror of the great IWW strike in Lawrence, Massachusetts, Lane declared, "I have a little grandchild. If anyone tried to starve her I would cut his throat. Right there is where I cease to be a Democrat and become an Anarchist." Just before election day, Lane pessimistically spoke to the prospects of his own middling constituents: "We find on one side a few men possessed of millions and on the other side the very poor and helpless and between these two a great class of people either striving to get into the first class or struggling to keep from being submerged into the second class until we have growing up in this country a great social unrest."[11]

To help counter the dominant order, Lane's own family generated an in-house radicalism. Lane actively supported his daughter Nina and her husband Isaac McBride in their vigorous participation in socialist politics. Although evidence is sketchy, Nina McBride embraced socialism before her father took office in 1913. Lane's blessing of the McBrides comes out not only in many tender letters between father and daughter but also in his hiring of Isaac McBride as his secretary and administrative assistant. Not many members of the United States Senate have had socialist chief secretaries at any time, much less with preparedness for war so prominent on the national political agenda. Yet McBride became a dynamic agitator against militarism at local socialist meetings even while serving under Lane. Upon IWW chief Bill Haywood's personal request as a "Fellow-Worker," McBride also helped arrange Lane's intervention in the attempt to prevent the execution of radical Wobbly Joe Hill. After Lane's death, McBride served as head of the

Washington office for the ardently pro-Bolshevik People's Council of America for Democracy and Peace.[12]

Harry Lane did not merely help to nurture young radicals within his own personal sphere. During the fateful period he served in Congress, he compiled a voting record that, according to the calculations of one scholar, made him the second most progressive Senate Democrat from 1911 to 1917. His current obscurity does make sense on the surface, though, for Lane sought more to serve as a conscience to the Senate than to insure that his name would be attached to successful legislation. Yet by sweeping politicians like Lane under the rug, we run the risk of dismissing one of the most powerful—and promising—political traditions in our history.[13]

"The most notable characteristic of his mind was its unshakable grasp of a few elementary principles of justice and humanity and the sudden and surprising aptness with which he applied them to the case in hand; if to the breaking down of ancient conventions or the shattering of ancient idols, so much the better." In this eulogy Lane's closest political friend, Portland attorney R. W. Montague, eloquently expressed both his constituents' attraction to Lane—and Lane's estrangement from many of his congressional colleagues. Lane often did, it must be noted, bring his fellow senators to laughter during his colorful speeches on topics ranging from the health qualities of apples (good) versus bananas (potentially very bad) to his experience mushing dogs in Alaska when the temperature hovered around forty-six below.[14]

Yet Lane much more frequently angered his fellow senators with his quixotic independence and scorn of rules. Lane insisted that *all* government business be done in the open so the public could see. He thus advocated doing away with the Democratic caucus just when Woodrow Wilson was attempting to tighten party regularity. Lane's idea that the Senate should bypass committees Francis Newlands called "revolutionary," and that was one of the nicer expressions used about Lane when he inspired senatorial ire. William Stone from Missouri, upset at Lane's holding up the Indian appropriations bill, began one speech: "To show how little the Senator knows about the thing he is talking about . . ." But Lane continued to thumb his nose at senators to the very end. In his last speech, given in great pain while he was dying just after the U.S. declaration of war in 1917, he suggested (with little humor intended), "We should surely do everything possible to ameliorate the conditions due to a lack of the food supply. I should like to ask the Senator from Missouri if he will not introduce a clause in the resolution to arm each member of the Senate with a hoe, so that if they begin work about 6 o'clock in the morning they could hoe up enough ground before noon, when they take up their duties in the Senate, to feed a good many soldiers." Perhaps it was Lane's endearing style that helped earn him a coveted spot on the Joint Select Committee on the Disposition of Useless Papers in the Executive Departments.[15]

Lane articulated a broad legislative agenda. As mayor, he had enthusiastically hosted the 1905 national woman suffrage convention, characterizing the model marriage as one "where the man helped the woman with the housework, and she helped him with public affairs." In turn, suffragists in Portland honored Lane with a grand fete just before he headed off to Washington. Once at the capital, Lane served as one of the most prominent advocates of suffrage in the Senate, introducing resolutions and speaking forcefully about the benefits of an expanded electorate. More generally, Lane favored government ownership of telephone and telegraph facilities, the merchant marine, and Alaskan coal-mining corporations.[16]

The distinctiveness of Lane's politics, however, came out most fully in his articulation of ideas relating to race, empire, capitalism, and democracy. Here Lane showed the depths of his passion for rule by the people, not just in Oregon, or even among white American voters generally, but without qualification in the Philippines and—most daringly—among the conquered Indian population within America's own borders.

Lane's racial views never did become fully egalitarian. While on the campaign trail, and again as senator, he pledged to work for the "rigid exclusion of coolie labor." Lane also declared, in the midst of one congressional debate, "I want to vote for any measure which will keep the Caucasian race in possession of its own country."[17]

That noted, Lane blazed a remarkable path toward genuine racial sympathy and enlightenment—with his progress toward egalitarianism flowing from his populist convictions. First, we have negative evidence. Despite Lane's strong concerns about immigration, which he feared would make life miserable for already exploited labor, he never said one word, at least in the public record, about any qualities that would mark Eastern Europeans, Asians, or African Americans as inferior—this in an age marked by the pervasiveness of such stigmatization.[18]

Lane spoke infrequently about blacks, generally conceding that part of the American racial dilemma to southern senators. Not always, though—and Lane at times quite effectively chided some of the era's most prominent white supremacists. When Lane challenged Georgia's Hoke Smith to recognize the successes of black southern farmers, Smith refused to let Lane speak any further. Once Lane regained the floor, he overtly protested the racial discrimination in the appropriation bill under debate. A month later, Lane confronted Nathan Bryan of Florida, who had claimed, "Only those people have a right to vote or ought to be permitted to vote who are intelligent, who are interested, and who will exercise the power." Lane complained that Bryan had broken faith with fundamental democratic principles because he wished, in establishing qualifications, to "set himself up in judgment" over his fellow black citizens.[19]

That Lane worked within the boundaries of white supremacy, but stretched these boundaries perhaps as far as they could go in the Progressive Era halls of Congress, comes through most clearly in an oration on immigration. Lane began with an extraordinary challenge to the predominant racial thinking of the period:

> We hear from gentlemen on each side of the Chamber, intelligent men, preening themselves upon the purity of the Caucasian race in this country and the greatness which it has achieved and the duty which we owe to the country and ourselves to keep that race unmixed and true to its traditions and to exclude those other peoples who are of differing races and hence less worthy morally and mentally, I assume, from participating in the governmental affairs of the Nation.
>
> They apply the argument to both the Atlantic and Pacific coasts, forgetting, it seems to me, that the past history of the country does not justify them in their assumptions of superiority.

Lane then narrated the history of slavery and the importation of Asian labor, linking them as part of the strategy of the Caucasian "governing class" to "secure cheap labor."[20]

Suspicion toward the motives of Caucasians, as well as capitalists, also led Lane to a strenuous critique of imperialism. When the issue of ill treatment of Americans at the hands of revolutionary forces in Mexico came before the Senate, Lane shared an "indignant" concern but emphasized that "there is a history back of this" involving the "bribery," "skulduggery," and "undue financial influence" by which U.S. citizens acquired "large tracts of immensely valuable properties in Mexico." That was Lane's public voice. In private, he was even more forceful, predicting that "persons who have large financial interests in Mexico" would begin arranging for the "cold blooded assassinations of not too prominent Americans" in order to force the nation into war.[21]

Lane even more emphatically denounced the American presence in the Philippines. Here he went considerably further than the traditional Democratic Party platform, which championed "an immediate declaration of the Nation's purpose to recognize the independence of the Philippine Islands as soon as a stable government can be established"—a goal realized in the Second Jones Bill of 1916, which, after considerable backsliding from Woodrow Wilson, guaranteed *eventual* independence for the Philippines.[22]

Lane, however, had no patience for the language of "as soon as" or "eventual." He demanded an immediate pull out from the archipelago. In his most eloquent speech on the issue, Lane directly confronted the entire justification for imperialism: "I am not favorably impressed with the theory advanced by those who contend that it is our duty to pilot the Filipinos up to some undefined standard of education, of citizenship, or capacity for self-government." They are "another people whose ways are not ours, yet a good people withal, but who love us not and have no reason to do so." And the populist principle of popular rule cut both ways. Lane was confident that "any time the vote is put to them on the direct question," "the mass and rank and file" of Americans "would gladly . . . let the Filipinos go about their business to govern their own country."[23]

Where had Harry Lane imbibed such lessons in militant anti-imperialism? From dinnertime conversations with his socialist daughter and son-in-law, perhaps. Yet well before that he had witnessed his own powerful homegrown example. The shameful treatment of Native Americans had made it clear how little of a white man's burden the country had the right to bear.

This was Lane's burning issue. Here lay the promise of America broken, battered, and betrayed. Lane savored his service on the Senate Indian Affairs committee, where according to one senator he "was jealous of the rights of the Indians, and opposed with all the power within him everything that to him smacked of wrong or injustice to them." Despite our instinct to debunk this kind of naïveté, such rhetoric turns out to be not so far from the truth. Lane never stopped providing numerous counts for an indictment of government policy toward Indians. He refused to say anything favorable about our "so-called civilization" of the Indians, stating, "I think the whole scheme of our management of the affairs of the Indian is a mistake. It is wrong; it is expensive to the Government; it is fatal to the Indians."[24]

Lane had one clear explanation for Indian poverty, and it had nothing to do with racial inferiority: "The Indians of this country are down; they are down upon their backs and the white man is astride them and is at work taking from them everything they have." The "criminal" system of Indian-white relations led "to poverty and hunger, even to death and to the ruination of a race of people who under proper handling and with proper treatment and encouragement might become one of the strongest factors in the civilization of this country." Not once did the junior senator from Oregon suggest that whites had *anything* to offer Indians.[25]

We can unfortunately only speculate about what caused such an extraordinary and incisive assessment of indigenous affairs. Regardless of Lane's inner motivation, he was offering a dramatic repudiation of his own ancestral heritage. Harry Lane had grown up with his grandfather, Joseph Lane, who had been, as Oregon's territorial governor, a crucial agent of native conquest. Joe Lane negotiated with the Cayuse in order to bring the killers of Narcissa and Marcus Whitman to trial, and he became a war hero not just in Mexico but in the mountains of southern Oregon as he helped during the 1850s to subdue the Rogues. Although Joe Lane opposed whites who advocated complete extermination, he was proud of his significant role in dispossessing Indians and gained much political capital from these activities. No direct evidence survives of the effect his grandfather's pioneering past had on Harry Lane, but we can be sure that growing up in this family—*somehow*—led not to the creation of yet more cant of conquest but instead to an often stunning critique of colonization.[26]

Even if Harry Lane's motivations must remain a mystery, his proposals for how to meet the Indian crisis need not. What he sought was simple: nearly complete control over Indian affairs by Indians. Early in his senatorial career Lane complained about Indians having "lands taken away from them without their consent" and asked that they "be fully advised" about legislative and bureaucratic plans. The government committed a grave disservice, according to Lane, in not allowing Indians to form political councils to discuss critical issues and decide how to spend their money. Even more daringly, Lane pressed for a radical extension of the Oregon System of direct democracy: "We should submit proposed legislation to the Indian and allow him to say whether he wants this or that thing done. But we do not do it. It is wrong." Such solicitude did not sit well with some of Lane's colleagues, with the vice president even having to intervene on one occasion to protect Lane from scurrilous abuse from Senator Thomas Walsh.[27]

In the spring of 1916, Lane moved beyond a defensive posture and formulated his own plan to free the Indians from tyranny. Lane introduced S. 4452 "for the abolishment of the Indian Bureau [and] the closing out of Indian tribal organizations." Getting rid of the Indian Bureau had long been a goal of Indian reformers, who hoped to save the government money upon the speedy completion of benevolent assimilation. Lane had a significantly different take on the issue, though, one more akin to the position taken by contemporary Indian activist Carlos Montezuma and many in the Society of American Indians. The government was the enemy, not a paternalistic ally, of the Indians, and Lane's language reflected his purpose: "the complete emancipation of the American Indian from the control, supervision, and management of the United States Government." Rather than a simple termination of government responsibility that would leave impoverished Indians twisting in the wind, Lane proposed the creation of a three-member independent commission of *Indians* that would conduct all relations between the United States government and Native Americans, "subject only to the control of Congress." The House and Senate would choose the three commissioners, but exclusively from a list of five candidates "selected by a council of all the Indian tribes." These commissioners would have "full and complete authority in the management of all Indian affairs." Lane's proposal was not fully developed, and begged crucial questions relating to continued tribal existence and the scope of federal governance. Still, Lane's call was a world away from the vision of the most influential Indian reformer of the era, president of the Indian Rights Association Herbert Welsh, who argued that Indians were "poor ignorant people whose real welfare depends on their being told." And at least some Native Americans themselves responded with considerable enthusiasm to Lane's proposal. Predictably, the IRA opposed the bill, but the Society of American Indians ran a poem in its magazine that proclaimed:

Let Lane's Bill swell the breeze,
And ring from all the trees,
Sweet freedom's song.[28]

The scholarship of Frederick Hoxie, the foremost scholar of national politics concerning Native Americans during this period, helps us to appreciate Lane's distinctiveness. "The Indian question had been transformed" in the first decade of the century, Hoxie writes; "optimism and a desire for rapid incorporation were pushed aside by racism, nostalgia, and disinterest." Harry Lane, however, repudiated the new Progressive consensus. Senator Marcus Smith, exasperated at Lane's opposition to an Indian appropriations bill, once even tried, unsuccessfully, to use the most primal of appeals to get through to the junior senator from Oregon:

MR. SMITH OF ARIZONA. . . . will he listen to the voice of reason and consanguinity for just about a minute?
MR. LANE. "Consanguinity"?
MR. SMITH OF ARIZONA. Yes; the Senator and I as white men now talking on this question.

Lane momentarily agreed to listen but then four times straight effectively told Smith where to stick his consanguinity when he upheld the rights of Indians over whites.[29]

Lane used almost every possible opportunity to comment on how similar Indians were to whites. When his colleagues complained about the failure of most Indians to become willing and successful farmers, Lane agreed but turned the issue around: "the majority of Indians do not take to the plow and the harrow, and I do not believe I blame them much. Most of the whites do not either." When asked if a Carlisle education "has a tendency to make the Indian a willing farmer," Lane answered: "I do not know that it does. I presume it gives him the aspiration, the same as it does a white child, for different things; but even so, he is afterwards placed under conditions where it would be almost impossible for him to advance." Coming from this era, such a statement is stunning in its simple, egalitarian expectations.[30]

Lane did, however, believe that Indians and whites were essentially different in one key respect. Indians were communists, and perhaps irredeemably so. Several times Lane enlightened his colleagues with such wisdom as "You are undertaking to individualize the Indian. The Indian is a communist. They hold their property in common. It is really with many members of their tribe a part of their religion not to part with land to individuals."[31]

Official policy of this age, as described by Francis Prucha, was to "turn the Indian into a self-reliant, independent worker, individualized both as to his land and his money." Lane therefore could have shared the perspective on communism of (his nonrelation) Secretary of the Interior Franklin K. Lane, who maintained that the Indian "has a tradition of his own to which by blood and inheritance he is loyal and *we have to dig that up and overturn it, and substitute a new standpoint for the one that he has*, if we are going to make a new man out of him and fit him to a new life." Again, Harry Lane cultivated a different garden. For the junior senator from Oregon, communism was a good quality—one that he hoped Indians would infuse into white society. Speaking, for example, of the system of redistributing property within Northwest Indian tribes, Lane announced, "As a physician for 40 years I have tried to find the potlatch germ, the potlatch bug. I intend to secure it in order to inoculate it into the systems of some of the wealthier class of the white people of this country. I think it would be good if we could instill into them some idea of such a distribution."[32]

Harry Lane's views on Indian communism may well have involved some exoticizing of an "other." It is more compelling, however, to see Lane's ideas about property, class, and democracy as a seamless whole that equally influenced his perspectives on the Federal Reserve, as well as on reservations, on J. P. Morgan, as well as on Mexico. North Dakota's Asle Gronna understood this when he recognized why Harry Lane took "a real pleasure" in being a member of the Indian Affairs committee when so few of his colleagues did. Such service allowed Lane to prove "his hatred against granting special privileges to the strong for the oppression of the weak and unfortunate." We should thus recognize Lane's ideas—that seamless whole—as part of the grand tradition of democratic populism.[33]

Lane's experience in the hallowed halls of Congress did not temper his disdain for the rich and powerful. Lane garnered national headlines the time he regaled his esteemed colleagues in the Millionaires' Club with a tale of J. P. Morgan's experiences in the afterlife. When Morgan attempted to approach the pearly gates after his many "criminal" dealings, Lane related, "I suspect St. Peter reached behind a post and met him with a baseball bat."[34]

Lane further revealed the petit bourgeois nature of his thinking when he complained, during consideration of the Federal Reserve Act, about the consequences of having the country's finances in "the hands of a few with the power to use them as they wish for their own personal benefit at the expense of the many." Lane noted that this lack of monetary democracy resulted in the failure of most businesses "despite every effort and the hardest kind of toil upon the part of those who inaugurate them." He then continued his paean to small business: "It is not a good condition where 90 per cent of all men of necessity fail. It seems to me it would be a good country, or rather a much better one, a fairly good government, wherein the affairs of the people were placed upon a basis by which 90 per cent of them could succeed."[35]

Indeed, Lane articulated remarkably well an anticapitalist moral economy of the middle class. In the course of criticizing the Clayton Antitrust Act for its inability to catch "big business and the crooks" and its potential to harass millions of small business owners with petty regulations, Lane launched an eloquent condemnation of the very idea of competition. Looked at realistically, Lane contended, competition did not exist at the higher levels of the American economy, where "men of large business affairs . . . combine and cooperate and fat upon their less fortunate brothers, who, by force of circumstances, are compelled to compete with one another." Those who did compete with one another had "every inducement in such a struggle to be unfair"; more generally competition "develops cunning and cruelty and hardens human nature." If competition reached its logical conclusion, "All of the good and the unselfish and the kindly folk who make life worth living would perish off the earth."[36]

Unfortunately, with the advent of World War I the following month, events forced Lane to turn his considerations concretely to how to prevent the best of humanity from perishing from the earth. Besides matters involving Indians, war-related issues most fully engaged Lane. They also ultimately earned him his all-too-brief spot in the national political limelight.

From the onset of the war Lane consistently opposed all munitions exports, and he was the only Democrat to contest a war tax proposed soon after the outbreak of hostilities. In late 1915 Lane cosponsored with Socialist representative Meyer London a resolution calling on Wilson to convene a conference of neutral nations. Lane and London castigated the war-induced "state of fear" that "menaces the normal development of this Nation and beclouds the real issues which confront our generation by the artificial issue of preparedness against an invisible and unnameable enemy." Neutrals should demand of belligerents "evacuation of invaded territories," "gradual concerted disarmament," an international system of arbitration enforced by commercial boycotts, "removal of the political and social disabilities of the Jewish people," and more generally "liberation of oppressed nationalities." Jane Addams served as the star witness on behalf of the resolution. Lane also later sought to create a United States Commission for Enduring Peace. Even as the war crisis drew imminent after the resumption of German submarine warfare against neutral and Allied shipping, Lane refused to support the cutoff of diplomatic relations with Germany.[37]

Lane wove together his populist tapestry of class, race, and democracy one final time in his lonely opposition to Woodrow Wilson's request to arm American merchant ships at the end of the Sixty-Fourth Congress. Denouncing the millionaire profiteers carrying weapons and supplies across the Atlantic, Lane made it clear that providing food for hungry American children was much more important for national security than was Wilson's proposal, especially at a time when "the country has more money than any other nation has ever possessed in the history of the world, gained in large part by visiting death and suffering and misery on other people." The armed ships bill violated Lane's democratic instincts, because it would take away the right to declare war from the poor and starving people, represented in Congress, and place that power in the hands of the president. Most fundamentally, Lane cried out for Americans to resist the race hatred he believed lay at the foundation of war. And when Lane finished his forty-five minute speech just hours before adjournment, his role in this bitter debate was far from over. Having seen Senator Ollie James carrying a gun, Lane crept up on him as chaos enveloped the Senate floor. At least in Lane's own mind, the Kentucky solon was intent on assassinating Robert La Follette. Lane, possessing the deadly skills of a physician, was prepared, if necessary, to thrust his rattail file directly into Ollie James's heart in order to save the life of his dear friend.[38]

The ensuing attack on Lane, La Follette, and his fellow dissenters who hoped to block the extension of effective presidential war powers immediately became intense, indeed vicious. Woodrow Wilson made his famous statement, "A little group of willful men, representing no opinion but their own, have rendered the great Government of the United States helpless and contemptible." According to the *New York Herald*, Lane and his fellow senators would "be fortunate if their names do not go down into history bracketed with that of Benedict Arnold." Just as intolerant was the outcry at home in Portland, with the chamber of commerce leading the way. Lane's old nemesis proclaimed the actions of all the senators who opposed Wilson "cowardly, pusillanimous, traitorous." Lane himself deserved "our complete repudiation." "Never has the State been so aroused over anything," claimed the *New York Times* in writing of Lane's betrayal.[39]

The outcry shocked Lane, who was suffering from a grave illness, likely Bright's disease or arteriosclerosis, and who had already suffered spells of blindness at the time of his armed ship speech. He desperately tried to justify himself to friends and enemies alike, and in so doing he demonstrated profoundly republican fears of centralized power and the military. As early as 1916 Lane had told the citizens of Oregon, "I am opposed to the creation of a large standing army which in addition to being a burden on the people I fear will later along be used to override the liberty and rights of the citizens of this country." Instead he favored forming a "national defense army" that would pay "ruling wages" to up to a million men for short periods. This true citizens' militia would build roads two-thirds of the time and learn "rudimentary military tactics" two days a week at the most, while never being used for riot control or as strikebreakers. If combat with another nation did become necessary, Lane advocated first filling "the trenches . . . with men of 45 years and over up to 70, including public officials, if you please, Members of this body and of the other House of Congress and such like gentry, to stand the first brunt of the fighting." And in a terribly prescient letter to an Oregon legislator Lane declared that the right to declare war is sacred, belongs only to the people and not to the president, and "upon the people's unimpaired possession of it rests their lives, their liberty and their happiness. It is a right which if once lost will perhaps never be regained."[40]

The maligning of Lane led to further deterioration of his already precarious health. Against the advice of doctors, he insisted on going to the Senate floor to vote against the American declaration of war, although in the end he had to leave his blood-flecked speech unread. Only five other senators took such a position. "Commercialism is undoubtedly behind the war spirit," Lane commented publicly; to a constituent he wrote, "We will, I fear, be fighting under the flag of the 'house of Morgan.'"[41]

Lane's vilification continued nearly unabated, and almost all local political figures (including, in a mild fashion, unionist mayoral candidate Will Daly) spoke out to condemn Lane's position. Even at the height of war fervor, though, Harry Lane maintained some key supporters. Organized labor, and a few leaders of the Grange, spoke out in his behalf. Adah Wallace Unruh, a prominent activist in the Portland Woman's Christian Temperance Union and Prohibition Party, defended Lane's entire record as mayor and senator as well as his specific stand against the war. A Socialist paper chimed in, using the middling tradition to call Lane "one of the straightest and noblest men this nation ever produced," someone who always did his duty, "regardless of the mob, be it the upper ten thousand or lower."[42]

Lane's petit bourgeois allies maintained their loyalty as well. Kelley Loe, who later became editor of a magazine titled *Everybody's Business*, expressed his opposition to the war. So did William Deveny and Dan Kellaher, who helped defeat in the East Side Commercial Club an anti-Lane resolution similar to the chamber of commerce attack. Kellaher, an East Side grocer, was long an anticorporate gadfly on the city council; during the 1920s became the most influential political ally of the Portland Housewives' Council. The proprietor of the Broadway Hotel wrote to Lane acclaiming his "heroic defense of the People. . . . Your name will live in the memory of the common people." Albert Berni, a prescription pharmacist who sold rubber goods, trusses, and toilet sundries, wrote Lane to congratulate the senator on his antiwar stand "for humanity's sake," concluding, "Business good and all well." Even at this time of acute crisis, then, the junior members of capital refused to fall into line behind their patriotic elders—a habit they had industriously cultivated during the prewar period.[43]

The vote against World War I was Lane's last; he died en route to Portland a month and a half later. Most of Lane's contemporaries attributed his early death to the abuse he received for his opposition to the war. One senator eulogized him appropriately: "He was democratic in his manners and in his mental and spiritual make-up." Lincoln Steffens also noted this, remarking earlier in Lane's career that the Portland mayor was "a democrat (with a small d)." Indeed, Lane constantly celebrated the involvement of the people in their government. Lane was a pioneer in the Oregon direct democracy movement, serving in the leadership of the Non-Partisan Direct Legislation League from at least 1901 on. He was then closely associated with the Oregon People's Power League, the state's primary advocate of direct democracy, and served on that organization's executive committee during the 1908 and 1910 elections. In the national public sphere Lane fervently defended Oregon's experiment with the initiative, referendum, and recall, above all urging the vigorous use of the latter to keep officeholders in check. In his 1912 campaign he even mildly advocated the extension of direct democracy to national governance, and while in Washington Lane spoke on behalf of the Oregon System for the National Popular Government League.[44]

Yet if much of the heroism in Lane's life comes from his antimilitarism, what perhaps tells us more about the petit bourgeois roots of his worldview is his perspective on a mundane matter that begins our return from Washington, D.C., to the arena of Portland politics. An interviewer asked Lane in 1914 to name the major problem with American municipal government. "Decentralized power," Lane replied without hesitation. Lane went on to state, "A benevolent despot, if he is honest and capable, can manage a city better than can 50 men filling a dozen different offices. . . . I would run a big city or a little city with one, two, or three men at the most." Lane also consistently used a business metaphor to describe how government should operate. Here we finally seem to have the proverbial Progressive reformer exposed, someone who under the guise of populist rhetoric actually wished to professionalize the government in order to remove it from popular control.[45]

If we look at what else Lane said in the interview, however, we can see that Lane used the business metaphor in precisely the opposite way that historians have claimed. A government based on *small* business principles would be much *more* accessible to democratic participation and accountability than the current system:

> "I am an incorrigible and inveterate champion of a government by the people directly applied," Senator Lane continued. "No agent business for me, unless the agent is under a microscope all the time. We don't buy a store or a factory, turn it over to a superintendent and then let the investment lie dormant in our mind. We demand reports and we look over the books and we are in the office or thereabouts to see that the hired men are on their jobs."

Lane also eloquently denounced the entrenched idea that "government is a highly technical profession." Such a view was dangerous because "All men require supervision. The president of a railroad is under the scrutiny of his board of directors. So is the president of a bank." Through constant study and discussion, members of the working class could and did exercise such public supervision even more effectively than the elite. In Oregon, according to an approving Lane, "railway men, carpenters and stone masons have a better understanding of the subjects on which they are voting than do business men and the members of the University Club." Why the necessity of centralization? "Then the eyes of the people would be on a single spot," Lane argued; "Nobody can watch a dozen rat holes simultaneously."[46]

So Lane's political theory was, no thanks to Lenin, a kind of democratic centralism. Repudiating expert or elite control of government, his vision of political reform and radical democracy came out of a profoundly personalistic conception of business. In turn, Lane's understanding of business practices—and the wisdom of workers as well—derived from the world of the Portland petite bourgeoisie, with its distinctive, and powerful, economic practices and ideology.[47]

Harry Lane represented, but surely was not fully representative of, Portland's middling folk. Few in Portland's middle class were as strenuous in their anti-imperialism. His antiracism was even more unusual. And how many small business owners in the Rose City ever once in their lives gave thought to an Indian reservation?

Still, Lane speaks quite tellingly of Portland's middle class, for he reveals the power and the promise of middle-class culture. His egalitarianism was an extension of theirs, his democratic dreams a deeper version of their own yearnings. In the end, we do have to remember that Portlanders elected him and accepted him—at least until the very end. Harry Lane was his own man. But we should give his constituents a good deal of credit for producing someone of his character—one might even say nobility.

PART II

THE POPULIST POLITICAL ECONOMY OF PROGRESSIVE ERA PORTLAND

If, moreover, we analyze that ill-defined conglomerate dubbed "civilization," we find that the elements of which it is made up lack any moral character.

This particularly holds good for the economic activity that always accompanies civilization. . . . We have replaced the stage coach by the railway, sailing ships by ocean liners, and small workshops by factories. All this expansion of activity is generally acknowledged to be useful, but there is nothing obligatorily moral about it. The artisan or small-scale industrialist who resists this general trend and stubbornly perseveres in carrying on his modest business fulfills his duty as much as the great manufacturer who covers the country with factories and assembles under his orders a whole army of workmen. The moral consciousness of nations is not deceived: it prefers a modicum of justice to all the industrial improvements in the world.

—EMILE DURKHEIM, *The Division of Labor in Society*

The originative part of America, the part of America that makes new enterprises, the part into which the ambitious and gifted workingman makes his way up . . . that middle class is being more and more squeezed out.

—WOODROW WILSON, *The New Freedom*

Private property based on the labor of the small proprietor, free competition, democracy . . . are things of the past.

—V. I. LENIN, *Imperialism: The Highest Stage of Capitalism*

The clue to the American democrat lies in his hybrid character. . . . He is a liberal of the small propertied type, vastly expanded in size and character by a set of incongruous strains: the peasant who has become a capitalist farmer [and] the proletarian who has become an incipient entrepreneur. . . . It is not hard to see why the term "petit bourgeois" loses its meaning in the case of a giant as rich, as complicated, and as various as this. When the European shopkeeper has absorbed practically the whole of the nation, what is to be gained by calling him a shopkeeper?

—LOUIS HARTZ, *The Liberal Tradition in America*

Confectionery at Burnside and Nineteenth, ca. 1917, located across from streetcar barns. It was operated by George Foss, retired streetcar motorman. (Courtesy Oregon Historical Society, #6702.)

In 1911, the well-known muckraker and future Pulitzer Prize–winning author Burton Hendrick came to Oregon to write a series of articles on the state's politics. He visited the Hood River Valley's family-sized fruit orchards, eastern Oregon's golden wheat fields, and those who had found homes and livelihoods in the state's metropolis. "The story of Oregon for the last ten years," Hendrick found, "is simply a story of the shifting of political power from the corporations, which had abused it for so many years, to the farmers, the small merchants, and the working classes."[1]

In this section of the book I explore the foundation of the anticorporate rebellion in Portland among Hendrick's alliance of workers and small property owners. After first showing the strength of a traditionally defined bourgeoisie and proletariat in the Rose City, I focus on the vitality of small capital in Portland and the ways we might fruitfully interpret the role of the petite bourgeoisie, or lower middle class, in a "republican political economy." I then sketch the contours of Portland's municipal politics, revealing how the power of printer and city commissioner Will Daly arose from the city's populist milieu.

Above all, I seek to redefine the way we conceive of the relationship between middle class and working class, noting the high degree of fluidity along the divides of white collar/blue collar, employer/employee, unionist/ business owner. In 1915, the *Portland Labor Press*, in an almost completely incidental manner, celebrated the success of one of the otherwise anonymous citizens whom we can generally only uncover through aggregate census data. "The friends of H. G. Parsons will be pleased to learn that he has gone into business for himself," wrote the newspaper. "Mr. Parsons was until recently employed by the Fitzgerald Cigar Co. He has been an active worker in the trade union movement." Such figures, peculiar—even alien—to us, were not at all unusual in Progressive Era Portland. Indeed, hundreds of otherwise unknown H. G. Parsonses lay at the heart of Portland's petit bourgeois radicalism. It is high time that we came to know them and their lost world.[2]

CHAPTER FOUR

THE CONTOURS OF CLASS IN PORTLAND

Portland is an ideal place to examine the politics and social life of middling folks, if only because both the lay and scholarly representations of the Rose City so resolutely depict a kind of middle-class utopia—perhaps the closest that Americans have been able to get to an urban Ecotopia. Like most myths, the idea that Portland is "middle class" is not completely wrong, but it does require considerable exploration. The result will be the discovery of new ways of looking at the middle class and its radicalism, not just as reflected through the heroic acts of extraordinary individuals such as Harry Lane, but also through the vitality of such mundane institutions as small printing enterprises.

"The middle class"—or at the very least, the great mass of middling folks—did indeed have an immense amount of political and cultural weight in Progressive Era Portland. Given our intellectual traditions, our usual tendency would be to think of a middle-class metropolis as a kind of individualistic, classless, and harmonious oasis. Instead, the historical record shows that a social fault line ran through Portland during this period, inspiring extraordinary popular struggles and political tumult. As Joseph Schafer, a prominent student of Frederick Jackson Turner, remarked in 1918, "although the populations of Northwestern cities are less complex than are those of Eastern and Middle Western cities, nevertheless one finds everywhere the deep social rift between the 'masses' and the 'classes' which constitutes the special problem of American democracy."[1]

Can the class relations and class conflicts of early-twentieth-century Portland, then, teach us anything valuable about American history as a whole? The simultaneous existence of broad middle-class power along with substantial class conflict was a peculiar combination, one that neatly distinguished Portland from proletarian homelands such as Lawrence, Massachusetts. Yet such deep contention amid apparent surface calm was not unique to the Rose City, and the patterns we see in Portland are also reflected in the histories of cities such as New York, Chicago, and Los Angeles.

The problem here is that scholars have been unwilling to analyze a patterning of class that departs from the comfortable distinction between proletariat and bourgeoisie. Our need to historicize and politicize the class categories that we use does not, however, mean that we must fall into a postmodern morass where identities are in a constant, unstable swirl. Indeed, in order most imaginatively to rethink the American middle class, we ironically need to rely on concepts that have seen more than their fair share of mechanical scholarly treatment. When Burton Hendrick placed the alliance of "farmers, the small merchants, and the working classes" at the center of Progressive Era Oregon politics, he alerted us to the necessity of exploring the relationship between small property holders and working people. Drawing from Hendrick's insight, I focus particularly on the small business owners who formed the core of what we might well call a *petite bourgeoisie*, or more broadly, a *lower middle class*. Almost completely neglected in American history, the petite bourgeoisie and lower middle class have been crucial categories in explanations of European social development. Many other different paths of entry are available into the problem of the American middle class. But used flexibly, the idea of a petite bourgeoisie/lower middle class brightly illuminates the contingent nature of class structure, class identities, and class politics.

East versus West: Economy, Population, Geography

No other city came close to competing for primacy with Portland, the clear economic powerhouse of Oregon. The city's population increased from 17,577 in 1880 to 258,288 in 1920; Portland was the third fastest growing city in the country between 1890 and 1910. Portland, though, was not merely, or even primarily, a "western" boom city. Portland's economic history was more analogous, as Carl Abbott has noted, to "solid and sober river cities of middle America" like St. Louis and, for more general comparative purposes, to "the two dozen or so regional centers in the second rank of the urban hierarchy." Much of the political action in early-twentieth-century America occurred in places like Portland. As Judith Sealander has noted, "as late as 1920, there were still only nineteen cities in the country with more than 250,000 residents. The cities that probably were the real crucibles for progressive reform were not the few very large ones, but rather the medium-sized ones."[2]

In an age of industry, Portland practiced commerce. Although located more than one hundred miles from the Pacific down the Columbia and Willamette Rivers, as a port the city served as an export and financial center for much of the Pacific Northwest. Even after it lost premiere status in the region to Seattle by the turn of the century, Portland continued to maintain financial domination over a wide hinterland. Founded initially as a trading center for gold and liquor, Portland built its modern economic base by shipping fruit, wheat, fish, and most of all lumber to domestic eastern and overseas markets. In 1912 the city ranked as the fourth leading exporter of all goods in the country.[3]

Transportation, trading, and financial institutions thus took prominence in

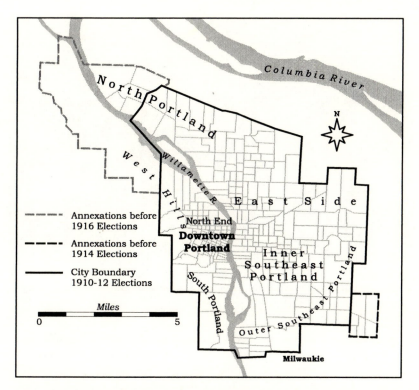

Portland, 1910–22. All maps composed by Paul Fyfield.

Portland, while industrial production lagged. (In 1910 the city, although twenty-eighth in the nation in population, ranked only fifty-fifth in manufacturing value.) The general prosperity of the Rose City stood out to contemporaries. Some authorities even listed Portland as the third wealthiest intermediate-sized city in the country. According to Herbert Croly, who came to Portland to study the city's architecture, the Rose City's affluence made it "better equipped than is any city of corresponding size in the country" with the office buildings and warehouses necessary to transact business affairs.[4]

An uncommonly uniform populace resided in Portland. As Kimbark MacColl notes, Oregon had "one of the most homogeneous populations in the country . . . overwhelmingly white, Anglo-Saxon and Protestant." Portland experienced more diversity than the rest of the state, with significant pockets of Chinese, Italians, Japanese, and Jews, but even during the heyday of the "new immigrants" the vast majority of its inhabitants traced their ancestry to northern Europe.[5]

As in any other human settlement, demographics played themselves out in Portland's geographic landscape. Founded in 1843, Portland began as a

Small factories on the banks of the east side of the Willamette River in 1898, with only sparse settlement beyond. Mt. Hood towers in the distance. (Courtesy, Oregon History Society, #38708, #1532.)

small, tight-knit city bounded by the Willamette River and the hills rising steeply to the west. A true walking city as late as the coming of the railroad, the city expanded east of the river only through consolidation with the independent cities of Albina and East Portland in 1891. Bridge construction and streetcar expansion gradually led to the settlement of what became known as the East Side. A majority of Portlanders continued to reside on the downtown-oriented West Side for more than a decade, but the construction boom that the Lewis and Clark Fair of 1905 initiated, along with subsequent annexation, led to the triumph of the area east of the river. At the turn of the century the West Side numbered nearly two-thirds of the city's residents. Around 1906, however, the East Side's population surpassed that of the West, and by 1916 outnumbered it 120,000 to 86,000. In one year alone, 1910, Portlanders built 3,000 houses on the East Side of the River and only 132 on the West Side. In less than two decades population ratios reversed, and by 1920 71 percent of Portlanders lived on the East Side.[6]

Beyond numbers, the social characteristics of the two sides of the river were of fundamental importance to Progressive Era Portland. In spite of the diversity of neighborhoods within each area, certain patterns clearly differentiated the West Side from the East Side. The economic and political center of the city remained on the West Side, and members of the city's elite lived almost exclusively downtown or in the West Hills.[7] Although segregation weakened a bit by the end of the teens, almost all Asian residents lived within a few blocks near downtown's rough-and-tumble "North End." Nearly

View of Portland two decades later, looking east from atop the West Side's hills. In the foreground are the tall commercial buildings of downtown, on the west bank of the Willamette. Beyond them lies the middling-class East Side. (From H. B. Van Duzer, "My Portland," *Old Colony Magazine,* November 1920, 11; courtesy Science, Industry, and Business Library, The New York Public Library, Astor, Lenox and Tilden Foundations.)

all blacks lived close by. Similarly, South Portland and other relatively un-assimilated ethnic neighborhoods provided the West Side with a cosmopoli-tan flavor, and poverty, lacking on the East Side.[8]

Property ownership clinched the differences between East and West. Even though the West Side contained a number of well-to-do sections, the per-centage of homeowners in 1910 was only 30 percent, in contrast to the East Side's 58 percent—with upwards of two-thirds in some of the more recently developed sections. In many ways, then, Portlanders saw the East Side as something of a middling-class suburb within the city, with fluid class lines contributing to the area's attraction. As the editor of the *Oregon Labor Press* noted, East Side merchants "have their homes with the homes of the East Side union families. Their children attend the same schools. East Side mer-chants rub shoulders with East Side union men as neighbors and friends." And the constantly increasing power of the East Side had a great influence

The Montavilla district in 1911, in the city's far East Side. The community was as much agrarian as metropolitan. At least two dairies are visible, as well as a feed store and livery stable, and a merchandiser whose roof advertises flour and overalls. Montavilla voters consistently supported radical direct democracy measures, the single tax, and antivaccinationism. (Courtesy Oregon Historical Society, #37952.)

on Portland's politics. Harry Lane, who owned a home on the southwest corner of Holgate and Twenty-eighth, as well as his fellow populists Will Daly, William U'Ren, and Lora Little, all called the East Side home, and this area also served as the basis for all the grand insurgencies that shook Progressive Era Portland, from the single tax to antivaccinationism.[9]

Contours of Class I: The Elite

Only when we factor in class can we understand the most important dynamics of social relations in early-twentieth-century Portland. And despite the middle-class veneer of the city, the quality of Portland's class relationships that contemporary commentators most commented upon was the dominance of an aggressive, self-conscious *upper class*. As journalist Dean Collins, himself a spokesperson for the elite, frankly acknowledged, the pioneers came "and established the dynasties that still rule Portland." By 1925, he remarked, their families had "achieved the suavity of manner that comes with the habit of aristocracy." "This self-conscious elite," according to the most prominent historian of Portland, E. Kimbark MacColl, quite willingly exercised its power and was cohesive enough that it continually threatened to become an effective ruling class. As Carl Abbott has observed, "Portlanders at the top of the economic structure . . . ran the city, and they assumed that to do so was their privilege and responsibility." So, clearly, Portland had its *bourgeoisie*. But this elite was in no way "middle class."[10]

The most critical facts about the Portland upper class were its extreme wealth compared to that of its fellow citizens; its farsighted ability to maintain control over the city's economy in the arenas of transportation, banking, and real estate; and its comfortable and increasingly symbiotic relationship with large corporations controlled by outside capital. First, certain numerical measures will indicate the wealth of members of Portland's elite. By 1903, the *Financial Redbook of America* recorded seventy-four Portland citizens owning assets of more than three hundred thousand dollars, effectively meaning multimillionaires in today's world. Those seventy-four rich Portlanders outnumbered their colleagues in similarly sized cities ranging from Los Angeles to Omaha, from Paterson to Seattle. In turn, the concentration of property in Portland was extreme. For instance, in 1918 less than 1 percent of the population garnered 63 percent of Multnomah county's taxable income.[11]

More important than counting tycoons, however, is exploring their methods of wealth procurement and the overall grip that the Portland elite held on the city's economy. Large fortunes in Portland derived from commerce, with limited forays into manufacturing. Portland's elite, moreover, rapidly diversified in order to control all the primary institutions of trade. The most important of these was the Oregon Steam and Navigation Company and its successor, the Oregon Railway and Navigation Company. Together, these corporations maintained a monopoly on much of the Pacific Northwest's transportation until the coming of the transcontinental railroad in 1883 and helped to create much of the Portland elite's riches.[12]

Similarly, Portland's status as the leading financial center of the Pacific Northwest had its material basis in the banks, such as the Ladd and Tilton and the U.S. National, that the primitive accumulation of the Portland frontier capitalists had financed. As the construction boom of the early twentieth century intensified, the Portland elite also preserved its grasp on the real estate market. As early as 1871, Simeon G. Reed had written, "Now we do know the values of Real Estate and if we put our money into that we can manage and control it." Control it the elite did, as prominent citizens such as William S. Ladd purchased huge tracts of land on the East Side, waiting until property values rose before subdividing and developing them. When Chester Moores, Portland's leading realtor in the early 1930s, looked back upon the evolution of the Portland upper class he asked, "In the entire history of Portland, do you know any individual who has ever made a fortune in the stock market—and kept it? No, the great personal fortunes of Portland originated into full stature through profits in real estate." As an example, when Henry W. Corbett died in 1903, he left an estate worth more than $2 million. His widow and three sons then watched as Corbett's $625,000 in downtown property investments appreciated fivefold by the end of the decade.[13]

Overall, then, it is crucial that we recognize—as did Portland's anticorporate activists like the single taxers—just how much the economic foundation of the Rose City's ruling class lay in real estate, banking, and transportation. Even if the city's commercial magnates did not command the wealth that came from giant industrial corporations, they had a continuous talent for ensuring the profitability of their investments.

Consider the relationship between eastern corporate capital and Portland's ruling class. "Colonial" economic relations did have some force in Oregon as a whole during the late nineteenth century. As David Johnson remarks, Oregon "became a tributary state to a series of foreign railroad syndicates, not the least of which was the Southern Pacific." Yet the Portland bourgeoisie hardly suffered from the intervention of these outside forces. As Gordon Dodds, the foremost exponent of the Oregon as colony argument, has commented, the goal of Portlanders "was not to throw off colonialism but to assert themselves and secure its advantages."[14]

Once it became clear that the city's further expansion necessitated it, the most effective way for the Portland elite to win the pseudocolonial economic game was actually to invite the railroads in—and then monopolize the opportunities that the new mode of transportation presented. When railroad construction engineer John Gates became mayor in 1885, he symbolized the beginning of the tight connections between national corporations and the Portland Establishment. During the new century the Southern Pacific, Union Pacific, and Great Northern railroads came to the city, and Portland's leading business owners continued to profit with them and through them. As Kimbark MacColl has noted, if the Portland elite "could not fight the railroads, it joined them, and drew whatever profits it could from the arrangement."[15]

The symbiosis between national corporate development and the Portland upper class proceeded in other areas as well. In 1907, for instance, William M. Ladd needed to sell the powerful Ladd and Tilton Bank to his brother-in-law, Frederick Pratt. In turn Pratt, from Brooklyn and heir to a major portion of Standard Oil, kept management in local hands until near the end of the bank's life in 1925. Portland elite member and "the state's leading banker" Abbott Low Mills, cousin of New York City mayor and National Civic Federation leader Seth Low and cousin-in-law to Wall Street financiers William Augustus and Alfred M. White, maintained analogous arrangements as the primary executive at First National Bank.[16]

The most significant example of the inextricable relationship between eastern-dominated corporations and Portland's upper crust was the Portland

Railway, Light, and Power Company (PRL&P). As the name indicated, the PRL&P was an all-purpose utility. Its most lucrative operations originated in a monopoly over East Side passenger rail service, and the corporation thus became a visible embodiment of the geography of power and class in Portland. By 1909 the PRL&P had become, according to MacColl, "the largest property owner in the city, with holdings worth twice those of the major railroads combined." Also by far the city's largest employer prior to the coming of shipyards during World War I, the corporation employed more than four thousand workers. Eastern investors, particularly E. W. Clark and Company of Philadelphia, did hold over 80 percent of the stock in the gargantuan regional monopoly. But basic control of the most visible economic institution in Progressive Era Portland remained in local hands. All in all, throughout the early twentieth century as before, the Portland elite continued to prosper greatly from its junior partnership in economic semicolonialism, even if its most important business was formally "in thrall to outside forces."[17]

Ordinary Portland citizens contested the economic and political power of the city's elite throughout the Progressive Era. We must recognize at this point, though, the economic and political rehabilitation of the Portland bourgeoisie in age of corporations. Some new blood entered the elite's ranks, but as late as the 1910s the "sons, grandsons, and relatives of the city's pioneer merchants" continued to dominate its leadership. The *Oregonian*, the state's leading newspaper, served as the house organ for the ruling class, and social organizations such as the Arlington Club became crucial, according to Carl Abbott, to the ways "the elite set themselves apart from Portland's middle classes." "By compromise and adaptation to the absentee-ownership of the city's largest corporations," Kimbark MacColl and Harry Stein conclude, the Portland Establishment "had retained its power and perpetuated its cherished allegiance to that private enterprise system which had so richly rewarded it."[18]

Contours of Class II: The Working Class

In addition to a self-conscious, widely recognized, and easily identifiable ruling elite, and the professionals who were so critical to the fate of *Muller v. Oregon*, Portland also had a large body of residents who fit within the broad category we have most familiarly come to know as "working class." A Portland proletariat is a surprising find, because historians have viewed the city as a deviation from the dominant trends of industrialization, conflict, and radicalization during this period. One of the state's earliest historians developed this interpretation of Oregon and its chief city as an exception, not fully mature according to the standard of the day. F. G. Young, editor of the *Oregon Historical Quarterly* and a Progressive reformer, rather ineloquently argued before the United States Commission on Industrial Relations in 1915:

Excepting in a few of the trades, the conditions are rather primitive—that is, there are no fully developed conditions into the classes of the employers and the employees. There is no marked class consciousness of distinct interest or how to handle their condition—antagonistic interests, if they are conscious of it; that is, Oregon in its industrial development is somewhat in the condition which the older countries in the eastern part of the Nation was in before the factory stage arrived. Of course, we have the lumber industry and others that have been somewhat developed—industrial development, the capitalistic system of organization—yet we are an undeveloped state. So that there is no close organization as between the capitalistic class and the laboring class.[19]

Although Young's interpretation of the city's economy was on the mark, he unfortunately missed much of the class consciousness of Portland workers. For in Portland an economic structure conducive to small business actually nurtured a vigorous strain of populist class radicalism among the city's skilled workers. Theirs was an insurgency that generated both utopian visions of a noncapitalist future and a nearly successful political threat to the rule of Portland's elite.[20]

Union membership figures are difficult to come by, but two independent sources give the figure of eight thousand in the years before World War I, out of a total of over 110,000 wage laborers. Approximately 7 percent of Portland's wage earners organized at the height of the Progressive Era, then, compared to a national average of 10 percent. Fragmentary evidence points to the relative success of the city's labor movement. Symbolically, Portland mill owner, workingmen's advocate, Democrat/Populist, and future mayor Sylvester Pennoyer declared the nation's first legally recognized Labor Day in 1887 by his authority as governor of Oregon. In the material realm, in the aftermath of World War I the eight-hour day was a nearly universal fact in the skilled trades throughout Oregon, despite the great struggle that this goal occasioned nationally. One early scholar attributed the comparatively peaceful coming of the eight-hour day to its institutionalization on municipal public works in 1912 through the initiative process, as well as to its enforcement on the part of the national government during the war. Furthermore, the wages for skilled workers increased at the fastest rate of any of the nation's thirty largest cities during the decade from 1915 to 1925. The pioneering role that Portland and Oregon played in protective labor law during this period also points to the strength of the city's unions. All in all, sociologist William Fielding Ogburn—a resident of the city—had good reason to pronounce in 1916, contrary to later historians' wisdom, that "the trade unions are strong" in Portland.[21]

Such success by no means derived from a polite moderation on the part of the city's working class and its leaders. Despite some qualitative evidence of Portland's generally low strike rate, at least during the "revolutionary" era after the close of World War I Portland workers joined in the massive national strike wave just as readily as their comrades elsewhere. Portland craft unions also encouraged considerable labor radicalism. The leaders of the city's American Federation of Labor, for instance, cooperated with the IWW during its first regional strike in 1907. The AFL *Portland Labor Press* for several years had a "Department of Socialism" that on one occasion tried to explain to confused members of the "middle class" that socialists *did* believe in private property—just not in capitalism. Although Portland's labor leaders did not appreciate the appearance of the city's Soviet-inspired Council of Workers, Soldiers, and Sailors, the Central Labor Council did sponsor the 1923 appearance of Eugene Debs. Debs's visit came at a time when both mainstream AFL leaders and Communists alike were disrupting his attempts to rebuild the Socialist Party.[22]

In one critical respect, the mainstream Portland labor movement, despite its eclectic radicalism, rarely did break out of the traditional AFL mold. When John Commons pressed Portland Central Labor Council secretary E. J. Stack—one of the most important labor progressives in the city—about efforts the city's AFL had taken to organize the "common unskilled" workers, Stack had to admit that his unions had done almost nothing. As elsewhere, the unorganized constituted the vast bulk of the working class in Portland, and despite the advent of the new labor history, we still know hardly anything about them compared to their unionized counterparts.[23]

We can, though, recognize two distinctive qualities about the majority of the city's workers outside of the unions. The first is Portland's prominent role as an employer of Chinese labor. Although the leading historian of this issue has claimed that the "Chinese never constituted serious competition for white labor," Portland's white laborers did vigorously oppose their Asian brethren.[24]

Second, especially given the national role of Portland in protective labor legislation, it is important to note that the share of women in the city's workforce increased from 15 percent in 1900 to 24 percent in 1920. Fairly strict sexual segregation of the labor market prevailed. "Competition of women for positions usually filled by men seems to be very slight," reformer Caroline Gleason noted, with women concentrated in the manufacturing of clothing and fruit and vegetable processing as well as in domestic service and boarding. Women remained, in the main, unorganized, although by the end of the 1920s one-third of the labor bodies in the state did admit female members. Women also made significant inroads into the lower-level white-collar occupations. In 1910, for example, more than two thousand worked in the semi-professions of music, teaching, and nursing, and another six thousand were retail clerks or staffed the lower echelons of corporate bureaucracies. With this kind of difficult-to-classify worker, however, it comes time to begin the transition from "working class" to "middle class."[25]

Introducing the Lower Middle Class

The bulk of Portland workers, then, remained unskilled and organized. Still, the relative power, and radicalism, of the organized Portland proletariat, despite the strength of the city's bourgeoisie, points toward an unexpected complexity in the class relations of the Rose City. The surprises we can find grow even larger as we begin our exploration of this middle-class city's middling folks. When historians have looked for a middle class, they have far too often tended to allow a professional elite to serve as a proxy for the entire middle class. In Portland, however, the more numerous, and ultimately the more politically significant, part of the middling population was its lower segment. This "lower middle class" of small-scale merchants and manufacturers, clerical workers, and lower-level professionals had a solid material base in the city's economic structure. Its members are difficult to locate in the records that have come down to us. Still, the idea of a lower middle class, used flexibly, both demonstrates the distinctive nature of Portland politics and allows us to use Portland as an opportunity to rethink our entire conception of class relations and the middle class in modern America.

"The" lower middle class is a beast that has rampaged through the pages of world, and especially European, history. Although most historians agree that members of the lower middle class frequently played determinative roles in the great nineteenth-century revolutions, until recently scholars of all political and intellectual stripes have assigned to this analytical concept-turned-monster much of the responsibility for fascism and Nazism. Before census records and city directories from Portland can begin to speak in a different way about these dangerous people, it will therefore be necessary to reflect on the European historiographical record. For as Jim Scott has noted, the lower middle class has suffered (with the exception of the lumpen proletariat) "the worst press of any class."[26]

The Marxist Arno Mayer has most sweepingly argued for the importance of a coherent lower middle class in modern history. In an influential 1975 article Mayer maintained that the transatlantic lower middle class had throughout the nineteenth and twentieth centuries—and continues today—to have a unified culture and set of political behaviors that allowed it to hold a "crucial swing position" in "the battle for control of the modern state." Mayer challenged historians to see the United States not as the middle-class country of legend but as perhaps the most *lower*-middle-class country in the world. Yet scholars have unfortunately not engaged this daring reconceptualization of our national identity. Thus European and American history retain in this realm the exceptionalist disjunction that other scholars have worked so hard to undermine.[27]

How would we know "the" lower middle class if we set out to find it? Here is Mayer's "preliminary and tentative definitional statement":

the lower middle class can be said to be composed of individuals (1) who earn their living by work that is not preeminently manual labor requiring steady physical exertion and that demands a minimum of alphabetization; (2) who by objective criteria (of income, wealth, education, residence, etc.) are neither upper nor lower class; (3) who are singularly self-conscious about being neither one nor the other, but aspire upward; (4) who are inclined to be highly individualistic in their pursuit of upward mobility; (5) who consider private property to be sacrosanct; (6) who are glaringly susceptible to personal co-optation and patronage; (7) who are bent on protecting or improving the life chances of their children; (8) who ultimately and particularly in situations of stress are more fearful of sinking down or back into dishonorable trades or manual labor than eager to rise into the absolute middle class; and (9) who coalesce for concerted political action only in such times as severe stress.

Two occupational strains thus merge into the lower middle class—the independent small property owners such as master artisans, craftsmen, farmers, petty retailers, and small manufacturers often known as the "old" middle class (or petite bourgeoisie) and the lower level of the new middle class of "predominantly dependent clerks, technicians, and professionals." This much we could gather from a considerably shorter definition than Mayer provides; we would need only the first and second of the characteristics that he lists.[28]

As Mayer's extended definition implies, however, he and most other intellectuals have provided the lower middle class with an a priori culture and politics. No class, however, has a predetermined politics, and we therefore have to formulate a much more flexible conception of the lower middle class. Here the ideas of Richard Hamilton, the wisest and broadest scholar of this group, become helpful. Hamilton simply states that the loose "rule-of-thumb definition" of the lower middle class is "the less well paid segments of the middle class or white-collar population." Hamilton's insight provides the core for my own empirical insights about a category that Progressive Era Americans themselves used.[29]

Contours of Class III: The Small-Scale Universe of Portland Manufacturing

At least a part of the reason that American historians have shied away from using the concept of the lower middle class is because of contemporary census categories for occupations. These classifications almost always speak indirectly at best about the usual indices of class: position in the mode of production, wealth, and income. Still, we can infer from the census some evidence that strongly hints at the strength of the lower middle class in Portland. One not unexpected clue is that the percentage of clerical workers in the male workforce—a crucial core of the "new" middle class—went up nearly 30 percent in the decade of generally slow economic growth from 1910 to 1920.[30]

Much more striking evidence of lower-middle-class vitality, however, comes from the composition of Portland's manufacturing sector. Despite the primacy of commerce in the Rose City, manufacturing expanded considerably throughout the period. Over a quarter of the city's wage labor force found employment in the manufacturing sector in 1900, and more than a third (40 percent of all males) did so in 1910 and 1920.[31]

What made Portland's industrial base distinctive, and what explains the apparent discrepancy between the relative insignificance of manufacturing to the city's economy and its importance in employment, was the extraordinary strength of small-scale firms in most industries. By examining the structure of manufacturing in Portland, we can see that the city represented—at least as late as World War I, and in many ways through the 1920s—something of a small property holder's paradise.

The sheer number of manufacturing firms in Portland during the early twentieth century provides a key measure of the social weight of small business. As table 2 (in appendix 1) shows, more than a thousand manufacturing and mechanical enterprises existed in the city in 1899, including the types of "neighborhood" industries like construction that future censuses would unfortunately not include under the manufacturing category. Nearly twelve hundred firm members and proprietors owned these enterprises. Portland workers thus possessed a quite good opportunity to own an establishment. One out of every forty members of the workforce, and one out of every thirty-five members of the male workforce, owned a *manufacturing* enterprise (much less a business in another sector). Among only those members of the workforce in the manufacturing sector, nearly one out of every *seven* owned and operated a firm. A decade later, in 1909, the chance to become a small enterpriser had diminished by almost half, primarily as an artifact of the census redefinition of the manufacturing sector. Still, the fact that at least one out of every fourteen members of the industrial workforce owned and operated a firm remains impressive for an age that most immediately brings to mind Andrew Carnegie and John D. Rockefeller.[32]

The great majority of Portland's manufacturing firms were small. The Census Bureau reported firm-level data only for the state as a whole, but with caution we can let this information serve as a rough indication of the character of business enterprise in the state's leading metropolis. In both 1904 and 1909 the value of the products of more than a third of the state's manufacturing firms was less than five thousand dollars, over 70 percent of the firms had product values less than twenty thousand dollars, and over 90 percent less than one hundred thousand dollars. These figures hold for even the most highly capitalized industry in the state, lumber and timber products. Not surprisingly, then, Oregon manufacturing firms on the whole had a relatively small number of employees. In 1909 none employed over 1,000 wage earners, three employed over 500, and only sixteen in the entire state employed more than 250. On the other hand, more than one-tenth of the state's manufacturing firms employed *no* wage earners, more than half employed between 1 and 5 wage earners, and nearly 90 percent employed fewer than 20. Noncorporate ownership accompanied smallness in scale. In 1909 individuals or noncorporate firms operated 71.5 percent of the state's manufacturing enterprises, down only slightly from a figure of 74.5 percent in 1904.[33]

The remarkable persistence of small-scale enterprise in Portland manufacturing comes out even more compellingly when we examine industry-wide census data for the city itself. Although some firms in Portland of course got bigger in the early twentieth century, all the way through the 1920s no general qualitative leap in size occurred. Most industries consisted mainly of shops and small-scale factories with employees whom one could literally count on the fingers of one pair of hands—or perhaps two. As table 3 shows, the average number of workers per firm in the manufacturing and mechanical sector in 1899 was a mere 8.1. Over the next few years that figure more than doubled, but it then stabilized, so that the average firm size in 1929 was 20.2 employees—a level actually *below* that of 1909.

Even more impressive is the number of firms in industries with modest workforces. For example, as table 4 reveals, from 1899 to 1914 between 89 and 97 percent of all manufacturing firms were in industries where the average firm employed fewer than 25 workers. As late as 1929, that figure remained almost two-thirds. The flip side of these figures is that 80 percent of all manufacturing employees in 1899, and 70 percent in 1914, worked in industries with an average firm size less than 25 (see table 5). Large firms had taken a much more commanding position in the labor market by the end of World War I. Still, with the exception of lumber, which accounted for one-quarter of all manufacturing employment, *all* Portland non-war-related manufacturing employees in 1919 worked in industries where the average firm size was less than 100. And in the 1920s, the percentage of firms in industries with an average workforce higher than 50 was actually slightly *less* than in the previous decade.

Certain industries well illustrate the continued primacy of small-scale enterprise in the sector—manufacturing—where historians are least likely to look for it. Portlanders produced commodities ranging from candy to machine tools in small shops. In the sweet consumer age just dawning, confectionery manufacturers averaged under 7 employees per firm in 1899. Thirty years later, that figure had expanded only to 12.5. The far more technological world of foundry and machine shop products was of broadly similar size—12 workers per firm in 1900, decreasing to fewer than 9 per firm in 1914 (half that of the confectionery industry!), and reaching only 19.8 in 1929. Even the city's acclaimed lumber mills, far and away Portland largest employers, had an average workforce of just over 90 employees in both 1899

Fourteen employees in front of the Mt. Hood Soap Company in 1927. (Courtesy Oregon Historical Society, #13036.)

and 1909, with that figure nearly doubling by 1914. The industry did not, however, expand significantly in the aftermath of World War I. With fewer than 240 workers per factory in the city's largest line of business at the end of the 1920s, the Rose City was no Homestead on the Pacific.[34]

Nor, in the persistence of small-scale employment, was Portland out of line with economic trends in the modern age. As sociologist Mark Granovetter has established, most Americans throughout the twentieth century worked in small firms, and indeed "the size of the workplace has hardly changed since 1920." Little wonder, then, that old-time Portlanders remember their lives saturated with small enterprise. Sunnye Nicholson relived her nostalgia in a 1976 oral history interview, remembering the southeast neighborhood of Sellwood during the early twentieth century as "just full of small family businesses, and everybody seemed to know everyone else. . . . There were dry-good stores, bakeries, meat shops, and grocery stores—millinery shops—and everyone was friendly." Perhaps a rosy memory of childhood, with all its limitations, can turn out to be more accurate than the usual scholarly expropriation of the twentieth-century petite bourgeoisie.[35]

Miss Nellie E. Munger's Millinery, 748 Thurman, between 1907 and 1909. Munger is probably on the left. In 1914, eighty-five millinery businesses and 277 dressmakers operated in Portland (*CD, 1914*). (Courtesy, Oregon Historical Society, #51095, #1734.)

Triumph of the Petite Bourgeoisie:
The Printing Industry in Portland

The printing industry serves as the best illustration of the persistence and power of small-scale enterprise within Portland's manufacturing sphere. Printing is particularly significant, because the distinctive petit bourgeois milieu of the industry produced Will Daly, the prominent labor leader and small business radical who nearly became mayor in 1917.[36]

Despite the hoopla associated with Oregon's export-oriented industries, printing quietly secured for itself a position as the second leading employer within the manufacturing sector in both the state and the city of Portland in the predepression decades. In the role printing played within the city's economy, Portland was not terribly dissimilar to Chicago, the economic giant of the age, nor to New York, where printing remained the second largest industry throughout the teens and twenties. And during this period, printing was actually the largest industry in Atlanta.[37]

The dominant tone set by small-scale enterprise within printing is just as remarkable as the industry's overall prominence. As the Census Bureau reported for the state as a whole, in printing, as in baking, "the majority of the establishments are small and the work is to a large extent done by the proprietors or their immediate representatives." Firm-level data again provides a useful sense of size. Although certain printing establishments got quite large in the course of the early twentieth century—the *Oregonian* was already by the 1880s one of the largest nontransportation employers in the entire region—the average number of employees in Portland printing firms remained small. The average number of wage earners per firm expanded from 5 in 1899 to 7.4 a decade later and then stabilized at just about that figure all the way through 1929. Salaried clerks made up a considerable part of the printing labor force, constituting more than half the employees in the newspaper and periodical printing sector by 1914. Yet even counting them, the total average workforce engaged in printing firms rose gently over the course of the period, from 7.1 in 1899 to 12.7 in 1909, and then up only to 16.0 in 1929. The printing business was the crown jewel in the industrial structure of a city that provided extraordinary opportunity for productive small property ownership.[38]

Female participation in the printing workforce was relatively high, possibly because of the small-scale nature of employment within the industry. Data in table 8 indicate that the percentage of female wage earners in the printing industry as a whole never rose above 13 percent, although in 1919 it did get close to 20 percent in the smaller-scale book and job sector. Still, a comparison to the lumber and flour industries is instructive. In 1919, a minuscule 103 out of 4,266 workers in the former and 18 out of 440 workers in the latter were women. Figures for the clerical workforce also indicate the potential for (relative) egalitarianism in the printing industry. By 1919 over one-third of the clerks within Portland printing as a whole, and fully 54 out of 117 in the book and job sector, were women. A comparison with the composition of labor in the baking industry tentatively confirms that it was the small-scale nature of printing enterprises that was a factor in the high level of female participation in that industry's workforce. In 1919, the sixty-one highly proprietary bakeries in Portland employed just under 20 workers per firm. Over 30 percent of both clerical and wage labor was female.[39]

The reasonably high level of involvement of women in Portland's printing enterprises was not the result of the exploitation of low-wage labor within the industry. Although we have hardly any direct evidence of the quality of relationships between employer and employees in Portland print shops, we can make some important inferences from what we do know about the printing business in the Rose City and elsewhere. When, for example, the counsel for the Commission on Industrial Relations asked the prominent Portland labor leader E. J. Stack to name the best organized unions in the city, Stack listed the printers and cigar makers. "They have what they call a 100 percent

Workers at the Modern Printing Company, 86½ Broadway. (Courtesy Oregon Historical Society, #29142.)

organization," Stack replied. Closed-shop status enabled printers to gain, along with the men's clothing trade, the most favorable hours of any industry in the entire state. The Portland printing unions had won the eight-hour day, with apparently little opposition from employers, in 1904. Meanwhile, the number of women in Multnomah Typographers Union No. 58, the main printers local in Portland, increased from 185 in 1903 to 350 less than a decade later.[40]

Moreover, the strength of unionism in the Portland printing industry did not arise from any persistent antagonism. After a lockout during the 1880s, no major struggles affected the industry. If evidence from other cities is a reliable guide, then excellent labor relations in the printing industry grew directly out of the mutual regard of small employers and their workers. Ava Baron, for example, has noted that in the mid–nineteenth century many printers "sympathized with the problems of their employers who worked alongside them, rather than view them as class enemies. These journeymen saw the large-scale capitalist, not their petty bourgeois employer, as their enemy." These "class" relations were by no means simply an artifact of an artisanal economy on its deathbed. Irene Tichenor has demonstrated how small-scale New York printers, in the aftermath of a bitter 1906 strike, broke ranks with the open-shop employers' association and formed a rival and ultimately more successful Printers' League that insisted on the closed shop, the eight-hour day, and systematic arbitration largely as a matter of "justice." Such a relation of solidarity between petit bourgeois employers and their employees must have profoundly shaped the life and politics of Will Daly.[41]

Portland's Small Businesses in Comparative Perspective

Perhaps Portland's status as a small business paradise was an anomaly. In order to investigate—and, as it turns out, overturn—such a claim, we must place Portland's petite bourgeoisie in comparative perspective. It is difficult to do so, because historians, who have understandably been dazzled by the growth of corporations, have not yet provided systematic evidence of this era's urban business structure. Still, we can begin to note both some of the distinctiveness of the economic world of Portland's petite bourgeoisie as well as the ways in which Portland conformed to surprising national trends.

By many standards, the crucial role that small enterprise played in Portland looks like a minor exception to the dominant trends in the American economy, best articulated in Alfred Chandler's classic statements of the late-nineteenth-century corporate revolution. James Livingston, for example, provides data pointing to the "eruption" of corporate capitalism as it supplanted a competitive entrepreneurial market system in just six to eight short years around the turn of the century. Less than 1 percent of all manufacturing establishments in 1905 controlled over a third of all capital and employed more than a quarter of all wage earners in the manufacturing sector; 10 percent of the establishments controlled 80 percent of the capital and 70 percent of the wage earners. Four years later less than 5 percent of all manufacturing firms employed nearly two-thirds of the workers. Out of the "wreckage" of small business, Livingston argues, "the large industrial corporation had become the dominant structural element in the American economy" no later than 1909.[42]

The economists David Gordon, Richard Edwards, and Michael Reich offer local evidence to clinch the point. As early as 1850 in Philadelphia, for instance, more than 40 percent of all workers labored in firms with more than 51 employees, and that figure went up to nearly two-thirds by 1880. Roughly comparable figures from Portland show that as late as *1929* only *one-fifth* of wageworkers worked in industries where the average firm size was over 50 (see table 5). And in the twentieth century the size of most Philadelphia industries dwarfed those in Portland. The average Philadelphia iron and steel firm employed 333 workers at the turn of the century; the largest employer in Portland, the lumber industry, employed just over 90 up through 1909. Across the nation, Mansel Blackford points out, "By 1914, nearly a third of all industrial workers found employment in plants with 500 or more in their labor forces, and another third in those with 100 to 499." Even more overwhelming evidence comes from the size of the nation's largest

George Skoog's grocery at 631 Mississippi, ca. 1917. (Courtesy Oregon Historical Society, #7214.)

factories, which rose from around 1,500 workers per establishment in 1880 to anywhere from 20,000 to 60,000 in the 1920s. Such factories were literally in a different universe from Portland's diminutive economic life.[43]

Yet all the world is not Philadelphia, and we must have the wisdom to resist the teleology of bigness that this kind of information apparently points toward. For the petite bourgeoisie did not merely survive during the coming of corporate capitalism; in many ways small business thrived. The best illustration of its persistence nationally comes from the late nineteenth century. Harold Livesay has argued that, in sectors outside of transportation, manufacturing, and banking, petty enterprises remained supreme. By the turn of the century, Livesay remarks, "the great majority of Americans went about their daily affairs dealing infrequently, if ever, with big business directly." He notes that "small businesses still supplied employment for nearly two-thirds of the 27 million Americans working in 1900." The creation of businesses exceeded the growth of the population, but the rate of business failure barely increased. Although a majority of workers employed in the manufacturing sector toiled in large firms, even many industrial fields remained impervious to concentration. And outside manufacturing, Susan Strasser has found that as late as 1923 two-thirds of all retail stores in the United States were small "mom-and-pop" operations. We can only imagine, then, the economic and cultural weight that the 728 grocery stores in 1914 (1,055 in 1926), or the 916 realtors and realty companies, or even the 351 music teachers, provided the Portland petite bourgeoisie.[44]

As these numbers indicate, no dramatic reversals of the economic position of small business occurred in the early twentieth century either, despite the concerns of contemporaries and later scholars about the triumph of Big Business. Self-employed business owners (other than farmers and professionals) more than doubled in number to 2.6 million over the entire period from 1880 to 1920, although their share of the total workforce, 8.2 percent in 1900, did decline to 6.5 percent two decades later. A different calculation, though, pushes the self-employment figures significantly higher. As table 9 shows, combining professionals and small business owners in the self-employed category of the *non*farm labor force allows us to see that it was only in 1920 that the ratio of self-employed in the urban workforce dipped below one in ten. Taking into account only men, the percentage of the self-employed outside the farm sector declined only from 13.5 in 1910 to 12.0 even as late as *1950.*[45]

Clearly, then, an expropriation of the petite bourgeoisie never took place in America, despite the constant cry of doom relating to small business. We might also take note, in terms of intellectual politics, that the number of histories of the unionized working class in the United States overwhelms that of self-employed business owners, despite the fact that the petite bourgeoisie rivaled, and often surpassed, the number of unionists. For example, in 1910 8.8 percent of the nonagricultural workforce was unionized, compared to a self-employment rate of 10.6 percent.[46]

With the weight of this data, the structure of business in Portland begins to look much more "normal," even if the glamour goes to the huge factories of the industrial heartland. And once we stop marginalizing small enterprises, they spring up phoenixlike in even the strangest of places. Again, take Chicago, where large-scale business supposedly had no rivals in the construction of a modern economy. Yet as Andrew Cohen has shown, a traditional "craft economy" linking small employers and unionists controlled wide swaths of the Windy City's economic life, particularly in the overwhelmingly proprietary areas of retailing, service work, construction, and teaming. Or take a look at the numbers for other great metropolises (see tables 10, 11, and 12). Cities like Cleveland, with an average manufacturing firm size rising from 45.9 in 1909 to 58.3 in 1927, had significantly larger businesses than the Rose City. Yet throughout this same period New York, Denver, and Los Angeles had average firm sizes comparable to Portland's, and by 1927 the average manufacturing business in these three cities employed *fewer* workers than in Portland. The portion of workers laboring in New York industries employing fewer than twenty-five workers actually *increased* by more than

150 percent, to 57.3 percent, between 1909 and 1927. In its "middle-class" petit bourgeois blandness, Portland was typical of a business structure we have simply not been willing to discover.[47]

This exploration of Portland manufacturing can, of course, provide us with only a glimpse into one small segment of the multifaceted world of the lower middle class. That segment is usually termed the "old middle class," old not just in relation to the new white-collar salaried bureaucratic work-force, but also because it was supposedly reaching the end of its useful life. Unfortunately, we do not have the same kinds of records available to study the composition of the "new" middle class—or, again, even the multitude of business owners in realms outside of manufacturing. Still, what we can learn from the strength of Portland's small business is that once we have labeled a city "middle-class," such naming tells us little—besides indicating our need to break out of hoary stereotypes. And once we have resurrected a dying petite bourgeoisie, we can turn to a dramatic reconceptualization of Portland's political economy that reveals not only a strong solidarity between middling folks and workers, but also even a middle-class spirit of anti-capitalism.

CAPITALISM, ANTICAPITALISM, AND THE SOLIDARITY OF MIDDLE CLASS AND WORKING CLASS

A Republican Political Economy in a Corporate Age

One critical conclusion arises from the exploration of Portland's class structure. As in almost all other cities in the United States, a simple polarization between "the business class" and "the working class"—to use the Lynds' terms from *Middletown*—much less between bourgeoisie and proletariat, simply does not describe the city's social relations. The simultaneous increase of corporate and elite power and the continued viability of small business, as well as the fairly solid organization into unions of skilled white male workers amidst a proletariat critically divided by race and gender, all point to the axis of class division and social conflict occurring along lines we can more accurately describe with the concept of a "republican political economy" than with liberal or Marxist models.

The concept of a republican political economy comes from scholars in political science who have drawn on recent work in social and labor history. Noting the vitality of republican ideology among workers and other subordinate groups in nineteenth-century America, these scholars have convincingly removed the inevitability from the coming of modern corporate America. Instead, as Gerald Berk has insisted, decisive political struggles at all levels of the government in the late nineteenth and early twentieth centuries, from the presidency and the Supreme Court on down, revolved around a conflict over whether "large-scale, centralized" industrial corporations, operating within national markets, or a "flourishing and innovative smallholder economy," based on regional markets and often cooperative principles, would triumph. And politics—not just technology or managerial organization—was crucial to the outcome of this struggle.[1]

From this perspective, the corporate and noncorporate sides were quite evenly matched. Republican economic visions remained viable, realistic alternatives that had constituencies ranging from struggling artisans to figures as powerful as Louis Brandeis. Victoria Hattam has made the most compelling argument about the qualities and strength of the republican outlook. According to Hattam, the late-nineteenth-century American labor movement split along intensely ideological lines. The eventual victor was the American Federation of Labor, with its exclusive class-conscious defense of workers' rights. In contrast, dominant in the labor movement throughout much of the post-bellum period was a "producers' vision" that animated such organizations as the Knights of Labor. Unlike the AFL, which ended up accepting a class structure with corporate capitalists at the top and a proletariat below, republicans such as the Knights sought to unite those who could maintain a middling propertied independence (whether in the form of skilled trade or petty productive capital) against the emerging corporate elite.[2]

Government policy based on this vision of a "republican political economy" promised to break up the monopolies that had supposedly come to control public lands, transportation, communication, and, most critically, money. Antimonopoly action would bring decentralized markets, with small firms in control of production. Indeed, an alliance between small manufacturers and skilled workers "lay at the heart of the producers' vision." A republican "middle class"—considerably different from any middle class in Gilded Age and Progressive Era history books—thus became the locus of resistance to corporate capitalism, and, perhaps, even to "capitalism" itself.[3]

The alliance between small business owners and workers is what contemporary trade unionists, as well as latter-day historians, pounced on as evidence of conservatism, and even delusion, on the part of labor reformers. Yet this idea of a republican political economy helps explain many characteristics of social relations in Portland—including petit bourgeois radicalism—that appear to us, a century later, as rather inexplicable.

The Solidarity of Middling Class and Working Class

Above all, the consistently high level of support that members of the Portland middle class gave strikers and labor unions throughout the Progressive Era, and beyond, demonstrates the continued strength of the "historical bloc" of republican petty producers that Jackson Lears has argued contended for but failed to gain hegemony in nineteenth-century America. Such solidarity occurred during a period when even those scholars most sympathetic to the republican alternative to corporate capitalism are sure the game was already up. In Portland, though, middling folks chose their allies in ways that greatly illuminate the continuities between nineteenth- and twentieth-century political economy.[4]

Unfortunately, the orthodoxy about the relationship between labor and the middle class, particularly its small business component, remains cut in Marxism and dried in ahistoricity. The radical economists Gordon, Edwards, and Reich, for example, point to a powerful early-twentieth-century coalition of small business owners, workers, Progressives, and Socialists that effectively mobilized against corporations. Yet on one rock alone the alliance was supposedly doomed to shipwreck. As Gordon and his colleagues remark, "big and small capitalists were united on one major issue: Both opposed unions and sought to limit or destroy them." Their argument is not surprising, since the three economists have figured out the essential motivation of all petty capitalists. Simply put, forever and ever: "Small businessmen dream of joining the ranks of big business, with its status."[5]

Such an outlook, however, does not at all represent social life in modern America. As Harold Vatter has noted, even the AFL, which welcomed the inevitability of the new corporate order, confined "its membership largely to the skilled workers in the small enterprise activities of the economy." David Brody explains that throughout the twentieth century unions helped petty enterprises rationalize their labor costs and organization, giving small business a fundamental advantage in the realm of labor relations. On the local level, Michael Kazin has argued that the strongest labor movement in the country during the Progressive Era, San Francisco's, depended on the vitality of a business environment dominated by small manufacturers producing for a regional market. As Kazin notes, "Proprietors of locally owned, long-existing firms knew that labor's aims were popular in the general community; even when employers fought a particular union, they usually defended the principle of unionism itself." And Andrew Cohen has made it clear that in Chicago, small businesses predominated in the most highly unionized sectors of the economy.[6]

The highest irony about these class relations is the surprise they continue to bring to historians. Because decades ago, Herbert Gutman plainly demonstrated the depth of community—indeed solidly middle-class—support for strikers during the Gilded Age. As early as 1966 Gutman questioned "the belief that urban property owners as a group shared a common ideology in responding to the severe dislocations resulting from rapid industrialization and in reacting to the frequent disputes between workers and factory owners." As Gutman insisted, "Because a grocer owned his business and a mayor presided over a bank, it does not mean they sympathized with the social policies of a large factory owner." Gutman's evidence for the density of support that shopkeepers, professionals, and other members of the middle class (and even local elites) provided striking workers was remarkable.[7]

Despite labor historians' general neglect of the relationship between middling folks and workers, some recent scholarship has demonstrated the widespread, and politically significant, support that strikers received from the middle class at least through the turn of the century. Most substantively, Lawrence Lipin has revealed the impressive nature of middle-class support for workers in Evansville and New Albany, Indiana during the Civil War and Gilded Age. In terms of larger cities, Sarah Henry has shown uniform and strong community support of the Knights of Labor among small property owners, professionals, and local politicians during a disruptive Brooklyn trolley strike in 1895. Similarly, Steven Piott has revealed how during the St.

Louis streetcar strike of 1900 there "developed a cross-class sense of community consciousness that was in many cases as remarkable as the examples of worker solidarity." Likewise, in Portland, Maine street railway workers had nearly complete public support during a bitter 1916 strike. In a more industrial realm, the *Chicago Socialist* noted during a 1902 strike against the city's packinghouses, "It . . . is certainly undeniable that most of the sympathizers who took an active part in the disturbances were well dressed people, many of whom from their appearance belonged to the little middle class. A canvas of the small store keepers undertaken by some of our party members, showed that this class was almost unanimous in favor of the strikers."[8]

What are we to make of these findings? Leon Fink fully recognizes the strong "petit bourgeois presence" in the Knights of Labor, and he properly celebrates the "blurring within it of sociologically determined class lines" as part of the order's "ambitious purpose to transform society, not just to improve the standing of one trade or another." James Livingston takes this analysis even further, arguing for the political, economic, and cultural centrality of the late-nineteenth-century producers' alliance among small business owners, skilled workers, and "jackleg farmers." "If there was a winner in the virtual class war of the 1880s and early 1890s," Livingston writes, "it was labor, not capital, mainly because strikers seemed always to have broad popular support from their communities." Both the small-propertied and the propertyless shared a "commitment to dispersed assets, competitive markets, and control of the property in one's labor power as the condition of self-determination"—in other words, "the political economy of republicanism." And the coming of the new corporate order completely depended, according to Livingston, on the purging and disciplining of this proletarian-friendly middle class.[9]

Livingston, however, presents no evidence of post-1900 petit bourgeois acquiescence. He, along with almost all other historians, simply assumes that they went over to the other side. Thus the testimony we have from Portland is all the more important, for it provides striking evidence of the support that the middle class continued to give to the working class, even at times of intense crisis, well into the twentieth century. Portland's middling folks did not, of course, support workers unanimously, but, given the prevailing scholarly orthodoxy, their attitudes and actions are still remarkable. The first important evidence comes from the earliest major labor conflict in the city's history. In 1890 workers in the building trades staged a general strike as part of a national effort to gain the eight-hour day. The work stoppage was big enough to be "crippling [to] the city's economy." Public support of the strikers, however, was nearly unanimous, as even the conservative *Oregonian* favored the workers' walkout. Many sympathetic contractors, including Sylvester Pennoyer, pulled out of their open-shop organization and organized a Master Builders' Association that sought to recognize the unions. With "the public's attitude in labor's favor," the carpenters, painters, plumbers, and trimmers gained their objective. Four years later, in a considerably different economic environment, Coxey's Army straggled through town, commandeering train equipment with the active blessing of now Governor Pennoyer. "On all these marching lines," contemporary chronicler Joseph Gaston noted, "the people sympathized with the marchers and furnished them food and shelter."[10]

Similar support continued to materialize well into the twentieth century. Many small employers sided with workers during a 1902 building trades strike. The public also gave its backing to female telephone operators during a bitter strike in the fevered year of 1919. Such solidarity could easily flow from the politics of the everyday. Or, at the very least, some workers and middling folks received confirmation of their mutual obligations on the Sabbath. In 1906, for example, Rev. C. S. Lapham of the East Side's Second Baptist Church "denounce[d] the oppressors of labor." The Reverend E. Nelson Allen of the Hawthorne Park Presbyterian Church went even further, contending that recent labor strikes "were the same as the struggle between the barons and their serfs" and that America's "aristocracy of wealth" was "more oppressive than any dividing line of birth that prevails in the old world."[11]

The Language of "Middle Class": Portland, 1916

Why did the Portland middle class, especially its small business owners, continue to show such solidarity with the working class? Beyond the supposed distinctiveness of Portland's social structure, the answer lies in the realm of ideology. Here an examination of the language of "middle class" that Portlanders articulated on just one occasion—in the midst of a major conflict in 1916 between small and large business—provides us with an impressive idea of the consciousness of those in the middle of the social order. And it bears noting how rarely even historians who choose to write about the middle class provide evidence that their subjects actually used the term, or had any other self-conception of themselves as "middle class," so once again the evidence from Portland is especially important.[12]

Latter-day historians who emphasize the monolithic conservatism of the American middle class had their counterparts in prewar Portland. Certainly, 1916 was not the safest of times to support labor. The economy was doing poorly, and World War I increasingly brought to the fore issues of preparedness and patriotism. Influential Portlanders had already begun to brand the leaders of the Central Labor Council with the label of treason for the CLC's militant opposition to preparedness. The CLC, for its part, went out of its way to cooperate with radicals, forging particularly harmonious relations with Socialists. With the local class war heating up, it makes sense that both extremes of the political spectrum recognized that the forces of order could count on the middle class. As the right-wing *Oregon Voter* assured its readers, "your real conservatives after all are largely represented in the middle classes, wage-earners and home-buyers." Patrick O'Halloran, a leader of Portland's tiny Socialist Labor Party remnant, agreed, albeit in different language— "Foolish and reactionary is the program of the middle class, who, to escape the power of concentrated wealth, attempt in vain to go back to the days of small-fry competition." No wonder that when Socialists put on a play about the current politics of the day, they cast not only Dick Welth, a Republican trust magnate, and Mary Drynow, a "Home Drudge," but Monroe Hasbeen, "Ex-Middle Class Democrat."[13]

Such clarity on this issue from both left and right, however, did not dissuade neighboring Clark County socialists from inviting to a summer picnic "their Portland comrades and business men." Nor did it prevent antimilitarists from feeling secure in their appeal for a producers' alliance against the war. In the Women's Department of the *Oregon Labor Press*, Lenna Stahl asked: "are the poor and middle classes expected to furnish dressings and bandages with the munitions of war sold to the belligerent nations by the greedy manufacturers of America"? The *Labor Press* reprinted a similar diatribe about the big-business foundations of war by a Chicago editor who declared, "Of course, the clerks, mechanics, laboring men, farmers, and the sons of the working and middle classes will have to man the battleships and fill out the ranks of the Army." Finally, the traditional paradigm about the middle class did not prevent the *Labor Press* from publishing a letter from an East Side physician a few weeks before the November elections. "Farmers, working men and women, and small business men," L. A. Kent beseeched, needed to vote against the "invisible government" of "big business."[14]

Labor's confidence in the petite bourgeoisie, and the middle class generally, arose not from a foolish belief in the American dream, but from concrete actions in the Portland drama of class struggle. During 1916 the recently formed Portland Chamber of Commerce, of which the Central Labor Council was initially a member, decided for the first time to take sides in a labor dispute. Refusing arbitration in a long-standing conflict between meatcutters and their employers, the chamber chose to use the occasion to press for the open shop. Instead of salivating at this enticing prospect, though, capital's junior members defected from the chamber and actively opposed what had become the principal organization of Portland's economic elite.[15]

In the midst of the confrontation, the editor of the *Labor Press* insisted that "thousands of small business men" had no voice in, and nothing to gain, from chamber policies. Fortunately for labor, small business owners also recognized the conflict of interests between themselves and associated large capital. In a referendum on its open-shop policy, the chamber received only one thousand replies from its forty-five hundred members, a response that union officials reasonably interpreted as a lack of support for the chamber's position at a time when former governor Oswald West and U.S. Senator George Chamberlain were actively denouncing the organization's actions. Tensions between small capital and large capital then burst into the open at the end of the year. As the populist *News* reported, "The Chamber of Commerce has declared war on the Grocers' and Merchants' association." The simmering dispute over the open shop resulted in jobbers and manufacturers who were chamber members declining to exhibit at the retailers' Food Fete because of the involvement of union carpenters. Mutual threats of "boycott" flew through the air as the grocers and merchants vowed to refuse to patronize open-shop jobbers and manufacturers. In turn, the president of the chamber of commerce threatened to retaliate against any business owners who attempted to split business ranks. Clearly the Portland petite bourgeoisie found unionization a principle well worth defending—and in a militant fashion.[16]

A letter to the *Labor Press* from one of the state's leading progressives, Judge Stephen Lowell, confirms the value Portlanders placed on fighting for the loyalty of those in the middle. The open-shop actions of the chamber of commerce infuriated Judge Lowell. Unions, according to this distinguished jurist, had a glorious history and fully benefited humanity generally as well as workers specifically. He then appealed to his fellows, declaring:

> May I suggest that the field of effort now by the members of the unions is not among business men, but to arouse the interest and sympathy of the great middle class, the vast majority of our population, who belong to neither the ranks of capital nor labor, as those terms are accepted. It is the men and women who are found there, who ultimately settle social and industrial problems. When aroused their numbers are such that they reflect the real public sentiment of a community, and public opinion in the last analysis controls in a republic.[17]

What Is Capitalism?

Judge Lowell's confidence in the ability of the middle-class public to assert itself in the context of strife between unions and big business may seem to skeptical historians like a deluded vision of social harmony. Yet put in the analytical perspective of a republican political economy, we can see that Lowell's statement, along with Portlanders' general language of class, spoke realistically to the role of middling folks in the struggle for power during the Progressive Era. And if we look even more deeply, we can see that some of the motivation for middle-class Portlanders' solidarity with workers likely flowed from a lack of consensus on the desirability of a capitalist social order. For even in the land of the Liberal Tradition, capitalism often lacked legitimacy, particularly among members of the petite bourgeoisie.

What, however, *is* capitalism? (And how could small business owners possibly be anticapitalist?) As with "middle class," "capitalism" is an essentially contested concept. Phyllis Deane remarks, capitalism's "definition—whether implicit or explicit—shows a chameleon-like tendency to vary with the ideological bias of the user." Even more bitingly, Arthur Schlesinger Jr. wrote long ago that "we might well banish the words 'capitalism' and 'socialism' from intellectual discourse. . . . They belong to the vocabulary of demagoguery, not to the vocabulary of analysis."[18]

Of course, many of the most important classical social theorists have quested for the true capitalism. In formulating my own definition, I draw, in an eclectic manner, upon the classical definitions and conceptualizations offered by Sombart, Weber, Tawney, and Schumpeter. With "class," I found an "anti-definition" most useful to unlock history. With "capitalism," however, I find most helpful a quite *peculiar* definition, one that asks us to make a sharp differentiation between an economic system based in private property and capitalism itself.[19]

First, it is important to recognize that the definition that relies most on common sense is one that emphasizes exchange. Peter Berger articulates this well when he states that capitalism is "production for a market by enterprising individuals or combines with the purpose of making a profit." Yet as Frederic Lane has written, "an exchange economy is not necessarily capitalistic. Not all commercial production is capitalistic production. One can distinguish between a simple commercial economy, or simple commodity production, and capitalistically organized production." Lane's insight is crucial to my conceptualization. For when we are defining capitalism, we must simultaneously—or even first—specify what it is *not*. The structural attributes we generally associate with capitalism, such as private property, distribution through abstract and generalized markets, the use of wage labor, and the pursuit of profit, do not necessarily lead to capitalism itself unless these attributes are given fairly free rein; for example, property rights need to be close to absolute, the pursuit of profit should be nearly unrestrained, and the use of wage labor should create a well-defined proletariat and bourgeoisie. As Alan Macfarlane writes, "The ethic of endless accumulation, as an end and not as a means, is the central peculiarity of capitalism." In turn, economic systems—no matter how involved in the truck and barter of an exchange economy—are not necessarily capitalist, if they simultaneously circumscribe what Robert Heilbroner characterizes as "the nature and logic of capitalism"—a process of ceaseless market competition whereby a small minority gains "domination . . . of the great majority who must gain 'employment.'"[20]

We can then view political economies heavily influenced by small business as—potentially—forms of Lane's *noncapitalist* simple commodity production. Ever since Louis Hartz and Richard Hofstadter made their compelling arguments that, in the phrasing of the latter, "the typical American was an expectant capitalist," we have failed to see that many small business owners were, like Alfred Winslow Jones's depression-era Akronites, actually anticapitalist. Perhaps perversely, we might compare them to the slaveholders of the Old South in a way pointed out by Elizabeth Fox-Genovese and Eugene Genovese. Shopkeepers and small manufacturers too were frequently "in but not of the bourgeois world." And, as the Portland single tax movement demonstrates, these "capitalists against capitalism" could, even in a twentieth-century world dominated by corporations, continue to use their economic ideology to generate significant and radical political challenges.[21]

Two very different intellectual heavyweights support this curious, but crucial, distinction between a genuine capitalism and an economy more substantially governed by petit bourgeois imperatives. Fernand Braudel remains the giant among historians of capitalism, with his massive three-volume *Civilization and Capitalism* serving as the capstone of a search for the economic underpinnings of human life over the last one thousand years.[22] Braudel noted that early in his career he believed that capitalism was undefinable, but he never found an adequate substitute for the term. The great *Annaliste* consistently emphasized commerce as the key to capitalism, which he argued should be "identified as the realm of investment and of a high rate of capital formation." Braudel made it clear, however, that not all—in fact generally not *much*—of exchange deserved the label *capitalism*. The operator of a stall at a street market, or a small dress manufacturer, each operating under fairly strict laws of competition, were in the Middle Ages and remain at the dawn of our millennium part of what Braudel characterizes as a distinct stratum: "the economy," or "the market economy." In contrast, "capitalism" grows on top of this vigorous realm, constituting an "anti-market . . . where the great predators roam and the law of the jungle operates." Capitalism is "sophisticated and domineering" in contrast to the market economy's "transparent" nature. Inherently monopolistic (despite its reputation for competition), capitalism constitutes "the high-profit zone" at the "very summit of society" and depends on "exploiting international resources and opportunities." This contrast matters politically as well as intellectually. Personally, Braudel spoke of his "regret . . . as a man of my time" seeking "the ideal society" that both sides during the Cold War refused to recognize this crucial "distinction between capitalism and the market economy."[23]

Karl Marx shared none of Braudel's romance with the market economy. Yet even more forcefully he argued that an economic system dominated by petty producers was *not* capitalism. To be sure, Marx did not primarily have in mind urban small business owners when he made this argument; he was addressing the "primitive accumulation" that expropriated peasants from their property holdings during colonization. Yet the discussion in the final chapter of the first volume of *Capital* makes clear that Marx completely scorned those who did not recognize that small property holders who relied primarily on their own labor were *not* capitalists. Marx begins:

> Political economy confuses on principle two very different kinds of private property, of which one rests on the producers' own labour, the other on the employment of the labour of others. It forgets that the latter not only is *the direct antithesis of the former*, but absolutely grows on its tomb only.

Societies in which producers controlled their own labor were "diametrically opposed" to and the "contrary" of "the capitalist regime." As long as workers remained in control of their means of production, Marx wrote, "capitalist accumulation and the capitalistic mode of production are *impossible*." Non-waged American farmers and artisans were a prime example of this kind of "queer people" who spread an "anti-capitalistic cancer." Marx ended volume 1 emphatically: "the capitalist mode of production and accumulation, and therefore capitalist private property, have for *their fundamental condition* the annihilation of self-earned private property; in other words, the expropriation of the laborer."[24]

For Marx, such an annihilation of the petite bourgeoisie would soon be complete. Yet we now know that this did not happen. And it still has not happened. When we define capitalism as Braudel and Marx have, as an economic system whose core is extensive wage labor employed by large enterprises seeking high profit by exercising their quasi-monopolistic privileges in the market, then most small business owners simply do not make it aboard the ship. We therefore continue to have a petit bourgeois "anti-capitalistic cancer" to diagnose. Queer indeed.[25]

Moral Economy: Not Just for Peasants Any More

> In the present strife between labor and its employer . . . the greater number of employers which the labor organizations come in conflict with do not comprise capitalists and never have had any right to think that they were capitalists. . . .
>
> Because a sheet metal worker works constantly and steadily for a number of years and saves from those years of privation and hard labor a small sum of money sufficient to buy a few tools and start a shop, [does that] make him a capitalist? . . .
>
> These men in Oregon who, in a small way, are accumulating a little money, should not run away with the idea that they are capitalists, or that their interests are any different on a final show down from the laborer.
>
> —*Portland Labor Press*, 1903

Now hold on a minute, the skeptical reader might say. All of the above represents theoretical sleight-of-hand, using fuzzy wordplay about capitalism to obscure the fact that the Babbitts of American history were hardly prepared to proclaim the petit bourgeois Commune. And even if we concede that Braudel and Marx are correct, we are still left with the American middle class's apparent belief in "the sanctity of private property, the right of the individual to dispose of and invest it, the value of opportunity, and the natural evolution of self-interest and self-assertion," that capitalist package which Richard Hofstadter arraigned for its creation of a "democracy in cupidity rather than a democracy of fraternity."[26]

True enough—to some degree. Braudel himself correctly asserts that "capitalism is unthinkable without society's active complicity." In the past, as well as today, most small business owners clearly have had a strong streak of acquisitiveness. (Is not the same true of most "workers," and even professors?) However, we need to convert into an *empirical* question the extent to which small enterprisers engaged in capitalist behavior, participated in capitalist economic structures, and—most crucially—gave their political assent to the capitalism all around them. To do this, we must first reverse course and set sail for America, that famous land where "capitalism came in the first ships," and examine the controversy about the transition to capitalism in early American history.[27]

Unless one is a rural historian, most scholars of the twentieth century have believed it safe to ignore the most vigorous debate about capitalism within the literature of American history. Why should we care about peasants from so long ago? Precisely, it turns out, because they help clarify the peculiar nature of capitalism in *all* of American history, especially as we think about small-propertied middling folk.

For more than two decades historians have focused on the *mentalité* of family farmers, exploring the extent to which exchange networks were communal or generalized, the degree to which familial imperatives reined in the profit motive, the ways in which accounts were kept and interest charged (or, quite often, not charged), and the reach of wage labor relations in the countryside.[28] Needless to say, scholars have been sharply at odds over these issues. James Henretta, Carolyn Merchant, Allan Kulikoff, Christopher Clark, Nancy Osterud, and many others have maintained that a "moral economy" effectively stymied capitalism until at least the late eighteenth century, and, according to Clark and Osterud, well into the nineteenth century. Just as firmly Stephen Innes, Winifred Rothenberg, Joyce Appleby, and Gordon Wood point to the expansive nature of market relations from the seventeenth century through the era of the early Republic, and they point to the enthusiasm with which Americans embraced what they characterize as an often-liberating capitalism.[29]

Can we reconcile these diverse viewpoints? Without denying their substantive differences, we should recognize the common ground that both sides do, reluctantly, share. Innes, for example, emphasizes that Puritan economic culture, although thoroughly imbued with capitalism, represented a communitarian and anti-"liberal" mix of "interest-motivated and altruistic-motivated action." New Englanders created "what some would call an oxymoron: moral capitalism." Religion, speaking in the name of justice, insured that "the ethics of the marketplace were never unchallenged." Joyce Appleby likewise emphatically marks the difference between her—Jeffersonian and democratic—capitalism and the later exploitative industrial variety. Capitalism, fresh and new in the 1790s, brought freedom, independence, and "a vision of classlessness," not a "hard-fisted, mean-spirited drive for profits." Even Gordon Wood, who is most corrosive in his criticism of the academic ethic and the spirit of anticapitalism, forcefully argues that what made capitalism possible was a vigorous civil society that helped "to temper and civilize the stark crudities of a market society" and that prevented full-blown profit maximization.[30]

If this moral, just, communitarian, antiliberal, tempered, civilized, classless, and democratic kind of economy deserves the name of capitalism, then perhaps there is not really so much to fight about in these historiographical wars after all. Even the scholars who argue for an alternative to capitalism in the early American countryside rarely deny rural folks' commitment to private property and their involvement in the market. As Daniel Vickers puts the case most sensibly, early American farmers attempted to balance competition with the goal of a "competency": a comfortable familial independence. This they defined as "the possession of sufficient property and skill to ensure free access to the means of production" so that they would not be forced to work in a continuous wage labor relationship. Commerce in and of itself was by no means an enemy of economic independence, then, but "monopoly," "privilege," and those—especially creditors—who irresponsibly used their power to oppress were.[31]

Vickers asserts that the idea of a competency based on propertied independence eventually died with industrialization. Yet the remarkably Jacksonian language of his pre-Revolutionary Americans should make us wary of such declension. Moreover, the economic philosophy of the Portland single taxers displays a striking continuity with these eighteenth-century sentiments, from a focus on propertied independence down to the shared dislike of land speculators and lawyers. The moral economy would outlast its agrarian context; it is truly not just for peasants any more.[32]

"Capitalists" against Capitalism

Progressive Era Portland was not Puritan New England, and we must be careful to note the differences of context. Still, we should begin to imagine Babbitt as a peasant. Or to put matters a bit more cautiously, it will be fruitful for us to think of the millions of small business owners in American history as rough equivalents of the early American "small producers" so much under scholarly scrutiny. And just as we can legitimately classify these rural folk as anticapitalist, so too can we begin to explore the possibilities of petit bourgeois anticapitalism.[33]

Arguably the most forceful, and certainly the most unconventional, voice in the debate over the transition to capitalism can help us bring this debate into the twentieth century. Michael Merrill asks us to return to the original definition of capitalism—a term unknown to Adam Smith and employed by Karl Marx only in unpublished form. First used extensively in radical working-class circles in the late nineteenth century, *capitalism* had a distinctly political connotation, for it meant an economy ruled by "capitalists" (a much older term, and one that referred to rich merchants and the financial aristocracy). Therefore small enterprisers, even though committed to a market-based "commercial society," could serve as an effective political counterweight to the development of capitalism by placing "as much emphasis on equality as . . . on accumulation." The smallholders' democratic triumph, the American Revolution, brought "to power a self-conscious class of small property holders who would resist dispossession and proletarianization for more than a century." As Merrill argues, before the Civil War small property owners "were not interested in encouraging the unlimited accumulation of private fortunes, or in expanding the most dependent forms of wage labor, or in increasing the financial opportunities available to the wealthy, or in commodifying everything. But they did want to protect the relatively widespread distribution of private property, to ensure that wage labor could continue to serve as a stepping stone to independent proprietorship, and to increase the financial opportunities available to the many." Merrill wisely comments, "commerce does not have to be organized to benefit only the Few, . . . [and a] commercial system run by or in the interests of farmers, mechanics and laborers deserves to be called something" other than capitalism.[34]

America's anticapitalist tradition, then, began with the people whom we have always seen as small-scale "capitalists." Alas, Merrill too kills off this petit bourgeois economy with the demise of the Populist remnant. This is a mistake, for small business owners who economically wished to balance competition with a competence, and who politically desired "to democratize property and to de-centralize power" have continued to play decisive roles in shaping the modern American political economy.

Nineteenth-century Americans often insisted on the distinction between middling folks and "capitalists." Consider, for example, the printer John Keogh of Fall River, Massachusetts, who forcefully took umbrage at the capitalist label. In 1883 Keogh testified before the United States Senate's Committee on Labor and Capital:

Q. Conducting business for yourself?

A. Yes, sir.

Q. Are you a capitalist?

A. No, sir. I was an operative for eleven years in the mills in Fall River.

Q. But you have a little establishment of your own now?

A. Yes.

Q. You are a capitalist then, to that extent you control yourself and your own money, and do your own business as you please?

A. Yes, but I do not consider myself a capitalist.[35]

The historian who has most impressively documented the material strength of such peculiar "capitalists" is Philip Scranton. In publications that have transformed the study of modern American economic history, Scranton has documented "a mature 'small business' alternative to industrial gigantism." According to Scranton, Philadelphia textile manufacturers had one supreme goal: in the parlance of the time, a "competence." The competence was the sign of "a curious sort of capitalist, one for whom accumulation had a determinate goal, a limit, a moment when one might . . . say 'Enough!'" Such a limit to accumulation had a direct effect on the quality of labor relations within the proprietary mode. Unlike the image of desperation-induced exploitation of workers often attached to petty capital, Philadelphia small business owners created for at least a good part of the nineteenth century a "paradise of the skilled workman by granting workers considerable autonomy, and by paying them well."[36]

Capitalism and the Populist Ideology: A Halfway Covenant

All that said, did these "capitalists against capitalism" go beyond their localistic economic strength and actually develop a substantive political *ideology* that was antagonistic to capitalism? Even Christopher Lasch, the most ardent defender of petit bourgeois anticapitalism, declared that the populist tradition "has generated very little in the way of an economic or political theory—its most conspicuous weakness."[37]

Yet this is simply not true. As scholars are finally beginning to recognize, nineteenth-century farmers, workers, and middling folk, with agrarian radicals in the lead, created not just economic counterinstitutions such as cooperatives but also a coherent set of alternative economic ideals. The Populists, above all, generated an impressive body of reflections on political economy that we can point to as the crowning achievement of middling anticapitalist thought. We still, however, filter too much of our thinking about Populist ideology through the lens of Richard Hofstadter's indictment of the agrarian myth. Because the farmers who were the backbone of the movement supposedly suffered from a "rampant, suspicious, and almost suicidal individualism," Hofstadter easily dismissed Populist politics as "petty capitalist" and simply "another episode in the well-established tradition of American entrepreneurial radicalism." And *The Age of Reform* has had a long shadow. As political theorist Richard Ellis describes the scholarly consensus, "Much is often made of Populism's 'propertied consciousness.' Chained to the Lockean rock, the Populists were unable to forge a fundamental alternative to capitalism."[38]

Yet if we look anew at the Populists' political economy from the perspective of Michael Merrill, not to mention Braudel, Marx, and the Portland labor movement, then we can reinterpret the Populists' dedication to small-scale property and moral market relations as an expression of—at the very least—an unfriendly critique of "capitalism" if not an outright repudiation of many of that beast's most important characteristics. Granted, almost all Populists believed in profit and property rights and were opposed to socialism. Listen, however, to W. S. Morgan: "Life is more sacred than property always and everywhere if the two are in peril, life should be saved if property perish. Capitalism places property above life, thereby declaring war upon humanity. This war must not cease until capitalism is vanquished and property becomes the servant, not the master of man."[39]

Most Populists did not use language as straightforward as Morgan's, but they did make clear their commitment to a small-scale moral economy that reined in competition, was critical of the system of wage labor, and was sympathetic to unionism. Perhaps above all, Populists denounced unlimited gain. As Ignatius Donnelly asserted, it was "right and wise and proper for men to accumulate sufficient wealth to maintain their age in peace, dignity, and plenty" but also desirable to "establish a maximum beyond which no man could own property." A North Carolinian reiterated the idea of a competence when he declared that Populists did "not wish to be rich but only want a reasonable chance that we may be able to go decent and respectable and educate our children."[40]

In turn, small-scale acquisitiveness dictated small-scale enterprise. Here the Populists made their biggest conceptual leap. To advance the cause of the petit bourgeois moral economy, the state would have to become much more active in economic affairs. Thus, when Marion Butler defended nationalization of the railroads, he maintained that the framers of the Constitution "took the position that any business that affected all or a great portion of the people, under circumstances where there could be no successful competition by men of small capital, was a *government function* and should be owned and operated by the government, at cost, for the benefit of all the people alike." Populists in this way created a two-tiered economic system. Most commerce would be small and market-based, but the trinity of land, transportation, and money would be subject to direct government ownership and control in order "to further legitimate the principle of popular determination, and to support nonmarket social ethics." In this way, the Populists assured that their petit bourgeois ideology would remain relevant for the twentieth century.[41]

Do we need to be concerned about the proper name for this "radically egalitarian critique of competitive individualism" that the Populists themselves called the Cooperative Commonwealth? The most significant scholars of Populist economic thought, Norman Pollack and Bruce Palmer, have wrestled with this problem and placed a tight hold on the Populists' embrace of "capitalism." Smartly using C. B. Macpherson's concept of a "simple market society" of small property owners who did not engage wage labor, Palmer agrees that these agrarian radicals were certainly no Rockefellers and Carnegies. Still, almost all Populists "accepted what they understood to be the basic American economic system—a simple market society with private property, profit, and economic competition among small producers." Palmer concludes, then, that the Populists "remained ultimately unwilling to surrender the fundamental premises of a capitalist society."[42]

Pollack is even more insistent on contending that the Populists were essentially moderate reformers, not radicals, because of their unwillingness to escape the Hartzian capitalist consensus. Yet Pollack does a terminological rain dance to keep his Populists inside the proper category. Populists articulated an economic faith in "direct opposition [to] the existing system of capitalism." Pollack calls the Populist vision "a public-centered capitalism," "a nonprivileged capitalism," and "a humanly fulfilling capitalism." He ends up calling them not only "capitalists of a subdued kind" but "American capitalists of the wrong sort." Queer people indeed, these Populists. Whatever we end up calling them, we must admit that the Populists—in forging such an effective halfway covenant—had fallen far away from the preachings of the capitalist clergy. In doing so, they made sure that the Question of Capitalism remained open at the turn of our century, even if scholars are only too willing to close down the shop.[43]

CHAPTER SIX

PETIT BOURGEOIS POLITICS IN PORTLAND AND WORLD HISTORY

Did the somewhat abstract issues of republican political economy, alliances between workers and middling folks, and the Question of Capitalism make a difference in the mundane realm of Portland's political arena? They did, as we can see through an exploration of the basic outlines of Portland's tumultuous municipal politics, which culminated in the near victory in the 1917 mayor's race of a remarkable petit bourgeois radical, Will Daly.

And these issues mattered far beyond the local level. They also proved to be some of the foundation stones for national politics. For example, the most important analysis of early-twentieth-century American political economy, Martin Sklar's *The Corporate Reconstruction of American Capitalism,* argues that advocates of small-propertied republicanism effectively stymied the restructuring of the governmental and legal system upon which successful corporate expansion depended. Victory came to the corporations only after compromise with small manufacturers and businessmen and the effective wooing of the new class of salaried white-collar employees. Even though Sklar in the end emphasizes the uprooting of the petite bourgeoisie, he effectively points out that the triumph of corporations occurred in spite of the powerful *opposition* of a middle class whose relationship to capitalism was truly up for grabs and which was prepared to exercise its democratic prerogatives.[1]

We need to follow up on that profound insight, extending the chronology beyond 1914 (where Sklar ends his story), preferably in local settings that will allow in-depth investigation of the way ordinary middling citizens experienced and attempted to reshape their changing social and political worlds. Yet the idea of a democratic modern lower middle class is so fundamentally at odds with our intellectual assumptions that we must first wrestle with the received wisdom on these matters that comes from the traditions of European historiography. Then, once we have banished at least some of the spectre of fascism from our supposedly common sense about the petite bourgeoisie, we can turn to a genuine reckoning with what should no longer seem like such an oxymoron: a *radical middle class.*

Rethinking the Folks Who Brought You Fascism:
The Historiography of Petit Bourgeois Politics

Earlier we saw that scholars such as Arno Mayer have defined the lower middle class as having an inherently reactionary politics. Antonio Gramsci laid out the indictment, alongside his savage scorn, as well as anyone: "In this its latest political incarnation of 'fascism,' the petty bourgeoisie has once again shown its true colours as the servant of capitalism and landed property, as the agent of counter-revolution. But it has also shown itself to be fundamentally incapable of accomplishing any historical task whatsoever. The Monkey-People make news, not history. They leave their mark in newspapers, but provide no material for books."[2]

Scholars such as Mayer and Hal Draper do give the petite bourgeoisie some credit for hostility to both bourgeoisie and proletariat; as Draper puts it, this intermediate class "is inherently Janus-like." Mayer praises the lower middle class for its democratic role in the great European revolutions up to 1848. Yet during and after 1848, and certainly by 1871, "the petite bourgeoisie increasingly looked in one direction only: backward." Mayer insists that lower-middle-class politics flows directly out of a "singularly cohesive" culture with hostility toward the working class at its heart. For both self-employed and salaried white-collar workers "the manual worker became the indispensable negative reference point." The resulting "*individual anxiety* and *collective fear* of downward mobility," according to Mayer, produces a "panic [at] the root of the erratic and intermittently frenzied politicization of the lower middle class."[3]

Mayer ends his indictment, indeed demonization, of the lower middle class with the statement: "Although it may waver along the way, in the final analysis the lower middle class resolves its ambiguous and strained class, status, and power relations with the power elite above and the underclass below in favor of the ruling class. It is this inner core of conservatism, ultimately revealed in moments of acute social and political conflict, that is common to all segments of the lower middle class and that justifies treating them as a coherent phenomenon and as a significant historical problem." In this reading, still the dominant one among intellectuals, Nazism almost becomes the least of the horrible problems for which we can pin responsibility on the lower middle class—the entire inegalitarian structure of modern life rests on the cramped aspirations of these middling folks. No wonder that that arbiter of current intellectual fashion, Pierre Bourdieu, can so easily deride millions of people when he declares: "The petit bourgeois is a proletarian who makes himself small to become bourgeois. . . . It is no accident that the adjective *petit* (small) or one of its synonyms can be applied to everything the petit bourgeois says, thinks, does, has or is, even to his morality."[4]

We must, however, escape what Brazilian political theorist Roberto Unger has called this "false necessitarianism" that has for a century structured intellectuals' thinking about petit bourgeois politics. As Peter Bailey has written, "putting the boot in on the lower middle class has long been the intellectuals' blood sport, an exorcism, so we are told, of the guilty secret so many of us share as closet petit bourgeois denying our own class origins." Richard Hamilton points the way toward a new intellectual future, showing how the entire "lower-middle-class thesis" that Mayer's article exemplifies is one of the most problematic "social misconstructions of reality" in all of academe. Hamilton argues convincingly that no evidence—*none*—has ever been produced to support the idea of an inherent lower middle class or petit bourgeois conservatism. What sources scholars have used when "derogating" the lower middle class have generally been either recycled uncritically or simply made up. Articles such as Mayer's "inject an element of hostility scarcely matched anywhere in the entire social science or historical literature." We may look, then, to Mayer for provocation—but ultimately not for intellectual guidance.[5]

Fortunately, a growing band of scholars has gone beyond Mayer's misconstruction of petit bourgeois reality to suggest some of the historical complexities of lower-middle-class politics. Jonathan Wiener, for instance, responded to Mayer by demonstrating that Marx, and even at times Lenin and Trotsky, emphasized that the lower middle class could, for all its shortcomings, prove a valuable ally in the proletarian struggle. European historians have similarly argued that the politics of the lower middle class was at the least indeterminant, and often strongly inclined toward the left wing of the political spectrum. Philip Nord has argued that organized small shopkeepers in Paris were by no means "liberal," but rather until the 1890s mobilized out of a populist radical republican tradition. The Parisian petite bourgeoisie's shift to the right at the end of the nineteenth century had as much to do with the Left's abandonment of the smallholder ideal as it did with the shopkeeper's desertion of the working class, and the resulting conservatism was neither bitter nor permanent.[6]

More generally, Geoffrey Crossick and Heinz-Gerhard Haupt have done pioneering work in opening up the contingencies of petit bourgeois politics in Europe. They confirm that shopkeepers and master artisans (the classic petite bourgeoisie) played widely different political roles in different European countries. In Britain, small property holders became key supporters of the reigning regime of laissez-faire liberalism. In nineteenth-century France, in contrast, the petite bourgeoisie's commitment to leftist politics was so extensive that the lower middle class "was a central element in defining what the left actually was." Members of the French petite bourgeoisie defended such values as hard work, family discipline, and small-propertied independence "more against the ravages of the rich and powerful than against the threat from the propertyless." The involvement of the petite bourgeoisie in the labor and socialist movements extended to Denmark, and even Germany.[7]

Of course, fascism presents the most imposing roadblock for those who wish to argue for the complexity, much less the promise, of modern lower-middle-class politics. Until recently, scholarly agreement about this subject has been close to absolute. The frustrations, the anxieties, the familial authoritarianism, and the petty resentments of the lower middle class were the fundamental causes of the genocidal rage of Nazism. As early as 1933 Harold Lasswell had formulated the basic theme: "Insofar as Hitlerism is a desperation reaction of the lower middle classes it continues a movement which began during the closing years of the nineteenth century. . . . The psychological impoverishment of the lower middle class precipitated emotional insecurities within the personalities of its members, thus fertilizing the ground for the various movements of mass protest through which the middle classes might revenge themselves." Other scholars, in particular Seymour Martin Lipset in his classic *Political Man*, then codified this wisdom as one of the pillars of a Cold War social science that had as a central defining feature fear of the masses.[8]

Over the last generation, however, the scholarly consensus over the culpability of the lower middle class for fascism has dramatically unraveled. During the 1980s, scholars like Thomas Childers and Richard Hamilton effectively began, through systematic analysis of the Weimar electorate, its class structure, and voting patterns through 1933, to contest the dominant analysis. In Childers's words, "By 1932 the NSDAP [the Nazis] had mobilised an extraordinarily heterogeneous social coalition, becoming a remarkably successful catch-all party of protest." In the 1990s this revisionism became even more forceful, as historians William Brustein, Conan Fischer, Detlef Mühlberger, and above all Jürgen Falter demonstrated that members of the German elite, the upper middle class, and the working class all played critical roles in the Nazi ascent. For example, Fischer argues for the size (40 percent of Nazi voters) as well as the geographical and occupational diversity of the working-class Nazi electorate. Even erstwhile Marxists shifted their votes to the Nazis in significant numbers; in 1932 more workers voted for the Nazis than for the Socialists or the Communists. Thus, proletarian Nazi voters were hardly marginal or atypical of their class, arguments often made by the defenders of the lower-middle-class thesis. Surely, plenty of lower-middle-class people supported Hitler, and we must never forget that. Still, assigning them sole blame for Nazism has been an act of stunning scholarly irresponsibility, with critical consequences for the way we think about class and democracy throughout modern history.[9]

Given the significance, and now the complexity, of scholarship on the European lower middle class, it is astonishing that historians have almost completely failed to use this concept to investigate the American past. Unfortunately, those isolated scholars who have ventured into the area have presented only a uniformly conservative lower middle class. Nancy MacLean, drawing on the insights of Hal Draper and refusing to engage those of Richard Hamilton, uses a mechanical model of the lower middle class to argue for its reactionary populist, even fascist, predisposition. More generally, Walter Nugent explicitly recognizes the lower middle class as a critical actor throughout the whole course of American history. Yet Nugent caricatures small property holders just as relentlessly as do Mayer and MacLean. He argues that the wrenching transformation from rural to urban occurred without fundamental economic political disruption because of the persistence of those "who owned little property, yet did own some, or could." Following Tocqueville, Nugent maintains that petty property holders—even owners of mere appliances—functioned "to stabilize society and make it almost impervious to revolution." Nugent rhetorically recapitulates the thesis of petit bourgeois conservatism: "Why fight when you already had some control anyway? Why risk losing your 'scanty fortune' in a revolution when all you wanted was some upward change?"[10]

Municipal Politics: Elite Rule, Racist Resistance

Nugent and MacLean at least can envision an American lower middle class. And the equation of property ownership with defense of the status quo is, after all, part of our culture's common sense. Still, it is the burden of this book to establish that property ownership, small-propertied values, and membership in the lower middle class can inspire some of the most expansive democratic thought and political radicalism imaginable.

Portland politics during the Progressive Era provide ample evidence for this argument. To be sure, the petit bourgeois radicalism whose social foundation was an alliance between middling and working-class Portlanders was most apparent *outside* the boundaries of mainstream politics. Such democratic populism, however, also served as a central defining feature of the mainstream political culture in the Rose City. Municipal politics in Portland from the 1880s to the 1920s revolved around a fairly constant struggle and stalemate between the city's elite, which attempted to gain support for its procorporate policies, and a reform movement that had much of its base of support among workers and middling folks. Fortunately, we have a tremendously detailed reconstruction of the nitty-gritty of the elite's corporate politics thanks to the investigative and analytical skills of Kimbark MacColl and Harry Stein. Their perspective frankly acknowledges the power of the Portland "ruling class" and thus goes a long way toward explaining civic life in the Rose City during this period. Their emphasis on elite control, however, tends to obscure the substantial oppositional role that many middling folks, and small business owners in particular, played in municipal politics.[11]

Members of the would-be Portland ruling class did not hide their power. Over the course of the entire late nineteenth century, at least one, and at times, two Rose City elites held seats in the U.S. Senate. The city's Republican political boss in the first decade of the century, and the man who replaced Harry Lane in the mayor's office, was the state's premiere railroad attorney, Joseph Simon. The structure of Portland city government itself encouraged elite control and corruption. With a weak mayoralty, nonelectoral administrative bodies dominated policymaking long before the supposedly undemocratic municipal reforms of the Progressive Era. In 1903, the city created a ten-member executive board, made up exclusively of those "prominent in Portland's business and professional life," with all municipal expenditures and franchises subject to the board's approval.[12]

As elsewhere, elite corruption and corporate control generated moral outrage and a reform movement beyond the control of the Establishment. At least some of the opposition to privileged Portlanders had its foundation, as befit a republican tradition that was so often exclusionary, in racism and xenophobia. Much of the racist revolt, in turn, drew on middling-class language, revealing the social base of petit bourgeois ideas as well as their potentially reactionary nature.

For example, the most acute racist event in Portland before the Klan era of the 1920s was the anti-Chinese agitation of the 1880s. Although not nearly as intense as the similar uprising in Washington Territory, where the governor declared martial law, much of union labor avidly supported the expulsion of Chinese workers. Antielite sentiment saturated the movement, as the city's Establishment actively attempted to contain the crusade. In calling for a boycott of businesses that continued to hire Chinese labor, the principal speaker at a rally in early 1886 warned, "We may be able to shake even the First National Bank on its foundation." Also springing into action was the "East Portland Encampment No. 4 of the Merchants' and Laboring Men's Anti-Coolie League."[13]

Prominent Portland manufacturer Sylvester Pennoyer helped foment the drive to rid the city of the Chinese, arguing in classic middling fashion that "the great producing and laboring classes of our state are being ground down between the upper and nether millstones of corporate power and cheap servile labor." Soon, he cautioned, "the Willamette Valley will be the home only of rich capitalists and Chinese serfs." Pennoyer's reward was his election in 1886 to the governorship. Speaking the language of republican political economy as well as Jacksonian democracy in a Labor Day speech in Portland in 1888, Pennoyer rallied his constituency by railing against combinations of capital and special privilege. "It is plainly seen," he argued, "that national legislation has been prostituted for the purpose of enriching the rich, and of taxing, beyond the dictates of justice, the middle and poorer classes."[14]

A considerably more subterranean operation in Portland during the following decade was the American Protective Association. Although not much evidence survives of its activities, we do have some clues about the people to whom these nativists directed their appeals. Writing to J. H. Hayne, a Portland APA leader, the president of the California chapter advised, "Our effort is to secure the middle class, the men who have property interests and can be relied upon for hard work and a zeal caused by patriotic impulses."[15]

Individuals on the border between the middle class and the working class responded warmly to this type of campaign. The president of the APA in Chicopee Falls, Massachusetts, wrote to Hayne to ask about the job situation in Portland. Charles Nute was a married man with a wife and two little girls, as well as "a Very Pretty Home partly Paid for." But business was tough in the Northeast, and the rubber shop for which he had labored six years was in receivership. Nute wanted to head out west, hoping to be able "to open up a Shop to repair Pneumatic Tires" but willing to work as a craft worker or "a Shipping Clerk for some Manufacturing Company." Unfortunately, we do not know what then happened to Nute. Yet we can tell that such ordinary and usually anonymous Portlanders who congregated around the fluid line separating white collar from blue collar and property owner from the non-propertied played a fundamental role in determining the shape of the city's politics.[16]

Contrary to the prevalence of such concerns in current scholarship, however, it was not invocations of racism or nativism that energized most members of the middling world in Portland. Certainly concerns about cheap labor were rarely far from the surface, and the mobilization of such sentiments always possible. For example, Oregon State Federation of Labor president T. H. Burchard warned in 1913 that European and Asian "serfs" would be swarming to the Pacific Coast after the opening of the Panama Canal, and he made a clear distinction about who would support and benefit from this immigration: "The smaller employers of labor are as antagonistic to this class of immigration as the actual laborers, but no assistance or relief may be expected from the class styling themselves as 'Employers' Associations." Such racism, however, was by no means an *inherent* part of lower-middle-class radicalism, and—as the example of Harry Lane indicates—members of the Rose City's middling sorts spent the great bulk of their energy treading much more hopeful and more generous paths of resistance.[17]

Redemocratizing the Commission Form of Government

Harry Lane's prominence in municipal politics provides us with just one indication of the political clout of middling folks in Portland—as well as with a new and distinctive way of reexamining middle-class politics. A more direct measure of the power of the petite bourgeoisie is the composition of the city council during the late nineteenth and early twentieth centuries. Despite the great power of the Portland Establishment, small business owners continuously formulated municipal policy. The first sixteen-member council elected after the consolidation of Portland with Albina and East Portland in 1891 consisted overwhelmingly of nonelite business owners. According to MacColl and Stein, this inaugurated a pattern: "From 1892 until the end of the century, no Arlington Club members would serve in elective city government. . . . The city council became the domain of small merchants, tradesmen and corporate agents, rather than managers or owners."[18]

Harry Lane's election in 1905 also brought to the council no members of the elite, but instead a realtor, "a druggist, an undertaker, a farm-implement executive, a transfer company owner, a jeweler, and a brick manufacturer" as well as four lawyers, all of whom usually opposed Lane on important issues. Lane's two dependable allies were, in turn, the grocer Dan Kellaher and Allan Rushlight, a plumbing contractor from the East Side. When Rushlight became the mildly reformist head of city government in 1911, he appointed his small business comrades to positions on the executive board. The last city council elected in Portland, in 1913, had an even more overwhelmingly petit bourgeois composition. And elite control of politics only continued to decline in the decade after the change to the commission form of government in 1913.[19]

The occupational status of council members did not, of course, dictate their politics in any unmediated fashion. Generally, the city councils voted in a procorporate manner. Still, the political strength of small business, at a time when corporate elites and modernizing professionals were supposedly gaining such power, is remarkable. In fact, even the municipal reform that historians of the era have most often viewed as undemocratic may have, instead, been something of a triumph for Portland's loose alliance between working and middling folks.

Portland shifted, by referendum, to a city commission form of government in 1913. The most basic change was from a council numbering fifteen, with ten members elected by districts and five at large, to a commission with a mayor and four commissioners, all elected at large. The elite-dominated appointive executive bodies lost much of their power under the new government. Many, although not all, in the city's upper class pushed for this transformation in governmental structure. Labor was by turns suspicious and supportive, saying simply (and accurately) that the commission form "can either be democratic, plutocratic, or imperialistic" but that "there need be no departure from democracy."[20]

Labor was correct. The change in government was not itself *structurally* undemocratic. Instead, the commission form of government represented a new institution where it became possible—indeed in many ways easier—for "groups at all levels of the social structure" to monitor city government, organize their constituencies, and form effective electoral coalitions. Perhaps this is why the Portland Establishment was so profoundly divided over the issue, with more liberal members enthusiastically supporting the idea and more conservative, corporate-oriented advocates such as Joe Simon and Abbot Mills opposing it. The staunchest foe of the commission proposal was in fact millionaire grain merchant Gay Lombard, and those who would continue to oppose the commission form of government after its approval were wealthy members of the Establishment such as B. S. Josselyn and Simon Benson.[21]

Overall, the split over commission government was too complex to fall easily into simple class categories. What is clear, however, is that the outcome of the election did not exhibit unchallenged elite, corporate, or professional power, as James Weinstein, Samuel Hays, Martin Schiesl, David Thelen, and others contend was the principal result of municipal reform in the late nineteenth and early twentieth centuries. As Thelen has argued, "These new city charters of the early twentieth century thus represented the fullest expression of the bureaucratic tradition of municipal reform as they enacted the values of efficiency, nonpartisanship, planning, centralization, hierarchy, administration, and expertise."[22]

In contrast, the Portland experience—where the inclusion of the initiative, referendum, and recall was taken for granted even by those who opposed these devices and where at-large elections promised to favor an East Side that had previously suffered from malapportionment—demonstrated that middling- and working-class people could benefit considerably from municipal reform. By a small margin the West Side voted down commission government, but the "white-collar" East Side's support was more than enough to carry the measure to victory, making Portland the third largest city in the United States to adopt this innovation. Thus Carl Abbott accurately remarks that the new municipal charter of 1913 "represented middle-class and working-class reform, with the margin of victory coming from the east side. Commission government meant government for homeowners, small businessmen, professionals, skilled workers, and the other members of Portland's great middle class."[23]

The evidence that most strongly confirms the potentially democratic nature of the commission reform, however, is the result of the subsequent election for mayor and city commission. Rather than diluting the strength of organized labor and the petite bourgeoisie, these constituencies instead gained the most effective and concentrated voice in municipal government they had ever had. For the top vote-getter in the 1913 election would, as city commissioner, largely dictate the tone of municipal politics over the next four years. Yet he is a person almost completely unknown even to local historians. His name is Will Daly.

CHAPTER SEVEN

WILL DALY

The Petit Bourgeois Hero of Labor

Historians relying on conventional wisdom might find it difficult to think of Will Day at the time of his election to the city commission as a prime candidate for radicalism, precisely because he was so "middle class." A prosperous small business owner, Daly managed his own printing enterprise until his election to the city commission. The chief plank of his platform was hardly revolutionary; Daly simply called for economy in municipal expenditure. Yet Daly was no upstanding, quiescent burgher. Instead, he came to his printing firm directly out of a career as the most powerful labor leader in Oregon. Daly was also an active direct democrat distinctly sympathetic to socialism. If any one person in Portland illustrates the complex ways in which individuals and groups straddled the fluid line between working class and middle class in a way that requires reconceptualization of both categories, it is Will Daly. And in his vindication of both small property and the class struggle, Daly confounds in equal measure the scholarly followers of both Karl Marx and Louis Hartz.

Appropriately, Will Daly arrived in Portland in 1902, the year that the state launched its experiment in direct democracy. He was thirty-three at the time, born in the aftermath of the Civil War in Springfield, Missouri, in 1869. During his political career, the Portland public knew only sketchy details about his early life. If Daly's supporters cultivated an image, it was one of semirags to respectability. In his case, the image was true to the reality. As the *Portland Labor Press* wrote of Daly's hardscrabble life in 1913, he was "Left fatherless at age of 8," and "All his early life was an uphill fight against the most severe odds to glean an education. After he had finished his day's work he would study at night and on Sundays." Daly entered the printing business at the tender age of ten, picking up his union card seven years later during the tumultuous year of 1886. In 1892 he married, and he and his wife, the former Daisy Flannery, up and moved to Oregon a decade later.[1]

Such public biographical information is often bound to keep silent much that is significant about any person's life, and so it was with Will Daly. Daly was born into and for many years lived a life rooted in a precarious immigrant working-class world. His father Patrick was born in Ireland; his mother Lucy's family, on the other hand, had lived in the South for at least two generations. Lucy and Patrick had their first child, Kate, when Lucy was only fifteen, Will followed four years later, and his sister Mary arrived last, in 1871. Patrick was a shoemaker, a long-time resident of Springfield, and "a skillful workman, and in his dealings with the world . . . upright and generous."[2]

At least we learn this much from the report of Patrick's 1876 suicide. Patrick overdosed on morphine while coming off a drunk. "The weak point in his nature was a love of strong drink in which he sometimes indulged to excess," a local paper reported, between the marriage listings and a notice about the city's orchestra. (Will would have actually been *six* when this happened, not eight as later reported by the *Labor Press*.) Widowed at the age of twenty-three, Lucy went to work as a carpet weaver to support the family. She died of heart trouble in 1901 at the age of fifty. We do not know of the inner turmoil caused by the relatively early deaths of Will's parents. What we do know is that by the time of Lucy's death the thirty-one-year-old Will had already toiled in the printing business for over two decades. His maternal uncle was a "well known job printer," and Will himself had become foreman of the *Springfield Leader-Democrat*. Married for almost ten years, Will and Daisy apparently decided that, upon the death of his mother, the time had come to make a twentieth-century trek westward.[3]

The Dalys spent their first months in Oregon in the state capital of Salem and moved soon thereafter to the Rose City. Given his later political career, it is ironic that Daly got his first printing job in the city working for the *Oregonian*, as a linotype operator. He became an employee of the Portland Linotype Company in 1907. A successful member of his craft, Daly hit the ground running in the union arena as well. Less than a decade after his arrival in Oregon, Daly became the state's most powerful labor leader. In 1908 Daly was elected president of both the Portland printers' local and the Oregon State Federation of Labor, a position to which he was reelected three times. In 1910, Daly became president of the Portland Central Labor Council, arguably an even more important position than head of the state organization. He was the first person to hold the presidencies of both the OSFL and the CLC simultaneously.[4]

As chief labor official of Oregon, Daly did not distinguish himself with any policy achievements out of the ordinary for a mainstream AFL official. He conducted a successful legislative campaign for a liability law favorable to employees, advised progressive governor Oswald West on convict labor, and cultivated closer ties between organized labor and the Grange and Farmers' Union. Yet his sympathies were much broader than those of the average business unionist of the era. In his last address as president of the state federation of labor, Daly defended the role of unions in the *Los Angeles Times* bombing case and decried the "great clamor from all quarters that the labor unions should be purged of the radical element: that they should be converted into admiration societies and pink tea socials; that they should aban-

Will Daly, president of the Oregon State Federation of Labor and Portland Central Labor Council, small business owner, and city commissioner, 1913–17. (*The Oregonian* © unknown, Oregonian Publishing Co. All rights reserved. Reprinted with permission.)

don by a policy of indolence and passiveness the great objects for which they have striven for half a century."[5]

Daly consistently provided solid support for radicalism within the labor movement. In 1909 three thousand Portlanders attended a mass meeting organized by the militant painters' union, to protest developments in the case of the Danbury Hatters. Those marching included women's unions, regular AFL organizations, and the "Workers of the World, or Socialists." Newspapers estimated one-quarter of the crowd to be red. The featured speaker was Big Bill Haywood, whose statements according to the *Oregonian* "bordered on the incendiary." Will Daly enthusiastically introduced Haywood as "the man who has suffered more in the cause of organized labor than any other in the United States." OSFL president Daly kept his remarks brief, but he did express his delight at the large socialist turnout. The strength of socialism, according to Daly, "showed there was a growing conviction among the people the old parties should be abandoned and that all should unite in a movement for real freedom in the United States."[6]

Yet Daly moved easily between the worlds of radicalism and mainstream politics. He stepped into the municipal political arena in 1911 when, at the behest of the Workingmen's Political Club, he ran for the Portland City Council. Daly's platform was hardly left-wing: "I will during my term represent the whole people and contend against special privileges to any one. Am against present excessive taxation." Nevertheless, Portland's labor press stated, "One of the best reasons why you should vote and work for the nomination of Will Daly is that not a single stone is being left unturned by the Employer's Association and their crowd of union hating open-shoppers to defeat him. They are ably assisted by the big corporations and the machine politicians because they object to his progressive ideas." In contrast, the voice of labor argued that "small home owners and working men" were Daly's natural constituency. Organized labor therefore cheered when its most important official became the first recognized union officer in Portland's history to serve on the council. Despite "considerable industrial disturbance" during the campaign, Daly was the top vote-getter for the five at-large positions, beating out his nearest rival, George Baker, by nearly three thousand votes. The 1911 election would not be the last battle between Daly and Baker.[7]

All of the information about Daly's life presented so far leads to the conclusion that Portlanders would have recognized Daly as, if anything, a kind of *working-class* hero. Nothing distinguished him as in any way "middle class," unless that term is stretched mercilessly. Yet in 1911, while he was *still* president of the Oregon State Federation of Labor and the Portland Central Labor Council, and while he was *still* organized labor's recognized voice on the city council, Will Daly's career took a profoundly non-working-class turn. Daly established his own business. He became the manager and owner of the Portland Monotype Company. Daly located his new shop at the same address as that of his former employer, 227½ Stark in the heart of downtown; his ex-bosses had presumably helped him set up in business. The enterprise soon prospered. Daly did not have "a speculative or daring business temperament," but his salary soon jumped from thirty dollars a week as an employee to as much as forty-five hundred dollars a year, with no substantial reverses. Now Will Daly was a solid member of the middle class.[8]

Or is this kind of categorization so simple? Despite his move to the employing side of the class divide, Daly remained the most powerful labor leader in the state; no move was made or even contemplated to oust him for being a traitor to the proletarian cause. Of course, we could view Daly's career as the epitome of true business unionism, with business owners actually running the unions! The problem is that, if anything, Daly became a more vigorous and outspoken advocate of populist democracy and working-class interests *after* he became a certified member of the petite bourgeoisie. In evaluating his political career in 1917, the conservative *Oregon Voter* remarked that Daly had "stood first, last and all the time for the interests of union labor." Unionists agreed. Petit bourgeois politics in Portland clearly was refusing to follow its supposedly inevitable path of pinched conservatism and ingrained hostility to the proletariat.[9]

After the establishment of the city commission form of government in 1913, Daly attempted to institutionalize his power even further by running for a seat on the new governing body. Again, he did not campaign on a distinctive, much less radical, platform. The *Portland Labor Press* trumpeted Daly's business success, proudly noting that he had established the Portland Monotype Company, "of which he is the sole proprietor and which he has made one of the substantial small foundries in the city." The voice of organized labor proclaimed Daly's fairness: "No other man in the race has shown such strength among trade unions, business men, professional men, women, and all who strive for better government." Labor's enthusiasm was rewarded. Out of a field of seventy-five, Daly again received more votes than any other candidate. Even though the Establishment had carefully recruited candidates in order to insure its power under the new system of government, the figure who most epitomized the alliance between organized labor and small business in Portland had now gained substantial power under the reorganization of city government.[10]

Even the *Oregonian*, declaring Daly "a successful business man" and agreeing with public sentiment that favored labor's representation on the commission as a functional interest group, pronounced itself satisfied with Daly's victory. Daly did not, however, stay in the good graces of the Establishment for long. Under the revamped municipal administrative system, Will Daly became commissioner of public utilities, arguably the most powerful position in the new government, as well as president of the commission. By early 1914 the *Oregonian* had become annoyed at Daly for a number of reasons, chief among them his attempts to appraise more accurately the Portland Railway, Light, and Power Company and his desire to install water meters in all Portland homes and businesses. The unionist commissioner also vigorously defended unions' rights to display boycott banners in public, which infuriated the Portland Employers' Association. Daly enjoyed a fair amount of success in getting the commission to pass measures like an eight-hour, three-dollar day on municipal public works, and he established a strong record in support of municipal ownership of utilities. With "Big business . . . after Daly's scalp," these were the issues on which the powerful laborite staked his record, continually dodging "willful malicious and brutal assaults."[11]

The *Oregon Voter* wrote in 1917 that Daly "controlled the city commission to a considerable extent during [his] first two years." Daly's chief ally on the commission was department store manager C. A. Bigelow. As with Daly, organized labor and East Side business owners provided Bigelow with his chief constituency. When Bigelow's term was up, the *Oregon Voter* wrote that, except for the ugly ducklings on the wrong bank of the Willamette, "Business men . . . are almost unanimous in dreading and opposing his [re]election." Daly was thus no political freak; his power flowed directly out of Portland's dominant class coalition.[12]

The issue that most made Daly's reputation, and that most infuriated corporate public utilities, was his forceful advocacy of jitneys. This literally drove the Establishment to the wall. Privately operated automobiles that served as a kind of quasi-public transportation, jitneys carried passengers wherever they pleased, often right alongside existing streetcar tracks. More than just a novel use for a new technology, jitneys compellingly raised the issue of self-employment and the ability of members of the working class to own small businesses. They were thus the perfect issue for the petit bourgeois laborite Daly.

Jitneys came to Portland in 1914, in the midst of a depression that brought 20 percent unemployment. They provided jobs for some of this massive number of the unemployed. Jitneys also skimmed significant amounts of traffic away from the PRL&P's streetcar monopoly, leading to outrage on the part of corporate officials. The question of regulating the jitneys came continuously before the city commissioners, and the public, between 1915 and 1917. From the start of these debates Daly served as the leading spokesperson for the jitney drivers. Eventually Mayor Russell Albee stripped Daly of control over transportation because of his vocal promotion of their interests.[13]

Jitney drivers themselves articulated their grievances in the language of what we might call proletarian petty proprietors. At the height of jitney fever 363 jitney drivers looped through the streets of Portland. Once it became clear how much hostility they faced from the city commission, the great majority joined a union affiliated with the Central Labor Council. This action simultaneously perplexed and infuriated the *Oregonian*, which announced that the "jitney drivers, who are not employes [sic], but proprietors, have organized a labor union. . . . It is a popular idea that labor unions are composed of wage earners, but apparently there is no bar to affiliation of proprietors' unions with labor unions—at least under certain conditions." The jitney union took its case to the public at such forums as the Alberta Women's Improvement Club, where its leader shared the limelight with the most prominent local socialist. Meanwhile, the chair of the PRL&P board, visiting from Philadelphia in order to campaign against jitneys, "advanced the idea that the popular form of government enjoyed by the people of this state had something to do" with his corporation's problem.[14]

The *Oregon Labor Press* ardently defended the jitneys, applauding their ability to "compete with Eastern capital invested in Portland." Jitney drivers

Earl V. McCreary in December 1911, when he worked for Neate and McCarthy autos. During the years of heavy jitney activity in Portland later in the decade, McCreary was listed in city directories as an apparently self-employed "chauffeur." (Courtesy Oregon Historical Society, #021105.)

dared to "own their own jobs and have unionized to protect themselves," according to the newspaper. No language could have better symbolized the merging of the interests of the petite bourgeoisie and the working class against the corporate order. Daly also explicitly defended the jitneys in class terms while arguing against regulation that would drive them out of business. "It would be as reasonable to forbid or deny all small merchants the right to do business within the city because the department stores have already made adequate investment and provision to serve this public," he stated, "as it would be to deny the public the jitney service for the sole reason that it would compete with the established street railway system." Daly's lessons in political economy went even further when he proclaimed: "It is said that jitney competition is unfair. Where has there ever been competition that is fair? Competition means the survival of the fittest; there is nothing fair about it." Daly meant this as a protest—not an endorsement— of economic Darwinism.[15]

Will Daly did not limit his domain to the often mundane existing world of municipal politics in Portland. He dreamed as well of what might be, becoming one of the most fervent advocates of direct democracy in Oregon. The *Oregonian* continually, and accurately, associated Daly with the most prominent populist in Portland, William U'Ren. By 1910 Daly was on the executive board of U'Ren's People's Power League (PPL). He was also a prominent member of the closely related single tax movement. Daly laid his cards on the table in 1916 when he endorsed the most thoroughgoing single tax measure to appear on the Oregon ballot. A mere six months later his enemies would gleefully repeat, over and over, Daly's words in the voters' pamphlet:

> Opportunity is knocking less and less at the door of the average citizen. The proposed Land and Loan Measure will broaden the field of opportunity for every industrious man to make a living for himself and family, even under our vicious competitive system. It will accomplish this by abolishing land monopoly and leaving the Earth in Oregon free to those who want to use it.
> Will H. Daly,
> Commissioner of Public Utilities for Portland[16]

In the very days during which Harry Lane underwent the most intense phase of his martyrdom, in March 1917, Will Daly became a candidate for mayor of Portland. The election was in June, and the campaign thus took place in the heated first months of the war, in a political culture in which issues of radicalism and disloyalty stood at the forefront of public concern. The *Oregonian* virulently attacked Daly at every opportunity. Typical was its assessment that Daly's election "would be notice that Portland has turned to radicalism. . . . It would be an irretrievable disaster."[17]

Most of this invective preceded the bombshell that the *Oregonian* and its companion Republican paper, the *Telegram*, dropped on the citizenry of Portland less than two weeks before the election. The newspapers announced that Daly had given his blessing to a scheme of left-wing unionists to stage a general strike in order to bring the shipbuilding industry to heel and to make Portland a closed-shop city. Despite vigorous denials from both Daly and organized labor, the *Oregonian* continued to trumpet Daly's role in the general strike. Meanwhile, the imagined conspiracy grew larger. With Daly's help, the unionists planned to neutralize the police department and the city's legal machinery, as well as the streetcar system. Then the plans for the strike spread to the entire Pacific Coast. Daly's election would thus play into the hands of the Kaiser. Ultimately, the *Oregonian* proclaimed: "the issue the people of Portland will decide by their ballots" is: "Shall Portland be turned over to the radical labor agitator, the walking delegate and I. W. W.?"[18]

Despite such attacks, Daly continued to garner considerable public support. The Democratic *Journal* continued its promotion of Daly's candidacy, maintaining that Daly's "efficiency and economy" and fights against the vice interests under the old council system most recommended him for the job. Beyond such mainstream support, the author of a letter to the editor, who spoke for "the people, or small home owners," contended, "If the people want a representative democratic administration it is up to them to support men with democratic ideas, men who have the nerve to defy the autocrats when it is necessary to do so in order to protect the people, men who fight to reduce the tax burden of the people and give them the benefits of some of the immense profits reaped by public service corporations." William U'Ren also endorsed Daly as a "safe" politician who had "consistently and persistently stood for every possible increase in the people's power over government."[19]

Daly himself stuck to a discussion of pragmatic policies, denied that what he had advocated while in city government was "radical," affirmed his pride in his union membership, and emphasized his ability to be fair to all citizens, especially workers. Daly's campaign ads touted his honesty and integrity while asking, "Shall the home-owners and workers of the city be represented or misrepresented in the city hall?" Daly's advocates also spoke directly to the class alliance that shaped his personal life and that served as his most effective constituency. In particular, the eclectic populist daily *News*—a member of the Scripps chain—consistently cheered Daly on. One of the newspaper's lead editorials asserted, "Daly will get the vote of the workers, the progressive business men and most of the women." Most succinctly, the *News*—without any sense of contradiction—presented what immediately appears to us as an oxymoron: "Daly can go to labor, because he himself is a union man. And he can present to labor the employers' side, because he is himself an employer."[20]

Perhaps the strangest irony that history played on Portland during 1917 came in the person of Daly's chief opponent. George Baker, like Daly an owner of an independent business, had also in his time toiled in the ranks of organized labor. Indeed, the similarities in their careers are extraordinary. Baker was born in 1868, Daly the following year; Baker's father worked as a shoemaker and deserted his family, while Daly's father practiced the same trade before committing suicide; Baker quit school at the age of nine, Daly at ten; both took pride in their working-class Irish ancestry. By 1917, though, Baker did greatly outperform Daly in the category of voluntary organization membership—with twenty-two fraternal ties to Daly's ten. (Besides his union connections, Daly belonged to groups as diverse as the Improved Order of Redmen and the Portland Bowling Club.)[21]

A "Horatio Alger character," George Baker was the impresario of a nationally renowned theatrical company. Yet early in his career he had also "been one of the leaders in the movement for the unionization of the theatre employees." A longtime holdover from the old-style politics, in which he had served repeatedly as city council president, Baker had by 1917 distanced himself from organized labor even though he had earned its endorsement during a successful campaign for city commission just two years earlier. Baker "always ran with strong Republican backing," according to Kimbark MacColl, and he "counted most of Portland's important business and banking executives as supporters," particularly the president of the PRL&P. Not

Future Portland mayor George Baker (1917–33), during his days in the world of business and labor. (Courtesy Oregon Historical Society, # 48540.)

surprisingly, between 1915 and 1917 Baker and Daly went head to head on a number of issues as each positioned himself for a run at the mayoralty.[22]

The most astute contemporary observer of George Baker's career noted in 1926 that the big business organizers of Baker's campaign effectively made "the real issue" of the 1917 race Daly's "radicalism," even though Baker himself stuck to the theme of economic growth. Still, the unions' favorite appeared to be the public's clear choice as well. As Baker's biographer stated, "until the very day before [the] election, Daly's election looked like a foregone conclusion."[23]

That is until June 3, 1917, when Portland's equivalent of the *Los Angeles Times* bombing occurred. Or perhaps Watergate is the more appropriate analogy. Several days earlier a mysterious break-in disturbed the peace at Daly's East Side residence. The thieves took no valuables but did ransack Daly's files. The Sunday *Oregonian* published the major discovery: a reproduction of Will Daly's December 1910 application for membership in the Socialist Party. The newspaper claimed that Daly had been a Socialist ever since.[24]

With the election two days hence, no time remained for Daly or his supporters to respond. After the election the *Journal* admitted that Daly had joined the SP in a fit of disgust at the "reactionary control" of both of the regular parties. But the newspaper maintained that Daly had never believed in "the radical doctrines of that party" and that he soon returned to the Republican fold, ever since that time suffering attacks from extremists among the Socialist leaders. We will probably never know the details, but Daly did reregister as a Republican in January 1912. Technicalities held little importance anyway; the *Oregonian* used its new knowledge mercilessly. Especially in conjunction with Daly's 1916 single-tax attack on capitalism as "vicious," the *Oregonian* asserted that its discovery "confirms everything that has been said about his radicalism [and] emphasizes anew the Socialist trend of his official acts as Commissioner." As Portland voters prepared to go to the polls, the *Oregonian* editorialized:

> If the people elect Daly, we shall have a Socialist for Mayor. He will jitneyize the city government. The era of the soap-box will be installed. The fight for single tax, often lost, will be renewed with stronger support. The firm hand of authority over the elements of disorder will be weakened. There will be encouragement for strikes and countenance of industrial agitation for the sake of agitation. The radicals will have a friend in the City Hall, and the investor, just now again looking to Portland, will be discouraged. We shall have a mayor for one class, and not a mayor for all the people.[25]

On election day, Portlanders came closer to fulfilling the *Oregonian's* worst nightmare than anyone could have imagined. Will Daly had almost everything going against him. He advocated the cause of unions in a conservative "middle-class" city. A onetime Socialist, he had his membership exposed at the worst possible time, in what Philip Silver characterized as the "coup of 1917." The most important cultural organ in the city bitterly opposed him. And the context for all this: a wave of war-related intolerance. Yet Will Daly lost to George Baker by fewer than two thousand votes out of more than forty-eight thousand cast.[26]

Portland had a preferential voting system with roots in the direct democracy movement. Voters could designate their top three candidates, and their second and third choices would be added to the first-place tally if no candidate received a majority of first-place votes. This happened in 1917, and Baker's total plurality counting all of the first-, second-, and third-place votes numbered 1,575. His margin over Daly in first-place votes alone was even lower, with Baker receiving 20,219 to Daly's 19,508, for a bare 50.9 percent majority. Daly won 175 of the city's precincts; Baker gained victory in only 2 more.[27]

Will Daly therefore came perilously close to becoming mayor of Portland in 1917, and the support he maintained in the face of the conservative onslaught is quite telling. We can best analyze the social foundation of the election by examining precinct-level voting data. Baker's strength was on the West Side, the home of the city's richest and poorest residents. Baker swept 87 out of 109 precincts there and garnered 63 percent of the vote. In turn, Daly's home turf in what Carl Abbott has called the "new middle-class city east of the Willamette" remained loyal to him. He won 155 out of 234 precincts on the East Side, with an overall 53.6 percent majority.[28]

The geography of class in this voting corresponded remarkably closely to the pattern on many of the initiatives and referenda that I analyze in the remainder of the book. Daly had no important pockets of support on the West Side except for immigrant South Portland. Yet he prevailed in 31 straight precincts in a southeastern part of the city that included the neighborhoods of Sellwood, Woodstock, Woodmere, Lents, Mt. Tabor, and Creston. Likewise, Daly almost universally swept the rest of the mixed working-class and lower-white-collar areas on the East Side, for instance taking 63 of 69 precincts in the north and northeastern parts of the city. Baker did, however, pick up significant but highly specific sections of the East Side, in particular, almost all of the posh upper-middle- to upper-class neighborhoods of Laurelhurst and Irvington (the home of U.S. Senator George Chamberlain).[29] Two precincts serve as good examples. In contrast to Daly's generally overwhelming support on the East Side, precinct 202 in the heart of Laurelhurst and precinct 228 in the middle of Irvington favored Baker by respective tallies of 231 to 40 and a resounding 123 to 5.[30]

The patterns of class that determined the election of 1917 were also apparent in the most important initiative on the municipal ballot, an "anticonspiracy" ordinance that would have "made it impossible to boycott, picket, or display a banner in any labor dispute." Many prominent liberal reformers spoke out against the measure, which in roughly similar form Portland voters had consistently turned down in previous elections. The *Journal*, the *News*, and organized labor spoke out against the initiative as a fundamental violation of free speech. Those who favored banning "picketing and the violence done in its name" included the *Oregonian*, the *Telegram*, the Portland Chamber of Commerce, the Portland City Club, and the Employers' Association of

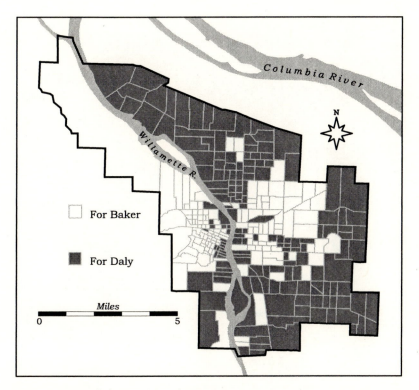

Voting in mayoral election, 1917, by precinct

Oregon. Noticeably absent from the list of the initiative's supporters were the East Side business organizations that had proven to be such thorns in the side of the capitalist Establishment.[31]

During the initial phase of the campaign, the anticonspiracy ordinance did not play into mayoral politics. With the *Oregonian*'s alarms about the impending general strike, however, the two bitter campaigns became, according to Philip Silver, "inextricably interwoven, affecting Baker's and Daly's candidacies so basically as to perhaps constitute the determining factor in the campaign." Portland voters approved the anticonspiracy initiative by the narrowest of margins—less than five hundred votes, with a solid majority of precincts actually rejecting the measure. Neighborhood voting patterns closely followed those in the mayor's race. Nearly 80 percent of pro-Baker precincts throughout the city favored the initiative, while close to 90 percent of pro-Daly precincts rejected it. Concerns about the ecological fallacy might cause some caution about going to a higher stage of interpretation. Quite clear, though, is the fact that in the midst of a concerted antiradical and

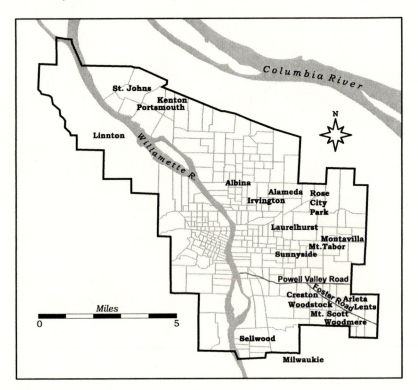

North and East Portland neighborhoods

antilabor offensive, during a war-induced wave of intolerance, middling folks maintained their solid support for labor.[32]

These results, and the ones that follow in the rest of the book, indicate that class remained a critical determining factor of politics even in a city as fundamentally "middle class" as Portland. No bourgeoisie and proletariat squared off against one another, but that happened rarely enough anywhere. Instead, the class conflicts in Portland continued to occur along a republican axis: rhetorically the people versus the interests, but concretely middling and home-owning working folks versus a professional, upper middle class and the corporate elite. Many Portlanders, like the editor of the *News* during Daly's run for mayor, recognized this and took the Rose City's class struggle for granted. We can use their insights in order to reimagine class in far less narrow and polarized terms.[33]

Will Daly's fate after his important moment in history perhaps mirrors the general invisibility of the petite bourgeoisie in American history. Daly almost immediately faded into insignificance. He returned to management of his

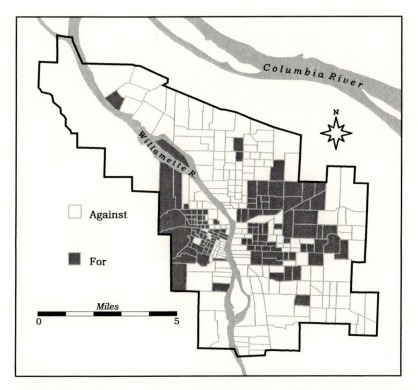

Voting on trade conspiracy initiative, 1917, by precinct. Those voting against the initiative were prounion.

business and moved out to a "ranch" along the Base Line Road on the southeastern outskirts of the city. In March 1918 Daly ran unsuccessfully for the Multnomah County Commission on a plank of administrative consolidation and parsimony. Two years later, in early 1920, A. Mitchell Palmer appointed Daly as federal food price commissioner for Oregon. Daly resigned two months into the job, disgusted at federal red tape and worried about the press of "his private business." That same year the *Oregonian* proudly reported Daly's endorsement of Baker's reelection. In his last public statement, Daly characterized Baker's as "a splendid administration."[34]

Daly died in 1924 at the age of fifty-four, leaving his wife and four children. A longtime member of the Campbellite Rodney Avenue Christian Church, where he had served as deacon and trustee, he received a funeral appropriate to one who had achieved such prosperity and respectability. Labor mourned "a valiant champion," and the *Oregonian* gave him credit for his central role in Portland's political life while obliquely referring to "the severe political conflicts" that Daly had engendered.[35]

The flag at City Hall returned to the top of its staff after Will Daly's burial in the Mt. Scott cemetery (ironically, in earth once owned by—and named for—*Oregonian* editor Harvey Scott). In the following days and years Daly's legacy continued in unassuming but concrete ways. Upon his election to the city commission in 1913, Daly had abandoned administration of his printing enterprise to his son John. John had served as an apprentice in the shop while continuing to live with his parents. He married in 1915 and established his own residence, although it would be long before he and his wife Mabel settled in one place. (By 1930 John had remarried, for reasons unknown.) Upon his return to private life, Will Daly resumed oversight of the Portland Monotype Company, apparently taking in John as an employee. Upon Will's death John again took over the company's management, although Daisy Daly became the official owner of the enterprise. She maintained at least legal oversight over the firm well into the 1930s, when John took over both ownership and control. In the 1940s John took his sister Hazel Arndt into the firm as a partner. By 1950, the year that Daisy died at the age of seventy-nine, the Portland Monotype Company had, however, dissolved, with John having left the city. Hazel Arndt lived with her mother until the latter's death, after which she carried on, as a compositor with the firm of Abbot Kerns and Bell, the family trade bequeathed to her by her father.[36]

The skeletal history of a business that eventually "failed" may not seem an appropriate place to end this story. Yet in the multitude of such unrecoverable entrepreneurial actions, based in family enterprise, the Portland petite bourgeoisie forged much of its powerful culture. That generally quiet, but always potentially radical, way of life reached its highest political expression in dramatic—even world historic—debates over declarations of war on the floor of the United State Senate and shocking revelations of applications for membership in the Socialist Party. These events, and the configurations of social life that served as their foundation, profoundly shaped the direction of local and national social change during the early twentieth century.

PART III

"THE MOST COMPLETE DEMOCRACY IN THE WORLD"

The Populist Radicalism of Direct Democracy

> If, as some political philosophers have argued, democracy is an "essentially contested" concept whose definition is never neutral but always entangled in competing moral and political commitments, then democratic politics is in fundamental respects a never-ending politics of discourse. In such a politics dissenting voices from the past can be silenced by the loss of cultural memory, and it is important, at the very least, to ensure that the more powerful of these voices are not dropped from the conversation or misheard.
>
> —ROBERT B. WESTBROOK, *John Dewey and American Democracy*

> No questions are more difficult than those of *democracy*.
> —RAYMOND WILLIAMS, *Keywords*

Despite his dedication to the cause of direct democracy and his prominence in the organization, Will Daly did not hold the contract to print the literature of the Oregon People's Power League. That honor went to a now obscure citizen named George Orton, who served as one of the longest-lasting foot soldiers for the grand cause of rule by the people. From the mid-1890s Orton, an East Side resident as well as manager and part-owner of the Multnomah Printing Company in downtown Portland, served on the executive board—and from 1901 until his death in 1921 as vice president—of the various organizations that sought to extend popular democracy.[1]

Born in California, Orton moved to Portland before his first birthday. After finishing public school, Orton became a printer's apprentice in 1881, at the age of seventeen. "Closely associated" with William U'Ren, Orton pushed for the Australian ballot and, ultimately, all the other reforms associated with direct democracy. He also quickly became caught up in early union struggles in Portland, becoming president of the Portland Federated Trades Council in 1901 and then the first president of the Portland Central Labor Council. From that post he went on to become one of the most powerful political voices for Oregon workers over the next two decades after his election in

George M. Orton, labor leader, print shop owner, and leader of direct democracy movement, ca. 1903. (Courtesy Oregon Historical Society, #103490.)

1900 and 1902 to the state house of representatives, where he served as one of the three main sponsors for the protective labor legislation that several years later led to *Muller v. Oregon*. Orton also gained statewide renown as the president of the Columbia River Salmon Protective Association, an organization that fought against "the power and influence of the few rich men owning fish wheels in the upper Columbia." Prominent in the civic affairs of the Rose City, Orton served in 1919–20 as president of the Portland school board, where he protected the rights of Catholic employees against mounting prejudice. George Orton was yet another petit bourgeois working-class hero.[2]

George Orton does not play much of a role in the rest of this book. Yet like his comrade Will Daly, he perfectly symbolizes much of the political energy and passion at the heart of one of the greatest populist experiments in

American history—the construction of the Oregon System of direct democracy. For Orton also found it no contradiction to own his own printing business at the same time that he toiled as one of the most valiant champions of the cause of labor. Once again, the fluidity between "working class" and "middle class" brought not confusion, much less quiescence, in Progressive Era Portland; it produced dramatic, and nationally significant, democratic activism.[3]

People's Power advocates made many compromises to advance their cause, and the class alliances underlying direct democracy were complex and ever-changing. Nor did their commitment to full popular rule always remain consistent. Still, what made the Oregon System distinctive—and what allowed the state to have a legitimate claim on being "the most complete democracy in the world"—was the strain of petit bourgeois radicalism at its core.

Amidst so many defeats, direct legislation was the most concrete triumph of middle-class radicalism in early-twentieth-century Oregon, and it is important to understand the victories won in the battles for the initiative and referendum, the recall, the direct primary, the direct election of senators, a corrupt practices act, and other measures that ultimately helped change the basic structure of electoral law throughout the United States. Even here, though, the *failed* initiatives of the People's Power League are more telling. Understanding populist democracy therefore requires an exploration not just of the successes, but also the expansive utopian visions, of the main architect of people's power, William U'Ren. U'Ren and his allies sought to create an ever more complete democracy through unicameralism, proportional representation, an administrative reorganization of the state government, and, finally, a system of occupational representation that would have brought women as well as workers to full political power.

I argue that such dreams of radical democracy fit into one of our most important, but neglected, political traditions: what we might call a living antifederalism. They also were not merely political: the populist vision of direct democracy included a very concrete dream of a petit bourgeois economic utopia. Yet in our current intellectual climate, we must ironically begin by asking whether we should even view direct democracy as democratic at all.

CHAPTER EIGHT

DIRECT DEMOCRACY
AS ANTIDEMOCRACY?

The Evolution of the Oregon System, 1884–1908

The American cultural and political Establishment has recently decreed, with a remarkable degree of consensus, that the People have gotten out of hand. Liberals in particular have sought to delegitimize direct popular control of government through the initiative and referendum. In the process they have needed to "anxiously conjure up the spirits of the past to their service and borrow from them names, battle slogans and costumes in order to present the new scene of world history in [a] time-honored disguise." Prominent liberal scholars Alan Brinkley, Nelson Polsby, and Kathleen Sullivan, for example, have gone so far as to pen *The New Federalist Papers*, in large part to defend against the supposed populist "challenge to deliberative democracy." Likewise the influential journalist Peter Schrag, a confirmed advocate of the welfare state and affirmative action, finds it necessary to remind us of the perils that dangerous majorities have presented in world history. In the course of painting a comprehensive portrait of the direct democracy dystopia that is post–Proposition 13 California, Schrag makes sure that we recall the Terror of the French Revolution. He even summons our dark fears of fascism by titling a chapter "March of the Plebiscites." Let us return to representative government as the Constitution intended, Schrag pleads, and reclaim—via that ardent defender of the welfare state and affirmative action Edmund Burke—the virtues of a conservative political system.[1]

Could a spectre be haunting the intellectual landscape of America? And is the name of that spectre direct democracy?

Until relatively recently, many—perhaps most—intellectuals would have used their liberal convictions to support the granting of more power to the masses. After all, the essence of democracy is popular rule, and the more the better. Yet in an age of post-Reagan democracy, bigotry against immigrants and homosexuals, and peasants with pitchforks, the People have become the Problem. As Robert Wiebe has noted, the concept of "majoritarian dangers to democratic rights, an oxymoron in the 19th century . . . became national-class dogma in the 20th"; David Thelen likewise remarks on liberals' "deep suspicion of majority rule." Conservatives have therefore become the most ardent defenders of direct democracy in the new millennium, and left-of-center academics and activists increasingly use their energy to explain their fears of rule by the rabble.[2]

Appropriately, historians have turned to the origins of the present crisis to explain how things could have gone so terribly wrong. A new consensus is developing that the original sin of antidemocracy was, ironically, embedded in direct democracy from its very beginnings in the Progressive Era. Paul Kleppner articulates recent scholarly wisdom well when he blames the primarily western virus of direct democracy for bringing to modern America many of its political woes. The initiative, referendum, and other reforms do not even deserve the label *democratic*, Kleppner argues, because they helped loosen the bonds of party and mass voting, leading in turn to the loss of any institutionalized opportunity for organized working-class political power. Westerners thus "opted for the appearances and illusions of democracy, for sporadic manifestations of the general will, instead of concrete political institutions through which modal public opinion could be expressed continuously."[3]

Michael Paul Rogin makes such condemnation even more explicit, stating that "direct democracy reforms were not meant to introduce direct democracy at all. . . . The people were required only to recognize and select expert and efficient leaders and to follow their lead on legislation. Direct democracy was an alternative to organization at the grass roots; yet it was an alternative from the point of view of elite autonomy, not 'populism.'" Or, without any substantive consideration of the direct democracy reformers themselves, Philip Ethington claims that, through their lack of a genuine tolerance for ethnoracial diversity, "the 'direct democracy' reforms of the Progressive Era institutionally empowered a theory of representation that virtually guaranteed an ethically barren public discourse." Arthur Lipow has most forcefully developed this leftist critique of direct democracy reformers. "Designed to prevent participation," direct democracy provided citizens merely "the right to ratify or reject issues" proposed by elites. Ultimately, for Lipow direct democracy is a "fraudulent" plebiscitarian "sham" only one step away from fascism. And, naturally, the middle class—and the petite bourgeoisie in particular—is to blame.[4]

Despite their condemnation of the populist virus, none of these scholars has paid any sustained attention to the location of the first effective and widespread use of direct democracy. During the first two decades of the twentieth century Americans most commonly referred to the entire package of electoral reforms such as the direct primary, direct election of United States senators, the recall, and direct legislation as the "Oregon System." Such a failure to explore the era's most significant manifestation of democratic radicalism has led to a crucial "dedemocratization" of Progressivism, where figures as ideologically diverse as Gabriel Kolko and Michael McGerr bemoan a one-dimensional triumph of conservatism and decline of popular politics.[5]

When, however, we examine what Oregonians called People's Power, we see that middling-class Portlanders developed some of the most utopian democratic visions in all of American history. Many contemporaries considered Oregon, again in Frederic Howe's words, "the most complete democracy in the world." Nurtured in an environment particularly hospitable to petit bourgeois radicalism, citizens of the Rose City did more to imagine how the People might rule than did perhaps any other twentieth-century social movement. To be sure, the early twentieth century left many antidemocratic legacies in the realms of politics, science, race, and the economy. Still, with our eyes open to the middle-class radicalism of Portland, we urgently need to reclaim the Progressive Era as the birthplace of modern populist democracy.[6]

The Creation of the Oregon System, 1884–1908

In 1915 Benjamin Parke DeWitt wrote, "The initiative, the referendum, and the recall . . . have been more widely discussed, more bitterly condemned, and more loyally praised than almost any other measures connected with the whole progressive movement; and the attention which they have attracted has been largely due to the fact that they have been greatly misunderstood." A fundamental part of this misunderstanding has been the failure to come to grips with the plebeian roots of these reforms.[7]

In turn, historian Joseph Schafer wrote in 1918, "Much has been said and written about the abnormal and foolish radicalism of the Northwest, particularly Oregon." "The basis of Oregon's reputation in that regard is found in her adoption of the so-called 'Oregon system' of direct legislation," he continued, and "the fact is that this legislation is almost wholly ascribable to influences running back twenty-five years to the populist agitation, and to a leadership which the populist movement evoked." Schafer was correct. When one seeks a neat and clean historical and historiographical break between insurgent Populists and modernizing Progressives, Oregon—and Portland—are simply not the places to look. George Mowry wrote a half century ago that "most progressive leaders had been violently opposed to the nineteenth-century agrarian radicalism of William Jennings Bryan and the Populists," and this statement has rarely been challenged. Yet in Oregon the Populists and Progressives were often the very same people, and they proudly shaped an era of populist progressivism.[8]

The first quiet calls for the initiative and referendum in Oregon came during the 1880s. The *Oregon Vidette and Antimonopolist*, advocate of "the interests of the producing and industrial classes," pushed a legislative program "to defend a citizen's rights against injustice by powerful corporations."

Published in Salem and Portland, the newspaper supported organization of all "toilers" and the six-hour day as well as proportional representation, woman suffrage, and the single tax. The *Vidette* did not, however, consider direct democracy to be the most important electoral reform; instead the newspaper's platform called for compulsory voting for both sexes to prevent the destruction of republican government.[9]

During the 1890s powerful dissenting forces attached themselves to the somewhat inchoate ideas of the *Vidette*. The Oregon People's Party became the major vehicle behind initiative and referendum agitation during this turbulent decade. A budding alliance of political organizations representing workers and farmers joined the Populists. The Portland Chamber of Commerce having turned down an invitation, the Oregon Farmers' Alliance, the Grange, Portland Federated Trades, Portland Central Labor Council, and the Knights of Labor united in 1894 under the leadership of William U'Ren to form the Joint Committee on Direct Legislation.[10]

Claiming that the legislature was composed of "the representatives of the monied and monopolistic classes," the committee distributed more than fifty thousand pamphlets showing how direct democracy would "make it impossible for corporations and boodlers to obtain unjust measures by which to profit at the expense of the people." Oregon could then follow in the path of the middle-class paradise of Switzerland, which had "no beggars, paupers, nor home-made millionaires." Harvey Scott, the cantankerous and influential editor of the *Oregonian*, well described the Populist impulse (and well forecast its eventual trajectory) when he warned that these would-be socialists "think that if they can get a direct vote on money, wages, interest, rents, profits, and the general scheme of business that has grown up among men, they will be able to set aside the whole of that science known as political economy." Indeed, everything would be up for grabs, for under this initial blueprint for direct democracy the referendum would be *compulsory*. Every law that the legislature—or any municipal or county governing body— passed would go to the voters for automatic review, and the Supreme Court would lose its right to declare such popular legislation unconstitutional.[11]

The fortunes of the Oregon Populists declined rapidly after 1896, but, in the words of Joseph Gaston, "they retired only to re-appear in another form. In their brief career as a party the populists had made a wide acquaintance among farmers, union labor men and small tradesmen. They were the people, and they appealed, not to millionaires, and great corporations but to men of moderate or humble circumstances." Still, those at the core of the direct democracy movement ultimately realized that victory would require an alliance with, in the words of Lincoln Steffens, "leading citizens—bankers, railroad men, corporation attorneys, [and] corrupt politicians." The story of how William U'Ren made a series of possibly corrupt bargains with machine politicians in order to get a more limited initiative and referendum has become a staple of Oregon history ever since Steffens publicized it at the height of the muckraking era. In brief, U'Ren led a band of Populist legislators in holding up the election of a U.S. senator during the 1897 legislative session. Taking advantage of factional splits within the Republican Party over the next five years, he secured the agreement of some of the state's most powerful politicians to work on behalf of direct legislation. Oregon voters then heeded the radical rhetoric of George Williams, the president of the Direct Legislation League and one of the honored pioneers of Oregon politics, when he warned that "in these days, when corporations and combinations of corporations have become so powerful, it seems to us that this amendment is necessary to protect the people from the aggressions of the money power of the country." At the 1902 election, Oregonians made their state the first in the union to adopt a fully functioning initiative and referendum law by the overwhelming vote of 62,024 to 5,668.[12]

After "this revolution," as U'Ren called it, the Oregon System grew in a fairly consensual manner through 1908. Court rulings twice threatened to derail the initiative and referendum, but eventually the United States Supreme Court put its stamp of approval on direct legislation in *Pacific States Telephone and Telegraph v. Oregon*. More significantly the *Oregonian*, which had switched from opposition to a "non-commital" [*sic*] stance toward the new democratic toolkit, remained ambivalent about "that darling device of populism." Yet this organ of the Portland Establishment learned to live with direct democracy, even at times offering support for the referendum until the end of the decade, when its old hostility returned. The paper then complained that "there is a reaction all over the country against the system as exemplified in Oregon. . . . Our state seems to be undergoing crucifixion for redemption of all the rest."[13]

The flowering of popular democracy in Oregon during the first decade of the twentieth century remains truly remarkable. A cascade of laws brought considerable national attention to the direct democrats who organized what they, in 1905, named the People's Power League in order to give recognition to their ultimate purpose. In 1904 U'Ren and his allies passed a direct primary law, which included a highly original pledge system that effectively insured, for the first time anywhere in the country and well before the Seventeenth Amendment, the popular election of U.S. senators. Candidates for the Oregon legislature were required to state on the ballot if they would, or would not, guarantee their vote in the legislature for the people's choice for senator. This "Statement Number One," according to the PPL, promised to drive "the knife to the very soul of political machines." Two years later voters passed a PPL measure extending direct legislation to local governments and authorizing the publication of a voters' pamphlet containing the text of, and arguments for and against, all initiatives and referenda. The 1908 election saw the passage of the recall, a strengthening of the provisions for direct election of senators, a law making proportional representation constitutional, and a corrupt practices act that limited and publicized campaign expenditures as well as authorized, in its most distinctive feature, the state to pay for "a large part of the candidates' and parties' distribution of literature."[14]

The People's Power League avalanche had, however, come at the expense of much of the populist impulse behind direct democracy. U'Ren had of necessity worked hard, as he declared in 1901, "to disarm the fears of the conservative elements that oppose us now." He trumpeted support from Portland's elite and assured a national readership that his cause "was not in any sense a class movement." In 1904 he went further, arguing that "capitalists and business men" considered the initiative and referendum "ample insurance against any revolutionary laws." Accepting U'Ren's assurances, wealthier and more powerful champions of the Oregon System such as Jonathan Bourne—elected in 1906 to the U.S. Senate with the support of U'Ren and many of his allies—came to consider direct legislation "the safest and most conservative plan of government ever invented."[15]

Still, the populism that would emerge with much more force from U'Ren and his comrades in the second decade of the century continued to retain some of its hold on People's Power advocates even during this time of moderation and coalition building. The virtue of direct democracy, according to the liberal Democratic *Oregon Journal*, was overthrow of rule by "the 'class,' the 'organized minority,' the 'rich and powerful'"; the initiative and referendum were "of untold value to the masses, as a defense against corporate aggression." The editor of the *Portland Labor Press* maintained that under the direct primary, taxes would decrease dramatically for the "small business man's [and] mechanic's home." The intention of the Corrupt Practices Act was to "put the poor man on a footing of equality with his wealthy rival in aspiring to public office," and the PPL argued that "the right to spend large sums of money publicly in elections tends to the choice of none but rich men or tools of wealthy corporations to important offices, and thus deprives the people's government of the services of its poorer citizens."[16]

By 1908 the tenuous threads holding the multiclass coalition had become seriously frayed, and a radical language of class reappeared in the face of rising conservative opposition. U'Ren and several of his People's Power allies, in supporting a strengthening of the system of grand jury indictments against arbitrary district attorneys, warned that "the time will inevitably come when wealth and great interests will seek to shut the mouth of every man who is against them." That same year AFL general organizer C. O. Young reinvigorated the rhetoric of the 1890s when, according to headlines in the *Labor Press*, he declared that the "Laboring and Producing Masses Require and Must Have Immediate Relief From Growing Abuses. Force of Events Has Driven All The Middle Classes Together for Non-Partisan Protective Political Action."[17]

THE GLASGOW VOTER
(Scotland)
My city is governed by the Council
and my ballot contains just the single

THE DES MOINES (IOWA)
VOTER
My city is governed by a commission
of Five, and my ballot contains just

THE PORTLAND, OREGON
VOTER, WITH A BALLOT
THREE FEET LONG
My city, county and state are gov-

The Portland voter, suffering from the excesses of direct democracy. (Joseph Gaston, *Portland, Oregon: Its History and Builders* [Chicago, 1911], vol. 1, opp. 639; courtesy Oregon Historical Society, #11457.)

Overall, then, it is little wonder that so many Americans closely watched Oregon as a "political experiment station." Oregon was, in effect, the only state to use the initiative and referendum in the first decade of the century, with voters casting their ballots 23 times on various measures. (Oklahoma, the only other state to use direct legislation during this period, did so only once.) Citizens in Portland itself were even busier, voting 129 times on municipal matters between 1905 and 1913. The enthusiasm of Burton Hendrick could barely be contained: "these sixty or seventy thousand freemen who regularly engage in law-making every two years may be regarded as the 'composite citizen'—*a typical illustration of the middle-class American conscience*. For the first time in history, they furnish a detailed picture of the workings of this American mind."[18]

As the decade neared an end, it became clear that not everyone shared Hendrick's fervor for the Oregon System. Earlier, in the euphoric aftermath of direct legislation's passage, only extremist lone wolves had expressed their opposition. For example, Ralph Duniway, son of Portland's famous suffragist

Abigail Scott Duniway, went so far as to declare in 1904 that "if the initiative and referendum is in force, I predict that men will be shot in the streets of Portland, that a state of anarchy will exist in Oregon, and that it will be necessary to call out the Federal troops." As the Oregon System gained national renown, though, the ranks of its opponents grew to include presidents of both Harvard University and the United States. Local resistance sprouted as well, particularly from the Republican Party, which starting in 1907 attempted to reconstruct its machine by holding nominating "assemblies" meant to circumvent the direct primary. Charles Carey, a prominent local corporation attorney and leader in the Republican machine, called direct democracy "utterly subversive of [the] essential feature of the American plan." Overall, "devastating assaults" effectively put "the reform movement in Oregon . . . on trial for its life."[19]

The democratic dreamer who met this ruling-class challenge to the People's Power was William Simon U'Ren.

CHAPTER NINE

DIRECT DEMOCRACY'S MECHANIC

William S. U'Ren

Paul Douglas, the staunchly liberal U.S. senator from Illinois, tells a story in his memoirs. A graduate student at Harvard during the teens, he became fast friends with the prominent economist F. W. Taussig. Douglas unfortunately also had a professor whose best days were behind him. C. J. Bullock, supposed to teach a course on pre-Smithian economic theory, instead "spent most of his time in virulent attacks on Woodrow Wilson, Jane Addams, and William S. U'Ren, the Oregonian who was the father of the initiative and referendum and of direct popular government in the United States."[1]

Progressive Era citizens would have well understood the inclusion of U'Ren in Bullock's unholy trinity. Like Wilson and Addams, U'Ren was in the front ranks of progressive democracy in Progressive America. And while not nearly as influential as presidents, he certainly did have their ear. In what might seem a trivial interaction, Theodore Roosevelt and U'Ren were conversing on a train when TR heard a distinctive birdsong. U'Ren identified the melody as the song of the western meadowlark. As a result TR credited U'Ren with giving him faith that "the radical democratic movement" could bring to America not just justice and equality, but also a higher level of appreciation of the spiritual and cultural dimensions of life.[2]

More substantively, influential editor Norman Hapgood related in his autobiography that Woodrow Wilson, once he "had seriously put his mind" to an issue, *never* changed his opinions—with one exception. The subject was popular government, the agent of change U'Ren. Wilson above all believed in the necessity of full and fair deliberation in government, and he regarded Congress as the best embodiment of such politics. Yet U'Ren, who had worked with Wilson on behalf of the short ballot, convinced the most eminent Calvinist politician of the day that the people as a whole were truly the best hope for thoughtful political decisions. The radical democrat from Oregon thus produced "the biggest change in [Wilson's] thought made by anybody."[3]

These examples point to William U'Ren as the most robust national symbol of populist democracy during the first decades of the twentieth century. As George Mowry put it during the 1950s, when the memory of U'Ren had yet to be extinguished, the Oregonian was "perhaps more responsible in an indirect way for influencing the political life of the several states than any other man in the nation." Still, U'Ren was fundamentally a local hero. He electrified politics in Progressive Era Portland as, in the words of Stewart Holbrook, "the most powerful man in Oregon." Orthodox populists might have scorned him, declaring this longtime lawyer a parasite on the republican body politic. Yet U'Ren actually served as the literal as well as ideological embodiment of the world of male producerism carried from the nineteenth century into the corporate era. He illustrates perhaps better than anyone the democratic possibilities of petit bourgeois radicalism as it came to grips with—and shaped—the modern age.[4]

If the eugenicists prominent in the early part of the twentieth century had sought to create the perfect petit bourgeois radical, they would have tried to isolate the genes of William Simon U'Ren. Both his mother and father taught him strict lessons of poverty and independence, justice and politics. Born in Lancaster, Wisconsin, in 1859, William was the second of five children born to the Welshman William Richard U'Ren and the former Frances Jane Ivey.[5]

William the elder emigrated from Cornwall early in the century, becoming dissatisfied, as a socialist, with the old country. When economic conditions permitted, he exercised his considerable skills at blacksmithing, labor he performed as a "strict union man," and this was the trade that he bequeathed to his son. Yet the senior U'Ren "had a head and he 'hated a boss.'" Above all, as Lincoln Steffens relates the story, he "wanted to work for himself." So William R. U'Ren inflicted upon his family a drifting, hardscrabble, and generally unsuccessful career as a Great Plains farmer. As his son later put it, "I was brought up in the fear of the poor . . . the terrible fear of poverty." The father of the Oregon System also learned politics from his own father, imbibing a deep thirst for reform from *Greeley's Paper* as well as hard-hitting family discussions. Himself an avid financial supporter of direct legislation efforts in Oregon, William R. late in life continued to inspire his son with such wisdom as "the United States Senators are a lot of leeches bleeding the whole nation of producers for the interest of the idle *rich*." This insight came in a 1908 letter in which father pleaded with son not to run for the Senate. By continuing the fight at home in Oregon for "Reform measures and wholesome laws," William S. could do so much more for "the labouring people . . . the producers . . . the ever down trodden *masses*," in other words "our class."[6]

Yet William and Frances U'Ren had come to the United States not just to seek economic success, but also to live a holier life as followers of John Wesley. Indeed, his mother had a strong claim on young Will's mind, raising her children "in an atmosphere of mysticism and devotion to God" that followed a three-centuries-long family Dissenting tradition. With only one full year of formal schooling, the Bible became the young U'Ren's "education." "I was especially fond of the Old Testament leaders, Moses and the rest," he told a 1928 interviewer; "I suppose it's because they were never satisfied with things as they were, but were always kicking." While his father told him of the evils of the "slave interest," U'Ren's mother told stories of "poor little black children sold away from their mothers." As Steffens recounted, "just as some boys want to be Napoleon, so young U'Ren dreamed that when he grew up he would be like Moses, the giver of laws that should lead the people out of Darkness into the land of Promise."[7]

William S. U'Ren would, however, be forced to wander in the wilderness before arriving in the promised land of Oregon at the age of thirty. After toiling in his father's shop and joining the Grange, U'Ren went out into the world at the age of seventeen, finding work in Colorado first as a laborer and then as a miner. Realizing that would-be legislators needed to understand the law, U'Ren attended evening law school, along with night classes at Denver Business College, before his admission to the bar at the age of twenty-one. He practiced in Aspen, Gunnison, and Tin Cup, serving as a newspaper editor in the latter village while also dabbling in Colorado Republican politics. Yet U'Ren came down with tuberculosis on top of his chronic asthma, and a doctor sent him off to seek a warm climate in the slight hope that he might have more than a few months to live. "I went to Honolulu to die," U'Ren later related. Instead, during his travels he encountered Henry George's *Progress and Poverty*, regaining his will to live so that he one day might serve the cause of the single tax and political democracy.[8]

U'Ren moved to his parents' ranch in eastern Oregon upon his return from Hawaii in 1889, landing a job as a stock hand but possessing the burning goal of laboring so that the state "would no longer be boss-ridden and corporation controlled." He quickly jumped into the reform cause, working in the early 1890s with Edwin Bingham on a successful fight for the Australian ballot. After hooking up with the Seth, Sophronia, and Alfred Luelling family of Milwaukie, Oregon, at a spiritualist séance, U'Ren took up the orcharding business with this prominent Populist family. He threw himself into the cause of direct legislation, using to great effect his position as secretary of the state Populist Party (a post he retained from 1894 until at least 1900) and as the leader, from his seat in the Oregon House of Representatives, of the 1897 Populist legislative caucus. He began his ascent toward national visibility in 1898 with election to the executive committee of the National Direct Legislation League. U'Ren finally stopped moving around after a trip, in the midst of the Boer War, to South Africa, where he settled the estate of his brother and worked outdoors in a sunny climate in order to relieve his asthma. He established a law practice with fellow Clackamas County reformer Christian Schuebel and, in early 1901, married Mary Beharell. His new wife, a widow from Ashland who taught for many years in southeast Portland's Brooklyn Elementary School and, late in their lives, served as her husband's secretary, was herself politically active. Mary U'Ren served as a state officer of the Oregon Women's Club early in their marriage and later was appointed, with her husband, to the Clackamas County library board.[9]

As he entered the most prominent phase of his political life, from 1902 to

William S. U'Ren, architect of direct democracy. (Courtesy Oregon Historical Society, #81789.)

1914, William U'Ren brought to his radical visions a background that covered nearly the entire occupational grounding of the American petite bourgeoisie, and this vocational diversity had critical consequences for his political ideals. U'Ren had served his time as an unskilled laborer and miner, had both grown up on a farm and run an orchard, had taken his turn at the artisan's bench, and had finally became an independent lawyer in his own firm. In an intriguing self-description, U'Ren wrote to the *Direct Legislation Record* that he "never graduated at any college; never distinguished myself particularly." That level of ambition was perfectly fine for someone who clearly imbibed the spirit of the petit bourgeois competence. As U'Ren told Lincoln Steffens in 1908, "my earnings average about $1,800 a year. . . . I haven't any money, but I haven't any wants either."[10]

We can, then, clearly label U'Ren a "middle-class" Progressive. But in the age of organization, U'Ren continued to draw his political ideals not from corporate white-collar work or the emerging professions, but from the rough-hewn world of the crafts. "Blacksmithing is my trade," he declared, and "it has always given colour to my view of things." This "citizen in politics" drew a tight connection between economics and public life. He pointed out that "in government, *the common trade of all men* and the basis of all social life, men worked still with old tools, with old laws, with constitutions and charters which hindered more than they helped." U'Ren then asked Steffens, "Why had we no tool makers for democracy?" Invoking the nineteenth-century artisanal universe, with its common roots in both the petite bourgeoisie and the proletariat, U'Ren elegantly stated the purpose behind his crusade for direct democracy: "You see, I saw it all in terms of the mechanic."[11]

With the victory of the initiative and referendum in 1902, U'Ren gained his claim to fame—and the attention of later historians. U'Ren recorded a remarkable string of victories as he extended the Oregon System during the first decade of the century. During this time, his power in Oregon politics was immense. As the *Oregonian* complained:

> Mr. U'Ren proposes to draft a law regulating the use of money in political campaigns. Will it be enacted? Of course it will. In Oregon the state government is divided into four departments—the executive, judicial, legislative and Mr. U'Ren— and it is still an open question which exerts the most power. One fact must be considered in making comparisons. That the Legislature does not dare to repeal the acts of Mr. U'Ren, the executive has no opportunity to veto them, and thus far the judiciary has upheld all his laws and constitutional amendments. On the contrary, Mr. U'Ren has boldly clipped the wings of the executive and legislative departments, and when he gets time will doubtless put some shackles on the Supreme Court. To date, the indications are that Mr. U'Ren outweighs any one and perhaps all three of the other departments.

U'Ren also played regular hardball politics, managing the successful 1906 campaign of Republican Jonathan Bourne for Senate as well as Bourne's unsuccessful bid for reelection. U'Ren had returned to the Republican fold after the demise of Populism, but he made it clear that his partisan attachment was thin. To Bourne he wrote, "the party collar does not bind me any closer than it does you, and if necessary to strengthen the People's Power I shall vote and talk for a Democrat." As for the party of Bryan and Wilson, U'Ren wrote to Bourne, "The Democratic Party cannot be as progressive as the . . . Republicans until the negro question is settled." U'Ren's politics clearly had a radical edge that transcended garden-variety Progressive antipartisanship. As he wrote to one of his confidantes in 1904, "I think if I were disposed to take any vigorous party action I would fall in with the socialists. That is a growing party and really stands for some live issues, while it seems to me that the economic development of the government has already carried us far beyond most of the issues raised by the Omaha platform."[12]

U'Ren avidly supported woman suffrage, speaking to enthusiastic audiences at the national suffrage conventions in 1905 and 1908 and in general "warmly advocat[ing] the right of women to participate in government and law." He was a much-sought-after speaker at union forums and Labor Day celebrations, serving the workers' cause as an attorney and drafter of legislation on such matters as the minimum wage and employers' liability. For two weeks in 1908 U'Ren threw his hat in the race for U.S. senator, withdrawing after pushing one of his Republican rivals to declare more forcefully his support for the popular election of the Senate. U'Ren's platform included advocacy of national direct legislation as well as his declaration, "I will most loyally support President Roosevelt in his rebellion against government of the United States by Standard Oil and its allies." That same year, Lincoln Steffens wrote, "I believe that [Oregon] will appear before long as the leader of reform in the United States, and if it is, W. S. U'Ren will rank in history as the greatest lawgiver of his day and country."[13]

U'Ren continued to garner national honors, becoming vice president of the Short Ballot Association under Woodrow Wilson in 1909 and a member of the executive committee of the National Progressive Republican League in 1911. U'Ren also served on the Committee of Fifty that set up the National Popular Government League to coordinate efforts for direct legislation throughout the United States. Immediately after the 1912 election, U'Ren made his most dramatic move to secure power in his own state, announcing his candidacy for governor. "I am going to get the radical vote," he proudly predicted. U'Ren first announced as an independent candidate and then also accepted the Prohibition nomination until the secretary of state ruled that he could not list two affiliations. U'Ren's platform included extension of the ·Oregon System, prohibition, "abolition of most of the Commissions," and good roads. It was that seemingly mundane last plank that drew the most opposition, for U'Ren not only intended to pay for the roads with a graduated inheritance tax but wished to require the state to employ "every citizen of Oregon who is in need of employment and demands the work" at wages "sufficient to care for and educate" a family.[14]

"It is for these measures that plutocracy hates him with a bitterness that cannot be expressed in words," announced U'Ren's trusted comrade Alfred Cridge. Cridge did not exaggerate. U'Ren's full-employment plan inspired considerable debate with the *Oregonian*, which decried the scheme's "utter impracticability, its sheer insanity." "Mr. U'Ren is dismayed by no Socialistic adventure, however dangerous, unprecedented or revolutionary," the newspaper declared; his "measure is in essence the last word in communism." U'Ren formulated a rebuttal true to the deepest impulses of middle-class radicalism. Public schools, bridges, and ferries are "socialistic," U'Ren noted in declaring that a nonissue. Even more expansively, the gubernatorial candidate maintained that "if the state has the right to punish a citizen for being idle, it is also the duty of the state to offer him a job at some honorable employment before convicting him of vagrancy. . . . Is it anything less than a crime against the laws of thrift and public welfare for the state to permit any citizen to remain idle who wants to work?" U'Ren disputed the charge that his inheritance tax would drive wealth out of the state, but then asked in inimitable middling fashion: "suppose there should be no estates above $50,000? Possibly there would not then be any unemployed. There are men now living who can remember when there was not an estate above $50,000 in Oregon, and neither was there an unemployed problem." U'Ren therefore disagreed with the *Oregonian* that he was "promoting class warfare," for "All my effort in politics is and has been for measures tending to remove the causes that produce class hatred and warfare. . . . No one class can make the law in Oregon now. It was not so before the initiative and referendum were adopted." This is indeed middle-class classlessness. But it is worlds away from the inegalitarian liberalism that intellectuals use to indict the middle-class political imagination.[15]

Campaigning in the name of The People, U'Ren gained the endorsement of organized labor and the populist *Portland News*. As the *Labor Press* proclaimed, "The working man or woman, the farmer, the business man, the professional man, who does not have some interest with the big corporations, expresses confidence in Mr. U'Ren." Not enough confidence, though, for U'Ren suffered the most humiliating defeat of his career. He finished fourth in the governor's race, behind even the Socialist candidate. The following year conservative commentator C. C. Chapman offered a genuine compliment: "Some day pilgrims may visit the home of U'Ren as a shrine, for today he is possibly known more widely throughout the world than any other citizen of Oregon, and his name will thunder down the ages as the founder of the Oregon system." Still, such talk of memorialization meant that the age of U'Ren was effectively over.[16]

Defeat did not deter U'Ren. He moved to southeast Portland from Oregon City immediately after the election and set up a new law practice. U'Ren maintained his single-tax agitation for two more years, and his active tinkering with the machinery of Oregon's government until 1923. He became an even more constant friend of labor, serving as the attorney of choice for strikers or other workers in trouble with the law. U'Ren polished up his government employment scheme again in 1919, persuading future governor Walter Pierce to introduce it in the legislature. This inspired the C. C. Chapman to offer a different characterization of U'Ren, this time as the "high priest of Oregon radicalism." The *Oregonian* protested his "pale pink version of bolshevism."[17]

U'Ren put his ideas about class and radicalism on the line most boldly in

William U'Ren defending Communist Labor Party members in 1920 criminal syndicalism trial. (Courtesy Oregon Historical Society, # 009663.)

the 1920 trial of three Communists, the first offenders prosecuted under the state's criminal syndicalism law. U'Ren made it clear that "the 'dictatorship of the proletariat' to my mind is the rankest nonsense." Still, he told jurors, "Christ was an agitator, if you remember," and he announced that the "beautiful dreams" of the defendants were peaceful and harmless. In turn, U'Ren compared Mayor George Baker's attempt to prevent a public talk by Portlander Louise Bryant to the czar's suppression of free speech in Russia. U'Ren even insisted that "there is much commendable in the communist state the communist labor party seeks to install in America." Finally, U'Ren used the trial to show that his populist language of class was by no means fully incompatible with his clients' more modern Marxism. As the *Oregonian* reported,

> By "industrial proletariat," U'Ren explained, was meant all workers, whether with brain or brawn, wearers of white collars or not. Incidentally, all the defendants in the trial wear white collars. . . . "The 'proletariat' might even include lawyers and judges," said U'Ren, smiling. In his judgment it included virtually all men who work, excluding idle millionaires and others who toil not.[18]

U'Ren's commitments remained the same for the next thirty years, but after 1920 he bowed out of the limelight. He popped up occasionally with plans to outlaw all American "wars of aggression, whether for conquest or collection of debts or for avenging insults and injuries." U'Ren also stepped up his activities for civil liberties, becoming by the depression the "locus of ACLU power in the city." He continued his service on the interlocking directorate of national reform organizations, serving as a member of the American Civil Liberties Union national committee and on the executive committees of the National Single Tax League and National Popular Government League as well as a vice president of the National Short Ballot Organization and the American Proportional Representation League.[19]

Seeking to amend the direct primary law and "drive the loan sharks from the state through limiting their interest charges to reasonable rates," U'Ren gained the Republican nomination for the Oregon House of Representatives in 1932 and 1934 but suffered defeat in the general election. Initially a supporter of FDR, U'Ren turned bitterly against the New Deal, assailing its paternalism. In its place, U'Ren proposed abolishing "involuntary unemployment by providing unlimited opportunity for voluntary, co-operative self supporting and productive labor." The incorruptible Corps of Engineers would supervise an "American Industrial Army" that any citizen could enlist for or resign from at any time. The army would operate with minimal bureaucracy and would not create any burden on taxpayers. Enlisted members would fill almost all "positions of authority and leadership," but without additional remuneration, working toward the goal of "the largest practicable measure of self-government" by the workers themselves. "Our government by the people cannot long endure if citizens who are able and willing to work are forced to exist on the government dole," U'Ren proclaimed, "instead of being enabled to support that government and themselves by their own labor. Political freedom is impossible without economic independence." U'Ren predicted the disappearance not just of government relief but of private charity as well upon the adoption of his plan.[20]

U'Ren's petit bourgeois goals thus remained constant throughout his long life. As he put it just two months before his death, he demanded "a job for everybody and proprietary interest in the job." No romantic who wished to do away with wage labor, U'Ren nevertheless insisted that individual economic independence and radical democracy were the proper goals of political life and that centralized power of any sort was the enemy. As journalists such as Richard Neuberger sounded him out on the occasion of his ninetieth birthday in 1949, they found that U'Ren "is afraid that political authority has become too concentrated in Washington, D.C. He also worries over what he calls the 'growing influence of the military' in government. Yet he thinks business also has become too big and endorses any 'constitutional' efforts to shackle corporate monopolies." Big labor came in for scorn as well because of its rampant jurisdictional disputes and dictatorial leadership.[21]

William Simon U'Ren went to his death on March 8, 1949, then, a firm believer that populists could seek a radical path that transcended the dependencies of both the liberal welfare state and laissez-faire capitalism. It is therefore fitting that just a few years earlier Czech visitors seeking a third way between capitalism and communism came to consult U'Ren on their peculiar dilemma.[22]

Yet was U'Ren simply an unsullied radical democrat, holding throughout his long life an unshaken confidence in popular rule? Here the comparison with Moses is not completely inappropriate. For U'Ren too had his various crises of faith in the people. Perhaps knowing that, ultimately, he would not reach the promised land, U'Ren at times grew angry with the stiff-necked populace in ways that compromised his democratic convictions. In coming to grips with U'Ren's legacy—and that of the democratic populism that he represents—we must, then, evaluate U'Ren's occasional turning away from a full and complete confidence in all of The People.

The earliest evidence of William U'Ren's betrayal—if that is not too strong a word—of radical democracy might come in a blueprint for direct legislation that the Oregon legislature considered in 1896. This plan included a literacy test for voting. It is impossible to tell, however, whether it was U'Ren or some legislator who inserted the clause. The case against U'Ren becomes much more compelling when we consider a 1910 statement from direct democracy advocates. Extolling the virtues of the Oregon System, U'Ren and his staunchest allies approvingly noted that "in what are called the slum districts and precincts the vote on measures is commonly a comparatively small percentage of the vote for officers." Or the clinching piece of evidence: U'Ren, alone, declaring in 1907 that

> in all our work we have found the great value of well-known names attached to our measures as officers or members of committees. Though not all of our friends were able to give much time, their names worked for them. You see, the average man is either too indolent, too busy, or too distrustful of his own judgment to study or decide for himself upon the details of a law on a great public question. People always ask of a proposition to enact a principle they approve, "Who is back of it?"

It is this specific statement that antiplebiscitarian Arthur Lipow jumps on to unmask the direct democrats. "Where in this is the rational and the educated citizen, or 'faith in the people' which latter-day historians have attributed to the Progressive mind by way of explaining their naivete?" Lipow legitimately asks. He continues: "Naive? Hardly. Shrewd and manipulative, certainly."[23]

The problem with this kind of debunking of the Progressives is that it lacks the complexity that we need to understand the democratic impulse that, almost with a will of its own, struggled to escape from the bad faith of antidemocracy. U'Ren displays this ambivalent, seemingly contradictory, way of thinking in the same year—even in the same article. In 1907, for example, U'Ren both noted that "woman suffrage and the local option law received the highest percentages of votes, showing that men do not vote on questions they do not understand" *and* vigorously argued that "the people of Oregon have learned that to get the best results they must do their own governing every day." Over and over U'Ren celebrated the active, delibera- tive, educational, and public qualities of direct democracy in ways and quan- tities that easily overwhelm his more antidemocratic statements. Most impor- tantly, U'Ren emphatically—if not consistently—included the lowest of the low in his conception of the political universe. At a Central Labor Council smoker in 1910 U'Ren proudly proclaimed that "no blacker Republican ex- isted than himself" and declared that "it is now up to the mudsills to legis- late." Three years later U'Ren expressed concern that if a higher percentage of signatures was required for initiative and referendum petitions, it would be- come "almost impossible to submit any measure that is desired in the inter- ests of the common people, or those who have little money or none at all besides what they earn by a day's wages." By 1919 U'Ren was supporting a universal compulsory voting bill—not a measure designed to warm the hearts of a terribly high number of progressive disfranchisers.[24]

In the end, U'Ren fundamentally believed that "the people can not depend on any man or a few men to confer any kind of freedom upon them." That he acted with mixed motives, and at times thought in a way that contra- dicted his primary convictions, does not remove him from the noble populist pantheon. After all, we live in an imperfect world, and arguably any radical democrat must eventually experience some crisis of faith in the masses. How a democrat recovers from these lapses then becomes the key question. We can witness William U'Ren's confidence in The People even more clearly as we explore his most daring democratic experiments—first, a dramatic reor- ganization of the state government, and, finally, a plan to overthrow the ruling class by installing housewives at the center of Oregon's political life.[25]

CHAPTER TEN

FROM THE GRAND REORGANIZATION TO A SYNDICALISM OF HOUSEWIVES

Feminist Populism and the Other Spirit of '76

William U'Ren and his comrades diluted their class hostility and democratic radicalism in the movement to extend the Oregon System from 1902 to 1908, but their populism returned to the fore during the most critical years of Progressivism. From 1909 to 1914, when the fate of reform was most fundamentally at stake, the advocates of People's Power attempted a much more drastic restructuring of Oregon's government than most liberals could tolerate or most Americans could even envision. This time, they met defeat. Still, many components of their blueprint for a true people's democracy continue to speak compellingly to us today, arising as they do from a dissenting tradition that goes back to the contested nature of our nation's founding. Moreover, U'Ren and his allies went beyond a simple reinvigoration of Anti-Federalism to innovatively blend into their democratic populism a feminist ideology that, while initially tentative, blossomed into another remarkable manifestation of middle-class radicalism.

The Grand Reorganization, 1909–1914

Charles Beard called the grand reorganization of the state government sought by U'Ren and his allies "one of the most suggestive documents to be found in recent American political literature." U'Ren had toyed with the idea of unifying the multitude of unaccountable state boards and commissions under one board of directors at least since 1906. The People's Power League commenced work along these lines during the summer of 1909 by requesting comments on what many considered a completely new constitution for the State of Oregon. U'Ren and his associates modified their proposals several times over the next few years, placing portions of their "revolutionary" designs on the ballot in 1910, 1912, and 1914.[1]

On first glance the organizational vision of U'Ren, the chief author, appears to be strikingly antidemocratic. One of the primary goals of his new civic design was to model state and county governments after business corporations, so that their conduct "may be made as efficient and economical as the management by the citizens of their private business." A highly centralized administration would anchor the new state government. The governor would have sole authority over all boards and commissions, would introduce all appropriations bills, and would appoint almost all of his cabinet as well as a state business manager to supervise the financial affairs of the state. As U'Ren explained, "on the executive side there must be undivided responsibility—one mind." Legislative terms would be six years. Overall, the enemies of populist democracy had apparently won a complete victory where it was least expected; as U'Ren put it, "no one has ever said there is victory in a multitude of generals, or business success in a crowd of general managers."[2]

But first glances are, in this case, deceptive. U'Ren's initial defense of the plan against charges that it was "monarchical" was simply that the people, under their expansive powers of direct democracy, could well defend their own liberties. U'Ren argued also that an easily identifiable and responsible chief executive would in many ways be more amenable to carrying out the public will than a logrolling, gerrymandered legislature precisely because it would be so easy to pin blame and responsibility on the governor—an argument that historians have unfairly dismissed.[3]

Most importantly, the grand reorganization included mechanisms to insure not just the maintenance, but also the extension, of democratic rule. First, U'Ren and his allies wished to limit the governor to one term and, crucially, strip the executive of the veto. State courts would also lose their power of judicial review. The tools of direct democracy would always be at the ready, as the governor could order the referendum on any piece of legislation that either he or the legislature proposed. As U'Ren noted, "there can be no danger of placing too much executive power with one man, if he is directly responsible to his employers, the people. The recall should be made much more easily workable than it is now." Indeed, the powers of the recall would extend to dissolution of the entire legislature. Not without good reason did the advocates of People's Power claim that "this plan *centralizes the state executive power towards the people*."[4]

To insure full popular access, an elected board of full-time "People's Inspectors of Government" would keep permanent watch on the government from seats on the floor of the legislature. The inspectors would publish all documents and commentary relevant to the functioning of government at all levels in an official state gazette sent to voters six times a year. The gazette would be necessary because "the citizens and taxpayers have no authentic information; no exact knowledge, nor any practical means of informing themselves about the doings of their public officers." It would be the ideal forum for deliberative democracy, becoming "a medium in which any citizen who has criticism, suggestion or news to offer concerning any department or office of government, or any measure, can submit his thought to every voter and taxpayer in the state, county, city, or district, as the case may be." A new set of checks and balances based on full and active citizenship would replace the clunky traditional system. "Every voter," proclaimed the People's Power

League, "should have knowledge and interest every day and all the time in his government; a great interest for three or four weeks of a 'hot campaign' once in two or four years is not enough."[5]

And despite his use of the corporate model, U'Ren voiced a strikingly anticorporate vision of the relationship between politics and society. Responding to some of Herbert Croly's commentary on the Oregon reorganization plan, U'Ren waxed philosophical—in a highly subversive mode:

> Citizens are the chief and most valuable product of government. The success of any government is to be judged by the poorest, least efficient and least useful able bodied citizen it produces, in comparison with what that citizen might have been worth to the state and to himself if he had been given every possible advantage by the state.
>
> A government is entitled to be called good, better, or best, in proportion to its success in obtaining the following results:
>
> That no child shall toil beyond its years and strength;
>
> That no adult shall ever be hungry or cold or want of food, clothing, or shelter;
>
> That no citizen shall ever suffer involuntary disemployment for so much as one day (That any man should have to hunt a job is high treason by the government against the man.);
>
> That jobs at good wages shall always be seeking men and women.
>
> That every citizen shall get all he earns, and earn all he gets.[6]

So, despite initial appearances, both the structure of, and the motivation for, the People's Power League grand governmental reorganization were substantively democratic. Contrasting U'Ren's vision with those of two of the period's most prominent Progressive political theorists underscores this point. Herbert Croly praised the Oregon plan and devoted more than a chapter to it in his 1914 book *Progressive Democracy*, in many ways a more systematic exposition of his philosophy than the earlier acclaimed *The Promise of American Life*. Yet Croly's angle of vision was in certain critical areas completely opposed to U'Ren's. To begin, Croly believed that the strengthening of Oregon's executive was a systematic corrective to, not a fulfillment of, direct democracy, which he felt had almost completely debilitated the legislature. Although he supported proportional representation, a key component of the reorganization, Croly made no mention of the People's Inspectors of Government. Most significantly, Croly vigorously opposed any expansive use of the tools of direct democracy, coming very close to saying that the initiative and referendum were merely veneers necessary to make the all-powerful governor more palatable to the citizenry, "negative safeguards, the existence of which may help to reconcile popular opinion to the more powerful organization of the fighting forces of a democratic state." In a similar manner, Charles Beard welcomed the Oregon plan as a sign that the friends of efficiency and the friends of democracy might finally agree on a system of government. At the same time, he and the New York Bureau of Municipal Research repudiated initiatives as "futile" and irresponsible.[7]

Unfortunately, the only recent scholarly treatments of the Oregon plan conflate U'Ren's grand reorganization with the ambivalence, if not hostility, toward majoritarianism of political theorists such as Croly and Beard. Daniel Rodgers, for one, interprets the "startling shrinkage in the number of elective offices" under the reorganization proposals as a sign of a great discomfort with the hurly-burly of decentralized and pluralistic democracy. Even more forcefully, Arthur Lipow again takes U'Ren (along with Croly) to task for his scheme to centralize state executive power and weaken the legislature. Political scientist Dwight Waldo, however, was more on the mark in 1948 when he noted that U'Ren's blueprints actually represented a genuine if at times subtle victory for "Management by the People" over "Management for the People."[8]

If a concern for administration did not submerge democratic dreams, neither did an emphasis on efficiency. "Efficiency" is one of the dirty words of Progressivism, and in many ways properly so, as the term so often masked managerial drives to dominate workers and elite efforts to regain control over popular politics. Yet a desire for efficiency could easily serve populist ends as well. When U'Ren proclaimed that government "must be so organized that it shall always obtain the highest degree of efficiency in all its departments and at least 100 cents of value in public service for every dollar of money that is collected from the tax-payers," he spoke compellingly to middling and working-class folks for whom supplying the public purse was a significant burden. The same impulse led Walter Weyl to articulate a plebeian enthusiasm for efficiency in *The New Democracy*:

> We must have a glass-house government; a government standardized and systematized; a government with double-entry bookkeeping; with conspicuous heads; with the line of responsibility leading straight and clear from the obscurest suboffi-cial to the responsible chief. Obscurity works in the interest of special classes; clarity in the interest of the people. If the people are to rule, they must not be made to waste their vision, enthusiasm, or indignation in vain attempts to determine who is to blame or what it is all about.[9]

Unicameralism and Proportional Representation

Beyond the basic governmental structure envisioned in the grand reorganization, two other features distinctive to the People's Power League governmental designs from 1909 to 1914 also point toward its radical democratizing tendencies. Little known today, unicameralism and, especially, proportional representation were important reforms in the Progressive landscape. U'Ren and his comrades were staunch advocates of both, believing that these institutional changes were crucial to the coming of people's power.

THE ASSAULT OF THE VICIOUS SEVEN.

A political cartoon from the *Oregonian* on the lunacy of direct democracy. Here the conservative voter takes aim at unicameralism, proportional representation, and other 'U'Renisms." (*Oregonian,* September 28, 1914, 1; courtesy Oregon Historical Society, #103491.)

In 1912 the People's Power League sponsored an initiative to abolish Oregon's upper house, and two years later the Grange, Farmers' Union, and Oregon State Federation of Labor joined forces in the unicameral cause. Getting rid of "the lobby-ridden, expensive, interfering, utterly useless State Senate" promised less cost, greater efficiency, and above all a dramatic reduction in the opportunity for logrolling and corruption. The state senate, like the national Senate and the House of Lords before that, was illegitimately intended, in U'Ren's words, "to represent the wealth of the country." Appealing to the successful experience of other unicameral countries, the populists asked Oregon voters to act in the spirit of the British, who had recently rendered the Lords largely powerless. Oregonians, however, were not willing to join U'Ren in this crusade. Only 30.3 percent of voters supported unicameralism in 1912, with a slight increase to 33.6 percent in 1914. Still, even that level of support could be reckoned something of a success. As a scholar later wrote about the 1912 election: "the fact that more than 30,000 ballots were cast in its favor shows an amount of approval that is surprising if we consider the weight of tradition, the special interests, and the prejudices that naturally oppose the unicameral system."[10]

A much more important part of the populist agenda was proportional representation. The complicated mathematical computations involved in PR's implementation often overshadowed the simple idea at its core. Under proportional representation, the election of the legislature would occur through a method by which any party, or other type of group, would garner the same percentage of seats as its percentage of votes statewide. The goal driving proportional representation advocates: replacing effective disfranchisement with genuine representation.

Why was PR necessary? And what were the dimensions of the problem? Elementary calculations best told the story. In the 1907 Oregon legislature, fifty-nine Republicans and one Democrat sat in the House of Representatives. Yet the percentages of the vote earned by each party would have actually translated into a bare majority of thirty-three Republicans, along with twenty Democrats, four Socialists, and three Prohibitionists. Although extreme, such malapportionment occurred frequently across the United States. Peter Argersinger has shown, for example, that although Democrats cast between 32 and 40 percent of the vote for Kansas congressional seats during the 1880s, they never elected a single candidate. Richard Oestreicher further suggests the power of different systems of electoral representation when he writes, "the 6 percent Socialist vote in 1912 gave the American Socialist party no congressional seats. In December 1910 the British Labour party received 6.4 percent of the national vote and elected forty-two members of Parliament." And, of course, Labour was ruling Britain less than four decades later. No wonder that Congressman, and future Republican president, James Garfield complained in 1870 how American voting rules left "a large portion of the voting people . . . permanently disfranchised."[11]

How to change this drastically antidemocratic system? Primarily by transforming the way Oregonians cast and, especially, counted their ballots. Many different methods of proportional representation exist, and the People's Power League chose slightly different procedures at the three elections when it placed PR proposals before the people. In 1910, for example, U'Ren's basic idea involved having legislative candidates nominated from traditional geographic districts (single-member for most of the state, with some multimember, especially for large cities) but providing voters throughout Oregon with the chance to vote for any candidate in the state. A Prohibitionist from Portland could thus place a sticker on the ballot for a fellow party member from Hood River County, and a Democrat from Newport could write in one of her comrades running from Fairview. Votes would be tallied statewide for both individual candidates and parties as a whole. For each one-sixtieth of the vote (or quota) that a party received for the sixty-member House, that party would receive one legislative seat. The candidates from each party with the highest number of votes would then claim their parties' seats.[12]

Most fundamentally, the People's Power League believed that every minority should have full representation in the political process. If a party received 17 percent of the vote, it deserved 17 percent of the seats. Yet beyond such precision, U'Ren and his associates also connected proportional representation to the rest of their populist radicalism. Not only would different parties secure legislative seats under PR, the composition of the legislators themselves would dramatically change. In 1914 U'Ren contended that proportional representation would lead to the "organization of the state government and legislature on industrial instead of purely political lines. . . . There will be fewer lawyers and doctors, but more mechanics and school teachers." And, in a talk at the Unitarian Church in 1911, U'Ren "included women as well" in his scheme to represent "interests," regretting that "one-half of the people are absolutely disfranchised, and the other half so largely misrepresented."[13]

The People's Power League hoped that its distinctive politics of class and democracy would lead to victory in the struggle for proportional representation. The PPL also sought to ride the wave of PR adoptions sweeping through much of the rest of the democratic world in these years. As two contemporary scholars noted, "it is little short of remarkable that this plan of electing representative assemblies, having made only a modicum of progress throughout the sixty or more years of its agitation, should suddenly have been widely accepted in Europe almost without disputation." North Americans were also experimenting with PR, even if in a much more limited fashion. By 1922 most cities in western Canada employed proportional representation in their municipal elections, and seven municipalities in the United States, including Cleveland and Cincinnati, adopted PR in the decade after Ashtabula, Ohio, became the first PR city in the country in 1915.[14]

Even though the People's Power League anticipated these pioneering achievements by several years, U'Ren and his comrades had good reason to think that their push for proportional representation might also be successful in the Beaver State. In 1908 Oregon voters passed, with a 58.9 percent majority, an initiative legalizing proportional representation. The legislature not only refused to act on this expression of the popular will but, to the contrary, submitted a referendum for the 1910 ballot that would have effectively outlawed PR. U'Ren and his partners received considerable comfort when the people rebuked this legislative referendum by a 30.1 to 69.9 percent margin. On the same ballot, voters also gave proportional representation (embedded in the governmental reorganization plan) a substantial 45.5 percent tally in favor of what the *Oregonian* labeled the "most dangerous of all measures submitted" in the election. Finally, PR advocates won a crucial victory when Portland voters adopted a form of commission government in 1913 that included a form of proportional representation.[15]

Election figures show that proportional representation and the grand reorganization were issues of class as well as democracy. In Portland, support for the initiative combining PR and many parts of the PPL's reorganization plan closely followed the neighborhood contours apparent in the 1917 Will Daly election, as well as in a number of other populist measures. The most basic divide again lay between the West Side and the East Side. On the West Side a greater margin than in the state as a whole, 47.8 percent, actually voted for the measure, even though thirty-one of fifty-five precincts rejected the initiative. Yet on the East Side the foot soldiers of direct democracy gave the initiative a full 56.7 percent of the vote, with eighty-five of ninety-nine precincts voting in favor. Proportional representation swept to victory in every single precinct in southeastern neighborhoods such as Sellwood, Woodstock, Woodmere, Montavilla, and Mt. Scott, as well as in all of North Portland. On the East Side, the initiative faltered only in the posh Alameda and Irvington areas, where the measure met defeat in ten of seventeen precincts, as well as in three of six precincts around upper-middle-class Laurelhurst.[16]

Despite the promising signs from the 1910 election, proportional representation went down to defeat by much larger margins in the next two elections.[17] The advocacy of PR, however, speaks tellingly to the democratic impulses at the foundation of People's Power. For the most important criticism of direct democracy is that it results in majority tyranny over unpopular and powerless minorities. Yet this condemnation, in historical perspective, unfairly isolates the initiative and referendum from the entire constellation of utopian electoral reforms envisioned by populists such as those in Progressive Era Portland.

Without a doubt, the People's Power League passionately yearned for the

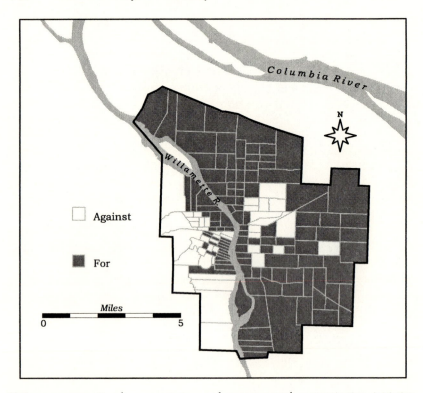

Voting on proportional representation and governmental reorganization initiative, 1910, by precinct

majority—the people—to regain its birthright and reclaim its government. Still, U'Ren and his comrades also made it clear that proportional representation, as an integral element of the Oregon System, would also preserve minority rights much more effectively than had the traditional American structure of governance. As they wisely argued in the 1910 voters' pamphlet, "the divided majority composed of many minorities has a right to representation." The People's Power League, after all its pioneering work in bringing direct democracy to Oregon, even used proportional representation to launch a defense of the potential of representative government, maintaining that PR "will eliminate, to a large degree, the necessity for using the initiative and referendum because there must, and always will be a fair discussion in the legislative assembly of minority party measures. Such debate will be led by representatives of the minorities who believe in the principles they advocate."[18]

The Oregonians' reasoning on this issue is firmly in line with the thinking of present-day advocates of proportional representation. Lani Guinier, for example, notes that PR is the most promising way to bring genuine empowerment to a wide variety of self-defined minorities, and political theorist Cass Sunstein champions proportional representation above all because it will improve the deliberative qualities of democracy. PR, according to Sunstein,

> would ensure that diverse views are expressed on an ongoing basis in the representative process, where they might otherwise be excluded. . . . proportional representation is designed to increase the likelihood that political outcomes will incorporate some understanding of the perspective of all those affected. For this reason proportional representation may be the functional analogue to the institutions of checks and balances and federalism, recognizing the creative functions of disagreement and multiple perspectives for the governmental process.

William U'Ren could not have said it better. The concluding moral: Populist radicals seeking a stronger democracy have not always been crypto-Jacobins or protofascists seeking, at their first opportunity, to trample civil liberties and minority rights.[19]

The Conundrum of Woman Suffrage

The Oregon direct democrats, with their vigorous populist radicalism, clearly deserve a much greater hearing than they have received before the court of history. Yet they might still face indictment on charges relating to the Woman Question. For it remains difficult to figure out their relationship to the supreme achievement of Progressive Era democratization, woman suffrage. After five previous attempts, Oregon in 1912 finally passed equal suffrage, becoming the seventh state in the nation to enfranchise women. In critical ways, though, the two movements operated in parallel universes. Direct democrats consistently supported woman suffrage, and suffragists regularly expressed their enthusiasm for the initiative and referendum. Both sets of reformers, however, only rarely engaged each other in any substantive fashion. Small producer patriarchy clearly did not prevent these populists from upholding the most important women's movement of the day. Why, then, did they not make a more effective connection to the suffragists? In turn, why did the woman suffragists have so little concern for petit bourgeois radicalism? The answer, in a complex way, seems to be largely a matter of class.[20]

The National American Woman Suffrage Association held its annual convention in Portland in 1905 to celebrate the Lewis and Clark Centennial and the associated world's fair. Yet the atmosphere was heady not because of the historical ceremonies, but because of the momentum of the Oregon System. Suffragists looked to the initiative and referendum with great hope and excitement, and the two movements appeared to hold a shared destiny. So great was the melding that Florence Kelley, upon her return from the NAWSA convention, noted that "it is a curious fact that a man is the head and front of this suffrage campaign, a Mr. U'Ren, a leading citizen of Portland."[21]

Kelley spoke inaccurately about the lines of authority among the state's suffrage leadership, but she was correct about the support of suffrage by Oregon direct democrats. The most prominent Portland populists lent their names to the suffrage cause, provided advice to the movement, and spoke powerfully of the justice of granting women the right to vote. Newly inaugurated mayor Harry Lane welcomed the national suffrage convention to the Rose City in 1905, and William U'Ren and C.E.S. Wood (who would subsequently marry suffragist Sara Bard Field) figured prominently among the speakers at the proceedings. The next year influential People's Power League member E.S.J. McAllister spoke at the final suffrage rally, and H. W. Stone, who would later serve on the PPL's executive committee, also gave a stirring address. In future elections Will Daly and Alfred Cridge added their names to the illustrious roster of direct democrats endorsing woman suffrage.[22]

These architects of the Oregon System not only endorsed the reform but also seemed—at least at times, and often in retrospect—to have conceived of woman suffrage and direct democracy as part and parcel of the same grand movement of the people against the oppressors. H. W. Stone, for example, warned the suffragists in 1906 that "the conservative corporations and financial institutions invariably opposed reform." The president and secretary of the Oregon State Federation of Labor agreed, arguing in the same year that suffrage was "destined to become one of the strongest factors in the solution of the economic struggle of the common people against plutocratic oppression." After the 1912 triumph, William U'Ren proudly noted: "We gained equal suffrage, which is a great victory." U'Ren later routinely included women's full citizenship in his list of "some of the things the people of Oregon have done . . . under the so-called Oregon System." And after his crushing defeat for governor in 1914, U'Ren still took heart in the wisdom of the people, reflected in "our past victories for initiative, referendum, recall, equal rights for women, employers' liability and worker's compensation."[23]

In turn, suffragists both national and local showered praise on the Oregon System. Susan B. Anthony, attending her last NAWSA convention months before her death, proclaimed: "the people of Oregon have inaugurated the initiative and referendum, perhaps the most salient movement of modern times for the emancipation of the masses from the power of the bosses. And this institution, we are sure, is the hope of women, and the many men who are with us." After U'Ren's speech at the 1905 convention, NAWSA "enthusiastically" passed a Carrie Chapman Catt resolution praising the initiative and referendum, "contrary to the habit of the association to consider only subjects relating directly to women and children." Local activists agreed. "The most powerful defense of the people is the initiative and referendum," according to the Oregon Equal Suffrage Association, and antisuffragists opposed direct democracy because "it is the increased vote of the laboring citizens that the millionaire classes fear."[24]

Oregon suffragists therefore showed, in what proved to be their most hard-fought campaign, just how readily the language of suffrage could flow into a populist language of class. Portland suffragist Sarah Evans complained about the unprecedented mobilization of "the upper and lower classes of anti-suffragists" in the 1906 campaign. After all, even the *Oregonian* recognized that the funding and organizational support behind the antisuffrage cause was coming from the "leading business men of Portland." Suffragists responded by turning their crusade into a genuine episode of class conflict. "A Working Woman" complained to the *News* that the antisuffragists came from the "non-producing faction of society." The OESA protested "the liquor interests, the corporations and the society ladies" employing, through attempts to manipulate voters, "the same old past method by which capital wrings from labor the millions which it enjoys." The most powerful Portland suffragists, Abigail Scott Duniway and Viola Coe, censured the opposition, "armed to the teeth with ballots, corporate power and capital." Elsewhere, Coe promised to mobilize the grand populist alliance, "the poor and the middle classes," in the cause of justice.[25]

But . . . that was that. The woman suffragists and direct democrats had been speaking almost precisely the same language in the ultimately unsuccessful 1906 suffrage campaign. The Oregon Federated Trades Council best expressed this blended rhetoric when it unanimously passed a resolution, offered by Lucy White and May Keegan of the Garment Workers' Union. "The recent protest by the corporate interests of Portland against equal rights for men and women," the resolution declared, "shows that the big corporations, the enemies of the people, are also the enemies of justice to women." After this election, though, the two movements increasingly took separate paths. As Sarah Henry has noted, direct democrats did on occasion give aid to woman suffrage, but they "never elevated it to equal status with their other reform proposals." On the other side, Duniway and her allies no longer spoke about empowering the masses in their struggle against corporate exploiters. In fact, two years after another stinging defeat in 1908, the OESA rejected its universalism and actually submitted a *taxpayers'* suffrage amendment, "bitterly fought by labor and fraternal organizations." In the elections following 1906 the suffragists—rarely—condemned the "women who are supported in idleness and luxury," but by the time of their final campaign in 1912, they were much more likely simply to mention that "there is always an element that resents change," thus draining their rhetoric of any class antagonism.[26]

One of the genuine ironies of this disjunction between an increasingly liberal suffrage movement and an increasingly populist direct democracy movement is that, quite possibly, the two crusades missed a major opportunity to unite on behalf of radical reform. Once again, precinct voting totals supply some intriguing information to help fill in a gap left by a lack of correspondence or letters to the editors—the kinds of sources necessary to get into the heads of the main players making strategic decisions for each movement.

The Oregon suffragists came to believe they had made serious mistakes in the 1906 campaign. Yet they actually did significantly better in that year, winning 43.9 percent of the vote statewide, than they did in 1908 and 1910, when their share of the vote dipped to 38.6 percent and then 37.4 percent. Suffrage consistently did worse in Multnomah County than anywhere else in the state. The key to gaining victory, then, in many ways lay in convincing Portland voters to support equal suffrage. Understanding this, the suffragists could have recognized that their most fertile source of support lay on the east side of the Willamette. As with so many other populist measures, the middling East Side favored woman suffrage significantly more than did the class-riven West Side. In 1906, for example, only 29.8 percent of West Side voters approved woman suffrage, but that figure went up to 40.6 percent on the East Side. When the suffragists dropped their rhetoric of class, however, they could not maintain their electoral base. East Side voting tallies sank to 32.7 percent yes in 1908 and 33.9 percent in 1910.[27]

Oregonians finally pushed woman suffrage over the finish line in 1912 by a narrow 51.8 percent to 48.2 percent margin. Even if we cannot explain the reasons for this reversal of voting trends solely by reference to class, it is intriguing that the East Side provided such firm support in the final campaign—as the suffragists themselves had predicted.[28] A full 54.8 percent of East Siders approved the measure, while only 46.8 percent of those on the West Side voted in favor of the amendment. The East Side thus delivered more than half of the statewide majority for suffrage. The measure carried 77 of 107 precincts on the East Side (with one tie), while on the West Side only 12 of 57 precincts registered a majority of yes votes. In most neighborhoods that were bastions of direct democracy in the outer southeast, such as Woodstock, Woodmere, and Mt. Scott, every precinct voted favorably. Interestingly, though, suffrage also did fairly well in the more posh East Side neighborhoods around Laurelhurst that usually voted down populist reforms. In turn, some of the more proletarian areas in the inner southeast that traditionally had carried direct democracy measures were not particularly enthusiastic about woman suffrage. Just as the leaders of populist democracy and woman suffrage did not mesh as well as they might have, then, neither did their electoral foundations completely match up. Still, the patterns in Portland compare well to support for the victorious suffrage campaign the year before in California, strongest—according to one leader—among "the comfortable, hard-working American middle class and in the upper organized laboring group."[29]

We return, then, to the conundrum. If direct democrats and suffragists

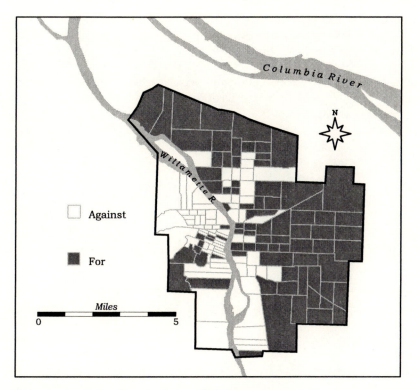

Voting on woman's suffrage initiative, 1912, by precinct

could at times make alliances, share constituencies, and speak the same language, then patriarchal imperatives simply do not explain their general mutual neglect. Sarah Henry has offered an intriguing solution to this problem, arguing that woman suffrage was "potentially more disruptive of the status quo" because of its radical subversion of the male majority. Robert Wiebe, on the hand, blames the suffragists. He claims that American suffragists, "Instead of challenging the world that white men made, . . . affirmed virtually all of it. As hierarchies appeared, its leaders spoke hierarchically." Both formulations, however, are a bit one-sided. After all, the woman suffrage movement actively moved away from more radical economic positions as it moved toward victory in 1912. At the same time, the male-dominated people's power movement showed its relative unconcern for women's rights. Both insurgencies, then, should share responsibility for the failure to bring both sexes fully into the grand populist alliance.[30]

Carrie Chapman Catt herself called woman suffrage a "bourgeois movement with nothing radical about it," "representative of the most coherent, tightest-welded, farthest reaching section of society—the middle." Recent scholarship, however, has considerably opened up the suffrage movement, showing its differing social bases and complex political possibilities as well as the survival of egalitarian alliances amid a growing conservatism. What, then, might have happened in the heady world of American progressive democracy if middling populists and feminists in Oregon, indeed throughout the country, had continued to work together for their mutual empowerment? Might these activists have doomed suffrage to even further delay? Or could they have taken a huge gamble and won an even larger jackpot as they watched both Woman and The People advance hand in hand?[31]

Occupational Representation: A Syndicalism of Housewives

> The idea of an actual representation of all classes of the people by persons of each class is altogether visionary.
> —ALEXANDER HAMILTON, *The Federalist Papers*, no. 35

> Oregon listened to a young lawyer, W. S. U'Ren, rather than to Alexander Hamilton.
> —FREDERIC[K] C. HOWE, "Oregon: The Most Complete Democracy in the World"

Historians will long argue over the legacy of suffrage. Yet I suspect that few historians would disagree with Eileen McDonagh when she states that "adding women's right to vote to the Constitution without necessary complementary legislation guaranteeing women's equality in society at large . . . testifies to a lack of support in the Progressive Era for increasing women's access to the public sphere." Once again, William U'Ren and his comrades—despite their relative lack of attention to woman suffrage—offer a particularly innovative way of further envisioning these crucial questions of gender and class. They thus also again help us reimagine the promise of radical democracy, this time by showing us the genuine possibilities of what we might call feminist populism. For these advocates of petit bourgeois radicalism, "dormant for several years" after 1914, regrouped in one last symbolic offensive that speaks volumes about their democratic motivations and the expansiveness of their populist visions.[32]

In 1920 U'Ren conceived another plan for reorganizing the state government. In the postwar era, U'Ren—who had just finished his defense of members of the Communist Labor Party—wrote with an angry tone, full of class hostility and with no masking of radical intent. U'Ren got most of his old allies, including the heads of the state's Federation of Labor, the Portland Central Labor Council, the Farmers' Union, and the Grange to support his "magnum opus," as the *Oregonian* unkindly called the plan. "Probably no more fantastic governmental structure ever was evolved by the human brain, outside of Russia," added C. C. Chapman.[33]

"The People's Power League proposes to complete the abolition of our Lawyers Soviet Government and its control by the manufacturer and capitalist master," an introductory letter began. The method of purging the accumulation of lawyers from the legislature (a perennial concern of the American citizenry, of course) was to have every Oregonian register and vote by *occupation*, rather than by party and territory, for his or her representative in a unicameral legislature. If one out of seven people in the state were farmers, as in the 1910 census count, then one out of seven legislators would be farmers; likewise with professionals, merchants, and specific occupations within the working class, such as printers. Even actors would likely earn one seat in the halls of power. Candidates would be listed on the ballot not only with their occupation but with their union affiliation (or disaffiliation) as well.[34]

The People's Power League envisioned a legislative charivari. Currently, "more than two-thirds of the whole number of senators and representatives, are members of the trading and professional classes who live chiefly on profits or on fees paid by the profiteers." The moral was simple: "This certainly is government of the people of Oregon by the combined capitalists, manufacturers, merchants and lawyers. It cannot by any stretch of imagination be called government of the people or by the people." Under the new system, "more than two-thirds of the members of the legislature will be farmers and wage workers." Beyond that, "a large majority of the members will be men and women who are living in poverty on wages or small farms." Such a legislature would also see "every small business . . . as fairly represented as any big business." As the *Oregonian* complained, the proposal for occupational representation "would develop what the radicals call class consciousness, which leads to class hatred. The troubles of the past would be as a ladies' tea-fight compared with those of the U'Renic millennium." Perhaps this helps explain why the left-leaning Seattle Central Labor Council and Washington State Federation of Labor endorsed the U'Ren plan and started preparations to place it on the ballot in the Evergreen State the year after the Seattle general strike.[35]

In the continued spirit of political revolution, the numerically dominant group in the proposed one-hundred-person legislature would be the thirty-four to thirty-eight "housewives," elected under rural and urban categories. For identification purposes, these women would be listed on the ballot not just as housewives, but also under their occupations before marriage, along with their husbands' current occupations. U'Ren and his fellows—and indeed, they were all men—made explicit, through their capitalization if nothing else, that "the proposed method makes the WOMEN EQUAL WITH MEN IN THE POWER of government." The *Oregon Labor Press*, in announcing full Central

Labor Council support for the plan, trumpeted its feminism: "One feature of the proposed plan is different from any that has been proposed in any country on earth in that it gives women equal representation on sex lines. This is a recognition of house work and home-making as being a business or occupation paramount to all others." The PPL was emphatic that "Men no more fairly represent women in the legislature than they formerly represented women at the polls."[36]

With female wageworkers voting under separate categories in gender-specific jobs as well as eligible to run in male-dominated categories, women would constitute a near if not actual majority of the legislature. Besides the housewives, the People's Power League expected two female factory workers, three representatives of pink-collar occupations such as clerks and saleswomen, and even one domestic servant to serve the Oregon citizenry. U'Ren and his allies even made a mild but not insignificant nod to ethnic diversity in their sample ballot for urban housewives by including Rosa Ann Gonzalos (the first candidate listed), Bridget Ann McGuire, and Roberta M. Cohen. Such a populist recognition of women as equal producers, rather than as victims and objects to be cared for, represented a major movement away from the professional-class project of protective legislation.[37]

This stunning proposal for equality for women, what we might call a "syndicalism of housewives," fits into a larger tradition. Recent scholarship has emphasized how small-propertied men have avidly sought to be "masters of small worlds"—ultimately motivated by a need to exercise total patriarchal control over their wives, their children, and their slaves or employees. As Robert Wiebe asserts, "men at the class margin . . . placed an unusually high premium on removing the women under their control from the labor market and maintaining them in a home." Yet while for yeoman and their ideological descendants the natural place for women after marriage was generally in the home, the most expansive populists in theory granted women's household and community work, as well as wage labor, the same value as male "productive" work. More concretely, the Knights of Labor actively sought to extend equal treatment to women wageworkers, and a rough equality between women and men was a hallmark of the Grange and more radical farmers' organizations. Populism does not have a perfect record on the woman question, but contrary to its castigation by many Marxists and feminists, it does have one of the best.[38]

The People's Power League drew on these traditions not only to advocate change in the composition of the legislature, but also explicitly to turn the state's politics upside down in the name of populist domesticity. They declared that

> a large majority of the representatives elected will be men and women who are trying to make HOMES, and who believe the home to be the most important work of mankind.

> The undersigned expect such legislators and governors to make and administer the laws, first, for the welfare of the children; second, for the welfare of the women; third, for the rights of men; fourth, for the rights of property; and last, for the rights of profit. "Involuntary" poverty and unemployment would also disappear.

At the same time, U'Ren took a crucial step away from essentializing women, declaring that female politics would be distinctive only "in matters of juvenile and moral laws, since women have as widely diversified interests from an economical standpoint as men." Overall, this is a kind of populist male feminism that historians have barely begun to explore.[39]

The People's Power League plan received significant, if not substantial, local comment. Two conservative editorials, in particular, cast illuminating light on U'Ren's vision. First, C. C. Chapman, editor of the *Oregon Voter*, noted that by making voting a function of occupation, the plan "Implies recognition of the fact that every hobo, leech, lazy rich and parasite loafer should not have a vote." U'Ren and his comrades did not respond directly to this criticism, but they did later insist that with occupational representation, "involuntary poverty and unemployment can be abolished and that kind of legislature will find the way. It is possible to provide profitable employment for all citizens who cannot make their own jobs, including those who have gray hair and more than forty-five birthdays."[40]

Second, the *Oregonian* basically refused to take the proposal seriously, although the language the paper adopted to rule it out of the bounds of legitimate discourse is quite important. The voice of Portland's Establishment labeled U'Ren's plan "grossly materialistic," indicting its consideration of voters' identities as "loggers and clerks and professional men," but not as baseball fans, fishermen, and movie aficionados. "Work and production are the least of our worries," the editors declared; "on with the dance." This was a deft response to a radical republican tradition that had consistently conceived of work as the core of one's (male) identity. U'Ren and his allies were simply unable to offer a response that demonstrated an understanding of the material and emotional lures of the new corporate age of leisure and consumption.[41]

Yet even if elite Oregonians succeeded in marginalizing U'Ren's plan, the People's Power League proposal did receive serious and sustained attention from intellectuals outside of the state. For the occupational plan fit into a powerful transatlantic intellectual discourse regarding the state, methods of representation, and political reconstruction. U'Ren himself cited as his inspiration only a radical young John Commons, who in 1900 envisioned an occupational electoral scheme. Another likely influence was Harry Allen Overstreet's "The Government of To-Morrow" from 1915, which advocated eliminating the "tyranny of the lawyer" and proposed solving "the whole vexed problem of sex difference in relation to political participation" by the representation of housewives.[42]

Other Progressive Era political thinkers, such as Moisie Ostrogorski and

Charles Beard, also tinkered with, in Beard's words, "representation of various economic and social interests that cut athwart territorial lines." Mary Parker Follett took this line of thinking farther than any other American intellectual of the time. Although she ultimately rejected occupational group representation in favor of the cultivation of a vigorous neighborhood life, Follett's 1918 book *The New State* is in large part a dialogue between her "group principle" and what she recognized as the extremely powerful intellectual movement for vocational representation. In turn, Paul Douglas declared in 1923 that "one of the most striking of the newer political theories that are being advanced today is that of occupational representation." Douglas respectfully referred several times to William U'Ren's proposal while instead making the case for proportional representation.[43]

The most profound rethinking of political representation at a time of liberal crisis came in Europe. Whether fascists trying to supplant representative institutions, Bolsheviks attempting to link the state directly to workers' councils, syndicalists trying to do away with the state altogether, or guild socialists and other self-conscious "pluralists" (most prominently, G.D.H. Cole and Harold Laski) forging a radical middle ground between all these alternatives, political philosophers and activists made occupational representation one of the burning issues in political theory in the immediate postwar period. The most prominent advocate for the creation of corporate occupational groups in order to strengthen social solidarity and electoral representation was Emile Durkheim. "What we particularly see in the professional grouping," Durkheim wrote in the second preface to *The Division of Labor in Society*, "is a moral force capable of curbing individual egoism, nurturing among workers a more invigorated feeling of their common solidarity, and preventing the law of the strongest from being applied too brutally in industrial and commercial relationships."[44]

Despite its transatlantic significance, and its supporters' initial gathering of petition signatures, U'Ren's proposal to destroy what he called the "invisible government" of bankers and manufacturers never appeared on the Oregon ballot. But even given this inglorious fate, the international intellectual history of occupational representation confirms that William U'Ren's final reconstruction of class and gender relations held a place in a dissenting heritage that we neglect only if we are willing to constrain our intellectual vision—and our democratic hopes.[45]

The Spirit of '76 and the Other Founders

> Thus were engrafted upon the Constitution of the State of Oregon
> the ideas of Rousseau, Mirabeau, Tom Paine, and Franklin, which
> many men tried in vain to incorporate in the written constitution

of the State of Pennsylvania and of the United States itself, and
might have succeeded had it not been for the sober counsel and
clear thought of Madison and Jefferson.
—L. B. Smith, "A Little Patriotism for a Change:
A Political Review of the Oregon System"

But can one doubt, if there had been telegraphs and railroads to
bring the people near together, and a modern ballot system, that
the single-chamber democrats in Pennsylvania would have carried
their theories to their logical conclusion and introduced direct
government in some form in that State?
—Ellis Paxson Oberholtzer, *The Referendum in America*

A contemporary commentator on the Portland direct democracy crusade has
provided us with perhaps the best way to evaluate the movement as part of a
long dissenting tradition worthy of our intellectual engagement and political
respect. When stalwart conservative Ellis Oberholtzer published the second
edition of his massive *The Referendum in America* in 1912, his main purpose
was to defend balanced government against what he called "these Western
invaders of our institutions." In the forefront nationally of the Rousseauistic
mobocracy that he condemned were the "junta of theorists" and "mentally
unstable citizens" associated with the supposedly socialist Oregon People's
Power League.[46]

Despite his zeal to protect America's sacred representative institutions, Oberholtzer's insights into William U'Ren and his followers remain crucial to
our ultimate understanding of the Oregon System. For the People's Power
League did indeed attempt "the thorough renovation of society." Moreover,
Oberholtzer explicitly recognized that the tradition from which the People's
Power League drew reached back to the radically egalitarian Pennsylvania
constitution of 1776, the most democratic frame of government in eighteenth-century America. In fact, during that similar short-lived democratic
moment a movement of radical small property holders—a combination of
middling and lower sorts—joined to design a government remarkably akin
to the vision of U'Ren and his followers.[47]

The most basic demand that the Pennsylvania radicals shared with the
People's Power League was the unicameral legislature. Eighteenth-century
unicameralism was, according to Willi Paul Adams, "one direct consequence
of increased self-confidence among the 'middle class of men.'" Both revolutionary Pennsylvanians and Progressive Era direct democrats saw a second
house as a bulwark for aristocratic, propertied interests; Benjamin Rush
"thought it only sensible for men of 'middling fortunes' to combine their
forces in one chamber to defend their interests against the rich." As in
the U'Ren grand reorganization, the (plural) Pennsylvania executive held no

veto powers, self-consciously making the legislature the supreme governing body.[48]

As was customary in colonial America, the Pennsylvanian constitution called for annual elections and rotation in office; the Oregon recall was the functional equivalent to these bulwarks against political privilege. The main safeguard to counter governmental tyranny and corruption in revolutionary Philadelphia, though, was "by far the most interesting and unique feature" of the constitution. Or, as the conservative Allan Nevins complained, it was the document's "crowning eccentricity." The Council of Censors, a popularly elected body deputed to launch a full-scale investigation into the operation of the government every seven years, was responsible for preserving the integrity of the constitution. Given the lack of other known precedents for his distinctive People's Inspectors of Government, it is quite possible—indeed, likely—that William U'Ren received inspiration for his ideas from the revolutionary middling ferment of 1776 Pennsylvania.[49]

Even U'Ren's proposal for occupational representation found powerful advocates among those present at the creation of the American republic. No eighteenth-century statesmen advocated placing housewives in the legislature. Yet many shared John Adams's insistence that a legislative assembly "should be in miniature an exact portrait of the people at large. It should think, feel, reason, and act like them." Support for direct occupational representation was particularly strong among those Gordon Wood labels "populist" and "grassroots" Anti-Federalists. "Federal Farmer," for example, declared, on behalf of the "middle and lower classes," that any fair government ought "to allow professional men, merchants, traders, farmers, mechanics, etc. to bring a just proportion of their best informed men respectively into the legislature."[50]

The direct democrats of the People's Power League did not particularly care for precedent, and they did not claim a distinguished lineage from the political theory of the new nation. Still, given how extreme and eccentric many of their measures appeared at the time—and continue to appear to us today—it is important to recognize that their ideas came out of a fertile American soil of dissent. The more we work to rehabilitate the creativity of this middling heritage, and the more we allow those whom Saul Cornell has recently called the Other Founders to speak, the better the chances that our own democratic hopes will live up to the legacy that they have bequeathed to us. Perhaps it has come time to compose *The New Anti-Federalist Papers*.[51]

CHAPTER ELEVEN

THE POLITICAL ECONOMY OF POPULIST DEMOCRACY

The Single Tax Movement in Portland, 1908–1916

Historian Richard Hofstadter's fundamental critique of direct democracy, which he drew from Herbert Croly, was that "the impulse toward popular rule was without meaning whenever it was divorced from a specific social program." Yet the challenge of Portland populism did not lie merely in the political realm, in what we might call structural reform designed to change the rules of the electoral game. Drawing on the middle-class moral economy, the Portland direct democracy movement also gave birth to one of the most dramatic expressions of middle-class anticapitalism during the Progressive Era in its battle for the single tax. All the radical leaders associated with the People's Power League—William U'Ren, Will Daly, George Orton, Alfred Cridge, E.S.J. McAllister, and C.E.S. Wood among them—were avid single taxers. And the proposals that they, as well as an alliance of small business owners and labor union officials, initiated to prevent the private appropriation of unearned profit unleashed by far the most bitter political conflicts in Oregon during the pre–World War I era. The mechanics of direct democracy very much hoped to use their tools to forge a new society.[1]

In fact, the single tax movement represented a genuine class struggle as well as a battle for the political soul of middling folks. Fundamentally at stake were the loyalties of small property holders. Single-tax activists appealed to Portland's petite bourgeoisie and middling homeowners by directly challenging the economic power of the city's ruling class. Single taxers articulated a utopian vision of a modern small-enterprise economy where the relationship between wage labor and self-employment remained fluid—and where, therefore, wage slavery would be eliminated. The people, not a corporate elite, would govern this petit bourgeois economy, radically extending the sphere of the ballot box. Far from being a mere revolt against high taxes, the struggle for the single tax inspired a modern critique of imperialism as well as a trenchant antimodern assessment of the pioneer heritage. The democratic vision of the single taxers met defeat, but not without confirming the survival of anticapitalism as a surprisingly strong minority viewpoint within the broad constellation of middle-class ideas of political economy. Here was direct democracy in action.

The Single Tax: Henry George and His Legacy

The single tax was the brainchild of Henry George, the most prominent middle-class radical of the late nineteenth century. In his 1879 masterpiece, *Progress and Poverty*, George theorized that the extreme inequality fostered by capitalist development resulted from monopolies in natural resources, particularly land. George sought to place all taxes on one source—publicly created land values. The tax was *single* because, in the words of the chief Portland single taxer William U'Ren, it would "exempt all vocations, all land improvements and personal property from taxation." George and subsequent single taxers held that elites secured, and maintained, their power by buying up potentially valuable pieces of land and withholding them from development until population growth caused their market value to skyrocket. They sought what was effectively an annual 100% capital gains tax on increases in land value.[2]

For example, Portland single taxers consistently targeted an essentially undeveloped block that *Oregonian* empire builder Henry Pittock owned. They claimed, accurately, that Pittock had purchased the land for a pittance and had watched the city grow until his land was worth more than half a million dollars. George and his followers insisted that a tax that would equal the full rental value of land such as Pittock's would not only fill government coffers but would break up land monopoly, leading to more development, more jobs, and more land available for the poor. With the government confiscating all rent, Pittock and his fellow capitalists would lose much of their incentive to amass large property holdings, thus creating a much more egalitarian, and small-scale, economic structure. And the tax was completely moral, since Pittock had not labored one bit to create the extra value of his land. As U'Ren put it, "Ground rent is the surest and safest method yet invented by which one person gets the product of another's labor and gives nothing in return."[3]

In terms of technical economics, the single tax appeared to many as an esoteric panacea. Yet Henry George's vision helped inspire some of the most substantial challenges to industrial capitalism during the Gilded Age. His picture of a nation riven by classes and exploitation and saturated with illegitimate wealth and power proved crucial in forging working-class movements as well as cross-class alliances. George himself came close to winning the New York mayoralty in 1886. The tensions in George's philosophy were, however, considerable. The status of private property, manufacturing, labor unions, and socialism became highly contentious issues within the single tax movement. Also, George's fiery radicalism was forged in the crucible of white supremacy, and George himself was one of the most prominent anti-Chinese agitators in nineteenth-century California. By the time of George's death in

1897, his grand dreams, despite limited and partial victories in cities such as Detroit, lay in shambles.[4]

After a hiatus of a little more than a decade, however, the single tax showed renewed strength, becoming a companion to many Progressive issues such as trustbusting and the fight against political corruption. New York City voters elected Henry George Jr. to Congress. Renowned Cleveland reform mayor Tom Johnson ardently advocated the single tax, as did many of his advisers, such as Frederic Howe (who, along with several other single taxers, went on to serve in the Wilson administration). In the second decade of the century, the state of Missouri and several cities in Colorado voted on various single tax measures; the Georgeites obtained a victory in Pueblo in 1913. In San Francisco the strongest municipal labor movement in the country endorsed the single tax. In the Northwest, Seattle witnessed two hard-fought campaigns over the issue in 1912 and 1913, and although the measures lost, a mayor championing the single tax took office in 1912. The land taxers had even more success in Everett, winning two elections in that bitterly divided industrial city. Many Socialists advocated full land value taxation as a partial step to the cooperative commonwealth, and the biggest state socialist organization in the country—Oklahoma—drew much of its strength from a blend of Georgist and Marxist tenets. As Benjamin Parke De Witt noted in 1915, the single tax principle was an integral part of "the social phase of the progressive movement."[5]

The Birth of the Movement: Portland, 1908

American single taxers mounted their most important and their most hard-fought campaign in the state of Oregon—and, specifically, in Portland. Every general election during the mature years of Progressivism in the state—from 1908 to 1916—witnessed a vigorous crusade for land taxation and against monopoly. Previous scholars have attributed these campaigns to the novelty of the initiative process, along with, in the words of the contemporary editor of the *Oregon Historical Quarterly*, a "compact group of astute and determined adherents to the Henry George idea in its most radical and revolutionary form." Yet the single tax fight in Portland has a much greater significance for historians, for it became a crucial part of the broad Progressive Era conflict over the development of corporate capitalism. Again, we find what we originally were least looking for—a radical middle class imbued with the spirit of anticapitalism.[6]

In 1908 the meaning of the Oregon System was up for grabs. Vivid reminders of the gross corporate abuses that had inspired the passage of direct legislation remained in the air. Most visibly, the Oregon land fraud trials continued until 1910. These prosecutions, which had brought down a United States senator and shaken the entire Portland Establishment, graphically reminded citizens of how, in the words of the state land agent ten years earlier, "Our laws taken as a whole, might be denominated very fitly as 'land monopoly made easy.'" Just two weeks before the May election chief prosecution informer S.A.D. Puter published his *Looters of the Public Domain*, a massive retelling of the land fraud conspiracies.[7]

In this setting H. D. Wagnon, a Portland fire insurance salesman, and Alfred Cridge, a Rose City journalist and union activist, led the single tax forces into battle. The initiative "aroused great interest" and was "vigorously discussed" throughout the state. Wagnon and Cridge proposed a "peculiar" form of single tax, one that would increase land value taxes by two to four cents per thousand dollars of assessed value while exempting from taxation most productive personal property, ranging from machinery to craftsmen's tools, as well as improvements relating to manufacturing. The constitutional amendment's supporters, however, fought the campaign on the merits of single tax as a whole.[8]

Under the banner of the Oregon Tax Reform Association, the single taxers consistently emphasized the positive benefits of removing taxation from "industry." They quoted Henry George to promise not so much equalization of resources as a growth atmosphere in which jobs, income, and other riches would flow out of new manufacturing. Yet while they assured the public that their measure was "no appeal to class or personal interests," the single taxers carefully noted that it did not exempt from taxation timber and "business buildup, merchandise, cash, improvements or public service corporations." Implicitly casting aspersion on those forms of wealth, Cridge and Wagnon promised that "the farmer, workingman, manufacturer, merchant and, in short, every producer" would benefit when "the various special interests and monopolies" were forced to stop leeching from the present tax system. Single taxers would develop such a language of class much more thoroughly in future campaigns.[9]

Although some critics assumed that the 1908 single tax initiative would bring "a violent reversal of the established system of private ownership," the Wagnon/Cridge measure received only mild opposition. When Oregonians went to the polls to consider the most far-reaching economic proposal ever put to them, the results "surprised its most sanguine supporters." Although the measure lost statewide nearly two to one, woman suffrage (which would triumph four years later) did only marginally better. In Portland, the results were heartwarming. With the measure carrying forty-four of ninety precincts, a change in only 175 votes out of 19,000 cast would have spelled victory within the city. On the rapidly growing East Side of the Willamette, with nearly three-fifths of Portland's voters, the single tax actually won. The initiative swept Ward 6, in working-class South Portland, and won eight of ten precincts in Ward 10 (working-class Albina and north Portland). Numerous precincts in the mixed residential areas of the southeast voted for the measure. The single taxers clearly had a mass base, a constituency that looked like it would grow as the city continued booming in population, driving up land prices and perhaps encouraging the energetic Oregon citizenry to look more closely at monopoly.[10]

Single Tax "Victory" in 1910

At the next election the single taxers were indeed victorious—even if under dubious circumstances. In 1910 single tax advocates decided to take a different tack. Instead of fighting for a land tax, effort went into passing a constitutional amendment that on the surface had nothing at all to do with the single tax.

The amendment proposed to eliminate poll taxes (still a live but minor issue), to give counties complete control over taxation methods, and—most dramatically—to strip the legislature of its power of taxation and thus to require that all taxation laws be passed by referendum. The Grange and organized labor initiated the constitutional amendment. The latter's brief argument in the voters' pamphlet simply alluded to the "experiments" that the amendment would facilitate, and only minimal discussion of the measure popped up in the pages of Portland's newspapers. Yet every voter in the state received a 128-page booklet called *People's Power and Public Taxation*, in which U'Ren, Cridge, and W. G. Eggleston went to great lengths to show how land value–based (although not "single") taxes would be substantially lower for the great majority of the population. The pamphlet's authors argued, most significantly, that the measure applied the spirit of popular rule to matters of taxation—in contrast to what one opponent called the "universally accredited practice" of having an "expert" prepare the state tax system.[11]

The single taxers soon faced the charge of deception for their supposed tactic of using the poll tax as an entering wedge, but almost all contemporary academic commentators agreed that the public clearly understood their motives.[12] In any case, with the law's passage, the "jubilant" single taxers had earned further maneuvering room. The measure received a narrow victory statewide, with Portland again proving even more receptive. Gaining over 54 percent of the vote in the city, the amendment won on both sides of the Willamette. All but one municipal ward had a majority of precincts pass the measure, and 113 of the city's 155 precincts approved it. Populist radicalism had swept The People into power in matters of the purse; now was the time to launch a major single tax campaign.[13]

The 1912 Election: Armageddon in Oregon

Princeton professor A. N. Young called the 1912 land value initiative "probably the most extraordinary measure which single taxers have ever submitted"

Voting on single tax initiative, 1910, by precinct

anywhere in the country. National single tax ideologues and organizations poured money and energy into what they believed to be their best-ever opportunity. Joseph Fels, multimillionaire Philadelphia soap manufacturer and nominal head of the American single taxers, provided a forty-thousand-dollar war chest. In the meantime, opponents of the measure spent one hundred thousand dollars. The leader of the conservative forces, himself from Seattle, admitted "in desperation" one night that "the money came from the wealthy men of Portland."[14]

Every Portland newspaper agreed that the most contentious issue of the year—more important even than the grand battle for the presidency between Roosevelt, Wilson, Taft, and Debs—was the single tax. And although eastern money financed the 1912 campaign, a purely inside agitator turned out to be the most effective single tax propagandist. William U'Ren had been nurturing the Georgist idea even before moving to Oregon, and he later acknowledged that he designed his electoral reforms in large part to forward the single tax cause. Despite what its opponents claimed, however, U'Ren and his colleagues did not formulate the 1912 Graduated Single Tax constitutional amendment as a pure Henry George measure. Instead, its sponsors openly composed the initiative to appeal to small property owners, departing from accepted single tax theory by admitting progressive taxation. The proposed tax applied only to owners of land values of over $10,000 in one county. The initial tax rate was $2.50 per $1,000 for land value between $10,000 and $20,000 and increased steadily until reaching a maximum rate of $30 per $1,000 for value over $100,000. The law would subject corporate franchises to taxation on the same basis as land. In turn, the measure exempted all personal property and improvements on land from state taxation. U'Ren and his allies left all other existing taxation intact. Companion countywide single tax measures appeared on the ballot in Coos, Clackamas, and Multnomah Counties, where the single taxers had the most confidence of a favorable outcome.[15]

For the first time, the Oregon single taxers articulated a full-blown populist language of class. They clearly identified Portland's ruling corporate elite as economic exploiters. In turn, they upheld the middling- and working-class alliance that undergirded their vision of a small-scale republican political economy. They focused above all on those who owned their own homes. The elite, in turn, fought back against the single tax by bluntly castigating its appeal to class interests and destruction of the institution of private property.

The two sides disagreed most fundamentally about the meaning and scope of private property. The single taxers believed in the right to tax property for reasons other than governmental finance, as well as in complete and direct popular sovereignty over the wealth that society created. As U'Ren argued, "single taxers expect that people will some day take all that is their own." He defended this principle in the largest public debate over the single tax, arguing that while the current measure stopped short of confiscation, if it proved satisfactory there would be nothing to prevent "adding a little more to the tax on land values until all the rent would be absorbed in taxes."[16]

The single taxers did not, though, believe in state ownership of land, much less of the entire means of production. U'Ren maintained in the debate that "we cannot maintain our present civilization without private ownership." Rather, the single taxers held to the tenets of the populist conception of moral economy, especially, that the only legitimate wealth was earned through work. Land was the chief element of their attack because increases in land values resulted not from "labor for labor but labor for privilege." If an improvement that a citizen labored to produce increased the value of property, then the citizen deserved to keep that increase. But if population alone drove up the price of land, then the commonwealth deserved that increase. As U'Ren stated, "In a word my object is to help make such laws in Oregon that no man can get a dollar without working for it, and no man shall produce a dollar of value by his labor without getting it."[17]

In turn, this labor theory of value dictated the desirability of an economy based on a rough equality of producers. As the editor of the *Portland Labor Press* stressed, "legitimate business will greatly profit by the law, as it will remove unnatural barriers which now serve as a means of creating a large idle speculative class of men who live, not by useful labor, but entirely off the products of labor." While the single taxers neglected the unearned values created in factories, they focused particularly effectively on economic values more easily open to public scrutiny. Thus not only land, but public service corporations with their valuable municipal franchises, were subject to the graduated tax. These would in fact be the law's primary targets. The gigantic utility monopoly, the Portland Railway, Light, and Power Company; the Southern Pacific Railroad land grant; and other companies associated with the "Water Power Trust" would all suffer great increases in their taxable property and tax rates.[18]

The single taxers went beyond popular resentment of such utilities to target as well all the large urban landholders who benefited disproportionately from an expanding economy—banks, department stores, breweries, and the estates of Portland's pioneer capitalists. They consistently used their criticism of unearned land values to delegitimize the Rose City's "powerful men and powerful interests" on behalf of "the plain people." The single taxers named names—and rarely were they outsiders like Rockefeller and Carnegie. The Ladds, the Corbetts, the Failings, and other members of the Portland aristocracy consistently appeared in the papers attached to the value of their monopolized land holdings, and single taxers released a list of the 232 largest landowners in Multnomah County.[19]

The single taxers' focus on land values therefore enabled them to target the Portland ruling class with remarkable accuracy. As noted earlier, real estate, transportation franchises, and public utilities (along with banks) functioned as the critical material foundations for elite rule in a city with a small manufacturing sector. Indeed, if the single taxers had been successful, the Portland ruling class—finding almost all its wealth expropriated—would have simply withered away. The single taxers thus recognized what historian Thomas Mc-Craw has recently noted: "Even down to the present day, more Americans have probably made fortunes from the appreciation of real estate values than from any other source." In turn, Daniel Rodgers argues that reforms such as municipal utility ownership and city planning "hardly threatened property itself; like other progressive inventions, they worked on the market economy's edges and margins." In contrast, the single tax solution went right to the heart of modern urban inequality.[20]

The single taxers placed these Portland elites and large corporate interests in conscious opposition to the heroes of their drama—homeowners and homemakers. As H. D. Wagnon, in 1912 the single tax candidate for Multnomah County assessor, contended, "no home owner would pay one cent" of the graduated tax. A favorite metaphor touched on the sacred familial circle:

"If you believe the land hog should be taxed and not your baby's crib, vote for single tax." The idea of home ownership encompassed a host of symbols, such as thrift, temperance, and independent citizenship. A letter to the editor from Heck Smith and Per O'Brien spelled this out, contrasting Jim Smith, who "beautified his home and gave tone to his neighborhood," and Tom Jones, who got drunk. Each got the same fine—Smith from the assessor and Jones from the municipal judge. Smith and O'Brien drew the moral: "It is cheaper to get drunk and paint the town red, under the present system of taxation, than to be an industrious and law abiding citizen." If the present tax system remained in place, warned the *News*, "it will be impossible for the average man to own a home in the city."[21]

We can speculate on why this appeal to small home ownership was so conducive to a single tax coalition composed of voters, some of whom identified themselves as "working class" while others thought of themselves more fundamentally as "middle class." (The Portland Central Labor Council gave its full support to the initiative, and Will Daly was one of the measure's chief advocates.) For skilled blue-collar workers as well as for those who wore white collars, the "home" represented a domestic realm that united the private and public worlds of independent citizens. Home ownership involved stability, roots in the community, and even a personal statement against the speculation and free play of the market. Thus owning a home could represent a turn away from relentless upward striving and toward security. Ultimately, it energized the family identity near the center of middling-class self-conception and made that self-conception political, transforming private virtues into a public challenge of corporate power. Rather than serving as a narcotizing brake on class consciousness, home ownership could in fact inspire political radicalism—just as the "homestead ethic" inspired backcountry political rebellions in the eighteenth century. As U'Ren would argue in 1916, under the single tax "every man will then have something better than a boarding house or a rented farm to fight for."[22]

Not surprisingly, home ownership was at the core of the strong plebeian class identity that the single taxers articulated. Editorials and letters to the editors frequently blended references to persons and abodes, speaking of the "workingman, the small home owners, and other average men," "the little worker, the small business man, the homes of the poor," or "the homes and small business men" that suffered from excessive taxation. In two missives to the *Journal* "B. T. S." articulated this middling-class identity most forcefully: "How about our own idle—those who decorate corners and fringe streets, to say nothing of those lolling in ease? These two classes come from the same source. What one earned and didn't get, the other is using not only to command workers, but to prevent employment." "The big business octopus" produced "parasites that have been exploiting" the "common people," particularly through a tax system that oppressed "the small home owner" and "the middle class."[23]

The opponents of the single tax well recognized the measure's fundamental appeals. The chair of the State Tax Commission decried the measure's indefensible "class appeal to the small land owners against the large owners." Anti–single taxers moved well beyond their elite base, however, to fashion arguments that would be persuasive to the middle-class swing vote in Portland. In fact, those opposed to the single tax were probably in the end victorious because of their ability to subtly invert the single taxers' appeals, arguing that a regime of corporate capitalism could best protect small property ownership.[24]

For example, the Tax Payers League emphasized that the single tax exempted "the favorite accumulations of very wealthy men" in capital and personal property such as stocks and bonds. The Oregon Equal Taxation League ran large ads in the *News* warning that the single tax would absorb all land into the state, "not only the large land holder's land but the small lot owner's land as well." The man who voted yes would vote "to have the state, in course of time take your home from you and make you a tenant." George McCoy perfected this appropriation of symbols in a letter to the editor, writing, "To the average family the home is the most paramount and sacred possession. Love of wife and children prompts men to build homes for their loved ones." McCoy sought to inspire women to do all they could to fight against the single tax, which by placing the entire tax burden on land was an "organized onslaught on the homes of the people."[25]

After such a bitter battle over the economic role of small property and the political allegiance of middling folk, the outcome of the election proved anticlimactic. The single tax initiative recorded the second highest number of total votes among the record thirty-seven measures facing the electorate, but a mere 27.8 percent of Oregon's voters approved the single tax. Portland's citizens proved only marginally more supportive. Just 18 of 155 precincts voted favorably, 16 of those on the East Side. The stunning defeat surprised everyone. As a neutral Massachusetts political analyst put it several months later, "To this day the decisiveness of the defeat of the single tax is a mystery to many a close student of Oregon politics. On the eve of the election it was thought not improbable that it might succeed." That sense of urgency is perhaps what led the president of the Portland Chamber of Commerce to rejoice that the defeat represented "the greatest thing the people have ever done for the state."[26]

U'Ren and his comrades regrouped, taking heart that only one of seven tax measures that the State Tax Commission had referred to the voters passed. The single taxers actively opposed these liberal reforms, which progressive governor Oswald West supported in order to move the state away from the antiquated general property tax system and toward a tax structure more favorable to regulated corporate growth. Since Oregonians clearly did not approve of the changes in taxation that the governing elite proposed, the single taxers perhaps felt that another modification of their basic principle might find more favor with the electorate. Radicalism had not succeeded. It had, however, apparently produced stalemate.[27]

Signs of Hope: The 1914 Election

Two single tax measures appeared on the 1914 ballot, but only one received serious consideration. Similar to the 1908 version, the initiative emphasized the exemption of personal property, this time up to a fifteen-hundred-dollar limit. The law, however, applied only to individuals, not to corporations. Two major differences marked the campaign. One was U'Ren's independent candidacy for governor on a platform of the single tax, prohibition, and guaranteed full employment. The other was the economic slump that hit the Pacific Northwest particularly hard. A prominent single taxer, labor leader Eugene E. Smith, noted while running as a recall candidate for mayor the considerable "dissatisfaction among the middle class and working class." Hard times would now test the Oregon System.[28]

The most important new theme of the single taxers was how much the rich—especially those who held "mortgages and diamond"—dodged their taxes. U'Ren attacked the "corporation wolf" and stated that the Homes Tax Exemption, the measure's nickname, "does not apply to corporations. The great department stores will get nothing from this, neither will the skyscraper nor the railroads, but the little merchant may save something on his taxes." Opponents picked up on the theme of struggle between petite bourgeoisie and haute bourgeoisie. George Mason, head of the conservative Non-Partisan League, wrote in the *Voters' Pamphlet* that the single tax "would put out of business practically every enterprise in the State that employs over a dozen men." Another argument held that the fifteen-hundred-dollar exemption— three thousand dollars for a married couple—would help only "the middle chap" while the poor and rich both had their taxes hiked. Voters realized that the measure, even if not as systematically or as forcefully argued as in 1912, was a continuation of the single tax (class) struggle.[29]

Two weeks before the election R. E. Smith, president of the newly formed Oregon Rational Tax Reform Association and a leading opponent of the single tax, stated that the measure had a 60 percent chance of passing. That estimate may have been a bluff, but the amendment indeed did much better than in 1912. Although the measure was again defeated statewide two to one, the returns from Portland must have been encouraging after the previous crushing defeat. In the city as a whole, 42.7 percent of the voters approved the measure, with that figure going up to 45.5 percent on the East Side. The amendment swept to victory in whole neighborhoods in the southeastern and northern parts of the city.[30]

A remarkable pattern also connects the single tax with the prohibition

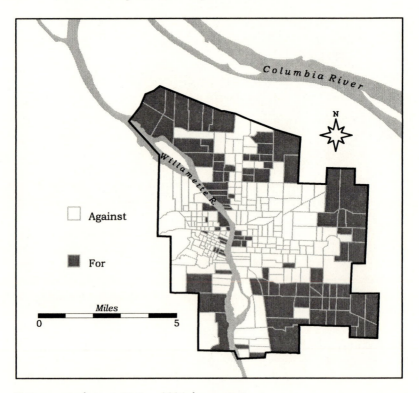

Voting on single tax initiative, 1914, by precinct

amendment on the same ballot. Oregon finally voted to close its saloons in 1914, and much of the dry rhetoric centered, like the single tax, around preservation of the home. As a supporter of both U'Ren's bid for governor and prohibition wrote to the *Labor Press*, it was "the middle and poorer classes who pay the bill" for liquor. Of the fifteen precincts that carried the single tax on the West Side, scattered in mostly immigrant and transient working-class areas, none passed prohibition. Of the sixty-nine pro-single-tax precincts on the East Side, however, fully fifty voted dry. Most wet East Side single tax precincts were in more proletarian sections of the inner south-east or in north Portland. Middling-class residential areas such as Lents, Mt. Scott, Woodmere, Creston, and Montavilla voted overwhelmingly in favor of both measures—for example, in precincts 111 through 132, only one op-posed single tax and none prohibition.[31]

The *Oregonian* gleefully reported after the election that "the disastrous U'Ren epoch has passed."[32] But these election returns instead provided en-couraging indications that Portland's middling home-owning neighborhoods had become, if anything, more willing to endorse the radical single tax idea

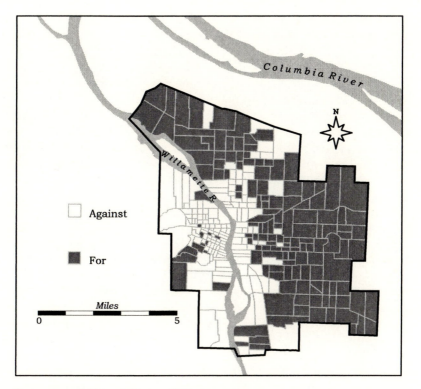

Voting on prohibition initiative, 1914, by precinct

of a moral economy. The single tax epoch would therefore not die without one final grand campaign.

Antimodernism, Antiwar, Anti-imperialism, and Anticapitalism: The 1916 Land and Loan Initiative

"The hardest times our people have seen in twenty years" had hit Portland by 1916. The chamber of commerce took advantage of the economic decline to fight for the open shop. In turn the city's labor unions, which had consistently supported the single tax, officially took over the campaign. For these workers, the single tax still retained its associations with small enterprise and the home, but its specific purpose in 1916 was to abolish poverty and unemployment (or "disemployment," as unionists significantly referred to it). The measure was "a thoroughbred single tax measure of stronger brand than any ever before," with the campaign more militant.[33]

The philosophy of the 1916 single taxers stretched to its limits the radicalism of the Georgist philosophy. Their last heroic resistance blended antimodern impulses and advocacy of industrial unionism, patriotic republicanism and alliance with socialists. Most profoundly, the single taxers creatively attempted to imagine a world in which the realms of the proletariat and the petite bourgeoisie had few boundaries. Their thinking, fully in the middle-class anticapitalist tradition, represented a formidable political—and moral—challenge to a country about to enter total war.

The Full Rental Value Land Tax and Homemakers' Loan Fund Amendment came out of an intensive series of caucuses organized by the Portland Central Labor Council, and it received the endorsement of the national AFL executive board. The constitutional amendment declared that "all citizens of Oregon are equally entitled to exclusive possession, for their personal use, of land enough for their homes and to yield a living by their labor, without paying any person for the right to live and labor on the land." Beyond the standard single tax mechanisms, the initiative would have set up a state loan fund to "help persons with no capital but their labor and character to make homes and farms." As the voters' pamphlet argument put it, "this law differs from the so-called single tax only in that it does not prohibit inheritance, income or license taxes," along with its inclusion of an option for the local taxation of improvements.[34]

A small-scale competitive market system without an exploitative class structure remained the goal of the single taxers—the laborite contingent included. An editorial in the *Labor Press* rearticulated many themes of nineteenth-century populist radicalism:

> Many confuse capital with monopoly. While capital is an aid to production, monopoly is an exploiter of wealth producers. In a competitive market the capitalist cannot "enslave" anybody; but give the capitalist a privilege—a monopoly—not in the possession of others, and he is enabled to use his capital to his private profit and to the public's detriment. For monopoly abolishes all equality in bargaining.

Eugene E. Smith, now president of the Portland Central Labor Council and a successful radical candidate for the legislature in 1918, even remarked that "we hope this [the loan fund] will grow and develop so that in time we will not have any private banks in Oregon." In turn, single taxers asserted that "the interests of the farmer, the small business man and the laboring man are identical. One and the same."[35]

U'Ren, who drafted this "People's Land and Loan" initiative for the unions, stepped up his attack on the elite. He crusaded against "all the predatory interests, all the big business interests speculating in land" as well as "the Master class" that was "exploiting its citizens for a profit." Comparing the United States to Britain, U'Ren predicted that "Americans will be no better if we do not stop coining the lives of our workingmen, women and children into profits for their millionaire masters." He later declared, "private ownership of ground rent is like chattel [sic] slavery."[36]

Despite his class hostility, U'Ren's vision remained petit bourgeois, albeit updated for the age of wages and, in the process, radicalized for the modern corporate era. U'Ren refused nostalgia; he knew that most workers would need to work for wages. Yet what differentiated between effective wage slavery and the possibility of true independence? As with eighteenth-century peasants, it was the substantive, and subversive, opportunity for self-employment.

U'Ren stated often in 1916 that the single tax would—mixing the language of labor and property—allow workers to "own their job." The loans would "give every man his choice all his life long between making his own employment on the land or accepting a job to work for wages." Almost all wageworkers would see their income double, because "then no person can be hired for less than he can make, working for himself." Even more critically, the "certainty of employment and the independence and freedom" that would come with the ability to leave a job at a moment's notice would infinitely empower "all useful labor . . . laborers, clerks, farmers, retail merchants, renters, [and] mechanics." The law would "add industrial freedom to the political liberty Americans now have," and would, according to U'Ren, "MAKE OREGON A STATE OF FREE MEN, INSTEAD OF A STATE OF [H]IRELINGS AND RENTERS WHO DEPEND ALTOGETHER ON THE PERMISSION AND SUCCESSFUL ENTERPRISE OF OTHERS FOR OPPORTUNITY TO EARN THEIR DAILY BREAD."[37]

Such sentiments may sound anachronistic to most historians, who fail to recognize the continued economic and political strength of the idea, and reality, of small business in an age of factories and industrial violence. Yet they made quite a bit of sense to Karl Marx, who wrote in *Capital*:

> The wage-worker of to-day is to-morrow an independent peasant, or artisan, working for himself. He vanishes from the labor market, but not into the workhouse. This constant transformation of the wage-labourers into independent producers, who work for themselves instead of for capital, and enrich themselves instead of the capitalist gentry, reacts in its turn very perversely on the conditions of the labor-market. Not only does the degree of exploitation remain indecently low. The wage-laborer loses in the bargain, along with the relation of dependence, also the sentiment of dependence on the abstemious capitalist.

U'Ren's ideas thus made perfect sense in a city that in many ways retained a republican political economy, a city where the following year radical petit bourgeois Will Daly would come so close to becoming mayor. It was therefore realistic for single taxers to believe, with John Stuart Mill, that "The industrial economy which divides society absolutely into two portions, the payers of wages and the receivers of them . . . is neither fit for, nor capable of, indefinite duration." Rather than retreating from the modern world, then, the Portland single taxers fully engaged it, and in doing so they pushed their radicalism to the very edge of public respectability. Moreover, advocates of the People's Land and Loan law linked their struggle with working-class militancy, antiwar activities, a general critique of American foreign policy, and a profoundly antimodern questioning of private property in land.[38]

Given its emphasis on land, it is easy to categorize Georgism as an "agrarian" philosophy. Yet the Portland single tax leaders were proud members of the American Federation of Labor. At the same time, the labor leaders who led the Portland single tax movement the same year challenged fundamental craft orthodoxy by passing a resolution that urged the AFL to embrace industrial unionism. Modern conditions and recent offensives by the Employers' Association, labor leaders argued, required broader working-class solidarity. The Central Labor Council put this theory into practice by actively cooperating with Portland Socialists, and even IWW members, at unemployment rallies and within organizations. In turn, the leader of the local Socialists, C. W. Barzee, endorsed the "immense ideal" in the Land and Loan measure. Oregon Socialists had opposed the single tax before, especially in 1908, but Barzee wrote that the 1916 measure "could not have been better planned had a committee from the Socialist party framed it." In turn, the labor council endorsed more Socialist legislative candidates than those from any other party.[39]

With World War I looming ever more closely over the horizon, the single taxers also chose to place their struggle firmly in a global context. In October 1915 the Portland Central Labor Council passed a resolution condemning militarism taught in the schools as despotic, undemocratic, murderous, brutal, and counter to the interests of all toilers. The council's antipreparedness stance enraged the *Oregonian*. Seven weeks later the Oregon Single Tax Association went further when it unanimously denounced the military program proposed by President Wilson and George Chamberlain, Senate Military Affairs Committee chair (and, ironically, a Democrat from Portland). "No matter how well prepared," the single taxers declared in the finest middling fashion, "no nation is safe which contains millionaires on the one hand and paupers on the other." More generally, the *Labor Press* condemned an American "dollar imperialism" that exploited the labor and resources of dependent countries. One ardent single taxer commented that for those who believed in the Oregon System, where citizens ran and controlled the government, it was contrary to democratic American traditions to deny subject people self-rule. William U'Ren himself praised Pancho Villa's "war cry of 'The land for the Peons.'"[40]

Although fully engaged, then, with some of the most destructive tendencies of the modern world, a distinctive set of premodern sentiments also energized the single taxers. U'Ren, for example, believed that divine will authorized the single tax, since "God ma[d]e the land for all the people." The *Labor Press* approvingly quoted Tecumseh and Black Hawk on the nondivisibility of land. Commentator "Opti Mist" quoted God's injunction to Moses and the Jews not to sell the land, a favorite single tax verse (Lev. 25:23). Stating that the imperial drive for land caused World War I, Opti Mist mused:

> Truly we have wandered far from the ways of our Lord. I have always been curious to know why the Old Testament was cast aside by us moderns—
> And why it was necessary that we kill off the noble red man—
> But it's all plain now—
> It was the land question.
> And I reckon some of the descendants of the early landgrabbers will feel just the same towards the proponents of the People's Land and Loan Measure as did their ancestors towards the noble red man—
> And the land.[41]

Opti Mist was correct. The Land and Loan measure drew "more opposition than any other measure on the ballot," and its enemies consistently targeted its threat to Anglo-Saxon civilization. Paul Murphy, vice president of the Laurelhurst Company, stated in a letter to the editor that "what distinguishes English-speaking men from others is their land hunger." Lawyer M. C. George wrote that Indians were the "original Henry Georgites," declaring the single tax wrong for the same reason communal tribal ownership was wrong. Henry Reed, Multnomah County's assessor, expressed this argument most emphatically. Reed, who had been the chief organizer of the 1905 Lewis and Clark World's Fair, possessed an all-consuming passion against the single tax. He felt that it called into question the entire Oregon pioneer heritage. In a remarkable twenty-page article for the *Oregon Voter* Reed waxed eloquent about the hardship the pioneers faced in order to make "their journey, which has no parallel in history." Nearly two thousand whites died to establish American sovereignty over the Oregon country, with "women and children suffering every outrage which the fiendish imagination of savage Indians could devise." The pioneers never would have crossed the plains knowing that the future held the single tax. Reed was implicitly declaring that the descendants of the pioneers would not allow themselves to be expropriated by these latter-day savages.[42]

The *News* opined before the election that the People's Land and Loan bill had no chance; only when "a large part of the public gets over its fear of such terms as 'single tax' and 'socialism'" would it recognize the necessity for such a piece of legislation. Early in the campaign U'Ren had hoped that the measure would "touch the hearts of the people, instead of merely appealing to them for the saving of a few dollars of taxes." But after the election labor officials admitted that "at no time did we believe" the measure would carry. Even these realistic supporters of the measure, though, did not expect the extent to which Oregonians repudiated the home-grown radicalism of the single tax. Utterly swamped statewide, the measure received less than a quarter of the vote in Portland. A lonely six precincts approved the amendment, with only two of those on the East Side. The question appeared again on the ballot in 1920 and 1922, but few people took those measures seriously. The single tax had finally died in Oregon.[43]

What are we to make of such overwhelming defeat? For those who firmly believe in the Liberal Tradition in America, such an outcome simply confirms what we have known all along. Alternatives to capitalism in the United States are not viable. Other scholars might be more inclined to historicize the issue and argue that while the producerist tradition generated anticapitalist ideology during the nineteenth century, it had clearly become anachronistic by the twentieth. Declension then becomes the headline story. Except for a few beleaguered Communists scurrying around in the underbrush, modern America has simply not witnessed any significant anticapitalist politics.

We can, however, look at the cup as one-quarter full, rather than as totally empty. Obviously, we must recognize the fundamental fact of the single taxers' defeat. Still, in every election nearly one out of four Portlanders voted for the single tax, and at times that figure reached much higher. In 1910 the single taxers achieved victory, albeit under peculiar circumstances, and in 1908 and 1914 they successfully convinced majorities in many Portland neighborhoods to join their cause. Conservative editor C. C. Chapman thus correctly pointed in 1919 to the "heavy votes by our citizens" on single-tax measures.[44]

Rather than interpreting the electoral verdict as proof of the hopelessness of the anticapitalist cause, then, we should recognize that the Question of Capitalism came into the twentieth century open enough that thousands of citizens were willing to vote in favor of a truly radical measure that expressed substantial discomfort with capitalism, indeed overt hostility to it. Those middle-class sentiments did not just disappear. As I will argue in the book's conclusion, they continued in a subdued fashion to inform the populist struggles over political economy that have shaped modern America, providing hope that we might yet find a viable and democratic alternative both to the dependencies of the social democratic welfare state and the inequalities of corporate capitalism.

PART IV

A POPULISM OF THE BODY

The Rationality and Radicalism of Antivaccinationism

> A good deal of our politics is physiological.
> —Ralph Waldo Emerson, "Fate"

> Indeed, people don't just become ill out of the blue. For the whole of a body to be affected its equilibrium must have already been disrupted. That's true for all illnesses. It's painfully obvious for illnesses said to be of the immune system. But all illnesses are, in fact, since being ill comes down to being unable to distance oneself from pathogenic agents.

> So why do we have this proliferation of terminal illnesses at a period of civilization as developed as ours? My hypothesis is that it's this very civilization that continuously submits our minds and bodies to stresses and strains and thus gradually destroys our immune systems. I'm surprised doctors aren't saying this.

> To cure someone is fine, but prevention is better. Medical intervention in someone's life is a break-in to their world. In a way, it's a violation of their world that turns them into dependents. It also takes away their right to speak, because ill people often understand nothing of the medical jargon or reasoning behind a particular diagnosis or treatment.
> —Luce Irigaray, *je, tu, nous: Toward a Culture of Difference*

We easily recognize that taxes, the home, and the school—all important subjects in this book—can energize middle-class politics. Yet matters relating to health and the body have also long been of primary concern to middling Americans. The historian Charles Sellers, for example, speaks of the "self-making middle-class obsession with health"—and he does not mean this kindly. Such criticism of the supposedly agonized relationship between middle-class Americans and their bodies crosses the political spectrum. Note H. L. Mencken's complaint about "that innumerable caravan of middling, dollar-grubbing, lodge-joining, quack-ridden folk which . . . the politicians slobber over as the bulwark of our liberties."[1]

Yet opportunities to examine intensively, from the grassroots, the ideologies of the body, health, and medicine of common people in the American past are all too rare. Fortunately, Progressive Era Portlanders have provided us with a rich but completely neglected set of sources for precisely this historical task. We can discover from the vigorous, and surprisingly successful, campaign against compulsory vaccination in the early twentieth century that middle-class Americans in fact cared deeply about issues of democracy, family, and community even while deeply absorbed in their own very personal concerns about the body.

In an age in which most Americans, especially those who consider themselves enlightened, take vaccination to be a scientific sacrament, events in the first two decades in Portland look either amazing or absurd. Antivaccination sentiment was so strong that parents opposed to both the practice itself and its compulsory nature effectively shut down public schools to prevent the vaccination of their children—and during epidemics at that. More importantly, a 1916 initiative to ban compulsory vaccination in Oregon lost by only 374 votes and actually received a substantial majority in Portland. Antivaccinationism had clearly grown into a mass movement—and, as we shall see, by no means only in Portland.[2]

So how might we evaluate these peculiar people? I argue in this chapter that the anti–compulsory vaccination movement arose out of Portland's middling milieu, quickly becoming a populist crusade that emphatically repudiated the authority of governmental and medical "experts" to define personal and public health. Plebeian Portlanders who opposed vaccination, moreover, went far beyond a simple defensive libertarianism to develop a comprehensive, and indeed radical, democratic ideology of health and the body that even today continues to be worthy of our respect and consideration. We can call such radicalism a middle-class populism of the body.[3]

CHAPTER TWELVE

A DELUDED MOB
OF IGNORANT FOOLS?

The Historiography of Antivaccination,
and the Risks of Vaccination

It is an understatement to note that my argument differs considerably from mainstream scholarly analysis of those who resisted vaccination. Invisible to nearly all historians, antivaccinationists receive their most insightful treatment from scholars willing to recognize some of their grievances while simultaneously denying the legitimacy of their ideas. At least that is better than the academic analysis that continues to use labels common at the time, calling those who resisted vaccination—as has one recent scholar—"the deluded, the misguided, the ignorant, the irrationally fearful."[1]

Yet we should first admit that we know almost nothing at all about the antivaccinationists. Historians who concentrate on the Progressive Era have neglected their conduct or ideas. The one exception is William Reese's excellent but brief treatment of opposition to school health reform in Toledo, Rochester, Kansas City, and Milwaukee. Reese wisely understands that "the vaccinator became one of the most hated men in American cities in the Progressive era." He suggests what I hope to confirm: "The history of school vaccination is not a saga of how heroic physicians used the tools of modern science to rescue little children from disease and premature death. It is largely a tale of conflict between the school and the home, one of the most striking controversies of the Progressive era." Otherwise, antivaccinationists remain locked outside of Progressivism's dramas, even though a prominent contemporary radical, B. O. Flower, argued that the antivaccination movement represented part of the era's great "conflict between privilege and the people in the healing art." Indeed Flower, editor of the reform journal *Arena*, noted that the regular medical profession was "probably the most dangerous monopoly-seeking class in our land to-day."[2]

If historians of Progressivism have neglected a critical source of popular struggles during their period, historians of medicine have not forgotten those who opposed vaccination. Interest, however, hardly implies sympathy—or even respect. For example Martin Kaufman, in the only study of the national movement, simply wrote off their arguments as "specious." In turn, John Duffy, one of the most distinguished historians of American public health, wrote in 1974 that the "main ranks" of the antivaccination movement "were filled with cranks, extremists, and charlatans." A bit more generously, he later declared that those who opposed vaccination were "supported by the element in any population that will cling to traditional ideas at all costs."[3]

In the last two decades, though, a new kind of medical history has blossomed, one much more concerned about those who disagreed with or contested the onward march of orthodox medicine in the twentieth century. Influenced by social history, several historians have begun to treat episodes of resistance against vaccination with something approaching a blend of respectful objectivity and analytical rigor. Judith Walzer Leavitt was the first historian of American medicine to use this approach in discussing mass protest against smallpox-related public health measures. In her study of the politics of health reform in Milwaukee, Leavitt analyzed the vigorous opposition to vaccination, isolation hospitals, and quarantine of smallpox carriers among predominantly poor German and Polish immigrants. Leavitt is alert to the real hazards of vaccination and the genuine grievances of these people. Still, she almost wholly attributes their massive defiance of public expertise to a *defensive* posture. Health reform simply "contradicted accustomed behaviors and added to personal suffering." Apparently no positive ideology motivated those who opposed conventional medicine.[4]

Two local case studies more successfully explore the ideas of the antivaccinationists, even if in the end they too suffer from similar analytical problems. Joan Retsinas, a sociologist, has examined the powerful opposition to vaccination in Rhode Island, where antivaccinationists scored impressive legislative victories in 1895 and 1902. Retsinas wishes to rescue these antivaccinators from the charge that they were merely "misguided obstructionists arguing against science." She employs Thomas Kuhn's notion of scientific paradigms to argue that neither those who advocated nor those who opposed vaccination were more "enlightened." Given the then incomplete and uncertain victory of the germ theory of disease, both sides simply saw the world in incommensurate terms. The catch with Retsinas's Kuhnian analysis, however, is that the old worldview becomes completely irrelevant under the regime of the new "normal" science. Thus, Retsinas ends her article riding the scientific wave of inevitability, claiming, "The antivaccinators were by 1900 old men clinging desperately to old ideas." "Indeed," she writes, antivaccinationists "were simply out of place in the twentieth century."[5]

To the contrary, antivaccination sentiment remained strong, and intellectually compelling, well into the twentieth century. For instance, Paul Bator has written about the massive resistance to compulsory vaccination in Canada between 1900 and 1920. Bator greatly advances our understanding of the North American antivaccination movement by analyzing its social basis and its ideological commitments in Toronto, where two mayors denounced vaccination, the school board in 1906 removed vaccination regulations, and the city council in 1919–20 refused to allow city health officials to carry out Ontario's law requiring vaccination of all citizens. As I will also show for Portland, Bator argues that the crusade "could rightly describe itself as a mass movement. Its membership appears to have come from the city's workers and middle class." Socialists and female reformers joined in the condemnation, contending that workers and children suffered the most from vaccination. Yet even Bator, despite his success in rediscovering the antivaccinationists, in the ends tucks them safely into the bed of history, from which most subjects never awake. The opponents of vaccination merely served the purpose of forcing health reformers to refine their crude vaccinating techniques and their dictatorial bedside manner. Like Leavitt, Bator deems the ultimate triumph of compulsory vaccination an unproblematic benefit, as long as health officials had enough "sensitivity." In the process, those who protested vaccination become—even in the hands of the most respectful scholars— once again carriers of ignorance, instead of sources of challenging, even profound, ideas still possibly relevant to our own search for a democratic medicine.[6]

Plebeian Puritans, Anti-imperialists, and Populist Victorians: A Brief International History of Antivaccination

Historians' lack of attention to antivaccinationism is all the more remarkable given the high level of antivaccination activism in global history. Even with the new currents of historical thinking in the past few decades that validate the recovery, and even the celebration, of deviance and marginality, historians seem to have inoculated themselves against paying attention to folks who are both thoughtful and just *too* far beyond the bounds of current rationality. Yet crusades to protest medical treatment of smallpox have been widespread and transatlantic—indeed worldwide—in scope. Their plenitude should remind us at the very least of the considerable contest that attended, and continues to attend, the establishment of orthodox medical authority in the modern world.[7]

The deep origins of popular protest against vaccination in America date to a famous episode in Puritan Boston. During a smallpox epidemic in 1721–22, the introduction of inoculation to America by Cotton Mather brought with it what Perry Miller characterized as "a grim struggle for the mastery of New England's soul," as well as, ultimately, an assassination attempt on Mather. "Class antagonism" abounded, as often illiterate "Leather Apron Men"—artisans and shopkeepers—challenged the scholarly elite pushing inoculation. Throughout the rest of the eighteenth century, Carl Bridenbaugh notes, "communities . . . split asunder over the issue of inoculation," with a substantial class divide at the heart of the conflicts. Several years before the Revolution, inoculation sparked two anti-Crown riots in Norfolk, Virginia, and in Massachusetts lower-class resistance to inoculation became entangled with Whig politics just before Lexington.[8]

Sporadic protests against vaccination itself continued in the antebellum period. For example, many among the free black community of Baltimore refused vaccination during an 1827 epidemic, and this continued to be a long-standing tradition among free blacks. Perhaps it was in such an atmosphere that Frederick Douglass originally developed his lifelong enmity for compulsory vaccination. Possibly stretching this tradition, we can better understand why Malcolm Little (no known relation to Portland antivaccination heroine Lora Little) received a prison transfer because "I refused to take some kind of shots, an inoculation or something."[9]

During the closing decades of the 1800s, the opposition to vaccination achieved the status of a genuine and effective, if intermittent, mass movement. Even that symbol of the heartland, Muncie, Indiana, witnessed great resistance to public health officials' attempts to institute compulsory vaccination and isolation. Most protest nationwide centered on the efforts of health authorities to establish compulsory vaccination for schoolchildren. As John Duffy reports about Massachusetts, "enforcement was in the hands of local school boards, some of whom were forcefully opposed to vaccination and many more of whom were apathetic." As a result vaccination "became a perennial issue in local school elections," and in the process "the laws often became dead letters."[10]

The burgeoning immigrant population served as one of the largest sources of resistance to vaccination in the late nineteenth century. In the mid-1890s, Polish resistance led to one of reform mayor Hazen Pingree's most intense political crises. Racial politics also got mixed up with the vaccination issue. Even during deadly epidemics many traditional Pueblo and Hopi Indians refused vaccination in the 1890s, the latter because of a fear of "extermination." An army colonel sent around the same time to the Texas-Mexico border region in order to quash revolutionary activity, while complaining about "the weird pharmacy and therapeutics of the border," noted of the local Tejano population that "it is difficult to get any of these people to consent to vaccination." This in turn elicited a vigorous defense of resistance to vaccination by the anonymous "El Bien Publico" publishing house, representing the "mexican people" of the Rio Grande Valley. Two decades later, a captain for the Texas Rangers "got all shot to pieces in Laredo when they attempted to force the Mexicans to be inoculated with vaccine and they wouldn't stand it."[11]

As a result of the enormous opposition to vaccination in late-nineteenth-century America, vaccination rates remained low throughout most of the country. For instance, Minnesota's state health officer reported that fully half to three-quarters of that state's children went unvaccinated, as did half of New York children. Across the nation, seven states—California, Illinois, Minnesota, West Virginia, Wisconsin, and Utah (the latter the site of a distinctively

Mormon hostility to vaccination)—repealed compulsory vaccination statutes. As Martin Kaufman somberly recognizes, "The anti-vaccinationists of this period were terribly successful."[12]

Steadfast opposition to vaccination continued in the new century. In 1905, the year that the U.S. Supreme Court upheld the legality of compulsory vaccination laws in *Jacobson v. Massachusetts*, only eleven states had such statutes, and no state actually *forced* vaccination on anyone, instead using other penalties for those who refused to comply. Left-wing Progressivism blended seamlessly into antivaccination politics. Robert La Follette vetoed a vaccination bill in Wisconsin in 1901, and Martin Freidrich, chief health official under renowned Cleveland reform mayor Tom Johnson, banned compulsory vaccination in the same year. Johnson, who opposed "shooting people full of poison against their will," clearly approved. Nor did all such conflicts proceed peacefully. One North Carolinian wrote that universal vaccination would not happen in his state without military force, and a New York City newspaper commented that "vaccination is always accompanied only by force in the Lower East Side." Western states witnessed the greatest antivaccination successes. A robust 55.8 percent of Arizonans voted against compulsory vaccination in a 1918 initiative, and the legislatures in California and Washington repealed compulsory vaccination laws in 1911 and in 1919 respectively. Beyond this, the same 1919 Washington legislature that abandoned compulsory vaccination passed a liberal statute legalizing all kinds of drugless healers, and the legislature two years later confirmed its antivaccination stand and went even further by allowing parents to exempt their children from physical inspection at school.[13]

As the result, renowned public health official Charles Chapin despaired in 1913 of the United States' status as "the least vaccinated of any civilized country." By the 1930s four states (Arizona, North Dakota, Minnesota, and Utah) had laws prohibiting compulsory vaccination, and only nine states and the District of Columbia had compulsory vaccination legislation. The central and western states almost completely rejected coercion. In 1945 Wilson Smillie was still complaining that vaccination was "gradually losing ground. Its enforcement meets with constant opposition from the general public." As late as 1970, the year before the CDC decision to end smallpox vaccination in the United States, agitation against vaccination continued.[14]

The United States joined the rest of the world in having robust antivaccination movements. Take the most spectacular example: Brazil, 1904. In November more than a week of deadly riots wracked Rio de Janeiro as citizens fought against the national government's plans to impose compulsory vaccination in the city. The opposition to vaccination came from "a cross-class alliance of the urban poor, working class, and petty bourgeoisie" that bitterly resented government plans to displace residents as part of an urban redevelopment scheme. Vaccination opponents left Brazil's capital "in shambles." And they were successful—the government rescinded compulsory vaccination as the result of the resistance.[15]

Opposition to vaccination reached epidemic proportions in colonial contexts, linking the most subaltern actors in global history with their white middle-class comrades in Portland. In colonial Ceylon and India opposition to vaccination became a potent rallying force against the forces of imperialism tampering with beliefs relating to Sitala, the smallpox deity; with caste, in the case of arm-to-arm vaccination; and with cows, the original source of the vaccine material. (Indeed, substantial resistance to vaccination continued beyond independence in India up to the very conclusion of the smallpox eradication campaign, perhaps inspired to some extent by Gandhi's example as an antivaccinationist.) Resistance to vaccination was successful, at least on a small scale, in nineteenth-century colonial Malaya. Algeria witnessed resistance to French colonial attempts to "pollute" Arab society through vaccination; the anticolonial Mumbo cult in Kenya mobilized in opposition to vaccination campaigns starting in 1913; Belgian Congolese soldiers revolted against the administration of vaccination during World War I; and in colonial Ghana "the arrival of the vaccinator in a village was sometimes a signal for a general exodus." One careful scholar has noted the rationality of resistance to vaccination in the Philippines under Spanish rule. In turn Puerto Ricans resisted American colonial compulsory vaccination policies, as did Sinn Fein in the Irish context. And a major part of the expansion of the nineteenth-century Japanese state occurred as it sought to extend vaccination to the northern frontier of Ezo; this Tokugawa policy in turn inspired considerable resistance on the part of the local Ainu population.[16]

Australia also saw vigorous antivaccination movements in the nineteenth century. Only two of the six Australian states adopted compulsory vaccination, and "conscience clauses" there "reduced the proportion of newborn infants vaccinated each year to less than 10%." In western Europe, the French Catholic Church "consistently refused to endorse" vaccination. Holland and Switzerland, the latter by a referendum vote, had by the early twentieth century outlawed compulsory vaccination. "Tremendous opposition in Germany" came within one vote of having the Reichstag pass a conscientious objection clause in 1914—this three decades after the emperor himself refused to vaccinate his children. As J. N. Hays notes, "passive resistance to the procedure was probably widespread everywhere in the Western world."[17]

The location of the most sustained and most successful movement was England, where "vaccination has been the subject of more controversy than any other procedure used by the medical profession." Such agitation ultimately won the right to conscientious objection in 1898 and even further liberalization in 1907. Powerful radical Liberal politicians such as John Bright led the antivaccination movement in Parliament, while the labor movement pressed for improved urban conditions and a more just distribution of wealth rather than vaccination as means of combating infectious diseases. In various localities, these "populists" represented an alliance akin to the one in Portland, with the most powerful opposition coming from "towns with a strong lower middle and working class who had a powerful voice in the local political culture—against the state, against London, and against anonymous professional authority." Antivaccinationists also had direct connections to the feminist campaign to repeal the Contagious Diseases Acts. Josephine Butler served in the Mothers' Anti-Compulsory Vaccination League, and poet Mary Hume-Rothery blasted the vaccination laws as part of "the unnatural dominance of females by the Male State."[18]

Let the People Decide: The Comparative Risks of Smallpox and Vaccination

The strength of the antivaccination tradition by no means disproves the dangers of smallpox, nor the evidence that points to the effectiveness of vaccination in preventing the disease. Any glance at a picture of a full-blown case of smallpox would convince anyone at the very least of the utterly grotesque nature of the disease. Yet an important irony crops up here. Antivaccinationist sentiment was, in the United States as well as other parts of the world, often strongest in areas where epidemics were *most* severe. Therefore those opposed to vaccination could hardly claim ignorance of the harm that the disease could inflict. Rather, individuals demanded the right to investigate for themselves, and their families, the risks and advantages of vaccination before reaching their own decision. To understand the rationality of their choices, we must explore briefly the costs and benefits involved in smallpox prevention.[19]

Smallpox epidemics have occurred for centuries—likely, for millennia. Although only moderately contagious, smallpox was quite deadly. Before the twentieth century, the case fatality rate during epidemics was generally around 25 percent. Blindness and other maladies beyond the dreaded scarring could also occur. Even if epidemics occurred only at irregular intervals, smallpox remained a constant concern for much of the world's population.[20]

The modern history of medical attempts to control smallpox in America began in colonial Massachusetts when Cotton Mather and Zabdiel Boylston began the process of *inoculation* to prevent the disease. Inoculation involved the transmission of live smallpox virus, in the form of pus or powdered scabs from a previous patient, into a healthy patient's skin. The recipient of the inoculation, if all went well, would develop a minor smallpox infection and thereby gain immunity to the disease. All did not go well, however, for the 3 percent of inoculees (including, apparently, Jonathan Edwards) who died from the procedure. *Vaccination*, by contrast, proved a much safer means of

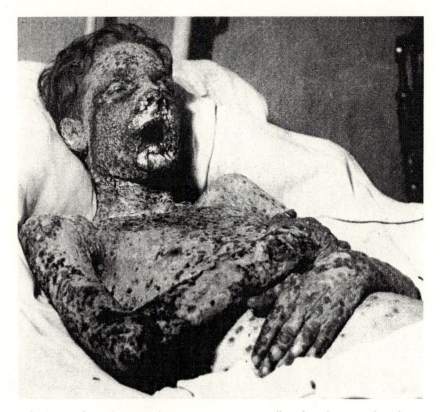

A fatal case of variola major. (From C. W. Dixon, *Smallpox* [London, 1962], 19.)

producing what was intended to be the same kind of immunity. Introduced in 1796, vaccination involved inserting into the skin cowpox virus, thus precipitating a much weaker infection in the individual and nearly eliminating the stage where those who had received inoculations were contagious.[21]

Many Americans, including Thomas Jefferson, hailed vaccination as a means of eradicating smallpox from the face of the earth. Indeed, the disease declined dramatically during the nineteenth century. Although smallpox continued to be a killer, the periods between epidemics grew longer and the epidemics themselves became less virulent. John Duffy has gone so far as to argue, "Smallpox was never a major threat in the United States in the nineteenth century."[22]

Public health reformers marshaled statistics to attribute this decline directly to vaccination, as in many cases more highly vaccinated populations suffered considerably less from the disease than nonvaccinated groups. Understandably, modern historians have tended to accept the claims of the health reformers at face value. Still, we must recognize that no historical study has attempted to isolate any of the many causes—particularly improved nutrition and sanitation—that could have been responsible for the weakening of smallpox in nineteenth-century America. Nor has any scholar publicly pondered just why the disease significantly weakened and then eventually died out in an American population far from universally vaccinated. Looking at this same problem across the Atlantic, historian E. P. Hennock has used comparative immunization rates in turn-of-the-century England and Germany, to make a compelling argument that universal vaccination was not necessary to "conquer" smallpox. By 1921 only 40 percent of English infants were receiving smallpox vaccinations, whereas rates in Germany never fell below 80 percent. Yet after 1906, the death rates in both countries became "equally insignificant." This was a lesson that the World Health Organization eventually learned when, late in its successful smallpox eradication campaign, it gave up on universal vaccination in order to concentrate on, in the manner of the early-twentieth-century English, "surveillance, containment and selective vaccination of contacts." Hennock does not discount vaccination's role in the overall decline in smallpox but even more firmly makes it clear that compulsion was absolutely not essential to the disease's disappearance.[23]

And if it is still possible to question vaccination in the twenty-first century, people found it much easier to be skeptical a century ago. As Joan Retsinas notes, late-nineteenth-century Americans lived in a world where "Vaccination proponents could not claim that vaccination had eradicated smallpox—the United States suffered epidemics in 1871 and 1888. Records suggested that even vaccinated people did not escape smallpox." Furthermore, beyond the issue of efficacy, significant dangers accompanied vaccination. Advocates and opponents could agree on at least some of the hazards involved. Vaccine safety increased throughout the nineteenth century, but at no time did the medical profession eliminate risk. In the decades just after Edward Jenner's discovery, no one could question the crudity of the vaccination process. As Stuart Galishoff admits, "Vaccination as first practiced had too many pitfalls to gain universal acceptance. The vaccines used were unreliable and the operation was risky." Bacterial contamination from both the vaccine and its method of administration long remained a major problem. Until the 1870s and 1880s, "humanized" virus served as the chief source of the vaccine. As Wilson G. Smillie's 1955 public health history textbook acknowledged, the "method of vaccination was from arm to arm, with all its attendant difficulties and dangers. Many outbreaks of syphilis occurred, which were due directly to transmission by vaccination. Frequent transmission of erysipelas and other virulent human infections resulted from arm-to-arm vaccination, and thus this method of prevention became justifiably unpopular." Even John Duffy acknowledged, "The early opponents of vaccination had tangible evidence on which to base their position."[24]

Problems continued well after the much-heralded introduction of bovine vaccine in the late nineteenth century. Galishoff notes that "the new vaccine had almost as many liabilities as the old one." The absence of any regulatory controls led to the proliferation of entrepreneurs who provided cheap rather than safe vaccine; dust, hair and even dung often remained in this commodity that was equally a product of the barnyard and the laboratory. As late as 1902 medical literature confirmed dozens of cases of tetanus, the main source of vaccine-related death. Streptococcal and staphylococcal infections resulted from vaccinators not cleansing patients' dirty arms. In the words of Hennock, "although it might indeed be true that the benefits of infant vaccination outweighed its risks, as its advocates insisted, those risks could loom so large as to make calculations of probability appear irrelevant to the individual parent."[25]

Injuries accompanied infection. Again according to Galishoff, "even when stringent precautions were taken, persons undergoing vaccination sometimes developed incapacitating arm sores requiring from four to eight weeks to heal." Bator found that in Ontario "the most common complaint of adults about vaccination was that it produced an infected arm which disabled them for weeks and prevented them from working." Beyond that, great pain could result from what was essentially minor surgery, for "the crude techniques then in use involved making a much larger abrasion than is the case today." Clearly, neither proletarians nor middling folks needed to understand contests over the germ theory to be upset about vaccination.[26]

The safety of vaccines improved greatly at the turn of the century. Storage in glycerin sterilized the virus, and the supervision of vaccine manufacture by states and the federal government either brought responsibility to or simply eliminated the marketplace. In the context of other twentieth-century improvements, Galishoff voices the common wisdom when he states that "smallpox was to linger on in the United States until medical science and government action rendered vaccination a completely safe and dependable procedure." Yet Donald Hopkins and Allan Chase, two staunch defenders of vaccination, caution us against the idea that the procedure ever became danger-free. Hopkins remarks that "excessive bacterial contamination remained a problem until the mid–twentieth century." Even perfectly microbial-free vaccine could still, albeit rarely, cause "adverse and even fatal complications following the vaccination of certain children and adults." Between 1949 (the year of the last smallpox case in the United States) and 1972, for example, an estimated 3,000 severe complications and 150 deaths occurred as the result of the smallpox vaccine. In 1968 alone, the vaccine caused at least 572 complications, with 16 of the 153 major complications leading to encephalitis and 9 to death, leading the doctors reporting these findings in the *New England Journal of Medicine* to "reaffirm the fact that the morbidity and mortality associated with smallpox vaccination in the United States are consider-

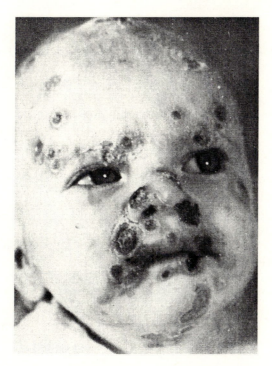

A child's reaction to the smallpox vaccine, quite palpable to parents. (From C. W. Dixon, *Smallpox* [London, 1962], 19.)

able." In 1971, the United States Public Health Service finally recommended the termination of smallpox vaccination because of "the extremely rare, but serious, residual complications of vaccination." One researcher has argued that the replacement of universal mass (i.e., compulsory) vaccination with vaccination only of high-risk groups and those in contact with the infection during this period could have cut vaccine-related deaths by 70 percent. (Just as today, public health officials warn of a minimum of 150 deaths and more than four thousand serious injuries—such as permanent brain damage—in the event of the mass reintroduction of smallpox vaccination in the face of a bioterrorism threat.)[27]

So, overall, throughout the nineteenth century smallpox was unquestionably a dread disease. Vaccination could prevent smallpox but had clearly recognizable hazards. Moving into the early twentieth century public health reformers began—with considerable justification—to tout the substantial, although not complete, safety of vaccines. Thus the turn of the century marks a critical divide in the question of the rationality of decision making about vaccination. During the nineteenth century those who argued that death, disfigurement, sore arms, syphilis, and even the loss of a critical few days at work were an integral part of the vaccination process had their facts right, regardless of the benefit we might ascribe to the procedure. Yet in the twentieth century, it would take quite an irrational leap of faith indeed to argue that the dangers of vaccination trumped those of smallpox. Or would it?[28]

The trick was that the terror of the disease also, justifiably, lost much of its hold on the American population right at the very beginning of the century. For indiscernible reasons a new strain of mild smallpox, *Variola minor*, effectively displaced the true mass killer, *Variola major*. Introduced into the United States in 1896, *V. minor* spread to the entire country by 1899. Most of those who became ill with the milder form of smallpox did not even know that they had the disease; only 20 percent ended up going to the doctor. Symptoms almost universally were far less serious. From 1900 to 1930 the number of *V. minor* cases outnumbered those of *V. major* by at least twenty to one. The potential for death from smallpox declined rapidly as one form of the disease displaced the other. The case fatality rate "dropped from 20 percent in 1895 and 1896, to 6.2 percent in 1897, 4 percent in 1900 and 0.6 percent in 1906," where it hovered from that time on. Furthermore, *V. minor* conferred permanent immunity to *V. major*.[29]

The twentieth century therefore saw a much safer vaccine chasing after a much less dangerous disease. As always, the public itself had substantive reasons to consider the costs and benefits of vaccination specifically as well as the expertise of medical officials generally. Indeed, in the only systematic quantitative study of the risks associated with both immunization and the disease itself, Maisie May has demonstrated that "the risk [of death] from smallpox for any random non-immune individual was less than that from vaccination" in England and Wales during the interwar period—even in areas hardest hit by epidemics. The decision not to vaccinate, May argues compellingly, was a completely rational one.[30]

We can conclude from this review of the literature in medical history that vaccination could in fact represent a genuine threat to citizens' personal health. "Ignorance has been the cultural factor which has exaggerated the fear of the danger resulting from vaccination," medical sociologist Bernhard Stern wrote in 1927. Without a doubt, however, the ideology of antivaccinationists went far beyond sheer ignorance.[31]

CHAPTER THIRTEEN

SHUTTING DOWN THE SCHOOLS

Parents and Protest in Mt. Scott

Ultimately we can only address the basic philosophical question raised by global antivaccinationists—the issue of democratic coercion versus democratic respect for individual rights—in public conversations about citizenship and its attendant obligations. As sociologist Peter Baldwin has noted, preventative public medicine casts up "the basic problem of reconciling individual and community in the most fundamental, pressing and unavoidable of terms." I will refrain here from engaging in that kind of philosophical reflection. Answers to more historical questions, however, are possible. Where did the ideas of the antivaccinationists come from, and what did they mean in practice?[1]

In Portland, it is impossible to separate the antivaccinationists from the milieu of radical direct democracy at the center of the city's politics in the first two decades of the twentieth century. Twice the opponents of compulsory vaccination placed the question on the statewide ballot, in 1916 and 1920. Mass agitation also occurred at the municipal level. The foundation of antivaccination was, again, the class alliance of workers and middling folks that also served as the backbone of radical electoral reforms in the Rose City.

The most vigorous episodes of local resistance to vaccination in Portland came in 1914 and 1920. Both affairs involved the city health officers' attempts to require vaccination for school attendance during epidemics. Both became the occasions for massive defiance of the medical officials' prerogatives, as parents essentially closed neighborhood schools to protest vaccination regulations. And in both protests, middling Portlanders demonstrated that their self-conceptions as citizens linked domestic and public concerns to create yet another innovative variety of democratic middle-class radicalism.

Prior to the 1914 protests, smallpox had not created much of a serious public health issue in the Rose City; the city suffered only nine smallpox-related deaths between 1898 and 1917. No record of opposition during the nineteenth century has come down to us, but both Portland and Oregon did enter the twentieth without a compulsory vaccination law. Occasional quiet stirrings of resistance to vaccination then began to appear in the city's newspapers. When the first signs of an epidemic hit Portland in 1902, the chief city medical officer acknowledged that some "scientists and physicians" opposed vaccination.[2]

Resistance to vaccination remained shadowy throughout the first decade of the century but clearly had grown strong enough to warrant periodic warnings of doom from the regular medical profession as well as from the editorial writers of the city's leading newspapers. In 1907 Esther Pohl-Lovejoy, Portland's chief medical officer, wrote that Montavilla, a neighborhood in the far southeastern part of the city, was "a community particularly averse to vaccination." The following year parents in Clinton-Kelly school refused to allow their children to be vaccinated during an outbreak of smallpox. Also in 1908 the state board of health spoke out against a pamphlet entitled "The Oregon Osteopath," which argued that both smallpox vaccination and diphtheria antitoxin were "relics of barbarism." Nor was love lost for the rare individuals who wrote into the newspapers to state their dissenting views on the subject. The *Oregonian* described antivaccinationists as "crazy," "misguided," "singularly senseless and cruel," and "desperate." Their message, full of "bigotry," contained "nothing rational" and attempted to "retard progress." Vituperation of this magnitude would continue until the antivaccinationists no longer represented a threat to the city's Establishment.[3]

The first organized opposition to vaccination came gradually onto the scene in precisely the same period in which the Oregon direct democrats made their most vigorous push for the single tax, proportional representation, and other electoral innovations. Health reformers claimed to have garnered victories against compulsory school vaccination as early as 1911. That year Lora C. Little, who would become the primary leader of the Portland antivaccinationists, also made her first public appearance. Little's initial communication to the *Oregonian* warned that even though antivaccinationists did not advocate violence, "We have sometimes stood off the vaccinator with a gun at the moment of attack." Little voiced twin objections: "it is a violation of the blood and when performed upon a man against his will is a personal assault of exceptionally outrageous character." Also in 1911, the "Health Defense League of Portland," very likely led by Little, petitioned against a ruling that forbade the holding of hands by children in public schools, which the school board passed in order to prevent the spread of contagion from "Orientals and other foreigners."[4]

For the next six years, Lora Little became a prominent player in the democratic underground of Portland politics. In January 1913, when no epidemic threatened the city, the Mothers' Club of the Woodstock neighborhood arranged for a debate between Little and Dr. Calvin White, secretary of the state health board. Held at the Woodstock Methodist church, the "sizzling" contest did not adhere to the rules of mainline Protestant decorum. "The audience gasped" as each speaker flung accusations of dishonesty at the other. Little accused "slick" doctors, with their strong "corporation spirit," of lying about statistics so that they could continue to reap the large amounts of money involved in the state-sponsored vaccination complex. White in turn proclaimed that "there was not one word of truth" in Little's statistics, arguing that vaccination was completely safe and effective. Smallpox had declined concomitantly with vaccination, Little responded, because of improvements in municipal and personal cleanliness. The vaccine itself was "morbid animal poison, and in one of the vaccine plants I saw the serum drawn from a dead calf." Dr. White, "hurling himself to the middle of the floor" and "advancing toward the speaker and shaking his finger in her face" amid cries of "Sit down!" and "Put him out!" then proceeded to denounce this "woman without any education or without any means or qualifications."[5]

Oregon still at this time had no compulsory vaccination legislation, even during epidemics. Researchers from the Bureau of Municipal Research in New York complained in 1913 that quarantine and vaccination went unenforced in the Rose City. However, city and state law, as well as the authority of the school board, did give municipal health officers in Portland the power to exclude unvaccinated children from school for two weeks during an outbreak of smallpox. After several cases of the illness came to light during the summer of 1914 in the southeastern part of the city, city health officer M. B. Marcellus exercised his discretion at four East Side elementary schools and Franklin High School just after the September start of classes. The result was a massive showdown between Marcellus and parents. A local editor proclaimed: "The entire Mt. Scott district has been shaken the past week, from Fortieth to Ninetieth street." Estimates varied, but at least two-thirds and perhaps as many as four-fifths of all students absented themselves from classes for the entire ten days of the vaccination order. The parents and their children had effectively shut down the schools. Teachers and students who remained gave up on the educational process and waited for the unvaccinated schoolchildren to return.[6]

The parents, however, refused the opportunity to take an extended family vacation. As the *News* put it, "the vaccination fight is growing so fast that it will soon be as noisy as the European war." Ordinary citizens rallied to overturn Marcellus's order and worked to readmit the children to school without vaccination. Mayor Russell Albee upheld Marcellus and soon had to contend with 100 angry parents, led by Reverend V. E. Willings of the Laurelwood Methodist church and W. O. Powell, head of the local Pacific College of Chiropractic, before a meeting of the city commission. A few days into the crisis the mayor tried to broker a compromise, whereby only those children who had actually been exposed to smallpox would need vaccination in order to attend school. The parents rejected this agreement, as did the school board, which insisted on the original order excluding all unvaccinated children. At least 235 parents, "exclusive of numerous children present," attended "an indignation mass meeting" to combat "the drastic and arbitrary order." The assembly appointed a committee to represent it before public officials and in legal proceedings; the group of five included neighborhood resident Lora Little.[7]

"The storm that has been raging over vaccination in the city schools" escalated the next day when the eccentric "populist" judge Henry McGinn ruled in the parents' favor in a case that W. O. Powell brought to force admission of his children to Creston Elementary. McGinn issued a temporary injunction preventing school officials from keeping unvaccinated children out of school. The city attorney vowed to appeal McGinn's ruling, and Marcellus gave indications that he would not obey it. The ruling came close enough to the end of the two-week period, however, that the legal fight proceeded no further. Both sides legitimately claimed victory. Marcellus had kept the unvaccinated children out of school and had avoided a formal legal judgment on compulsory vaccination. More significantly, the parents had forced Marcellus to back down on almost all fronts, and they therefore ceased their agitation in this particular case. Most of the primary instigators of the Mt. Scott disturbances then regrouped under the banner of the Health Defense League, promised to continue to do battle with the city health department, and implied support of the effort currently under way to recall Mayor Albee.[8]

The mix of arguments that the parents used to uphold their position blended an interesting set of political and medical ideas. Calls to preserve "our right and liberty" against the arbitrary, even illegal, power of Dr. Marcellus predominated; a declaration by the parents' committee simply stated, "we insist on our right of schooling for our children, regardless of their being vaccinated or not." Majoritarian sentiments corresponded with civil libertarianism. Reverend Willings stated, presumably correctly given school attendance figures, that "Four-fifths of the people of Mount Scott oppose vaccination," to which the chiropractor W. O. Powell added, "The majority in any case should rule. The majority of people in Mount Scott are opposed to vaccination. Why should they not rule?"[9]

Diatribes like that of Willings against "the health authorities and the 'medical trust'" easily led to a critique of orthodox views of smallpox and medicine generally. Parents emphasized the minimal danger of smallpox when compared to the hazards of vaccination. Mrs. E. H. Ingham stated before the mayor a view shared with at least several others. "Personally," she said, "I would rather have smallpox than be vaccinated. I know of many horrible results from vaccination." A "feature" of the largest mass meeting was the presentation of three girls to the audience. Two of the children, "bright and healthy looking," had contracted naturally occurring smallpox the summer before, while the other, Marian Howerton, had suffered from a partially paralyzed arm and general illnesses since her vaccination eighteen months earlier. Etta Welch also challenged the claims made for the efficacy of vaccination. If vaccination did provide immunity, Welch stated, then vaccinated children had nothing to worry about from a smallpox outbreak. Therefore, "Why not let those who believe in vaccination have their children vaccinated and let the others send their children to school and take chances of their getting smallpox?" "If I want to take a chance with my child," Welch declared, "why is it any of the health authorities' business?"[10]

Small businesses at SE Foster Road and Sixty-first Street in the Mt. Scott district of southeast Portland. (Courtesy Oregon Historical Society, #024299.)

It is possible to identify the family's main occupation for ten of the twelve individuals, besides Little, who either led the movement or spoke out during meetings. White-collar professions predominated, but the overall mix was a broad range of middling and working-class vocations. One lawyer, two pastors, one irregular physician, and the president of the city's chiropractic college set the tone for white-collar participation in the parents' protest. A real estate agent and a butcher represented those who were self-employed. The president of the Health Defense League, Charles Kitching, served as a clerk for the railway mail service. Etta Welch was married to a lineman, and Marian Howerton's father was a watchman. Marian herself perhaps had a lower-level white-collar position awaiting her if she recovered from her vaccination injuries; her two sisters and one brother held printing, clerking, and book-keeping positions. Three of the twelve individuals were women, although Lora Little was the only female among the official leadership.[11]

The Mt. Scott neighborhood, nearly eight miles from downtown and a relatively recent annexation to the municipality, was part of the broad southeastern swath of the city that served as the firm foundation for the most far-reaching of direct democracy reforms. In 1914, for example, every precinct but one in the Mt. Scott area provided majorities for the radical single tax scheme of William U'Ren and his allies. As the profile of the leaders of the antivaccination movement indicates, the neighborhood contained a broad mix of middle-class and working-class folks. A plethora of small businesses, a good number friendly to labor, filled the wide thoroughfare of Foster Road, and the many children who failed to return from the hop harvest when the public schools opened in September illustrate the proletarian character of the neighborhood. Entire families engaged in this harvest in order to get money for, among other things, textbooks. In the last years of his life Will Daly moved to Mt. Scott. When Daly mounted his radical challenge for the mayoralty in 1917, he garnered an impressive 70 percent of the vote in Mt. Scott precincts. And to prove that the 1914 antivaccination movement in Mt. Scott was no flash in the pan, *all* sixteen precincts in the district supported, by wide margins, the 1916 initiative that sought to ban compulsory vaccination. More than 66 percent of neighborhood voters favored the measure.[12]

The citizens who fomented the initial resistance to vaccination in Portland, then, were hardly marginal players in the politics of the Rose City, even if their neighborhood was off the cultural map of the city's elite. They were, in fact, at the heart of the populist direct democracy movement.

CHAPTER FOURTEEN

FROM THE DEATH OF A CHILD TO SEDITION AGAINST THE STATE

The Life and Ideology of Lora C. Little

The antivaccination uprising in Mt. Scott merely served as the prelude for the most sustained early-twentieth-century attempt by Portlanders—indeed by any Americans—to apply the methods of populist democracy to medical and scientific matters. The energy of activists who opposed vaccination soon went into the 1916 initiative, the brainchild of an obscure individual named Lora C. Little. Little had served as the most insistent and most articulate critic of orthodox medicine during the 1914 Mt. Scott protests. For example, to the sympathetic but not yet convinced editor of the *Mt. Scott Herald* she argued:

> it is unquestionable that smallpox, like other eruptive fevers, is an active effort to eliminate an excess of waste matter unable to find outlet by natural channels, and is therefore life-saving. Nor can it be gainsaid that vaccination is an artificial pollution of the blood with a virus that is capable of propagating itself in the system.
>
> This one is an effort of nature. The other is an artifice of the doctors. Trust nature, is a safer motto than trust the doctor. Nature does not contradict herself. Medical authority is a mass of contradictions.

To discover how Little could believe that smallpox was a health-producing disease, and what that says about middling folks' alternative ideas about medicine, we must first reconstruct, as best we can, her remarkable life—a life previously unknown to historians.[1]

At the time of the Mt. Scott antivaccination insurrection, Lora Little had lived in the neighborhood for approximately two years. She served as the teacher at her own School of Health Culture, also known as the Little School of Health. Despite the "Mrs." often attached to her name, she had no spouse during her six-year long residence in the Rose City. She was a confident member of the petite bourgeoisie as well as a vocal health reformer. At her school she promised: "Success in self-care of the health taught. Saves money, saves suffering, saves life. All diseases reached by my natural methods." A rare advertisement for her services proclaimed: "BE YOUR OWN DOCTOR. Run your own machine. You can do it better than another, being inside it. It pays YOU to keep well, to get well quickly when sick, to know how to take care of your family."[2]

Lora C. Little, editor, healer, antivaccination activist. (From *Medical Freedom*, June 1913, 9.)

Little quickly became known in the community for far more than the antivaccination campaign. She regularly gave talks to local citizens' groups, although not all of her ideas met with approval. When Little slammed sugar in front of "mother's clubs," she reported, "I have met with sour faces and ridicule." Perhaps this was because of her prohibitionist message that "the candyshop, as I have said time and again, is but little better than the dramshop." (She actually tolerated the dramshop.) Public authorities also presumably viewed her as a pest. After Little's departure from the city the *Oregonian* reported, "She always was present at budget sessions of the City Council, urging a decrease in the expenditures of the Bureau of Health or failing in this, demanding a drugless system in whole or in part as a substitute for present methods."[3]

What inspired her strict commitments is unclear. Born Lora Williams in a log cabin in Waterville, Minnesota Territory, in 1856, Little was a teacher, seamstress, printer, and housewife before becoming an activist. She sojourned up and down the East Coast prior to settling in the Twin Cities at the turn of the century. In 1900 she resided in Minneapolis alongside many white-collar neighbors. Her husband Elijah was a civil engineer with a specialty in bridge building, and the Littles shared their rented home with their niece, Luna Williams. Elijah disappeared from the city directories, and apparently from Lora's life, in 1906.[4]

Otherwise, the hints about Little's life before Portland are shadowy but intriguingly suggestive. She once praised home life and denounced "clubs and fashion" as a "delusion. . . . Take it from one who has seen more than enough of the inside of club work." She revealed a much more important part of herself when, in 1906, she wrote the muckraking-titled *Crimes of the Cowpox Ring*—"the most powerful campaign document yet produced" by antivaccinationists, according to one activist. In *Crimes* Little wrote movingly of the death of her only child, seven-year-old Kenneth. Kenneth, forced to get vaccinated in order to enter the Yonkers, New York, public schools in 1895, died as a result after developing measles and diphtheria.[5]

Little threw herself into the political life of Minneapolis as soon as she arrived in town. As early as 1899 Little criticized the local school board for requiring vaccination, disparaged the military's vaccination plan for soldiers in the Spanish-American War, and advocated cleanliness and ventilation in public health matters. Although she rarely spoke on issues explicitly oriented toward women during her years in Portland, in 1900 she vigorously defended woman suffrage.[6]

Little's most significant public activity during her Minnesota years came as publisher and editor, from 1902 to 1907, of the *Liberator*. Little's journal was, according to the chief organ of the British movement, "the brightest and ablest health and anti-vaccinist periodical in the United States." According to an advertisement, this "Monthly Journal of Health and Freedom Opposes the Vaccination Folly [and] Exposes the Medical Delusion that Health can be had by Means of Drugs." In the *Liberator* Little propagandized for women's dress reform and against high heels, for "Hindu-Yogi" breathing practices and against "the fundamental error that disease is a foe to be fought." She also took aim at "the ill-gotten wealth of a Gould, a Carnegie, or a Rockefeller," advocating "some painless (or fitting) way of getting rid of millionaires." Little was particularly emphatic about the evil of the Anthony Comstock mentality, celebrated "Sex—The Central Problem of Life," and maintained that "the woman who is really most attractive to her own as well as to the other sex, is the woman who is strongly sexed."[7]

Little's main concern lay with the tyranny of state medicine and the resulting "necessity for open, uncompromising hostility toward the [medical] profession as a whole." As secretary and organizer for the Minnesota Health

Kenneth Marion Little, 1889–1896. (From Lora C. Little, *Crimes of the Cowpox Ring: Some Moving Pictures Thrown on the Dead Wall of Official Silence* [Minneapolis, 1906], 9.)

League, Little dedicated herself to the fight for full personal freedom in the realm of health, including opposition to the "Segregation of Invalids." Little kept her readers posted, with meticulous detail, about the laws relating to compulsory vaccination. In fact, she herself made history in 1903 by instigating the passage of a Minnesota statute preventing public health authorities from requiring vaccination of children, except during an epidemic. She took her antivaccinationism in a fairly extreme direction, declaring resistance to compulsory vaccination fully legitimate and asking readers of the *Liberator* "to come to the aid of the man who lies in a Georgia jail awaiting trial for killing a man in the effort to protect his person from the official blood-poisoners." Little also decried the "brutal invasion" of a Philadelphia faith-healing church, in the middle of worship, by police intent on vaccinating congregants. How could this happen? Little's answer:

> it was a congregation of negroes. We used to talk of the Reconstructed South. It is time we had a Reconstructed North. I venture that hardly a reader of this account has not had his indignation modified on reading that negroes were the victims. If this is so, does it not show how wide reaching is the falling off from the true idea of freedom and equality before the law which has been the professed ideal of our government.[8]

By 1906 Little was traveling extensively as an antivaccination agitator. The next year she gave up editing the *Liberator*, pleading poverty ("I who do not know where my coal and other supplies for the coming winter are coming from") and hardship ("Nobody knows what privations and toil I have endured the past five years" because of "all but superhuman sacrifice"). She instead devoted herself to serving as a health teacher. She spent considerable time abroad, giving lectures and exercise classes as a "missionary" in London, Glasgow, Edinburgh, and the antivaccination Mecca of Leicester. By late 1908 she had returned to the United States, continuing her antivaccination campaign in Massachusetts. The following year found her crossing the continent and landing in Hood River, Oregon.[9]

By the time she reached Portland, Little had, by self-admission, been in poor health for a number of years, despite having been an avid student of water cure and phrenological journals from the age of seven. Little "was aware of my ignorance, however, and never ceased to search, inquire and study. The fault, I now know, was chiefly a matter of food." Eating and reading (particularly the latter) brought back her well-being. In contrast to the dominant nineteenth-century theoreticians of health reform, Little asserted, "Vegetarianism of itself is not enough, as I myself proved, remaining ill through years of it." Eventually, discovering the prominent critics of orthodox medicine Horace Fletcher and Bernarr Macfadden helped teach Little to give up breakfast in order to allow her system to clear itself out daily. Not until her discovery of Drs. E. R. Moras and J. H. Tilden, as well as Axel Emil

Gibson and Otto Carque, though, did Little finally understand "the food question." (Carque, an anti-imperialist fruitarian, authored—among other works—*The Foundation of All Reform*.) With the aid of these writers, "health became a simple matter."[10]

Soon Lora Little's perusal of the pages of health culture turned to an active involvement in the movement. She began propagandizing for whole wheat and contributing to various health magazines. Little remained tightly connected to the national and even international antivaccination community, but that did not prevent her from also throwing herself into local political activity. In addition to her antivaccination campaign, Little teamed up with the most important radical direct democrats in Portland to campaign against an involuntary sterilization act. In 1913 the Oregon legislature, at the behest of Dr. Bethenia Owens-Adair and Democratic governor Oswald West, enacted a law that authorized the State Board of Health to sterilize "habitual criminals, moral degenerates and sexual perverts" confined within state institutions. Thrice-convicted felons, rapists, sodomites and others who engaged in "the crime against nature, or [in] other gross, bestial and perverted sexual habits" could face the knife for the public good. Little, as vice president of the Anti-Sterilization League (an organization formed at the East Portland public library), collected enough signatures to refer the law to the voters in the 1913 special election.[11]

Organizations ranging from the Women's Good Government Club to the Oregon Civic League thoroughly debated the measure, making the issue the "most widely discussed" measure of the campaign. The *Oregonian* served as the chief proponent for the bill, arguing that the sterilization measure promised a clear eugenic benefit to the public. Even though generally staid organizations like the Portland Ad Men's Club announced their unanimous resolve to fight sterilization, the *Oregonian* in its main editorial on the Sunday before the election characterized the opposition as "led by panicky, supersentimental individuals who are always suspicious that some law will be warped to ignoble purposes."[12]

Opponents of sterilization above all appealed to the public's fears of arbitrary authority. The board of the Anti-Sterilization League included several citizens unknown for their activism as well as some of the leading lights of popular democracy. William U'Ren, Judge McGinn, and prominent lawyer C.E.S. Wood all lent their names to Little's crusade. They argued that the law would make it possible for only two men to perform, secretly, surgical mutilation on the most helpless members of society, and that it therefore did not "sufficiently guard the safety of the insane and feeble-minded and all prisoners in the state institutions." History demonstrated that people with this kind of power tended to abuse it. Wood went further: the philosophical anarchist and single taxer commented dryly, "I disapprove of the law because it accomplishes nothing, may be an engine of tyranny and oppression and is

ROT." The editor of the populist *News* agreed. The critics of sterilization also spoke of the bill's "cruel and inhuman" aspects, its misleading wording that could lead to brain surgery as well as sterilization, and its doubtful benefit to society. Little herself called the bill "the most vicious piece of legislation ever passed by a legislative assembly."[13]

On election day, Lora Little scored her first major Oregon victory, although she received almost no formal public recognition of her efforts beyond Owens-Adair's comment nearly a decade later that Little was the "most active among the enemies of the sterilization law." With nearly 93 percent of those who went to the polls casting their ballot on the measure, 56 percent of voters statewide and nearly 58 percent of voters in Multnomah County voted sterilization down—making it the only law of the five referred by the legislature in 1913 that the discriminating citizenry rejected. Following this demonstration of genuine populist libertarianism, Little continued in the political arena by securing the Oregon Progressive Party's nomination for state representative the following year on a platform assailing medical monopoly and upholding "the home, parental responsibility, and personal freedom." Without proportional representation, though, she stood little chance of election as a minor party candidate. After her defeat, Lora Little awaited events in the next session of the legislature before launching her most important petition drive, on the subject of compulsory vaccination.[14]

A Petit Bourgeois Ideology: Lora Little's Philosophy of Health and Life

Lora Little therefore became, two years after her move to Portland, one of the most important crusaders struggling to define the social and political meaning of direct democracy. Just as the ideas of the radical architects of the initiative, referendum, and other measures bear intensive critical scrutiny, so, it turns out, do Little's. And we will see that Little's populism of the body, like the ideas of U'Ren and his fellow direct democrats, arose from a radical petit bourgeois social milieu and cultural impulse.

Fortunately, Little felt it her duty to evangelize her "democratic epistemology" to the local community. For two years she penned a column for the *Mt. Scott Herald* entitled "Health in the Suburbs." In her weekly essays Little not only assailed the medical establishment and body fat, she warned of the dangers of everything from enemas to ice applied to a bruise. Positively, she upheld the virtues of brown rice and minimal meat eating. Her tone was firm, and at times haughty; nearly every prominent person in Portland or the nation who died between 1915 and 1917 received a moralistic autopsy based on the deceased's dietary and medical habits. In the end, though, Lora Little wished not to alienate but to win over her audience, which she considered to include mainly upstanding middling folks. In her first column, for example,

Little described Mt. Scott as a paradise "where the air is good, the water equal to the best, gardens the rule and wealth not overly plentiful." Here, she stated, "the external conditions for health are not far from ideal."[15]

We make a great error in thinking that opposition to compulsory vaccination simply represented a defensive libertarianism—"a deeply flowing belief," in the words of one historian of antivaccinationism, "in the importance of maintaining, at all costs, the 'freedom of the individual.'" As Little herself wrote, opposition to vaccination was much more than "purely a question of personal liberty"; it reflected great concerns about the commonweal as well. Little laid out a coherent and well-thought-out philosophy that (despite its many eccentricities and problematic extremities) mirrors many concerns Americans continue to have about medical authority.[16]

For Little, illness above all reflected individual immorality or a life out of balance. Little's process of thinking did not correspond with that of orthodox medicine, and neither did her conclusions. For instance, Little rejected specific diagnoses for specific illnesses, since "the same general principles underlie the cure of all forms of disease, and . . . the same general directions to rid one of one disease need only slight modification and adjustment to cure any other." Do not worry about the rising incidence of tetanus from rusty nails; "Eat right, live right, and all your injuries, of whatever kind, quickly disappear." Even "cancer is no more a local disease than any other." Simply put, "it takes a cancerous constitution to produce a cancer." Overall, for Little health was "all a matter of right living, of self-control and wise adjustment."[17]

However much we might debate the therapeutic value of such doctrines, they allowed Little to launch an all-out assault on the medical profession. Little considered doctors to be little more than power- and profit-hungry oppressors who, proceeding from faulty ideas, only made people sicker. Little's criticism of specialization and modernization in the medical profession grew particularly emphatic when her subject became experts, expertise, and reformers. She advocated, for instance, a wholesale expansion of lay power in medical decision-making:

> Supposing we begin by asking ourselves, "Is an intimate knowledge of anatomy, bacteriology, chemistry, materia medica and the like essential to health or healing?" Or, granting our premise above, put it this way, Must one know these sciences in order to be clean, temperate and useful?
>
> If so, how did the human race survive through the long pre-scientific ages? History and tradition unite in giving pre-scientific man credit for greater vigor and longer life than scientific man enjoys. Does this not hint at a misuse of science?

Above all, Little warned against "the learning that vaunts itself and proposes to tyrannize over the common sense of the common people."[18]

Little's critique of the reform impulse, much akin to that of John Dewey, arose directly from a vindication of popular rights and wisdom. For instance, eugenicists inspired this insightful portrait of the progressive improvers who engaged in what she elsewhere called "meddle mania":

> A bull in a china shop is a gentle, constructive creature compared with a lot of prim and more or less pious folks when they start in to clean up society and the world.
>
> Mr. Sudden Reformer sees something he does not like in some of his fellow citizens. Very likely it is a reprehensible thing. Plenty of evils exist in the lives and habits of all classes. This would be a thing of which Mr. Sudden Reformer is not himself guilty, therefore he hates it with a mighty loathing.
>
> Dwelling on it, he works himself into a frenzy. He would suppress, eradicate, exterminate and stamp out that evil instanter.

Instead, education and Christianity were proper voluntary social mechanisms. In addition to her hostility toward eugenics, Little was suspicious of prohibition, despite her distaste for alcohol. "I have much sympathy for the decent brewer, distiller and saloonkeeper in Oregon," Little explained, "because in this sudden and violent spasm of civic virtue they are the chief sufferers."[19]

If Little rebuked medical doctors specifically and reforming experts in general, she condemned just as vigorously the entire course of conventional modern "middle-class" life and aspirations. Thoreau represented the ideal of simplicity to which all should subscribe: "joining the mad race to keep up with Lizzie, by spending our money for disease-producing food, drinks, clothing and amusements" only brought sickness and death. "I see no solution except for our present overspecialized civilization to unscramble itself," Little declared. "To escape from the economic pressure that leads to this and many other ills, we will have to go back to the simpler life, where each family has its cow and its pig and its hens, and its garden patch—and raise our own food." More generally, Little declared, "The next great social movement in this country should be toward the renascence of the home."[20]

In addition to championing her favored method of agricultural production, Little advocated a general repudiation of the market and the modern division of labor, "for then we are not straining every nerve trying to get rich and retire, by producing all we can and selling it to the rest of the world." She argued that "a good many other defects in our present social state will be corrected by such unspecializing of industry." At the very least, destroying the division of labor "will make for all-round human development and culture, instead of making one-sided specialists. It will make for sanity, and health."[21]

As an example, Little explicitly connected the need for more whole grains with the general problem of industrial production. Whole flours quickly became rancid and wormy. Thus their processing had to occur "in comparatively small quantities so as to be marketed and consumed within a short

journals
We Wiley

time. This will decentralize the milling industry, returning it to something like old methods and proportions." Implicitly linking her philosophy to the politics of fellow Mt. Scott resident Will Daly, Little characterized this as "an example of a return to small businesses which can be prophesied as the result of the growing desire for sane and healthy living."[22]

Lora Little's sermons from Mt. Scott represent one of the most intriguing examples we have nationally of the ideas of those who in past generations believed in lay healing and alternative medicine. Little's editorials also provide a crucial context for understanding her ideas about vaccination. Little certainly articulated all the compelling medical reasons for opposing the procedure. She insisted on the mildness of smallpox, reviewed the dangers of vaccination, and questioned the still-disputed germ theory of disease. Still, Little above all had bedrock nonscientific beliefs that impelled her to hold medicine—indeed, all expert learning—accountable to individual, community, and polity.

Little marshaled a forceful scientific case against vaccination, stating that it could lead to diphtheria, meningitis, and tuberculosis, as well as cancer. She approved of Dr. Alexander Wilder's statement that "the propagation of disease, on the pretext of thereby arresting disease, is bad in logic, wicked in morals and futile in practice." In turn, Little's medical arguments blended seamlessly with her political objections. She found even the quarantining of disease carriers objectionable for two reasons—one, because contagion was an unproved theory, and two, because of the oppression involved. One beauty of a generalized system of quarantine, Little warned, "will be the absolute supremacy of the doctor." Democracy would die, for "once you are quarantined as a disease carrier, no power on earth can free you but the doctor. What can judges and juries and governors and presidents know about germs?" Little rued, "The public is gradually being trained to submission."[23]

The Oregon System, however, would "let the people themselves, for the first time in the history of this country, pass on the question of compulsory vaccination." Little predicted that a great "conspiracy of silence" would "be broken by a heavy thud shortly, when compulsory vaccination is thrown down hard at the polls by a people who like to think that they own the blood in their veins and feel it is their business what goes into it." The Oregon campaign would represent the first step in the general movement to "recover rights lost by the people of this country under the rule of an undemocratic and un-American system of State medicine." General medical freedom—the right to choose one's own health practitioner and mode of therapy—would soon follow.[24]

CHAPTER FIFTEEN

DIRECT DEMOCRACY AND ANTIVACCINATION

An Antivaccination Majority in Portland in 1916

The stakes were high as Little went about her duties both to save democracy and to use its tools by gathering, "largely single-handed[ly]," signatures as the chief petitioner for the anti–compulsory vaccination initiative in 1916. The initiative had its roots in the previous year's legislative session, when powerful senator Gus Moser introduced a bill to make it a felony for any school, employer, or public official to require vaccination. Lora Little, saying she "represented the mothers of Oregon," led the delegation that spoke for the bill in committee. Christian Science objection to conventional medicine also entered into the debate. A bitter fight ensued, with the bill in the end the bill losing by a margin of only nineteen to eleven.[1]

Little's initiative, identical to Moser's bill, received only limited discussion in the newspapers. Apparently opponents took the measure's defeat for granted. Calvin White, the state health officer, did write a long essay emphasizing the ravages of smallpox and the safety, purity, and effectiveness of vaccine. He again marshaled statistics and particularly appealed to the "unanimity of opinion on vaccination" within the medical profession. The *Oregonian* turned the measure into a referendum on the invulnerability of scientific expertise. Only "pseudo-physicians," "mountebanks," and the hyperignorant kept the antivaccination movement going. In the aftermath of the election, the *Oregonian* scoffed at the mere idea of common people's evaluation of science: "The anti-vaccination measure was in effect an effort to determine by popular vote whether science after a long series of painstaking observations and investigations had reached a correct conclusion. Persons who have neither investigated nor observed, very nearly decided that science had made a mistake."[2]

Once again Lora Little, with little visible public support other than the endorsement of the Portland Mothers' Congress/PTA and the Portland Central Labor Council, served as the spokesperson for the 1916 initiative. She focused on repudiating the omnipotence of scientific authorities. "It is easy to hurl the charge of ignorance at opponents," Little commented,

> but to claim anything like unanimity on this subject among doctors is to limit one's range of vision to one's own party. There is nothing on which doctors differ more widely.

As the humble opinion of a layman, I venture to say that a medical prescription which has been on trial for a hundred years and still requires a compulsory law to make people accept it can have little to recommend it. When doctors differ laymen must decide.

Little's best opportunity to reach the voters of Oregon came in the voters' pamphlet. She opened her one-page argument there with a quote from Daniel Webster: "Compulsory vaccination is an outrage and a gross interference in a land of freedom." She then proceeded to discuss the repulsive mode of vaccine production, jerked some tears in relating the 1915 deaths of two children from vaccination, listed the serious diseases that resulted from the procedure, and challenged the government methods for testing the purity of the vaccine. Even with uncontaminated vaccine, however, "Differences in individual constitution must forever make vaccination highly uncertain and dangerous." Those who wanted vaccination kept their rights under the initiative, just as antivaccinationists would keep theirs, and therefore the bill stood merely for "simple justice."[3]

More Oregonians than any official commentator imagined responded to these calls for justice and populist wisdom. With 74 percent of those who went to the polls voting on the measure, the initiative to ban compulsory vaccination garnered nearly 100,000 votes—just 374 short of passage. In Multnomah County, with 81 percent of voters deciding the fate of the initiative, Little's measure accumulated a 6,675-vote majority and 55 percent of the vote. As the *Vaccination Inquirer* proudly announced, "to secure 99,000 votes without any organization, without money, and without any campaign save in Portland, is an achievement not to be despised, and many who formerly treated Mrs. Little's work with a certain amount of contempt have changed their attitude." The mass movement that had begun in Mt. Scott, although in a narrow sense not successful, had clearly produced an astonishing number of votes against the dictates of organized medicine.[4]

Since so much of our evidence about antivaccination ideology in this election comes from one source, we must be cautious in seeking to discern the motivations of voters who supported the initiative. Once again, though, the breakdown of votes according to the rough geography of class in Portland provides an intriguing confirmation of the social basis of the anti–compulsory vaccination movement. As in the Mt. Scott uprising of 1914, and as with so many of the other proposals for direct democracy and radical economic restructuring that voters considered in Oregon during these years, the protest against compulsory vaccination came from those who, in their struggle against the development of organized expertise during the Progressive Era, represented an alliance of lower-middle-class and working-class citizens.

As in Multnomah county, just over 55 percent of Portlanders voted to ban compulsory vaccination. Yet that bland figure conceals some momentous differences within the city. The West Side actually voted the initiative down by a narrow margin, with only 49.7 percent of voters approving the measure. Still, even on the West Side, 65 precincts favored the measure and only 44 disapproved. On the East Side, where prosperous mixed middling and working-class neighborhoods engulfed pockets of the well-to-do, the initiative received much more substantial support, with 57 percent voting yes, and fully 84 percent (180 out of 214) of the precincts approving the proposal. The "yes" vote went up to 62.8 percent in more proletarian North Portland, with every one of the 21 precincts there supporting Little's plan for medical freedom.

Neighborhood support for the initiative also reveals the substantial class basis behind the vote. No hard and fast rule applies, as significant sections of downtown supported the measure, but the unanimity of certain areas in the southeast is nonetheless remarkable. For example, a run of sixty-four consecutive precincts, beginning in immigrant South Portland (on the West Side) and continuing on through Sellwood, Woodstock, Lents, Mt. Tabor, Sunnyside, and other parts of the southeast close to the Willamette, voted yes. This area included the Mt. Scott district, the initial base of the city's antivaccination movement. Seventeen successive precincts, centered in Montavilla and extending to the edges of the ritzy Laurelhurst neighborhood, all voted yes. (Irvington and Alameda proved once again to be the primary East Side holdouts.) Finally, in the broad northern sections of the city, extending out into the outlying neighborhoods of Kenton and St. Johns, a stunning 75 out of 76 precincts advocated the prohibition of compulsory vaccination. The British *Vaccination Inquirer* was perhaps not too far from the truth when it quoted Dr. C. S. Carr, who commented that in the United States, "The extreme lower classes, out of complete indifference, acquiesce in vaccination, while the extreme upper classes by overweening confidence in professional opinion also give ignorant consent. But the great middle class, which constitutes the brain and brawn of a bustling nation, have little or no confidence in vaccination."[5]

Lora Little's Departure

World War I brought a cessation of public antivaccination struggles, at least until one last battle in 1920. The war itself brought a dramatic change in the Portland antivaccination movement, as Lora Little left the Rose City, never to return. Engaged by the Medical Freedom Education Committee of Battle Creek, Little departed soon after the American declaration of war on "a tour that it is hoped will include the whole of the United States." Before taking leave of Portland, Little made sure to sign up as part of a women's committee endorsing Will Daly's run for mayor.[6]

By the end of March 1918, Little had been propagandizing for several

Voting on anti–compulsory vaccination initiative, 1916, by precinct

weeks in raving red North Dakota, where the state organization for medical freedom "included a number of prominent men." After authorities denied her access to public halls, she conducted house-to-house canvasses in Bismarck and Mandan, distributing the League for Medical Freedom's *Truth Teller*. The paper included articles attacking vaccination in the military "as a huge graft of the 'medical trust,'" profaning the bodies of helpless soldiers and even killing some of them. Little obtained close to one hundred women's signatures for a petition asking President Wilson to outlaw the compulsory vaccination of "these originally vigorous and healthy young men" in the armed forces.

She then reaped the same fruit for her efforts as did so many other radicals during the hysteria of World War I America—arrest for violation of the Espionage Act for her attempt to "cause insubordination, disloyalty and mutiny and refusal of duty" in the military. Little strenuously "denied making any effort to handicap the United States in the prosecution of the war" and in fact declared her full support for it. She did, however, blame "inflamed patriotism, prompted by medical malignity," for her arrest. All in all,

The petite bourgeoisie in the Lents neighborhood, adjacent to Mt. Scott, ca. 1925. Lents was a strong foundation for antivaccinationism, as well as for other radical direct democracy measures. Note the print shop in the left-hand corner, behind the Eagle Garage. (Courtesy Oregon Historical Society, #37294.)

Randolph Bourne's contemporaneous comment on "The State" remains instructive:

> Army and Navy . . . are the very arms of the State; in them flows its most precious lifeblood. To paralyze them is to touch the very State itself. And the majesty of the State is so sacred that even to attempt such a paralysis is a crime equal to a successful stroke. Even though the individual in his effort to impede recruiting should utterly and lamentably fail, he shall in no wise be spared. Let the wrath of the State descend upon him for his impiety!"

Lora Little, however, had the last laugh when the North Dakota Supreme Court overturned compulsory vaccination after a case resulting from her agitation.[7]

"If we have read her character aright," declared the *Vaccination Inquirer*, Lora Little "will be rather exhilarated than daunted by the storms she stirs up." Indeed, upon her release from North Dakota Little began to organize the Chicago-based American Medical Liberty League. She would serve as the AMLL's secretary and chief organizing force for the rest of her life. The AMLL consisted of "adherents of Christian Science, Allopathy, Homeopathy, Osteopathy, Chiropractic and other systems" who opposed such manifestations of state medicine as tuberculin testing of cows' milk, vivisection, the medicalization of public schools, and, of course, compulsory vaccination. The league even took a slap at imperialism, arguing in its pamphlet *Philippines Pus Punching* that "The Occident with all the pomp, panoply and gun play of arrogant Allopathy" should cease its medical tyranny abroad. Little herself authored *The Baby and the Medical Machine*, the heart-rending story of Oliver, a two-year-old Portlander ripped from his parents' arms in New York by that city's callous and arbitrary health authorities. The succinct AMLL propaganda attached to Little's pamphlet announced the organization's radical demands. "Laymen skilled in sanitary science at the head and in control of all health boards and bureaus"—certainly not a request most Progressive profession-alizing modernizers would have willingly complied with.[8]

Little displayed considerable solidarity with the downtrodden during her time in Chicago. She wrote a lengthy weekly column for the *Chicago Labor News* where she decried the tyranny of medical licensure, opposed the Shep-pard-Towner maternal and infant child welfare act because it would inspire a "medical inquisition" to hunt down supposedly syphilitic pregnant women, and alerted unionists about the ill effects of their chlorinated and thus "drugged drinking water." Little took on as well those in her own activist community who declared: "Oh, yes, it is all right for your family and mine to be free to choose, and free to refuse vaccination and medical inspection, but not those foreigners and other ignorant people." Declaring this philosophy un-American, she backed up her words with a forceful defense of two work-ing-class Polish breadwinners, one male and one female, whom the public health authorities had "kidnap[ped]" from their homes and incarcerated in the county hospital when they came down with tuberculosis. In a different case, Little's organization engaged Clarence Darrow to seek the release of a quarantined suspected typhoid carrier, a fight the famous lawyer ultimately took to the Illinois Supreme Court. The AMLL also worked with unionists such as Margaret Haley—antivaccinationist head of the Chicago Teachers' Federation—to help prevent employers from requiring the vaccination of workers. Overall, Little harassed the Chicago public health authorities with "pitiless pertinacity," with perhaps the biggest triumph of her career coming in January 1926. That month the Chicago City Council created a new mu-nicipal board of health but explicitly refused it authority to enforce com-pulsory vaccination.[9] Little called this "Our capital achievement."

Little remained a stinging nettle until the very end. The American Medical Association's Propaganda Department kept up surveillance of her activities throughout the 1920s, always happy "to swell our 'chamber of horrors'" with AMLL pamphlets and letters sent to the AMA by those on the lookout for quacks. No wonder that Little called it the American Machiavellian Associa-tion. Yet her defiance persisted, and at the age of seventy-three she began a new journal, the *Avalanche*, so that her organization would have an indepen-dent voice. Death came two years later, at 10:25 A.M. on October 30, 1931, from a kidney ailment. The international antivaccination community mourned one of its all-time heroines, "a woman of great ability, high courage, and indomitable will." "So glowing was her zeal, so quenchless her indefatigable

activity," according to the *Vaccination Inquirer*, that many surely found it difficult to imagine that Lora Little would no longer be wielding her considerable
talents in the struggle against State Medicine—a contest that no longer
seemed so quixotic as the result of her extraordinary efforts.[10]

The Last Hurrah: The 1920 Initiative

Another casualty of World War I, besides Lora Little's freedom, was the relatively benign public health policy of the City of Portland and the State of
Oregon. Soon after the war ended officials went on several provaccination
offensives. Opposition to the procedure remained vigorous, but in the end
the Portland antivaccination movement suffered a rout in 1920 from which it
never recovered.

During 1919 and 1920 city health officer George Parrish attempted
to push through compulsory vaccination requirements for municipal pen-
sioners, and then for all persons exposed to smallpox, and then finally for all
residents of the state. Failing in these efforts, Parrish and the city attorney
drafted a bill requiring vaccination for all students, regardless of exposure,
when smallpox came to town. In January 1920 the school board endorsed
Parrish's plan, and the period of benign neglect had officially ended. Now
parents and their children, as well as unvaccinated teachers, had during
smallpox incidents a choice between vaccination and twenty-one days out of
school during the incubation period.[11]

Parrish's strategy soon provoked considerable resistance. Three weeks after
the promulgation of the new school board policy, the *Oregonian* headlined,
"Women Aroused by Vaccination Order." Again the southeastern part of the
city, including the Creston district that served as one of the bases for the Mt.
Scott revolt six years earlier, provided the foundation of antivaccination protests. A committee, headed by an individual identified only as "Mrs. Harvey,"
visited the school board, the district attorney's office, and Dr. Parrish. The
group received, at least from the city health officer, a simple response—
contempt. In response, Mrs. P. E. Alger, president of the Clinton Kelly PTA,
asserted that two-thirds of the children had absented themselves from
school, and she warned that "some talk was current that the mothers would
take their children to school Monday and try force as a means of getting
them back."[12]

This mothers' strike against the condescending paternalism of the health
authorities received the full support of the Health Defense League of Oregon,
with acting president George Morris assuring parents that his organization
would aid anyone deprived of legal rights. State health officer David Roberg
responded by restating the root of the matter: "These laymen . . . now pro-
fess to know more than the medical profession about health matters." In
turn, the antivaccinationists wanted even more control over public health, as

they planned to draft a city and state amendment that would make health officers elective and much less powerful. The "Public School Protective League" then announced its intention of circulating an initiative petition similar to one in California.[13]

Those responsible for proposing the 1920 initiative represented yet another middling crusade against compulsory vaccination. The president of the Public School Protective League at the time of the circulation of the petitions was W. H. Malloy, city manager of the Pacific States Fire Insurance Company; the new president in the fall was Naomi Stengel Armstrong, a teacher at Couch School. Josephine Fritz, a bookkeeper at the F. E. Taylor real estate company, served as secretary-treasurer along with vice president C. L. McKenna, supreme secretary of the United Artisans, a fraternal lodge and insurance company. Their ballot measure proposed to prohibit "vaccination, inoculation or other medication" as a requirement for school or job.[14]

The phrase "other medication" would cause the antivaccinationists many problems in the 1920 campaign, although the league may very well have chosen its words with care. The arguments for and against vaccination itself did not change much compared to the 1916 campaign. The *Oregonian* and medical officials, however, warned that with the distinctive language of the 1920 measure, the initiative would totally destroy the capacity for *any* governmental public health measures, including quarantine. Dr. Andrew Smith, acting state health officer, showed typical humility about his role when he noted that "Regulations of the health board which this measure would destroy, serve as the sole protection to the health of the people of this state." Such a statement was an ideological universe away from Lora Little's populist ideas about self-care. Thus the conflict over vaccination in 1920 became, as it had four years earlier, as much a struggle over the public application and power of expertise as over pus and pox. Prominent national medical official Milton Rosenau asserted that the initiative "would put civilization back into the dark ages."[15]

The most powerful, and the most important, argument in favor of the initiative again came in the voters' pamphlet. There the members of the Public School Protective League put before the electorate their fears of arbitrary authority, their beliefs about health, and even to some extent their ideology of state and society. First, the league made clear its general purpose, the protection of schoolchildren from "medical exploitation." Public health officials had begun an unprecedented assault on the public, even threatening those who refused vaccination with jail.[16]

Against this compulsion, the advocates of the initiative set out a philosophy of democratic familial rights. Compulsory vaccination, they argued, "violates the principles of democracy and is antagonistic to American ideals." The Public School Protective League asked, "What would you think of an order that would compel all to worship according to one church? Would you favor it? Of course you would not. Neither are you in favor of compelling all to patronize one school of healing, or submit to one kind of medical treatment." The measure's supporters also touched on general issues of fundamental importance in a liberal society, and they spoke out powerfully. "The public school is and must always be subordinate to the home," the league declared at a time of increasing state intrusion on domestic life; "The medical oversight of the child is primarily and fundamentally a function of the home, which cannot be safely delegated to any other institution." The league ended with the kind of populist message that two years later would resonate with considerable force in the Ku Klux Klan–supported compulsory public-schooling bill: "keep a free child in a free school, thereby guaranteeing the right to life, liberty and the pursuit of happiness."[17]

In fact, in the same year that William U'Ren introduced his plan for a syndicalism of housewives, the father of direct democracy also spoke out forthrightly in favor of medical freedom. U'Ren, an admirer of the health reformer and advocate of thorough mastication Horace Fletcher, explained his views in a letter to the editor shortly before the election. Of the amendment, he asked simply, "suppose it does give every person the right to say what medical or surgical treatment he or she will take. Is there anything wrong with that?" U'Ren stated, with dubious evidence, that "all the lawyers" agreed that the measure would not restrict state power to quarantine. The bill would prevent, U'Ren declared in no uncertain terms, "any fool doctor who happens to be the health officer from issuing his ukase compelling every person to wear a rag over his nose, or a muff on his ear, because of alleged bugs existing only in the imagination of the aforesaid." After this attack on both arbitrary public health power and, implicitly, the germ theory of disease, U'Ren worried about only one thing. That was the reach of the measure. He feared that the courts would strictly interpret the law to prohibit *only* vaccination. U'Ren apparently wanted the bill to represent a full public embrace of personal liberty in all matters relating to health.[18]

Although both opponents and proponents of compulsory vaccination spoke out with as much power and certainty as they had in 1916, the end results were strikingly different. Statewide the bill got swamped by a margin of 63,018 to 127,570. This time Portland did not differ much from the rest of the state, with the amendment receiving only 35.5 percent of the citywide vote. Neighborhoods generally did not significantly vary in their vote, even though one southeastern precinct favored the initiative sixty-six to two. A good one-third of Portland citizens in 1920 still demonstrated their willingness to challenge medical and scientific authority in a radical, populist manner, but the great majority of the city's inhabitants supported compulsory vaccination.[19]

Or did they? The proponents of vaccination were much more vocal in 1920 than in 1916, and a large part of their efforts went into making claims about the initiative, the truth of which it is perhaps impossible to discern. That the measure would deprive public authorities of all power to regulate health certainly does not come directly out of the language of the proposed amendment. Confusion and caution thus likely played crucial roles in the measure's defeat. For example, the political committee of the Portland Central Labor Council, which had endorsed Little's 1916 initiative, recommended the defeat of the bill but made it clear that "it was not favorable to compulsory vaccination." Labor's chief fear was that the measure's passage would "make it impossible to enforce other health regulations without which the public health would be constantly menaced." Similarly, that defender of the little person, the *Portland News*, issued no recommendation on the bill even though "We do not like compulsion." The editor simply threw up his hands: "The arguments by experts on both sides bewilder us."[20]

Even if we must be cautious about interpreting the vote, we can once again uncover the social basis of the 1920 anti–compulsory vaccination movement. As with the Mt. Scott revolt of 1914, it is possible to identify leaders, spokespersons, and petitioners involved either in the election campaign or in the earlier agitation over public school policies. Of the thirty-one names (other than U'Ren and B. S. Josselyn) listed in Portland newspapers, the city directory documents the primary occupation of the individual or family in every case. The fifteen women and sixteen men committed to promoting their cause of medical and familial freedom represented once again a plebeian alliance solidly anchored in the world of lower-level white-collar work. Four of the men held jobs of either a proletarian or artisanal nature, while the other twelve had middling-class positions ranging from co-owner of the Hawthorne St. Metal Works to solicitor to chiropractic physician. Interestingly, the eleven married women involved in the crusade had much more working-class backgrounds, with their husbands holding jobs such as blacksmith, boilermaker, conductor, printer, brakeman, and shipworker. The movement's four independent women were, on the other hand, solid white-collar workers—two bookkeepers, a cashier, and a teacher. One of the intriguing features of the movement is the many white-collar workers at the Pacific States Fire Insurance Company involved in the opposition to compulsory vaccination. Whether voluntarily or not, the cashier, the assistant manager, the secretary and manager, and the city manager of the firm made it into the public record as antivaccinationists.[21]

Along with the radical direct democracy movement, the Portland antivaccination movement faded from view in the 1920s. The last time organized antivaccination sentiment made it into the newspapers was in January 1922, when Dr. George Parrish once again warned of the dangers of a new epidemic. This time, however, his tone admitted defeat as much as power. He noted that "vaccinations against smallpox have been largely neglected despite the constant warnings of the health officer. Campaigns against vaccination and false propaganda have served to keep the public from taking advantage of this almost sure preventative." Although Parrish retained the right to exclude unvaccinated children from school for twenty-one days, he admitted that "The parents of a child have a constitutional right and if they do not want their child vaccinated, he does not have to be vaccinated." On that ambiguous note the organized antivaccination movement in Portland ended. Perhaps it is appropriate, though, that the *Producer's Call*, voice of populist democracy in Portland during the early 1920s, receive the last mention for its opposition to compulsory vaccination during the fall of 1922.[22]

Echoes of the battle for medical freedom, however, continued to be audible in Portland throughout the remainder of the decade. Compulsory vaccination never again appeared on the ballot, but an initiative to legalize naturopathy—an increasingly prominent school of alternative medicine—received 38 percent of the vote in 1924. (In 1919 the Oregon House had narrowly defeated, by only two votes, a legal code for naturopathy.) The League for the Conservation of Public Health, formed to fight "cults," bemoaned the hold of irregular medicine over the deluded populace. Portland continued to support a large and thriving school of chiropractic, and Oregon generally "was being ravaged by 'several hundred' unidentified pretenders who, by 'masquerading as 'doctors' . . . are carrying on immoral practices to an almost unbelievable extent.'" In Portland alone, in 1920, 140 female nonmedical "healers" practiced their trade, a rapid expansion from the 39 in 1910. And in 1926 the city health officer continued to lament his legal and political inability to implement compulsory vaccination in the Rose City. Stalemate, not defeat, is thus the proper way to characterize the achievements of the Portland antivaccination movement.[23]

CHAPTER SIXTEEN

THE SUCCESS AND RADICALISM OF ANTIVACCINATION

What kind of overall evaluation should we offer for such a strange, but strong, mass movement? First, we have to recognize the movement's true power, well beyond its victories in European countries. In the United States, despite the movement's many formal defeats and its gradual dispersal, the campaign to prevent compulsory smallpox vaccination was in crucial ways spectacularly successful. It is difficult for us to imagine today how a movement so antagonistic to the spirit as well as the ideology of modern medicine and science could have so effectively stymied the authorities who represented these icons of modernity. Even in Portland and in Oregon, in the face of setbacks at the hands of the voters, the antivaccinationists helped keep in place what to us looks like a remarkably tolerant (or foolish, depending on one's perspective) policy by keeping the public health authorities continually on the defensive. Opponents of vaccination directly challenged "the Progressives' twin deities, science and bureaucratic efficiency," and they often triumphed.[1]

Furthermore, the antivaccination effort continues to hold social and ideological meaning for us. As we have seen, the idea that those who opposed vaccination must have come from ignorant, deluded, and marginal populations remains prevalent among academics. This is an old view that traditional leftists have shaped and shared. For example, Friedrich Engels once remarked that the early Christians had their modern counterpart in

> those who have nothing to look forward to from the official world or have come to the end of their tether with it—opponents of inoculation, supporters of abstemiousness, vegetarians, antivivisectionists, nature healers, free-community preachers whose communities have fallen to pieces, authors of new theories on the origin of the universe, unsuccessful or unfortunate inventors, victims of real or imaginary injustice who are termed "good-for-nothing pettifoggers" by the bureaucracy, honest fools, and dishonest swindlers—[and] all throng to the working class parties in all countries.

(Note Seymour Martin Lipset's revealing comment on this quote. He claims that "it is often men from precisely these origins who give the fanatical and extremist character" to and "form the core of believers" of dangerous totalitarian crusades.) Similarly Morris Hillquit noted that American prewar radicals represented a motley and ideologically bankrupt—because non-Socialist—crew that included "men with flowing ties and pioneers of the female bob; iconoclasts, malcontents, sentimentalists and faddists of all imaginable hues," as well as "pacifists, feminists and anti-vaccinationists."[2]

Yet even if Engels's and Hillquit's curt dismissals of the opponents of vaccination do not provide much insight, their observation that antivaccinationists formed a core segment of nineteenth- and early-twentieth-century radicalism helps us to clarify their significance in Portland. For in that city, home to all kinds of daring democratic experiments, the antivaccination movement indeed represented a genuine populist crusade with its roots firmly in the world of the middle class. As happened with radical direct democracy and the single tax, members of the petite bourgeoisie and the proletariat joined together to combat powerful forces that threatened their autonomy. More positively, the hundreds of parents who actively supported the movement and the thousands who passively aided it by keeping their children home rather than having them vaccinated forcefully demanded that science and its experts remain democratically accountable. These almost completely anonymous citizen-parents, with the help of Lora Little's leadership, used Oregon's direct democracy in the way that William U'Ren and his People's Power League advocates had intended—to reshape the world through direct rule by the people.[3]

Beyond Portland, the agitation against vaccination speaks to some of the most pressing issues of our time, even to how we define reality itself. Lora Little had a comprehensive ideology of individual and social well-being. Although it had few if any overtly spiritual dimensions, her philosophy falls well into the broad range of metaphysical healing systems that William James discussed in *The Varieties of Religious Experience*. These nonmedical methods, James noted, give "to some of us serenity, moral poise, and happiness, and prevent certain forms of disease as well as science does, or even better in a certain class of persons." According to Robert Fuller, what made the groups that advocated unorthodox health doctrines "so significant in James's opinion was that they overthrew the pretension of positivistic science as the sole method for defining reality."[4]

Little, along with her comrades in Portland, also tried to overthrow another disturbing legacy of the Progressive Era—what Christopher Lasch challengingly characterized as the "proletarianization of parenthood." In an age in which, as Lasch put it, experts in private corporations and public bureaucracies have effectively socialized child-rearing skills in order to return them to increasingly powerless and dependent parents in the form of mystified knowledge, we should view the antivaccinationists' insistence that they had the experience, skills, and insight to keep their children healthy as part of a truly radical and democratic struggle to limit the power of the new professionals. In the process, they came to serve as articulate opponents of the "high-modernist ideology" that James Scott convincingly argues has led to much misery for twentieth-century humanity. More positively, the antivaccinationists sought what sociologist-philosopher John O'Neill has called a "familied politics," one that seeks to "enhance *the communicative competence of citizen democracy*" by reinvigorating "the common-sense *bioknowledge* of persons and families whose lives are otherwise administered by the modern corporate economy and its therapeutic state." Or put more simply: Lora Little and her allies sought what intellectuals almost by definition view as unattainable, what sociologist John Gaventa calls a "knowledge democracy."[5]

Nor are these various struggles over, despite the master narrative in the history of medicine that assures us that orthodox scientific medicine uprooted its competitors early in the century. Only several states currently legally allow nonallopathic medical practitioners, despite their impressive popularity with even well-educated professionals. The antivaccination movement, although largely unaware of its deep roots in American history, continues to gain strength today. Times have changed considerably, however, and the Portland anti–compulsory vaccination movement, which promised a populism of the body as well as a democracy of the middling family, provides us with a convincing example of what transformations have occurred to influence our current prospects. It is now almost inconceivable for us to imagine parents who rejected not only vaccination, but quarantine as well, actually *demanding* that their unvaccinated children be allowed into public schools in the midst of an epidemic of what was once one of humanity's most feared diseases. Until we can see more than irrationality in this, we are not prepared to understand popular, indeed staunchly middle-class, ideologies prevalent only one lifetime ago.[6]

PART V

THE USES OF POPULISM
AFTER PROGRESSIVISM

The 1922 School Bill and the Triumph
of the Ku Klux Klan

> Here is a state composed of eighty-five percent native Americans. It
> has no race problem. It is predominantly Protestant in faith, the
> Catholics forming but eight percent of the population. It is not
> torn by industrial conflict. It is not threatened by radicalism in any
> form. It has progressive laws, an admirable educational system, less
> than two percent illiteracy. Yet this typical American state has been
> completely overrun and, for a time at least, politically dominated
> by a secret oath-bound organization preaching religious bigotry
> and racial animosity and seeking primarily its own political
> aggrandizement. One asks how this is possible.
> —JOHN MOFFATT MECKLIN, *The Ku Klux Klan* (1924)

> The great danger overshadowing all others which confronts the
> American people is the danger of class hatred. History will
> demonstrate the fact that it is the rock upon which many a
> republic has been broken and I don't know of any better way to
> fortify the next generation against that insidious poison than to
> require that the poor and the rich, the people of all classes and
> distinction, and of all different religious beliefs, shall meet in the
> common schools, which are the great American melting pot, there
> to become . . . the typical American of the future.
> —PORTLAND ATTORNEY WALLACE MCCAMANT, DEFENDING THE
> COMPULSORY PUBLIC SCHOOL INITIATIVE

The eyes of the political nation returned to Portland and Oregon—for at least a
disdainful glance—once more after World War I. Having distinguished itself for
its patriotism during bond drives and red scares, the Rose City witnessed what
appeared to be the natural culmination of postwar political reaction. Fiery
crosses burned from Mt. Scott and Mt. Tabor on the East Side, thousands of
Portlanders rushed to join the new secret organization in town, and by the
beginning of 1923 most observers felt that the Ku Klux Klan was substantially in
charge of the legislature, and—with good reason—perhaps even the Portland

mayoralty and the governor's office. Portland had become one of "the hooded capitals of the nation."[1]

Progressive Oregon, once the shining beacon of hope for direct democracy, became during the early 1920s one of the trio of seemingly lily-white states—the others were Indiana and Colorado—to witness the brief reign of the Invisible Empire. The influence of the Klan, which was centered in Portland, climaxed in 1922 when the KKK collaborated with the Scottish Rite Masons in use of the direct legislation process to pass an initiative requiring the attendance in public school of every child between the ages of eight and sixteen. The bill would have outlawed all private and parochial schools. According to John Higham, it "was perhaps the last and certainly one of the most severe of the Americanization laws" of the postwar period.[2]

Despite the many horrors that the Klan was responsible for in the postwar period, despite the lynching, the night-riding, and the brutal bigotry, we (against our best instincts) need to avert our eyes—temporarily—from the men with white hoods in order to most fully understand middle-class politics during the 1920s. For it is simplistic to view the triumph of the School Bill, its common contemporary label, as pure bigotry. Rather, the Bill represented a subtle, but crucial, transformation of middle-class populism. Not just, or even primarily, anti-Catholic, many of the school initiative's proponents spoke powerfully to concerns about the power of elites and the prospects for equal social opportunity in modern America. They thus captured many voters who might have otherwise disdained the Klan. Yet in doing so the spokesmen for the bill—mainly non-Klansman—reformulated such populism away from the issues of egalitarian small property and direct democracy that were foremost in the minds of Oregon System radicals.

The ideology that advocates of the School Bill promulgated was instead a distinctly liberal, and ultimately classless, variant of populism. Such liberal populism, as we might call it, resonated with the social concerns of the same bloc of low-level white-collar workers, small entrepreneurs, and skilled blue-collar workers that had mobilized behind small-propertied radicalism in Portland. Liberal populism spoke to the increasingly tenuous place this set of Americans held in an unequal society. What School Bill defenders ended up demanding, though, was an equal opportunity for all to enter an unequal society through compulsory public education—not the transformation of hierarchy itself. In essence, School Bill proponents thus embraced the new corporate order by addressing the problem of the market skills of individual workers, not the property owned by various classes or the expertise lodged in bureaucratic institutions. Even that political movement was stillborn, however, as the United States Supreme Court soon declared the School Bill unconstitutional and the Klan quickly faded away. Still, the battles over the School Bill and the Ku Klux Klan in 1920s Portland show the continued strength of lower-middle-class populism, as well as how that political impulse could always serve antidemocratic as well as democratic ends.

CHAPTER SEVENTEEN

SCHOOL BOARDS AND STRIKES

Petite Bourgeoisie against Elites

The first signs of the movement that eventually blossomed into the School Bill crusade came during the most mundane of political affairs, the June 1921 Portland school board elections. This annual event did not often generate much attention, because it occurred separately from the city and state elections. In 1921, however, a surge of interest resulted in the largest vote in the history of the city's school elections, with more than twice as many voters going to the polls as in the previous year. At stake was control of the majority of the school board. The state had authorized the expansion of the board from five to seven members, and four positions were vacant. In a move symbolic of the changing political culture in Portland, longtime single taxer, unionist, small business owner, and radical officer of the People's Power League George Orton declined to seek reelection.[1]

On the surface, the results of the election appear easy to interpret. In a rare display of unity, the three most influential newspapers of the city enthusiastically supported the same slate of candidates. Yet in a tide of religious enthusiasm, an anti-Catholic slate beat the quasi-official ticket by a two-to-one margin. As the terse statement of the four winning candidates asserted, their success was "a victory of the great majority of the people in this city who believe in maintaining our free public school system on a strictly nonsectarian basis as against a certain minority who by their thorough organization eternally persist in meddling with our educational institutions."[2]

All the newspapers in the city credited the "strong religious faction" and "the solid support of the A.P.A. or anti-Catholic voters" with the upset. Also at work, however, was the peculiar form of class alliance between small business owners and skilled workers that played such a prominent role in Portland politics. Without a doubt, the losing candidates represented the city's commercial and professional elite. A subcommittee of the exclusive Portland City Club selected the ticket. The instructions for the subcommittee were to choose "two substantial business men, a lawyer and a woman, who would be representative of the women's clubs." The *Oregonian* cried out: with "so much strife and so many religious issues injected of late," "there is a demand for substantial business heads on the board."[3]

Three out of the four candidates on the winning ticket were indeed good, solid, upstanding businessmen. W.J.H. Clark was a managing officer of the

Northwest Automobile Company, J. E. Martin had for many years been in the wholesale machinery business, and George P. Eisman was top executive at Eisman Hardwood Floor company. Clark, Martin, and Eisman were not, however, the kind of businessmen that the newspapers and the City Club had in mind for the exercise of civic rule. All three candidates endorsed a strong tenure law for teachers, a contentious issue in the previous legislature. Each of them also supported the right of teachers to organize a union, an issue on which Clark was "very emphatic." The *Oregonian*, on the other hand, felt that in the increasingly open-shop environment of Portland, teacher unionization was not even a proper issue to discuss in a school board campaign. The heads of organized labor in Portland were particularly enthusiastic about Eisman, who in 1922 became vice president of the East Side Business Men's Club. According to the *Oregon Labor Press*, Eisman "for a number of years has been in the good graces of organized labor due to the fact that under all conditions he ran a union establishment and has figured the salaries of his men on a basis considerably above the scale." The pesky pro-proletarian Portland petite bourgeoisie was again on the prowl.[4]

For all these reasons, the three candidates had publicly accepted positions on a labor-backed ticket. The fourth position on their slate went to W. E. Kimsey, direct democrat and secretary of both the Portland Central Labor Council and the state labor federation. This ticket, the *Labor Press* announced, "is pledged to make of the schools free institutions where knowledge may be disseminated without the censorship of commercialism." By the time the brief campaign ended, however, a dispute over the number four spot on the ticket arose. Mysterious forces supporting George B. Thomas, a school board member running for reelection and former Port of Portland commissioner, hijacked the three business owners and, according to the *Labor Press*, put them on a Protestant ticket against their will. The apparent protests of Clark, Martin, and Eisman notwithstanding, it was the Thomas slate that carried the day at the election—perhaps, the *Oregonian* speculated, with the help of the heavy turnout of women voters.[5]

Thus, in this instance, the alliance between small business and skilled workers was tenuous. Still, given the three candidates' pledges about teachers' rights, this victory of the petite bourgeoisie over Portland's civic elite clearly represented something beyond a mere triumph of reactionary nativism. Above all, the 1921 school board election illustrated the continuing fluidity of class relations in Portland. Once again, as during the peak years of the Oregon System, the city's elite had to respond to a powerful, insurgent alliance of members of the lower middle class and skilled workers. We cannot understand the battle over the compulsory public education initiative without an appreciation of this social context.[6]

Contemporary commentators and later historians have puzzled over the considerable anomaly of the Klan coming to such a supposedly clean and quiet place as Oregon. Earl Pomeroy has well expressed the dominant view of this period, writing that the state "had no significant problems of racial or economic conflict." Yet upon closer examination, during 1922 an upstart petite bourgeoisie was just a piece of the social turmoil that pervaded the consciousness of much of official Portland. Although certainly not as traumatic a year as 1919, when Mayor George Baker appealed to "the great middle class" to "forget selfish purposes and interests and harness our activity to purge the country of the evils of Bolshevism," class conflict never strayed far from the minds of Portland's citizens. How different parts of the city responded to such crisis during a national recession, when the export wheat market crashed and when the Wobblies proclaimed a "Revolution in Portland"—and the mayor believed them—is also crucial to an explanation of the meaning of the School Bill and the Klan. For, as we will see, the loyalty of the great middle class remained very much up for grabs.

Besides the Klan, the numerous strikes that took place in Portland served as the key nonelectoral issue distilling middle-class political identity during 1922. Across the country over 1.6 million workers walked off the job that year in actions that, despite their impressive display of working-class solidarity, were ultimately defensive and defeated. In Portland, middling-class support for strikers, for the labor movement, and even, tentatively, for radicals and radicalism remained vigorous, vociferous, and sustained.[7]

News of the 1922 strikes, whether among longshoremen in the spring, railroad workers in the summer, or waterfront employees in the fall, frequently made its way to the front pages of Portland's newspapers. Although hardly bloody by the standards of the day, these struggles were marked by violence, arrests, and injunctions. *Oregonian* readers woke up on election day, for example, to a page one story, "Another Near-Riot at Docks Quelled." IWW involvement in the longshore struggles particularly incensed the governing elite. Mayor Baker announced that the IWW was planning "to take control of Portland" and work toward "the overthrow of law and order, the ruination of industry, and the Russianizing of the world." Then Baker warned of the twenty-five thousand Wobblies set to descend on the city in a nationally coordinated invasion. That many did not materialize, but after "a thorough ransacking of the city," several hundred were arrested, with many deported from the Rose City. Governor Ben Olcott also promised to help crush the Wobblies.[8]

During his diatribes Baker applauded AFL members for their conservative patriotism. The heads of the state and city labor federations promptly challenged city policy and told Baker that the conflict was an International Longshoremen's Association strike, with IWW aid gladly—albeit suspiciously—accepted. The mayor responded that if the AFL had indeed allied with the IWW, "then I must be against organized labor" and "it is the beginning of the end for the American Federation of Labor." The *Telegram* chimed in: "There can be no compromise—no middle ground—between law and anarchy."[9]

In light of all of this antirevolutionary bombast, and the chilling effect it had on radicals and the general political environment nationally, one would expect that the mayor would have the full support of the community, especially its middle classes. On the contrary, criticism of Baker's policies and support for the strikers suffused the public realm. An examination of the reaction to the strikes and strikers, both off-the-cuff and philosophical, provides a critical means of exploring the continuing openness of the ideological relationship between middle class and working class.

During the first longshore strike, the police targeted IWW members for arrest. Even the *Telegram* complained about this policy, on the grounds that it denied citizens equal protection under the law. The strikers also had allies among the police force. More significantly, the Oregon State Board of Conciliation attempted, in the middle of the conflict, to arbitrate the strike. The arbitration board consisted of a representative of business; the president of the state federation of labor, Otto Hartwig; and William Woodward, a representative from "the public." Woodward, a prominent business owner, a member of the school board, and soon to be the most prominent spokesperson for the School Bill, hammered out an agreement that effectively met the union's demand for a neutral hiring hall. Both the ILA and the United States Shipping Board, a third party in the strike, agreed to the settlement. The employers, however, refused even to consider it. The *News* provided a sense of why labor would receive such an attentive hearing in the mind of the public. In a front-page editorial the newspaper quoted Henry George on the decline of wages under capitalism and insisted that "Labor is not only the man in overalls. It is the merchant, the clerk, the bookkeeper—all who work to live!"[10]

As the summer wore on labor received even more support, this time from important religious leaders. Rev. W. T. McElveen of the First Congregational Church of Portland, for example, unstintingly defended striking railroad workers. The *Oregonian* remarked that McElveen's "intemperate denunciation" was "likely to encourage outbreaks of mob violence." In September the Episcopalians joined in, as their Church League of Industrial Democracy held its convention in Portland. Over twenty-five hundred people crowded the municipal auditorium to hear Mary Van Kleeck utter "progressive, radical—almost revolutionary" views on the subject of her talk, the "attitude of the public" toward the labor movement. Her fellow speaker, Dr. W. Russell Bowie of Richmond, told the audience, "Today Jesus is on trial, modern materialism is as Pontius Pilate." The relationship between church and labor further solidified the day before the election when the Portland Ministerial Association appointed official delegates to the city's Central Labor Council. Labor leaders were delighted to welcome McElveen, Rev. W. A. Stevenson, and Rev. T. H. Gallagher—the latter one of the foremost clerical supporters of the Portland Ku Klux Klan.[11]

CHAPTER EIGHTEEN

LIBERAL POPULISM

The Compulsory Public School Bill

The social atmosphere in Portland surrounding strikes, unions, and labor radicalism does not merely furnish local color for an analysis of the 1922 election. Rather, showing that politicians, newspaper editorialists, business owners, and religious leaders gave their support to workers whom civic officials classified as revolutionary provides a tantalizing glance at how fluid the relationship between the middle class and the working class remained. The background of the compulsory public school initiative was therefore a public arena in which class alliances were in the process of continuing negotiation, where the relationship between community and capitalism remained much less settled than most portraits of the 1920s depict. One of the fundamental purposes of the School Bill was the attempted settlement of such class relationships in the direction of a liberal populism that rhetorically challenged elites while ultimately refusing to confront corporate power and social relations.

A fixation on education is supposedly at the heart of the middle-class mentality. Reformers still hold—although in today's heady free-market atmosphere much less so than in the past—that the common school is the true basis of American political and social democracy. William Graebner, for example, points out "the ability of the rapidly expanding public schools to articulate a vision of a classless, egalitarian, conflict-free, meritocratic, homogeneous society." Revisionists often maintain, on the other hand, that the ideology of the public school since the mid–nineteenth century has exemplified a middle-class hegemony that masks elite privilege.[1]

Actual history has been much more complicated than this. The Portlanders who most forcefully articulated the ideology of education that led to the passage of the School Bill did not simply speak some monolithic, timeless, "middle-class" vision but rather reformulated the thoughts, hopes, and desires about education and social life held by various middling Portlanders. In a social environment in which class conflict, petit bourgeois radicalism, and the potential impermanence of corporate power were still quite tangible parts of the political landscape, the School Bill helped remake Portland's middle class, again through an intensely political process.[2]

Some of the supporters of compulsory public schooling in Portland did, to be sure, wear white hoods. The Klan consistently linked passage of the public schools bill with preservation of the purity of the white race and Americanizing immigrants, and the KKK's notoriety allowed it to gain considerable credit for the passage of the bill. Racism also pervaded the editorials of the *Sunnyside Gazette*, the weekly for one of the southeast Portland neighborhoods staunchest in its support for direct democracy. "America's public school educational system," the *Gazette* declared, "is all right and if operated as it should be as a fundamental American institution it would prevent the scum of Southern Europe and Mexico from becoming a menace to our form of government. Compulsory public school education offers the only answer to the question 'What shall be done to Americanize the foreigner?'" Celebrating the measure's passage, the *Gazette* proclaimed that "on November 7 the message of victory was flashed back over the trail to the beginning of the race in Asia Minor. Oregon is true to Anglo-Saxon civilization."[3]

Given such sentiments, it may seem perverse to argue that racism played an almost completely insignificant *public* role in the passage of the compulsory school bill. It was, however, not the Klan but the Scottish Rite Masons who introduced the School Bill and most thoroughly advocated its passage. These other supporters of the School Bill relied on substantially more egalitarian arguments that, as one student of the bill has written, had much in common with the democratic strains in the thought of Horace Mann and John Dewey.[4]

The significance of egalitarian political ideology and class relations in explaining the meaning of the School Bill perhaps comes out most forcefully through its most prominent supporter: none other than William Woodward, the prolabor head of the state arbitration board. A self-made business owner who had worked his way up into Portland's Establishment without benefit of corporate connections, Woodward had also earned the great respect of Portland's unionists. In June 1922, when the battle over the School Bill had just begun, the Central Labor Council invited him to speak on the topic, "Save the Children." According to the *Oregon Labor Press*, Woodward received one of the warmest receptions the unionists ever granted to a nonworker, for ultimately "he became to his hearers the personification of the public school system."[5]

Why did Woodward embody so well for these workers the spirit of the public schools—and by extension much of the spirit of democracy? Essentially, it was because he successfully represented and spoke, as a petit bourgeois who had made it to the top and still cared about workers, for a capitalist social system that promised fairness and equality. Unlike radical "capitalists against capitalism," however, Woodward did so without speaking to the inequalities in property relations that undergirded the corporate social order. He was therefore a perfect incarnation of the School Bill and what it represented for the transformation of democratic hopes in Portland: the creation of a liberal, and no longer subversive, populism.[6]

William F. Woodward, proponent of compulsory public schooling and "egalitarian capitalist." (Courtesy Oregon Historical Society, #018458.)

In the most prominent debate over the School Bill, Woodward took on William Wheelwright, former president of the city's chamber of commerce, before the Portland Ministerial Association. Woodward did insist that immigrants needed to be Americanized. The genuine villains in his story, though, were not foreigners, but native Americans—particularly the rich—who avoided their duty to mix in society. Private schools of any kind undercut the very basis for the common citizenship upon which the nation depended; only public schools blended all children "without regard to birth, creed, race or affiliation." Almost in passing, Woodward noted that some of those who criticized the public schools were religious—Methodist, or Catholic, or Seventh Day Adventist. The chief sentiment that Woodward deplored derived not from religion, but from the mentality of the family man, who having "accumulate[d] a little," sent his children to the private schools "where the sons of the wealthy and the well-to-do go." There "they will be separated from the common herd" and go to school only with their "own class." Such a situation was intolerable, according to Woodward, because "the citizenship of a nation" must make "no distinction . . . between classes." Telling his audience to disregard the condemnation of the public schools by "the wealthy, the rich," Woodward ended by declaring that "within the school house and on the public school playground rests today the only pure democracy under the sun."[7]

Despite his censuring of the rich, William Woodward gave no indication that he advocated *any* kind of restructuring of the economic system, much less the kind that Oregon System radicals had championed. Most other arguments for the bill followed this pattern: a linking of the public schools with an egalitarian society, a castigation of the rich, and a vigorous rhetorical defense of democracy. It would be unwise to view this public ideology as merely a gloss on anti-Catholicism. At the same time, it is important to remember that most School Bill supporters refused to address wider social inequalities.

The argument for the School Bill in the state voters' pamphlet was the one most readily accessible to citizens, and it was also the one that most tangibly displayed a fear of immigrants. It began simply: "Do you believe in our public schools?" You did if you believed in the creation of "true citizens" as well as in the "assimilation and education of our foreign born." Rather than leaving the job of Americanization to social workers or other experts, it was the duty of the entire public to create the American melting pot. "Mix the children of the foreign born with the native born, and the rich with the poor," the eleven authors declared, and out came "the finished product—a true American." Nothing was more important than egalitarian unity: "Our children must not under any pretext, be it based upon money, creed or social status, be divided into antagonistic groups, there to absorb the narrow views of life as they are taught. . . . A divided school can no more succeed than a divided nation." This was the kind of argument that ex-governor and Senator George Chamberlain would use in defending the law before the U.S. Supreme Court. As Chamberlain explained in the celebrated case of *Pierce v. Society of Sisters*, "I feel that the average voter [supported the law] because it brought the child in contact and touch with rich and poor alike, and with those of different religious faiths, and taught him when he went out into the world to be tolerant of the views of others, whether political, sectarian, or otherwise. . . . It was adopted . . . not to Americanize particularly, but to democratize the children, and to cut out this social and group class feeling that exists when they attend any sectarian or private school."[8]

The chief sponsors of the compulsory public schooling initiative, the Scottish Rite School Committee, proceeded along the same lines in the campaign's most widely distributed flyer. This broadside argued in classic liberal fashion that the "public school is DEMOCRATIC. It receives and treats all alike; wealth does not count, poverty does not hinder." Hard work could equalize any inequality, and thus the "only aristocracy is that of learning, of application, of good conduct." Thus the public school was a representation of "the United States in miniature," providing young children a "DEMOCRATIC BAPTISM." The Masons did have some vague enemies: they spoke out against unnamed but "vicious, un-American elements that hate the public school because it REALLY TEACHES THE CHILDREN." Yet in another prominent ad, the Masons were only able to conclude with a rather subdued populist moral: "Do we want a nation of red-blooded men, women and children, or do we want a nation of blue-bloods?"[9]

Therefore there was indeed an implicit conflict between races in the eyes of School Bill advocates. Rather than being a nativist struggle between foreign and native born or between nonwhites and whites, however, the conflict was instead a battle between Americans with real blood in their bodies and artificial would-be aristocrats. The editor of the *Oregon Teacher's Monthly* amplified the transformed populism that, along with an archetypal American denial of classes, underlay the School Bill. She stated that the initiative's most basic purpose was to "make the democracy of the public school an antidote for the inevitable class consciousness and possibly lopsided or snobbish private school attitude." All American children would receive the same education in ethics and "equality," so that "there shall be no classes." Teachers learned—or confirmed their suspicion—that "of the men most hated, feared, caricatured in American history, for their selfishness, their greed, most of them have been class-consciously marked; either along self-made selfish lines, or else the product of exclusive privileges." Both the uneducated "Boss Crokers" and the selfish "Morgans" represented prime examples of what happened to those who received no public education. Between the Crokers and the Morgans lay a virtuous middle class ready to do battle for what was now a constricted version of American democracy.[10]

The social basis of the School Bill corresponded closely to this middling populist rhetoric. The School Bill passed statewide by a margin of 115,506 to 103,685, with 52.7 percent of the vote, even though five days before the election the *Oregonian* stated that the measure was "on its last legs and likely to be defeated." The initiative's support came generally not from the state's rural areas, but rather from the cities that dotted the Willamette Valley. Five thousand of the initiative's 12,000-vote majority came from Portland, where the measure garnered 53.5 percent of the vote. In the Rose City the bill "brought out the largest registration in the history of the community," and the *Oregonian* noted, "Not since women were given the ballot in Oregon have so many attended the polls in Multnomah County as yesterday. The women were aroused by the religious issue and the school bill." Countywide, 72 percent of registered voters went to the polling place, and fully 68 percent of the registered electorate decided the fate of the bill. This is in stark contrast to the nationwide turnout of 42 percent during the 1922 off-year elections.[11]

Nearly twice as many precincts in Portland carried the measure as voted it down, and it is the precinct breakdown of the vote totals that best demonstrates the distinctive class pattern to the School Bill vote. The most basic demarcation lay in the familiar division between the east and west sides of the Willamette. On the West Side, the measure suffered a substantial defeat, receiving only 42.4 percent of the vote. Thirty-one precincts supported the measure, while seventy-five voted it down. The measure highly engaged the electorate, with over 93 percent of those who voted for governor voting on the initiative. A remarkable string of thirty-six precincts, extending from the more posh residential neighborhoods in the West Hills to parts of downtown, rejected the bill.[12]

The contrast with Portland's East Side could hardly be greater. The interest in the School Bill on this side of the river was even more intense. Eight percent *more* voters cast their ballots on the issue than decided to exercise their suffrage in the governor's race, an almost unheard of phenomenon. The East Side as a whole passed the measure with a comfortable 56.5 percent of the vote. More telling was the count of precincts; 226 favored the School Bill and only 55 opposed, a more than four-to-one margin.

Specific neighborhoods supplied the backbone of School Bill electoral support, and analysis of them displays an important pattern. An extraordinary congruence exists between the areas that supported compulsory public schooling in 1922 and those mixed middle-class/working-class districts that had provided the staunchest support for the single tax and prohibition in 1914, as well as antivaccinationism in 1916. The residential precincts starting in Sellwood in the inner southeast and running along through Woodstock and Lents, on to Montavilla, and back down through Mt. Tabor and Sunnyside provided solid backing for the bill. More than 60 percent of Sunnyside's voters endorsed the measure. Sellwood residents approved the initiative by a more than two-to-one margin, as did the voters in a consecutive string of forty winning precincts in the outer southeast. Likewise, over two-thirds of the voters in a continuous segment of precincts in North Portland, including predominantly working-class St. Johns, Portsmouth, and Kenton, approved

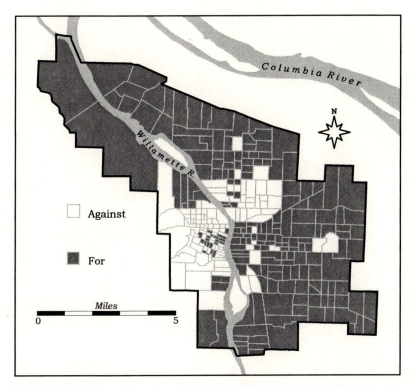

Voting on compulsory public education initiative, 1922, by precinct. Note that Linn-ton, in the far northwest, was a heavily forested precinct that, in terms of social characteristics, had much more in common with the East Side than the West Side.

compulsory public schooling. Once more, upper-middle-class Alameda and Irvington bucked the East Side trend.

Whatever other hidden ethnocultural variables this crude electoral analysis might neglect, it points to the centrality of class to the outcome of the compulsory public school election. The School Bill appealed to a solid combination of people in the middle, with those living in mixed working-class and middle-class residential areas providing overwhelming support for the initiative. The ban on private schools clearly appealed not just broadly to the same type of people who had provided the foundation for anticorporate radicalism, but presumably to many of the very same voters in the very same neighborhoods. This middling bloc had once again challenged the Portland political Establishment through the electoral arena and, at least temporarily, come out victorious.

CHAPTER NINETEEN

CORPORATE TOOLS

The Middling World of the Portland Klan

Middle-Class Populists? The New Historiography of the Second Klan

White supremacist Lothrop Stoddard declared in 1919, "One of the most interesting and perhaps momentous developments of this momentous time is the 'Middle Class Movement.'" Indeed, the fact that the School Bill fit snugly into the traditions of middle-class populism should be no surprise to scholars of the 1920s. For one of the most important recent revisions of this period has highlighted both the "middle class" and the "populist" nature of the Ku Klux Klan. No longer simple rednecks alienated from a modern society they barely understood, the new Klan has gone mainstream with a vengeance.[1]

But does this interpretation work for the Portland Klan?

The answer is partially yes—but primarily no. The Klan in the Rose City did, it seems, have a middling foundation, but its politics were actively anti-populist. Before reviewing the evidence from Portland, however, it will prove illuminating to evaluate the arguments of the new generation of Klan scholars in order to most effectively highlight the complexity of using the category "middle class," and the inadvisability of using the word *populist*, to apply to—at the very least—the Portland Klan.

For three decades historians have convincingly demonstrated that the post–World War I Invisible Empire, despite its virulent strains of racism, was not merely another mouthpiece for backwards, rural, fundamentalist, marginal folk whom modernity forgot to whisk into the twentieth century. Kenneth Jackson, in his landmark *The Ku Klux Klan in the City*, pioneered the current approach, and since the publication of his book local studies of the Klan have become something of a cottage industry, despite the oft-heard protestation that the Kluxers do not receive the attention they deserve. The old view of the purely reactionary Klan remains entrenched in various synthetic accounts of the period, but the monographic scholars have adopted a new and even fairly unified perspective on their subject.[2]

Leonard Moore has stated the synthesis most forcefully. In a review article, Moore noted that recent inquiries have shown that the typical set of white hoods functioned "as a kind of interest group for the average white Protestant who believed that his values should be dominant in American society." Not terribly violent or even intimidating, more interested in prohibition and other moral concerns than race, the second Ku Klux Klan in fact deserved the label *populist*. The KKK provided a wide conglomeration of coreligionists a means to "resist elite political domination and attempt to make local and even state governments more responsive to popular interests." Likewise, although she has a substantially different political lesson to teach from that of Moore, Nancy MacLean also views the second Klan as a populist (albeit "reactionary populist") movement in her study of the KKK chapter in Athens, Georgia.[3]

The new mode of interpretation of the Klan has brought much insight to an area often dominated more by moral grandstanding than concern for historical context. Yet this paradigm has its own weaknesses. To begin, the intensive local studies suffer from the myopia common to social history. They do not examine the "non-Klan" part of the localities with much depth, do not spend enough time exploring competing social and political movements of the period, and most critically do not extend their chronological frame much beyond the all-too-brief years in which the Klan rose to power. The new studies (MacLean is a partial exception) therefore tend be anchored somewhat weightlessly in the 1920s, without effective placement within the long-range transformations wrought by capitalism and democracy or without substantial connections to the ideological struggles that characterized American history during the nineteenth and early twentieth centuries—or even during 1922. Thus *populism* becomes a dehistoricized term, defined simply as an "interest in exerting a greater measure of popular control over social and political affairs" without a comparison with the many various designs of that era's radicals and reformers, who of course had just that same abstract goal. As I will show in contrast, if the Portland Klan had any connection to populism, it came through hijacking the grand tradition of Portland's direct democrats rather than serving as a vehicle for combat with elites.[4]

The reinterpretation of the Klan as populist is closely connected to scholars' recent emphasis on the relationship between class and the Klan. In this matter both sides agree that the Klan had a significantly "middling" nature, but they disagree fairly heatedly on the conclusions to draw from that finding. An examination of their competing claims will show that we can use the insights of both sides of the debate, as well as evidence from Portland, to help construct a more contingent way of conceptualizing the relationship between the Ku Klux Klan, the middle class, and populism.

Most analysis of the class origins of Ku Klux Klan members ultimately derives from the demonization tradition. The idea of an inherent connection between marginal members of the middle class and intolerant social movements molds itself equally well into the frameworks of liberals and leftists. Kenneth Jackson here represents the former, going out of his way to contest the darker implications of a mass society/status anxiety framework while in the end not escaping it himself. In his classic treatment, Jackson declares without qualification that "the secret order was a lower-middle-class movement." Jackson does not systematically spell out what he means by this in terms of occupation, but he does note from the partial membership records of four cities that the Invisible Empire included "a substantial minority" of white-collar workers and a great majority of blue collars. (Jackson unfortunately does not discuss how his proletarians qualify as "lower middle class.")[5]

Nancy MacLean, on the other hand, represents the leftists, and in her hands Jackson's rather benign lower middle class becomes an avenging devil, the twentieth-century "petite bourgeoisie" incarnate. In her book MacLean finds that members of the city's ruling class at the top and unskilled urban workers and rural laborers at the bottom were underrepresented in the Klan. The majority of Kluxers were men who came from "old" petit bourgeois occupations such as shopkeeper or farmer and "new" ones such as white-collar salaried employee. Overall, the predominance of "the broad middle" of the class structure was the result of an effective Klan appeal to these folks' worst populist resentments against blacks, women, and workers as well as, in diluted form, against big capitalists. Given that MacLean does not compare the preponderance of white-collar members of the Athens Klan with the occupational distribution of the entire eligible population, however, it is impossible to determine whether petit bourgeois people (however defined) were truly overrepresented in the Klan. MacLean's thesis thus risks falling like a house of cards on this methodological problem alone.[6]

MacLean's Marxism promises precision in class terminology, but her new creature becomes as much of a spongy monolith as Jackson's entity. MacLean's petite bourgeoisie includes almost all those in between the area's elite and its unskilled workforce. Skilled workers, conveniently, become unproblematically petit bourgeois due to their artisanal heritage and their work in small-scale employment settings, and even tenant farmers and factory workers are infected with the petit bourgeois virus through their family connections to small property (as well as their own desire for it). "Middle class" and "petite bourgeoisie" thus turn out to be interchangeable categories— except for the political implications each contain. Via an uncritical borrowing from Arno Mayer and Hal Draper, we relearn the old news that the petite bourgeoisie has "an obsession with respectability" and is always prone to anti-Semitism and detestation of the proletariat. In the end, MacLean gravely announces, we are simply fortunate that the petite bourgeoisie/middle class did not more effectively harness its reactionary populism, destroy American democracy, and institute fascism during the turbulent interwar period. It *could* have happened here, and we know who would have been responsible.[7]

Given the simultaneous rigidity and imprecision of the Kenneth Jackson and Nancy MacLean models, should we simply throw away the idea of a connection between the Klan and the middle class? That is the moral of much of the other recent scholarship on the Invisible Empire. Consciously disputing Jackson's lower-middle-class thesis, it holds that members of the Klan were a remarkable cross-section of white, Protestant society. Robert Goldberg, in his pioneering examination of the Invisible Empire in Colorado, was the first to argue that a great "diversity," rather than a foundation in any one group, characterized the social basis of the Klan. William Jenkins and Leonard Moore have also joined the chorus, maintaining that Klan members "belonged to all social strata" and represented "a wide cross section of Indiana's occupational spectrum." In all of these new revisionist accounts, class explains very little about Klan motivation, ideals, and politics.[8]

Fortunately, the classic and the revisionist interpretations need not necessarily speak at cross-purposes. If historians stop insisting that class analysis depends on linking the Klan with one particular solidly categorized class—an assumption shared on both sides of the debate—the findings of all the studies become much more commensurate. We can then see that the second KKK represented yet another zone of contestation where those at the intersection of the middle class and the working class struggled to define their political and social relationships, even to define their very class identities.

For example, those scholars who conceive of the Klan as a quintessentially lower-middle-class or middle-class movement have an awfully large number of blue-collar "working-class" Klan members to explain. According to Jackson's limited sample, blue-collar workers constituted the clear majority of Klan members—70 percent in Knoxville, Tennessee, and nearly 75 percent in Winchester, Illinois. In MacLean's sample, skilled workers made up 19 percent of the Klan in Athens, "the largest general category after lower white-collar workers and petty-proprietors and managers." Some skilled workers were among the leaders of the chapter. Semiskilled and unskilled workers, including mill operatives, made up another 15 percent of the chapter. Thus a fastidious class categorizer could easily argue that working-class participation in the Athens Klan was a full one-third. As all the other studies show, participation of the proletariat in the Klan was vital, and sometimes overwhelming.[9]

On the other side of the debate, historians are so intent on arguing that the Klan represented a cross-section of the Protestant population that they tend to obscure the critical middling nature of the movement. Goldberg, Moore, and Jenkins have all discovered that elites and unskilled workers joined the Klan at rates considerably less frequently than their more "ordinary" neighbors. Modifying his bolder generalization, Moore argues that the Indiana Klan "did not represent a pure cross section" of society, but rather that "low-level white-collar workers and skilled blue-collar workers joined the Klan slightly more often than members of other occupations."[10]

The way to reconcile these different interpretations is to realize that, once smoothed of their rough edges, they are complementary. Jackson and Mac-Lean are correct in their insistence on the importance of those in the middle to the Klan, although ultimately their theses are reductionist. Goldberg, Jenkins, and Moore, on the other hand, are correct in their observation of the broadly representative nature of Klan membership. They fail to come to grips, however, with the significance of the tendency of the elite and the unskilled—historically the opponents of populist social movements—not to affiliate with the Invisible Empire. What we learn from both sides is that the backbone of the Klan, north and apparently south, was a powerful combination of skilled blue-collar workers and lower-level white-collar workers. As Shawn Lay argues, the 1920s Klan was "in its essence and in the broadest sense of the term, a middle-class social movement." What we need to understand, however, is that no group ("middle class" or "lower middle class" or "petite bourgeoisie") brought with it any inherent politics to the KKK. Rather, the Invisible Empire functioned, in complex and complicated ways, to politically mediate—and even help define—the middle of the social order.[11]

The Middling World of the Portland Klan

The alliance between those at the intersection of the petite bourgeoisie and the proletariat, of course, proved crucial to the fate of radical populist movements in Portland. Unfortunately, sources related to Klan membership in the City of Roses are quite limited. What they do tentatively tell us is that members of this same middling bloc served as the foundation of Klan politics. Yet the confirmation of middling involvement in the Portland Klan does not bring in its train a concomitant labeling of the Rose City's KKK as "populist." Instead, the Klan in Portland actively worked to disconnect those in the middle from antielitist politics of any kind, whether reactionary or radical.

No membership records exist for the Portland KKK, rendering impossible the intensive investigation historians have elsewhere made of the organization's occupational basis. The only extant list of Portland Klan members contains thirty-two names, most of whom do not appear in the city directory. Contemporary comments on the social support of the Klan are likewise scattered and vague. The *Oregonian*, which essentially tolerated the Klan once it became powerful, noted that induction ceremonies for over two thousand Klansman in February and April 1922 drew "from all the important walks of life in the city. There were doctors, lawyers, business men of all kinds, railroad men, clerks and citizens from other professions and employments." The *News*, a vociferous opponent of the Klan, agreed, commenting, "Professional and business men, clerks, citizens from every walk of life" had joined. Waldo Roberts sounded more specific, remarking of Oregon: "Not the bad people of the State, but the good people—the *very* good people—are largely responsible for the transformation of the Oregon commonwealth into an invisible empire." Yet his oft-quoted statement actually said nothing directly about class; Roberts simply meant to indict the many Protestant clergy who had become active Kluxers.[12]

More helpful, although indirect, was the statement of Frank Davey, whom Governor Olcott appointed to examine the issue of Japanese landownership in Oregon, a key Klan issue. Davey, former speaker of the Oregon House, asserted in 1920 that although business owners seeking trade opportunities were tolerant, there was a "strong antipathy against the Japanese among small farmers, mechanics, laborers, and salaried classes in general. A large part of this antipathy is racial and does not depend on economic facts." David Horowitz also cautiously notes that the social makeup of the Klan statewide generally was a combination of working class and middle class. With such consistent findings from other cities, it is relatively safe to assume that the Portland Klan membership did not significantly differ from its middling base elsewhere.[13]

Even if the Klan masses remain elusive, we know much more about their leaders. Moreover, it is clear that the they were individuals crucial to the articulation of social relationships between skilled workers and those more firmly in the middle of the class structure. KKK leaders therefore illustrate again the critical political consequences of the fluidity of the collar line. For the most powerful Klansman in Portland were ex-unionists who had held significant power within the ranks of organized labor *and* had worked as at least middle level managers for large oligopolistic corporations.

Fred Gifford, Exalted Cyclops of the Portland Klan, exemplified this pattern. Born in Minnesota, Gifford moved with his parents to the Rose City in 1889 at the age of eleven. After graduating from high school he acquired, according to C. C. Chapman, "a technical education in electrical engineering lines that might be the envy of many a college graduate." Gifford first put this increasingly valuable knowledge to work as a telegraph operator with the Southern Pacific. Gifford proved of such great worth to the railroad that he soon received a promotion to supervisor of repairs all the way from Portland to Dunsmuir, California.[14]

Eventually Gifford secured a series of positions that involved more and more authority within the world of corporate public utilities. He went from the Southern Pacific to the Portland phone company and became wire chief for the city; in the middle of his stint the Bell system put him in charge of construction and maintenance in the eastern sections of both Oregon and Washington during the corporation's expansion into that region. In 1913, Gifford migrated to the Northwestern Electric Company, which was at that time poised to compete against the Portland Railway, Light, and Power Company. Gifford started with Northwestern as chief of distribution, and by the time he joined the Klan he had become superintendent for transmission. Chapman, who well understood the local corporations and who was hardly in agreement with Gifford's politics, commented that Gifford's "duties were exceedingly important from a technical standpoint and the company valued his services very highly."[15]

Gifford's biography so far places him firmly within the world of the professional middle class. Allegations that Gifford's value to Northwestern Electric went well beyond his engineering skills, though, started to fly fast after he became powerful in the Klan, allowing us to learn about the complexities of his class identity. For Fred Gifford had not only held high managerial positions within corporations; he had also been a labor leader of at least medium stature. In this peculiar world of early-twentieth-century Portland, where white-collar unionists were not at all unusual, Gifford rose to prominence within the house of labor. First he became, in 1911, business agent for the Electrical Workers' local. The following two years Gifford served as the local's president, at least nominally overseeing walkouts against the Home Telephone Company as well as the first "girls" operators' strike.

When Gifford took over leadership of the Portland Klan, he was a prominent Mason, but he had played no role in earlier nativist organizations. Gifford had, however, achieved renown in a different realm—for his alleged role in the 1919 strike against the phone company. Here introduction is necessary of Gifford's two most powerful allies in the Portland Klan, Grand Titans Charles N. Hurd and W. D. (Ole) Quinn. Hurd and Quinn were also electricians, with Hurd serving as president of the local in 1919 when not only the electricians, but also female phone operators, began a walkout. The union sent Hurd to San Francisco to negotiate with the representatives of the Portland public service corporations, and he returned advocating settlement at existing wages. Even though he later presided at the meeting at which the Portland local decided to go along with the coastwide strike, Hurd decided to testify on behalf of the employers in front of the State Board of Conciliation. He characterized the strike as Bolshevik-inspired, illegal, and unconstitutional. Hurd also objected to any organization of the female operators, arguing that they had loose morals and were incapable of self-governance.

For his betrayal of the workers' cause, the union stiffly fined Hurd, and he thereafter became known as the "$1,000 Scab." Gifford and Quinn apparently supported Hurd in his actions and picked up similar reputations as "political manipulators" for the corporations. Patronage rewards for their actions in the strike evidently came quickly. Gifford received a promotion at Northwestern Electric. Pacific Telephone and Telegraph—the same corporation that earlier in the century had contested the legality of the Oregon System—appointed Hurd superintendent of its Tabor Exchange and Quinn superintendent of installation for the city. Hurd, by 1924 Gifford's "power behind the throne," and Quinn remained on the payroll at the telephone company throughout their affiliation with the Klan.[16]

Overall, Gifford, Quinn, and Hurd thus had "middling" biographies akin in some ways to those of Will Daly, George Orton, and William U'Ren. They were comfortable in both the world of unions and in the world of employers. Yet their allegiances were strikingly different from these radical direct democrats; their loyalties ultimately went to the corporations responsible for employing and promoting them. These renegade proletarians—or were they true-hearted members of the middle class?—therefore perfectly foreshadowed the political role of the Portland Klan.

Opponents of the Klan and the School Bill

We can also see the function that the Klan played in post–Progressive Era Portland politics, and particularly the Klan's middling nature, by way of its articulate opponents. Although antagonism toward the Klan and the School Bill did come from those who had formerly advocated a small-propertied direct democracy, such resistance proved sporadic. As early as 1921, soon after the Klan's first appearance in the city, Charles Rynerson, editor of the *Oregon Labor Press*, went on the offensive against the Invisible Empire. Rynerson wrote of the Klan: "everywhere it is anti-labor and anti-liberal. In any community where dominating commercial interests find opposition to their control the organization of a Ku Klux Klan is a convenient way of ridding the community of the opposition and intimidating all who are inclined to stand for justice." Luther Powell, then head of the Portland Klan, responded in classic First Klan fashion by telling Rynerson that he "would be a fit subject for a Vigilance Committee." In an ironic application of a statute that organized labor opposed, the *Labor Press* declared Powell's letter "an open violation of the state syndicalism law" and initiated grand jury proceedings in the matter.[17]

Meanwhile William U'Ren, counsel to the Central Labor Council, noted that the Klan's white hoods violated a state antimask law. As one who had spent more than a generation working for the public and political regeneration of society, being able to work with socialists and even communists but not Wobblies, U'Ren also issued the most damning epithet possible against the secret order: its members, because of their flaunting of the law, were "anarchists." Yet because of an actual or threatened boycott, the *Labor Press* suddenly ceased any mention of the Klan, and the organization disappeared from the pages of the paper during all of 1922. U'Ren, in turn, worked on behalf of KKK-supported candidate Charles Hall in an unsuccessful recount effort after the 1922 Republican gubernatorial primary.[18]

Likewise, when the Portland Klan attempted to take on the mantle of the Oregon System by forming the Oregon Good Government League and holding a Progressive Party convention, some old-line progressive activists came out to witness the meeting's results. It soon became apparent that Fred Gifford and his allies would run the organizations with an iron hand. H. P. Lee, an old Roosevelt Progressive, protested to no avail that "the money power, otherwise profiteering, is a more important issue than parochial schools." Twice the seasoned radicals, including single taxer H. D. Wagnon, Robert Duncan, Frank Myers, and others associated with the *Producer's Call* organized counterconventions. At the first they adopted a simple two-plank platform: endorsement of the U'Ren occupational plan and "government ownership of 'all economic sources of value'"—issues of no interest to the KKK. Nothing substantive came out of either assembly, though, and neither issued a formal condemnation of the Klan.[19]

In fact, the *only* explicit radical condemnation of the School Bill came from C. W. Barzee, the Portland socialist most closely affiliated with the radical direct democrats. Responding to those advocates of the initiative who stressed its "strike . . . at autocracy or class education in private schools, not mixed with the common herd," Barzee declared that "money (wealth) and not education is the class line of demarkation [sic]." The bill was tyrannical because of its anti-Catholicism as well as because of the educational monopoly it would set up. Barzee also protested against the progovernmental standardized curriculum that would result. "Think not that we have free thinking public schools," he stated; "Our schools are privately directed by the 'invisible government' through [the] Morgan-Rockefeller directorship of the Columbia University." Even Barzee's straightforward blast against the "reactionary" bill, though, turned out to be tarnished. A month earlier Barzee had written to Walter Pierce, promising Socialist Party support for the Democrat's gubernatorial bid, and adding, "I am in close touch with the Ku Klux Klan through some of my best friends who are very influential." Everyone, it appears, had dirt on their hands.[20]

Everyone, that is, except members of Portland's old-line ruling class, the same people who had been in the forefront of opposition to radical direct democracy and, at times, to any form of direct legislation at all. Besides the directors of private schools and churches that the School Bill directly affected, like those of the Catholics and Lutherans, the most vocal opponents of the initiative came from those who constituted the cream of the Portland elite. The committee organized to combat the initiative "on principle" included "prominent business men" such as W. L. Brewster, Judge Charles H. Carey, W. M. Ladd, Robert H. Strong, W. B. Ayer, Richard W. Montague, C. B. Moores, and J. B. Kerr, as well as Henrietta Failing and Mrs. Sol Hirsch. The leader of the anti–School Bill forces was William D. Wheelwright, "one of the city's most distinguished elder business leaders." The Portland ruling class was not completely united on the issue. For example, Robert Smith, president of the Lumberman's Trust Company and longtime foe of radical taxation measures, was the leader of the Scottish Rite petition drive that put the School Bill on the ballot, even though he afterwards faded out of the campaign. Still, it is clear that Portland followed the pattern that other historians of the Klan have identified, with those at the top of society staying furthest away from organized nativism, at least during the years in which crosses blazed. And the elite was forceful in its defense of inequality. As J. P. Kavanaugh, arguing before the U.S. Supreme Court in the *Pierce* case asked, why should Oregon and the Soviet Union be the only governments "to have a monopoly of education, to put it in a straitjacket, by the fixing of unalterable standards and thereby to bring their people and their citizens to one common level?"[21]

Corporate Tools: The Antipopulist Politics of the Portland Klan

The Ku Klux Klan began recruiting in Oregon during the spring of 1921, and soon Portland became the center of an increasingly powerful state organization. The most reasonable estimates of Klan membership place the statewide total at anywhere between fifteen thousand and thirty-five thousand at any one time, with at least nine thousand in Portland at the peak of the Empire's influence. Predictably, some analysts—particularly national ones—attributed Klan strength, and ultimately passage of the School Bill, to the racist rural rednecks who constituted what the *New York Times* called the "backwoods" majority vote in the 1922 election. According to Waldo Roberts, in Oregon "the 'thinking people' are in a hopeless minority. People in the mass don't think, they feel."[22]

In actuality, the Oregon Klan was "essentially urban," and from early on the Portland chapter played a sophisticated role in both city and state politics under Fred Gifford's leadership. Rumors of Mayor Baker's involvement with the Klan abounded. In the May 1922 election, the Klan and its allies came out the clear winners, nearly knocking off incumbent governor Ben Olcott in the Republican primary. The Klan also took credit for the victory of twelve of the thirteen Republicans for the Multnomah County delegation to the lower house of the legislature. (These candidates then went on to win the general election.) The *Oregon Voter* proclaimed that "Religiously, the election was a torrid encounter. . . . May 19 may pass into history as the Dawn of the Nightshirt Era in Oregon politics."[23]

Klan influence in the November general election is somewhat more difficult to clarify, since the Federation of Patriotic Societies, another influential nativist society, competed with the KKK. The School Bill, of course, was the main Klan achievement, even if the KKK's role in passage of the initiative is difficult to discern, and likely overrated. Switching its allegiance to the minority Democrats, the Klan through its front organizations endorsed the triumphant gubernatorial candidate, Walter Pierce, as well as the first Democrat to win an Oregon congressional seat since 1879, Portlander Elton Watkins.

Commentators calculated a Klan majority in the house of representatives and a substantial minority in the senate, with house speaker Kaspar K. Kubli aptly symbolizing the power of the Invisible Empire.

The ambition of the Klan legislative program during the 1923 session, however, considerably exceeded the authority the Invisible Empire could ultimately command. Only statutes preventing public school teachers from wearing religious garb in the classroom and an antialien landownership bill aimed at the Japanese became law, while proposals that did not pass included the proscribing of sacramental wine, forbidding the employment of aliens in public works, repealing the tax exemption of religious bodies, and requiring all foreign owners of businesses to post their nationality on their buildings. All in all, the claim of Waldo Roberts in 1923 that "the past two years have witnessed a *complete* political revolution in the State of Oregon" was rather overblown. Still, no one could deny that in the twelve months following the spring of 1922 the Ku Klux Klan acquired significant political power and turned local and state politics topsy-turvy.[24]

Despite its general emphasis on nativism, the policies and ideologies of the Klan also articulated—albeit often obliquely—stands on the issues at the heart of the Progressive Era reconstruction of Oregon politics: corporate power and alliances between working class and middle class. David Horowitz, the leading scholar of the Oregon Klan, even goes so far as to suggest, in accord with current revisionism, that "a complex mixture of nativism and populism" undergirded the order, and that Klansmen "unwittingly mounted a radical critique of the emerging social and cultural features of the postwar world."[25]

Ultimately, however, Horowitz's thesis turns out to suffer from the same problem as the general argument about national Klan populism. An investigation into the Klan's relationship to and ideas about the social and economic power of corporations provides almost no evidence of an insurgent democratic force, and many indications of a movement that did not even live up to the basic premises of the liberal populism that other School Bill advocates embraced. The Portland Klan instead essentially served as a corporate tool that sought to suppress populism through its advocacy of an aggressive capitalism and its antagonism to direct democracy.

During the early twentieth century political actors across the ideological spectrum threw accusations of corporate intrigue and corruption at their opponents with often wild abandon. Interestingly, the Rose City's KKK did not, eschewing the language of republican political economy. The Invisible Empire's adversaries, on the other hand, made frequent, and compelling, allegations of the ties between the leaders of the Klan and specific corporations as well as the corporate order generally. The quote that occurs most frequently in the historical literature is succinct, and comes from "one of the most perceptive contemporary students of the secret order." Journalist Robert

Duffus wrote, "The Klan leadership in Oregon is closely allied with certain of the electric light and power corporations, and it is common gossip among politicians that it was organized, or encouraged, as a counter-irritant against reform movements which might impair the corporate interests." Local commentators of different ideological stripes were remarkably consistent in their agreement on this issue, even though they were not able to provide smoking guns.[26]

Yet did the Klan appeal to populist yearnings, even if its political connections were apparently reactionary? The answer to this question is clearly no. An examination of the ideology that the Portland Klan promulgated reveals the fundamentally antidemocratic nature of the Invisible Empire. In fact, the Rose City Klan instead used a language that, like the actions of Gifford, Hurd, and Quinn, actively attempted to detach workers and middling folk from anticorporate politics.

The *Western American*, with Lem Dever as editor, was the chief mouthpiece of the Portland Klan. Few copies of the newspaper exist, but those that do speak eloquently to Klan social ideals. Tellingly, the School Bill receives almost no attention. The *Western American* did weakly voice some of the same liberal rhetoric that predominated in the campaign for the initiative. "A greater, grander America, free from greed and graft, where an equality of opportunity shall be the secure right of every loyal citizen, irrespective of race, religion, or color," was, according to the newspaper, the Klan's foremost aspiration. Only the most veiled mentions of the pernicious effects of social inequality, however, ever appeared in the publication. Instead, readers learned of the magic transformative effects of the Klan dominion, where the fellow with wealth "relinquishes his millions, and Lazarus his rags. The poor man here is as rich as the richest and the rich man as poor as the pauper. He knows but one distinction and that is unsullied manhood. His symbols are the Fiery Cross and the scintillating, stainless Flag."[27]

In affairs outside the Empire, every Klansman devoted himself—by the very act of signing his membership card—to a "Closer relationship between Capital and American Labor," particularly by "Preventing unwarranted strikes by foreign labor agitators." Dever told his comrades that he had personal knowledge of the plans of Lenin to lead the colored hordes of the world in battle against America. It is therefore not difficult to understand why Fred Gifford, in the name of the Klan, supported Mayor Baker's repressive policy against the IWW during the fall longshore strike. At the same time, the *Western American* thought of itself at times as a self-appointed voice for the white working class and energetically advanced what it called "justice for the farmers . . . and the cause of labor." Dever stated that the newspaper refused "much" advertising from open-shop businesses and stood uncompromisingly for workers' rights "as upheld by the A.F.L., under its conservative and law-abiding leadership."[28]

Happily welcoming the AFL to Portland for its 1923 national convention, Dever launched into an oration that echoed the radicalism of previous Portland producerism. Dever noted the Klan's stand on behalf of "the eight-hour day standard, and for wages as high as economic conditions will permit. The demand is made continually for economic reforms of such a sweeping character as to assure the farmers and working folk the greatest possible share of the wealth which their industry and enterprise create. Through the Klan, it is believed, the solidarity of the producers of America can be brought about, to the end that right and justice shall triumph over wrong, and then the problem of involuntary poverty shall be solved." After the 1923 AFL convention passed a resolution repudiating the Klan, the *Western American* combined its attacks on the "gang of Kaseys and Abies" who supposedly controlled the national leadership of the union with a more radical appraisal of the organization. Proclaiming that it was time for a "white Man's Labor Federation," Dever argued that all AFL leaders were "overfed grafters" in league with open-shop "Big Interests."[29]

Yet all this was not only the start, but also the end of the *Western American's* critique of capitalist social relations. Despite its purported concern for "the solidarity of the producers of America," the Portland Klan failed to mention any nonproducers against whom its heroes could mobilize. And the commonwealth that the Klan intended to defend was clearly corporate, as well as white. The Klan's prescription for a good economy had nothing to do with breaking up inequalities, but rather involved continuing full-steam ahead with constant growth. The *Western American* congratulated the Portland Chamber of Commerce for its leading role in economic development campaigns. Klan beliefs about public utilities also meshed well with those of the chamber. Dever praised voters in neighboring California for repudiating a hydroelectric initiative sponsored by "the Communist-minded originators of the public ownership delusion." Since hostility toward utility corporations was the sine qua non of urban populism, it is hardly helpful to consider the Portland Klan as a manifestation of such a phenomenon.[30]

The Portland Klan's ideas about government are even more conducive to labeling the movement as reactionary *non*populism, for the KKK repudiated the democratic hopes of the Oregon System. Especially in one remarkable article, the *Western American* declared war on all the assumptions that underlay even moderate direct legislation. Responding to the Plumb Plan of government railroad ownership, and to national discussion about the recall of judicial decisions, the newspaper argued that the battle was now on between republican rule as set out in the Constitution and democratic rule by majorities. The Klan stood squarely against the latter.

"Demos Always Tyrannical" was one section in this sustained assault on popular rule. Dever proclaimed: "We have had enough legislation for direct rule by Demos." Speaking in a manner that would have made Harvey Scott warm in his grave, the Klan editor stated, "The complex problems arising in civilized government cannot be solved by popular vote, and the worst of all forms of despotism is the united and unrestrained will of the majority." Revolutionary France and Soviet Russia were the nightmares that lurked in the future of the United States unless the masses were taught that the American government, with the full blessing of Madison, Hamilton, and Washington, placed sharply circumscribed limits on the popular will. Christ, Socrates, and Galileo were poignant examples of how "Chaos and despotism would follow the direct rule of the herd—the autocracy of the hoi polloi—which always has been cruel, narrow, unjust, tyrannical, wicked, and brutal." Klansman learned that "The majority is always thoughtless and slothful, incapable of intelligent decision and action." The solution to the problem of democracy was at hand, however, even "recognizing the thoughtless masses for what they are." Besides the vigorous enforcement of the Constitution, with the Klan serving as the document's Praetorian Guard, "the movement toward centralizing all power and responsibility" was quickly gaining momentum. The Klan cheered on this trend, since "Our great stupid multitude needs masterful leadership."[31]

Although the mass of Kluxers in Portland were not vicious nightriders intent on murder and intimidation, the organization was in the end no harmless defender of prohibition and other "Protestant" moral values. Stanley Coben claims that "Everywhere, the Klan fought to overcome the power of business and professional elites." But in Portland the Klan represented no threat to "modernizing elites" whatsoever. Instead, the Portland Klan played a key role in forging the relationship between working class and middle class as well as between capital and labor. The KKK helped turn the widespread sentiment for a liberal populism, as expressed in the School Bill, into an even more conservative movement that reinforced elite authority. The Ku Klux Klan may have launched populist crusades in other localities. Ultimately, though, the Portland Klan above all attempted to repudiate the Oregon System by attaching its adherents among skilled workers and lower-middle-class folks to a vision of racist, hooded corporate Americanism rather than to open, participatory democracy.[32]

CHAPTER TWENTY

The Producer's Call and the Portland Housewives' Council

The Tenuous Survival of Petit Bourgeois Radicalism

Despite the Klan onslaught, left-wing populism in Portland did not die out. For also launched in 1922 was the appropriately named *Producer's Call*. The *Call* provided a continuing voice for the small-propertied radicalism that had sustained the most serious Progressive Era radicalism in the Rose City. This populist newspaper served as the mouthpiece for a successful anticorporate recall effort in 1922. It was also the official organ of the Housewives' Council, during the 1920s Portland's most bitter foe of public utilities. The *Producer's Call* and its associated crusades provide further confirmation that even if the two ideologies had broadly similar social bases, small-producer radicalism remained substantially different from—and much more democratic than—the liberal populism of respectable School Bill advocates as well as the pseudopopulism of the Portland Klan. And bringing the *Producer's Call* and the Housewives' Council back into the historical record requires that we seriously rethink the standard story of twentieth-century American populism's inevitable rightward movement. Democratic dreams declined while intolerance roared during the twenties, but by no means did they disappear.[1]

The *Producer's Call* originated in Oregon City at the start of 1922 as the "Champion of the Farmers and Wage Earners" of Oregon. M. J. Brown was editor, while Frank Myers—one of Harry Lane's closest confidantes—served as business manager. The paper advocated an income tax, impartial assessments, clean politics, lower governmental expenses, equal justice for all, and "the full rights of the producers of wealth from the humblest to the highest."[2]

The newspaper served as a reunion space for many activists who had formed the radical backbone of the Oregon System. Alfred Cridge, the oldest veteran in this struggle, wrote his last columns in the *Producer's Call*, completing an almost forty-year career in Oregon fighting for direct democracy before dying three months into the paper's run. Cridge continued advocating his old standbys, proportional representation and the single tax, as well as a ban on bonded indebtedness and an initiative requiring that four-fifths of the people approve any new state office or debt. To the very end, Cridge believed that the people "by going to the ballot-box are empowered to establish peace on earth and good will of one to another." C. W.

Barzee, former leader of the Oregon Socialist Party and now at least a part-time farmer who belonged to the Lents Grange, also contributed many articles, carrying on crusades against German war reparations and for supplanting "capitalist-prostituted institutions" with "the truth which Jesus taught would make us free." The paper spoke out against the death penalty, and even against the spanking of children, which it linked to the electric chair. Naturally, the *Producer's Call* also continued the grand tradition of opposition to compulsory vaccination.[3]

The *Producer's Call* did not, however, much discuss either the Ku Klux Klan or the School Bill. Its editors certainly did not have the courage to oppose either one directly. The paper noted in passing mass inductions of Klansman, and as election day approached implied its disapproval of the "open scrap fight of race and religion" into which the Klan and Federation of Patriotic Societies had converted the election. Letters to the editor were about evenly split on the School Bill. The strongest stands on compulsory public education the newspaper took were brief editorial comments that "the school bill should be considered entirely separate from the governorship" and "leave politics and religion out of it. The issue is taxation."[4]

If the *Producer's Call* propounded a rather murky stance on nativism, the social base for which the newspaper spoke was not at all unclear. The paper upheld the rights of "the people" versus the corporations, and workers and small business owners versus big business. Above all, the *Call* spoke for taxpaying small property owners. In its hesitant endorsement of Walter Pierce for governor, for example, the newspaper argued that "Farmers, merchants and home owners must know the big corporations are slipping out of a big part of their taxation." What stature of business owners the editors had in mind became clear with the *Call's* complaint about advertising, which only large concerns could afford, while "the middle-class merchant, the 'little fellow,'" got left out in the cold.[5]

The *Producer's Call* also—and very much unlike the Klan—expressed an impressive solidarity with the working class, even if its perspective was far from proletarian. The editors, for instance, labeled "a means of settling rightly the differences between employer and employee" as "the biggest problem that has ever menaced the world." The paper took the side of the strikers in all of the year's labor struggles, characterizing Mayor Baker's vision of a Wobbly revolution as bunk and insisting that full civil liberties be available to members of the IWW. The newspaper did fear the strength of unions if they exercised their power in a manner hostile toward business. "Employers ought not to have to stand for a union of men telling them how to run their business," the newspaper declared, just as workers should not have to fight off scabs just to keep their jobs. Yet the solution to this problem was not to persecute labor; the *Producer's Call* considered injunctions worse than Wobblies. Instead, the newspaper recommended that the government require all employers to open their books for compulsory arbitration during strikes. Overall, "predatory Big Business" was the main enemy of middling folks.[6]

Nor was the control of corporations that the *Producer's Call* advocated merely rhetorical. The newspaper served as the organ of the successful May 1922 recall effort against two state public service commissioners, F. G. Buchtel and F. A. Williams. The reasons behind the recall were complicated, involving personal intrigue and organizational disputes between the Klan and the Federation of Patriotic Societies, as well as the official cause of protesting a rate increase that the commission granted to the Pacific Telephone and Telegraph Company. To recall leader (and School Bill supporter) Robert Duncan, though, the results were anything but complex: "Monopoly is fallen. Wall Street is in the dust. The corporations are kicked out of Oregon politics. Hereafter the people will have something to say about the tributes they pay to Big Business." Even if the results of the recall were not quite so dramatic, at the very least the *Producer's Call* kept public service corporations alive as a viable political issue at a time when almost all the other Portland newspapers had tried to remove them from the realm of civic discussion.[7]

Active in the debate over public utilities was the Portland Housewives' Council. In the early 1920s William U'Ren dreamed of housewives running the government. At the same time, a group of actual housewives organized under the banner of small-propertied radicalism in order to continue the contest against monopoly. The Housewives' Council originated in a series of public meetings that the U.S. attorney called in 1919 in order to fight the High Cost of Living, but the organization soon declared its independence and became a thorn in the side of the postwar authorities. The council instigated inquiries into the sugar trust, the price of bread, and the high cost of rentals; conducted a boycott of potatoes; and pushed for an expansion of Portland's public market.[8]

In 1922 the Housewives' Council began to intervene in the affairs of public utilities, pushing its concern about household economy in an anticorporate direction. Although Robert Duncan was the brash and outspoken head of the 1922 recall movement, it was actually the Housewives' Council that had reactivated the crusade in February after a hiatus of some period. Following its triumph in the May election, the Housewives' Council filed a complaint requesting that the public service commission cut the PRL&P streetcar fares from eight to five cents. The Housewives' Council was especially attentive to the criticism of the proposed fare reduction from the Central Labor Council, which feared a cut in wages, and the women suggested all kinds of decreases the corporation could make without affecting the incomes of workers. The council's president, Josephine Othus, ran unsuccessfully for the city commission on an antiutility platform. The Housewives even advocated the reintroduction of jitneys, which had not been seen on the streets of Portland since their defeat in the 1917 municipal elections.[9]

For three years the state Public Service Commission promised the House-wives' Council a hearing on the five-cent fare before finally ruling against the reduction. This infuriated the council, which threatened to abolish the PSC by vote of the people. Instead, the Housewives' Council decided to launch an even more radical initiative, which became, according to one contemporary commentator, "the first state-wide movement for public power to attract general attention." The Housewives' plan, as it came to be known, provided for a five-person commission empowered to issue government bonds up to 5 percent of assessed state valuation in order to build public electric and water generating and distribution facilities. The Establishment did not take this violation of the rights of private enterprise sitting down, outspending the measure's proponents $75,058.47 to $1,217.13. The *Oregonian* pronounced, "we have had alarming measures, silly measures, impractical measures, revolutionary measures; but nothing heretofore put up to the people compares with this astounding proposition in audacity, in novelty, and in potential consequences of failure and ruin." Nor did traditional public power advocates support the Housewives, as both organized labor and Walter Pierce abandoned the scheme, despite claims that the governor had helped draft the initiative. Only the *News* quietly endorsed what the *Oregon Voter* characterized as "this extraordinary measure," and, predictably, an electoral landslide buried the proposal.[10]

The Housewives' Council apparently disappeared from the public arena, amid much internal conflict, just before Franklin Roosevelt took office. Yet its final pronouncement points to the survival of small-producer radicalism well after its supposed demise. In 1931, the council proposed a $4 billion fund of new legal tender, known as "public improvement currency," designed to reinflate the money supply and relieve "the burdens of the home." The Housewives demanded that their representatives "cease to play this game of taking away from the toiling masses to enrich the classes," instead beseeching Congress to enact "such legislation as will take the control of public improvements from the money brokers."[11]

In the overall sweep of Portland politics during the early twentieth century, the Housewives' Council and the activists associated with the *Producer's Call* seem like fairly marginal players, although even that is disputable given the overwhelming victory of the 1922 recall. At the very least, these 1920s populists do effectively highlight the stark contrast between small-producer radicalism and the ideology promulgated by School Bill proponents, whether of respectable or Klan ilk. The key demarcation was a willingness to combat the power of corporations in the name of a populist alliance of farmers, workers, and middling folks. Still, the historical connections between these ideologies go well beyond simple opposition. Above all, the near silence of the *Producer's Call* on the question of compulsory public education, and even the Klan, demonstrates what was perhaps most crucial about the politics of class in 1922 Portland: the effective neutralization of any radical middle-class critique of the School Bill's liberal populism, much less of the KKK's bigotry.

The Hard Work and Difficult Politics of Middle-Class Classlessness

Overall, then, what effect did the School Bill, and its nefarious companion the Klan, have on the reconstruction of middling-class politics in Portland? Even if he downplayed the specific purpose behind the School Bill, Waldo Roberts correctly characterized the atmosphere of the 1922 election in Portland and in Oregon generally when he noted that "a blind, unorganized, and somewhat incoherent spirit of revolt was the strongest political sentiment in the State at the time of the election." Specifically, an insurgent, populist coalition—middling folks politically and socially still allied to working-class people—had again formed an alliance that promised to bring equality back to American society, through the abolition of private and parochial schools. For the most part, though, those in the middle had detached their revolt from questions of property, democracy, and the prevailing corporate power structure. Beyond that, the Klan actively promulgated an antidemocratic, elite-friendly politics. Ultimately, liberal populism and its bigoted companion produced a momentarily triumphant but twisted politics of classlessness—the quintessential characteristic of supposed American exceptionalism.[12]

Most historians and intellectuals hold that a classless vision and politics has been the mother's milk of the American middle class. Other scholars have argued in a more complex fashion that middle-class and working-class people during at least the nineteenth century worked together to produce the social relations and ideology of classlessness. For example Brian Greenberg, in a study of working-class consciousness in nineteenth-century Albany, New York, has pointed out that various mediating voluntary organizations, such as the Odd Fellows, often led workers and those in the middle class to unite in the exaltation of a free labor ideology that denied conflict between labor and capital. Sociologist Mary Ann Clawson has similarly argued that nineteenth-century fraternal orders essentially served as cross-class associations that provided white male members of the working class with a crucial alternative to an identity based primarily on the workplace. In a disruptive age of capitalist industrialization, such organizations offered a harmonious realm for the celebration of the figure of the precapitalist artisan, who symbolized the unbifurcated goals of workers' mutuality and small proprietors' egalitarianism.[13]

Portland's School Bill campaign helps us to extend these insights. Fraternal orders were crucial in the drafting and passage of the initiative. Scottish Rite Masons originated the idea and served as its chief public sponsors, despite the conflicts this caused within the larger world of Masonry. And, of course, the Ku Klux Klan was arguably the most successful fraternal society in America during the 1920s. On the surface, then, the School Bill represented yet another manifestation of the vision of working class and middle class united in harmony that Greenberg and Clawson have noted as the hallmark of fraternalism.[14]

At a deeper level, however, advocates of the School Bill, ranging from William Woodward to the Masons to Lem Dever, could not help dragging out the issue of class in at least a mildly unharmonious manner. In the decade between Harry Lane's election to the Senate in 1912 and the blazing of crosses on top of the East Side's hills in 1922, Portland politics had changed dramatically. Yet during a year of revolutionary strikes and petit bourgeois school board insurgencies, the intensity of the relationship between "the middle class," particularly its lower segment of small business owners and salaried white-collar employees, and those above and below them had not dampened. School Bill supporters, KKK kleagles, *Producer's Call* proponents, and Housewives' Council comrades shared one goal: to struggle in the political arena for their vision of a middle-class society. In the short term, School Bill advocates, and the thousands of voters who agreed with them—were the most successful, effectively transforming populism from an anticorporate radicalism to a liberalism that recognized, and then proceeded to blur, class distinctions. The creation of "middle-class classlessness" in Portland, then, did not occur at night behind closed lodge doors, accompanied by secret handshakes and jolly fraternal pats on the back. Rather, classlessness was an intensely public and political activity that actively, albeit ironically, involved substantial numbers of working-class people. This was hard work, full of contest; middle-class classlessness, even in America, has never come naturally. Nor was, or is, classlessness the only possible rhetoric of class available to those in the middle.

The triumph of the KKK and the School Bill was not only tentative, it was also temporary. Both died quick deaths. By 1923 Portland's Klan chapter was in disarray, the next year irreparably split, and by 1925 completely spent as a political force. That same year the United States Supreme Court, in the pathbreaking case of *Pierce v. Society of Sisters*, struck down the School Bill as a violation of religious freedom and familial choice. It thus became the province of politicians like Oregon governor Walter Pierce, who went on to become a staunch New Dealer in Congress, to create a synthesis of new and old politics, fighting corporate power with some of the surviving ideological resources of small-producer radicalism while accommodating to, as well as informing, modern liberalism.

There were few political heroes in 1920s America. We should certainly never forget that the movement for the School Bill demonstrates just how much middle-class insurgency in Portland had lost, since the heyday of the Oregon System, its democratic and egalitarian impulse to recreate the world. Still, the ability of populism to persist through a decade of such limited political possibilities, never coming close to succumbing to anything akin to fascism, proved crucial in allowing middle-class radicalism to redeem itself in more hopeful, and more democratic, times.[15]

PART VI

CONCLUSION

Populism, Capitalism, and the Politics of
the Twentieth-Century American Middle Class

> My husband doesn't have a college education, so he's a blue-collar
> worker. So he's got to kind of bust butt to get ahead.
> Unfortunately, we don't get a break. We're that middle class.
> —WOMAN FROM NEW JERSEY

> Most people do not have any idea how the median family lives.
> —CHRISTOPHER JENCKS, HARVARD UNIVERSITY, 1999

> To throw some light on discussions about the "people," . . . one
> need only bear in mind that the "people" . . . is first of all one of
> the things at stake in the struggle between intellectuals.
> —PIERRE BOURDIEU

Just one week after the compulsory public schooling initiative succeeded at
the polls, readers of the *Portland Telegram* had the opportunity to contem-
plate two of the most important ideological themes of twentieth-century
American class politics. What the newspaper's subscribers read flowed directly out of their own experience of local and national politics. The articulation of the dominant theme came in the editorial "Are You Producing?" Here
the *Telegram*'s editor declaimed against the large parasitical percentage of
Portland's population whose existence came from the productive labor of
others. Those who were "living by their wits" instead of through hard work
included all too many lying lawyers, duplicitous doctors, salaried lodge officials, "labor union parasites," and—of course—governmental officials.[1]

This language we can understand all too easily in our cramped and constrained political culture. We may not find the editor's explanation attractive
or compelling—he blamed, in classic republican fashion, the love of amuse-
ment and decadent luxury. If the rise of the Silent Majority and the subsequent Reagan Revolution accomplished anything, however, it was in reinstill-
ing into American politics this rhetoric of pseudoproducerism.

Yet the readers of the front page of the *Telegram* might have noticed a
different, though closely related, ideological foundation of contemporary politics. There a national dispatch told of the plans for the organization in Con-

gress of a "new progressive" or "people's bloc" to replace the narrow farmers' coalition. Led by insurgent Republicans like William Borah and Robert La Follette, this bloc would "stand for advancement of the interests of the farmer, of labor, of small merchants and of middle class workers."[2]

There, in plain language, is one of the primary but far-too-often suppressed realities of twentieth-century politics. For while the middling coalition that flowered in Progressive Era Portland substantially changed during the transition from direct democracy to the Ku Klux Klan, it no more disappeared after the 1920s than it vanished after the supposed dissolution of populism and effective anticorporate rebellion after 1896. We continue to live today in a world in which populist politics still in many ways sets a significant part of the agenda for our commonwealth. Millions of Americans use this populism to negotiate their identities as simultaneously "middle class" and "working class" while continuing to articulate a staunchly democratic, and at times even anticapitalist, political worldview. Thus the radical middle class in Progressive Era Portland, Oregon, becomes not merely an exotic archeological discovery, but—much more importantly—it becomes a lens through which we can glimpse our own current prospects. And perhaps even help restore our hope in a redemptive democratic politics.

CHAPTER TWENTY-ONE

THE LOWER MIDDLE CLASS IN THE AMERICAN CENTURY

Messing Up the Middle

Even as ardent a defender of the populist political heritage as Christopher Lasch believed that the heroic days of the radical middle class had largely passed by the end of the Progressive Era. Yet the reality is much more complicated. Once again, we can uncover our complex past only by moving away from staid stories of declension, finally fully acknowledging the tenacious political messiness of American ideas about the class structure. For example, the most important question about twentieth-century Americans' language of class is not its supposed absence but, according to historian Margo Anderson, why Americans characterize as "middle class" the great mass of people who by so many standards are working class. Yet we will not be able to proceed with this issue unless we first recognize just how mixed-up class categories became in twentieth-century America. When trying to fathom the meaning of the American middle class, confusion can, ironically, become clarity.[1]

As Anderson suggests, we might perhaps best explore this conundrum by trying to understand the rhetoric of prominent twentieth-century unionists. These men could have attempted to promulgate a language of class based on the category of labor, but instead the most prominent sounded the tocsin of consensus. Take CIO president Philip Murray, who argued in the midst of a huge strike wave, "We have no classes in this country; that's why the Marxist theory of class struggle has gained so few adherents. We're *all* workers here. And in the final analysis the interests of farmers, factory hands, business and professional people, and white-collar toilers prove to be the same."[2]

Does Murray's quote mean that the working class simply sold out, buying into the grand bazaar of consumption in Cold War America? This is a complication question. What scholars particularly need to recognize is that the ideas of "middle class" among working people have often significantly diverged from those of most intellectuals. As Anderson demonstrates, the terms *middle class* and *labor* are commonly intertwined in the minds of the American public. White-collar "public employees, teachers, nurses, as well as auto workers, construction workers, and teamsters feel themselves to be both part of the 'labor' movement and part of the middle class." Anderson, although unable to explain this combination, wisely understands that this represents not a contradiction, or false consciousness, but rather a genuine attempt by the mass of Americans to explain their distinctive middling social situation.[3]

Thus Philip Murray was not merely voicing a simplistic vision of "class-lessness" while combating foreign radicalism. He was also rearticulating the nineteenth-century producers' alliance. Here Michael Kazin's analysis of the language of the United States labor movement is useful. Kazin maintains that since the late 1800s the leaders of labor have resolutely refused to speak a vocabulary of class that would have little meaning for them or their followers. Rather, they have spoken in the name of "the broad middle of the polity, 'the people.' Located above this 'hard-working' majority were lazy and/or exploitative businessmen, large property owners, and others who did not labor honestly; while below was a lower class mired in criminality and poverty, for reasons only partly attributable to economic injustice." Even seasoned business unionists like George Meany and Walter Reuther continued to express antielitist sentiments that had their ideological roots in the Knights of Labor and the Populists, who "equated civic virtue with the broad middle class of 'producers,' particularly small farmers, craftsmen and shopkeepers."[4]

Anderson and Kazin help us grasp, then, just how much middle-class politics and culture throughout the twentieth century remained intimately connected with the prospects and struggles of the working class. Middle-class radicalism may rarely have been as powerful as in Progressive Era Portland. Yet the ways such populism helped to create a powerful modern American lower middle class by combining and reworking working- and middle-class identities by no means stopped with the start of the Great War, much less with the demise of the Ku Klux Klan. Rather, we should see—in one of the great continuities of American history—how our country's deep strain of egalitarian politics has been continually nourished by an always potentially subversive middling-class consciousness, from the Anti-Federalist period to the present.[5]

Sociologists on the American Lower Middle Class

Historians have almost completely ignored the problem of the relationship between the working class and the middle class. What historians have decided not to see, though, sociologists have written about in abundance, understanding that a politically constituted lower middle class has played a central role in American politics and social life. The best of this sociological work has come in the course of intensive studies of specific communities and business firms. We can mark the inauguration of scholarly consideration of the relationship between petite bourgeoisie and proletariat with the 1955 publication of Eli Chinoy's classic *Automobile Workers and the American Dream*. This study revealed a great yearning for small business ownership among mass-production employees at the height of the postwar economic boom, even if not many workers acted on their dreams. Chinoy remarked, "Paradoxically, the very process of alienation which Marx thought would transform industrial workers into class-conscious proletarians has instead stimulated their interest in small business and in small-scale private farming, institutions of capitalist society which Marx asserted were doomed to extinction." General Motors might have been in charge of the American Century, but the petite bourgeoisie wrote some of the era's most compelling hidden transcripts.[6]

Several years later Bennett Berger returned to the problem of the supposedly transformed lives of the postwar industrial working class, again focusing on autoworkers. His main interest lay in workers moving to suburbia and the extent to which this made them members of the middle class. The conclusions that Berger derived make his modest study one of the most brilliant but overlooked pieces of postwar social scientific literature.[7]

Berger returns us to the intricacies, and perhaps the impossibilities, of class categorization. His workers split fairly evenly in their class identification between working class and middle class, with one subject's "revealingly paradoxical comment" particularly relevant: "around here, the working class *is* the middle class." Berger made it clear that proletarians had ideas of middle-class-ness considerably different from cultural tastemakers. "To be 'middle class,' then, probably means to them not what sociologists mean by middle class, but rather *middle of the working class*," Berger wrote. This was the world of their possibilities as well as their hopes. Foremen, small business owners, and lower white-collar workers represented "the upper limit of their aspirational framework," while "the 'upper' middle class, white-collar worlds of engineers, junior executives, professionals, and would-be professionals are completely beyond their ken; this latter milieu is alien to them, beyond their limits of possibility." The age of the great American middle class, in other words, saw the development of at least two middle classes, with barely any mutual comprehension—but with a great potential for antagonism once the postwar consensus faded.[8]

Three excellent ethnographies from the mid-1980s further delineate the contours of the lower middle class, the relationship between the middle class and the working class, and the powerful and hard-edged populism of the middling bloc. Most compellingly, the sociologists David Halle, Jonathan Rieder, and Robert Zussman show the centrality of politics to the consciousness and life of those in the middle. They also confirm that no serious intellectual or politician can continue to ignore the influence of the lower middle class on American public life. In small worlds carefully examined we can thus see the continued, if subterranean, influence of the radical middle class.

In his study of northern New Jersey chemical workers, David Halle most explicitly takes on the entire range of intellectual problems surrounding the connection between the American middle class and the working class. Halle seeks to understand just how much the industrial blue-collar working class overlaps with both the lower and upper sectors of the white-collar middle class and, in a separate but related inquiry, how much the working class is integrated into an American political consensus.

Halle's findings require examining class on three distinct levels. On the job, at the point of production, he finds clear evidence of fairly traditional class consciousness. These chemical plant workers do not conceive of themselves as members of "the working class," but do very strongly as "working men." The class identity of the workers at the chemical plant "distinguishes them from big business and from the upper- and lower-white-collar sectors" and "implies serious moral criticism of the system of production under capitalism." Yet when workers leave their jobs behind—which they are more than willing to do—a whole new range of visions of class appear. *Outside* of work, the chemical plant employees' "identity centers on concepts such as being 'middle class' and 'lower middle class.' It implies a set of links with people at a certain income range and standard of living." Furthermore, when these workers do think of *class*, they think first and fundamentally of this consumption-oriented middle-class dimension to their lives.[9]

Such middle-class awareness in no ways represents a triumph of consensus. Many if not most of the workers feel that the middle class is getting "squeezed" or "screwed." The culprits are clear: the rich and the poor. As Halle remarks, "while they perceive the *middle* of this class structure as a graduated hierarchy, most perceive the top as a system of economic power that in many ways subverts and dominates political power." Homeownership is the centerpiece of middle-class and lower-middle class life, and taxation that "big business" enforces and hands over to those unwilling to work is its chief threat. Halle finds this "populism," which includes the attitude that major corporations run the country and that all politicians are out to exploit the people, so strong that he labels it as "a third class identity."[10]

Halle realizes that his findings have direct relevance for contemporary politics. He acknowledges the strains of racism, nativism, and exclusionary attitudes toward the poor among the chemical workers. Yet he finds that these middling folks could go the other way. For example, given the high level of "class conflict" on the job, the possibility exists of an alliance between blue-collar workers and lower-level (conceivably even upper-level) white-collar workers against employers. The "politics of homeownership" so important to these workers will likewise draw them into alliances with a broad range of those in the middle. And these members of "the middle class or lower middle class" base their politics not on inherently reactionary premises, but rather on the perspective of "an extreme democrat." Even if some intellectuals would like to see in them the harbingers of fascism, these workers, despite their many flaws, have no use whatsoever for anything resembling dictatorship. Rather, their "classic democratic vision" is one where the will of the people is carried out in an unmediated manner. Thus it should not be surprising that one of Halle's workers came close to endorsing William U'Ren's plan for occupational representation:

> Agh! Business run the country. It always has. . . . [Busing is] a General Motors conspiracy. . . .
>
> What we need is a parliament that is representative. There are too many lawyers. There are about six doctors in Congress, but how many welders are there? We need a Congress with people who will represent the working man.[11]

Robert Zussman, in turn, looks at the other side of the collar divide in his study of engineers in two New England firms. Zussman's concern is to investigate the new middle class, which he calls "loosely the 'middle levels.'" Despite the professionalism of his subjects, he comes to conclusions strikingly similar to those of Halle. Zussman's "accountants, technicians, officials, administrators, and middle managers of all sorts who work as salaried employees in industry and government" and who form "the upper reaches of white-collar employment" now constitute about a quarter of the working population. Classical class differences remain salient at the workplace, but have come to matter much less in the nonproduction realms such as residence, consumption, and citizenship. Here engineers place themselves firmly in "the middle class," although that term again demands redefinition to fit the self-conceptions of ordinary Americans. As Zussman states: "this is not a middle between capital and labor. Rather, to adopt the variant a few of the engineers used, it is a "working middle class," a broad middle between the extremes of independent wealth and dependent poverty. . . . Most important, it is a middle that includes blue-collar as well as white-collar workers."[12]

Thus Zussman chooses in the end to adopt the category of some of the engineers to describe them as a whole: they are a "working middle class." He admits that this term is "jarring" and that some will be tempted "to dismiss the idea of a working middle class as little more than an example of bourgeois false consciousness, a gloss on persistent inequalities between the middle levels and the working class." Yet the realities of property taxes, schooling, and welfare state institutions have provided the material basis for a potentially powerful alliance between working and middling folks, anchored in homeownership and suspicious of those below and above them in the class structure.[13]

With Jonathan Rieder's study of the Jews and Italians of the Brooklyn neighborhood Canarsie, we move beyond abstract categories to the flesh and blood of the recent politics of what Rieder often calls "the middle-income classes." Here is where we can most concretely see the survival of lower-middle-class populist ideologies even among those whose ancestors had not arrived on these shores during the Populist insurgency. If anyone doubts that our era is a time of true and bitter "middle-class consciousness," Rieder's *Canarsie* will immediately dispel such a notion.

Rieder speaks frankly and casually of his subjects as lower middle class. He frequently notes their marginal white-collar occupations and incomes. Writing of the "cramped quality of lower middle-class life," Rieder declares, "The basic fact of life for the residents of Canarsie was the precariousness of their hold on middle-class status." Their own self-identification is equally clear. As Rieder puts it, "Canarsians did not identify with the Olympian heights of the professional upper middle classes." One Canarsie woman marking herself off from her fellow residents spoke this way of the gradations of status within her neighborhood:

> I would say I'm middle and not lower middle class. I'm different because I'm educated. I'd say the middle class is more snobbish. Take my brother. He lives in Great Neck, and he looks down on Canarsie, because the people are lower middle class and uneducated.[14]

The lives that these people experienced as the result of the social movements of the 1960s and the 1970s were ones of torment and travail. Previously at the heart of the New Deal coalition, Canarsie's white ethnics turned heartily to backlash politics, with their sense of themselves as middle-class victims at the heart of their consciousness. "Canarsie is up against the wall. That's what the lower middle and middle classes feel pressing on them." A conservative Democrat spoke explicitly in class-conscious terms: "It's okay to talk about the welfare classes, but the real problem is the middle-class squeeze. You get it from top and bottom. It's not only the welfare, but the multinational corporations who are ripping us off, taking our jobs away and sending employment to the South and the West. The middle classes are the lost people."[15]

What do we make of all of this? Rieder presents considerable racism and selfishness, and so we have to be less than hopeful about these developments in middle-class political life. Most of the time Rieder himself formulates this issue the old-fashioned way, asking if we can detect in all this talk "an ominous harbinger of fascism" and giving Lipset's "classic formulation" of right-wing populist extremism a respectful hearing. Yet Rieder also notes another little-noticed dimension of lower-middle-class populism. An Italian police officer, for instance, spoke of his neighbors' lack of Christian compassion during the busing crisis. He got very angry at a congressional candidate who exalted "the white middle class." As the cop put it:

> The phrase "white middle class" is a racist statement to me. Of course it's okay for blacks to move next door. The question is one of intrusion and the problems that come with the intruders, not because they are black, but because they are not middle class. That goes for everything between black and white. This is primarily a

class struggle, and the people of Canarsie are trying to save what they have. They are trying to remain middle class.

Statements like these lead Rieder to contend that a "strain of biracial populism, a local version of the national black and white coalition assembled by Jimmy Carter in 1976, remained a submerged yet latent and probably growing current in Canarsie life."[16]

More programmatically, Rieder notes, "An alliance of middle-income blacks and whites might not remedy the plight of the black underclasses; it risked replacing the meanness of race with the meanness of class. But at least the common interests between the races could provide a foundation on which to reconstruct a politics of generosity." He emphasizes how quickly Canarsie's backlash played itself out, and how impermanent was the move toward conservatism upon the part of these lower-middle-class ethnics. The other half of the equation, and one that Rieder presses hard in his analysis, is that the lower middle class did not just give up on egalitarianism, but that Democratic Party activists consciously deserted middling folks. In the process, these "left-liberals abandoned much of the traditional base" of the party as their ideology "hardened into an orthodoxy of the privileged classes."[17]

If any moral comes out of the sophisticated sociological studies of Rieder, Zussman, and Halle, it is that in many ways America still has a politicized class structure that continues to strongly resemble the populist republican political economy of a century before. Far from being an atypical Pacific outpost, Progressive Era Portland then instead becomes a crucial key for deciphering the politics of class at the dawn of the twenty-first century. Obviously the relationship between middling folks and working people remains highly complex. Still, we can, indeed must, see the potential for a solid alliance between—and even a partial merging—of working class and middle class, anchored in populism.

The Revival of the Petite Bourgeoisie

When looking for a typical member of the lower middle class today, one thinks of a salesman like Willy Loman, or perhaps a homeowning factory operative like Archie Bunker. The lowly white-collar worker and the prosperous skilled worker have for many replaced the independent business owner as the core symbol of the American middle class. Still, we should remember that Archie Bunker eventually opened his own bar. Figures such as this should help us realize that even the petite bourgeoisie, which served as the fundamental anchor of an earlier populist political economy, has failed to disappear from the American social and political landscape.

No study illustrates this better than George Steinmetz and Erik Wright's remarkable 1989 examination of self-employment in the postwar era. Steinmetz and Wright (the latter, the foremost Marxist theoretician of class in America) are upfront about what *should* have happened to the petite bourgeoisie according in orthodox Marxist theories: sickness unto death. Self-employment has of course declined considerably since the nineteenth century, when the proportion of the self-employed in the workforce reached nearly 42 percent in 1870 and 1880. That figure now stands at between 10 and 15 percent, but Steinmetz and Wright convincingly argue that, given the common predictions of the fate of the petite bourgeoisie, these figures are "indeed high." What is most striking, though, is not just the persistence of this class, but even more "the rise of the petite bourgeoisie" since 1976. The historic pattern has been reversed, and the rate of self-employment in the economy is climbing, as much as 15 to 20 percent in less than one decade. This is in large part the result of sectoral changes toward a postindustrial service economy, but older industrial areas have also witnessed the increase. Self-employment in European industrial nations has either held steady or increased as well.[18]

Steinmetz and Wright do not even attempt to describe the historical trajectory of "small business"—a much larger category. They do note, however, that "most small employers are indeed very small—in 1980 over 50 percent of all employers employed fewer than five employees." They also fail to disaggregate their statistics between the agricultural and nonagricultural sector, a task crucial if one is to chart the historical patterning of urban class relations. As I showed earlier, American nonfarm self-employment was 12.6 percent in 1880, a figure very similar to Steinmetz and Wright's inclusive calculations for a century later. That figure declined to 8.9 percent by 1920. The slow strangulation of family farming, therefore, may have masked even more of a tale of nonagricultural petit bourgeois survival and revival than even Steinmetz and Wright realize.

The implications of the endurance, and increase, of self-employment are enormous. As Steinmetz and Wright recognize, being one's own boss remains a "deeply held ideal in American culture" and "is not a complete fantasy." Besides the approximately one-tenth of the population that is currently self-employed, an additional one in six members of the labor force (one in five for men) has at some time been self-employed. Therefore, "at least a quarter of the total labor force, and a third of the male labor force, either is or has been self-employed." Simply comparing those figures to contemporary rates of unionization makes it easy to see how academics' romance with the labor movement can in critical ways obscure our vision of the class structure. And by adding in parents and close friends, that figure pushes up to two-thirds of Americans who have a strong "personal linkage" to self-employment. Two-thirds. These numbers are not mere abstractions. They represent the overwhelming *majority* of Americans whom historians have abandoned, or more accurately, never thought it worth the effort to get to know.[19]

Once we abandon our tropes of declension—whether they involve the decline of the petite bourgeoisie, the uprooting of populism, or the fall of the middle class—we can turn to much more substantive questions. What, then, might the history of middling folks tell us about our continuing hopes for a renewed democratic future? And might we even use the surprising survival of the petite bourgeoisie in our own day to bring back to the table the relationship between small property and moral economy? Do we dare even now reopen the Question of Capitalism?[20]

CHAPTER TWENTY-TWO

THE FATE OF POPULISM

Moral Economy and the Resurgence
of Middle-Class Politics

The Moral Economy of the Twentieth-Century
American Middle Class

The petite bourgeoisie has survived the vigorous attempts by modern intellectuals to kill it. Despite occasional flare-ups, however, its anticapitalism was
eclipsed as an oppositional ideology during the American Century of growth-
oriented welfare state corporate capitalism, from roughly the 1930s through
the 1960s. For example, Alan Brinkley has convincingly established the
exhaustion of Huey Long and Charles Coughlin's populist ideas during
the 1930s, and he has also effectively explored the foreclosure of the antimonopoly ideal at the level of federal New Deal policy. The depression set
the example for the rest of the Fordist era, when the most severe conflicts
over political economy became struggles over the extent of government and
union control over corporations—not whether those economic behemoths
were legitimate in the first place.[1]

Still, we must keep in mind that historians have not been interested in the
actual ideas about capitalism that the mass of Americans held during the
twentieth century. Even at the height of the corporate era, it turns out, petit
bourgeois concerns continued to energize workers' political responses, including some of the most left-leaning. Lizabeth Cohen, for example, has
shown in her study of interwar Chicago that immigrant workers who turned
to the CIO and the New Deal sought a "moral capitalism." Much of their
economic vision originated from the welfare capitalism of the 1920s, but
Cohen also shrewdly remarks that "long-standing expectations about America, particularly workers' own desire to acquire property" proved crucial to
these workers' politicization. Even the famous *Fortune* pollsters who so
proudly claimed in 1940 that all Americans were middle-class at the same
time emphatically argued that "nothing could be more false than the idea
that U.S. ambition, as of the year 1940, vaults beyond the hopes of a modest
competence. The man on the street wants more income than he has, but no
more than that of many a government clerk."[2]

Now that we have passed into the "post-Fordist" era, and as the legitimacy of
corporations has returned as an important political issue, petit bourgeois ideals

have again begun to animate significant economic criticism. Michael Walzer, for example, has written compellingly of the essential justice of petit bourgeois economic activity and its accompanying culture of competence. More broadly, various political theorists have pointed to a line of philosophers, ranging from John Stuart Mill to John Rawls, who have upheld a "property-owning democracy" as the fairest and most egalitarian economic system possible. Richard Krouse, Michael McPherson, and Jonathan Riley persuasively argue that the most just economy is one that uses markets to allocate *earned* reward but that assures, especially through steep inheritance taxes and the confiscation of unearned rent from natural resources (particularly land), that members of each generation begin with a relatively equal set of property holdings. Such an "egalitarian market society" would be far superior to the liberal welfare state, which tolerates gross inequalities of property and then seeks to redistribute wealth—almost always in the most mild of fashions. Indeed, although one could characterize their ideal kind of economy as, in Riley's words, a "classless version of capitalism where most are at once workers and owners of capital," Krouse and McPherson persuasively argue, in our endless terminological debate, that a system that prevents the "division of society into propertied and propertyless classes" is fundamentally *anticapitalist*.[3]

Nor are such utopias unattainable. In terms of cultural attitudes, "The distinction between 'earned' and 'unearned' incomes is loaded with more ethical content in our culture than the contrast between high and low incomes." Even though this statement was written by scholars nearly half a century ago, I strongly suspect that this moral vision continues to hold, potentially serving as a resource for a more just economy and not just for blind opposition to welfare queens. In the material realm, Charles Sabel, Michael Piore, and Jonathan Zeitlin have created something of a school of political economy that has demonstrated the economic viability of small-scale production within flourishing, democratic economic networks. Historically, Sabel and Zeitlin reconstruct and rehabilitate a craft-based alternative to mass production, an alternative that had impressively strong roots in various cities and regions throughout the nineteenth-century transatlantic world. Flexibility and constant innovation in specialized production formed the foundation for a labor process that revolved around skilled workers. High wages flowed to these firms' employees, with owners and workers often attaining a solidarity difficult for us to imagine as part of business relations. And despite the many defeats this small-scale alternative met at the hands of both capitalist and social democratic advocates of a mass-production economy, it did not disappear but merely went underground, showing a remarkable resurgence since the 1970s. Especially strong in western Europe, "flexible specialization," or "small firm networks," provide a contemporary living model of what Michel Albert has aptly characterized as "Capitalism against Capitalism."[4]

And, as counterintuitive as it may seem in the era of Bill Gates and the juggernaut of globalization, we should bring our visions of political economic contingency up to the current day. Clearly, the present-day American populace is no seething hotbed of anticapitalist radicalism, nor—despite the battle in Seattle and the implosion of Enron—will the masses storm the barricades any time soon. On the other hand, citizens of the United States have far from given up on economic justice, even if the political space in which they can express their visions has considerably shrunk in past decades. Americans are, and will likely always be, firmly attached to most of the institutional components of a market economy, as loath as leftists are to admit this. Yet, to discomfort those on the right, this does not mean that capitalism will have a free ride in the future. Perhaps far from it, we can expect—as well as hope.

As the political theorist Richard Ellis has argued, "although Americans are overwhelmingly committed to the institution of private property, they are deeply divided about what constitutes a fair distribution of private property and whether the community should decide how the individual disposes of that property." Political scientists Herbert McClosky and John Zaller, in the most systematic survey of the public's attitudes toward capitalism, are much more convinced of the power of the liberal tradition than Ellis. Still, even they—writing at the height of the Reagan era—note the "ambivalence with which the craving for wealth is regarded." Americans, they contend, have "always harbored values that tended to keep the quest for profit within certain limits." The economic motivation of a great majority derives from the idea of a competence, as "Seventy percent of the general public say that security is more important to them than advancement." And petit bourgeois utopias still inform the day-to-day economic ideas of ordinary Americans. As McClosky and Zaller put it: "Questions rarely arise about the social desirability of the small, individually owned or family business, such as a neighborhood store or small manufacturing plant; but as a business grows and takes on the characteristics of 'big business' and large-scale capitalism, it awakens anxieties among many Americans. . . . Thus, for example, when Americans are asked whether business has 'too much power' in American life, only about 35 percent say yes. But when they are asked about 'big business,' the figure rises to 82 percent. The term *capitalism* itself seems even less well regarded."[5]

Ambivalence and subterranean utopias may be a difficult basis upon which to build an effective social movement. Yet those genuinely interested in economic justice must not give up on the middle class, and its petit bourgeois visions. Middling folks continue to have an extremely complex relationship to capitalism, one very much worth understanding, and building upon.

Alan Wolfe has most compellingly made this argument. In a systematic set of in-depth interviews with suburbanites, Wolfe has discovered that middle-class people are fairly implacable enemies of what passes for contemporary capitalism. They seek what he characterizes as a "balanced capitalism," where people can combine work, family, and community responsibilities in a moral way. Tellingly, middle-class folks have in their heart a "soft spot for unions," even if they view them as largely irrelevant, and they are "increasingly hostile to corporations." During the depression, only a quarter of the population refused to affirm a basic commonality of interest between employer and employee, but according to Wolfe, "By 1994, when unions and class consciousness were in steep decline, the percentage of those who believed that employers and employees had opposite interests had increased to 45 percent, while those who thought they were the same had decreased to 40 percent. There are, many middle-class Americans believe, no alternatives to capitalism. But a form of capitalism that sets up individuals in situations of intense conflict with each other is corrosive of the ideal of a society in which people are understood to share a common fate." Almost none of Wolfe's interviewees want to get rich, because "wide-scale differences in pay" violate "a moral as well as an economic ideal. . . . Too much wealth is like too much of anything else: a bad thing." Wolfe concludes: "Support in America for a conception of capitalism that includes a prominent role for economic justice is remarkably broad and is as likely to be shared by conservative Christians as by East Coast liberals."[6]

Wolfe has the intellectual bravery to break out of the social misconstruction of reality that has so hindered our view of the relationship between the middle class and capitalism. We have, at last, a vivid portrait of the fin de siècle moral economy of the middle. Petit bourgeois radicalism it may not exactly be. Yet we can be confident that, in some complex fashion, the American moral economy in the twenty-first century is the *legacy* of the many struggles that have informed middling folks' quest for an ideal economy in past times.

In this way, Revolutionary Era farmers, small-scale nineteenth-century "capitalists against capitalism," the Populists, and even the Portland single taxers still speak compellingly to us in the present—if we will listen. As historians, we need to understand these connections in a much more systematic fashion. As citizens, we need to recognize how ethically compelling and politically powerful the moral economy remains, not just in the margins of American life—there it continually renews itself—but also in the very middle-class mainstream where Hartz, Tocqueville, and so many other brilliant intellectuals have told us that the Question of Capitalism is forever closed.[7]

The Prospects of Populism

Despite capitalism's great triumphs during the decade, the 1990s saw a return of the radical middle class to the center of national politics. Populist discourse, flowing out of a conflictual idea of "the middle class," not only inspired influential challenges to the two-party system; in various forms it proved to be the very lifeblood of the decade's presidential campaigns. Bill Clinton announced his attention to "the forgotten middle class," Al Gore and Joe Lieberman promised to fight for the hard-working middle class, and George W. Bush took office with a "Blueprint for the Middle Class." Yet despite the many ways that these appeals meshed with the most mainstream, even banal, of American values, the candidates' invocation of the middle class did not mean a simple capitulation to well-off and well-educated white suburban voters comfortably wired into the New Economy. Rather, the revival—by even the top figures of the political establishment—of the middle class as a contested political category reveals how fundamentally the American political realm at the turn of the twenty-first century continues to play out patterns of class and democracy established at the eighteenth-century founding. In so many essential ways, the fate of democratization in our country remains a matter of the political choices made by those in the always potentially radical middle.

The idea of the middle class, linked with the working class in a grand alliance against elites, had a difficult time after the Progressive Era. But the radical middle by no means died out. In 1934 agrarian insurgent Lynn Frazier, senator from North Dakota, complained about discrimination against "working people, farmers, and small business men." Even as proletarian an agitator as John L. Lewis declared in 1939 that "the millions of organized workers banded together in the CIO are the main driving force of the progressive movement of workers, farmers, professional and small business people and of all other liberal elements in the community." As populist resentments degenerated during the era of Joe McCarthy, however, public expressions of a coalition of productive middling and working people largely disappeared. The heyday of growth-oriented politics much more easily produced a classless vision, particularly one that spoke of the embourgeoisification of the working class under the benevolent rule of corporate elites. Insofar as populists spoke of the middle class, they tended to give that category an exclusivist construction, as in the complaint even before World War II from one of William Borah's constituents about liberal social legislation: "Is this doctrine of class hatred to go on until the great middle class, which really constitutes the backbone of the country, is to be submerged, and labor and the have-nots are the only ones to receive consideration at the hands of the government?"[8]

That spirit of exclusion maintained considerable strength during the revival of populism in 1968 and after, as the poster politician for the crusading masses became George Wallace. With a vengeance, Wallace rekindled the language of the radical middle class. Wallace thundered about how "the destruction of the middle class is a big thing." "Rising taxes and inflation were the scourges of the middle class, who carried on their backs the non-producers and welfare loafers," wrote Wallace; "middle-class stability and hard work had produced the social health of the nation." On *Meet the Press*, Wallace told of politicians soon to be steamrolled "by this average man on the street, this man in the textile mill, this man in the steel mill, this barber, this beautician, the policeman on the beat . . . and the little businessmen." At a 1972 Tallahassee rally, Wallace asserted that "we're sick and tired of the average citizen being taxed to death while these multibillionaires like the Rockefellers and the Fords and the Mellons and the Carnegies go without paying taxes. . . . We've got to close up these loopholes on those who've escaped paying their fair share so we can lower taxes for the average citizen—the little businessman, the farmer, the elderly, the middle class."[9]

The 1990s witnessed a reintensification of this language of class, with conservatives taking great advantage of the reawakening of populist upset. Celebrating the Republican takeover of Congress in the 1994 elections, Ross Perot said that "the working class, the folks who work for a living, the middle class, the people who make this country go have taken their country back." It is Pat Buchanan, of course, who has done the most to stir up the body politic in recent years. When asked on CNN who exactly *were* his peasants with pitchforks, he replied, "working class, middle class folks who don't have any voice in Washington." The Republicans needed to reclaim "the middle class and working class who don't have lobbyists on K Street or on Capitol Hill"; the GOP had to become a "more inclusive party, more middle-class, working-class, small business rather than so beholden to these corporations." Even echoing Lora Little, Buchanan declared that "wisdom is not to be found in the think tanks or the experts but in the experience of the people."[10]

So we have traveled from the Anti-Federalists to Pat Buchanan: from tragedy to farce (or worse)? Scholars such as Michael Kazin and Catherine McNicol Stock have written eloquently of the noxious nativism and patriarchal imperatives that have so often fueled populism. Yet the standard view on the academic liberal-left, that at least twentieth-century populism was *inherently* racist and sexist is, I think, far from proven. Prominent pundits such as Thomas and Mary Edsall, Kevin Phillips, and E. J. Dionne have made the compelling case that both liberals and the Left purposefully abandoned middling folks and their populist languages of class. As Dionne has put it, starting in the 1960s "many liberals even lost faith in their own political base, the broad middle classes whom Democrats once proudly referred to as 'the working people.' They came to believe that 'populism' was only something that hucksters such as George Wallace engaged in. The slogan 'trust the people,' once a liberal sentiment, fell to George Wallace and the right by default."[11]

Therefore, we should view the future of American populism as contingent, with little—indeed nothing—inherently reactionary about it, and with much depending on the hard work of political activism. We can confirm this by looking at the more generous, if still problematic, uses of the term *middle class* during the 1990s, up to and including the fateful 2000 election. Take the flawed master of end-of-the-century politics, William Jefferson Clinton. While wrapping himself in the mantle of centrism, Clinton accepted the Democratic nomination in 1992 "in the name of all those who do the work, pay the taxes, raise the kids and play by the rules—in the name of the hard-working Americans who make up our forgotten middle class." Clinton proclaimed, "I am a product of that middle class," proudly recalling his mother's struggles to become a nurse and, even more, his grandfather's country store in the town of Hope. Noting that his grandfather dispensed credit to hard-working poor folks without regard to race, Clinton appealed emphatically to the most broad-minded petit bourgeois egalitarianism:

> My grandfather had a grade-school education. But in that country store he taught me more about equality in the eyes of the Lord than all my professors at Georgetown; more about the intrinsic worth of every individual than all the philosophers at Oxford, and he taught me more about the need for equal justice than all the jurists at Yale Law School. You want to know where I get my commitment to bringing people together without regard to race? It all started with my grandfather.[12]

Clinton then warned "the forces of greed and the defenders of the status quo: your time has come . . . and gone." After his election, and when his political fortunes looked bleakest in the wake of the 1994 triumph of Newt Gingrich and the Republican Contract with America, Clinton rebounded with a set of tax cuts and incentives labeled a "Middle Class Bill of Rights."[13]

Clinton's gentle, and ultimately perhaps even disingenuous, populist rhetoric did not translate into many successful proposals or policies. It did, however, provide a template for much of the political rhetoric of the 2000 election. That election, in turn, demonstrated how solidly anchored was the return of the populist middle class in the mainstream American electoral landscape. We might even say that the twentieth century had in some ways turned full circle, beginning with an insurgent Progressive radical middle class, and ending with—at the very least—substantial echoes of a working middle class at the heart of political rhetoric.

Take Al Gore's bid for the White House, which ultimately generated populist language more hard-edged than Clinton's had ever been. In terms of policy Gore focused, in a fairly conventional manner, offering "tax cuts for the middle-class families." Yet his rhetoric edged toward the classic radical populist formulation, coming as close to linking up with the proletariat as an establishment politician of our era is likely to get. He vowed to "fight for middle-class families and working men and women" and argued that those who have "the hardest time paying taxes, the hardest time making ends

meet" are "the working men and women of this country, middle-class families." By the last days of the campaign, Gore predicted that George W. Bush's
tax plan would lead to "a massive redistribution of wealth from the middle
class to the wealthiest few. It is in fact a form of class warfare on behalf of
billionaires."[14]

Al Gore won the majority of citizenry over to his "mellowed-out version"
of populism, with its lack of any radical policy prescriptions. Yet, due to the
Federalist electoral structure, he lost out to a candidate who courted the
middle class more aggressively than any Republican candidate since Richard
Nixon. George W. Bush promulgated, in his most important domestic policy
statement, a "Blueprint for the Middle Class." Repudiating Gore's "class warfare," Bush instead sought to lay out a milder "agenda for middle America,
which is sometimes overlooked in our national debate." His "real plans for
real people" focused on a "cradle to grave" program of Social Security reform,
prescription drug benefits, and above all increased educational opportunities
and tax reductions. Bush did at times use class language: "my tax cut helps
the middle class and hard-working families." His goal, though, was not to
question the class system, but rather "to increase access to the middle class
for hard-working families."[15]

George W. Bush's victory did not represent a triumph of the radical middle
class. Yet the level of middle-class talk, and middle-class upset, during the
last three presidential elections—culminating in Bush's presidency—discloses how American politics has been reoriented toward a genuine engagement with what we might call middle-class class conflict. Such conflict
comes in many different forms, ranging from the entirely rhetorical, to a
seeking after a hypercentrist "radical middle," to a struggle to deepen American democracy through a substantive critique of corporate power, economic
inequality, and the decline of citizen power.[16]

Ralph Nader's candidacy represented this kind of truly democratic populism. At the speech announcing his candidacy, Nader reached back to the
history of the radical middle to explain how abolitionists, rebellious farmers,
and unionists "helped mightily to make America and its middle class what it
is today." Nader envisioned a middle class consisting primarily not of wired
stock-holding soccer moms and latte-drinking bourgeois bohemians, but
rather of workers on the edge, linked to those below them. As in days of old,
Nader promised to "break the grip of today's oligarchs" who "subordinate
democracy to plutocracy." His goal, however, went well beyond romantic
proletarianism, to reinvigoration of the middle class through "innovations
helping to disperse ownership and establish local control over local wealth."
Quoting Jefferson and Brandeis on the need to tame the money power,
Nader called for "a renewed commitment to wider ownership of capital resources and a subordination of manic mercantilism to democratic values."
The result of this "new populism"—this middle class moral economy—

would be a "deep democracy" where the participation of ordinary citizens would flourish.[17]

Nader received a minuscule—albeit in the end crucial—2.7 percent of the vote. How do we reckon with this meager electoral tally? Does it mean that populism has spiked and has begun a decline as we enter a new age of political stability? I doubt it. The great public disenchantment over government, and elites in general, means at the very least that the present remains an era pregnant with political possibilities—populist or otherwise. That Nader indirectly pushed even George W. Bush to talk about middle-class egalitarianism points to an opposite conclusion: that, quite likely, middle-class radicalism has become an important structural part of the mainstream of American national politics. In all likelihood populism will suffer defeat after defeat, at least as conventionally defined. Yet it, and angry and anxious middle-class concerns more generally, will persist. Today's moderates will view such populism as a chronic backache, hoping it will go away but probably learning, in the style of Al Gore, to deal with it at a rhetorical level. Meanwhile many on both the left and the right will hope that populism will supply the swing votes necessary to further their quite different antiestablishment goals. Populism, then, has joined liberalism and conservatism as fundamental parts of our political mosaic.[18]

We should still ask, though: would we even want more middle-class populism if we could get it? Above all, this book has sought to show that the middle-class populist legacy contains within it one of the great American traditions of political, economic, social, and even intellectual democratization. Still, one of the momentous unresolved questions about populism is whether it can support a program of full racial emancipation at a time of heightened conflict over issues such as affirmative action and immigration. More generally, can a political philosophy premised on the expansion of majoritarianism ever truly grasp the oppression of minorities? Certainly Ralph Nader's unwillingness to speak out forcefully on racial issues does not offer much hope for the rapid resolution of this primal populist dilemma, although his candidacy deserves much credit for effectively neutralizing, at least in the short term, the bigoted populism of Pat Buchanan. If, however, we look to the past, the career of Harry Lane reminds us of how our history includes heroic, if lonely, figures who have been able to connect racial and economic populism to produce a genuinely inclusive middle-class radicalism. And in any case, whether we like it or not, we have no other choice than to trust that middling folks will, ultimately, respond to egalitarian appeals. Bill Clinton eloquently, if defensively, noted this during his first presidential campaign. At the same meeting where Clinton denounced Sister Souljah, a member of Jesse Jackson's Rainbow Coalition asked him: "how can you reassure us that appeals to the, quote, 'middle class' is not a new code word for avoiding the issue of racial justice?" Clinton responded, "If trying to restore the middle class in this country is a code word for racism, we are in deep trouble. We might as well fold our tent and go home."[19]

A considerably different criticism of traditional populism is that it foments class antagonism at the expense of more universal political ideals. Stanley Greenberg and Theda Skocpol adopt this perspective in *The New Majority: Toward a Popular Progressive Politics*, a collection that advocates instead a "family populism" that might unite "middle-class and less-privileged working families in a broad, winning electoral alliance." Like so many northeastern academics and beltway insiders, Skocpol and Greenberg hope to have a well-controlled and genteel populism, one that accomplishes what its masters seek without rocking the boat *too* much. Yet as attractive as their vision of a new majority is, it seems doubtful that progressive politics will move forward without unleashing some of the bitterness and intensity of middle-class class conflict. Whether that can happen within the Democratic Party is an excellent question; whether or not the Democratic Party can continue with its modest post-Reagan comeback without turning to class seems unlikely.[20]

In turn, effective class appeals must be truly innovative, moving well beyond standard categories and assumptions. Above all, advocates of a renewed class politics in America will need to embrace the middle class, as strange as that seems in the preeminent land of middle-class classlessness. Those on the left still dream of bringing together what Michael Zweig has recently characterized as "the working class majority." As with so many Marxists, Zweig is able to shrink the middle class with a wave of the magic wand of objective sociological categorization, without a moment's concern for how ordinary citizens might construct their own complicated class identities.[21]

Such reasoning, although in a somewhat more flexible way, provides the foundation for Ruy Teixeira and Joel Rogers's influential *America's Forgotten Majority*, the book credited with moving Al Gore toward a more class-oriented appeal during the 2000 campaign. Teixeira and Rogers likewise turn 75 percent of American adults into an unproblematic "working class." Although they are persuasive that blue-collar—and, even more, low-level white-collar—workers without the credentials of higher education have been the crucial swing vote in the last decade's elections, Teixeira and Rogers falter in trying to connect the Democratic Party to the proletarian line. No matter that, according to their own analysis, many of their workers fall right in the middle of the nation's income distribution, that they are intensely concerned about what they consider the "raw deal" given "the middle class," and that they want, above all, "a fair shot at a dignified, reasonably prosperous and secure life—in short, a middle-class life as it once was understood." Such messiness does not really matter as long as a one can continue to proclaim: The Old Working Class is Dead. Long Live the Working Class! "Everybody likes to believe they're in the middle class," Joel Rogers remarked in an interview, but to him that only shows that "people are very uncomfortable in America with the notion of class."[22]

We need to turn the tables, though, and ask: why are academics and activists, especially those on the left, so uncomfortable with the actually existing class categories that ordinary people use? Why this fear of engaging middling folks on their own terms? Of course, part of the reason is a legitimate upset at the lack of scholarly and popular recognition that many even in the middle *do* in fact still think of themselves as working class. Furthermore, given the amorphous nature of the category, the term *middle class* is particularly amenable to what two sociologists have wisely labeled a cynical "politics of false inclusion," with politicians often mercilessly stretching the middle class to include 99 percent of the population. Those who appeal to the middle class by no means always express democratic convictions.[23]

At base, though, the disdain of the middle class arises from a sense that once an individual or group has adopted the designation *middle class*, the game is up. Since middle-class politics can be only moderate at best, middling folks can never threaten the system. This is, admittedly, an assumption that the political mainstream plays up with a vengeance. Bill Bradley voices the timeless Aristotelian wisdom as well as anyone: "In many ways, the middle class has given America a stability that other nations lack. It serves as the ballast in our ship of state. It is a force for moderation." In turn, leftist Michael Zweig voices the grand fear of middle-class conservatism in a particularly bald form:

> My insistence on identifying a working class is not a word game. It is not just a matter of semantics to say that workers are in the working class, not the middle class; it is a question of power.
>
> To exercise power, you need to know who you are. You also need to know who your adversary is, the target in the conflict. When the working class disappears into the middle class, workers lose a vital piece of their identity. *In political, social, and cultural terms, they don't know who they are any more.* To make matters worse, they also lose a sense of the enemy, as the capitalist class vanishes among "the rich."

Yet the truth is that even after people label themselves, or more significantly are labeled, as working class, middle class, or something else, the real task of social analysis has only just begun. The categories, these abstractions, do not speak to dreams, to visions, to hopes—that is, to our deepest commitments.[24]

Many in the middle, of course, do simply seek after security and pander to the privileged. We have plenty of evidence—for the Establishment so generously doles it out—that middle-class folks can be selfish and inegalitarian, racist and resentful.[25] History, however, can strengthen our spirit as we struggle against such meanness. We have a whole host of past middle-class radicals alive among us, providing us inspiration not only when we visit the Lincoln Memorial and when we celebrate Martin Luther King Jr. Day, but when we remember the deeds and thoughts of Tom Paine, David Walker, Frederick Douglass, Susan B. Anthony, William Lloyd Garrison, John Brown, Jane Addams, Ida B. Wells-Barnett, Eugene Debs, W.E.B. Du Bois, Betty Friedan, César Chávez, Tom Hayden, and many, many more. My modest contribution is to have added Harry Lane, Will Daly, William U'Ren, and Lora Little to this pantheon of hope. Not just them, of course, but also the thousands of middling folks who made Portland during the early twentieth century the most complete democracy in the world. We honor their memory by learning from their lives to temper our intellect—and, then, by dreaming the most daring of democratic dreams ourselves.

APPENDIX 1

TABLE 1
Major Divisions of Portland Workforce, 1900–1930

		Professional Services (%)	Domestic and Personal and Services (%)	Trade and Transportation (%)	Manufacturing and Mechanical (%)	Extractive (%)	Total Workforce
1900	Total	6.7	32.3	30.8	26.9	3.3	47,575
	Men	5.7	30.5	32.3	27.7	3.8	40,389
	Women	12.3	42.7	22.0	22.7	0.3	7,186
1910	Total	6.7	14.2	39.3	36.4	3.4	110,891
	Men	5.1	9.9	40.9	40.1	4.1	91,344
	Women	14.3	34.1	32.1	19.3	0.2	19,547
1920	Total	8.0	12.5	39.7	35.9	3.9	120,608
	Men	5.8	8.5	38.3	42.3	5.0	92,102
	Women	15.2	25.2	44.1	15.2	0.3	28,506
1930	Total	9.4	14.7	42.6	30.0	3.3	145,435
	Men	6.7	9.2	42.6	37.1	4.4	105,711
	Women	16.6	29.2	42.6	11.3	0.2	39,724

Sources: U.S. Census Office, Department of the Interior, *Twelfth Census of the United States: 1900* (Washington, D.C.: GPO, 1902–4), 20:686–89, table 43; U.S. Bureau of the Census, Department of Commerce and Labor, *Thirteenth Census of the United States: 1910* (Washington, D.C.: GPO, 1914), 4:194–206, table 3; U.S. Bureau of the Census, Department of Commerce, *Fourteenth Census of the United States: 1920* (Washington, D.C.: GPO, 1922–23), 4:1201–4, table 2; U.S. Bureau of the Census, Dept. of Commerce, *Fifteenth Census of the United States: 1930, Population*, vol. 4, *Occupations, by States* (Washington, D.C.: GPO, 1933), 1370–72, table 12.

TABLE 2

Opportunity to Own Manufacturing Enterprise in Portland, 1899–1914

	1899	1909	1914	1919
Total Workforce	47,575	110,891		
Number of firms	1,064	649	837	846
Ratio of proprietors and firm members to total workforce	1:40.3	1:145.3		
Total male workforce	40,389	91,344		
Ratio of total male workforce to proprietors and firm managers in manufacturing sector	34.2	119.7		
Total manufacturing workforce	8,572	10,845	14,421	
Ratio of total workforce to proprietors and firm members in manufacturing sector	7.3	14.2	17.2	

Sources: U.S. Census Office, Dept. of Commerce and Labor, *Special Reports: Occupations at the Twelfth Census* (Washington, D.C.: GPO, 1901), 686–89; U.S. Census Office, Dept. of Commerce and Labor, *Census Reports*; vol. 8, Twelfth Census of the United States, Taken in the Year 1900, part 2, *States and Territories* (Washington, D.C.: GPO, 1902), 738; U.S. Bureau of the Census, Dept. of Commerce and Labor, *Thirteenth Census of the United States: 1910, Population* (Washington, D.C.: GPO, 1913), 4:194; U.S. Bureau of the Census, Dept. of Commerce and Labor, *Thirteenth Census of the United States: 1910, Abstract of the Census with Supplement for Oregon* (Washington, D.C.: GPO, 1913), 668; U.S. Bureau of the Census, Department of Commerce, *Census of Manufactures: 1914* (Washington, D.C.: GPO, 1916), 1268.

TABLE 3
Average Workforce per Firm in Manufacturing Sector in Portland, 1899–1929

	1899	1909	1914	1919	1919ª	1921	1923	1925	1927	1929
Total workforce	8,572	14,891	14,421	26,813	12,929	15,436	21,534	20,318	20,318	21,380
Number of firms	1,064	649	837	846	665	837	793	861	766	1,039
Average workforce	8.1	22.9	17.2	31.7	19.4	20.2	27.2	23.3	26.5	20.6

Sources: U.S. Census Office, Dept. of Commerce and Labor, *Census Reports*, vol. 8, Twelfth Census of the United States, Taken in the Year 1900, part 2, *States and Territories* (Washington, D.C.: GPO, 1902), 738–41; U.S. Bureau of the Census, Dept. of Commerce and Labor, *Thirteenth Census of the United States: 1910, Population*, vol. 4 (Washington, D.C.: GPO, 1913), 194; U.S. Bureau of the Census, Dept. of Commerce and Labor, *Thirteenth Census of the United States: 1910, Abstract of the Census with Supplement for Oregon* (Washington, D.C.: GPO, 1913), 665, 668; U.S. Bureau of the Census, Dept. of Commerce, *Census of Manufactures: 1914*, vol. 1 (Washington, D.C.: GPO, 1918), 1268–71; U.S. Bureau of the Census, Dept. of Commerce, *Fourteenth Census of the United States: 1920, Population* (Washington, D.C.: GPO, 1923), 4:1201–4; U.S. Bureau of the Census, Dept. of Commerce, *Census of Manufactures: 1919* (Washington, D.C.: GPO, 1923), 1256–59; U.S. Bureau of the Census, Dept. of Commerce, *Biennial Census of Manufactures, 1921* (Washington, D.C.: GPO, 1924), 1578; U.S. Bureau of the Census, Dept. of Commerce, *Biennial Census of Manufactures, 1923* (Washington, D.C.: GPO, 1926), 1437; U.S. Bureau of the Census, Dept. of Commerce, *Biennial Census of Manufactures, 1925* (Washington, D.C.: GPO, 1928), 1435; U.S. Bureau of the Census, Dept. of Commerce, *Biennial Census of Manufactures, 1927* (Washington, D.C.: GPO, 1930), 1477–78; U.S. Bureau of the Census, Dept. of Commerce, *Fifteenth Census of the United States, Manufacturers: 1929*, vol. 1 (Washington, D.C.: GPO, 1933), 302.

ªNon-war-related: Eliminates categories of wooden shipbuilding, structural ironwork, and "All other industries," which includes three large shipyards (see James N. Tattersall, "The Economic Development of the Pacific Northwest to 1920," Ph.D. diss. University of Washington, 1960, 239).

TABLE 4

Frequency of Various Sizes of Workforce in Portland Manufacturing Firms, Selected Years, 1899–1929

Average Size of Workforce for Firms in Industry	1899	1909	1914	1919	1919[a]	1921	1927	1929
0–25	97.3%	89.4%	94.7%	60.8%	77.3%	69.7%	56.1%	65.9%
25.1–50	1.4%	3.4%	2.6%	5.7%	7.3%	27.7%	36.3%	32.0%
50.1–100	1.3%	6.5%	1.3%	29.5%	12.5%	0.4%	5.5%	0.3%
100.1–250	0.0%	0.8%	1.4%	4.0%	2.9%	2.2%	0.0%	0.5%
250 or more	0.0%	0.0%	0.0%	0.0%	0.0%	0.0%	2.1%	1.3%

Sources: U.S. Census Office, Dept. of Commerce and Labor, Census Reports, vol. 8, Twelfth Census of the United States, Taken in the Year 1900, part 2, States and Territories (Washington, D.C.: GPO, 1902), 738–41; U.S. Bureau of the Census, Dept. of Commerce and Labor, Thirteenth Census of the United States: 1910, Population, vol. 4 (Washington, D.C.: GPO, 1913), 194; U.S. Bureau of the Census, Dept. of Commerce and Labor, Thirteenth Census of the United States: 1910, Abstract of the Census with Supplement for Oregon (Washington, D.C.: GPO, 1913), 665, 668; U.S. Bureau of the Census, Dept of Commerce, Census of Manufactures: 1914, vol. 1 (Washington, D.C.: GPO, 1918), 1268–71; U.S. Bureau of the Census, Dept. of Commerce, Fourteenth Census of the United States: 1920, Population (Washington, D.C.: GPO, 1923), 4:1201–4; U.S. Bureau of the Census, Dept. of Commerce, Census of Manufactures: 1919 (Washington, D.C.: GPO, 1923), 1256–59; U.S. Bureau of the Census, Dept. of Commerce, Biennial Census of Manufactures, 1921 (Washington, D.C.: GPO, 1924), 1578; U.S. Bureau of the Census, Dept. of Commerce, Biennial Census of Manufactures, 1927 (Washington, D.C.: GPO, 1930), 1477–78; U.S. Bureau of the Census, Dept. of Commerce, Fifteenth Census of the United States, Manufacturers: 1929, vol. 3 (Washington, D.C.: GPO, 1933), 440.

Note: Figures represent the percentage of firms that are in industries in which the average workforce is in the specified range. In 1899, for example, 97.3% of all firms were in industries in which the average firm's workforce was 25 or less.

[a]Non-war-related industries.

TABLE 5

Percentage of Workers in Portland Manufacturing Industries with Various Average Sizes of Workforce, Selected Years, 1899–1927

Average Size of Workforce for Firms in Industry	1899	1909	1914	1919	1919[a]	1921	1927	1929
0–25	80.3%	62.7%	69.9%	14.5%	30.0%	40.9%	24.3%	30.5%
25.1–50	5.7%	7.2%	5.1%	5.8%	12.0%	40.7%	42.8%	50.0%
50.1–100	14.1%	26.3%	6.5%	56.4%	32.1%	17.2%	12.1%	1.2%
100.1–250	0.0%	3.5%	18.5%	23.2%	25.9%*	17.2%	0.0%	2.9%
250+	0.0%	0.0%	0.0%	0.0%	0.0%	0.0%	20.8%	15.5%

Sources: Same as table 4.

[a]Non-war-related: Lumber Only.

TABLE 6

Largest Manufacturing Industries in Portland, 1914 and 1929

Industry	Invested Capital		Valued Added by Manufacture		Persons Engaged in Industry	
	1914	1929	1914	1929	1914	1929
Lumber	$8,707,728		$3,123,165	$8,717,698	2,664	3,460
Printing	$2,486,100		$2,933,299	$8,429,411	1,673	2,435
Flour	$4,648,208	na	$5,300,068	na	258	na
Foundry and machine shops	na		na	$7,818,667	na	2,118

Sources: U.S. Bureau of the Census, Dept. of Commerce, *Census of Manufactures: 1914* (Washington, D.C.: GPO, 1916), 1270–71; U.S. Bureau of the Census, Dept. of Commerce, *Fifteenth Census of the United States, Manufacturers: 1929*, vol. 3 (Washington, D.C.: GPO, 1933), 440.

TABLE 7

Structure of Employment in Portland Printing, Selected Years, 1899–1929

	Firms	Persons Engaged	Proprietors and Firm Members	Wage Earners	Salaried Officials and Clerks	Wage Earners per Firm	Persons Engaged per Firm
1899	77	544	78	385	81	5.0	7.1
1909	132	1,681	311	981	418	7.4	12.7
1914	136	1,663	111	943	619	6.9	12.2
1919	137	1,855	102	987	766	7.2	13.5
1929	152	2,435		1,181	1,254	7.8	16.0

Sources: Same as table 3, plus U.S. Bureau of the Census, Dept. of Commerce, *Fifteenth Census of the United States, Manufacturers: 1929*, vol. 3 (Washington, D.C.: GPO, 1933), 440.

TABLE 8

Composition of Portland Printing Workforce, 1899–1919, by Sex

	Female Wage Earners	Male Wage Earners	Percentage Female Wage Earners	Female Clerks	Male Clerks	Percentage Female Clerks
1899	48	321	13.0			
1909	100	869	10.1	89	238	27.2
1914	86	867	9.0	121	400	23.2
1919	129	916	12.3	218	401	35.2

Sources: Same as table 3.

Note: Based on workers sixteen years of age or over.

TABLE 9
Self-Employment in the American Nonfarm Population, 1880–1920

Year	Number of Self-Employed, Including Professionals	Percentage of Self-employed
1880	1,394,000	12.6
1890	1,969,000	12.1
1900	2,513,000	12.0
1910	3,049,000	10.6
1920	2,969,000	8.9

Source: Recalculated from Mansel G. Blackford, A History of Small Business in America (New York: Twayne, 1991), 36.

TABLE 10

Employment in Manufacturing Sector in Portland and Five Other Cities, Selected Years, 1909–27

	1909	1914	1921	1927
Portland				
Total workforce	14,891	14,421	15,436	20,318
Number of firms	649	837	837	766
Average workforce	22.9	17.2	20.2	26.5
Atlanta				
Total workforce	15,091	15,504	12,660	18,583
Number of firms	483	423	490	428
Average workforce	31.2	36.7	25.8	43.4
Cleveland				
Total workforce	98,686	122,758	103,336	131,146
Number of firms	2,148	2,345	2,256	2,251
Average workforce	45.9	52.3	45.8	58.3
Denver				
Total workforce	15,037	14,412	13,348	15,054
Number of firms	766	885	716	730
Average workforce	19.6	16.3	18.6	20.6
Los Angeles				
Total workforce	21,875	31,540	42,161	66,608
Number of firms	1,325	1,911	2,210	2,965
Average workforce	16.5	16.5	19.1	22.5
New York				
Total workforce	680,510	732,790	536,665	552,507
Number of firms	25,938	29.621	26,801	27,076
Average workforce	26.2	24.7	20.0	20.4

Sources: U.S. Bureau of the Census, Dept. of Commerce and Labor, *Thirteenth Census of the United States: 1910, Population,* vol. 4 (Washington, D.C.: GPO, 1913), 194; U.S. Bureau of the Census, Dept. of Commerce and Labor, *Thirteenth Census of the United States: 1910, Abstract of the Census with Supplement for Oregon* (Washington, D.C.: GPO, 1913), 665, 668; U.S. Bureau of the Census, Dept. of Commerce and Labor, *Thirteenth Census of the United States: 1910, Manufactures,* vol. 9 (Washington, D.C.: GPO, 1912), 104, 126, 236, 886, 992; U.S. Bureau of the Census, Dept of Commerce, *Census of Manufactures: 1914,* vol. 1 (Washington, D.C.: GPO, 1918), 126, 162, 284, 1068, 1212, 1268; U.S. Bureau of the Census, Dept. of Commerce, *Biennial Census of Manufactures, 1921* (Washington, D.C.: GPO, 1924), 1524, 1539, 1544, 1553, 1563, 1578; U.S. Bureau of the Census, Dept. of Commerce, *Biennial Census of Manufactures, 1927* (Washington, D.C.: GPO, 1930), 1417, 1431, 1436, 1448, 1460, 1477–78.

Note: Years shown in comparative tables differ from those in tables for Portland alone because of the available data.

TABLE 11
Frequency of Various Sizes of Workforce in Manufacturing Firms in Portland and
Five Other Cities, Selected Years, 1909–27

Percentage of Firms in Industries with Average Workforce of	1909	1914	1921	1927
Portland				
0–25	89.2%	94.7%	69.7%	56.1%
25.1–50	4.6%	2.6%	27.7%	36.3%
50.1–100	6.5%	1.3%	0.4%	5.5%
100.1–250	0.8%	1.4%	2.2%	0.0%
250+	0.0%	0.0%	0.0%	2.1%
Atlanta				
0–25	45.8%	49.4%	60.8%	42.1%
25.1–50	46.2%	35.9%	32.2%	11.0%
50.1–100	8.1%	13.0%	7.1%	44.6%
100.1–250	0.0%	0.9%	0.0%	2.3%
250+	0.0%	0.7%	0.0%	0.0%
Cleveland				
0–25	45.0%	47.1%	47.1%	46.8%
25.1–50	15.1%	13.9%	16.8%	10.2%
50.1–100	34.7%	32.3%	29.3%	31.0%
100.1–250	4.6%	4.4%	5.9%	9.8%
250+	0.7%	2.3%	1.0%	2.2%
Denver				
0–25	96.0%	98.1%	92.6%	94.1%
25.1–50	2.9%	0.0%	4.5%	3.7%
50.1–100	0.5%	0.5%	2.2%	1.5%
100.1–250	0.0%	0.9%	0.0%	0.0%
250+	0.7%	0.6%	0.7%	0.7%
Los Angeles				
0–25	83.1%	87.3%	82.9%	70.6%
25.1–50	14.8%	10.0%	15.7%	24.5%
50.1–100	1.4%	1.8%	1.0%	3.2%
100.1–250	0.5%	0.4%	0.2%	1.5%
250+	0.3%	0.4%	0.1%	0.2%
New York				
0–25	40.7%	59.0%	84.9%	81.1%
25.1–50	55.2%	35.5%	11.4%	13.0%
50.1–100	3.9%	4.9%	3.2%	5.3%

TABLE 11
continued

Percentage of Firms in Industries with Average Workforce of	1909	1914	1921	1927
100.1–250	0.1%	0.6%	0.3%	0.5%
250 +	0.2%	0.0%	0.2%	0.1%

Sources: U.S. Bureau of the Census, Dept. of Commerce and Labor, *Thirteenth Census of the United States: 1910, Population,* vol. 4 (Washington, D.C.: GPO, 1913), 194; U.S. Bureau of the Census, Dept. of Commerce and Labor, *Thirteenth Census of the United States: 1910, Abstract of the Census with Supplement for Oregon* (Washington, D.C.: GPO, 1913), 665, 668; U.S. Bureau of the Census, Dept. of Commerce and Labor, *Thirteenth Census of the United States: 1910, Manufactures,* vol. 9 (Washington, D.C.: GPO, 1912), 104, 126, 236, 886–90, 992–94; U.S. Bureau of the Census, Dept. of Commerce, *Census of Manufactures: 1914,* vol. 1 (Washington, D.C.: GPO, 1918), 126–30, 162–64, 284–86, 1068–76, 1212–16, 1268–70; U.S. Bureau of the Census, Dept. of Commerce, *Biennial Census of Manufactures, 1921* (Washington, D.C.: GPO, 1924), 1524, 1539–41, 1544, 1553–55, 1563–67, 1578; U.S. Bureau of the Census, Dept. of Commerce, *Biennial Census of Manufactures, 1927* (Washington, D.C.: GPO, 1930), 1417, 1431–33, 1436–37, 1448–50, 1460–63, 1477–78.

TABLE 12

Percentage of Workers in Industries with Various Average Sizes of Workforce, in
Portland and Five Other Cities, Selected Years, 1909–27

In Industries with Average Size of Workforce in	1909	1914	1921	1927
Portland				
0–25	62.7%	69.9%	40.9%	24.3%
25.1–50	7.2%	5.1%	40.7%	42.8%
50.1–100	26.3%	6.5%	1.2%	12.1%
100.1–250	3.6%	18.5%	17.2%	0.0%
250+	0.0%	0.0%	0.0%	20.8%
Atlanta				
0–25	20.5%	20.6%	28.9%	14.3%
25.1–50	61.9%	43.3%	54.4%	8.4%
50.1–100	17.6%	23.3%	16.9%	70.4%
100.1–250	0.0%	2.7%	0.0%	7.0%
250+	0.0%	10.1%	0.0%	0.0%
Cleveland				
0–25	12.0%	10.8%	12.3%	10.6%
25.1–50	11.7%	9.6%	15.1%	6.6%
50.1–100	52.5%	48.3%	41.0%	39.3%
100.1–250	15.3%	10.9%	23.0%	23.2%
250+	8.4%	20.5%	8.5%	20.3%
Denver				
0–25	82.2%	77.9%	66.3%	70.7%
25.1–50	3.8%	0.0%	6.8%	6.4%
50.1–100	1.7%	2.0%	10.0%	6.4%
100.1–250	0.0%	5.9%	0.0%	0.0%
250+	12.3%	14.3%	16.8%	16.6%
Los Angeles				
0–25	59.2%	60.8%	56.8%	40.1%
25.1–50	24.5%	19.1%	27.6%	36.9%
50.1–100	4.7%	6.4%	4.3%	10.0%
100.1–250	2.8%	4.4%	2.9%	8.8%
250+	8.9%	9.4%	8.4%	4.3%
New York				
0–25	22.1%	35.0%	64.1%	57.3%
25.1–50	65.6%	49.4%	19.4%	19.8%
50.1–100	9.6%	12.1%	10.5%	16.2%
100.1–250	0.3%	3.0%	2.2%	3.2%
250+	2.4%	0.6%	3.8%	3.4%

Sources: Same as table 11.

TABLE 13
Rank of Printing among All Manufacturing Industries as Measured by the Number of Persons Employed, in Portland and Five Other Cities, 1909–27

	1909	1914	1921	1927
Portland	2nd	2nd	3rd	2nd
Atlanta	1st	1st	1st	1st
Cleveland	5th	5th	6th	6th
Denver	1st	2nd	2nd	2nd
Los Angeles	2nd	1st	4th	3rd
New York	2nd	2nd	2nd	2nd

Sources: Same as table 11.

APPENDIX 2

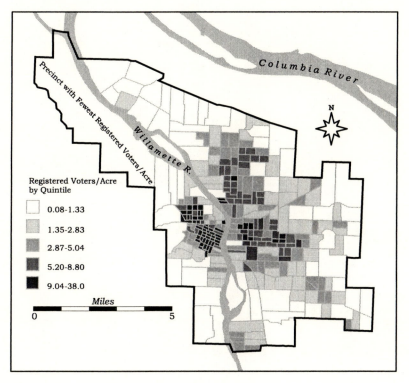

Voter registration density by precinct, 1916

Abbreviations

Abstract	"Abstract of Votes," Multnomah County, Oregon State Archives, Salem, Oregon
AMA	American Medical Association, Chicago
CD	*Polk's Portland City Directory* (Portland, annually)
CR	*Congressional Record*
DLR	*Direct Legislation Record*
JAH	*Journal of American History*
MSH	*Mount Scott Herald* (Portland)
News	*Portland News*
OHQ	*Oregon Historical Quarterly*
OHS	Oregon Historical Society
OHSMA	Oregon Historical Society, Manuscripts and Archives Department
Jour.	*Oregon Journal*
OLP	*Oregon Labor Press*
Oreg.	*Oregonian* (Portland)
OSL	Oregon State Library, Salem
OV	*Oregon Voter*
PC	*Producer's Call*
PLP	*Portland Labor Press*
RLN	Richard L. Neuberger Papers, Special Collections, University of Oregon, Eugene
SCUO	Division of Special Collections and University Archives, University of Oregon
SPARC	Stanley Parr Archives and Records Center
Tel.	*Evening Telegram* (Portland) and *Portland Telegram*
VP	State of Oregon, *A Pamphlet Containing a Copy of All Measures . . . or Proposed Constitutional Amendments and Measures . . .* (Salem, 1908–26)
Vac. Inq.	*Vaccination Inquirer*

NOTES

PREFACE

1. I take inspiration from Dorothee Kocks's blending of political passion and the historian's craft in her brave *Dream a Little: Land and Social Justice in Modern America* (Berkeley, 2000); I have also learned much from the provocative argument for the return of moral and political concerns to history in David Harlan, *The Degradation of American History* (Chicago, 1997).

2. I have therefore taken seriously James Livingston's challenge to stop writing populist tragedy; instead, this is very much an attempt to write populist comedy. See James Livingston, *Pragmatism, Feminism, and Democracy: Rethinking the Politics of American History* (New York, 2001), 39–48.

3. Indeed, I believe that my intellectual method is a highly democratic one. As Daniel Boyarin explains the purpose of his own "extensive citation and discussion of others' work," he has sought to "signal the intellectual debts that I have and to indicate that any project of thought takes place in a community of thinkers and is part of a social process. The references should also help readers who wish to follow further any particular aspects of the argument or the materials under discussion to find their way to other writers and, furthermore, to help them to dispute and argue against me when they so wish. *It is rather the text that just 'tells the story' that insists on its own authority, while an 'academic' text gives ample room and provides equipment for others to contend with it and contest it.*"

See Daniel Boyarin, *Unheroic Conduct: The Rise of Heterosexuality and the Invention of the Jewish Man* (Berkeley, 1997), xii (emphasis added). Likewise, Mary Ryan reckons that "such straightforward contention can be a useful mode of discourse in a democracy"; *Civic Wars: Democracy and Public Life in the American City during the Nineteenth Century* (Berkeley, 1997), 18.

4. James Goodman, "For the Love of Stories," *Reviews in American History* 26 (Mar. 1998): 266 (emphasis added); Norman Mailer, *The Executioner's Song* (Boston, 1979); Mikal Gilmore, *Shot in the Heart* (New York, 1994), 107–12, 122–35, 217–18; Susan Orlean, "Figures in a Mall," *New Yorker*, Feb. 21, 1994, 48–63, reprinted in Orlean, *The Bullfighter Checks Her Makeup: My Encounters with Extraordinary People* (New York, 2001), 245–55.

For a glimpse of the contemporary middle-class populist impulse of the area, listen to one of Harding's supporters in 1994: "There are plenty of people who think we're scum because we live out here on the east side. Well, I live in a very non-scum neighborhood. It's actually a so-called good neighborhood, but it's always going to be thought of as trash, because it's east side. . . . It's a class difference—that's what all this mess is about Tonya" (Orlean, *Bullfighter Checks Her Makeup*, 250).

5. *Hood River News*, May 1, 1985; Allan Nevins, *John D. Rockefeller: The Heroic Age of American Enterprise* (New York, 1940), 1:188, 183. For the fullest treatment of my ancestors, see Allan Nevins, *Study in Power: John D. Rockefeller, Industrialist and Philan-*

thropist (New York, 1953), 1:12–36, and Nevins, *John D. Rockefeller*, 1:182–91; see also Ron Chernow, *Titan: The Life of John D. Rockefeller, Sr.* (New York, 1998), 60–63, 77, 83–88. Also useful are the obituaries of James Clark and his brother Maurice in *Cleveland Leader*, Sept. 2, 1905; and *Cleveland Plain Dealer*, Mar. 10, 1901.

6. Michel Foucault, "Nietzsche, Genealogy, History," in *The Foucault Reader*, ed. Paul Rabinow (New York, 1984), 90.

7. Wilbur Hall, "Portland the Spinster," *Collier's Weekly*, May 19, 1917, 30–31; "Working of the Oregon System," *Nation*, Apr. 23, 1914, 452.

8. Dorothy O. Johansen, *Empire of the Columbia: A History of the Pacific Northwest*, 2d ed. (New York, 1967), 299, and "A Working Hypothesis for the Study of Migrations," in *Experiences in a Promised Land: Essays in Pacific Northwest History*, ed. G. Thomas Edwards and Carlos A. Schwantes (Seattle, 1986); Gordon DeMarco, *A Short History of Portland* (San Francisco, 1990), 35.

For the most systematic statement of the Portland myth, see Terence O'Donnell and Thomas Vaughan, *Portland: An Informal History and Guide* (Portland, 1984); see also William Toll, *The Making of an Ethnic Middle Class: Portland Jewry over Four Generations* (Albany, 1982), 88; Carl Abbott, *Portland: Planning, Politics, and Growth in a Twentieth-Century City* (hereafter *Portland*) (Lincoln, 1983), 30–31; and Richard Maxwell Brown, "Rainfall and History: Perspectives on the Pacific Northwest," in Edwards and Schwantes, *Promised Land*, 13–27. For the thesis of middle-class moderation applied to Oregon generally, see especially Gordon B. Dodds, *Oregon: A Bicentennial History* (New York, 1977). The most complex work within this tradition is Carl Abbott, *Greater Portland: Urban Life and Landscape in the Pacific Northwest* (Philadelphia, 2001).

9. On Reed, see Robert A. Rosenstone, *Romantic Revolutionary: A Biography of John Reed* (New York, 1975), especially 7–22. I interrogate the myth of Portland further in "Historical Invisibility and the Myth of the Harmonious City: Will Daly, Lora Little, and the Hidden Face of Progressive-Era Portland," *OHQ* 99 (Fall 1998): 248–97. For a work that steadfastly resists this myth, see David Peterson Del Mar, *What Trouble I Have Seen: A History of Violence against Wives* (Cambridge, Mass., 1996).

10. On the fruitful concept of public culture, see Thomas Bender, "Wholes and Parts: The Need for Synthesis in American History," *JAH* 73 (June 1986): 120–36; Frederic[k] C. Howe, "Oregon, the Most Complete Democracy in the World," *Hampton's Magazine*, Apr. 1911, 459–72.

PART I
Rehabilitating the American Middle Class

1. Robert N. Bellah et al., *Habits of the Heart: Individualism and Commitment in American Life* (Berkeley, 1985), viii; Benjamin DeMott, *The Imperial Middle: Why Americans Can't Think Straight about Class* (New York, 1990).

CHAPTER ONE
Rethinking the Middle Class: Politics, History, and Theory

1. Robert Rives La Monte, "The American Middle Class," *Arena* 39 (Apr. 1908): 436–40, literally passim; he uses the vampire and sycophant image four times in four pages.

2. Max Weber, "The Protestant Sects and the Spirit of Capitalism," in *From Max Weber: Essays in Sociology*, ed. H. H. Gerth and C. Wright Mills (New York, 1946), 302–22 (quote on 308); David J. Saposs, "The Role of the Middle Class in Social Development: Fascism, Populism, Communism, Socialism," in *Economic Essays in Honor of Wesley Clair Mitchell* (New York, 1935), 395–424 (quotes on 414–15); Charles Henry Melzer, "The Intermediate Millions," *North American Review*, Feb. 1919, 226; Sinclair Lewis, *Babbitt* (New York, 1922). As Weber's example indicates, caricatures of the middle class were hardly limited to the United States. For the depth of antibourgeois sentiment in nineteenth-century Europe, see Peter Gay, *The Bourgeois Experience, Victoria to Freud: Education of the Senses* (New York, 1984), 17–44.

3. Lewis Corey, *The Crisis of the Middle Class* (New York, 1935), 124, 134, 47, 141, 239, 283. For a more sympathetic reading of Corey, see Michael Denning, *The Cultural Front* (London, 1997), 99–101. Depicting Hitler and Mussolini as the embodiment of *American* middle-class hopes and dreams was not unique to Corey. As Norman Thomas put it, "Fascism is the last stand not only of capitalism, in an economic sense, but of the whole middle-class culture and prestige." Thomas forecast the "probability" in the United States of a successful fascist "middle-class revolution." See Thomas, *The Choice before Us: Mankind at the Crossroads* (New York, 1934), 53, 186. Other depression-era radicals, though, most prominently John Dewey, Reinhold Neibuhr, and Alfred Bingham, did foresee the democratic potential of the middle classes; see Robert B. Westbrook, *John Dewey and American Democracy* (Ithaca, 1991), 443–44, 527; Alfred Bingham, *Insurgent America: The Revolt of the Middle Classes* (New York, 1935); and Donald L. Miller, *The New American Radicalism: Alfred M. Bingham and Non-Marxian Insurgency in the New Deal Era* (Port Washington, N.Y., 1979).

4. C. Wright Mills, *White Collar: The American Middle Classes* (New York, 1951); Cornel West, *The American Evasion of Philosophy: A Genealogy of Pragmatism* (Madison, 1989), 135; Mills to William Miller, May 30, 1949, in *C. Wright Mills: Letters and Autobiographical Writings*, ed. Kathryn Mills with Pamela Mills (Berkeley, 2000), 38; Mills, *White Collar*, 233 and xvi.

5. E. Franklin Frazier, *Black Bourgeoisie: The Rise of a New Middle Class* (New York, 1957), sec. 2, 86 and passim, 217, 26; Deborah Gray White, *Too Heavy a Load: Black Women in Defense of Themselves, 1894–1994* (New York, 1999), 189. Frazier's shadow stands over studies of the African American middle class as does Mills over the white; for an overview see Bart Landry, *The New Black Middle Class* (Berkeley, 1987). For a recapitulation of this perspective, see Harold Cruse, *The Crisis of the Negro Intellectual* (New York, 1967): "no class in the world ever sells out so cheaply as the black bourgeoisie" (91); "The black bourgeoisie is self-seeking but in a shortsighted, unsophisticated, unpolitical and cowardly fashion" (178), etc.

6. Lipset, *Political Man: The Social Bases of Politics* (Garden City, N.Y., 1963 [1960]), esp. 127–79, is the most succinct statement of this view. In a similar vein, Daniel Bell and Richard Hofstadter palmed off all sorts of retrograde social movements, ranging from antievolutionism to the John Birch Society, on the "old middle class" and "the less educated members of the middle class." See Bell, "The Dispossessed" (1955) in *The Radical Right* (New York, 1963), 24; and Hofstadter, "The Pseudo-Conservative Revolt" [1955], in *The Radical Right*, 77. See also William Kornhauser, *The Politics of Mass Society* (Glencoe, 1959). These theorists, though, hardly believed that the au-

thoritarian American working class was more democratic than the middle class. See Michael Paul Rogin, *The Intellectuals and McCarthy: The Radical Specter* (Cambridge, Mass., 1967).

7. Bellah et al., *Habits of the Heart*, 152.

8. Mike Davis, *Prisoners of the American Dream: Politics and Economy in the History of the U.S. Working Class* (London, 1986), 71, 303–6. Davis is more compelling in his indictment of reactionary middle-class "Sunbelt Bolshevism" in *City of Quartz: Excavating the Future in Los Angeles* (London, 1990), 151–219 (quote, 156).

9. Barbara Ehrenreich, *Fear of Falling: The Inner Life of the Middle Class* (New York, 1989), 11, 250. Paul Lyon comments, "One could not find a better shorthand to the irrelevancy of much of the American left than Ehrenreich's contempt for the lives of most middle-class people." See Paul Lyons, *Class of '66: Living in Suburban Middle America* (Philadelphia, 1994), 227–28. For an explanation (that comes close to a ratification) of the "illustrious tradition of associating the middle class with cultural emptiness and spiritual poverty," see Catherine Jurca, *White Diaspora: The Suburb and the Twentieth-Century American Novel* (Princeton, 2001), 17.

10. For an important meditation on this problem, see Gorman Beauchamp, "Dissing the Middle Class: The View from Burns Park," *American Scholar*, Summer 1995, 335–49.

11. The key text recognizing the connection between simple respect for the American middle class and social theory about it is a brilliant letter from Richard Hofstadter to C. Wright Mills concerning the presuppositions of *White Collar*. Irving Louis Horowitz quotes the letter extensively in *C. Wright Mills: An American Utopian* (New York, 1983), 250–52; Olivier Zunz also discusses it in *Making America Corporate: 1870–1920* (Chicago, 1990), 3–4. Perhaps the most fair-minded history of the American middle class is Cindy Sondik Aron, *Ladies and Gentlemen of the Civil Service: Middle-Class Workers in Victorian America* (New York, 1987).

12. Speech of Patrick Henry in the Virginia Ratifying Convention, June 5, 1788, in *The Complete Anti-Federalist*, ed. Herbert J. Storing (Chicago, 1981), 5:219; "Mr. Martin's Information to the General Assembly of the State of Maryland" (1788), in Storing, *Complete Anti-Federalist*, 2:71; see also Saul Cornell, "Aristocracy Assailed: The Ideology of Backcountry Anti-Federalism," *JAH* 76 (Mar. 1990): 1148–72; Leon Fink, *Workingmen's Democracy: The Knights of Labor and American Politics* (Urbana, 1983), 13; "The Omaha Platform" (1892), in *The Populist Mind*, ed. Norman Pollack (Indianapolis, 1967), 60.

13. Richard F. Hamilton, *Class and Politics in the United States* (New York, 1972). Ironically, one of the founders of the countertradition was a now non-Marxist Lewis Corey, who argued that the middle class could and should play a crucial role in the destruction of monopoly capitalism and the creation of democratic socialism. Corey, "Problems of the Peace: IV. The Middle Class," *Antioch Review* 5 (Mar. 1945): 68–87.

14. Barbara and John Ehrenreich, "The Professional-Managerial Class," originally published in 1977 in *Radical America*, is more accessible as the lead article in *Between Labor and Capital*, ed. Pat Walker (Boston, 1979), 5–45; Barbara Ehrenreich, "The Professional-Managerial Class Revisited," in *Intellectuals: Aesthetics, Politics, Academics*, ed. Bruce Robbins (Minneapolis, 1990), 173–85 (quote on 185). The most systematic use of the PMC concept in a historical work is Richard Ohmann, *Selling Culture: Magazines, Markets, and Class at the Turn of the Century* (London, 1996).

15. Mark E. Kann, *Middle Class Radicalism in Santa Monica* (Philadelphia, 1986).

16. Louis Hartz, *The Liberal Tradition in America: An Interpretation of American Political Thought since the Revolution* (New York, 1955), 52.

17. Richard Sennett, "Middle-Class Families and Urban Violence: The Experience of a Chicago Community in the Nineteenth Century," in *Nineteenth-Century Cities: Essays in the New Urban History*, ed. Stephan Thernstrom and Sennett (New Haven, 1969), 414 and 418; Sennett, *Families against the City: Middle Class Homes of Industrial Chicago, 1872–1890* (Cambridge, 1970), 207, 217, and 237; Burton J. Bledstein, *The Culture of Professionalism: The Middle Class and the Development of Higher Education in America* (New York, 1976), 334. For a later work that follows in these footsteps, see Loren Baritz's *The Good Life: The Meaning of Success for the American Middle Class* (New York, 1989).

18. Paul E. Johnson, *A Shopkeeper's Millennium: Society and Revivals in Rochester, New York, 1815–1837* (New York, 1978), 8. Nancy Hewitt's companion book on women's activism in nineteenth-century Rochester is the most effective scholarship we have showing that divisions within the middle class, and political struggles between different kinds of middling folks, have been crucial to opening up American sexual and racial politics. See Nancy A. Hewitt, *Women's Activism and Social Change: Rochester, New York, 1822–1872* (Ithaca, 1984). Lori D. Ginzberg, *Women and the Work of Benevolence: Morality, Politics, and Class in the Nineteenth-Century United States* (New Haven, 1990) is, in contrast, another book that ends by completely deradicalizing the middle class, which, "cornered . . . in a defense of privilege," is interested above all in "social control" (211–12).

19. Mary P. Ryan, *Cradle of the Middle Class: The Family in Oneida County, New York, 1790–1865* (New York, 1981), 147. For another community study, see John S. Gilkeson Jr., *Middle-Class Providence, 1820–1940* (Princeton, 1986).

20. Karen Halttunen, *Confidence Men and Painted Women: A Study of Middle-Class Culture in America, 1830–1870* (New Haven, 1982).

21. Even more explicit condemnations of a simultaneously sexually repressed and sexually repressive hegemonic "bourgeoisie" come from Carroll Smith-Rosenberg, *Disorderly Conduct: Visions of Gender in Victorian America* (New York, 1985) and Charles Sellers, *The Market Revolution: Jacksonian America, 1815–1846* (New York, 1991). A firm exception to such denigration is Gordon S. Wood's celebration of the democratic triumph of middling people in *The Radicalism of the American Revolution* (New York, 1991). Yet Wood's analysis simply mirrors Sellers's explanation for the rise of the market; in both accounts the middle class is unproblematically the world historical purveyor of economic liberalism.

22. Kevin Mattson, *Creating a Democratic Public: The Struggle for Urban Participatory Democracy during the Progressive Era* (University Park, Pa., 1998), 11; Glenda Elizabeth Gilmore, *Gender and Jim Crow: Women and the Politics of White Supremacy in North Carolina, 1896–1920* (Chapel Hill, 1996), xix; James Goodman, *Stories of Scottsboro* (New York, 1994), 60. Judith Weisenfeld expresses this same impulse when she argues against those who see middle-class African Americans as less "authentic" than poorer blacks; *African American Women and Christian Activism: New York's Black YWCA, 1905–1945* (Cambridge, 1997), 6–7.

It is an intriguing issue in intellectual politics why scholars have found it easier to be more positive about nonwhite middle classes than the supposedly normative white middle class. See, for just a few examples, Richard A. Garcia, *Rise of the Mexican American Middle Class: San Antonio, 1929–1941* (College Station, 1991); Nick Salvatore, *We All Got History: The Memory Books of Amos Webber* (New York, 1996); Christopher Robert Reed, *The Chicago NAACP and the Rise of Black Professional Leadership, 1910–1966* (Bloomington, 1997); and, especially, the self-conscious break from Frazier in Adam Green, "The Rising Tide of Youth: Chicago's Wonder Books and the 'New' Black Middle Class," in *The Middling Sorts: Explorations in the History of the American Middle Class*, ed. Burton J. Bledstein and Robert D. Johnston (New York, 2001), 237–55.

23. Stuart M. Blumin, *The Emergence of the Middle Class: Social Experience in the American City, 1760–1900* (New York, 1989); 9–10. For a perceptive critique of Blumin's analysis of the supposedly wide gap between workers and white-collar folks, see Maris A. Vinovskis, "Stalking the Elusive Middle Class in Nineteenth-Century America: A Review Article," *Comparative Studies in Society and History* 33 (July 1991): 582–87. A book that closely follows Blumin's theoretical lead is Andrew C. Holman, *A Sense of Their Duty: Middle-Class Formation in Victorian Ontario Towns* (Montreal, 2000); for one example of replication, without evidence, of the Giddens/Blumin argument about classlessness as part of a general attack on an essentialized middle class, see Nan Enstad, *Ladies of Labor, Girls of Adventure: Working Women, Popular Culture, and Labor Politics at the Turn of the Twentieth Century* (New York, 1999), 27 and passim.

24. Zunz, *Making America Corporate*, 201, 147. For a more complex perspective on middle-class corporate life, see Clark Davis, *Company Men: White-Collar Life and Corporate Cultures in Los Angeles, 1892–1941* (Baltimore, 2000).

25. Richard Hofstadter, *Age of Reform: From Bryan to F. D. R.* (New York, 1955), 238, 241–42. For a recent brief reflection by Blumin on the supposed lack of middle-class politics in the nineteenth century, see Glenn C. Altschuler and Stuart M. Blumin, *Rude Republic: Americans and Their Politics in the Nineteenth Century* (Princeton, 2000), 8–10

26. Jurgen Kocka, *White Collar Workers in America, 1890–1940: A Social-Political History in International Perspective* (Beverly Hills, 1980); Alan Brinkley, *Voices of Protest: Huey Long, Father Coughlin, and the Great Depression* (New York, 1982).

27. Catherine McNicol Stock, *Main Street in Crisis: The Great Depression and the Old Middle Class on the Northern Plains* (Chapel Hill, 1992), 10, 1, 42, 53, 47. For other studies that effectively highlight the complexities of middle-class politics see Lary May, "Movie Star Politics: The Screen Actors' Guild, Cultural Conversion, and the Hollywood Red Scare," in *Recasting America: Culture and Politics in the Age of the Cold War*, ed. May (Chicago, 1989), 125–53; Andrew Hurley, *Environmental Inequalities: Class, Race, and Industrial Pollution in Gary, Indiana, 1945–1980* (Chapel Hill, 1995); Kathryn Kish Sklar, *Florence Kelley and the Nation's Work: The Rise of Women's Political Culture, 1830–1900* (New Haven, 1995); Daniel J. Walkowitz, *Working with Class: Social Workers and the Politics of Middle-Class Identity* (Chapel Hill, 1999); Sylvie Murray, "Rethinking Middle-Class Populism in the Postwar Era: Community Activism in Queens," in Bledstein and Johnston, *The Middling Sorts*, 267–79, and Murray, *The Progressive Housewife: Community Activism in Suburban Queens, 1945–1965* (Philadelphia, 2003).

For speculation about a global middle-class tradition of "apolitical politics," see

Brian P. Owensby, *Intimate Ironies: Modernity and the Making of Middle-Class Lives in Brazil* (Stanford, 1999), 234; for a much more complex meditation on middle-class politics than we have in United State historiography, see Michael F. Jiménez, "The Elision of the Middle Classes and Beyond: History, Politics, and Development Studies in Latin America's 'Short Twentieth Century,'" in *Colonial Legacies: The Problem of Persistence in Latin American History*, ed. Jeremy Adelman (New York, 1999), 207–28.

28. Christopher Lasch, *The True and Only Heaven: Progress and Its Critics* (New York, 1991). Lasch's earlier views of the middle class were significantly different. In *The New Radicalism in America: The Intellectual as a Social Type, 1889–1963* (New York, 1965), xiii, 168, he forthrightly used *middle class* "simply as a synonym for *bourgeoisie*," noting also that "the middle class as a whole had for some time instinctively preferred order to anarchy, regularity to uncertainty and risk."

29. E. P. Thompson, *The Making of the English Working Class* (New York, 1966 [1963]), 9–11. The best analysis of Thompson's preface, and theory of class generally, is William H. Sewell Jr., "How Classes Are Made: Critical Reflections on E. P. Thompson's Theory of Working-Class Formation," in *E. P. Thompson: Critical Perspectives*, ed. Harvey J. Kaye and Keith McClelland (Philadelphia, 1990), 50–77. It is important to note the genuine intellectual hostility to Thompson's ideas on the part of many social scientists. See, for example, John Hall's introduction to a collection of sociological class analysis, where he argues that Thompson's "repression of theory . . . offers *no help* in sorting through the alternative conceptual approaches to class analysis." John R. Hall, "Introduction: The Reworking of Class Analysis," in *Reworking Class*, ed. Hall (Ithaca, 1997), 9; emphasis added.

30. This observation applies generally to the most important book series on the subject, The Working Class in American History, published by the University of Illinois Press.

31. Thompson, *Making*, 11, emphasis added. For a promising attempt "to use the analytical inadequacy of 'class' as a rallying point," see Wai Chee Dimock and Michael T. Gilmore, eds., *Rethinking Class: Literary Studies and Social Formations* (New York, 1994), 2.

32. For an excellent study that takes class as an issue to be investigated rather than as a given, see Sara Maza, "Luxury, Morality, and Social Change: Why There Was No Middle-Class Consciousness in Prerevolutionary France," *Journal of Modern History* 69 (June 1997): 199–229; see also David Garrioch, *The Formation of the Parisian Bourgeoisie, 1690–1830* (Cambridge, 1996) for a salutary emphasis on politics in class formation.

33. J. H. Hexter, "The Myth of the Middle Class in Tudor England" (1950), in *Reappraisals in History: New Views on History and Society* (New York, 1961), 72. For an older view that contains some of the same warnings about our inability to categorize the middle class, see G.D.H. Cole, "The Conception of the Middle Classes," in *Studies in Class Structure* (London, 1955), 78–100.

34. My emphasis on human agency by no means implies that *individuals*, through conscious self-definition, create classes. Rather, class is a dialectical process involving communal life as well as individual consciousness. If anything, group ideas matter much more than an individual's own labeling. If Bill Gates wishes to call himself middle class, that won't hold much water if 99 percent of Americans disagree. Therefore polls, such as the classic one from *Fortune* (Feb. 1940, 14) showing that a vast

majority (actually, only a plurality of 47 percent) of Americans characterized themselves as some variant of "middle class" are notoriously susceptible to misinterpretation. Even if "all" Americans supposedly thought of themselves as middle class, their fellow citizens would not necessarily agree with that categorization, and—more significantly—what each individual *means* when invoking the term *middle class* might well vary substantially from person to person. Therefore, when we call the United States a middle-class country, we have only begun to explore the nation's political and cultural complexities.

35. Adam Przeworski, "Proletariat into Class: The Process of Class Formation," in *Capitalism and Social Democracy* (Cambridge, 1985), 69, 66, 70; Przeworski, "Class, Production, and Politics: A Reply to Burawoy," *Socialist Review* 89 (Apr.–June 1989): 94 (emphasis added); Przeworski, "Proletariat into Class," 71. Both Przeworski and Löic Wacquant (see below) are writing in reaction to sociologist Erik Olin Wright, the most prominent contemporary theorist of class. Despite the fact that Wright decisively rejects "history [as] . . . conceptually constitutive of the concept of class itself," his agenda has long been the same as mine. He recognizes that the fundamental task of reconstructing class analysis is to bring the middle class back in, and his primary political concern is the potential for class alliances between working class and middle class.

Yet Wright is so determined to fit his social analysis into elegant theoretical boxes that he ends up creating categories that have almost no connection to the real social consciousness of the actually existing masses. Thus Wright's impressive models can often explain, at least over a limited amount of time, the comparative level of support for the welfare state among his "nonskilled managers" and "expert supervisors." Yet I dare any historian to write a meaningful, synthetic history using the "contradictory locations within class relations" that, according to Wright, are the only basic reality to the "middle class." His elaborate "twelve-location class-structure matrix" will surely baffle any scholar interested in either change over an extended period of time or in exploring the lives (particularly the consciousness, culture, and politics) of ordinary people. Erik Olin Wright, *Class Counts: Comparative Studies in Class Analysis* (Cambridge: Cambridge University Press, 1997), 495; Erik Olin Wright, ed., *The Debate on Classes* (London, 1989), 347; Wright, *Class Counts*, 24–25. See also Wright's original landmark, *Classes* (London, 1985).

36. Löic J. D. Wacquant, "Making Class: The Middle Class(es) in Social Theory and Social Structure," in *Bringing Class Back In: Contemporary and Historical Perspectives*, ed. Scott G. McNall, Rhonda F. Levine, and Rick Fantasia (Boulder, 1991), 57–58; Franklin Charles Palm, *The Middle Classes: Then and Now* (New York, 1936), 3.

37. Dror Wahrman, *Imagining the Middle Class: The Political Representation of Class in Britain, c. 1780–1840* (Cambridge, 1995), 245, 339; D. S. Parker, *The Idea of the Middle Class: White-Collar Workers and Peruvian Society, 1900–1950* (University Park, Pa., 1998); Sanjay Joshi, *Fractured Modernity: Making of a Middle Class in Colonial North India* (New York, 2001), 2. Joshi's book, despite a reduction of middle-class politics and culture to domination over subalterns, is the best synthesis of the international historiography of the middle class. Any analysis of class and politics like mine or Wahrman's owes a fundamental debt to Gareth Stedman Jones's controversial "Rethinking Chartism," in *Languages of Class: Studies in English Working-Class History, 1832–1982* (New York, 1983).

38. Bruce Laurie, "'Spavined Ministers, Lying Toothpullers, and Buggering Priests': Third-Partyism and the Search for Security in the Antebellum North," in *American Artisans: Crafting Social Identity, 1750–1850*, ed. Howard B. Rock, Paul A. Gilje, and Robert Asher (Baltimore, 1994), 98–119; and Bruce Laurie, "'We Are Not Afraid to Work': Master Mechanics and the Market Revolution in the Antebellum North," in Bledstein and Johnston, *The Middling Sorts*, 50–69. See also Tony A. Freyer, *Producers versus Capitalists: Constitutional Conflict in Antebellum America* (Charlottesville, 1994). For an argument that nineteenth-century English popular radicalism appealed to "a Middling Class which was . . . neither Middle Class nor Working Class," see R. S. Neale, "Class and Class Consciousness in Early Nineteenth Century England: Three Classes or Five?" in *History and Class: Essential Readings in Theory and Interpretation*, ed. Neale (New York, 1983), 158.

39. For a creative exploration of a twentieth-century "middle majority market . . . located along the border of working class and middle class," see Andrew Hurley, *Diners, Bowling Alleys, and Trailer Parks: Chasing the American Dream in the Postwar Consumer Culture* (New York, 2001), 13. For a book that seeks to bring the histories of both middle class and working class together, but that still sees each class having diametrically opposed values, see William E. French, *A Peaceful and Working People: Manners, Morals, and Class Formation in Northern Mexico* (Albuquerque, 1996).

40. Here I have learned from the radical nominalist argument of William Reddy, even if I am not willing to go as far down the path of methodological individualism as he is. See William M. Reddy, *Money and Liberty in Modern Europe: A Critique of Historical Understanding* (Cambridge, 1987), esp. chapter 1, "The Crisis of the Class Concept in Historical Research."

CHAPTER TWO
Curt Muller and the Capitalist Middle Class: Social Misconstructions of Reality

1. *Muller v. Oregon*, 208 U.S. 412. The decision is reprinted in Louis D. Brandeis and Josephine Goldmark, *Women in Industry* (New York, 1969) repaginated at the end of the book, 1–8. Citations from Brewer's decision will be to *Women in Industry*.

2. Robert H. Wiebe, *The Search for Order, 1877–1920* (New York, 1967), 166, 128, 111, and more generally "A New Middle Class," 111–32. The idea that the Progressives "were not in the least proletarian" but rather "middle-class to the core" dates back to the participants in the movement; see William Allen White, *The Autobiography of William Allen White* (New York, 1946), 482. Historians who have tried to break the connection between the middle class and Progressivism include Morton Keller, James J. Connolly, and David Thelen. Thelen, despite his compelling interest in the radically democratic elements in the early-twentieth-century reform tradition, unfortunately rules out of bounds any attempt to find class identities in the new "consumer" age. See Morton Keller, *Regulating a New Society: Public Policy and Social Change in America, 1900–1933* (Cambridge, Mass., 1994), 3; James J. Connolly, *The Triumph of Ethnic Progressivism: Urban Political Culture in Boston, 1900–1925* (Cambridge, Mass., 1998), 9; David P. Thelen, *The New Citizenship: Origins of Progressivism in Wisconsin, 1885–1900* (Columbia, Mo., 1972), and, even more, David P. Thelen, "Social Tensions and the Origins of Progressivism," *JAH* 56 (Sept. 1969): 323–41. A daring rethinking of this issue comes in Benjamin Heber Johnson, *America's Unknown Rebellion: The Plan de*

San Diego Uprising and the Forging of Mexican American Identity (New Haven, forthcoming). Johnson uncovers a "Tejano Progressivism" with a strong petit bourgeois orientation.

3. *CD*, 1912, 1914, 1905; funeral program, Hans Curt Muller, in possession of Barbara Whisnant; *Jour.*, Oct. 18, 1932; Elaine Gale Zahnd Johnson, "Protective Legislation and Women's Work: Oregon's Ten-Hour Law and the *Muller v. Oregon* Case, 1900–1913," Ph.D. diss., University of Oregon, 1982, 236–39 (quote, 239). Ronald K. L. Collins and Jennifer Friesen, "Looking Back on *Muller v. Oregon*," *American Bar Association Journal* 69 (1983): 294–98 (part 1) and 472–77 (part 2) is a popular account of the case that contains additional undocumented material about Muller.

4. *CD*, 1906–40; *Jour.*, Oct. 18, 1932.

5. Melvin I. Urofsky, *A Mind of One Piece: Brandeis and American Reform* (New York, 1971), 40; Nancy Woloch, *Muller v. Oregon: A Brief History with Documents* (Boston, 1996), vii; *Oreg.*, Feb. 26, 1908, 8; Leonard Baker, *Brandeis and Frankfurter: A Dual Biography* (New York, 1984), 16; Philippa Strum, *Brandeis: Beyond Progressivism* (Lawrence, Kans., 1993), 63. The author of the editorial in the generally conservative *Oregonian* was almost certainly the socialist C. H. Chapman, an honorary vice president of the Oregon Consumers' League; see N.A., *Report of the Social Survey Committee of the Consumers' League of Oregon* (Portland, 1913), 2.

6. Woloch, *Muller v. Oregon*, 4; *Muller* decision, Brandeis and Goldmark, *Women in Industry*, 6–7; *Jour.*, Feb. 24, 1908, 6.

7. Alice Kessler-Harris, "Law and a Living: The Gendered Content of 'Free Labor,'" in *Gender, Class, Race, and Reform in the Progressive Era*, ed. Noralee Frankel and Nancy S. Dye (Lexington, 1991), 95; Alice Kessler-Harris, *Out to Work: A History of Wage-Earning Women in the United States* (New York, 1982), 185; Deborah L. Rhode, *Justice and Gender: Sex Discrimination and the Law* (Cambridge, 1989), 41; Joan Hoff, *Law, Gender, and Injustice: A Legal History of U.S. Women* (New York, 1991), 201.

For sympathetic feminist readings of *Muller*, see Kathryn Kish Sklar, "The Historical Foundations of Women's Power in the Creation of the American Welfare State, 1830–1930," in *Mothers of New World: Maternalist Politics and the Origins of Welfare States*, ed. Seth Koven and Sonya Michel (New York, 1993), 75; Vivien Hart, *Bound by Our Constitution: Women, Workers, and the Minimum Wage* (Princeton, 1994). For critiques of the Brandeis brief as well as the actual court decision, see Blanche Crozier, "Regulation of Conditions of Employment: A Critique of *Muller v. Oregon*," *Boston University Law Review* 13 (1933): 276–92; Ann Corinne Hill, "Protection of Women Workers and the Courts: A Legal Case History," *Feminist Studies* 5 (Summer 1979): 271; and Nancy S. Erickson, "*Muller v. Oregon* Reconsidered: The Origins of a Sex-Based Doctrine of Liberty of Contract," *Labor History* 30 (Spring 1989): 247–48. Crozier, arguing that "women are not today controllable as though they were machines for the producing and rearing of children" censured *Muller* as "certainly one of the most conservative opinions ever written" (291). For an attempt to "go beyond simply condemning the legislation for 'stereotyping' women, on the one hand, or blessing it for reforming an industrial abuse," see Susan Lehrer, *Origins of Protective Labor Legislation for Women, 1905–1925* (Albany, 1987), 11; for another balanced feminist treatment that focuses on the pernicious effects of *Muller* as a legal precedent, see Judith A. Baer, *The Chains of Protection: The Judicial Response to Women's Labor Legislation* (Westport, Conn., 1978), 66.

For an argument about the negative effects of protective legislation on women's unionization in Oregon, see Johnson, "Protective Legislation," 323, 332–36, 348–49, 386, 390, 398. It is worth noting that one of the important minimum-wage cases to come out of Oregon, *Stettler v. O'Hara* 243 U.S. 629, actually combined two cases, one from a Rose City box factory owner, Frank Stettler, and another from his employee, Elmira Simpson (*Simpson v. O'Hara* 70 Ore. 261). Just as we need to explore more of the lives of business owners like Muller and Stettler, we very much need to learn about what motivated workers like Simpson. See also Sister Miriam Theresa [Caroline J. Gleason], *Oregon Legislation for Women in Industry* (Washington, D.C., 1931), 25.

8. Urofsky, *Mind of One Piece*, 170–71 n. 80; Nancy S. Erickson, "Historical Background of 'Protective' Labor Legislation: *Muller v. Oregon*," in *Women and the Law: A Social Historical Perspective*, ed. D. Kelly Weisberg, vol. 2, *Property, Family, and the Legal Profession* (Cambridge, Mass., 1982), 155–86; *Woman's Tribune*, Aug. 11, 1906, 62.

9. "Brief for the Plaintiff in Error," in *Landmark Briefs and Arguments of the Supreme Court of the United States: Constitutional Law*, ed. Philip B. Kurland and Gerhard Casper, vol. 16 (Arlington, Va., 1975), 6, 16, 13, 30–31; Appellants' Brief, in the Supreme Court of the State of Oregon, March Term 1906, *Oregon v. Muller*, Supreme Court Files, Case no. 6412, Drawer no. 67, 41, 51, 39, Oregon State Archives, Salem; "Brief for Plaintiff in Error," 23–24. Historians who have recognized the virtues of Muller's arguments include Hoff, *Law, Gender, and Injustice*, 199–200; Erickson, "Historical Background," 161–62; and especially Woloch, *Muller v. Oregon*, 33–35. Woloch reprints portions of Muller's federal brief, 133–44.

10. Erickson, "Historical Background," 161; "Appellants' Brief," 17; "Brief for Plaintiff in Error," 18; Woloch, *Muller v. Oregon*, 34.

11. Joseph Gaston, *Portland, Oregon: Its History and Builders* (Chicago, 1911), 3:170–71; "Labor Unions," undated, William D. Fenton Papers, OHSMA, MSS 1507, Belles Lettres Essays Folder, 1, 3. Unionists claimed that the Citizens' Alliance supported Muller's legal case; *PLP*, Jan. 26, 1906, 1.

12. "Appellants' Brief," 7; Peter Boag, "Sex and Politics in Progressive Era Portland and Eugene: The 1912 Same-Sex Vice Scandal," *OHQ* 100 (Summer 1999): 158–81. McAllister served, with Fenton, as Muller's attorney from the earliest stages of the case through Muller's state appeal, but he bowed out for unknown reasons in the middle of 1906 before the case advanced to the federal level. See Stipulation, In the Supreme Court of Oregon, State of Oregon vs. Curt Muller, March 15, 1906 and Petition for Writ of Error, In the Supreme Court of the State of Oregon, August 1906, Supreme Court Files, Oregon State Archives, Salem. For the role of the laundry owners' association, see *Jour.*, Jan. 21, 1906, 5; and *Tele*, June 27, 1906, 8.

13. Edwin V. O'Hara, *A Living Wage by Legislation: The Oregon Experience* (Salem, 1916), xviii; City of Portland, Police, Arrest Dockets, A2001–073, vols. 48–51, 1910, SPARC; *Stettler v. O'Hara*, 243 U.S. 629; O'Hara, *Living Wage*, xviii; Johnson, "Protective Legislation," 347; Elizabeth Brandeis, "Labor Legislation," in *History of Labor in the United States, 1896–1932*, ed. John R. Commons, vol. 3 (New York, 1935), 511–12; Victor P. Morris, *Oregon's Experience with Minimum Wage Legislation* (New York, 1930), 214; *OV*, Nov. 20, 1915, 93. For an excellent study that notes the split between small and large capital over this issue, as well as the larger class politics of *Muller*, see Johnson, "Protective Legislation," especially 243–46, 279.

14. O'Hara, *Living Wage*, xxi–xxii.

15. *Oreg.*, Nov. 1, 1913, 10; Gleason, *Oregon Legislation for Women*, 30. Ironically, O'Hara's meliorative liberalism led to admiration from the Ku Klux Klan, which in Portland shared many of his economic views. See J. G. Shaw, *Edwin Vincent O'Hara: American Prelate* (New York, 1957), 60–61, and chapter 19 of this book.

I do not mean to imply that support for protective legislation came only from professionals and the corporate elite; far from it. In fact, maximum hours and minimum wage legislation passed by overwhelming legislative margins—in the case of the statute that led to *Muller*, unanimously. See *The Journal of the House of the Twenty-second Legislative Assembly of the State of Oregon* (Salem, 1903), 527; and *The Journal of the Senate of the Twenty-second Legislative Assembly of the State of Oregon* (Salem, 1903), 636. Furthermore, labor representatives introduced the maximum hours law, hoping to obtain legislation covering both women and men, and unions consistently supported the Industrial Welfare Commission. The worker-oriented *News* hailed *Muller* as "a big victory" for "Oregon labor," even though unions did nothing to defend the statute during the appeals process. Johnson, "Protective Legislation," 94, 300, 383; Caroline J. Gleason, "For Working Women in Oregon," *Survey*, Sept. 9, 1916, 585–86; *News*, Feb. 25, 1908, 1; Johnson, "Protective Legislation," 247.

16. For the governing board of the OCL, see *Report of the Social Survey Committee*, 2; for its role in Oregon, see Maud Nathan, *The Story of an Epoch-Making Movement* (Garden City, N.Y., 1926), 198–205.

17. Karl Polanyi, *The Great Transformation: The Political and Economic Origins of Our Time* (Boston, 1944), 133.

18. Louis M. Hacker, "The Anti-capitalist Bias of American Historians," in *Capitalism and the Historians*, ed. F. A. Hayek (Chicago, 1954), 64–92; Francis Fukuyama, *The End of History and the Last Man* (New York, 1992); for just one example among many, Marcus Rediker, *Between the Devil and the Deep Blue Sea: Merchant Seamen, Pirates, and the Anglo-American Maritime World, 1700–1750* (Cambridge, 1987).

19. Alexis de Tocqueville, *Democracy in America* (New York, 1956), 2:253.

20. Richard F. Hamilton, *The Social Misconstruction of Reality: Validity and Verification in the Scholarly Community* (New Haven, 1996).

21. Hamilton, *Social Misconstruction of Reality*, 267 n. 33; Alfred Winslow Jones, *Life, Liberty, and Property: A Story of Conflict and a Measurement of Conflicting Rights* (Philadelphia, 1941). See also Richard F. Hamilton, *Restraining Myths: Critical Studies of United States Social Structure* (Beverly Hills, 1975), esp. "The Politics of Independent Business," 33–98.

22. Jones, *Life, Liberty, and Property*, 226, 227.

23. Jones, *Life, Liberty, and Property*, 350, 228–34, 233. Another confirmation of the ideological divide between the lower middle and upper middle classes during the depression comes from Arthur W. Kornhauser, "Analysis of 'Class' Structure of Contemporary American Society—Psychological Bases of Class Division," in *Industrial Conflict: A Psychological Interpretation*, ed. George W. Hartmann and Theodore Newcomb (New York, 1939). Kornhauser shows that the lower middle class differed sharply from its superiors in its "strong labor sympathies" and support for the "socialization of industry" (254). See also 236, 250–54.

24. Wright, *Classes*, 262–63. For a contrasting sociological claim that small businessmen play "a significant role in the ideological servicing of contemporary capital-

ism," see Frank Bechhofer and Brian Elliott, "Petty Property: The Survival of a Moral Economy," in *The Petite Bourgeoisie: Comparative Studies of the Uneasy Stratum*, ed. Bechhofer and Elliott (London, 1981), 182–200.

CHAPTER THREE
Harry Lane and the Radicalism of Middle-Class Reform

1. An exception is Timothy R. Mahoney, *Provincial Lives: Middle-Class Experience in the Antebellum Middle West* (New York, 1999).

2. Stewart H. Holbrook, *Lost Men in American History* (New York, 1946), 319. Steven J. Diner, *A Very Different Age: Americans of the Progressive Era* (New York, 1998), 212; and John Whiteclay Chambers II, *The Tyranny of Change: America in the Progressive Era, 1890–1920*, 3d ed. (New York, 2000), 159, both misidentify U'Ren as governor of Oregon, an office he never held, and neglect to mention his actual political role.

3. O'Donnell and Vaughn, *Portland*, 52; Ruby Fay Purdy, *The Rose City of the World: Portland, Oregon* (Portland, 1947), 85; Elaine S. Friedman, *The Facts of Life in Portland, Oregon* (Portland, 1993), 11. The appellation *Rose City*, however, seems to predate Lane's mayoralty; see Rinaldo Minton Hall, "Portland, the Rose City," *Pacific Monthly* 13 (June 1905): 362.

4. Thomas W. Ryley, *A Little Group of Willful Men: A Study of Congressional-Presidential Authority* (Port Washington, N.Y., 1975), 33.

5. James B. Morrow, "Harry Lane Tells James B. Morrow His Life Story," *Oreg.*, Aug. 2, 1914, VI, 4.

6. Paul S. Holbo, "Senator Harry Lane: Independent Democrat in War and Peace," in Edwards and Schwantes, *Promised Land*, 244–45; Oswald West, "Reminiscences and Anecdotes: McNarys and Lanes," *OHQ* 52 (Sept. 1951): 149; Fred Lockley, *History of the Columbia River Valley from the Dalles to the Sea* (Chicago, 1928), 2:874; *Jour.*, Nov. 14, 1933, 12. In light of my argument about the radicalism of nonorthodox healing in Progressive Era Portland, I should make it clear that Lane did not think that "quacks" had anything to contribute to medical knowledge (Morrow, "Harry Lane," 6).

7. Holbo, "Senator Harry Lane," 245; E. Kimbark MacColl, with Harry H. Stein, *Merchants, Money, and Power: The Portland Establishment, 1843–1913* (Portland, 1988), 382; *Oreg.*, Mar. 13, 1908, 10; Lockley, *Columbia River Valley*, 1:461.

8. MacColl and Stein, *Merchants, Money, and Power*, 390–91, 418–19; Craig Wollner, *Electrifying Eden: Portland General Electric, 1889–1965* (Portland, 1990), 74–80. For Lane's support among the middle class, see Dodds, *Oregon*, 173; and Carl Abbott, *Portland: Gateway to the Northwest* (hereafter *Gateway*) (Northridge, Calif., 1985), 91.

9. Holbo, "Senator Harry Lane," 249; "Address Delivered by Harry Lane at Dinner Tendered Dr. Wise at the Commercial Club, October 10th, 1906," RLN, Box 38, Folder 42, 5–6; G. Thomas Edwards, *Sowing Good Seeds: The Northwest Suffrage Campaigns of Susan B. Anthony* (Portland, 1990), 239.

10. "Dear Sir," Aug. 9, 1912, Neuberger Papers, Box 38, Folder 40; *Jour.*, Nov. 1, 1912, 24; *Jour.*, Mar. 23, 1912, in Clipping Folder, Frank S. Myers MSS, OHSMA; *Jour.*, Oct. 26, 1912, 2; *Jour.*, Oct. 31, 1912, 1–2.

11. "Lane Denounces Tariff System," *Oreg.*, n.d., Clipping Folder, Myers MSS; Holbo, "Senator Harry Lane," 249.

12. Poem of Nina Lane McBride in a 1912 clipping from a New Orleans socialist paper, RLN, Box 38, Folder 43; clipping from *Public Ownership*, Jan. 8, 1916, RLN, Box 38, Folder 43; William Haywood to I. McBride, Sept. 27, 1915, Joe Hill Folder, Lane Papers, OHSMA; assorted clippings in RLN, Box 38, Folder 43; "Minutes of the Twelfth Regular Meeting of the Organizing Committee of the People's Council of America, July 12, 1917," People's Council of America Records, Swarthmore College Peace Collection, Microfilm Reel 3.1. For the People's Council, see C. Roland Marchand, *The American Peace Movement and Social Reform, 1898–1918* (Princeton, 1972), 266–322.

13. Howard W. Allen, "Geography and Politics: Voting on Reform Issues in the United States Senate, 1911–1916," *Journal of Southern History* 27 (May 1961): 225. Lane trailed Wisconsin senator Paul Husting by only one percentage point for the top spot.

14. Lockley, *Columbia River Valley*, 2:877; *CR*, Senate, Sixty-Third Congress, First Session (hereafter *CR* followed by Congress number and session number), Aug. 16, 1913, 3447; *CR*, 63-1, Aug. 16, 1913, 3447; *CR*, 63-2, Jan. 21, 1914, 2041; *CR*, 64-2, Feb. 22, 1917, 3878.

15. *CR*, 63-2, Dec. 15, 1913, 895; *CR*, 63-2, Jan. 29, 1914, 2510; *CR*, 63-2, Jan. 13, 1914, 1563; *CR*, 63-1, June 17, 1913, 2028; *CR*, 63-3, Mar. 1, 1915, 4900; *CR*, 65-1, Apr. 6, 1917, 441; *CR*, 63-3, Feb. 2, 1915, 2834.

16. Edwards, *Sowing Good Seeds*, 236–37; undated *Oregonian* clipping, Lane Papers, OHS; *CR*, 63-1, July 31, 1913, 2947; *CR*, 63-2, Mar. 17, 1914, 4954; *CR*, 64-2, Feb. 22, 1917, 3876; *CR*, 64-2, Feb. 28, 1917, 4476; *New York Times*, Jan. 13, 1914, 8; *CR*, 63-2, Aug. 11, 1914, 13859; *CR*, 63-2, Jan. 12, 1914, 1518. For Lane's pioneering appointment of women to the positions of chief city health officer and head of a separate women's police division, of which he spoke proudly in Congress, see Gloria E. Myers, *A Municipal Mother: Portland's Lola Greene Baldwin, America's First Policewoman* (Corvallis, 1995); *CR*, 63-2, Mar. 17, 1914, 4954.

17. Harry Lane to Nina Lane McBride, Mar. 15, 1907, Nina Lane Faubion Papers, SCUO; *Jour.*, Nov. 1, 1912, 1; *New York Times*, Aug. 22, 1916, 4; *CR*, 64-2, Dec. 12, 1916, 218.

18. For examples of Lane's views on immigration, see *CR*, 63-2, May 29, 1914, 9435 and *CR*, 63-3, Dec. 31, 1914, 7901. In his commitment to restricting contracted "coolie" labor rather than Asian (or other) immigrants themselves, Lane followed in the working-class tradition laid out by Andrew Gyory in *Closing the Gate: Race, Politics, and the Chinese Exclusion Act* (Chapel Hill, 1998). On contemporary racial attitudes, see Matthew Jacobson, *Whiteness of a Different Color: European Immigrants and the Alchemy of Race* (Cambridge, Mass., 1998); and Robert G. Lee, *Orientals: Asian Americans in Popular Culture* (Philadelphia, 1999), 106–44; for the not always ignoble antiracist traditions of the Populists, see C. Vann Woodward, *Tom Watson: Agrarian Rebel* (New York, 1938); Lawrence C. Goodwyn, "Populist Dreams and Negro Rights: East Texas as a Case Study," *American Historical Review* 75 (Dec. 1971): 1435–56; and Manning Marable, "Black History and the Vision of Democracy," in *The New Populism: The Politics of Empowerment*, ed. Harry C. Boyte and Frank Riessman (Philadelphia, 1986), 198–206, which also highlights the radical black petit bourgeois tradition.

19. *CR*, 64-2, Jan. 30, 1917, 2243; *CR*, 63-2, Feb. 5, 1914, 2945, 2948; *CR*, 63-2, Mar. 3, 1914, 4200.

20. *CR*, 64-2, Dec. 12, 1916, 218.

21. *CR*, 63-1, July 22, 1913, 2600; Harry Lane to C. E. S. Wood, Aug. 27, 1913, Wood Papers, Box 161 (41), Huntington Library; this item reproduced by permission of The Huntington Library, San Marino, California.

22. Peter W. Stanley, *A Nation in the Making: The Philippines and the United States, 1899–1921* (Cambridge, Mass., 1974), 179, 215–25. Lane served on the Senate Committee on the Philippines; *CR*, 64-1, Dec. 13, 1915, 233.

23. *CR*, 64-1, Jan. 31, 1916, 1803; *CR*, 64-1, Aug. 16, 1916, 12722. The contrast between Lane and the mainstream of the anti-imperialist movement, which argued against the U.S. hold on the Philippines on racist grounds, is profound. For the latter, see Lee, *Orientals*, 106–13.

24. *CR*, 65-1, Sept. 16, 1917, 7215; *CR*, 63-2, June 22, 1914, 10840; *CR*, 63-2, June 24, 1914, 11037.

25. *CR*, 63-2, June 18, 1914, 10652; *CR*, 64-2, Jan. 27, 1917, 2109; *CR*, 64-1, May 8, 1916, 7573.

26. For Joseph Lane's career, see James E. Hendrickson, *Joe Lane of Oregon: Machine Politics and the Sectional Crisis, 1849–1861* (New Haven, 1967). We do know that Harry Lane professed at least a fictive family relationship with the descendants of the Indians his grandfather had helped conquer. His daughter Harriet told of Harry's camping trip to southern Oregon, when he came across a number of Indians named Lane, including a "Joe Lane, who permitted his photograph to be taken by Mrs. Lane on the Doctor's claiming kinship with him." Harriet Lane, "General Joseph Lane and His Relation to the History of Oregon between the Years 1849 and 1853," B.A. thesis, University of Oregon, 1909, SCUO, 14 n. 2.

27. *CR*, 63-2, June 6, 1914, 9933; *CR*, 63-2, July 24, 1914, 12603; *CR*, 63-2, June 17, 1914, 10593; *CR*, 63-3, Mar. 2, 1915, 5087–90, 5107–8. The chair of the Indian Affairs Committee spoke to Lane's effectiveness when he gave Lane credit, along with those who would become his fellow antiwar insurgents La Follette and Asle Gronna, for killing an Indian appropriation bill; see George F. Sparks, ed., *A Many-Colored Toga: The Diary of Henry Fountain Ashurst* (Phoenix, 1962), 39. On La Follette's progressive stance on Indian policy, see Nancy Unger, *Fighting Bob La Follette: The Righteous Reformer* (Chapel Hill, 2000), 91, 145, 150; for federal Indian policy more generally during the Progressive Era, see Francis Paul Prucha, *The Great Father: The United States Government and the American Indians*, combined edition (Lincoln, 1995), 763–89; and Keller, *Regulating a New Society*, 282–93.

28. *CR*, 64-1, May 5, 1916, 7442; William T. Hagan, *The Indian Rights Association: The Herbert Welsh Years, 1882–1904* (Tucson, 1985), 256; *American Indian Magazine*, Jan./Mar.—Apr./June 1916, 112, Jan./Mar.—Apr./June 1917, 64. For Native American hostility toward the Indian Bureau, see Peter Iverson, *Carlos Montezuma and the Changing World of American Indians* (Albuquerque, 1982), 102–19, 145–53, 178–85; for Montezuma's apparent endorsement of Lane's bill, see Carlos Montezuma to R. H. Pratt, Mar. 20, 1916, the Papers of Carlos Montezuma (microfilm edition, Reel 4, Correspondence). For Welsh and the mainstream "friends of the Indians" more generally, see Frederick E. Hoxie, *A Final Promise: The Campaign to Assimilate the Indians, 1880–1920* (Lincoln, 1984).

29. Hoxie, *A Final Promise*, 113; *CR*, 63-3, Mar. 1, 1915, 4898–99. Harry Lane thus also knocks holes in the supposedly monolithic power of the ideology of whiteness during the Progressive Era. On the need for historians to open up space beyond whiteness, see Eric Arnesen's effective critique, "Whiteness and the Historians' Imagination," *International Labor and Working-Class History* 60 (Fall 2001): 3–32.

30. *Hearings before the Committee on Indian Affairs, U.S. Senate, 64th Congress, 1st Session, on S. 793, a Bill Modifying and Amending the Act Providing for the Disposal of the Surplus Allotted Lands within the Blackfeet Indian Reservation, Montana, April 11, 1916* (Washington, D.C., 1916), 10; *CR*, 63-3, Feb. 27, 1915, 4836. Lane therefore fell within the "nuanced, sympathetic, and humane vision" that Sherry Smith has identified among certain writers of the period. See Sherry Smith, *Reimagining Indians: Native Americans through Anglo Eyes, 1880–1940* (New York, 2000), 14.

31. *CR*, 63-3, Mar. 1, 1915, 4900.

32. Prucha, *The Great Father*, 767; Keith W. Olson, *Biography of a Progressive: Franklin K. Lane, 1864–1921* (Westport, Conn., 1979), 93 (emphasis added); *CR*, 63-2, June 24, 1914, 11037.

33. *CR*, 65-1, Sept. 16, 1917, 7217. For a similar argument about the strength of this tradition of radical democracy, see Benjamin Heber Johnson, "Red Populism: T. A. Bland, Agrarian Radicalism, and the National Indian Defence Association," in *The Countryside in the Age of the Modern State: Political Histories of Rural America*, ed. Catherine McNicol Stock and Robert D. Johnston (Ithaca, 2001), 15–37.

34. *CR*, 63-2, Jan. 31, 1914, 2646. The *New York Times*, Feb. 1, 1914, II, 1, featured Lane's accusations under the headline "Senate in Turmoil on Morgan Charges," crediting Lane with "one of the liveliest sessions the Senate has seen for many months." The *Times* recorded a slightly different version of the Oregon senator's "sarcastic references to the probable fate in the hereafter of the late Mr. Morgan," adding concluding words that the *Congressional Record* stenographer either did not hear or suppressed: "I don't know, but he ought to [have]."

35. *CR*, 63-2, Dec. 15, 1913, 894.

36. *CR*, 63-2, July 2, 1914, 11540–41.

37. *Oreg.*, Nov. 16, 1915; *New York Times*, Jan. 28, 1916, 20; *Jour.*, Oct. 18, 1914, 1; Holbo, "Senator Harry Lane," 250; *CR*, 64-1, Dec. 13, 1915, 228; "Congress of Neutral Nations," *Hearings before the Committee on Foreign Affairs, House of Representatives, Sixty-Fourth Congress, First Session on H.J. Res. 38* (Washington, D.C., 1916), 3; "Conference of Neutral Nations," *Hearings before the Committee on Military Affairs, United States Senate, Sixty-Fourth Congress, First Session, Relating to Conference of Neutral Nations* (Washington, 1916); *Oreg.*, Nov. 16, 1915; *CR*, 64-1, Jan. 5, 1916, 490; John Milton Cooper, *The Vanity of Power: American Isolationism and the First World War, 1914–1917* (Westport, Conn., 1969), 170.

38. *CR*, 64-2, Mar. 4, 1917, 5002–4. On the would-be assassination, Holbo, "Senator Harry Lane," 252, questions whether or not Lane's physical and emotional exhaustion might have been at the root of the episode, although he grants the possible reality of the event. Thelen, on the other hand, accepts the story without qualification; see David P. Thelen, *Robert M. La Follette and the Insurgent Spirit* (Madison, 1985), 133–34. See also the neutral stance of Unger in *Fighting Bob La Follette*, 245. Ryley, *Little Group*, 127, wisely notes that we have no corroborating evidence; the best information we have comes from recollections of George Norris and Robert La Follette Jr.,

who report Lane's telling them about the episode. Bella Case La Follette and Fola La Follette, *Robert M. La Follette* (New York, 1953), 1:620; Senator George W. Norris to Fola La Follette, Feb. 15, 1939, La Follette Family Papers, Container E78, Manuscript Division, Library of Congress.

39. Thelen, *Robert M. La Follette*, 134; John F. Kennedy, *Profiles in Courage* (New York, 1956), 198; Richard L. Neuberger and Stephen B. Kahn, *Integrity: The Life of George W. Norris* (New York, 1937), 92; *New York Times*, Mar. 6, 1917, 1. For the chaotic ending of the 64th Congress, see Arthur S. Link, *Wilson: Campaigns for Progressivism and Peace, 1916–1917* (Princeton, 1965), 360–66.

40. Holbo, "Senator Harry Lane," 255; Richard L. Neuberger, "Time Vindicates a Prophet from Oregon," *Oreg.*, Sept. 29, 1935, 4; *CR*, 64-1, Apr. 18, 6360–61, 6341; Lane to Hon. Samuel H. Garland, Mar. 29, 1917, Correspondence File, Lane Papers, OHSMA. For the diagnosis of Bright's disease (a kidney ailment now generally known as glomerulonephritis) and the course of his illness, see Nina McBride, Diary Entry, Mar. 25, 1917, Correspondence File, Lane Papers, OHSMA; and Neuberger and Kahn, *Integrity*, 76, 94, 105, 108; Steven J. Peitzman, "From Bright's Disease to End-Stage Renal Disease," in *Framing Disease: Studies in Cultural History*, ed. Charles E. Rosenberg and Janet Golden (New Brunswick, 1992), 3–19; National Institutes of Health, "Glomerular Diseases," 2000, (http://www.niddk.nih.gov/health/kidney/pubs/glomer/glomer.htm).

41. Neuberger and Kahn, *Integrity*, 124; *Jour.*, Apr. 5, 1917, 1; Lane to E. W. Eastman, Apr. 4, 1917, RLN, Box 38, Folder 40. At the end of the month Lane attempted to go to the Senate floor to vote against conscription but could not make it and soon thereafter left Washington; *Jour.*, Apr. 27, 1917, 1; Apr. 29, 1917, 1. For the populist congressional opposition to imperialism and Wilsonian foreign policy, see David A. Horowitz, *Beyond Left and Right: Insurgency and the Establishment* (Urbana, 1997), 20–24.

42. *OLP*, Mar. 10, 1917, 4; *Jour.*, Mar. 5, 1917, 1–2; unidentified clipping, Lane Papers, OHSMA.

43. *Jour.*, Apr. 2, 1917, 6; Neuberger, "Time Vindicates," 4; Josef Matschiner to Lane, Mar. 5, 1917, in Correspondence on Armed Forces Neutrality Bill Folder, Nina Lane Faubion Papers, SCUO; Albert Berni to Lane, Mar. 24, 1917, Lane Papers, Correspondence File, OHSMA; *CD*, 1917.

44. *CR*, 65-1, Sept. 16, 1917, 7215; Lincoln Steffens, "The Taming of the West," *American Magazine*, Oct. 1907, 598; Tony Howard Evans, "Oregon Progressive Reform, 1902–1914," Ph.D. diss., University of California, Berkeley, 1966, 265; *Oreg.*, Nov. 17, 1901, 10; 1908 *VP*, 100; 1910 *VP*, 167; *Jour.*, Nov. 1, 1912; Judson King to William S. U'Ren, Dec. 16, 1913, Judson King Papers, Box 2, Folder General Correspondence Oregon, Manuscript Division, Library of Congress. For the moving eulogies of Lane's dear friends George Norris and Robert La Follette, along with those from other senators (only partially available in the *Congressional Record*), see *Senate Documents*, 65th Congress, Third Session, Dec. 2, 1918–Mar. 4, 1919, vol. 10 (Washington, 1920).

45. Morrow, "Harry Lane," 4.

46. Morrow, "Harry Lane," 4.

47. Lane's congressional speeches on his philosophy of government strengthen my interpretation of his democratic views of politics. He was a staunch opponent of

government bureaus, especially regulatory commissions, that would operate *outside* the view of the people and without democratic accountability. See *CR*, 63-1, Sept. 25, 1913, 5190; *CR*, 63-2, Dec. 15, 1913, 893; *CR*, 63-2, Jan. 13, 1914, 1565; *CR*, 63-2, Aug. 4, 1914, 13222–24; *CR*, 64-1, Aug. 8, 1916, 12293; *CR*, 64-1, June 26, 1916, 9837. Elizabeth Sanders argues compellingly that such antagonism to bureaucracy came out of an agrarian vision hostile not to the state itself, but rather to the state exercising undemocratic discretion. See *Roots of Reform: Farmers, Workers, and the American State, 1877–1917* (Chicago, 1999), 9, 387–89.

PART II
The Populist Political Economy of Progressive Era Portland

1. Burton J. Hendrick, "Law-Making by the Voters: How the People of Oregon, Working under the Initiative and Referendum, Have Become Their Own Political Bosses," *McClure's*, Aug. 1911, 435.
2. *PLP*, Jan. 14, 1915, 1.

CHAPTER FOUR
The Contours of Class in Portland

1. Joseph Schafer, *A History of the Pacific Northwest*, rev. ed. (New York, 1918), 300.
2. MacColl and Stein, *Merchants, Money, and Power*, 336, 443; Abbott, *Portland*, 11, 22; Judith Sealander, *Grand Plans: Business Progressivism and Social Change in Ohio's Miami Valley, 1890–1920* (Lexington, 1988), 12.
3. Earl Pomeroy, *The Pacific Slope: A History of California, Oregon, Washington, Idaho, Utah, and Nevada* (Seattle, 1973 [1965]), 138; Johansen, *Empire of the Columbia*, 436, 329–30; Carl Abbott, "Regional City and Network City: Portland and Seattle in the Twentieth Century," *Western Historical Quarterly* 23 (Aug. 1992): 293–322.
4. Ellwood P. Cubberly, *The Portland Survey: A Textbook on City School Administration Based on a Concrete Study* (Yonkers-On-The-Hudson, 1915), 103, 107; Herbert Croly, "Portland, Oregon: The Transformation of the City from an Architectural and Social Viewpoint," *Architectural Record* 31 (June 1912): 592.
5. E. Kimbark MacColl, *The Growth of a City: Power and Politics in Portland, Oregon, 1915 to 1950* (Portland, 1979), 139. For explorations of the complexities of Portland's demographic composition, see William Toll, "Permanent Settlement: Japanese Families in Portland in 1920," *Western Historical Quarterly* 28 (Spring 1997): 19–43; Elizabeth McLagan, *A Peculiar Paradise: A History of Blacks in Oregon, 1788–1940* (Portland, 1980), Charles F. Gould, "Portland Italians, 1880–1920," *OHQ* 77 (Sept. 1976): 238–60; Toll, *Ethnic Middle Class*; and Ellen Eisenberg, "Transplanted to the Rose City: The Creation of an East European Jewish Community in Portland, Oregon," *Journal of American Ethnic History* 19 (Spring 2000): 82–97.
6. Abbott, *Portland*, 55; MacColl, *Growth of a City*, 38. Suffragist Sara Bard Field nicely explained the freedom of buying a modest home on Portland's East Side around 1910 in "To Portland," in chapter 13, "Growing Disharmony," Amelia R. Fry, *Sara Bard Field: Poet and Suffragist*, Regional Oral History Office, Bancroft Library, Univer-

sity of California, Berkeley, 1979, http://sunsite.berkeley.edu:2020/dynaweb/teiproj/oh/suffragists/field/@Generic_BookView.

7. The maps in this book are based on Multnomah County Court, "Boundaries of Election Precincts of Multnomah County, State of Oregon" (Portland, 1914); and "Election Precincts . . . as Established by the County Court" (Portland, 1912, 1917), Multnomah Public Library, Portland, Oregon.

8. Abbott, *Portland*, 54; MacColl, *The Shaping of a City: Business and Politics in Portland, Oregon, 1885 to 1915* (Portland, 1976), 17.

9. Abbott, *Portland*, 55; *OLP*, May 6, 1916, 5. For the more settled nature of African American life on the East Side, see William Toll, "Black Families and Migration to a Multiracial Society: Portland, Oregon, 1900–1924," *Journal of American Ethnic History* 17 (Spring 1998): 52–53.

For sketches of Portland's neighborhoods and the city's general geography of class, see Abbott, *Portland*, 3, 23–29, 54–55, 89–90; and Abbott, *Gateway*, 2–3, 57. For the ways in which this basic geographic divide continues to structure Portland politics and culture, see a journalist's comment: "Ask an east-sider to describe the west side and you can expect to hear the following: It's rich; snooty; where the status seekers begin their climb. . . . Ask a west-sider for an opinion of the east side, and the tune will go something like this: It's poor, it's middle class; it's flat; it's *dangerous*." Keith Moerer, "West Side/East Side," *Willamette Week*, June 11–17, 1984, 1, 7, cited in Nancy Kimball McFadden, "House and Home in Portland, Oregon: A Study of Ordinary Houses in Some Southeast Portland Neighborhoods at the Turn of the Century," Ph.D. diss., University of Oregon, 1993, 72 n. 20.

10. Dean Collins, "Pilgrim's Progress," in *The Taming of the Frontier*, ed. Duncan Aikman (New York, 1925), 166–67; MacColl and Stein, *Merchants, Money, and Power*, xv; Abbott, *Gateway*, 67. My interpretation here follows the compelling "ruling class perspective" laid out by E. Kimbark MacColl in his excellent trilogy of books. See MacColl and Stein, *Merchants, Money, and Power*, 450. For a convincing argument for historians to distinguish between the bourgeoisie and the middle class, see Sven Beckert, "Propertied of a Different Kind: Bourgeoisie and Lower Middle Class in the Nineteenth-Century United States," in Bledstein and Johnston, *The Middling Sorts*, 285–95.

11. *Oreg.*, Oct. 14, 1903, 12; *OV*, Oct. 12, 1918, 41.

12. MacColl and Stein, *Merchants, Money, and Power*, xvi.

13. MacColl and Stein, *Merchants, Money, and Power*, 283–84; MacColl, *Growth of a City*, 1; MacColl and Stein, *Merchants, Money, and Power*, 360–61.

14. David Alan Johnson, *Founding the Far West: California, Oregon, and Nevada, 1840–1890* (Berkeley, 1992), 274; Dodds, *Oregon*, 136.

15. MacColl and Stein, *Merchants, Money, and Power*, 251, 250.

16. MacColl, *Growth of a City*, 201–2; MacColl and Stein, *Merchants, Money, and Power*, 364 (quote), 271–72.

17. MacColl, *Growth of a City*, 34, 119; Wollner, *Electrifying Eden*, 87.

18. MacColl and Stein, *Merchants, Money, and Power*, 450–51; Abbott, *Gateway*, 69; see also Christopher Lasch, "The Moral and Intellectual Rehabilitation of the Ruling Class," in *The World of Nations: Reflections on American History, Politics, and Culture* (New York, 1973), 80–99. For another interpretation of the period that emphasizes corporate power, see William G. Robbins, *Landscapes of Promise: The Oregon Story, 1800–1940* (Seattle, 1997).

19. United States Commission on Industrial Relations, *Final Report and Testimony Submitted to Congress by the Commission on Industrial Relations*, 64th Congress, 1st Sess., Senate Document No. 415, 1916, 11 vols., 3:4575.

20. Scholars who have pointed to the conservatism of Portland workers include Dodds, *Oregon*, 140; Carlos A. Schwantes, *Radical Heritage: Labor, Socialism, and Reform in Washington and British Columbia, 1885–1917* (Seattle, 1979), 16–17; MacColl and Stein, *Merchants, Money, and Power*, 240.

21. Gaston, *Portland, Oregon*, 1:627; Commission on Industrial Relations, *Final Report and Testimony*, 3:4583–84. Schwantes, *Pacific Northwest*, 250; Harvey Elmer Tobie, "Oregon Labor Disputes, 1919–1923: A Study of Representative Controversies and Current Thought," Ph.D. diss., University of Oregon, 1936, 332; MacColl, *Growth of a City*, 38; William F. Ogburn and Delvin Peterson, "Political Thought of Social Classes," *Political Science Quarterly* 31 (1916): 305. In 1916 the *Oregon Labor Press* spoke of ten thousand union men in Portland (Apr. 1, 1916, 7).

22. Johansen, *Empire of the Columbia*, 481; Tobie, "Oregon Labor Disputes," 324–25; *OLP*, Sept. 8, 1913, 8 and July 26, 1919, 1; Theodore Draper, *The Roots of American Communism* (New York, 1957), 139; James Weinstein, *The Decline of Socialism in America, 1912–1925* (New Brunswick, 1984 [1967]), 199; J. Robert Constantine, ed., *Letters of Eugene V. Debs, 1874–1926* (Urbana, 1990), 3:400–401. In 1908 ten thousand people attended one of Debs's speeches in Portland; see Jeff Johnson, "The Heyday of Oregon's Socialists," *Oreg.*, Dec. 19, 1976, magazine section, 15. Historians arguing for Portland's low strike rate include MacColl, *Growth of a City*, 38; and Toll, *Ethnic Middle Class*, 88.

23. Very helpful in this area will be D'mitri Palmateer, "Along the Itinerant Frontier: Mobility, Class, and Social Reform in Portland, Oregon, 1890–1920," Ph.D. diss., Binghamton University, in progress.

24. Robert Edward Wynne, "Reaction to the Chinese in the Pacific Northwest and British Columbia, 1850 to 1910," Ph.D. diss., University of Washington, 1964, 104.

25. Gleason, *Oregon Legislation for Women*, 8; Abbott, *Gateway*, 81. For an argument about how female clerical workers during this period occupied a middle zone between working class and middle class, see Ileen DeVault, *Sons and Daughters of Labor: Class and Clerical Work in Turn-of-the-Century Pittsburgh* (Ithaca, 1990).

26. Jim Scott, "Socialism and Small Property—or—Two Cheers for the Petty Bourgeoisie," *Peasant Studies* 12 (Spring 1985): 185.

27. Arno J. Mayer, "The Lower Middle Class as Historical Problem," *Journal of Modern History* 47 (Sept. 1975): 415; on the United States, 422–23. Richard F. Hamilton provides a heroic intellectual history of the "problem" of the reactionary lower middle class in *Who Voted for Hitler?* (Princeton, 1982), 9–36.

28. Mayer, "Lower Middle Class," 424, 411.

29. Hamilton, *Who Voted for Hitler?* 35. The category "lower middle class" is therefore not an abstract or alien social scientific concept with no relationship to the language of contemporary Americans. An example is University of Wisconsin professor W. I. King, who in 1919 divided the American population into the poor, the lower middle class, the upper middle class, and the rich. See Willford Isbell King, *The Wealth and Income of the People of the United States* (New York, 1919), passim but especially 78. In the same year, but from the world of advertising, the J. Walter Thompson agency classified consumers in a similar manner—"wealthy, upper middle,

lower middle, poor, illiterate (negroes or foreigners)." See Jennifer Scanlon, *Inarticulate Longings: The Ladies' Home Journal, Gender, and the Promises of Consumer Culture* (New York, 1995), 221. Or take H. L. Mencken's 1920 observation, in the best demonization tradition, that "the United States has never developed a true proletariat. . . . Instead it has simply developed two bourgeoisies, an upper and a lower. Both are narrow, selfish, corrupt, timorous, docile and ignoble; both fear ideas as they fear the plague." Mayo DuBasky, ed., *The Gist of Mencken: Quotations from America's Critic* (Metuchen, 1999), 13.

30. Toll, *Ethnic Middle Class*, 145.

31. See appendix, table 1. The portion of the workforce involved in manufacturing fell to 30.0 percent in 1930, with the portion of the female workforce in manufacturing decreasing continually from 1900 to 1930, from 22.7 to 11.3 percent.

I have not done the extensive work with the manuscript census that would be necessary to analyze the racial background of the petite bourgeoisie. Yet William Toll has provided important evidence of the considerable strength of the petite bourgeoisie among African American men and women and Japanese men; see his "Black Families and Migration," 45, 48, and "Permanent Settlement," 36, 42–43.

32. In 1914 the census also ratcheted up its standard for inclusion of manufacturing establishments from those with outputs valued at five hundred dollars or more to five thousand dollars or more, thus striking as much as a third of the Portland petite bourgeoisie from this historical record with the stroke of a clerk's pen. See Anthony Patrick O'Brien, "Factory Size, Economies of Scale, and the Great Merger Wave of 1898–1902," *Journal of Economic History* 48 (Sept. 1988): 644–45.

33. U.S. Bureau of the Census, Department of Commerce and Labor, *Thirteenth Census of the United States: 1910, Abstract of the Census with Supplement for Oregon* (Washington, D.C., 1913), 656, 658–59, 657.

34. U.S. Census Office, Department of Commerce and Labor, *Census Reports*, vol. 8, *Twelfth Census of the United States, Taken in the Year 1900*, part 2: States and Territories (Washington, D.C., 1902), 738–41; U.S. Bureau of the Census, Department of Commerce and Labor, *Thirteenth Census of the United States: 1910, Abstract of the Census with Supplement for Oregon* (Washington, D.C., 1913), 665, 668–69; U.S. Bureau of the Census, Department of Commerce, *Census of Manufactures: 1914* (Washington, D.C., 1916), 1268–71; U.S. Bureau of the Census, Department of Commerce, *Census of Manufactures: 1919* (Washington, D.C., 1923), 1256–59; U.S. Bureau of the Census, Department of Commerce, *Fifteenth Census of the United States, Manufacturers: 1929*, vol. 3 (Washington, D.C., 1933), 440.

The work of James Soltow on the persistence of small businesses in the metalworking industries is of note here; see for example his "Origins of Small Business and the Relationships between Large and Small Firms: Metal Fabricating and Machinery Making in New England, 1890–1957," in *Small Business in American Life*, ed. Stuart Bruchey (New York, 1980), 192–211, and "Structure and Strategy: The Small Manufacturing Enterprise in the Modern Industrial Economy," in *Business and Its Environment: Essays for Thomas C. Cochran*, ed. Harold Issadore Sharlin (Westport, Conn., 1983), 81–99.

35. Mark Granovetter, "Small Is Bountiful: Labor Markets and Establishment Size," *American Sociological Review* 49 (June 1984): 323; Christine Ermenc, *Voices of Portland* (Portland, 1976), 31. For a contemporary liberal recognition of the survival of small

property ownership, see Walter E. Weyl, *The New Democracy* (New York, 1912), 176–77; for the same insight from a socialist on the political importance of "the persistence of the petty retail stores, and of petty industries," see John Spargo, "The Influence of Karl Marx on Contemporary Socialism," *American Journal of Sociology* 16 (July 1910): 39.

36. My argument thus differs from what is arguably the classic work in the field, where Seymour Martin Lipset, Martin A. Trow, and James S. Coleman argue that small printing shops retarded rather than encouraged union and political activism. See *Union Democracy: The Internal Politics of the International Typographical Union* (Glencoe, Ill., 1956), 150–97.

37. For figures, see appendix, table 13. Printing was the third largest employer in Chicago in 1919, behind only slaughtering/meatpacking (where firms employed an average of 608 employees per firm compared to printing's 20) and men's clothing. The value of printing's products was second only to slaughtering/meatpacking, and the 1,381 printing firms dwarfed the number in all other industries. Lizabeth Cohen, *Making a New Deal: Industrial Workers in Chicago, 1919–1939* (New York, 1990), 14–15. Where, then, are all the books on the printing industry in Chicago to compare to the fine works on steel, railroads, and meat?

38. Appendix, table 7; U.S. Bureau of the Census, Department of Commerce and Labor, *Thirteenth Census of the United States: 1910, Abstract of the Census with Supplement for Oregon* (Washington, D.C., 1913), 653, 668.

39. U.S. Bureau of the Census, Department of Commerce, *Census of Manufactures: 1919* (Washington, D.C., 1923), 1256.

40. Commission on Industrial Relations, *Final Report and Testimony*, 3:4580; U.S. Bureau of the Census, Department of Commerce and Labor, *Thirteenth Census of the United States: 1910, Abstract of the Census with Supplement for Oregon* (Washington, D.C., 1913), 655–66; *PLP*, Labor Day Issue, Sept. 1, 1913, 8; Johnson, "Protective Legislation," 418.

41. *PLP*, Sept. 1, 1913, 8; Ava Baron, "Women and the Making of the American Working Class: A Study of the Proletarianization of Printers," *Review of Radical Political Economics* 14 (Fall 1982): 28–29; Irene Tichenor, "Master Printers Organize: The Typothetae of the City of New York, 1865–1906," in Bruchey, *Small Business*, 175, 190, 187–88. For the experiences of one printing industry worker in the early twentieth century, see Laurence Pratt, *I Remember Portland, 1899–1915* (Portland, 1965), 10–45.

42. James Livingston, *Origins of the Federal Reserve System: Money, Class, and Corporate Capitalism, 1890–1913* (Ithaca, 1986), 56–57; Alfred D. Chandler, *The Visible Hand: The Managerial Revolution in American Business* (Cambridge, 1977); see also for critical statistics Harold G. Vatter, *The Drive to Industrial Maturity: The U.S. Economy, 1860–1914* (Westport, Conn., 1975), 170–71.

43. David M. Gordon, Richard Edwards, and Michael Reich, *Segmented Work, Divided Workers: The Historical Transformation of Labor in the United States* (New York, 1982), 117; Mansel G. Blackford, *A History of Small Business in America* (New York, 1991), 36, 133; Gordon, *Segmented Work*, 133.

44. Harold C. Livesay, "Lilliputians in Brobdingnag: Small Business in Late-Nineteenth-Century America," in Bruchey, *Small Business*, 341–43; Susan Strasser, *Satisfaction Guaranteed: The Making of the American Mass Market* (New York, 1989), 65–66, 230; *CD*, 1914, 1926. Livesay's definition involves a simple managerial and owner-

ship structure rather than a small firm size. For a similar argument for the period 1820–70, see Jeremy Atack, "Firm Size and Industrial Structure in the United States during the Nineteenth Century," *Journal of Economic History* 46 (June 1986): 463–75.

45. Blackford, *Small Business*, 27; Matthew Sobek, "Work, Status, and Income: Men in the American Occupational Structure since the Late Nineteenth Century," *Social Science History* 20 (Summer 1996): 202 n. 26. Kurt Mayer long ago noted that "if the opportunity to become an independent producer has lost much of its factual basis, this has occurred in farming rather than in business." See Mayer, "Small Business as a Social Institution," *Social Research* 14 (1947): 340. Jane Jacobs also noticed the growth of urban small businesses between 1900 and 1959; see *The Death and Life of Great American Cities* (New York, 1961), 147–48. For an important rethinking of the question of the decline of small property, set in an earlier period, see Gordon Darroch, "Class in Nineteenth-Century Central Ontario: A Reassessment of the Crisis and Demise of Small Producers during Early Industrialization, 1861–1871," *Canadian Journal of Sociology* 13 (Winter–Spring 1988): 49–71.

Other important figures come from Harold Vatter, who has calculated that in 1904 over three-quarters of all business establishments were small and unincorporated, and that number even excludes the multitude of enterprises where there was employment of self (and family) and no other. The number of business firms in the United States grew by over a third from 1899 to 1919. Interestingly, a *decline* in the average numbers of wage earners per establishment from 9.73 to 6.15 accompanied the gradual growth in the number of noncorporate firms between 1904 and 1919. See Harold G. Vatter, "The Position of Small Business in the Structure of American Manufacturing, 1870–1970," in Bruchey, *Small Business*, 147, 143, 148.

46. Gerald Friedman, "New Estimates of Union Membership: The United States, 1880–1914," *Historical Methods* 32 (Spring 1999): 75–86. Fine exceptions to this seeming iron rule of academe are Ewa Morawska, *Insecure Prosperity: Small-Town Jews in Industrial America, 1890–1940* (Princeton, 1996); Robert C. Kenzer, *Enterprising Southerners: Black Economic Success in North Carolina, 1865–1915* (Charlottesville, 1997); Wendy Gamber, *The Female Economy: The Millinery and Dressmaking Trades, 1860–1930* (Urbana, 1997), which also breaks ground by addressing both entrepreneurs and wage workers as part of the same universe; and Sarah Deutsch, *Women and the City: Gender, Space, and Power in Boston, 1870–1940* (New York, 2000), 115–35. A good case study is Matthew W. Roth, *Platt Brothers and Company: Small Business in American Manufacturing* (Hanover, N.H., 1994); see also Melanie Archer's work, an example of which is "Family Enterprise in an Industrial City: Strategies for the Family Organization of Business in Detroit, 1880," *Social Science History* 15 (Spring 1991): 67–95; and Debra Michals, "Toward a New History of the Postwar Economy: Prosperity, Preparedness, and Women's Small Business Ownership," *Business and Economic History* 26 (Fall 1997): 45–56. For a rare linkage of small business with political activism, see Tiffany Melissa Gill, "'I Had My Own Business . . . So I Didn't Worry': Beauty Salons, Beauty Culturists, and the Politics of African-American Female Entrepreneurship," in *Beauty and Business: Commerce, Gender, and Culture in Modern America*, ed. Philip Scranton (New York, 2001), 169–94; for a study of the congressional politics surrounding small business, see Jonathan J. Bean, *Beyond the Broker State: Federal Policies toward Small Business, 1936–1961* (Chapel Hill, 1996). The best work

in a North American setting is David Monod's Canadian study, *Store Wars: Shopkeepers and the Culture of Mass Marketing, 1890–1939* (Toronto, 1996).

47. Appendix, table 10; Andrew Wender Cohen, "Obstacles to History: Modernization and the Lower Middle Class in Chicago, 1900–1940," in Bledstein and Johnston, *The Middling Sorts*, 189–200; and Cohen, "The Struggle for Order: Law, Labor, and Resistance to the Corporate Ideal in Chicago, 1900–1940," Ph.D. diss., University of Chicago, 1999.

CHAPTER FIVE
Capitalism, Anticapitalism, and the Solidarity of Middle Class and Working Class

1. Gerald Berk, "Constituting Corporations and Markets: Railroads in Gilded Age Politics," *Studies in American Political Development* 4 (1990): 134; Berk, "Corporate Liberalism Reconsidered: A Review Essay," *Journal of Policy History* 3 (1991): 81, 83; and Berk, *Alternative Tracks: The Constitution of American Industrial Order, 1865–1917* (Baltimore, 1994). Also see James Livingston's important "A Reply to Gerald Berk," *Journal of Policy History* 3 (1991): 85–89. Livingston amplifies his challenge to the general principles of this "populist" version of history in *Pragmatism and the Political Economy of Cultural Revolution, 1850–1940* (Chapel Hill, 1994). For a positive assessment of the current viability of a "republican political economy," see William H. Simon, "Social-Republican Property," *UCLA Law Review* 38 (Aug. 1991): 1340 and passim.

2. Victoria Hattam, "Economic Visions and Political Strategies: American Labor and the State," *Studies in American Political Development* 4 (1990): 91–92; Hattam, *Labor Visions and State Power: The Origins of Business Unionism in the United States* (Princeton, 1993).

3. Hattam, "Economic Visions," 94, 99 n. 51.

4. T. J. Jackson Lears, "The Concept of Cultural Hegemony: Problems and Possibilities," *American Historical Review* 90 (June 1985): 572, 575–76. For another argument about the contingency of the coming of corporate capitalism, see Gretchen Ritter, *Goldbugs and Greenbacks: The Antimonopoly Tradition and the Politics of Finance in America* (Cambridge, 1997). Although Ritter admits that antimonopoly alternative left lasting legacies, she states that it was no longer viable after the 1890s. On the supposed foreclosure of republican economic radicalism, see James L. Huston, *Securing the Fruits of Labor: The American Concept of Wealth Distribution, 1765–1900* (Baton Rouge, 1998). Gerald Berk is the only one of the "contingency school" of historical political scientists who sees any hope in the twentieth century; see especially his "Neither Markets nor Administration: Brandeis and the Antitrust Reforms of 1914," *Studies in American Political Development* 8 (Spring 1994): 24–59.

5. Gordon, *Segmented Work*, 110. For a powerful comparative argument that re-opens the issue of middle-class–working-class alliances, see Doowon Suh, "Middle-Class Formation and Class Alliance," *Social Science History* 26 (Spring 2002): 105–37.

6. Vatter, *Drive*, 184; David Brody, "Labor and Small-Scale Enterprise during Industrialization," in Bruchey, *Small Business*, 263–79; Michael Kazin, *Barons of Labor: The San Francisco Building Trades and Union Power in the Progressive Era* (Urbana, 1987), 19; Cohen, "Struggle for Order." See also Michael Santos, "Laboring on the Periphery: Managers and Workers at the A. M. Byers Company, 1900–1956," *Business*

History Review 61 (Spring 1987): 133–53. For a contrary view that stresses petit bourgeois despotism in the "preindustrial," "backward," "premodern," and "anachronistic" secondary manufacturing sector, see Steven Fraser, "Combined and Uneven Development in the Men's Clothing Industry," *Business History Review* 57 (Winter 1983): 547.

7. Herbert G. Gutman, "Class, Status, and Community Power in Nineteenth-Century American Industrial Cities: Paterson, New Jersey: A Case Study," and "A Brief Postscript: Class, Status, and the Gilded Age Radical: A Reconsideration," in *Work, Culture, and Society in Industrializing America: Essays in American Working-Class and Social History* (New York, 1976), 255–56. Ira Berlin, in the illuminating introduction to Gutman's posthumous essays, shows how even Gutman unfortunately shrank from the full implications of his evidence of solidarity between the middle and working classes. Still, Gutman's many loyal followers have had the opportunity to explore, revise, and extend his insights. Yet except for an occasional comment confirming Gutman's insights for small-scale industrial cities during the Gilded Age, labor historians have almost completely refused to engage this issue. One partial exception is Shelton Stromquist, *A Generation of Boomers: The Pattern of Railroad Conflict in Nineteenth-Century America* (Urbana, 1987), especially 142–87.

As Berlin notes, Gutman was himself the son of a Queens drugstore owner, and his family was deeply embedded in Yiddish socialist culture. Berlin's desire to call Gutman a member of the working class rather than the middle class is indicative of the difficulty intellectuals have in conceiving that members of the petite bourgeoisie can be radical and in solidarity with workers. See Herbert Gutman, *Power and Culture: Essays on the American Working Class* (New York, 1987), 17, 4.

8. Lawrence M. Lipin, *Producers, Proletarians, and Politicians: Workers and Party Politics in Evansville and New Albany, Indiana, 1850–87* (Urbana, 1994); Sarah M. Henry, "The Strikers and Their Sympathizers: Brooklyn in the Trolley Strike of 1895," *Labor History* 32 (Summer 1991): 329–53; Steven L. Piott, *The Anti-monopoly Persuasion: Popular Resistance to the Rise of Big Business in the Midwest* (Westport, Conn., 1985), 70, 103–4; Robert H. Babcock, "'Will You Walk? Yes, We'll Walk!': Popular Support for a Street Railway Strike in Portland, Maine," *Labor History* 35 (Summer 1994): 372–98; Babcock reports the same popular support in other Canadian and U.S. strikes on 376–77. See also David O. Stowell, *Streets, Railroads, and the Great Strike of 1877* (Chicago, 1999), which unfortunately provide a far too narrowly materialist explanation for middle-class support of strikers.

For a broader view of the strength of republican political alliances, see Nick Salvatore, *Eugene V. Debs: Citizen and Socialist* (Urbana, 1982); and Richard Jules Oestreicher, *Solidarity and Fragmentation: Working People and Class Consciousness in Detroit, 1875–1900* (Urbana, 1986), 237; for the work that takes the politics of cross-class alliances most seriously, see Richard Schneirov's *Labor and Urban Politics: Class Conflict and the Origins of Modern Liberalism in Chicago, 1864–1897* (Chicago, 1998). Jeffrey Haydu, "Two Logics of Class Formation? Collective Identities among Proprietary Employers, 1880–1900," *Politics and Society* 27 (Dec. 1999): 507–27, points to earlier cooperation between employers and employees but then sees only hostility after the late nineteenth century.

For evidence of the continued strength of community support for strikers after World War II, see George Lipsitz, *Rainbow at Midnight: Labor and Culture in the 1940s*

(Urbana, 1994), 115–16; for examples of solidarity between small business owners and other white-collar members of the middle class in the context of Cold War politics, see William C. Pratt, "Workers, Bosses, and Public Officials: Omaha's 1948 Packinghouse Strike," *Nebraska History* 66 (Fall 1985): 294–313; and May, "Movie Star Politics." For rural examples of such cross-class alliances, see Joe William Trotter, *Coal, Class, and Color: Blacks in Southern West Virginia, 1915–1932* (Urbana, 1990).

9. Fink, *Workingmen's Democracy*, 223–24; Livingston, *Federal Reserve System*, 34, 42. For the purging and disciplining, see also James Livingston, "The Social Analysis of Economic History and Theory: Conjectures on Late Nineteenth-Century American Economic Development," *American Historical Review* 92 (Feb. 1987): 84.

10. Abbott, *Gateway*, 66; Craig Wollner, *The City Builders: One Hundred Years of Union Carpentry in Portland, Oregon, 1883–1983* (Portland, 1990), 17–23 (quotes on 21–22); Jack E. Triplett Jr., "History of the Oregon Labor Movement Prior to the New Deal," M.A. thesis, University of California, Berkeley, 1958, 33–34; Gaston, *Portland, Oregon*, 1:627. Such a division in the ranks of employers repeated itself in a 1903 painters' strike; see *PLP*, Apr. 17, 1903, 4.

11. Tobie, "Oregon Labor Disputes," 194; *Eastside News*, Nov. 5, 1906, 2; Oct. 22, 1906, 4.

12. The historical book that takes the language of middle class most seriously is Owensby, *Intimate Ironies*.

13. *OLP*, Dec. 16, 1916, 4; *OV*, Sept. 18, 1915, 245; *Oreg.*, Oct. 8, 1916, III, 11; *OLP*, Oct. 16, 1915, 4. For more on the battle for the heart and soul of the middle class, see *OV*, Feb. 26, 1916, 112.

14. *News*, Aug. 30, 1916, 6; *OLP*, Mar. 11, 1916, 2; June 10, 1916, 5; Oct. 13, 1916, 5.

15. *OLP*, July 1, 1916, 1.

16. *OLP*, Dec. 23, 1916, 1; July 1, 1916, 4; July 8, 1916, 1; *News*, Nov. 24, 1916, 1. This episode marked the continuation of previous hostility between the city's elite and the Grocers' and Merchants' Association. The previous November Portland's Employers' Association had invited the state Retail Merchants Association to join them in an open-shop offensive, but the Rose City branch "absolutely opposed" the alliance, warning of "industrial warfare in Portland" and noting its members' consistent friendliness "toward organized labor" (*PLP*, Nov. 13, 1915, 1).

17. *OLP*, Aug. 26, 1916, 1.

18. Phyllis Deane, "Capitalism," in *The Social Science Encyclopedia*, ed. Adam Kuper and Jessica Kuper, 2d ed. (New York, 1996), 71; Arthur M. Schlesinger Jr., "Epilogue: The One against the Many," in *Paths of American Thought*, ed. Schlesinger and Morton White (Boston, 1963), 536.

19. Sombart, *The Quintessence of Capitalism*; Max Weber, *The Protestant Ethic and the Spirit of Capitalism*, trans. Talcott Parsons (New York, 1958); Weber, *General Economic History*, trans. Frank H. Knight (New York, 1966), 207–9; R. H. Tawney, *Religion and the Rise of Capitalism: A Historical Study* (New York, 1926); Joseph A. Schumpeter, *Capitalism, Socialism, and Democracy* (New York, 1942). For brief overviews of the development of the concept of capitalism, see Maurice Dobb, *Studies in the Development of Capitalism* (New York, 1947), 1–8; Fernand Braudel, *The Wheels of Commerce*, trans. Siân Reynolds (New York, 1985), 232–39; Raymond Williams, "Capitalism," in *Keywords: A Vocabulary of Culture and Society*, rev. ed. (New York,

1983), 50–52; Meghnad Desai, "Capitalism," in *A Dictionary of Marxist Thought*, ed. Tom Bottomore, 2d ed. (New York, 1991), 71–75.

20. Peter Berger, *The Capitalist Revolution: Fifty Propositions about Prosperity, Equality, and Liberty* (New York, 1986), 19; Frederic C. Lane, "Meanings of Capitalism," *Journal of Economic History* 29 (Mar. 1969): 6; Alan Macfarlane, *The Culture of Capitalism* (London, 1987), 226; Robert L. Heilbroner, *The Nature and Logic of Capitalism* (New York, 1985), 52. For a definition comparable but more expansive than Berger's, see Thomas H. McCraw, ed., *Creating Modern Capitalism: How Entrepreneurs, Companies, and Countries Triumphed in Three Industrial Revolutions* (Cambridge, Mass., 1997), 3–4; for a distinction similar to Lane's, see James O'Connor, "A Note on Independent Commodity Production and Petty Capitalism," *Monthly Review* 27 (May 1976), 60–63.

21. Hartz, *Liberal Tradition in America*, Richard Hofstadter, *The American Political Tradition and the Men Who Made It* (New York, 1948), 55; Elizabeth Fox-Genovese, *Within the Plantation Household: Black and White Women of the Old South* (Chapel Hill, 1988), 55. The most forceful contemporary defense of the Hartz-Hofstadter tradition comes from John P. Diggins, most recently in *On Hallowed Ground: Abraham Lincoln and the Foundations of American History* (New Haven, 2000), esp. 222–27.

22. Fernand Braudel, *Civilization and Capitalism, 15th–18th Century*, trans. Siân Reynolds, 3 vols. (New York, 1981–84).

23. Braudel, *Wheels of Commerce*, 231, 238–39, 231, 229, 230; Braudel, *Afterthoughts on Material Civilization and Capitalism* (Baltimore, 1977), 62, 111, 113, 63, 111, 114, 115. Marc Egnal comments that the value in Braudel's definition is that it "allows us to talk about capitalism as a system that embraced only part of a society"; *Divergent Paths: How Culture and Institutions Have Shaped North American Economic Growth* (New York, 1996), 205.

24. Karl Marx, *Capital: A Critique of Political Economy*, trans. Samuel Moore and Edward Aveling, ed. Frederick Engels, 3 vols. (1867–94), 1:838 (emphasis added), 838, 839, 838, 840 (emphasis added), 842, 846, 848 (emphasis added). See also Hal Draper's argument, closely following Marx, that members of the petite bourgeoisie "are not capitalists"; *Karl Marx's Theory of Revolution*, vol. 2, *The Politics of Social Classes* (New York, 1978), 289.

I follow here the lead of the most sophisticated historical study of the development of capitalism. Robert Brenner has long argued that small property holding served as the primary barrier to the development of capitalism in early modern western Europe; see his contributions in *The Brenner Debate: Agrarian Class Structure and Economic Development in Pre-industrial Europe*, ed. T. H. Aston (Cambridge, 1985). For a more general discussion, see Brenner, "The Origins of Capitalist Development: A Critique of Neo-Smithian Marxism," *New Left Review* 104 (July–Aug. 1977): 32–33, 36–37, 49–50.

25. For another treatise on the distinction between "capitalism" and "property," see Hilaire Belloc, *The Servile State*, 3d ed. (London, 1927).

26. Hofstadter, *American Political Tradition*, viii.

27. Braudel, *Afterthoughts*, 63; Carl N. Degler, *Out of Our Past: The Forces That Shaped Modern America* (New York, 1959), 1.

28. The best bibliography of this massive literature is in Paul A. Gilje, "The Rise of Capitalism in the Early Republic," in *Wages of Independence: Capitalism in the Early*

Republic, ed. Gilje (Madison, 1997), esp. 13–15 n. 4; see also the various essays in the Gilje volume, especially Christopher Clark, "Rural America and the Transition to Capitalism," 65–79. The most incisive review is Allan Kulikoff, *The Agrarian Origins of American Capitalism* (Charlottesville, 1992), esp. 1–33. For the twentieth-century rural moral economy, see Stock, *Main Street in Crisis*; Marilyn P. Watkins, *Rural Democracy: Family Farmers and Politics in Western Washington, 1890–1925* (Ithaca, 1995); and Brian Q. Cannon, *Remaking the Agrarian Dream: New Deal Rural Resettlement in the Mountain West* (Albuquerque, 1996).

29. James A. Henretta, *The Origins of American Capitalism: Collected Essays* (Boston, 1991); Carolyn Merchant, *Ecological Revolutions: Nature, Gender, and Science in New England* (Chapel Hill, 1989); Kulikoff, *Agrarian Origins*; Clark, *The Roots of Rural Capitalism: Western Massachusetts, 1780–1860* (Ithaca, 1990); Nancy Grey Osterud, *Bonds of Community: The Lives of Farm Women in Nineteenth-Century New York* (Ithaca, 1991); Stephen Innes, *Creating the Commonwealth: The Economic Culture of Puritan New England* (New York, 1995); Winifred Barr Rothenberg, *From Market-Places to a Market Economy: The Transformation of Rural Massachusetts, 1750–1850* (Chicago, 1992); Joyce Appleby, *Capitalism and a New Social Order: The Republican Vision of the 1790s* (New York, 1984); Gordon S. Wood, "The Enemy Is Us: Democratic Capitalism in the Early Republic," in Gilje, *Wages of Independence*, 137–53, and Wood, *Radicalism of American Revolution*. A book that firmly weighs in on the capitalist side of the debate is William Cronon, *Changes in the Land: Indians, Colonists, and the Ecology of New England* (New York, 1983); for a compelling statement of the anticapitalist argument that discusses both farmers and artisans, see George David Rappaport, *Stability and Change in Revolutionary Pennsylvania* (University Park, Pa., 1996). For the best overview of the concept of "moral economy," see E. P. Thompson, *Customs in Common* (New York, 1991), 185–351, which includes both his original 1967 article "The Moral Economy of the English Crowd in the Eighteenth Century" and an imaginative review of the global scholarly uses of the term. See also, in a very different context, James C. Scott, *The Moral Economy of the Peasant: Rebellion and Subsistence in Southeast Asia* (New Haven, 1976).

30. Innes, *Creating the Commonwealth*, 8, 7, 29, 31; Appleby, *Capitalism and a New Social Order*, 45–47, 78, 104–5; Wood, "The Enemy Is Us," 148. The most well known attempt to reconcile the two camps is James T. Kloppenberg, "The Virtues of Liberalism: Christianity, Republicanism, and Ethics in Early American Political Discourse," in *The Virtues of Liberalism* (New York, 1998), 21–37.

31. Daniel Vickers, "Competency and Competition: Economic Culture in Early America," *William and Mary Quarterly* 47 (Jan. 1990): 7, 14, 17, 20. See also Vickers, *Farmers and Fishermen: Two Centuries of Work in Essex County, Massachusetts, 1630–1850* (Chapel Hill, 1994), esp. 13–29. For a chronological extension of the "competency" as a powerful force circumscribing our usual ideas of "profit" see Sally McMurry, *Transforming Rural Life: Dairying and Agricultural Change, 1820–1885* (Baltimore, 1995), 45, 52–55. In 1852 Webster's *American Dictionary* defined *competency* as "Sufficiency; . . . property or means of subsistence sufficient to furnish the necessaries and conveniences of life, without superfluity" (McMurry, 52).

32. On lawyers and speculators, see Vickers, "Competency," 22. Note that Vickers, 15–20, disputes the use of the term *moral economy* on strict Thompsonian standards.

33. For an interesting connection of peasants with the modern American middle

class, see Rowland Berthoff, "Peasants and Artisans, Puritans and Republicans: Personal Liberty and Communal Equality in American History," *JAH* 69 (Dec. 1982): 592.

34. Michael Merrill, "The Anti-capitalist Origins of the United States," *Review: Fernand Braudel Center* 13 (Fall 1990): 469, 468, 494, 466; Merrill, "Putting 'Capitalism' in Its Place: A Review of Recent Literature," *William and Mary Quarterly* 52 (Apr. 1995): 322–23; Merrill, "'Capitalism' and Capitalism," *History Teacher* 27 (May 1994): 278.

35. Fink, *Workingmen's Democracy*, 10. Leon Fink, who uncovered this testimony, perceptively remarks, "In part, what 'being a capitalist' implied was disregard for the workers' self-respect, the open defense of the laws of classical political economy, the working assumption of labor as a commodity." In nineteenth-century France, the government classified such in-between people as *ouvrier-patrons*; one engraver declared, "when you ask an engraver: are you an employer, are you a worker? He replies: wait until tomorrow, perhaps I'll be able to give you an answer, because today I don't know what I am." Geoffrey Crossick and Heinz-Gerhard Haupt, *The Petite Bourgeoisie in Europe, 1780–1914* (London, 1995), 40, 78. In general, compare Nicos Poulantzas, *Classes in Contemporary Capitalism* (London, 1978), 151: "The petty bourgeoisie is not a bourgeoisie smaller than the others; it is not part of the bourgeoisie at all, since it does not exploit, or at least is not chiefly involved in exploiting, wage labor."

36. Philip Scranton, *Proprietary Capitalism: The Textile Manufacture at Philadelphia, 1800–1885* (Philadelphia, 1983), 3, 69, 314. This theme continues in Scranton, *Figured Tapestry: Production, Markets, and Power in Philadelphia Textiles, 1885–1941* (New York, 1989); for Scranton's magnum opus, see *Endless Novelty: Specialty Production and American Industrialization, 1865–1925* (Princeton, 1997). For the same pattern of harmonious labor relations, see David Bensman, *The Practice of Solidarity: American Hat Finishers in the Nineteenth Century* (Urbana, 1985); for a dissent emphasizing the capitalistic nature of small producers, see Donna J. Rilling, *Making Houses, Crafting Capitalism: Builders in Philadelphia, 1790–1850* (Philadelphia, 2001). On the importance of the idea of a "competence" to Christopher Lasch's social theory, see *True and Only Heaven*, 530; for a gendered reading of competency in the English context, see Leonore Davidoff and Catherine Hall, *Family Fortunes: Men and Women of the English Middle Class, 1780–1850* (Chicago, 1987), 198–228. For similar moral conceptions of property among European small businessmen, see Crossick and Haupt, *Petite Bourgeoisie in Europe*, 201–5.

37. Lasch, *True and Only Heaven*, 532. For an overview emphasizing the strength, as well as continuity, of populist economic ideas, see Thomas Goebel, "The Political Economy of American Populism from Jackson to the New Deal," *Studies in American Political Development* 11 (Spring 1997): 109–48. Scranton himself characterizes his business owners as capitalists, although his goal is to demonstrate "the possibilities of capitalism" and that "capitalism is [not] a unity" (*Endless Novelty*, 3–4). For the most forceful argument that the majority of small business owners were *not* capitalists and did not think of themselves as capitalists, at least in the antebellum period, see Freyer's superb *Producers versus Capitalists*, esp. 4–15, 35–40. See also Lasch, *True and Only Heaven*, 205, but compare the challenge from Joyce Appleby, "The Popular Sources of American Capitalism," *Studies in American Political Development* 9 (Fall 1995): 437–57.

38. Hofstadter, *Age of Reform*, 46, 44–45, 58; Richard J. Ellis, *American Political Cultures* (New York, 1993), 38.

39. Bruce Palmer, *"Man over Money": The Southern Populist Critique of American Capitalism* (Chapel Hill, 1980), 203.

40. Ellis, *American Political Cultures*, 40; Palmer, *Man over Money*, 37.

41. Palmer, *Man over Money*, 31; Norman Pollack, *The Humane Economy: Populism, Capitalism, and Democracy* (New Brunswick, 1990), 161, 108, 143.

42. Ellis, *American Political Cultures*, 41; Palmer, *Man over Money*, 31, 220.

43. Pollack, *Humane Economy*, 51, 71, 108, 167, 57, 64–65. For a discussion of the "communal, pre-bourgeois" economic character of the farmers who became Populists, see Steven Hahn, *The Roots of Southern Populism: Yeoman Farmers and the Transformation of the Georgia Upcountry, 1850–1890* (New York, 1983), 52.

CHAPTER SIX
Petit Bourgeois Politics in Portland and World History

1. Martin J. Sklar, *The Corporate Reconstruction of American Capitalism, 1890–1916: The Market, the Law, and Politics* (New York, 1988).

2. Antonio Gramsci, *Selections from Political Writings (1910–1920)*, ed. Quentin Hoare, trans. John Matthews (London, 1977), 374.

3. Draper, *Marx's Theory of Revolution*, 291; Mayer, "Lower Middle Class," 416, 425, 432, 434.

4. Mayer, "Lower Middle Class," 436; Pierre Bourdieu, *Distinction: A Social Critique of the Judgement of Taste*, trans. Richard Nice (London, 1984), 338.

5. Roberto Mangabeira Unger, *Politics: A Work in Constructive Social Theory*, part 1, *False Necessity: Anti-necessitarian Social Theory in the Service of Radical Democracy* (New York, 1987), 11; Peter Bailey, "White Collars, Gray Lives? The Lower Middle Class Revisited," *Journal of British Studies* 38 (July 1999): 274; Hamilton, *Social Misconstruction of Reality*, 146–70, 153. For Hamilton's dissection of Mayer's article, see 157–59.

6. Jonathan M. Wiener, "Marxism and the Lower Middle Class: A Response to Arno Mayer," *Journal of Modern History* 48 (Dec. 1976): 666–671; Philip G. Nord, *Paris Shopkeepers and the Politics of Resentment* (Princeton, 1986), especially the conclusion. Wiener applies his ideas about petit bourgeois populism to the American context in an excellent reading of Nate Shaw's autobiography; see his review of *All God's Dangers: The Life of Nate Shaw* in *Journal of Social History* 10 (June 1976): 170–78. Nord continues to stress "the centrality of an awakened middle class" to successful democratic institutions in "The Origins of the Third Republic in France, 1860–1885," in *The Social Construction of Democracy, 1870–1990*, ed. George Reid Andrews and Herrick Chapman (New York, 1995), 52.

7. Geoffrey Crossick and Heinz-Gerhard Haupt, "Shopkeepers, Master Artisans, and the Historian: The Petite Bourgeoisie in Comparative Focus," in *Shopkeepers and Master Artisans in Nineteenth-Century Europe* (London, 1984), 15, 9, 5. See also Crossick and Haupt, *Petite Bourgeoisie in Europe*; and Jonathan Morris, *The Political Economy of Shopkeeping in Milan, 1886–1922* (Cambridge, 1993).

8. Harold Lasswell, "The Psychology of Hitlerism," *Political Quarterly* 4 (1933): 374; Lipset, *Political Man*. Peter Baldwin, "Social Interpretations of Nazism: Renewing a Tradition," *Journal of Contemporary History* 25 (Jan. 1990), 5–37, is one of the last

confident statements of this line of thinking; a more complex treatment of the Nazis and the German heritage of middle-class populism is Peter Fritzsche, *Rehearsals for Fascism: Populism and Political Mobilization in Weimar Germany* (New York, 1990). For persuasive indictments of the scholarly inadequacies of this tradition, see Hamilton, *Who Voted for Hitler?* 9–36, and Hamilton, *Social Misconstruction of Reality*, 107–70. For an example of the acceptance of the Lasswell-Lipset formulation, even by a writer otherwise skeptical of the standard scholarly treatment of the middle class, see Kevin Phillips, *Boiling Point: Democrats, Republicans, and the Decline of Middle-Class Prosperity* (New York, 1994 [1993]), 235.

9. Thomas Childers, introduction to *The Formation of the Nazi Constituency*, ed. Childers (London, 1986), 2; Conan Fischer, conclusion to *The Rise of National Socialism and the Working Classes in Weimar Germany*, ed. Fischer (Providence, R.I., 1996), 237–43. For the earliest compelling criticisms of the received wisdom, see Hamilton, *Who Voted for Hitler?*; Thomas Childers, *The Nazi Voter: The Social Foundations of Fascism in Germany, 1919–1933* (Chapel Hill, 1983); Childers, "The Middle Classes and National Socialism," in *The German Bourgeoisie*, ed. David Blackbourn and Richard J. Evans (London, 1991), 318–37. Michael Kater, *The Nazi Party: A Social Profile of Members and Leaders* (Cambridge, Mass., 1983), also helped reveal the broader Nazi social appeal, although Kater remained more sympathetic to the older view. For the elaboration of revisionism, see William Brustein, *The Logic of Evil: The Social Origins of the Nazi Party, 1925–1933* (New Haven, 1996); Conan Fischer, *The Rise of the Nazis* (Manchester, 1995); Detlef Mühlberger, *Hitler's Followers: Studies in the Sociology of the Nazi Movement* (London, 1991); and Jürgen Falter, *Hitlers Wähler* (Munich, 1991). Translations of Falter are "How Likely Were Workers to Vote for the NSDAP?" and "The Young Membership of the NSDAP between 1925 and 1933: A Demographic and Social Profile," in Fischer, *Rise of National Socialism*, 9–45, 79–98. The essays about England, France, Denmark, Belgium, and even Italy in Rudy Koshar, ed., *Splintered Classes: Politics and the Lower Middle Classes in Interwar Europe* (New York, 1990) also provide critical evidence to uncouple the lower middle class from fascism.

10. Nancy MacLean, *Behind the Mask of Chivalry: The Making of the Second Klan* (New York, 1994), esp. 179–88 and 251–53; Walter Nugent, "Tocqueville, Marx, and American Class Structure," *Social Science History* 12 (Winter 1988): 328, 329, 339. I critique MacLean's analysis of the petit bourgeois composition of the Klan in chapter 19. Sam Bass Warner Jr., in *Streetcar Suburbs: The Process of Growth in Boston, 1780–1900*, 2d ed. (Cambridge, Mass., 1978), esp. 86–101, uses *lower middle class* in an innovative but unreflective manner; see also Roy Rosenzweig, "Boston Masons, 1900–1935: The Lower Middle Class in a Divided Society," *Journal of Voluntary Action Research* 6 (July–Oct. 1977): 119–26.

11. MacColl and Stein, *Merchants, Money, and Power*.

12. Paul Gilman Merriam, "Portland, Oregon, 1840–1890: A Social and Economic History," Ph.D. diss., University of Oregon, 1971, 44; MacColl and Stein, *Merchants, Money, and Power*, 218, 244, 344–45, 359.

13. MacColl and Stein, *Merchants, Money, and Power*, 239; Wynne, "Reaction to the Chinese," 103.

14. MacColl and Stein, *Merchants, Money, and Power*, 240; *Oreg.*, June 3, 1888.

15. George H. Derrick to J. H. Hayne, Feb. 3, 1898, in Manuscript 1511—Associations and Institutions, APA File, OHSMA.

16. Charles F. Nute to J. H. Hayne, Feb. 4, 1898, APA File, OHSMA.

17. *PLP*, Sept. 8, 1913, 16.

18. MacColl and Stein, *Merchants, Money, and Power*, 244–45, 288, 314.

19. MacColl and Stein, *Merchants, Money, and Power*, 285, 435; Abbott, *Gateway*, 86.

20. *PLP*, Apr. 28, 1910, 6.

21. Martin J. Schiesl, *The Politics of Efficiency: Municipal Administration and Reform in America: 1880–1920* (Berkeley, 1977), 24; MacColl, *Growth of a City*, 32–33. For the basic events surrounding the adoption of the commission form of government, see MacColl and Stein, *Merchants, Money, and Power*, 445–50. The most complex treatment is Sarah M. Henry, "Progressivism and Democracy: Electoral Reform in the United States, 1888–1919," Ph.D. diss., Columbia University, 1995, 212–19.

22. David P. Thelen, "Two Traditions of Progressive Reform, Political Parties, and American Democracy," in *The American Constitutional System under Strong and Weak Parties*, ed. Patricia Bonomi, James MacGregor Burns, and Austin Ranney (New York, 1981), 42. For the most prominent arguments that the commission form of government was undemocratic, see Samuel P. Hays, "The Politics of Reform in Municipal Government in the Progressive Era," *Pacific Northwest Quarterly* 55 (Oct. 1964): 157–69, reprinted in Hays, *American Political History as Social Analysis* (Knoxville, 1980); and James Weinstein, *The Corporate Ideal in the Liberal State, 1900–1918* (Boston, 1968), 92–116. See also Lynette Boney Wrenn, *Crisis and Commission Government in Memphis: Elite Rule in a Gilded Age City* (Knoxville, 1998). Sarah Henry, *Progressive Democracy: Remaking the Vote in the United States, 1888–1919* (New York, forthcoming), will greatly clarify this issue.

For an argument that supports my position, noting that labor radicals and even Socialists often supported structural electoral reforms like the city commission form, see Fink, *Workingmen's Democracy*, 227; for a much more complex perspective that notes significant union support for the commission government, see Bradley Robert Rice, *Progressive Cities: The Commission Government Movement in America, 1901–1920* (Austin, 1977). No longer is it tenable to argue, as does Amy Bridges, that "There is overwhelming evidence about the class difference in sources of support for machine and reform government. Everywhere, machine politicians claimed strong support from working-class voters, while municipal reformers could count on middle-class voters." See *Morning Glories: Municipal Reform in the Southwest* (Princeton, 1997), 24–25.

23. Abbott, *Portland*, 69; Abbott, *Gateway*, 93; MacColl and Stein, *Merchants, Money, and Power*, 449. That Portland was the third largest city in 1913 comes from Rice, *Progressive Cities*, appendix; by 1922 it was the sixth largest. The measure to adopt the commission form of government energized the electorate; 35.8 percent more citizens voted on that measure than elected the mayor. Richard W. Montague, "The Oregon System at Work," *National Municipal Review* 3 (Apr. 1914), 282.

CHAPTER SEVEN

Will Daly: The Petit Bourgeois Hero of Labor

1. *Oreg.*, Mar. 24, 1924, 1; *PLP*, May 19, 1913, 1.

2. 1880 Greene County Census transcript, 202; *Missouri Weekly Patriot*, Jan. 13,

1876. I wish to thank Inabell Williams of the Springfield Public Library for her work in tracking down information about the early life of Daly and his family.

3. *Missouri Weekly Patriot*, Jan. 13, 1876; *Springfield and North Springfield City Directory, 1884–1885*, 46; Springfield *Republican*, May 17, 1901.

4. *PLP*, May 19, 1913, 1; *CD*, 1903–11; Jack E. Triplett Jr., "History of the Oregon Labor Movement Prior to the New Deal," M.A. thesis, University of California, Berkeley, 1961, 92; *PLP*, May 16, 1908, 4.

5. *PLP*, Jan. 1, 1911, 1; Jan. 18, 1912, 1.

6. *Oreg.*, May 3, 1909, 1, 3.

7. *PLP*, Apr. 13, 1911, 1; Mar. 23, 1911, 1; May 4, 1911, 1; June 2, 1913, 1–2; June 8, 1911, 1. Samuel P. Hays sees the election of union leaders like Daly under reformed municipal government as a sign that "spokesmen for labor as an organized functional group replaced working-class community leaders as decision makers." Still, this trend need not imply, as does Hays, a decline of democratization; historians need to examine the actual politics and policies of such commissioners. See Samuel P. Hays, "Political Parties and the Community-Society Continuum" (1967), in *American Political History*, 323.

According to one relatively impartial contemporary observer, Daly from 1911 to 1913 was "recognized as the most fearless and incorruptible man on the council, taking a major part in the fight against domination by the public utilities." See Philip Silver, "George Luis Baker: An Inquiry into the Methods and Psychology of Municipal Leadership," B.A. thesis, Reed College, 1926, 46.

8. *OV*, May 19, 1917, 234, 237.

9. *OV*, May 19, 1917, 251. One historian who has identified an important pattern of unionists going into business for themselves, and then into office as labor-oriented politicians, is Kazin, *Barons of Labor*, esp. 280.

10. *PLP*, May 19, 1913, 1; May 26, 1913, 1–2; MacColl and Stein, *Merchants, Money, and Power*, 448.

11. *Oreg.*, June 5, 1913, 12; June 5, 1913, 10; *PLP*, July 14, 1913, 1; *Oreg.*, Feb. 15, 1914, III, 6; *Jour.*, Mar. 24, 1914, 6; *Oreg.*, Sept. 18, 1914, 7; Apr. 24, 1915, 9; *OLP*, June 12, 1915, 1; *Jour.*, June 4, 1915, 6.

12. *OV*, May 19, 1917, 251; May 29, 1915, 137; MacColl and Stein, *Merchants, Money, and Power*, 448–49.

13. Carlos A. Schwantes, "The West Adapts the Automobile: Technology, Unemployment, and the Jitney Phenomenon of 1914–1917," *Western Historical Quarterly* 16 (July 1985): 313; *Jour.*, Mar. 24, 1917, 6; *Oreg.*, May 20, 1917, I, 20. Daly articulates his position on jitney policy most clearly in *Jour.*, May 22, 1917, 4.

14. Wollner, *Electrifying Eden*, 102; *Oreg.*, Oct. 23, 1916, 8; Oct. 30, 1916, 9; Oct. 17, 1916, 12.

15. *OLP*, Nov. 2, 1916, 3; Nov. 25, 1916, 1; Nov. 10, 1916, 9. Jitneys remained an issue in Portland at least through 1918, when city voters rejected a conservative attempt at their regulation. *OV*, May 25, 1918, 8.

16. *Oreg.*, June 1, 1917, 12; 1916 *VP*, 14.

17. *Oreg.*, June 3, 1917, I, 1, 4.

18. *Tel.*, June 2, 1917, 15; *Oreg.*, June 3, 1917, I, 17; June 4, 1917, 8; June 3, 1917, I, 1, 4. Daly's denunciation of the allegations is in *Jour.*, June 1, 1917, 1–2.

19. *Jour.*, May 19, 1917, 6; May 27, 1917, I, 6; May 22, 1917, 8; *Oreg.*, June 3, 1917, I, 22.

20. *Jour.*, May 22, 1917, 4; *News*, May 31, 1917, 5; May 14, 1917, 4; June 2, 1917, 1.

21. Silver, "George Luis Baker," 16, 20; MacColl, *Growth of a City*, 140; *OV*, May 19, 1917, 231.

22. MacColl, *Growth of a City*, 140, 142; Silver, "George Luis Baker," 42.

23. Silver, "George Luis Baker," 48–50.

24. *Oreg.*, June 3, 1917, I, 2.

25. *Jour.*, June 6, 1917, 1–2; *Oreg.*, June 4, 1917, 10; June 3, 1917, III, 6. The one historian who has picked up on the significance of the *Oregonian's* action is Gordon Dodds, who devotes a paragraph to the race between Daly and Baker in 1917 (*Oregon*, 182). That paragraph is, unfortunately, the most sustained treatment of Daly in any work of scholarship.

26. Silver, "George Luis Baker," 51. The following electoral analysis comes from results in *Oreg.*, June 7, 1917, 8.

27. In this and other analysis of precinct-level data, calculations are based on first-place votes alone. I want to thank Greg Earhart for invaluable work with the voting results.

The method of voting in the 1917 election, now known as *instant runoff voting*, has received renewed attention in light of the 2000 election. See Tom Wicker, "Instant Runoff Voting: A New Way to Vote," http://www.tompaine.com/opinion/2000/09/26/7.html; Lila Guterman, "When Votes Don't Add Up: Mathematical Theory Reveals Problems in Election Procedures," *Chronicle of Higher Education*, Nov. 3, 2000, A18; Robert Richie, Steven Hill, and Caleb Kleppner, "Instant Runoff Voting and Full Representation: Keys to Fulfilling Democracy's Promise," in *Democracy's Moment: Reforming the American Political System for the Twenty-first Century*, ed. Ronald Hayduk and Kevin Mattson (New York, 2002), 143–57; and the general information at http://www.fairvote.org/irv/index.html.

28. Abbott, *Portland*, 54–55. Precinct locations are in *Oreg.*, June 4, 1917, 11.

29. See appendix 2 for precinct voting density.

30. *News*, Sept. 27, 1916, 2. For Daly's precinct streaks, see the results from precincts 105 to 132 for the southeast and 241 to 298 for the north/northeast; for Baker's in Laurelhurst and Irvington, precincts 198 to 236½. The *News* specifically attributed Daly's defeat to the heavy turnout in the lumpen proletarian North End as well as Laurelhurst and Irvington; June 6, 1917, 1. On Laurelhurst as an "elite, upper-class neighborhood," see McFadden, "House and Home," 76, 114–20.

31. Dodds, *Oregon*, 182; *News*, May 31, 1917, 3; June 2, 1917, 1; *Jour.*, May 23, 1917, 8; May 31, 1917, 4; *Oreg.*, June 3, 1917, I, 20.

32. Silver, "George Luis Baker," 47.

33. The voting studies of renowned social scientist William Fielding Ogburn, who began his academic career at Reed College, suffer from this narrow conception of class; see Ogburn and Peterson, "Political Thought"; and William F. Ogburn and Inez Goltra, "How Women Vote: A Study of an Election in Portland, Oregon," *Political Science Quarterly* 34 (Sept. 1919): 413–33. Ogburn came to conclusions opposite from mine, arguing generally that class was largely irrelevant to voting on initiatives

and referenda in the Rose City and in particular that "the middle class resembles the upper class more than it does the laboring class" ("Political Thought," 311).

Theoretically problematic, however, is Ogburn's following the common view that "the middle class" was distinct from "the working class." Empirically, Ogburn's choice of middle-class precincts is also suspect. First, he only selected three such precincts for the 1910 and 1912 elections, and five for the 1914 general polling. (Ogburn increased the number of middle-class precincts to sixty-five in his study of 1914 women's voting, but he unfortunately did not provide their numbers or locations ("How Women Vote," 429). Second, the precincts themselves are not representative of East Side voting patterns. Ogburn's middle-class precincts, located in the Rose City Park and Sunnyside neighborhoods ("Political Thought," 304 n. 1), supported proportional representation, woman suffrage, and prohibition at close to the same levels as the East Side as a whole. Yet these precincts voted much more negatively on proposals involving economic radicalism than did the rest of the middling East Side, giving the 1914 single tax initiative only 33.3 percent of the vote (compared to 45.5 percent for the entire East Side) and, in 1917, giving Will Daly only 29.4 percent of the combined number of Baker-Daly ballots when Daly received almost double that percentage throughout the East Side. So, even though much more detailed empirical research should be done on these rich electoral records, it is reasonable now to overturn Ogburn's conclusions about middle-class voting.

Richard Lehne attempted to improve on Ogburn's study, but his similarly small number of middle-class precincts came only from the West Side; see Lehne, "An Analysis of Popular Support for Initiative and Referendum Measures in Oregon, 1902–1916," B.A. thesis, Reed College, 1965, 60. Gary King highlights the historic nature of Ogburn's studies in *A Solution to the Ecological Inference Problem: Reconstructing Individual Behavior from Aggregate Data* (Princeton, 1997), 3, as does David John Gow, "Quantification and Statistics in the Early Years of American Political Science, 1880–1922," *Political Methodology* 11 (1985): 1–18.

34. *News*, June 6, 1917, 1; *Jour.*, Mar. 2, 1918, 2; *Oreg.*, Mar. 3, 1918, I, 4; Feb. 12, 1920, 1; Apr. 18, 1920, I, 1; Oct. 16, 1920, 4. The war years in Portland are probingly analyzed in Adam Hodges, "World War I and Local Change in America: Federal War Production and Class Relations in Portland, Oregon," Ph.D. diss., University of Illinois, 2002.

35. *OV*, May 19, 1917, 230; *Oreg.*, Mar. 24, 1924, 1.

36. *Jour.*, July 12, 1950, I, 7. I traced the history of the Daly family and its business in *CD*, 1912–50.

PART III
"The Most Complete Democracy in the World": The Populist Radicalism of Direct Democracy

1. Lute Pease, "The Initiative and Referendum—Oregon's 'Big Stick,'" *Pacific Monthly*, May 1907, 570; *Oreg.*, Nov. 17, 1901, 10; Feb. 16, 1908, 9. Orton even served as acting president of the People's Power League in 1912, just at the time when that organization was losing most of its elite members and was consolidating its plebeian base (1912 *VP*, 35).

2. *Jour.*, Nov. 25, 1921, 2; Evans, "Oregon Progressive Reform," 178 n. 71; William S. U'Ren to Daniel Kiefer, Sept. 6, 1909, Lincoln Steffens Papers, Rare Book and Manuscript Library, Columbia University, New York; *Journal*, Nov. 25, 1921, 2; Johnson, "Protective Legislation, 94, 234; 1908 *VP*, 108; Lawrence J. Saalfeld, *Forces of Prejudice in Oregon, 1920–1925* (Portland, 1984 [1950]), 64. For Orton's legislative record, see *PLP*, Feb. 26, 1903, 1; for the "cataclysmic" salmon politics of 1908, see Joseph E. Taylor III, *Making Salmon: An Environmental History of the Northwest Fisheries Crisis* (Seattle, 1999), 151, 156–65, 185–87; for the rarity of workers serving on school boards during this period, see George S. Counts, *The Social Composition of Boards of Education: A Study in the Social Control of Public Education* (Chicago, 1927), 60.

3. For a contemporary statement of how those broadly in the middle were forces for a "new democracy," see Weyl, *The New Democracy*, 235–39.

CHAPTER EIGHT
Direct Democracy as Antidemocracy? The Evolution of the Oregon System, 1884–1908

1. Karl Marx, *The Eighteenth Brumaire of Louis Napoleon* (New York, 1963 [1852]), 15; Alan Brinkley, Nelson W. Polsby, and Kathleen M. Sullivan, *The New Federalist Papers: Essays in Defense of the Constitution* (New York, 1997), esp. 23–27 and 148–50; Peter Schrag, *Paradise Lost: California's Experience, America's Future* (New York, 1998), 269, 188, 272. See also David S. Broder, *Democracy Derailed: Initiative Campaigns and the Power of Money* (New York, 2000), a book hostile to direct democracy but one that includes the first serious consideration of William U'Ren in decades. For a succinct statement of the elitist liberal position, see Nelson Tebbe, "Rethinking Referenda," *Tikkun*, Sept.–Oct. 1998, 23–24; for compelling progressive defenses of direct democracy, see Julia Bloch, "Reclaim Referenda," *Tikkun*, Sept.–Oct. 1998, 24–25; Kevin Mattson, "Taking Back the Initiative: Renewing Progressive Democracy," *Social Policy* 29 (Summer 1999): 21–27; Joseph F. Zimmerman, *Participatory Democracy: Populism Revived* (New York, 1986); Zimmerman, *The Initiative: Citizen Law-Making* (Westport, Conn., 1999); and Galen Nelson, "Putting Democracy Back in the Initiative and Referendum," in Hayduk and Mattson, *Democracy's Moment*, 159–70. For a refutation of the thesis that big money has taken over the direct democracy process, see Elisabeth R. Gerber, *The Populist Paradox: Interest Group Influence and the Promise of Direct Legislation* (Princeton, 1999). See also www.iandrinstitute.org for the most impressive source relating to both the history and contemporary use of direct democracy. Most criticism of direct democracy does not take account of this wisdom of Thomas McGraw: "That these devices do not guarantee freedom from . . . abuses is not the fault of the progressives. . . . Rather, the blame lies with subsequent generations, which have often endured abuses few progressives would have tolerated." See Thomas K. McGraw, "The Progressive Legacy," in *The Progressive Era*, ed. Lewis L. Gould (Syracuse, 1974), 187.

2. Robert H. Wiebe, *Self-Rule: A Cultural History of American Democracy* (Chicago, 1995), 200; David Thelen, *Becoming Citizens in the Age of Television: How Americans Challenged the Media and Seized Political Initiative during the Iran-Contra Debate* (Chicago, 1996), 42. Wiebe and Thelen offer bracing counters to the liberal lack of faith

in majoritarianism. On conservative support of direct democracy, see Michael P. Federici, *The Challenge of Populism: The Rise of Right-Wing Democratism in Postwar America* (New York, 1991). For vigorous defenses of the rationality and desirability of populist democracy, see Benjamin I. Page and Robert Y. Shapiro, *The Rational Public: Fifty Years of Trends in Americans' Policy Preferences* (Chicago, 1992); Kevin Phillips, *Arrogant Capital: Washington, Wall Street, and the Frustration of American Politics* (Boston, 1994), esp. 172–77 and 183–95; and especially the work of Benjamin R. Barber, in particular *Strong Democracy: Participatory Politics for a New Age* (Berkeley, 1984). For an intriguing recent example of a proposal to rewrite the Constitution in the direction of a populist direct democracy, see Kenneth M. Dolbeare and Janette Kay Hubbell, *U.S.A. 2012: After the Middle-Class Revolution* (Chatham, N.J., 1996). For an older liberal tradition of faith in the masses, see Henry Steele Commager, *Majority Rule and Minority Rights* (Gloucester, Mass., 1958).

3. Paul Kleppner, "Voters and Parties in the Western States, 1876–1900," *Western Historical Quarterly* 14 (Jan. 1983): 66–67; Paul Kleppner, "Politics without Parties: The Western States, 1900–1984," in *The Twentieth-Century West: Historical Interpretations*, ed. Gerald D. Nash and Richard W. Etulain (Albuquerque, 1989), especially 328–29.

4. Rogin, *The Intellectuals and McCarthy*, 197; Philip J. Ethington, "The Metropolis and Multicultural Ethics: Direct Democracy versus Deliberative Democracy in the Progressive Era," in *Progressivism and the New Democracy*, ed. Sidney M. Milkis and Jerome M. Mileur (Amherst, 1999), 193; Arthur Lipow, *Political Parties and Democracy: Explorations in History and Theory* (London, 1996), 15, 7; Lipow, *Authoritarian Socialism in America: Edward Bellamy and the Nationalist Movement* (Berkeley, 1991 [1982]), 116.

For a much more persuasive argument that, contra Kleppner, strong political parties have generally served the dictates of conservative corporate interests, and that the resulting growth of direct democracy in the West was therefore indeed a *democratic* development with implications for contemporary American politics, see Martin Shefter, "The Regional Receptivity to Reform: The Legacy of the Progressive Era," *Political Science Quarterly* 98 (Fall 1983): 459–83, esp. 471, reprinted in Martin Shefter, *Political Parties and the State: The American Historical Experience* (Princeton, 1994).

5. Gabriel Kolko, *The Triumph of Conservatism: A Re-interpretation of American History, 1900–1916* (Glencoe: Free Press, 1963), Michael E. McGerr, *The Decline of Popular Politics: The American North, 1865–1928* (New York, 1986). Mark Lawrence Kornbluh, *Why America Stopped Voting: The Decline of Participatory Democracy and the Emergence of Modern American Politics* (New York, 2000) follows in this tradition. For a meditation on the general theme, see Robert D. Johnston, "Re-Democratizing the Progressive Era: The Politics of Progressive Era Political Historiography," *Journal of the Gilded Age and Progressive Era* 1 (Jan. 2002), 68–92.

None of the most commonly used syntheses of the Progressive Era mention the Oregon System. See Wiebe, *The Search for Order*; Arthur S. Link and Richard L. McCormick, *Progressivism* (Arlington Heights, Ill., 1983); Nell Irvin Painter, *Standing at Armageddon: The United States, 1877–1919* (New York, 1987); and Diner, *A Very Different Age*. Older books generally at least give it a brief mention; see Samuel P. Hays, *The Response to Industrialism: 1885–1914* (Chicago, 1957), 155–56. Fortunately, scholarly neglect of the Oregon System is beginning to come to an end; see the important treatments in Thomas Goebel, *A Government by the People: The Initiative and Referendum in America, 1890–1940* (Chapel Hill, 2002); and Henry, *Progressive Democracy*. Sidney M. Milkis, another political scientist, is the first scholar to place the national movement for direct democracy at the center of the meaning of Progressivism, although he also neglects Oregon; see "Introduction: Progressivism, Then and Now," in Milkis and Mileur, *Progressivism and the New Democracy*, 1–39.

6. Howe, "Most Complete Democracy." One contemporary scholar who recognizes this is David P. Thelen; see in particular his defense of direct democracy in "Two Traditions," which follows his brief comments in *The New Citizenship*, 2–3. See also his forthright defense of direct democracy in *Paths of Resistance: Tradition and Dignity in Industrializing Missouri* (New York, 1986), 268–69.

7. Benjamin Parke Dewitt, *The Progressive Movement* (New York, 1915), 214–15.

8. Schafer, *History of Pacific Northwest*, 303; George E. Mowry, *The California Progressives* (Berkeley, 1951), v. Historians who have noted this distinctive aspect of Progressivism in Oregon include Pomeroy, *The Pacific Slope*, 196; and Evans, "Oregon Progressive Reform," 33.

I do not pretend to offer here a comprehensive history of the development of the Oregon System; for that, see the solid treatments of Paul T. Culbertson, "A History of the Initiative and Referendum in Oregon," Ph.D. diss., University of Oregon, 1941; Evans, "Oregon Progressive Reform"; and, especially, Henry, *Progressive Democracy*. For other studies of direct democracy during this period, see David B. Magleby, *Direct Legislation: Voting on Ballot Propositions in the United States* (Baltimore, 1984); Thomas E. Cronin, *Direct Democracy: The Politics of Initiative, Referendum, and Recall* (Cambridge, Mass., 1989); Lloyd Sponholtz, "The Initiative and Referendum: Direct Democracy in Perspective, 1898–1920," *American Studies* 1 (Fall 1973): 43–64; Steven L. Piott, "The Origins of the Initiative and Referendum in America," *Hayes Historical Journal* 11 (Spring 1992): 5–17; John M. Allswang, *The Initiative and Referendum in California, 1898–1998* (Stanford, 2000); and the most comprehensive treatment, Goebel, *Government by the People*. The fairest example of contemporary scholarship to explore direct democracy nationally, but with a focus on Oregon, is Arthur N. Holcombe, *State Government in the United States* (New York, 1916), 401–44; for a bibliography, Edith M. Phelps, *Selected Articles on the Initiative and Referendum*, 3d ed. (New York, 1914), xvii–xlii.

9. *Oregon Vidette and Anti-Monopolist* (Salem), June 16, 1883, 2; June 25, 1885, 2; Nov. 16, 1885, 1; June 2, 1883, 2; June 23, 1883, 2. The existing run of the *Vidette* is extremely limited. The claim to its being the first advocate of the initiative and referendum comes from Joseph Teal, "The Practical Workings of the Initiative and Referendum in Oregon," in *The Initiative, Referendum, and Recall*, ed. William Bennet Munro (New York, 1912 [1909]), 217; Cecil T. Thompson, "The Origin of Direct Legislation in Oregon: How Oregon Secured the Initiative and Referendum," M.A. thesis, University of Oregon, 1929, 11; and Richard Clark Frey Jr., "The Oregon Press and the Beginning of the Oregon System, 1890–1903," M.A. thesis, University of Oregon, 1963, 27–28.

Thompson and Frey also state that Alfred Cridge was assistant editor during the paper's radical years in the mid-1880s. Cridge went on to become one of the most prominent radical proponents of extension of the Oregon System, single tax, and regulatory labor legislation. Cridge, the son of spiritualists and radical abolitionists, himself took credit for being the first to advocate direct legislation as early as 1884 "through the then virile Knights of Labor" and the *Vidette*. See Alfred Cridge, "William S. U'Ren, Lawgiver of Oregon and Single Taxer," *Single Tax Review*, Mar.–Apr. 1910, 35. On Cridge's parents and their prominence in the worlds of nineteenth-century reform, see John C. Spurlock, *Free Love: Marriage and Middle-Class Radicalism in America, 1825–1860* (New York, 1988); and Ann Braude, *Radical Spirits: Spiritualism and Women's Rights in Nineteenth-Century America* (Boston, 1989). On working-class support for direct democracy, see David Montgomery, *Citizen Worker: The Experience of Workers in the United States with Democracy and the Free Market during the Nineteenth Century* (New York, 1993), 161.

10. On the direct democracy movement in the 1890s, see Thompson, "Origin of Direct Legislation"; Culbertson, "History of the Initiative"; Homer L. Owen, "Oregon Politics and the Initiative and Referendum," B.A. thesis, Reed College, 1950; Evans, "Oregon Progressive Reform," 34–74; Thomas C. McClintock, "Seth Lewelling, William S. U'Ren, and the Birth of the Oregon Progressive Movement," *OHQ* 68 (Sept. 1967): 196–220; and perhaps still the basic source, Burton J. Hendrick, "The Initiative and Referendum and How Oregon Got Them," *McClure's* 37 (July 1911): 234–48.

11. Joint Committee on Direct Legislation, "The Initiative and Referendum," 4th ed. (n.p., n.d. [1893/94]), pamphlet at OSL, 10, 6, 8, 3; *Oreg.*, Mar. 18, 1894, 4, quoted in Frey, "Oregon Press," 46; Joint Committee, "Initiative and Referendum," 7.

The *compulsory* nature of the referendum was an integral part of the program of the early direct democrats in Oregon. For reasons unknown, U'Ren had, however, changed his thinking by 1896, in that year inventing the "curious" "voluntary" referendum method requiring petition signatures. He intended this method to be used at both the state and national levels. See Culbertson, "History of the Initiative," 57; Eltweed Pomeroy, "The Direct Legislation Movement and Its Leaders," *Arena* 16 (June 1896): 40; *DLR* 33 (Mar. 1896), 16. At the national level, Populist congressman William Peffer advocated a compulsory national referendum; see Peter H. Argersinger, *The Limits of Agrarian Radicalism: Western Populism and American Politics* (Lawrence, Kans., 1995), 243–44.

For the divisions within the Oregon Populist movement, many of them relating to direct legislation, see Marion Harrington, "The Populist Movement in Oregon, 1889–1896," M.A. thesis, University of Oregon, 1935; Robert C. Woodward, "William Simon U'Ren: In an Age of Protest," M.A. thesis, University of Oregon, 1956, 43–54; and David B. Griffiths, *Populism in the Western United States, 1890–1900* (Lewiston, N.Y., 1992), 105–84.

12. Gaston, *Portland, Oregon*, 1:634–35; Lincoln Steffens, "W. S. U'Ren, the Law Giver," *American Magazine*, Mar. 1908, 527–40, reprinted in Steffens, *Upbuilders* (Seattle, 1968 [1909]), 298; *Oreg.*, May 14, 1902, 8. U'Ren suffered from occasional charges of corruption throughout his active public life, but there is no compelling evidence that he was guilty of such accusations.

13. *DLR* 2 (June 1895), 15; *Kadderly v. Portland*, 44 Or. 118, 74 P. 710 (1903); *Pacific States Telephone and Telegraph Co. v. Oregon*, 223 U.S. 118 (1912); extracts from the most relevant court cases are included in Charles A. Beard and Birl E. Shultz, eds., *Documents on the State-Wide Initiative, Referendum, and Recall* (New York, 1912), 304–14; *DLR* 10 (Sept. 1903), 46; *Oreg.*, Nov. 17, 1901, 4; Feb. 20, 1909, 10. For the twists and turns in Harvey Scott's thinking about direct democracy, see Frey, "Oregon

Press," 91–102, 108. Beard himself saw that the initiative, if made as easy to use as U'Ren had in Oregon, "was undoubtedly a revolutionary change from the American system of government as conceived by the framers of the Constitution." See Charles A. Beard, *Contemporary American History, 1877–1913* (New York, 1914), 286.

For a contemporary review of the legal issues involved in direct legislation, and arguments that the Supreme Court decided *Pacific States* incorrectly and that direct democracy is indeed a violation of the "republican" clause in the U.S. Constitution, see Julian N. Eule, "Judicial Review of Direct Democracy," *Yale Law Journal* 99 (May 1990): 1503–90; and Douglas C. Hsiao, "Invisible Cities: The Constitutional Status of Direct Democracy in a Democratic Republic," *Duke Law Journal* 41 (Apr. 1992): 1267–1310.

14. *Oreg.*, Feb. 18, 1906, 10; *Equity*, Apr. 1910, 56; 1908 *VP*, 103. For these laws see, generally, Culbertson, "History of the Initiative"; Evans, "Oregon Progressive Reform"; Henry, *Progressive Democracy*. For the popular election of senators, see George H. Haynes, *The Senate of the United States: Its History and Practice* (Boston, 1938), 100–103; for the voters' pamphlet, see George H. Haynes, "The Education of Voters," *Political Science Quarterly* 22 (Sept. 1907): 484–97; on the recall see Joseph F. Zimmerman, *The Recall: Tribunal of the People* (Westport, Conn., 1997); for corrupt practices acts nationally during the Progressive Era, see Holcombe, *State Government*, 227–39; and Earl Sikes, *State and Federal Corrupt-Practices Legislation* (Durham, 1928). For the significant democratic consequences of the "Oregon model" and the Seventeenth Amendment generally, see Sara Brandes Crook and John R. Hibbing, "A Not-so-Distant Mirror: The Seventeenth Amendment and Congressional Change," *American Political Science Review* 91 (Dec. 1997): 845–53; for a conservative scholar's case against the direct election of senators, see C. H. Hoebeke, *The Road to Mass Democracy: Original Intent and the Seventeenth Amendment* (New Brunswick, 1995). See also Richard B. Bernstein, with Jerome Agel, *Amending America: If We Love the Constitution So Much, Why Do We Keep Trying to Change It?* (New York, 1993), 122–28; David E. Kyvig, *Explicit and Authentic Acts: Amending the Constitution, 1776–1995* (Lawrence, Kans., 1996), 208–14.

15. *DLR* 7 (Dec. 1901), 60; *Arena* 29 (Mar. 1903): 273; W. S. U'Ren, "The Operation of the Initiative and Referendum in Oregon," *Arena* 32 (Aug. 1904): 131; *Arena* 38 (July 1907): 84. For further examples of moderate defenses of the Oregon System, see Jonathan Bourne Jr., "Initiative, Referendum, and Recall," *Atlantic*, Jan. 1912, 122–31, reprinted in Munro, *Initiative, Referendum, and Recall*, 194–215; Montague, "Oregon System at Work"; and Teal, "Practical Workings," 217–32. The three most prominent contemporary book-length studies fall into the same category: Allen H. Eaton, *The Oregon System: The Story of Direct Legislation in Oregon* (Chicago, 1912); James D. Barnett, *The Operation of the Initiative, Referendum, and Recall in Oregon* (New York, 1915); and Gilbert L. Hedges, *Where the People Rule; or, The Initiative and Referendum, Direct Primary Law, and the Recall in Use in the State of Oregon* (San Francisco, 1914), esp. 111–14.

16. *Jour.*, July 16, 1903, 6; Oct. 20, 1908, 8; *PLP*, Mar. 18, 1904, 4; *Arena* 35 (May 1906): 510; "Dear Sir," Letter 15007 (1907), People's Power League, Initiative and Referendum Folder, OSL; 1908 *VP*, 103.

17. 1908 *VP*, 117; *PLP*, Sept. 1, 1908, 1, 4.

18. Joseph Schafer, "Oregon as a Political Experiment Station," *American Monthly*

Review of Reviews, Aug. 1906, 172–76; Oregon Legislative Research, *The History and Development of the Initiative and Referendum in Oregon and Other States* (n.p., 1978), 13, OSL; Montague, "Oregon System at Work," 278–83; Hendrick, "Law-Making by Voters, " 441.

19. *Oreg.*, Dec. 12, 1904, 8; Woodward, "William Simon U'Ren," 153; Charles H. Carey, "New Responsibilities of Citizenship," *Yale Law Journal* 18 (June 1909): 600; Evans, "Oregon Progressive Reform," 197. Some important examples of the opposition to the Oregon System include Frederick V. Holman, "Results in Oregon," in *Dangers of the Initiative and Referendum*, ed. Civic Federation of Chicago (Chicago, 1911), reprinted in Munro, *Initiative, Referendum, and Recall*, 279–97; A. Lawrence Lowell, *Public Opinion and Popular Government* (New York, 1913); Elihu Root, *Experiments in Government and the Essentials of the Constitution* (Princeton, 1913), 24–39; William Howard Taft, *Popular Government: Its Essence, Its Permanence, and Its Peril* (New Haven, 1913), 52–55; George Kennan, "The Direct Rule of the People," *North American Review* 198 (Aug. 1913): 145–60; R. A. Ballinger, "A Discussion of the Oregon System," *OV*, Dec. 18, 1915, 213–26. The Portland *Spectator*, voice of the open-shop business elite, also consistently denounced direct democracy.

CHAPTER NINE
Direct Democracy's Mechanic: William S. U'Ren

1. Paul Douglas, *In the Fullness of Time: The Memoirs of Paul H. Douglas* (New York, 1972), 33.

2. Theodore Roosevelt, "The People of the Pacific Coast," *Outlook*, Sept. 23, 1911, 162. For Roosevelt's relationship to direct democracy, see Sidney M. Milkis and Daniel J. Tichenor, "'Direct Democracy' and Social Justice: The Progressive Party Campaign of 1912," *Studies in American Political Development* 8 (Fall 1994): 282–340; and Theodore Roosevelt, *Progressive Principles: Selections from Addresses Made during the Presidential Campaign of 1912*, ed. Elmer H. Youngman (New York, 1913), esp. "The Right of the People to Rule" and "A Charter of Democracy," 19–83.

3. Norman Hapgood, *The Changing Years: Reminiscences of Norman Hapgood* (New York, 1930), 237. For Wilson's own personal closeness to and crediting of U'Ren, see "An Address in New Haven, Connecticut, on Civil Service Reform," in *The Papers of Woodrow Wilson*, ed. Arthur S. Link, vol. 24, 1912 (Princeton, 1977), 175–76 and the reports of his 1911 trip to Oregon in *Papers of Woodrow Wilson*, vol. 23, 1911–1912 (Princeton, 1977), 61–79. See also "Wilson Urges Oregon System for New Jersey," *La Follette's Weekly Magazine*, Jan. 28, 1911, 8; and Woodward, "William Simon U'Ren," 136–41.

4. George E. Mowry, *The Era of Theodore Roosevelt and the Birth of Modern America* (New York, 1958), 77; Holbrook, *Lost Men*, 319.

5. Basic biographical information comes from Woodward, "William Simon U'Ren," which is boiled down in "William S. U'Ren: A Progressive Era Personality," *Idaho Yesterdays* 4 (Summer 1960): 4–10; Esther G. Weinstein, "William Simon U'Ren: A Study of Persistence in Political Reform," Ph.D. diss., Syracuse University, 1967; Steffens, "W. S. U'Ren"; *Jour.*, Nov. 18, 1927, 14; "William Simon U'Ren," in *Dictionary of American Biography*, ed. John A. Garraty and Edward T. James, Supplement 4 (New

York, 1974), 844–45; and "William Simon U'Ren," in *American National Biography*, ed. James A. Garraty and Mark C. Carnes (New York, 1999), 22: 121–23.

6. Evans, "Oregon Progressive Reform," 55; Steffens, "W. S. U'Ren," 290, 289, 291; Woodward, "William Simon U'Ren," 3; Steffens, "W. S. U'Ren," 293; Direct Legislation League, Financial Statement, n.d., Jonathan Bourne Papers, SCUO; William and F. J. U'Ren to William S. U'Ren, n.d. [1908], Lincoln Steffens Papers, Rare Book and Manuscript Library, Columbia University, New York.

7. Woodward, "William Simon U'Ren," 2; Evans, "Oregon Progressive Reform," 55, 58; Thompson, "Origin of Direct Legislation," 20; Steffens, "W. S. U'Ren," 288–89. The adult U'Ren remained unchurched and rarely spoke of spiritual matters; once he concluded a long Sunday evening talk at the Unitarian church: "I believe the very best religion is good politics, and the very best politics is good religion" (*PLP*, Nov. 23, 1911, 8). According to one account based on an interview with U'Ren's niece, U'Ren experimented with "nearly every variety of religion from Christian Science to theosophy, on one occasion even helping to finance a Hindu book." Scott Reed, "W. S. U'Ren and the Oregon System," B.A. thesis, Princeton University, 1950, 18.

8. *Jour.*, Nov. 18, 1927, 14; Woodward, "William Simon U'Ren," 1; Gaston, *Portland, Oregon*, 2:649.

9. *Jour.*, Nov. 18, 1927; McClintock, "Seth Lewelling," 203; Griffiths, *Populism*, 137; *Oreg.*, Apr. 13, 1900, 5; Woodward, "William Simon U'Ren," 55, 62, 64, 67; Weinstein, "William Simon U'Ren," 51–53; *Jour.*, May 1, 1949, A9; *Oreg.*, Sept. 3, 1914, 6.

10. *DLR* 5 (Mar. 1898), 19; Steffens, "W. S. U'Ren," 325.

11. Steffens, "W. S. U'Ren," 287, 294, 287–88 (emphasis added).

12. *Oreg.*, July 17, 1906, VIII, 4; Evans, "Oregon Progressive Reform," 254; Woodward, "William Simon U'Ren," 76–77 (quote, 142); U'Ren to L. H. McMahan, July 18, 1904, McMahan Papers, SCUO. U'Ren rarely spoke about racial issues. In a 1928 interview, however, U'Ren recounted how he learned about the corruption of politics when he attempted to intervene on behalf of Chinese immigrants during an 1880 riot that he later found out had been instigated by the Denver Republican Party; see Thompson, "Origin of Direct Legislation," 22–23.

13. Steffens, "W. S. U'Ren," 323; Edwards, *Sowing Good Seeds*, 230; Woodward, "William Simon U'Ren," 104; *Oreg.*, Apr. 6, 1908, 2; Weinstein, "William Simon U'Ren," 116; Culbertson, "History of the Initiative," 113, 121; *PLP*, Nov. 7, 1910, 4; *Jour.*, Sept. 6, 1908, I, 16; *Oreg.*, Feb. 25, 1908, 6; Evans, "Oregon Progressive Reform," 162–65.

14. Woodward, "William Simon U'Ren," 136; "William Simon U'Ren," in Garraty and James, *Dictionary of American Biography*, 845; Henry, "Progressivism and Democracy," 235; *Oreg.*, Oct. 14, 1914, 14; Aug. 1, 1913, 10; "My Platform," U'Ren Folder, Oregon History Vertical File, OSL; *Oreg.*, Feb. 8, 1914, 10. U'Ren's full employment scheme had much in common with Jacobin policy during the French Revolution; see Jean-Pierre Gross, *Fair Shares for All: Jacobin Egalitarianism in Practice* (New York, 1997), 146–53.

15. *PLP*, Sept. 28, 1914, 2; *Oreg.*, Mar. 11, 1914, 10; Feb. 25, 1914, 8; Feb. 28, 1914, 8; Aug. 27, 1914, 6.

16. *OV*, May 8, 1915, 47; *PLP*, Oct. 26, 1914, 4; *News*, Nov. 6, 1912, Second Election Extra, 1; *News*, Nov. 2, 1914, 1; *PLP*, Labor Day, 1913, 31; Evans, "Oregon Progressive Reform," 294–95.

17. *Oreg.*, Nov. 24, 1914, 6; *OLP*, Jan. 15, 1916, 1; *Tel.*, June 21, 1921, 1; June 22,

1921, 1; Tobie, "Oregon Labor Disputes," 245, 259; Arthur H. Bone, ed., *Oregon Cattleman/Governor/Congressman: Memoirs and Times of Walter M. Pierce* (Portland, 1981), 135; *OV*, Jan. 25, 1919, 14; *Oreg.*, Sept. 29, 1919, 3; Oct. 6, 1919, 8.

18. *Oreg.*, Mar. 9, 1920, 3; Mar. 12, 1920, 4; Mar. 3, 1920, 1; Mar. 16, 1920, 5; Mar. 12, 1920, 4. A few months after the trial James Martin, former U.S. consul-general to New Zealand, made the intriguing accusation that U'Ren was a "spy" for socialists, joining the Republican Party merely "to socialize it from within" (*Oreg.*, Aug. 28, 1920, 5). On U'Ren and the CLP, see Harry W. Stone Jr., "Oregon Criminal Syndicalism Laws and the Suppression of Radicalism by State and Local Officials," M.A. thesis, University of Oregon, 1933, 22–24.

19. *Jour.*, Apr. 12, 1925, 1, 16; *Oreg.*, Jan. 13, 1938, 5; Albert F. Gunns, *Civil Liberties in Crisis: The Pacific Northwest, 1917–1940* (New York, 1983), 204, 64; Woodward, "William Simon U'Ren," 155; John Chamberlain, *Farewell to Reform: The Rise, Life, and Decay of the Progressive Mind in America* (Chicago, 1965 [1932]), 73. Gunns claims that "there was little evidence that [U'Ren] took an active part in challenging the criminal syndicalism laws" (64–65), but this is clearly untrue given his role in the 1920 trial. Still, U'Ren does seem to have become reluctant to defend Communists by the 1930s (206, 213). For a confirmation of U'Ren's anticommunism of the 1930s, see Harry H. Stein, "Gus Jerome Solomon: A Biography," manuscript in the author's possession.

20. Weinstein, "William Simon U'Ren," 134–37; "W. S. U'Ren's Bill to Abolish Unemployment," appendix 4 in Reed, "W. S. U'Ren," 91–94; *Jour.*, May 12, 1935, 4; Otis L. Graham Jr., *An Encore for Reform: The Old Progressives and the New Deal* (New York, 1967), 68–69.

21. *Jour.*, Jan. 9, 1949, 3; *Oreg.*, Dec. 13, 1948, 9.

22. *Oreg.*, Oct. 3, 1946. U'Ren thus fits neatly into the tradition so well laid out in Horowitz, *Beyond Left and Right*.

23. *DLR* 3 (Dec. 1896), 46–47; C. B. Galbreath, comp., *Initiative and Referendum: Published for the Constitution of 1912* (Columbus, 1912), 73; Pease, "Initiative and Referendum," 574–75; Lipow, *Political Parties and Democracy*, 18. U'Ren applauds the effective disfranchisements of illiterates in "Six Years of the Initiative and Referendum in Oregon," *Chicago City Club Bulletin*, May 26, 1909, 465, 477. See also W. S. U'Ren, "Strength and Weakness of the Oregon System as Developed by Ten Years of Operation," *OV*, Jan. 15, 1916, 387–88. Alexander Keyssar surveys the antidemocratic implications of progressive electoral reforms in *The Right to Vote: The Contested History of Democracy in America* (New York, 2000), 117–72.

24. William S. U'Ren, "Results of the Initiative and Referendum in Oregon," *Proceedings of the American Political Science Association* 4 (1907): 193, 197; *PLP*, Jan. 13, 1910, 6; Barnett, *Operation of the Initiative*, 54; *OV*, Feb. 15, 1919, 316.

25. N.A., *Single Tax Conference Held in New York City, Nov. 19 and 20, 1910* (Cincinnati, 1911).

CHAPTER TEN
From the Grand Reorganization to a Syndicalism of Housewives: Feminist Populism and the Other Spirit of '76

1. Beard and Shultz, *Documents*, v; *Oreg.*, Dec. 22, 1906, XIII, 1; *Jour.*, May 25, 1912, 6.

2. C. H. Chapman, Lee M. Clark, Will Daly, et al., "Introductory Letter: Additional Explanation Bill for a Law and Suggested Amendments to the Constitution of Oregon" (1909), People's Power League Pamphlets, OSL, 1; *Equity*, July 1913, 164; Beard and Schultz, *Documents*, 351. There were several variations in this plan between the time it was introduced in 1909 and basically abandoned in 1914; see Chapman, Clark, and Daly, "Introductory Letter"; George M. Orton, E. S. J. McAllister, C. Schuebel, et al., *Please Read* (1910), People's Power League Pamphlets, OSL; and W. G. Eggleston, A. D. Cridge, and W. S. U'Ren, *People's Power and Public Taxation* (Portland, 1910). For coverage of the changes see George H. Haynes, "'People's Rule' in Oregon, 1910," *Political Science Quarterly* 26 (Mar. 1911): 32–62, and Haynes, "'People's Rule' on Trial: The Oregon Election, November 5, 1912," *Political Science Quarterly* 28 (Mar. 1913): 18–33. Unless otherwise noted, I have drawn my conclusions and quotations from the most accessible formulation of the plan, reprinted as an appendix to Beard and Schultz, *Documents*, 349–83. See also James D. Barnett, "Reorganization of State Governments," *American Political Science Review* 9 (Mar. 1915): 287–93; and Albert M. Kales, *Unpopular Government in the United States* (Chicago, 1914), 185–88.

3. Beard and Schultz, *Documents*, 350.

4. *Equity*, July 1913, 164; Beard and Schultz, *Documents*, 353 (emphasis added).

5. Beard and Schultz, *Documents*, 354; Eggleston, Cridge, and U'Ren, *People's Power*, 105; Beard and Schultz, *Documents*, 353–54. Under an initial version of the proposal, the inspectors would have full investigatory powers over all state, county, and municipal government (1910 VP, 181).

6. William S. U'Ren, "Remarks on Mr. Herbert Croly's Paper on 'State Political Reorganization,'" *Proceedings of the American Political Science Association* 8 (1912): 137 (replying to Herbert Croly, "State Political Reorganization," *Proceedings of the American Political Science Association* 8 [1912]: 122–35); U'Ren, "Strength and Weakness of the Oregon System," 387–88. Elisabeth Clemens warns against easy assumptions about the use of corporate organization models by farm, labor, and women's groups during the Progressive Era: "if organizational forms are part of a public discourse, business methods may be used by many actors for many reasons, including opposition to business interests. Fire may be fought with fire." Elisabeth S. Clemens, *The People's Lobby: Organizational Innovation and the Rise of Interest Group Politics in the United States, 1890–1925* (Chicago, 1997), 47.

7. Herbert Croly, *Progressive Democracy* (New York, 1914), 284–308 (quote, 308); Beard, "Reconstructing State Government," *New Republic*, Aug. 21, 1915, II, 1–16 (quote, 7). An examination of both the Oregon and the Croly reconstruction plans, favorable to both, is Walter F. Dodd, "Proposed Reforms in State Government," *American Political Science Review* 4 (May 1910): 243–51.

8. Daniel T. Rodgers, *Contested Truths: Keywords in American Politics since Independence* (New York, 1987), 182–84; Lipow, *Political Parties and Democracy*, 19; Dwight Waldo, *The Administrative State: A Study of the Political Theory of American Public Administration* (New York, 1948), 36.

9. U'Ren, "Remarks on Mr. Herbert Croly's Paper," 137; Weyl, *New Democracy*, 310–11. Even Samuel Haber, a historian highly critical of efficiency, has recognized that it was possible for efficiency to coexist with, and not just override, democracy. See *Efficiency and Uplift: Scientific Management in the Progressive Era, 1880–1920* (Chicago, 1964), xi, 116.

Similar reasoning underlay the People's Power League's support for the short ballot, an important part of the grand reorganization. Quoting its primary advocate, Richard Childs, U'Ren and his comrades argued that decreasing the number of candidates at each election allowed for "the maximum amount of concentrated public scrutiny at the election" and that

> the more elaborate and complex you make politics the fewer the people who can afford the time and energy to take part. Too much electing, therefore, leads toward oligarchy—the rule of the few.
>
> The simpler you make politics the more easily and the more surely will the whole people take part. Simplification, therefore, leans toward the rule of the many—democracy. (Orton, McAllister, and Schuebel, *Please Read*, 28, 30)

For a fuller defense of the short ballot, see Bernard Hirschhorn, *Democracy Reformed: Richard Spencer Childs and His Fight for Better Government* (Westport, Conn., 1997).

10. 1912 *VP*, 221; 1914 *VP*, 82–83; *PLP*, Sept. 21, 1914, 1; *Oreg.*, Sept. 3, 1914, 8; Alvin W. Johnson, *The Unicameral Legislature* (Minneapolis, 1938), 96.

During the teens, at least ten states seriously considered unicameralism, starting with Oregon and Ohio in 1912. A contemporary defense of unicameralism is Schuyler C. Wallace, "The Legislative Gauntlet," *Woman Citizen*, Feb. 23, 1924, 13–14. The best overview of unicameralism throughout American history is Johnson, *The Unicameral Legislature*; see also Daniel B. Carroll, *The Unicameral Legislature of Vermont* (Montpelier, 1933), esp. 1–11; Cronin, *Direct Democracy*, 32–34. The most prominent unicameralist in American history, after Benjamin Franklin and Tom Paine, was Harry Lane's dear friend George Norris; for the story of unicameralism's triumph in Nebraska, see John P. Senning, *The One-House Legislature* (New York, 1937); and Richard Lowitt, *George W. Norris: The Triumph of a Progressive, 1933–1944* (Urbana, 1978), 58–70. For an argument about how thoroughly undemocratic and "defective" the current structure of the Senate is, see Michael Lind, *The Next American Nation: The New Nationalism and the Fourth American Revolution* (New York, 1995), 316–18.

11. Orton, McAllister, and Schuebel, *Please Read*, 8; Peter H. Argersinger, "The Value of the Vote: Political Representation in the Gilded Age," *JAH* 76 (June 1989): 63; Richard Oestreicher, "Urban Working-Class Political Behavior and Theories of American Electoral Politics, 1870–1940," *JAH* 74 (Mar. 1988): 1270; Argersinger, "Value of the Vote," 63. U'Ren and his allies hoped to change all governing bodies to PR. U'Ren noted in 1905 that proportional representation would have converted the Portland city council from an all-Republican body to one including seven Republicans, three Democrats, three reformist Citizens Party members, one Socialist, and one Prohibitionist (*Oreg.*, Oct. 23, 1905, 6).

12. 1910 *VP*, 171–74; 1912 *VP*, 212–13, 1914 *VP*, 78–79. The People's Power League was therefore a "most ingenious adaptation" of the Party List (PL) PR method prevalent throughout Europe, with the crucial difference that voters would have voted for individual candidates, not slates selected by different parties. U'Ren did consider using the single transferable vote (or Hare) system of PR, which was more popular among American proportional representationalists, and it is unclear why the PPL decided against this method. The STV generally involved creating multimember districts where voters ranked their preference for candidates (1, 2, 3, and so on). Each number 1 tally that a winning candidate did not need, or that could not help a hopeless

candidate, was then switched to the candidate with the number 2 preference, and so on, until enough candidates had the necessary quota. See *Equity*, Jan. 1909, 31; *Oreg.*, July 15, 1910, 7. For clear and fuller contemporary and current explanations of PL and STV, as well as other PR methods, see Paul H. Douglas, "The Necessity for Proportional Representation," *Ethics* 34 (1923–24): 6–26; Douglas Amy, *Real Choices/New Voices: The Case for Proportional Representation Elections in the United States* (New York, 1993), 13–20, 225–33; and Kathleen Barber, *Proportional Representation and Election Reform in Ohio* (Columbus, Ohio, 1995), 67–82.

13. *Daily Oregon Statesman* (Salem), Oct. 22, 1914, 3; *PLP*, Nov. 23, 1911, 8.

14. Howard Lee McBain and Lindsay Rogers, *The New Constitutions of Europe* (Garden City, N.Y., 1922), 84; Douglas, "Necessity for Proportional Representation," 15; Leon Weaver, "The Rise, Decline, and Resurrection of Proportional Representation in Local Governments in the United States," in *Electoral Laws and Their Political Consequences*, ed. Bernard Grofman and Arend Lijphart (New York, 1986), 141. The classic history and defense of proportional representation is Clarence Gilbert Hoag and George Hervey Hallett, *Proportional Representation* (New York, 1926), followed by George H. Hallett and Clarence Gilbert Hoag, *Proportional Representation: The Key to Democracy* (New York, 1940). The best bibliographies are Lamar T. Beman, *Proportional Representation* (New York, 1925); and Amy, *Real Choices/New Voices*.

15. W. G. Eggleston, "The People's Power in Oregon," *World's Work* 22 (May 1911): 14356; Culbertson, "History of the Initiative," 112; *Oreg.*, Nov. 3, 1910, 12; Henry, "Progressivism and Democracy," 212–17. For an excellent review of PR, as well as its role in California politics, see Tom Sitton, "Proportional Representation and the Decline of Progressive Reform in Los Angeles," *Southern California Quarterly* 77 (Winter 1995): 347–64.

16. These election results are calculated from the precinct-level voting data in 1910 Abstract; precinct locations are from *Jour.*, Nov. 4, 1912, 6.

17. In 1912 the People's Power League combined proportional representation with parts of the grand reorganization, and the measure went down to defeat statewide by a margin of 30.4 to 69.6 percent. In 1914 proportional representation stood alone, and it garnered only 22.5 percent of the vote. In neither election did geographic voting patterns matter.

18. 1910 *VP*, 173; 1914 *VP*, 80.

19. Lani Guinier, *The Tyranny of the Majority: Fundamental Fairness in Representative Democracy* (New York, 1994); Cass R. Sunstein, "Beyond the Republican Revival," *Yale Law Journal* 97 (July 1988): 1588–89. For a compelling analysis of the political theory of group representation that advocates PR, see Melissa S. Williams, *Voice, Trust, and Memory: Marginalized Groups and the Failings of Liberal Representation* (Princeton, 1998), esp. 215–37; see also John Low-Beer, "The Constitutional Imperative of Proportional Representation," *Yale Law Journal* 94 (1984): 163–88; Amy, *Real Choices/ New Voices*; Arend Lijphart, *Patterns of Democracy: Government Forms and Performance in Thirty-Six Countries* (New Haven, 1999), 143–70; Mark Monmonier, *Bushmanders and Bullwinkles: How Politicians Manipulate Electronic Maps and Census Data to Win Elections* (Chicago, 2000), 136–49; G. Bingham Powell, *Elections as Instruments of Democracy: Majoritarian and Proportional Visions* (New Haven, 2000); Robert Richie and Steven Hill, *Whose Vote Counts?* (Boston, 2001). The best short statements are Hendrik Hertzberg, "Let's Get Representative," *New Republic*, June 29, 1987, 15–18;

and Michael Lind, "A Radical Plan to Change American Politics," *Atlantic*, Aug. 1992, 73–83; the most important current advocate of PR is the Center for Voting and Democracy, at http://www.igc.org/cvd/. Still the most forceful argument against PR is Ferdinand A. Hermens, *The Representative Republic* (South Bend, 1958). During the heyday of PR, African Americans, women, and Communists all saw increases in their levels of representation in Cleveland, Cincinnati, Toledo, and New York City; see Barber, *Proportional Representation in Ohio*, 66, 158, 300–302.

20. Sarah Henry first pointed to the complex relationship of the two movements in Oregon in "Progressivism and Democracy," 197–208; in *The Public City: The Political Construction of Urban Life in San Francisco, 1850–1900* (New York, 1994), 401, Philip J. Ethington also remarks that "the enfranchisement of women was an issue apart from the other major reform issues of the Progressive Era." For brief introductions to the Oregon movement, see Lauren Kessler, "A Siege of the Citadels: Search for a Public Forum for the Ideas of Oregon Woman Suffrage," *OHQ* 84 (Summer 1983): 117–49, and Kessler, "The Ideas of Woman Suffrage and the Mainstream Press," *OHQ* 84 (Fall 1983): 257–75.

21. *Washington Post*, Sept. 17, 1905, IV, 7.

22. Evans, "Oregon Progressive Reform," 132; Edwards, *Sowing Good Seeds*, 228–31, 236–37; *Jour.*, June 3, 1906, Scrapbook 89, 52, OHS; *Oreg.*, May 21, 1906, 14; 1910 *VP*, 167; *Oreg.*, Nov. 3, 1912, III, 12; Alfred D. Cridge, "Why So Many Measures in Oregon?" *Equity*, Oct. 1912, 133.

23. *Oreg.*, May 21, 1906, 14; *Tel.*, June 1, 1906, 9; Nov. 6, 1912, 1; U'Ren, "Strength and Weakness," 384; *PLP*, Nov. 9, 1914, 1.

24. *Jour.*, July 3, 1905, 9; Ida Husted Harper, ed., *The History of Woman Suffrage* (New York, 1922), 6:136; Boyer letter, Mar. 17, 1906, in Scrapbook 86, 14, OHS; OESA Circular to Clerics, Apr. 24, 1906, Scrapbook 90, 108, OHS; OESA, "Voters Read: Denial to Protest of Corporate Interests," *Oreg.*, June 1, 1906, 13.

25. Harper, *History of Woman Suffrage*, 6:543; *Oreg.*, May 17, 1906, 11; *News*, Sept. 7, 1910, Clippings Folder, Mary Sumner Boyd Papers, OHS; *Oreg.*, May 26, 1906, 1; June 1, 1906, 13; June 3, 1906, 11; Scrapbook 89, 27, OHS. Ruth Moynihan, Duniway's biographer, describes this owner of a millinery shop and small publishing company as "an agrarian reformer" and "an enthusiastic supporter of the Knights of Labor" with "populist leanings," although Thomas Edwards emphasizes Duniway's connections with the Portland elite. See Ruth Barnes Moynihan, *Rebel for Rights: Abigail Scott Duniway* (New Haven, 1983), 65, 163, 167; and Edwards, *Sowing Good Seeds*, 195. For confirmation that antisuffragists generally represented "the American aristocracy," "a privileged urban elite of extraordinary wealth, social position, and political power," see Susan E. Marshall, *Splintered Sisterhood: Gender and Class in the Campaign against Woman Suffrage* (Madison, 1997), 56, 5.

26. *Tel.*, June 1, 1906, 9; Henry, "Progressivism and Democracy," 204; Harper, *History of Woman Suffrage*, 6:544; 1910 *VP*, 4; 1912 *VP*, 5. On the 1910 taxpayer's suffrage amendment, which due to a printer's error would have actually allowed all women to vote, see Moynihan, *Rebel for Rights*, 214. Sara Hunter Graham notes that the same process played out at the national level in precisely these years, as between 1906 and 1910 the suffragists' highly democratic "visionary cause . . . transformed into an eminently safe program for middle-class club meetings" that refused to threaten elite interests. *Woman Suffrage and the New Democracy* (New Haven, 1996), 51–52.

27. Voting statistics here and in the following paragraph are calculated from Abstracts, 1906–12; precinct locations are in *Oreg.*, June 4, 1906, 8; *Jour.*, Nov. 4, 1912, 6.

28. According to the *Oregonian*, "all through the campaign the suffragists claimed that the East Side would carry the measure, if it was carried at all, in spite of an adverse total from the West Side" (Nov. 10, 1912, I, 13).

29. Gayle Gullett, *Becoming Citizens: The Emergence and Development of the California Women's Movement, 1880–1911* (Urbana, 2000), 192.

30. Henry, "Progressivism and Democracy," 205; Wiebe, *Self-Rule*, 166–67. Eileen L. McDonagh and H. Douglas Price, "Woman Suffrage in the Progressive Era: Patterns of Opposition and Support in Referenda Voting, 1910–1918," *American Political Science Review* 78 (June 1985): 431, makes an argument similar to Henry's, as does Philip J. Ethington's attempt to deny the explanatory power of class, "Recasting Urban Political History: Gender, the Public, the Household, and Political Participation in Boston and San Francisco during the Progressive Era," *Social Science History* 16 (Summer 1992): 301–301n.

31. Mari Jo Buhle, *Women and American Socialism, 1870–1920* (Urbana, 1981), 236. For scholarship that contests the older story of conservative declension found in works such as Aileen S. Kraditor, *The Ideas of the Woman Suffrage Movement, 1890–1920* (New York, 1965), see Nancy Cott, *The Grounding of Modern Feminism* (New Haven, 1987); Suzanne Lebsock, "Woman Suffrage and White Supremacy: A Virginia Case Study," in *Visible Women: New Essays on American Activism*, ed. Nancy A. Hewitt and Suzanne Lebsock (Urbana, 1993), 62–100; Gilmore, *Gender and Jim Crow*, 203–24; Ellen Carol DuBois, *Harriot Stanton Blatch and the Winning of Woman Suffrage* (New Haven, 1997); and Rosalyn Terborg-Penn, *African American Women in the Struggle for the Vote, 1850–1920* (Bloomington, 1998); as well as Graham, *Woman Suffrage*; and Suzanne Marilley, *Woman Suffrage and the Origins of Liberal Feminism in the United States, 1820–1920* (Cambridge, Mass., 1996). The most sophisticated treatment of the relationship between progressive politics and suffrage is Gullett, *Becoming Citizens*.

32. Eileen L. McDonagh, "Race, Class, and Gender in the Progressive Era: Restructuring State and Society," in Milkis and Mileur, *Progressivism and the New Democracy*, 164.

33. *Tel.*, May 26, 1920, 3; *Oreg.*, Apr. 5, 1921, 11; *OV*, June 5, 1920, 561. One of the PPL board members during these years was W. E. Kimsey, secretary of both the Oregon State Federation of Labor and Portland Central Labor Council. In 1922, Kimsey resigned his positions within the house of labor after purchasing an interest in the printing firm of Dempsey and Downs; *OLP*, Dec. 22, 1922, 1.

34. This frame of government changed in minor details while the People's Power League considered it from 1920 to 1923, but the essential components remained the same. My information comes from the reprinting of the first edition in the *OV*, June 5, 1920, 561–81 and the second edition of 1921, People's Power League Pamphlet no. 12, "Introductory Letter with Draft of Proposed Constitutional Amendment for Basing Election of Representatives on the Voters' Business Occupations Instead of Partisan Politics, Abolition of State Senate and Subordinating Executive Department," OSL (hereafter Draft Two). The quote is in *OV*, June 5, 1920, 574. Another provision of the plan that indicated continuity between this proposal and previous U'Ren ideas included a veto-less governor elected by the legislature, thus "subordinating the exec-

utive department" and making "the governor and legislature more directly responsible to the voters and more responsive to their will" (Draft Two, 1).

35. Draft Two, 8; *OV*, Jan. 1, 1921, 13, 51. Draft Two, 2, 9; *Oreg.*, Apr. 23, 1923, 8; *Seattle Union Record*, June 24, 1920, 2, 3; June 26, 1920, 3; June 28, 1920, 4.

36. Draft One, *OV*, June 5, 1920, 575; *OLP*, May 29, 1920, 1; *Seattle Union Record*, June 24, 1920, 9. The People's Power League at one point split the rural housewives' category into the spouses of farmers and farm tenants; *Seattle Union Record*, June 24, 1920, 9.

37. *Seattle Union Record*, June 24, 1920, 9; Draft Two, 7.

38. Wiebe, *Self-Rule*, 120. The most compelling statement of this position is Stephanie McCurry, *Masters of Small Worlds: Yeoman Households, Gender Relations, and the Political Culture of the Antebellum South Carolina Low Country* (New York, 1995); this general perspective is shared by MacLean, *Behind the Mask*.

For the most complex views on the subject, see Rebecca Edwards, *Angels in the Machinery: Gender in American Party Politics from the Civil War to the Progressive Era* (New York, 1997), 91–110; and Michael Goldberg, *An Army of Women: Gender and Politics in Gilded Age Kansas* (Baltimore, 1997). We can also reconstruct the tradition of feminist populism in Buhle, *Women and American Socialism*; Susan Levine, *Labor's True Woman: Carpet Weavers, Industrialization, and Labor Reform in the Gilded Age* (Philadelphia, 1984); Watkins, *Rural Democracy*; and Rebecca Edwards, "Playing a Straight Flush: Mary Lease and the Stories of Populism and Progressivism," paper presented at the Annual Meeting of the Organization of American Historians, 2001.

39. *OV*, June 5, 1920, 575; *Oreg.*, Apr. 22, 1923, 17.

40. *OV*, June 5, 1920, 561; Draft Two, 2, 11.

41. *Oreg.*, May 27, 1920, 10. For a sophisticated statement of the *Oregonian's* viewpoint, see Mary Follett's argument: "no one group can enfold me, because of my multiple nature. That is the blow to the theory of occupational representation." Mary Parker Follett, *The New State: Group Organization the Solution of Popular Government* (University Park, Pa., 1998 [1918]), 295. See also Read Bain, "A Socialized State," *Commonwealth Review of the University of Oregon* 3 (Jan. 1921): 107–8.

42. Originally appearing in John R. Commons, *Representative Democracy* (New York, 1900), "Representation of Interests" is reprinted in Commons, *Proportional Representation*, 2d ed. (New York, 1907), 355–63; Harry Allen Overstreet, "The Government of To-Morrow," *Forum* 54 (July 1915), 6–17 (quotes, 13). William Macdonald includes a mild proposal for occupational representation in *A New Constitution for a New America* (New York, 1921), 127–39; for a self-consciously antidemocratic application of the idea, see John Corbin, "The Industrial Republic," *North American Review*, 216 (Aug. 1922), 174–89. See also Felix Adler, "Far-Reaching Changes in the Government of Our Democracy," *Standard* 6 (Apr. 1920), 258–64; and Victor S. Yarros, "How Can the Senate Be Reformed? Convert It into a Soviet," *Public*, Aug. 23, 1919, 903–4. For the importance of Commons's ideas in the formation of pluralist theory in modern political science, see Mancur Olson Jr., *The Logic of Collective Action: Public Goods and the Theory of Groups* (Cambridge, Mass., 1965), 114–16; see also John R. Commons, *Myself: The Autobiography of John R. Commons* (Madison, 1964), 71–73. A Federalist-inspired opposition to occupational representation comes in William Seal Carpenter, *Democracy and Representation* (Princeton, 1925), 73–88.

43. M. Ostrogorski, *Democracy and the Party System in the United States: A Study in*

Extra-constitutional Government (New York, 1910), 453; Ostrogorski, *Democracy and the Organization of Political Parties*, vol. 2 (New York, 1970 [1902]), 700, 756; Beard, "Reconstructing State Government," *New Republic*, Aug. 21, 1915, II, 1–16 (quote, 9); Follett, *The New State*; Paul Douglas, "Occupational versus Proportional Representation," *American Journal of Sociology* 29 (Sept. 1923): 129–57. The best recent treatment of Follett is Mattson, *Creating a Democratic Public*, 87–104.

44. Emile Durkheim, *The Division of Labor in Society*, trans. W. D. Halls (New York, 1984), xxxi–lix (quote, xxxix); see also Durkheim, *Professional Ethics and Civic Morals*, trans. Cornelia Brookfield (Glencoe, Ill., 1957), 37–41, 96–97, 102–9. The most systematic and sympathetic treatment of this aspect of Durkheim's thought is Steven Lukes, *Emile Durkheim: His Life and Work: A History and Critical Study* (London, 1973), 536–42. The best contemporary overviews of the European political theory of occupations are McBain and Rogers, *New Constitutions of Europe*, 117–33; W. Y. Elliott, *The Pragmatic Revolt in Politics: Syndicalism, Fascism, and the Constitutional State* (New York, 1928); and Francis W. Coker, *Recent Political Thought* (New York, 1934), esp. 296–301.

A recent compilation of pluralist writings is Paul Q. Hirst, *The Pluralist Theory of the State: Selected Writings of G. D. H. Cole, J. N. Figgis, and H. J. Laski* (London, 1989); see also the companion defense of this perspective, Paul Q. Hirst, *Associative Democracy: New Forms of Economic and Social Governance* (London, 1994). Christopher Lasch began to rehabilitate this line of thinking, linking it with the fate of proprietorship, in *True and Only Heaven*, 296–342.

45. *Oreg.*, Apr. 16, 1923, 8; and People's Power League, Draft Two, 12. The Portland labor movement did not abandon U'Ren's plan until 1930 (*OLP*, Jan. 10, 1930, 1). For a recent proposal to create, by lot, a legislature that would represent an occupational cross-section of the United States, see Ernest Callenbach and Michael Phillips, *A Citizen Legislature: A Modest Proposal for the Random Selection of Legislators* (Berkeley, 1985); for a vigorous debate over the desirability of formally including associations in political representation, see Joshua Cohen and Joel Rogers, eds., *Associations and Democracy* (London, 1995).

46. Ellis Paxon Oberholtzer, *The Referendum in America, with Some Chapters on the Initiative and Recall*, 2d ed. (New York, 1912), 492, 97 n. 15. For Oberholtzer's life and elitist politics, see David Glassberg, *American Historical Pageantry: The Uses of Tradition in the Early Twentieth Century* (Chapel Hill, 1990).

47. Oberholtzer, *Referendum*, 511. On the Pennsylvania Constitution, see J. Paul Selsam, *The Pennsylvania Constitution of 1776: A Study in Revolutionary Democracy* (New York, 1971 [1936]); Gordon S. Wood, *The Creation of the American Republic: 1776–1787* (Chapel Hill, 1969); and, especially, Steven Rosswurm, *Arms, Country, and Class: The Philadelphia Militia and "Lower Sort" during the American Revolution, 1775–1783* (New Brunswick, 1987). The actual text can be found in Francis Newton Thorpe, ed., *The Federal and State Constitutions*, vol. 5 (Washington, 1909), 3081–92.

48. Willi Paul Adams, *The First American Constitutions: Republican Ideology and the Making of the State Constitutions in the Revolutionary Era* (Chapel Hill, 1980), 179–80 and more generally 262–66; Staughton Lynd, *Intellectual Origins of American Radicalism* (Cambridge, 1982 [1968]), 68–77. For a brief on behalf of unicameralism, see Richard N. Rosenfeld, *American Aurora: A Democratic-Republican Returns* (New York, 1997).

49. Selsam, *Pennsylvania Constitution of 1776*, 199; Allan Nevins, *The American States during and after the Revolution, 1775–1789* (New York, 1969) [1924], 152. The definitive work remains Lewis H. Meader, "The Council of Censors," *Pennsylvania Magazine of History and Biography* 22 (1898): 265–300; for a vindication of the censors, see Donald S. Lutz, *Popular Consent and Popular Control: Whig Political Theory in the Early State Constitutions* (Baton Rouge, 1980), 128–49. Lutz characterizes the censors as "an intermediate step toward initiative, referendum, and recall" (128).

For considerations of the recall during the revolutionary era see Adams, *The First American Constitutions*, 244; and Cronin, *Direct Democracy*, 42, 129. Cronin notes that "recall was thus a familiar concept to officials and political theorists in America's formative period. The need for the recall device in post-Revolutionary America was largely obviated by the then widespread support for short terms and rotation in office for all public officials" (42).

50. Wood, *Creation*, 165; Wood, *Radicalism of American Revolution*, 259; Jack N. Rakove, *Original Meanings: Politics and Ideas in the Making of the Constitution* (New York, 1996), 229.

51. Saul Cornell, *The Other Founders: Anti-Federalism and the Dissenting Tradition in America, 1788–1828* (Chapel Hill, 1999). For a powerful invocation of the 1776 Pennsylvania Constitution, see Jesse Lemisch, "Anti-impeachment Historians and the Politics of History," *Chronicle of Higher Education*, Dec. 4, 1998, B6. Further linkages are possible. Generally, Jennifer Nedelsky contends that the Anti-Federalists sought an "approximation of direct democracy." More specifically, Akhil Amar takes note of the Anti-Federalists' "suspicion of professionalism and the division of labor," which would certainly apply to antivaccinationist Lora Little. Amar also remarks that "the Anti-Federalists feared the emergence of a 'military-industrial complex,'" one of the main concerns of Harry Lane. See Jennifer Nedelsky, "Confining Democratic Politics: Anti-Federalists, Federalists, and the Constitution," *Harvard Law Review* 96 (1982): 343; Akhil Reed Amar, "Anti-Federalists, *The Federalist Papers*, and the Big Argument for Union," *Harvard Journal of Law and Public Policy* 16 (Winter 1993): 114. For a contrasting argument that, without evidence, sees a pluralist Madisonian perspective that denied class conflict as "an enduring formula for the ways in which middle-class Americans live and think of themselves," see Olivier Zunz, "Class," in *Encyclopedia of the United States in the Twentieth Century*, ed. Stanley Kutler (New York, 1996), 197.

CHAPTER ELEVEN
The Political Economy of Populist Democracy: The Single Tax Movement in Portland, 1908–1916

1. Hofstadter, *Age of Reform*, 265.

2. W. S. U'Ren, "Single Tax," *Annals of the American Academy of Political and Social Science* 58 (Mar. 1915): 222–27. George and his followers thus agreed with Karl Polanyi, who later noted, "What we call land is an element of nature inextricably interwoven with man's institutions. To isolate it and form a market out of it was perhaps the weirdest of all undertakings of our ancestors" (*The Great Transformation*, 178).

3. *PLP*, Jan. 26, 1911, 1–2; W. G. Eggleston, "Graduated Specific Tax and Exemption Amendment" (n.p., 1912), pamphlet at OSL, 12; U'Ren, "Single Tax," 225. The

single taxers' charge had a substantial basis in reality; on the Pittock Block, see Mac-Coll, *Growth of a City*, 186. For just one example of how such unearned values continue in our era, on an even grander—and more obscene—scale, see Davis, *City of Quartz*, 134.

4. David Scobey, "Boycotting the Politics Factory: Labor Radicalism and the New York City Mayoral Election of 188[6]," *Radical History Review* 28–30 (1984): 280–325; Robert E. Weir, "A Fragile Alliance: Henry George and the Knights of Labor," *American Journal of Economics and Sociology* 56 (Oct. 1997): 421–39; Elizabeth Blackmar, *Manhattan for Rent, 1750–1850* (Ithaca, N.Y., 1989), 265–67; Alexander Saxton, *The Indispensable Enemy: Labor and the Anti-Chinese Movement in California* (Berkeley, 1971); Don Mitchell, *The Lie of the Land: Migrant Workers and the California Landscape* (Minneapolis, 1996); Melvin G. Holli, *Reform in Detroit: Hazen S. Pingree and Urban Politics* (New York, 1969), 59–60.

My analysis of George and his followers is drawn especially from John L. Thomas, *Alternative America: Henry George, Edward Bellamy, Henry Demarest Lloyd, and the Adversary Tradition* (Cambridge, Mass., 1983); Daniel Aaron, *Men of Good Hope: A Story of American Progressives* (New York, 1951), 55–91; Ronald Yanosky, "Seeing the Cat: Henry George and the Rise of the Single Tax Movement, 1879–1890," Ph.D. diss., University of California, Berkeley, 1993; and Domenic Candeloro, "The Single Tax Movement and Progressivism, 1880–1920," *American Journal of Economics and Sociology* 38 (Apr. 1979): 113–27. For an imaginative placement of George's radicalism in a transatlantic philosophical context, see Ursula Vogel, "The Land Question: A Liberal Theory of Communal Property," *History Workshop*, n.s. 27 (Spring 1989): 106–35. Vogel cites J. A. Hobson's characterization of George's English followers as of the "lower-middle or upper-working classes" (128).

5. De Witt, *Progressive Movement*, 341, 357–60; Daniel Rodgers also recognizes the "disproportionately large number of single taxers in the early progressive crusades" in "In Search of Progressivism," *Reviews in American History* 10 (Dec. 1982): 123. For an overview of single tax activities during this period, see Arthur Nichols Young, *The Single Tax Movement in the United States* (Princeton, 1916), 184–230; Candeloro, "Single Tax Movement." For the locales, see Joseph Dana Miller, "The Single Tax and American Municipalities," *National Municipal Review* 3 (Oct. 1914): 737–41; Samuel Danziger, "The Singletax and American Municipalities," *National Municipal Review* 4 (1915): 616–21; Robert H. Bremner, "The Single Tax Philosophy in Cleveland and Toledo," *American Journal of Economics and Sociology* 9 (Apr. 1950): 369–75; Frederic C. Howe, *The Confessions of a Reformer* (Chicago, 1978 [1925]), esp. 224–30; Howe, *Privilege and Democracy* (New York, 1910), 255–75; Kazin, *Barons of Labor*, 159; and James R. Green, *Grass-Roots Socialism: Radical Movements in the Southwest, 1895–1943* (Baton Rouge, 1978).

6. Young, "The Single Tax Movement in Oregon," *American Economic Review* 1 (Sept. 1911): 644. For basic narratives of the Oregon single tax movement, see James H. Gilbert, "Single-Tax Movement in Oregon," *Political Science Quarterly* 31 (Mar. 1916): 25–52; and Robert C. Woodward, "W. S. U'Ren and the Single Tax in Oregon," *OHQ* 61 (1960): 46–63. See also Frank Parker Stockbridge, "The Single Taxers," *Everybody's Magazine* 26 (Apr. 1912): 507–22. Single tax advocacy in Portland reached back into the 1880s; see *Oreg.*, Dec. 7, 1889, 10; Dec. 10, 1889, 10; Dec. 12,

1889, 10; Feb. 19, 1891; and Mr. and Mrs. "Freeland" Gordon, *The People's Welfare, or The Solution of Hard Times* (Portland, 1884).

7. T. W. Davenport quoted in William Robbins, *Land: Its Use and Abuse in Oregon, 1848–1910* (Corvallis, 1974), 35; long review of Puter in *Oreg.*, May 23, 1908, 11. On the trials, see John Messing, "Public Lands, Politics, and Progressives: The Oregon Land Fraud Trials, 1903–1910," *Pacific Historical Review* 35 (1966): 35–66.

8. George A. Thatcher, "The Initiative, Referendum, and Popular Election of Senators in Oregon," *American Political Science Review* 2 (Nov. 1908): 603; *Review of Reviews* 38 (July 1908): 21; Young, *Single Tax Movement*, 169; 1908 *VP*, 65. On Wagnon, who had pioneer Oregon roots and was one of Henry George's political "lieutenants" in California, see *Jour.*, Mar. 16, 1924, I, 8.

9. 1908 *VP*, 65–69; *Jour.*, Oct. 15, 1908, 8. See also "Single Tax Supplement," *PLP*, May 12, 1908, 1–2.

10. Gilbert, "Single-Tax Movement," 228; *Oreg.*, May 10, 1908, III, 6; May 16, 1908, 8; May 17, 1908, III, 6; *PLP*, June 9, 1908, 1. These and all subsequent election results are calculated from the precinct level voting data in Abstracts, 1908–16.

11. For the wording of the amendment and the argument for it, see 1910 *VP*, 72, 24–25 (quote on 25); Eggleston, Cridge, and U'Ren, *People's Power*, 647.

12. The charge of duplicity came from, among others, F. G. Young, who stated that the single taxers' methods were "not unlike the fabled wooden-horse strategy ascribed to the Greeks in their taking of Troy" ("Single Tax Movement," 646). Recent historians have agreed with Young; see Gordon B. Dodds, *Oregon*, 170, and *The American Northwest: A History of Oregon and Washington* (Arlington Heights, Ill., 1986), 186. Contemporary scholars who specifically refuted Young's contention were Barnett, *Operation of the Initiative*, 42; Eaton, *Oregon System*, 177–78 n. 37; and Young, *Single Tax Movement*, 172–73. Gilbert, "Single Tax Movement in Oregon," 34–36, is neutral. In fact, Barnett himself (110–11) claims that state officers were equally if not more duplicitous in their successful 1912 measure to repeal the 1910 amendment. For the burden of the poll tax on workers, see *PLP*, Oct. 26, 1911, 4; for the single-taxer refutation of the charge of deception, see Alfred Cridge, "The People as Lawmakers in Oregon," *American Federationist*, Jan. 1911, 53; and for the most compelling evidence of the reality and significance of the poll tax, see David Elvin Lindstrom, "W. S. U'Ren and the Fight for Government Reform and the Single Tax, 1908–1912," M.S.T. thesis, Portland State University, 1972, 94–96.

13. Haynes, "People's Rule in Oregon, 1910," 56.

14. Young, *Single Tax Movement*, 175; *Jour.*, Oct. 25, 1912, 20; Woodward, "U'Ren and the Single Tax," 55; *Jour.*, Oct. 31, 1912, 11. Of note is Joseph Fels's work against medical as well as economic monopoly; see *Medical Freedom*, July 1913, 13.

15. "U'Ren and the Single Tax," 48–51; 1912 *VP*, 226–29.

16. *Oreg.*, Oct. 28, 1911, 8; Oct. 25, 1912, 18.

17. *Jour.*, Oct. 25, 1912, 20; Oct. 25, 1912, 20. The single taxers' labor theory of value helps explain U'Ren's opposition to an income tax, which he maintained would take away earned wealth (*Jour.*, Nov. 1, 1912, 8). On the same grounds John Stuart Mill, in arguing for an "egalitarian market economy" and against a liberal welfare state, opposed the income tax and supported a high land tax. See Richard Krouse and Michael S. McPherson, "The Logic of Liberal Equality: John Stuart Mill and the Ori-

gins of the Political Theory of Welfare State Liberalism," in *Responsibility, Rights, and Welfare: The Theory of the Welfare State*, ed. J. Donald Moon (Boulder, 1988), 144–45.

18. *PLP*, Jan. 12, 1911, 1; *News*, Oct. 30, 1912, 1; and 1912 *VP*, 230–32.

19. *Jour.*, Oct. 11, 1912, 8; Nov. 3, 1912, II, 12; Nov. 3, 1912, II, 12; Eggleston, "Graduated Specific Tax"; 1912 *VP*, 201; 1916 *VP*, 230–32. The single taxers consistently emphasized the local ruling class, never trying to make an anticolonial argument against eastern or "outside" interests. In this way they differed substantially from Huey Long and Charles Coughlin, who fought for a similar "small-scale capitalism" during the depression. See Brinkley, *Voices of Protest*, 144, 150, 159–60.

20. McCraw, "American Capitalism," in *Creating Modern Capitalism*, 303; Daniel T. Rodgers, *Atlantic Crossings: Social Politics in a Progressive Age* (Cambridge, Mass., 1998), 206. It is worth noting that even as staunch a Marxist as Mike Davis recognizes that "as a general rule, changing modes of land speculation have tended to determine the nature of Los Angeles's power structures" (*City of Quartz*, 105). Another leftist, Robert Fitch, provides a compelling case for the use of a confiscatory land value tax to help promote small business in contemporary New York City; see *The Assassination of New York* (London, 1993), 251–55, 264–66.

21. *Jour.*, Oct. 9, 1912, 6; *News*, Oct. 24, 1912, 1; *Jour.*, Oct. 11, 1912, 8; *News*, Oct. 11, 1912, 4.

22. Richard Maxwell Brown, "Back Country Rebellions and the Homestead Ethic in America, 1740–1799," in *Tradition, Conflict, and Modernization: Perspectives on the American Revolution*, ed. Brown and Don E. Fehrenbacher (New York, 1977), 73–99; *OLP*, Oct. 21, 1916, 2. I should note that all the public members of the official single tax movements in Portland were men, even though we have at least two brief mentions in the historical record of an Oregon chapter of the Women's Henry George League; see *Oreg.*, June 30, 1905, 12; and Harper, *History of Woman Suffrage*, 6:120.

My ideas here derive from a long lineage of scholarship about home ownership, family life, and middle-class politics. The best work in this tradition is Sylvie Murray, *Building a Better Life: The Citizens of Suburban Queens, 1945–1965* (Philadelphia, 2003). I recognize, however, that the politics of populist homeownership could in some times and places be antiliberal; see Thomas J. Sugrue, *The Origins of the Urban Crisis: Race and Inequality in Postwar Detroit* (Princeton, 1996), 209–29.

23. *Jour.*, Oct. 26, 1912, 4; *News*, Oct. 11, 1912, 4; Nov. 1, 1912, 1; *Jour.*, Oct. 12, 1912, 8; Oct. 15, 1912, 8. See also W. G. Eggleston and W. S. U'Ren, *Clackamas County Assessments and Taxes in 1910* (Portland, 1912), viii.

24. *Oreg.*, Oct. 9, 1912, 5. For the most influential statement opposing the 1912 measure, see Charles H. Shields, *Single Tax Exposed*, 3d ed. (n.p., 1912).

25. *Oreg.*, Oct. 29, 1912, 4; Nov. 3, 1912, sec. 1, 15; *News*, Oct. 21, 1912, 4; *Oreg.*, Nov. 2, 1912, III, 9.

26. Haynes, "People's Rule' on Trial," 22; *Oreg.*, Nov. 7, 1912, 14.

27. For the competing tax measures, see 1912 *VP*, 14–30, 167–201; "Rational Tax Reform vs. Single Tax" (n.p., 1912), pamphlet at OSL.

28. *Jour.*, Oct. 11, 1914, I, 11.

29. *Jour.*, Oct. 29, 1914, 2; *PLP*, Oct. 12, 1914, 6; 1914 *VP*, 64; *Jour.*, Oct. 21, 1914, 8.

30. *Jour.*, Oct. 17, 1914, 7.

31. *PLP*, Oct. 12, 1914, 6. Worth noting is the 1910 statement of Reverend W. F.

Reagon, pastor of Portland's First Christian Church, who declared that prohibition "has been a fight of the great middle class against the revolutionary anarchist of the slums, and the millionaire law-breaker of Fifth Avenue" (*Oreg.*, Nov. 14, 1910, 8). For an assessment of prohibition as populist politics, see Michael Kazin, *The Populist Persuasion: An American History* (New York, 1995), 79–106; for the movement in Oregon, see John E. Caswell, "The Prohibition Movement in Oregon, 1904–1915," *OHQ* 39 (Dec. 1938): 64–82.

32. *Oreg.*, Nov. 5, 1914, 10.

33. William S. U'Ren to W. G. Eggleston, Aug. 18, 1916, William S. U'Ren folder, William G. Eggleston Papers, Bancroft Library, University of California, Berkeley; *Oreg.*, Oct. 7, 1916, 10.

34. *OV*, Mar. 25, 1916, 252; 1916 *VP*, 7–11. It is possible that this single tax plan had its origins in the land-loan ideas of the Populists; see Jeffrey Ostler, *Prairie Populism: The Fate of Agrarian Radicalism in Kansas, Nebraska, and Iowa, 1880–1892* (Lawrence, Kans., 1993), 78.

35. *OLP*, Dec. 4, 1915, 4; *OV*, Mar. 25, 1916, 229; *OLP*, Mar. 18, 1916, 1. The *Labor Press* changed its name midway through 1915.

36. *OLP*, Jan. 29, 1916, 5; July 3, 1915, 5; July 24, 1915, 4; *Jour.*, Sept. 3, 1916, I, 5.

37. All quotations from U'Ren, "Oregon Voters Can Abolish Poverty in This State," *OLP*, Oct. 21, 1916, 2, except "then no person . . ." (*OLP*, July 3, 1915, 5). See also *OLP*, Jan. 29, 1916, 8.

38. Marx, *Capital*, 1:843; Mill quoted in Jonathan Riley, "Justice under Capitalism," in *Nomos XXXI: Markets and Justice*, ed. John W. Chapman and J. Roland Pennock (New York, 1989), 151. For a contemporary British argument about the "spiritual capitulation" involved in the move from an economy based on a wide distribution of property, which endorsed relatively egalitarian "wage-relationships" in contrast to an economy based on a "wage-system," see J. E. F. Mann, N. J. Sievers, and R. W. T. Cox, *The Real Democracy (First Essays of the Rota Club)* (London, 1913), 43. For a more modern consideration of "property rights in the job," see William H. Simon, "Social-Republican Property," *UCLA Law Review* 38 (Aug. 1991): 1383.

39. *OLP*, Feb. 1, 1915, 3; Feb. 8, 1915, 3; Feb. 15, 1915, 1; Feb. 26, 1916, 6; Oct. 28, 1916, 8. Frank Walsh, the leading advocate of industrial democracy in the Democratic Party, gave the Portland single taxers his active support (*OLP*, Nov. 6, 1915, 1). On Walsh, one of the key middle-class radicals of the Progressive Era, see Weinstein, *Corporate Ideal*, 172–213; and Shelton Stromquist, "Class Wars: Frank Walsh, the Reformers, and the Crisis of Progressivism," in *Labor Histories: Class, Politics, and the Working-Class Experience*, ed. Eric Arnesen, Julie Greene, and Bruce Laurie (Urbana, 1998), 97–124.

40. *OLP*, Oct. 2, 1915, 1, 4; Nov. 20, 1915, 3; June 3, 1916, 4; Nov. 25, 1916, 3; U'Ren, "Single Tax," 226. For the substantial involvement of single taxers in democratic anti-imperialism during the two decades after the Spanish-American War, see Jim Zwick, "The Anti-Imperialist League and the Origins of Filipino-American Oppositional Solidarity," *Amerasia* 24 (Summer 1998): 65–86; for the petit bourgeois nature of anti-imperialist radicalism during the 1920s, see Robert David Johnson, *The Peace Progressives and American Foreign Relations* (Cambridge, Mass., 1995).

41. *Oreg.*, Oct. 12, 1916, 10; *OLP*, Feb. 5, 1916, 6; Jan. 29, 1916, 4. For an earlier

Populist who drew on Indian communal landownership to formulate a radical theory of property, see Johnson, "Red Populism."

42. *Jour.*, Oct. 26, 1916, 10; *Oreg.*, Oct. 29, 1916, IV, 11; Oct. 22, 1916, III, 11; Henry Reed, "The Land Rent Tax Amendment," *OV*, Oct. 7, 1916, 299–300; *Jour.*, Sept. 26, 1916, 6. These arguments echo those of Senator Henry Dawes, the architect of late-nineteenth-century Indian land dispossession. Dawes commented that tribal landownership was "Henry George's system . . . under which there is no enterprise . . . there is no selfishness, which is at the bottom of civilization"; quoted in Yehoshua Arieli, *Individualism and Nationalism in American Ideology* (Cambridge, Mass., 1964), 331. For the conservative political uses of the pioneer heritage in Oregon, see Rick Harmon, "Thomas Condon and the 'Natural Selection' of Oregon Pioneers," *OHQ* 99 (Winter 1998–99): 436–71.

43. *News*, Nov. 4, 1916, 8; U'Ren to Dana Sleeth, Jan. 7, 1915, Sleeth Family Papers, courtesy of Peter Sleeth; *OLP*, Nov. 11, 1916, 1.

44. *OV*, Feb. 1, 1919, 10.

PART IV
A Populism of the Body: The Rationality and Radicalism of Antivaccinationism

1. Sellers, *The Market Revolution*, 253; DuBasky, *The Gist of Mencken*, 14.

2. Richard Moskowitz, "Vaccination: A Sacrament of Modern Medicine," *Homoeopath* 12 (Mar. 1992): 137–44. Those who opposed the *compulsory* nature of compulsory vaccination often differed from those who opposed vaccination itself. For convenience, however, I will use *anti–compulsory vaccination* and *antivaccination* interchangeably unless the distinction is important.

3. Part of the intellectual project of this chapter is to perform a rehabilitation of a "middlebrow" culture intensely critical of establishment science. As Andrew Ross smartly remarks in regard to subaltern-loving practitioners of cultural studies, "middlebrow culture, when it is not passionately denigrated is thought to be stable, flat, and unprofitable, its politics unremarkable." Intellectuals far too often "police the cultural order by deriding the sublegitimate middlebrow as only they can." See Ross, *Strange Weather: Culture, Science, and Technology in the Age of Limits* (New York, 1991), 8.

CHAPTER TWELVE
A Deluded Mob of Ignorant Fools? The Historiography of Antivaccination, and the Risks of Vaccination

1. Michael Bliss, *Plague: A Story of Smallpox in Montreal* (New York, 1991), 207.

2. William J. Reese, *Power and the Promise of School Reform: Grassroots Movements during the Progressive Era* (Boston, 1986), 232–33. For a model history of conflict over a progressive public health measure, see Jonathan Zimmerman, *Distilling Democracy: Alcohol Education in America's Public Schools, 1880–1925* (Lawrence, Kans., 1999); B. O. Flower, *Progressive Men, Women, and Movements of the Past Twenty-Five Years* (Boston, 1914; repr., Westport, Conn., 1975), 298, 316.

Compare Flower to Ivan D. Illich, who in *Medical Nemesis: The Expropriation of Health* (New York, 1976), 42, does battle with medicine's "radical monopoly." "A radical monopoly," Illich writes, "goes deeper than that of any one corporation or any one government. . . . Ordinary monopolies corner the market; radical monopolies disable people from doing or making things on their own. The commercial monopoly restricts the flow of commodities; the more insidious social monopoly paralyzes the output of nonmarketable use-values."

3. Martin Kaufman, "The American Anti-vaccinationists and Their Arguments," *Bulletin of the History of Medicine* 41 (1967): 471; John Duffy, *A History of Public Health in New York City*, 2 vols. (New York, 1968–1974), 2:152; Duffy, *The Sanitarians: A History of American Public Health* (Urbana, 1990), 200. For an older denunciation of "religious fanatics and ignorant superstitious people," see Ann Beck, "Issues in the Anti-vaccination Movement in England," *Medical History* 4 (1960): 317.

4. Judith Walzer Leavitt, *The Healthiest City: Milwaukee and the Politics of Health Reform* (Princeton, 1982), 8. Leavitt reluctantly admits the truth of most antivaccination concerns in "'Be Safe. Be Sure': New York City's Experience with Epidemic Smallpox," in *Hives of Sickness: Public Health and Epidemics in New York City*, ed. David Rosner (New Brunswick, 1995), 95–114.

5. Joan Retsinas, "Smallpox Vaccination: A Leap of Faith," *Rhode Island History* 38 (1979): 114, 123.

6. Paul Adolphus Bator, "The Health Reformers versus the Common Canadian: The Controversy over Compulsory Vaccination against Smallpox in Toronto and Ontario, 1900–1920," *Ontario History* 75 (1983): 349, 368.

7. For a reflection on historical resistance to orthodox medicine, see the introduction to Robert D. Johnston, ed., *The Politics of Healing: Essays in the History of Twentieth-Century North American Alternative Medicine* (New York, forthcoming). The most prominent argument for the "consolidation of authority" of the regular medical profession during the Progressive Era is Paul Starr, *The Social Transformation of American Medicine* (New York, 1982).

8. Perry Miller, *The New England Mind: From Colony to Province* (Cambridge, Mass., 1953), 361; Kenneth Silverman, *The Life and Times of Cotton Mather* (New York, 1984), 354, 346; Gary Nash, *The Urban Crucible: Social Change, Political Consciousness, and the Origins of the American Revolution* (Cambridge, Mass., 1979), 455 n. 23; Carl Bridenbaugh, *Cities in Revolt: Urban Life in America, 1743–1776* (New York, 1955), 327, 329–30; Patrick Henderson, "Smallpox and Patriotism: The Norfolk Riots, 1768–1769," *Virginia Magazine of Historical Biography* 73 (1965): 413–34; Ola Elizabeth Winslow, *A Destroying Angel: The Conquest of Smallpox in Colonial Boston* (Boston, 1974), 90–93; Christine Leigh Heyrman, *Commerce and Culture: The Maritime Communities of Colonial Massachusetts, 1690–1750* (New York, 1984), 304–29. My thanks to Elizabeth A. Fenn for her help with colonial inoculation politics; for an overview of resistance to inoculation see her *Pox Americana: The Great Smallpox Epidemic of 1775–1782* (New York, 2001). Inoculation is different, as I will explain below, from vaccination.

9. Donald R. Hopkins, *Princes and Peasants: Smallpox in History* (Chicago, 1983), 268; William Travis Howard Jr., *Public Health Administration and the Natural History of Disease in Baltimore, Maryland, 1797–1920* (Washington, D.C., 1924), 281; Retsinas, "Smallpox Vaccination," 122; Malcolm X, *The Autobiography of Malcolm X*, as told to Alex Haley (New York, 1964), 218.

10. William G. Eidson, "Confusion, Controversy, and Quarantine: The Muncie

Smallpox Epidemic of 1893," *Indiana Magazine of History* 86 (Dec. 1990): 374–98; Robert S. Lynd and Helen Merrell Lynd, *Middletown: A Study in Modern American Culture* (New York, 1929), 447–48, 454; John Duffy, "School Vaccination: The Precursor to School Medical Inspection," *Journal of the History of Medicine and Allied Sciences* 33 (July 1978): 345.

11. Holli, *Reform in Detroit*, 186–95; Richard H. Frost, "The Pueblo Indian Smallpox Epidemic in New Mexico, 1898–1899," *Bulletin of the History of Medicine* 64 (1990): 440–43; Robert A. Trennert, *White Man's Medicine: Government Doctors and the Navajo, 1863–1955* (Albuquerque, 1998), 43; Trennert, "White Man's Medicine vs. Hopi Tradition: The Smallpox Epidemic of 1899," *Journal of Arizona History* 33 (Winter 1992): 349–66; Jesus T. Recio, *War Against Peace, or a New Attila: Contemporaneous Episodes on the Frontier of Texas, attested by facts complied by "El Bien Publico's Publishers* (Rio Grande City, Tex., 1895), 27, 69; *Proceedings of the Joint Committee of the Senate and the House in the Investigation of the Texas State Ranger Force* (Austin, 1919), 1138. My gratitude to Ben Johnson for the Texas citations.

12. Philip Jordan, *The People's Health: A History of Public Health in Minnesota to 1948* (Saint Paul, 1953), 54; Duffy, *Public Health in New York*, 2:149; Duffy, *The Sanitarians*, 55, 182, 200; Duffy, *Public Health in New York*, 1:152–54, 565; Roy Porter, *The Greatest Benefit to Mankind: A Medical History of Humanity from Antiquity to the Present* (New York, 1997), 395; Kaufman, "American Anti-Vaccinationists," 464. Ward B. Studt, Jerold G. Sorensen, and Beverly Bunge, *Medicine in the Intermountain West: A History of Health Care in Rural Areas of the West* (Salt Lake City, 1976), discuss the "celebrated" repeal of compulsory vaccination of Utah but also notes the official provaccination policies of the Mormon hierarchy (32–34, quote, 34); see also Joseph E. Morrell, *Utah's Health and You: A History of Utah's Public Health* (Salt Lake City, 1956), 99–105.

13. Duffy, *Sanitarians*, 200; Harris L. Coulter and Barbara Loe Fisher, *DPT: A Shot in the Dark* (New York, 1985), 339; *Jacobson v. Massachusetts*, 197 U.S. 11 (1905); Samuel B. Woodward, "Legislative Aspects of Vaccination," *Boston Medical and Surgical Journal*, Sept. 15, 1921, 307–10; Bernhard J. Stern, *Should We Be Vaccinated? A Survey of the Controversy in Its Historical and Scientific Aspects* (New York, 1927), 110–11; Eugene C. Murdock, "Cleveland's Johnson: The Cabinet," *Ohio Historical Quarterly* 66 (Oct. 1957): 389; B. O. Flower, "How Cleveland Stamped Out Smallpox," *Arena* 27 (Apr. 1902): 426–29; William A. Link, *The Paradox of Southern Progressivism, 1880–1930* (Chapel Hill, 1992), 26; Elizabeth Ewen, *Immigrant Women in the Land of Dollars: Life and Culture on the Lower East Side, 1890–1925* (New York, 1985), 143; Charles Foster Todd, "The Initiative and Referendum in Arizona," M.A. thesis, University of Arizona, 1931, 69; Hopkins, *Princes and Peasants*, 292; Stern, *Should We Be Vaccinated?* 113; James C. Whorton, "Drugless Healing in the 1920s: The Therapeutic Cult of Sanipractic," *Pharmacy in History* 28 (1986): 16, 18. Advocates of medical freedom scored other significant victories during this period. For example, medical antimonopolists in the National League for Medical Freedom helped defeat Progressive Era health reformers' plans for a cabinet-level National Health Department. James C. Whorton, *Crusaders for Fitness: The History of American Reformers* (Princeton, 1982), 147–48.

James A. Tobey reprints the landmark *Jacobson* decision in his *Public Health Law*, 3d ed. (New York, 1947), 359–75. In an intriguing connection that points to the significant relationship between different kinds of professional class reform, Louis Brandeis used *Jacobson* as a crucial precedent for *Muller v. Oregon.* In his famous brief he cited only three cases—*Lochner* six times and *Jacobson* twice (Brandeis and Goldmark, *Women in Industry*, 9–10). For reflections on *Jacobson's* repressive features, from a scholar who approves of the decision, see Alan Hyde, *Bodies of Law* (Princeton, 1997), 241–51.

14. Hopkins, *Princes and Peasants*, 292–93; S. B. Woodward and Roy F. Feemster, "The Relation of Smallpox Morbidity to Vaccination Laws," *New England Journal of Medicine* 208 (1933): 317; Wilson G. Smillie, *Public Health Administration in the United States*, 2d ed. (New York, 1945), 118; Harry Wain, *A History of Preventive Medicine* (Springfield, Ill., 1970), 193. A 1930 White House–authorized survey found that only 21 percent of urban preschoolers and 7 percent of rural preschoolers had been vaccinated. See Samuel H. Preston and Michael R. Haines, *Fatal Years: Child Mortality in Late Nineteenth-Century America* (Princeton, 1991), 14.

15. Teresa A. Meade, *"Civilizing" Rio: Reform and Resistance in a Brazilian City, 1889–1930* (University Park, Pa., 1997), 91–113 (quotes, 112, 104); Teresa Meade, "'Civilizing Rio De Janeiro': The Public Health Campaign and the Riot of 1904," *Journal of Social History* 20 (Dec. 1986): 301; Jeffrey D. Needell, "The *Revolta Contra Vacina* of 1904: The Revolt against 'Modernization' in *Belle-Époque* Rio de Janeiro," *Hispanic American Historical Review* 67 (1987): 233–69. For an example of the global connections of the antivaccination movement, see Lora Little's coverage of the Brazilian revolt, *Liberator* 7 (Aug. 1905): 125–26.

16. David Arnold, *Colonizing the Body: State Medicine and Epidemic Disease in Nineteenth-Century India* (Berkeley, 1993), esp. 141–44; Frédérique Apffel Marglin, "Smallpox in Two Systems of Knowledge," in Frédérique Apffel Marglin and Stephen A. Marglin, *Dominating Knowledge: Development, Culture, and Resistance* (Oxford, 1990), 104–5; Mark Harrison, *Public Health in British India: Anglo-Indian Preventive Medicine, 1859–1914* (Cambridge, 1994), 82–87; Deepak Kumar, "Unequal Contenders, Uneven Ground: Medical Encounters in British India, 1820–1920," in *Western Medicine as Contested Medicine*, ed. Andrew Cunningham and Bridie Andrews (Manchester, 1997), 184–85; Dipesh Chakrabarty, "Postcoloniality and the Artifice of History: Who Speaks for the 'Indian' Pasts?" in *A Subaltern Studies Reader, 1986–1995*, ed. Ranajit Guha (Minneapolis, 1997), 288–89; Paul Greenough, "Intimidation, Coercion, and Resistance in the Final Stages of the South Asian Smallpox Eradication Campaign," *Social Science and Medicine* 41 (1995): 633–45; *Vac. Inq.*, Oct. 1, 1929, 183; Lenore Manderson, *Sickness and the State: Health and Illness in Colonial Malaya, 1870–1940* (Cambridge, 1996), 47; Anne Marcovich, "French Colonial Medicine and Colonial Rule: Algeria and Indochina," in *Disease, Medicine, and Empire: Perspectives on Western Medicine and the Experience of European Expansion*, ed. Roy MacLeod and Milton Lewis (London, 1988), 107–8; Marc H. Dawson, "Socioeconomic Change and Disease: Smallpox in Colonial Kenya, 1880–1920," in *The Social Basis of Health and Healing in Africa*, ed. Steven Feierman and John M. Janzen (Berkeley, 1992), 100; Luise White, *Speaking with Vampires: Rumor and History in Colonial Africa* (Berkeley, 2000), 103; K. David Patterson, *Health in Colonial Ghana: Disease, Medicine, and Socio-Economic Change, 1900–1955* (Waltham, Mass., 1978), 70; Ken De Bevoise, *Agents of Apocalypse: Epidemic Disease in the Colonial Philippines* (Princeton, 1995), 105, 102–17; José G. Rigau-Pérez, "Strategies That Led to the Eradication of Smallpox in Puerto Rico,

1882–1921," *Bulletin of the History of Medicine* 59 (1985): 81; Susan Cannon Harris, "Bodies and Blood: Gender and Sacrifice in Modern Irish Drama," Ph.D. diss., University of Texas, 1998; Brett L. Walker, "The Early Modern Japanese State and Ainu Vaccinations: Redefining the Body Politic, 1799–1868," *Past and Present* 63 (May 1999): 121–60. International resistance to vaccination continued through to the very end of the United Nations eradication program, particularly among older women generally and among the Amharas of Ethiopia specifically (Frank Fenner et al., *Smallpox and Its Eradication* (Geneva, 1988), 489). For a powerful meditation on the theme, see Sheldon Watts, *Epidemics and History: Disease, Power, and Imperialism* (New Haven, 1997).

17. Alan Mayne, "'The Dreadful Scourge': Responses to Smallpox in Sydney and Melbourne, 1881–1882," in Macleod and Lewis, *Disease, Medicine, and Empire*, 231; P. H. Curson, *Times of Crisis: Epidemics in Sydney, 1788–1900* (Sydney, 1995), 109–12; Fenner et al., *Smallpox*, 310; Jack D. Ellis, *The Physician-Legislators of France: Medicine and Politics in the Early Third Republic, 1870–1914* (Cambridge, 1990), 71; Hopkins, *Princes and Peasants*, 147–48; Richard J. Evans, *Death in Hamburg: Society and Politics in the Cholera Years, 1830–1910* (Oxford, 1987), 222 (Evans also notes anti-Semitic opposition to vaccination; see 500); Peter Baldwin, *Contagion and the State in Europe, 1830–1930* (New York, 1999), 303; J. N. Hays, *The Burdens of Disease: Epidemics and Human Response in Western History* (New Brunswick, 1998), 279. The most comprehensive history of European antivaccinationism is Baldwin, *Contagion and the State*, 244–354.

18. W. M. Frazer, *A History of English Public Health* (London, 1950), 372; Stern, *Should We Be Vaccinated?* 125–26, 71, 138; F. B. Smith, *The People's Health, 1830–1930* (New York, 1979), 169, 167, 166; Dorothy R. Porter and Roy Porter, "The Politics of Prevention: Anti-vaccinationism and Public Health in Nineteenth-Century England," *Medical History* 32 (1988): 240; Judith R. Walkowitz, *Prostitution and Victorian Society: Women, Class, and the State* (New York, 1980), 108, 129.

Along the lines of my own argument, Patrick Joyce, in *Visions of the People: Industrial England and the Question of Class, 1848–1914* (New York, 1991), 74, also sees the campaign against the Vaccination Acts as part of the "extreme or classical populism" that historians have ignored, while Dorothy Porter and Roy Porter note that the anti-vaccinationists appealed "to that cluster of populist and radical interests that paraded themselves as Davids ranged against the Goliath of the Victorian establishment." See Porter and Porter, "The Enforcement of Health: The British Debate," in *AIDS: The Burdens of History*, ed. Elizabeth Fee and Daniel M. Fox (Berkeley, 1988), 104. Richard D. French argues that the English antivaccination movement's foundation was in a "middle class" "in partnership with the socially-conscious working class, the labor aristocracy," and Iorwerth Prothero adds that "the bulk of the support" for antivaccination and related movements "tended to be from small tradesmen, shopkeepers, a few professionals, and, especially, artisans and other educated workmen." R. M. MacLeod, however, points to the class differences within the movement between northern and southern England. See French, *Antivivisection and Medical Science in Victorian Society* (Princeton, 1975), 237; Prothero, *Radical Artisans in England and France, 1830–1870* (Cambridge, 1997), 276; and R. M. MacLeod, "Law, Medicine, and Public Opinion: The Resistance to Compulsory Health Legislation, 1870–1907" (part 1), *Public Law* 1967:114–15. Nadja Durbach focuses on working-class politics in "'They Might as Well Brand Us': Working-Class Resistance to Compulsory Vaccination in Victorian England," *Social History of Medicine* 13 (2000): 45–62.

19. My primary argument in this section involves the *retrospective* rationality of the antivaccinationists. We cannot, after all, expect them to have had access to modern scientific evidence, although they did make some of the same points that I do a century later. The main purpose of the section, then, is not so much to get inside the heads of the antivaccinationists, but rather to use the historical method to show how far, in hindsight, antivaccinationists departed from their reputation as irrational and deluded.

20. Stuart Galishoff, *Newark: The Nation's Unhealthiest City, 1832–1895* (New Brunswick, N.J., 143); Fenner et al., *Smallpox*, 199–200. The standard history of smallpox in the United States, and indeed in the world, is Hopkins, *Princes and Peasants*, especially 234–94.

21. Wain, *History of Preventive Medicine*, 186; Hopkins, *Princes and Peasants*, 254. For a general history of vaccinations, see Susan L. Plotkin and Stanley A. Plotkin, "A Short History of Vaccination," in *Vaccines*, ed. Stanley A. Plotkin and Edward A. Mortimer Jr. (Philadelphia, 1988), 1–7.

22. Duffy, *The Sanitarians*, 55.

23. E. P. Hennock, "Vaccination Policy against Smallpox, 1835–1914: A Comparison of England with Prussia and Imperial Germany," *Social History of Medicine* 11 (Apr. 1998): 67, 69, 66; Hopkins, *Princes and Peasants*, 293. Hopkins, *Princes and Peasants*, 267–90, provides the most accessible data on the frequency and severity of epidemics in nineteenth-century America. He also provides the most transparent example of using very old sources to support the claim that vaccination was the primary reason for the decline of smallpox. Another illustration of this tendency is Preston and Haines, *Fatal Years*, 13–14, 18, where the chief evidence is a 1902 medical report. Historians have failed to recognize that such scientific public health reports were inevitably, because of the antivaccination controversy, political documents.

For compelling arguments that vaccination did play an important role in the rapid decline in death from smallpox in Europe, see A. J. Mercer, "Smallpox and Epidemiological-Demographic Change in Europe: The Role of Vaccination," *Population Studies* 39 (1985): 287–307; and Peter Sköld, *The Two Faces of Smallpox: A Disease and Its Prevention in Eighteenth- and Nineteenth-Century Sweden* (Umeå, Sweden, 1996). Even the ultraskeptical Thomas McKeown credits vaccination against smallpox (but not other vaccinations) with contributing to the decrease in mortality during the nineteenth century. See McKeown, *The Modern Rise of Population* (New York, 1975), 99–101, and McKeown, *The Role of Medicine: Dream, Mirage, or Nemesis?* (Princeton, 1979), 100–101. See also Fenner et al., *Smallpox*, 271–72.

24. Retsinas, "Smallpox Vaccination," 119; Galishoff, *Newark*, 145; Wilson G. Smillie, *Public Health: Its Promise for the Future: A Chronicle of the Development of Public Health in the United States, 1607–1914* (New York, 1955), 125; Duffy, *Public Health in New York*, 2:148–49.

25. Galishoff, *Newark*, 146–47; Duffy, *Public Health in New York*, 2:152; Allan Chase, *Magic Shots: A Human and Scientific Account of the Long Struggle to Eradicate Infectious Diseases by Vaccination* (New York, 1982), 75; Hennock, "Vaccination Policy," 61.

26. Galishoff, *Newark*, 147; Bator, "Health Reformers," 360; Duffy, *Public Health in New York*, 2:148.

27. Galishoff, *Newark*, 161, 145; Hopkins, *Princes and Peasants*, 301, 294, 85; Fenner et al., *Smallpox*, 309; Chase, *Magic Shots*, 76, 80; J. Michael Lane, Frederick L. Ruben, John M. Neff, and J. D. Millar, "Complications of Smallpox Vaccination, 1968," *New England Journal of Medicine* 281 (1969): 1207; Fenner et al., *Smallpox*, 309–10; Alex R. Kemper, Matthew M. Davis, and Gary L. Freed, "Expected Adverse Events in a Mass Smallpox Campaign," *Effective Clinical Practice* 5 (Mar.–Apr. 2002): 84–90; John F. Modlin, "A Mass Smallpox Vaccination Campaign: Reasonable or Irresponsible?" *Effective Clinical Practice* 5 (Mar.–Apr. 2002): 98–99; Gina Kolata and Lawrence K. Altman, "Smallpox Vaccine Stockpile Is Larger Than Was Thought," *New York Times*, Mar. 29, 2002. The most comprehensive discussions of vaccination complications are Fenner et al., *Smallpox*, 296–311; and Graham S. Wilson, *The Hazards of Immunization* (London, 1967), 157–78. Those who had been vaccinated could also serve as sources of smallpox for close contacts (Fenner et al., *Smallpox*, 1265).

It is also important to remember, as Claudia Huerkamp notes for Germany, that "improvements in the administration of the vaccine would probably have taken even longer without the pressure of the anti-vaccinationist movement." Such was presumably was also the case in the United States. See Claudia Huerkamp, "The History of Smallpox Vaccination in Germany: A First Step in the Medicalization of the General Public," *Journal of Contemporary History* 20 (1985): 630.

28. For the most compelling contemporary statement of the safety (and necessity) of vaccination, see a book in the series Harvard Health Talks, Benjamin White, *Smallpox and Vaccination* (Cambridge, Mass., 1924). White calls antivaccinationists "the priests of Baal" (70).

29. Hopkins, *Princes and Peasants*, 5–6, 287–91 (quote on 290); Fenner et al., *Smallpox*, 329–30. The transfer of immunity between the two types of the disease led one English physician to suggest, not unreasonably, that the best way to prevent the dangers of smallpox was not through vaccination but rather through encouraging the spread of *V. Minor*. See S. R. Maisie May, "Charles Value Chapin and Changes in the Type of Contagious Disease," paper presented to Yale University History of Science and Medicine section, 1998.

30. Maisie May, "'Should We Be Vaccinated?' Individual Risk Assessment and the Spread of Smallpox in England and Wales, 1919–1935," Msc. diss., Oxford University, 1996, 40–42 (quote, 41).

31. Bernhard J. Stern, *Social Factors in Medical Progress* (New York, 1927), 65.

CHAPTER THIRTEEN
Shutting Down the Schools: Parents and Protest in Mt. Scott

1. Baldwin, *Contagion and the State*, 2. For an imaginative exploration of the political theory of alternative healing, see Fred M. Frohock, *Healing Powers: Alternative Medicine, Spiritual Communities, and the State* (Chicago, 1992).

2. *Oreg.*, Feb. 4, 1902, 8. For an example of one of the Portland doctors who opposed compulsory vaccination, see P. L. McKenzie's letters, *Evening Journal*, May 26, 1902, 3, and *Oreg.*, June 3, 1902, 5.

The city averaged only 103.7 cases per year between 1898 and 1917, with the highest number being 299 in 1908. The overall smallpox case fatality rate in Progressive Era Portland was thus six-tenths of 1 percent. See City of Portland, Auditor,

Reports and Studies, A2001-058, Box 10–11, Annual Report of the Health Department, 1898–1917, SPARC. (Four of the next six annual reports are missing, making further analysis of smallpox incidence hazardous.)

3. City of Portland, Mayor, *Mayor's Message and Annual Reports of Officers*, A2000–002, Box 2, Annual Report of the Health Department, 1907, 212, SPARC; *Jour.*, Oct. 21, 1908, 10; *Jour.*, Feb. 1, 1908, 14; *Oreg.*, Mar. 13, 1910, III, 6; July 1, 1911, 8.

4. *Oreg.*, Oct. 30, 1913, 8; July 1, 1911, 8; *Medical Freedom*, Mar. 1911, 5.

5. *Jour.*, Jan. 4, 1913, 3; *Chiropractor*, Apr. 1913, 15, 18.

6. N.A., *Organization and Business Methods of the City Government of Portland, Oregon* (New York, 1913), 24; *MSH*, Sept. 24, 1913, 1. For attendance figures, see *Tel.*, Sept. 15, 1914, 1, 8; Sept. 16, 1914, 8; Sept. 18, 1914, 8; Sept. 26, 1914, 15; *Oreg.*, Sept. 16, 1914, 11. On the effective shutdown of the schools, see *Tel.*, Sept. 16, 1914, 8; Sept. 21, 1914, 14. The four schools were Arleta, Creston, Hoffman, and Woodmere. The previous year the editor of the *Labor Press* provided some sense of the class background of the protestors when he complimented the neighborhood mothers of Arleta, "women of moderate circumstances," including many wives of union men, for their communitarian work at local schools (*PLP*, July 28, 1913, 4).

Such resistance occurred in many other American localities. In Toledo, over two-thirds of children were absent in 1914 due to opposition to vaccination, and in 1905 parents kept half of the students out of the Bellingham, Washington, schools. Sentiment was so strong that citizens elected two antivaccinationists to the school board in Seattle in 1909 and two more in Los Angeles in 1911. *Medical Freedom*, Feb. 1914, 11; Blake Marcus Harrison, "The Antivaccination Movement in America: The Seattle Experience, 1850–1946," B.A. thesis, University of Washington, 1991, 171–72; *Medical Freedom*, Dec. 1911, 13.

7. *News*, Sept. 23, 1914, 2; *Tel.*, Sept. 18, 1914, 8; *Oreg.*, Sept. 18, 1914, 15; Sept. 22, 1914, 4; *Tel.*, Sept. 21, 1914, 14; Sept. 22, 1914, 6. Two years previously Powell had been a Prohibition Party candidate for the legislature; even then his reputation came primarily from his opposition to vaccination (*Jour.*, Oct. 22, 1912).

8. *Oreg.*, Sept. 23, 1914, 11; Sept. 24, 1914, 11; Sept. 25, 1914, 8; *Tel.*, Sept. 30, 1914, 8. The Health Defense League also brought suit against one of the doctors for injuries resulting from a vaccination performed on a seven-year-old without consent. The case resulted in a verdict for the defendant a year later, but not before Judge McGinn declared compulsory vaccination illegal (*MSH*, Oct. 14, 1915, 2). On McGinn, see MacColl, *Growth of a City*, 125–28 (quote, 127).

9. *Oreg.*, Sept. 20, 1914, I, 17; Sept. 18, 1914, 15; *Jour.*, Sept. 20, 1914, I, 7; W. A. Turner to H. R. Albee, Jan. 22, 1914, City of Portland, Mayor Albee, Subject Files, A2000-003, 6/72–89, "J," 1914, SPARC.

10. *Tel.*, Sept. 30, 1914, 8; *Oreg.*, Sept. 18, 1914, 15; *Tel.*, Sept. 18, 1914, 8; Sept. 22, 1914, 6; *Oreg.*, Sept. 22, 1914, 4.

11. The identification of individuals involved in the antivaccination movement comes from *Oreg.*, Sept. 18, 1914, 15; Sept. 20, 1914, I, 17; Sept. 22, 1914, 4; *Tel.*, Sept. 30, 1914, 8. I traced occupations through *CD*, 1913–15.

12. The social and cultural characteristics of the neighborhood come out most prominently in the *Mt. Scott Herald*. For Foster Road in 1916, see Charles S. Rosenblum, "Housing and Housing Reform in Portland, Oregon, 1900–1934: An Examina-

tion of the Response to Urbanization during the Progressive Era," B.A. thesis, Reed College, 1973, appendix, "Distribution of Retail Firms, Portland, Oregon"; and *PLP*, Dec. 4, 1915, 8. On hop picking, see *Tel.*, Sept. 16, 1914, 8. For the distance from downtown, see MacColl, *Shaping*, 490. For the precincts that defined Mt. Scott, and the electoral data on Daly, see *MSH*, June 7, 1917, 1. The 1914 and 1916 voting data were compiled from Abstract, 1914, 1916.

Chapter Fourteen
From the Death of a Child to Sedition against the State: The Life and Ideology of Lora C. Little

1. *Jour.*, Sept. 20, 1914, I, 7; *MSH*, Sept. 24, 1914, 1.

2. This information on Little comes from *CD*, 1909–18, and *MSH*, Mar. 11, 1915, 4; Sept. 14, 1916, 4.

3. *MSH*, Mar. 11, 1915, 4; Mar. 23, 1916, 4; *Oreg.*, Apr. 7, 1918, I, 9.

4. Death Certificate, Lora C. Little, Cook County, Illinois; *Liberator* 6 (Jan. 1905): 95; U.S. Bureau of the Census, *Twelfth Census of the United States*, 1900, Schedule No. 1, Manuscript Census, Minnesota, County of Hennepin, City of Minneapolis, Supervisor's District no. 5, Enumeration District no. 21, Sheet no. 9; Minneapolis City Directory, 1899–1908. Little's death certificate lists her as a widow. My immense thanks to Beth Johnston for genealogical research on Lora Little.

5. Lora C. Little, *Crimes of the Cowpox Ring: Some Moving Pictures Thrown on the Dead Wall of Official Silence* (Minneapolis, 1906), 9, 18, 71–75; *Liberator* 10 (Feb. 1907): 137. With the citation of *Crimes*, Martin Kaufman ("American Anti-Vaccinationists," 470) is the only historian to have ever mentioned Lora Little.

6. *Minneapolis Journal*, Aug. 25, 1899, 10; Feb. 26, 1902, 4; June 19, 1902, 4; Jan. 22, 1903, 4; Mar. 10, 1900, II, 4.

7. *Vac. Inq.*, Feb. 1, 1907, 183; Otto Carque, *The Foundation of All Reform: A Guide to Health, Wealth, and Freedom, a Popular Treatise on the Diet Question* (Chicago, 1904), rear advertising section; *Liberator* 8 (Jan. 1906): 93; 11 (July 1907): 110; 11 (Sept. 1907): 164; 2 (Jan. 1903): 112; 3 (Sept. 1903): 177; 2 (Oct. 1902): 20; 4 (Feb. 1904): 137–37; 5 (July 1904): 108; 6 (Jan. 1905): 96; 6 (Feb. 1905): 129.

8. *Liberator* 2 (Jan. 1903): 130; 8 (Feb. 1906), 138; 4 (Mar. 1904), 170–71; *Vac. Inq.*, Dec. 1, 1903, 171; *Liberator* 6 (Mar. 1905): 165; 4 (Dec. 1903), 79–80. Little turned out to be ambivalent about her antivaccination law. Although she later took much credit for this piece of pioneering legislation, at the time of its passage she called the law a "disgusting piece of legislative folly" due to its epidemic loophole. *Liberator* 3 (Aug. 1903): 318; 3 (May 1903), 233. Harvard public health professor Benjamin White, however, had no doubt about the law's success. He used Minnesota as the primary example of "the price paid for the neglect of vaccination. There the antivaccinationists prevail, and with the people their word bears greater weight than that of the health officials. In 1903 compulsory vaccination was abandoned" (*Smallpox and Vaccination*, 75).

9. *Liberator* 8 (Sept. 1906): 151; Little to John Pitcairn, Sept. 5, 1907, John Pitcairn Archives and Carriage House, Bryn Athyn, Pa.; *Vac. Inq.*, Apr. 1, 1908, 1; May 1, 1908, 38; June 1, 1908, 52; Aug. 1, 1908, 84; Jan. 1, 1910, 213.

10. *Liberator* 6 (Jan. 1905): 95; *MSH*, Sept. 21, 1916, 2; Sept. 24, 1914, 1; Carque,

Foundation of All Reform, esp. 53–66. On Macfadden and Carque, see Whorton, *Crusaders for Fitness*, 267–68, 296–303; see below for Fletcher. On the staunchly democratic origins of the kind of self-medical care ideology that these reformers advocated, see James H. Cassedy, "Why Self-Help? Americans Alone with Their Diseases," in *Medicine without Doctors: Home Health Care in American History*, ed. Guenter B. Risse, Ronald L. Numbers, and Judith Walzer Leavitt (New York, 1977), 31–48.

11. *MSH*, Jan. 4, 1915, 4; May 13, 1915, 4; Apr. 27, 1916, 2; May 4, 1916, 2; Dec. 7, 1916, 2; 1913 *VP*, 13–14; *Jour.*, July 16, 1950, n.p., Oswald West Papers, OHSMA; B. A. Owens-Adair, *Human Sterilization: Its Social and Legislative Aspects* (n.p., 1922), 71. Rapists convicted with only circumstantial evidence were not subject to the law. Little and the Anti-Sterilization League did not include any argument against the measure in the voters' pamphlet; for Owens-Adair's views see her *Human Sterilization* (Warrenton, Ore.?, 1910?); for a history of similar laws in American history, see Philip R. Reilly, *The Surgical Solution: A History of Involuntary Sterilization in the United States* (Baltimore, 1991); for the Oregon case, see Mark A. Largent, "'The Greatest Curse of the Race': Eugenic Sterilization in Oregon, 1909–1983," *OHQ* 103 (Summer 2002): 196–99.

For Little's long-standing opposition to compulsory sterilization, see *Liberator* 7 (May 1905): 48. Eugenics laws, she wrote, "are asked for by persons who think they can set themselves apart from their kind and make themselves dictators over their less fortunate fellows." Quoting poetry, Little proclaimed, "I am part of the things I despise, / Since my life is bound up by their common span." She called on the public to "banish the cruel pessimism that says the race to save itself must resort to the sterilization and prohibition of marriage" (*MSH*, Sept. 7, 1916, 2). Along the same lines, Little complained of the Darwinian tendency of compulsory medical inspection: "To deny the weakling an education, to make him an outlaw from school, is on the order of the old Spartan plan (only a shade less drastic) of destroying the unfit." Little, "Seeking Medical Freedom," *Open Door*, Nov. 1918, 12; my thanks to Nadav Davidovitch for this citation.

12. *Equity*, Jan. 1914, 40; *News*, Oct. 31, 1913, 9; *Oreg.*, Nov. 2, 1913, III, 10; Nov. 2, 1913, III, 6; Oct. 30, 1913, 8; Oct. 30, 1913, 8; *Medical Freedom*, Dec. 1913, 15; *Oreg.*, Nov. 2, 1913, III, 6.

13. Owens-Adair, *Human Sterilization*, 71–72; *News*, Oct. 22, 1913, 4; *Oreg.*, Nov. 2, 1913, III, 10; Owens-Adair, *Human Sterilization*, 72. On Wood, see Robert Hamburger, *Two Rooms: The Life of Charles Erskine Scott Wood* (Lincoln, 1998). The connection that Little made between coerced vaccination and coerced sterilization was a compelling one. The most infamous statement comes from Oliver Wendell Holmes's decision in *Buck v. Bell*, 274 U.S. 200 (1927): "The principle that sustains compulsory vaccination is broad enough to cover cutting the Fallopian tubes. . . . Three generations of imbeciles are enough."

By and large, scholars have not examined enough the *opponents* of sterilization and other such eugenics measures. It may very well be the case that populists have provided a strong core of resistance to these brutal and inhumane laws, in addition to the other "coalition of critics" that Daniel J. Kevles has identified in *In the Name of Eugenics: Genetics and the Uses of Human Heredity* (New York, 1985), 113–47. See also Margaret Canovan, *G. K. Chesterton: Radical Populist* (New York, 1977), 66–72; Steven Selden, *Inheriting Shame: The Story of Eugenics and Racism in America* (New York,

1999), 106–26; and Frank Dikötter, "Race Culture: Recent Perspectives on the History of Eugenics," *American Historical Review* 103 (Apr. 1998): 476.

14. Owens-Adair, *Human Sterilization*, 72. Voting figures come from Culbertson, "History of the Initiative and Referendum," 530 and 1913 Special Election Abstract. West Side and East Side voting figures show little difference (*Oreg.*, Nov. 6, 1913, 14). For Little's 1914 candidacy, see *MSH*, Sept. 24, 1914, 4, and *Medical Freedom*, May 1914, 14; for her platform, see *Vac. Inq.*, Dec. 1, 1914, 296.

15. Logie Barrow coined the term *democratic epistemology*, "a definition of knowledge as open to anybody," in *Independent Spirits: Spiritualism and English Plebeians, 1850–1910* (London, 1986), 146. The most extensive set of Little's autopsies, ranging from Edward Harriman to Harvey Scott, were in *MSH*, May 18, 1916, 2, where Little also forecast the early death of Theodore Roosevelt; for quote see *MSH*, Jan. 7, 1915, 4. Little's orientation toward the middle class did not prevent her protesting against the attempt by municipal authorities to vaccinate forcibly between one thousand and fifteen hundred unemployed men in 1914 (*Medical Freedom*, Apr. 1914, 12).

16. R. M. MacLeod, "Law, Medicine, and Public Opinion: The Resistance to Compulsory Health Legislation, 1870–1907" (part 2), *Public Law* 1967:211; Little, *Crimes of the Cowpox Ring*, 62. We should remember that a libertarian argument on such issues can move well beyond simple social irresponsibility. For one strong argument that links state coercive power over vaccines and AIDS transmission, and that asks us to dispute the entire concept of "public health" as part of a "medical model of society [that] is the conceptual engine of totalitarianism," see Richard D. Mohr, "AIDS, Gays, and State Coercion," *Bioethics* 1 (1987): 48–49.

17. *MSH*, Aug. 5, 1915, 2; Oct. 5, 1916, 2; July 1, 1915, 4; Dec. 7, 1916, 2; Aug. 5, 1915, 2.

18. *MSH*, July 15, 1915, 4; Aug. 24, 1916, 2; July 15, 1915, 4; May 18, 1916, 2. Little's views on doctors, and much more, were analogous to those of Gandhi; see, for example, M. K. Gandhi, *Nature Cure* (Ahmedabad, India, 1954).

19. Westbrook, *John Dewey*, 185; Little, *Crimes of the Cowpox Ring*, 6; *MSH*, Mar. 16, 1916, 2.

20. *MSH*, Jan. 7, 1915, 4; Sept. 23, 1915, 2; Feb. 4, 1915, 2. A report from the Portland Housing Association shows that Little's prescription was not anachronistic. The Housing Association noted that as late as 1918 the Woodstock neighborhood (adjacent to the Mt. Scott uprising) was "settled largely by persons who left the congested districts so that they might have yards and gardens and keep chickens, rabbits, and cows"; Rosenblum, "Housing and Housing Reform," 32. For a brief sketch of the undeveloped nature of Woodstock during this period, see Pratt, *I Remember Portland*, 68–69.

21. *MSH*, Sept. 23, 1915, 2. Little's philosophy appears to be a remarkable forerunner of the trenchant critique of medical utopianism offered by René Dubos. See, for example, Dubos, *Mirage of Health: Utopias, Progress, and Biological Change* (New York, 1959), 216: "We have eliminated from modern society some of the crudest forms of economic injustice; but we operate human relationships on a basis of aggressive competition and of endless striving for success. We have lavishly produced and made available to men a wealth of comforts and earthly goods; but we have denied to most of them the possibility of choosing and of participating creatively in the joy of production."

22. *MSH*, Apr. 13, 1916, 2. If such ideas seem excessively antimodern, it is important to remember how congruent they are with current "agrarian" thinking. Compare, for example, the philosopher and poet Wendell Berry's critique of "orthodox agriculture" and the overspecialization of modern life. His most accessible work is *The Unsettling of America: Culture and Agriculture* (San Francisco, 1986 [1977]). Berry sees great cultural dangers in vaccination (138).

23. *MSH*, Feb. 11, 1915, 4; July 1, 1915, 4; Sept. 2, 1915, 2; Jan. 21, 1915, 2; May 20, 1915, 2; Jan. 21, 1915, 2. Alexander Wilder was cofounder of the first national antivaccination organization in the United States and was also the "ideological godfather" of the Society for the Prevention of Premature Burial, a surprisingly strong movement closely linked to the antivaccinationists and their critique of expert medicine. See Martin S. Pernick, "Back from the Grave: Recurring Controversies over Defining and Diagnosing Death in History," in *Death: Beyond Whole-Brain Criteria*, ed. Richard M. Zaner (Dordrecht, 1988), 49. For the best analyses of the politics of quarantine, see Judith Walzer Leavitt, *Typhoid Mary: Captive to the Public's Health* (Boston, 1996); and Howard Markel, *Quarantine! East European Jewish Immigrants and the New York City Epidemics of 1892* (Baltimore, 1997).

24. *MSH*, May 13, 1915, 4; May 20, 1915, 2. Little noted that Oregon would be the first place on the globe, after the cantons of Switzerland, to have a popular vote on vaccination (*MSH*, Sept. 21, 1916, 2).

CHAPTER FIFTEEN
Direct Democracy and Antivaccination

1. *News*, Oct. 1, 1915, 1; *Oreg.*, Jan. 20, 1915, 5; Feb. 19, 1915, 6; *Jour.*, Jan. 20, 1915, 4 (quote); *Tel.*, Jan. 20, 1915, 4; Feb. 18, 1915, 8; Mar. 20, 1915, 1; *MSH*, Jan. 14, 1915, 4. Moser presumably introduced the bill at the behest of Little. For the text of the bill and the initiative, see *Oreg.*, Jan. 20, 1919, 5; and 1916 *VP*, 29. On Moser, who in the next session would serve as president of the Senate, see MacColl, *Growth of a City*, 155, 167, 225–27.

2. *OV*, Oct. 14, 1916, 337–41 (quotes on 339–40); *Oreg.*, Sept. 25, 1916, 8; Oct. 8, 1916, III, 6; Nov. 13, 1916, 8. The unpredictable *News* also quietly opposed the measure (Nov. 4, 1916, 8).

3. *News*, Oct. 16, 1916, 1; *Jour.*, Sept. 29, 1916, 6; *OLP*, Oct. 28, 1916, 8; *OV*, Nov. 4, 1916, 37; *Oreg.*, Oct. 8, 1916, III, 6; Sept. 25, 1916, 8; 1916 *VP*, 30.

4. *Vac. Inq.*, Feb. 1, 1917, 24. Statewide voting figures come from Culbertson, "History of Initiative," 532; these and the following city and county voting data were calculated from 1916 Abstract; precinct locations come from *Oreg.*, Nov. 5, 1916, I, 10.

5. *Vac. Inq.*, Dec. 1, 1903, 170. The Lents PTA had invited Lora Little to discuss the initiative at a community program just before the election (*News*, Oct. 18, 1916, 2).

6. *Vac. Inq.*, Sept. 1, 1917, 198; Daly campaign committee materials, undated (ca. early May 1917), Thomas Neuhausen Papers, Box 4, Political Correspondence, 1917 Portland Election, SCUO. Another interesting link between Will Daly and Lora Little, besides their common Mt. Scott residence, was their enmity to city health officer R. B. Marcellus. Daly attempted to get the health officer fired for mishandling a leprosy case

and engaging in petty corruption. See, among many stories in the press, *Oreg.*, Dec. 15, 1915, 7, where a physician linked Daly's indictment of Marcellus with similar attacks from antivaccinationists. For the records of the case, see City of Portland, Auditor, Collected Reports and Studies, 17/1–2, Investigation of Dr. M. B. Marcellus Leprosy Case, 1914–15, SPARC. Daly and Marcellus had tangled earlier over Daly's attempt to liberate Portland dogs after Marcellus's muzzling order during a rabies scare (*Tel.*, Sept. 30, 1914, 8).

7. *Oreg.*, Apr. 7, 1918, I, 9; *Bismarck Tribune*, Mar. 30, 1918, 1; *Vac. Inq.*, Aug. 1, 1918, 153; Randolph Bourne, "The State," in *War and the Intellectuals: Essays by Randolph S. Bourne, 1915–1919*, ed. Carl Resek (New York, 1964), 89; *Vac. Inq.*, May 1, 1919, 63. I am grateful to James A. Davis of the State Historical Society of North Dakota for tracking down the *Tribune* article. For Little's earlier opposition to the war, see *MSH*, Jan. 4, 1917, 3.

8. *Vac. Inq.*, June 1, 1918, 117; Jan. 1, 1919, 3; The Journal A.M.A. Propaganda Department to Mrs. Herman Haas, Mar. 7, 1921, Historical Health Fraud and Alternative Medicine Collection, AMA, courtesy, AMA Archives; "Platform Adopted at the Eight Annual Meeting of the AMLL" (ca. 1927), AMA, courtesy, AMA Archives; American Medical Liberty League, "Philippines Pus Punching" (Chicago, ca. 1919), Boston Medical Library of the Francis A. Countway Library of Medicine, Harvard University; Little, *The Baby and the Medical Machine* (Chicago, n.d.), 1, 6, 7. Little reprinted almost the same material from *Baby* in *Chicago Labor News*, Aug. 13, 1920, 2, thus making 1920 the likely publication date. Of interest, given Little's fate during World War I, is the fact that (according to the imprint on my copy of the pamphlet from the Library of Congress) *The Baby and the Medical Machine* ended up in the Army Medical Library. My thanks to Susan Lederer for passing along the AMA documents.

9. *Chicago Labor News*, Dec. 31, 1920, 3; Oct. 8, 1920, 2; Sept. 17, 1920, 2; Oct. 29, 1920, 2; Oct. 1, 1920, 4; *Vac. Inq.*, Apr. 1, 1920, 41; The People ex rel. Jennie Barmore, Relatrix, vs. John Dill Robertson et al. Respondents, No. 14123, Supreme Court of Illinois, 302 Ill. 422; 134 N.E. 815; 1922 Ill. Lexis 1243; 22 A.L.R. 835; *Vac. Inq.*, June 1, 1921, 70; June 2, 1924, 70; AMLL to Dear Sir, June 10, 1925, AMA, courtesy AMA Archives; *Vac. Inq.*, Dec. 1, 1922, 146; Nov. 1, 1927, 142; *Chicago Herald and Examiner*, Jan. 14, 1926, 1, 2; AMLL, "Report . . . to the Eighth Annual Meeting, Hotel Sherman, Chicago, Nov. 7–9, 1926," pamphlet in the author's possession.

10. Anonymous to Miss Josephine B. Timberlake, Sept. 25, 1929, AMA; Lora C. Little, "Know the Facts about Vaccination," American Medical Liberty League pamphlet, ca. 1918, Yale University, Cushing/Whitney Medical Library, 12; *Vac. Inq.*, Dec. 2, 1929, 214; Little Death Certificate; *Vac. Inq.*, Jan. 1, 1932, 3; *Chicago Tribune*, Nov. 1, 1931, 16. No library holds a copy of the *Avalanche*, but I was recently able to purchase the second issue from Ebay.com. It runs twenty-four pages and is glossier than Little's previous publications. The content includes the standard denunciations of State Medicine and vaccination. The novelty of the *Avalanche* lies in its advertisements for health food stores, alternative medicine books and pamphlets, and a variety of drugless healers, including the Sanatology Health School, with its slogan: "The whiter the bread the sooner you're dead; The more sugar you soak the quicker you croak" (*Avalanche*, Nov. 1929, 39).

11. *Oreg.*, Mar. 16, 1919, I, 18; *Jour.*, July 12, 1919, 3; July 23, 1919, 5; Jan. 4,

1920, I, 6 (quote); *Tel.*, Jan. 7, 1920, 1; *Jour.*, Jan. 8, 1920, 12; Jan. 16, 1920, 6; Jan. 25, 1920, III, 5. Parrish was apparently a wealthy property owner; see *OV*, May 29, 1915, 36.

12. *Oreg.*, Feb. 7, 1920, 19. Mrs. Harvey turned out to be Frankie Harvey, wife of printer James H. Harvey, and she was important enough even without a public first name to become secretary of the group of parents protesting at Arleta school. PTA involvement against the dictates of organized medicine is a bit surprising given the general political orientation of the group; see Molly Ladd-Taylor, *Mother-Work: Women, Child Welfare, and the State, 1890–1930* (Urbana, 1994), 43–73.

13. *News*, Feb. 7, 1920, 19; *Oreg.*, Feb. 8, 1920, I, 20; Feb. 9, 1920, 7; *Tel.*, Feb. 9, 1920, 9; *Oreg.*, Feb. 25, 1920, 4.

14. Names and ballot language come from 1920 *VP*, 21–22. Occupational identification here and in subsequent paragraphs, unless otherwise noted, comes from Portland *CD*, 1918–22.

15. *Oreg.*, Oct. 27, 1920, 8; *Tel.*, Nov. 1, 1920, 8; *Oreg.*, Oct. 25, 1920, 8; Oct. 24, 1920, IV, 10. The *Telegram*, Oct. 2, 1920, revealed that Metropolitan Life printed and distributed one hundred thousand circulars opposing the bill.

16. 1920 *VP*, 22.

17. 1920 *VP*, 22.

18. *Oreg.*, Oct. 31, 1920, IV, 8; Esther G. Weinstein, "William Simon U'Ren: A Study of Persistence in Political Reform," Ph.D. diss., Syracuse University, 1967, 53. On Fletcher, who believed that "Democracy has become an Oligarchy of Greed" and who hoped to eradicate poverty through his rather curious reforms, see Whorton, *Crusaders for Fitness*, 168–81 (quote on 171). U'Ren's reference to the rag over the nose was to the municipal health authorities' attempt to mandate the wearing of masks during the 1918 influenza epidemic. For Portlanders' massive resistance to health policies during the epidemic, see Dick Pintarich and Ray Stout, "Year of the Plague: The Swine Flu Pandemic of 1918," in *Great Moments in Oregon History*, ed. Win McCormack and Dick Pintarich (Portland, 1987), 118–24.

Inveighing against the "deception, mysticism, fetichism, misery, and sorrow" of vaccination, the Christian Scientist and prominent member of the Portland Establishment B. S. Josselyn also spoke on behalf of the initiative (*Oreg.*, Oct. 20, 1920, 10). On Josselyn, an ardent foe of Mayor Harry Lane, a staunch advocate of the city commission form of government, and "the head and front of the Employers' association," see MacColl and Stein, *Merchants, Money, and Power*, 415–16, 446–47; and *News*, Oct. 1, 1912, 1. Josselyn's arguments were nearly the only public expressions of religious ideas in the entire antivaccination conflict between 1914 and 1920.

19. Culbertson, "History of Initiative," 535; Portland data calculated from 1920 Abstract.

20. *OLP*, Oct. 16, 1920, 1; *News*, Oct. 30, 1920, 1.

21. Names come from *News*, Feb. 7, 1920, 10; *Oreg.*, Feb. 7, 1920, 19; Feb. 8, 1920, I, 20; Feb. 11, 1920, 20; Feb. 25, 1920, 4; Oct. 24, 1920, I, 14; Oct. 31, 1920, IV, 9; *Jour.*, Oct. 24, 1920, II, 3; *Tel.*, Oct. 30, 1920, 8.

22. *Oreg.*, Jan. 28, 1922; Jan. 31, 1922; *PC*, Nov. 15, 1922, 4.

23. Secretary of State, *Oregon Blue Book, 1959–1960* (Salem, 1959), 228; *OV*, Feb. 25, 1919, 335; Whorton, "Drugless Healing," 20, 16; U.S. Bureau of the Census, *Thirteenth Census of the United States, 1910: Population* (Washington, D.C., 1913),

4:206; *Fourteenth Census of the United States, 1920: Population* (Washington, D.C., 1921), 4:1203; *Portland Examiner*, Apr. 15, 1926, 3. The national census recorded 7,902 female healers in 1920; Joseph A. Hill, *Women in Gainful Occupations, 1870 to 1920* (Washington, 1929), 42.

The categorization of "healers" in the census is interesting. In 1910 both sexes are listed under this "semiprofessional" category, but in 1920 officials changed the terminology. Despite the 104 female physicians and surgeons in Portland in 1910, no female physicians were listed in 1920. On the other hand, no male "healers" were listed in 1920, despite the 18 of them in 1910. The 1920 category of healer specifically excluded "osteopaths and physicians and surgeons." Also intriguing are the 17 "fortune tellers, hypnotists, spiritualists, etc." listed in 1910—another category eliminated in 1920. In addition, the city directory listed eighty-seven Christian Science practitioners in 1920. Ronald L. Numbers reports that as late as the 1930s, "nearly a quarter of American healers were Christian scientists, osteopaths, chiropractors, or irregulars of some stripe." See Numbers, "The Fall and Rise of the American Medical Profession," in *The Professions in American History*, ed. Nathan O. Hatch (Notre Dame, 1988), 65.

Both the antivaccination and the naturopathy initiatives were part of what Richard Neuberger condescendingly termed the "fribble trumpery" that the Oregon System produced. See *Our Promised Land* (New York, 1938), 146.

CHAPTER SIXTEEN
The Success and Radicalism of Antivaccination

1. Allen M. Kraut, "Silent Travelers: Germs, Genes, and American Efficiency, 1890–1924," *Social Science History* 12 (Winter 1988): 379.

2. Friedrich Engels, "On the History of Early Christianity," in *Marx and Engels: Basic Writings on Politics and Philosophy*, ed. Lewis S. Feuer (Garden City, N.Y., 1959), 174; Lipset, *Political Man*, 178–79; *Survey*, Feb. 1, 1926, 562. Cott, *Grounding of Modern Feminism*, 274, initially directed me to the Hillquit quote. For the connection between radical political ideologies and critiques of conventional medicine in nineteenth-century France, see David S. Barnes, *The Making of a Social Disease: Tuberculosis in Nineteenth-Century France* (Berkeley, 1995), 217.

3. The Portland story might shed light on a link between populist radicalism and irregular medicine that historians have not yet uncovered. For traces of this, see Christopher Lasch, "The Decline of Populism," in *The Agony of the American Left* (New York, 1969), 13–15; Wiebe, *The Search for Order*, 14; and Thomas A. Bland, *How to Get Well and How to Keep Well* (Boston, 1896), 200–201, where the Populist and Indian reformer Bland concludes his treatise by calling on the people to "rise up in rebellion" against compulsory vaccination. On Bland, see Johnson, "Red Populism." Martin Pernick notes the background of antivaccinationists in the radical Garrisonian branch of abolitionism and comments that "anti-slavery continued to provide an important metaphor for their later crusades against the power of doctors" ("Back from the Grave," 50–51).

4. James, quoted in Robert C. Fuller, *Alternative Medicine and American Religious Life* (New York, 1989), 8. For James as a staunch medical democrat who compared discrimination against alternative medicine to anti-Semitism and "Armenian massa-

cres," see Eric Caplan, *Mind Games: American Culture and the Birth of Psychotherapy* (Berkeley, 1998), 85–87 (quote, 87).

5. Christopher Lasch, *Haven in a Heartless World: The Family Besieged* (New York, 1977), especially 12–21; James C. Scott, *Seeing Like a State: How Certain Schemes to Improve the Human Condition Have Failed* (New Haven, 1998); John O'Neill, *Five Bodies: The Human Shape of Modern Society* (Ithaca, 1985), 83, 67, 68; John Gaventa, "The Powerful, the Powerless, and the Experts: Knowledge Struggles in an Information Age," in *Voices of Change: Participatory Research in the United States and Canada*, ed. Peter Park, Mary Brydon-Miller, Budd Hall, and Ted Jackson (Westport, Conn. 1993), 21–40. For a compelling case study of this proletarianization, see Rima D. Apple, "Constructing Mothers: Scientific Motherhood in the Nineteenth and Twentieth Centuries," in *Mothers and Motherhood: Readings in American History*, ed. Apple and Janet Golden (Columbus, 1997), 90–110. Scott defines high modernism as a "muscle-bound version of the self-confidence about scientific and technical progress, the expansion of production, the growing satisfaction of human needs, the mastery of nature (including human nature), and, above all, the rational design of social order commensurate with the scientific understanding of natural laws" (4). Ironically, Scott marginalizes antivaccination and celebrates vaccination, even as he recognizes the valid local knowledge embedded in inoculation (*Seeing Like a State*, 77, 96, 325–26).

The antivaccinationists also help us create a historical tradition of "popular epidemiology," a concept that Phil Brown and Edwin J. Mikkelsen have formulated to analyze, and celebrate, the public struggles over scientific meaning and method arising out of debates about toxic waste. See *No Safe Place: Toxic Waste, Leukemia, and Community Action* (Berkeley, 1990), esp. 125–63. For compelling arguments advocating the rationality of increased lay participation in scientific policymaking, see Brian Wynne, "Misunderstood Misunderstanding: Social Identities and Public Uptake of Science," *Public Understanding of Science* 1 (1992): 281–304; and Richard E. Sclove, "Better Approaches to Science Policy," *Science* 279 (Feb. 1998): 1283; for a powerful study of democracy, expertise, and modern medicine see Steven Epstein, *AIDS, Activism, and the Politics of Knowledge* (Berkeley, 1996).

6. For the popularity of nontraditional healers among the contemporary American middle class, see Meredith B. McGuire, with the assistance of Debra Kantor, *Ritual Healing in Suburban America* (New Brunswick, 1988). For the surprising strength of current skepticism about vaccination throughout the American population, see Emily Martin, *Flexible Bodies: Tracking Immunity in American Culture, from the Days of Polio to the Age of AIDS* (Boston, 1994), 198–203; for its rationality see Anne Rogers and David Pilgrim, "The Risk of Resistance: Perspectives on the Mass Childhood Immunisation Programme," in *Medicine, Health, and Risk: Sociological Approaches*, ed. Jonathan Gabe (London, 1995), 73–90; Deborah Lupton, *The Imperative of Health: Public Health and the Regulated Body* (London, 1995), 86–87; and Kevin Dew, "The Measles Vaccination Campaigns in New Zealand, 1985 and 1991: The Issues behind the Panic," Victoria University of Wellington, Department of Sociology and Social Policy, Working Papers no. 10, 1995. The best place to gauge the current antivaccination movement is at the website of the National Vaccine Information Center (NVIC) at www.909shot.com; see also *Mothering* magazine. For a critical perspective, see Arthur Allen, "Injection Rejection," *New Republic*, Mar. 23, 1998, 20–23. For an example of the kind of medical experimentation that fuels antivaccination sentiments, see Alex-

ander Cockburn, "The Kevorkian in the White House," *Nation*, Oct. 14, 1996, 9–10, and Dorothy Roberts, *Killing the Black Body: Race, Reproduction, and the Meaning of Liberty* (New York, 1997), 145–48. On the danger that overmedicalization could cause epidemiological disasters in the future, see Laurie Garrett, *The Coming Plague: Newly Emerging Diseases in a World Out of Balance* (New York, 1994), which follows in the footsteps of René Dubos. Garrett documents the gigantic blunders of the 1976 swine flu immunization campaign, which led to much greater public suspicion of vaccination (153–91).

I wish to thank Anne Johnston for her help with the formulation of the conclusion, as well as for living antivaccination with me for so long.

Part V

The Uses of Populism after Progressivism: The 1922 School Bill and the Triumph of the Ku Klux Klan

1. Kenneth T. Jackson, *The Ku Klux Klan in the City, 1915–1930* (New York, 1967), 236. It is going much too far, however, to say that the Klan "took political control" of Portland, as Stanley Coben claims in *Rebellion against Victorianism: The Impetus for Cultural Change in 1920s America* (New York, 1991), 147.

2. John Higham, *Strangers in the Land: Patterns of American Nativism, 1860–1925* (New York, 1968 [1955]), 260.

Chapter Seventeen

School Boards and Strikes: Petite Bourgeoisie against Elites

1. *OLP*, June 24, 1921, 1; *Oreg.*, June 18, 1921, 1–2. The election was June 18; the first report of the Ku Klux Klan coming to Portland that I have found appears in *Tel.*, June 17, 1921, 1. No one, however, ever claimed that the Klan was behind the victorious 1921 school board ticket—only unnamed anti-Catholic forces.

2. *Oreg.*, June 21, 1921, 22. This was not the first time nativists had beaten members of the elite in a school board election. The Federation of Patriotic Societies candidate was also victorious against prominent public figures in 1916. See Malcolm Clark Jr., "The Bigot Disclosed: Ninety Years of Nativism," *OHQ* 75 (June 1974): 146.

3. *News*, June 20, 1921, 2; *OLP*, June 24, 1921, 1; *Tel.*, June 2, 1921, 1–2; *Oreg.*, June 12, 1921, 14; June 18, 1921, 1–2. For the tight grip of the capitalist class on American school boards during this era, see Counts, *Social Composition*, 50–75, 82–97.

4. *OLP*, June 10, 1921, 1; *Oreg.*, June 18, 1921, 8; Jan. 27, 1922, 9.

5. *OLP*, June 17, 1921, 1–2; June 10, 1921, 1; *Oreg.*, June 20, 1921, 2.

6. Even the *Catholic Sentinel*, Mar. 2, 1922, 4, argued that the 1921 election did not represented a nativist triumph. Although it recognized that "what appeared to be an A. P. A. ticket" carried the election, it chalked that slate's victory up to the fear the teachers and other unions had of "the so-called business ticket." For further evidence of elite disgust at the petite bourgeoisie on the school board, see *OV*, June 10, 1922, 42; June 17, 1922, 453; June 24, 1922, 485.

7. For the national scene, see David Montgomery, *The Fall of the House of Labor: The Workplace, the State, and American Labor Activism, 1865–1925* (New York, 1987),

407–10; Montgomery views "the hostility of the middle classes toward the strikers" as the norm during this period (328).

8. *Oreg.*, Nov. 7, 1922, 1; Oct. 18, 1922, 8; Oct. 19, 1922, 1, 14; *News*, Oct. 19, 1922, 1; *Oreg.*, Oct. 26, 1922, 14. For a listing of all the strikes in Portland as well as throughout the state during 1922, see Tobie, "Oregon Labor Disputes," 385–90.

9. *Oreg.*, Oct. 20, 1922, 8; Oct. 21, 1922, 1; *Tel.*, Oct. 16, 1922, 4.

10. *Tel.*, June 8, 1922, 4; *Oreg.*, May 12, 1922, 1; *Tel.*, May 11, 1922, 1; *News*, May 9, 1922, 1; May 23, 1922, 9; May 26, 1922, 1; July 27, 1922, 1.

11. *News*, July 15, 1922, 10; *Oreg.*, July 17, 1922, 8; Sept. 9, 1922, 13; Sept. 19, 1922, 8 (this editorial sets out the newspaper's contrasting view on "Labor's Solidarity with the Community"); *OLP*, Sept. 8, 1922, 1; *Oregonian*, Nov. 7, 1922, 22. McElveen strongly opposed the School Bill (Saalfeld, *Forces of Prejudice*, 75).

CHAPTER EIGHTEEN
Liberal Populism: The Compulsory Public School Bill

1. William Graebner, "Outlawing Teenage Populism: The Campaign against Secret Societies in the American High School, 1900–1960," *JAH* 74 (Sept. 1987): 412.

2. For a strikingly similar middle-class battle for obligatory public schooling in Chile in 1920, see Patrick Barr-Melej, *Reforming Chile: Cultural Politics, Nationalism, and the Rise of the Middle Class* (Chapel Hill, 2001).

3. *Sunnyside Gazette*, July 29, 1922, 2; Dec. 9, 1922, 2.

4. Stephen L. Recken, "A Reinterpretation of the Oregon School Bill of 1922: The Concept of the Common School in Progressive America," M.A. thesis, Portland State University, 1973; for a companion argument that a "radical rhetoric of class leveling, integration, and democratization" mattered as much, if not more, than "bias and religious bigotry" in explaining support for the School Bill, see Barbara Bennet Woodhouse, "'Who Owns the Child?': *Meyer* and *Pierce* and the Child as Property," *William and Mary Law Review* 33 (Summer 1992): 1001, 1035.

5. *OLP*, June 16, 1922, 1. While in the legislature, Woodward "made spectacular fights" for free textbooks and on behalf of his proposal to abolish property qualifications for voters in school board elections. See *OV*, Apr. 3, 1926, 34.

6. Among other roles he played in the Portland class structure, Woodward gave his outspoken support for minimum wage legislation for women, and representatives from both labor and business chose him unanimously to serve as chair of the State Board of Conciliation when that commission commenced operation in 1919. Gleason, "For Working Women," 585–86; Tobie, "Oregon Labor Disputes," 316.

7. A verbatim transcript of the debate appears in the *OV*, Oct. 7, 1922, 14–22. The *Voter* characterized the debate as bringing out "clearly the strongest arguments for and against" the bill by "the two ablest and most eloquent exponents." After the debate, the Ministerial Association tabled a resolution opposing the School Bill.

8. 1922 *VP*, 23; Woodhouse, "Who Owns the Child," 1103–4.

9. "Reasons Why You Should Support the Compulsory Education Bill" (Portland: A.&A.S.R. School Committee, 1922), flyer in Manuscript 646, Lutheran Schools Committee, Folder 3, OHSMA; *Oreg.*, Nov. 2, 1922, 19. Both ads appeared in many newspapers, see, for example, *Oreg.*, Nov. 5, 1922, I, 5.

10. *Oregon Teacher's Monthly*, Oct. 1922, 12.

11. Eckard Vance Toy Jr., "The Ku Klux Klan in Oregon: Its Character and Program," M.A. thesis, University of Oregon, 1959, 280; Pomeroy, *The Pacific Slope*, 228; *Oreg.*, Nov. 2, 1922, 8; Oct. 10, 1922, 1; Nov. 8, 1922, 8. Unless otherwise noted, the information on voting comes from analysis of precinct vote totals in 1922 Abstract; the polling places are listed in *Oreg.*, Nov. 6, 1922, 20. Registration figures are available only for Multnomah County, not Portland; see *Oreg.*, Oct. 29, 1922, I, 1; the national turnout figure is from McGerr, *Decline of Popular Politics*, 186. The specific Portland election figures in both Jackson, *Klan in the City*, 207, 285 nn. 22–23, and Saalfeld, *Forces of Prejudice*, 86–87, are generally incorrect. The anti–School Bill forces outspent its advocates $58,795.27 to $15,664.44; Sam A. Kozer, *Biennial Report of the Secretary of State* (Salem, 1923), 112.

12. The total vote cast on the initiative in comparison with the governor's race comes from "Abstract of Votes for Governor," Multnomah County, General Election 1922, Oregon State Archives, Salem.

CHAPTER NINETEEN
Corporate Tools: The Middling World of the Portland Klan

1. Lothrop Stoddard, "The Common People's Union," *World's Work* 39 (Nov. 1919): 102.

2. Jackson, *Klan in the City*.

3. Leonard J. Moore, "Historical Interpretations of the 1920s Klan: The Traditional View and the Populist Revision," *Journal of Social History* 24 (Winter 1990): 353; MacLean, *Behind the Mask*. Moore provides an excellent bibliography of scholarship both old and new, reprinted with minor revisions in *The Invisible Empire in the West: Toward a New Historical Appraisal of the Ku Klux Klan of the 1920s*, ed. Shawn Lay (Urbana, 1992), 17–38.

4. Moore, "Historical Interpretations," 355 n. 9. Moore's equally spacious definition of populism in his monograph is "promoting the ability of average citizens to influence the workings of society and government." Leonard J. Moore, *Citizen Klansmen: The Ku Klux Klan in Indiana, 1921–1928* (Chapel Hill, 1991), 11.

Almost all recent published studies, beginning with Jackson's, suffer from these chronological and thematic limits. See particularly Robert Alan Goldberg, *Hooded Empire: The Ku Klux Klan in Colorado* (Urbana, 1981); Larry R. Gerlach, *Blazing Crosses in Zion: The Ku Klux Klan in Utah* (Logan, 1982); Shawn Lay, *War, Revolution, and the Ku Klux Klan: A Study of Intolerance in a Border City* (El Paso, 1985); and William D. Jenkins, *Steel Valley Klan: The Ku Klux Klan in Ohio's Mahoning Valley* (Kent, Ohio, 1990); and Shawn Lay, *Hooded Knights on the Niagara: The Ku Klux Klan in Buffalo, New York* (New York, 1995), 148. For an exception to the rule of chronology, see Glenn Feldman, *Politics, Society, and the Klan in Alabama, 1915–1949* (Tuscaloosa, 1999), which otherwise presents a traditional interpretation.

5. Jackson, *Klan in the City*, 240–42.

6. MacLean, *Behind the Mask*, 57, 54, xii. For another work that looks at the Klan as an expression of a much more fluid middle-class politics, see Chris Rhomberg, "White Nativism and Urban Politics: The 1920s Ku Klux Klan in Oakland, California," *Journal of American Ethnic History* (Winter 1998): 39–55.

7. MacLean, *Behind the Mask*, 69–73, 97, 65–67, 136–38, 186–88. MacLean claims to reject "fatalistic readings of the proclivities of the petite bourgeoisie," arguing instead that "contingency" and "culture and politics" are key to explaining lower-middle-class behavior. Yet this does not mean that the petite bourgeoisie has any democratic heritage of its own; instead, it has been the responsibility of labor unions and "anti-fascist forces" to restrain the natural white male middle-class "commitment to enforce the subordination of whole groups of people" (186–87, 67, xiii). Compare this to MacLean's important corrective to a fellow scholar's "belittl[ing]," "scorn[ful]," and "somewhat condescending" analysis of the black bourgeoisie, where she wisely argues against "the way the term middle class functions as a subtle epithet . . . to close off further investigation" ("Race-ing Class, Historicizing Categories," *Labor History* 41 (Feb. 2000): 76).

8. Goldberg, *Hooded Empire*, ix–xi, 45–46, 174–78; Jenkins, *Steel Valley Klan*, xi, 52; Moore, *Citizen Klansmen*, 61. Also confirming this point are Christopher N. Cocoltchos, "The Invisible Empire and the Search for the Orderly Community: The Ku Klux Klan in Anaheim, California," in Lay, *Invisible Empire*, 97–120, and Kenneth D. Wald, "The Visible Empire: The Ku Klux Klan as an Electoral Movement," *Journal of Interdisciplinary History* 11 (Autumn 1980): 217–34.

9. Jackson, *Klan in the City*, 242. In Chicago (108) white collars were 60 percent of the membership, but Jackson notes that the figure is biased in the direction of white collars because of the condition of the records. MacLean, *Behind the Mask*, 57, 54. Jenkins and Moore show that skilled blue collars were proportionally *more* likely to join (Jenkins, *Steel Valley Klan*, 82–84, 86; Moore, *Citizen Klansmen*, 63, 66). For a confirmation that, at least in two Pennsylvania counties, "membership lists often show the importance of skilled workers and foremen as well as petit bourgeois groups such as shopkeepers," see Philip Jenkins, *Hoods and Shirts: The Extreme Right in Pennsylvania, 1925–1950* (Chapel Hill, 1997), 72. Also, blue-collar workers predominated in the Rhode Island Klan; see Joseph W. Sullivan, "Rhode Island's Invisible Empire: A Demographic Glimpse into the Ku Klux Klan," *Rhode Island History* 47 (May 1989): 74–82. Alan Dawley, for one, does not shy away from the fact that "the Klan included plenty of wage earners," in *Struggles for Justice: Social Responsibility and the Liberal State* (Cambridge, Mass., 1991), 491 n. 35.

10. Goldberg, *Hooded Empire*, 36–37, 45–46, 174–77; Moore, *Citizen Klansmen*, 62, 69.

11. Lay, *Hooded Knights*, 148. I should add that MacLean displays the best evidence for the ways the Klan helped politically constitute "the middle class," since she does have impressive sources pointing to the reactionary nature of Klan leaders' concern about the fate of those in the middle (see, for example, *Behind the Mask*, 160). This makes it all the more unfortunate that *Behind the Mask*, the most intellectually challenging history of the American petite bourgeoisie that we have, is so inflexible (and, I might add, undemocratic) in its interpretation.

12. *Salem Capital Journal*, Oct. 20, 1922, 7; *Oreg.*, Feb. 28, 1922, 5; Apr. 18, 1922, 4; *News*, Feb. 23, 1922, 7; Waldo Roberts, "The Ku-Kluxing of Oregon," *Outlook*, Mar. 14, 1923, 491.

13. Davey, quoted in Toy, "Klan in Oregon," 26; David A. Horowitz, "The Klansman as Outsider: Ethnocultural Solidarity and Antielitism in the Oregon Ku Klux

Klan of the 1920s," *Pacific Northwest Quarterly* 80 (Jan. 1989): 12–20; see also Horowitz, "Social Morality and Personal Revitalization: Oregon's Ku Klux Klan in the 1920s," *OHQ* 90 (Winter 1989): 364–84.

14. Unless otherwise indicated, the information on Gifford's life comes from an invaluable brief biography in the *OV*, Mar. 25, 1922, 358.

15. *OV*, Mar. 25, 1922, 358. Gifford remained on the payroll at Northwestern at least until the end of 1921, significantly after his attention to the Klan had become full-time. He eventually set up Klan offices at the Northwestern building in downtown Portland.

16. *OLP*, July 12, 1919, 1; July 19, 1919, 1; C. Easton Rothwell, "The Ku Klux Klan in Oregon," B.A. thesis, Reed College, 1924, 135, 122–25; Clark, "The Bigot Disclosed," 178, 159–60, 188 n. 125. On some of the issues behind the 1919 telephone strike, see Tobie, "Oregon Labor Disputes," 166–97. In another telephone company strike in 1920, Hurd advocated the maintenance of a company union; see Tobie, "Oregon Labor Disputes," 225.

17. *OLP*, July 29, 1922, 4; Aug. 5, 1921, 1–2; Aug. 12, 1921, 1.

18. *Oreg.*, Aug. 4, 1921, 10. My thanks to Eckard Toy for this reference. The antimask ordinance that U'Ren uncovered later served as the legal basis for a proclamation by Governor Ben Olcott against the Klan. The only comment from U'Ren about the Klan I have been able to find from 1922 is an ad for Republican gubernatorial candidate Ike Patterson where U'Ren declared that "stirring up religious strife is the oldest trick of princes and politicians to make the people forget about taxes. Catholics and Ku Klux will both cool off after the election, but taxes will be with us yet." See *News*, May 17, 1922, 2.

19. *Oreg.*, Sept. 6, 1922, 22; Aug. 20, 1922, 1, 4; Sept. 7, 1922, 1; Sept. 17, 1922, 18; Sept. 24, 1922, sec. I, 1–2; *Salem Capital Journal*, Aug. 21, 1922, 1, 8; Sept. 6, 1922, 1, 5.

20. *PC*, Oct. 12, 1922, 2; Barzee to Pierce, Sept. 3, 1922, quoted in Bone, *Oregon Cattleman/Governor/Congressman*, 168.

21. *Oreg.*, July 20, 1922, 6; MacColl, *Growth of a City*, 160; David B. Tyack, "The Perils of Pluralism: The Background of the Pierce Case," *American Historical Review* 74 (Oct. 1968): 93. All the individuals listed in this paragraph can be identified in Mac-Coll's books as members of the city's Establishment. On Robert Smith, see Saalfeld, *Forces of Prejudice*, 73. The high-society voice of the open-shop Portland elite, the *Spectator*, also vociferously opposed the School Bill and the Klan.

22. Toy, "Klan in Oregon," 272, 35 n. 46; *New York Times*, Dec. 3, 1922, II, 8; Roberts, "Ku-Kluxing of Oregon," 491. Similarly, Dartmouth sociologist John Mecklin attributed the triumph of the Oregon Klan to "a singular lack of independent, critical public sentiment" and noted that "it seems to indicate that the mass of Americans are still medieval in their thinking"; John Moffatt Mecklin, *The Ku Klux Klan: A Study of the American Mind* (New York, 1924), 50–51.

23. Rothwell, "The Klan in Oregon," 122; *OV*, May 27, 1922, 356.

24. *OV*, Jan. 27, 1923, 130–31; Feb. 10, 1923, 206–8, 222; Feb. 17, 1923, 234–35; Roberts, "Ku-Kluxing of Oregon," 490. For the general political activities of the Klan I have relied primarily on Toy's pioneering "Klan in Oregon," and Saalfeld, *Forces of Prejudice*.

25. Horowitz, "Social Morality," 369, 379–80; see also Horowitz, "The Klansman

as Outsider." For the Klan's racism, see especially Clark, "The Bigot Disclosed," and for a fascinating examination of the anti-Semitic British-Israel doctrine of prominent Portland Klan minister Rueben Sawyer, see Michael Barkun, *Religion and the Racist Right: The Origins of the Christian Identity Movement* (Chapel Hill, 1994), 21–26.

26. Jackson, *Klan in the City*, 117; Robert L. Duffus, "The Ku Klux Klan in the Middle West," *World's Work* 46 (Aug. 1923): 363–72, 371–72; Lem A. Dever, *Confessions of an Imperial Klansman* (Portland, 1924), 43, 23, 36; *News*, May 17, 1922, 12; *Capital Journal*, Oct. 23, 1922, 2; *OV*, May 12, 1923, 213–14. My general argument does not so much depend on direct evidence of Klan/corporation connections as it does on placing the Klan's ideology and actions in the context of contemporary Portland politics. In that sense, proved conspiracy is far less important than contemporary perception and comparison with other movements. It is important to remember Eckard Toy's comment that "there were allegations that the Klan leaders used their political influence, particularly in Multnomah County, to preserve the favored position of the public service corporations. The evidence, however, is purely circumstantial" ("Klan in Oregon," 44).

27. *Western American*, Nov. 30, 1922, 4; Dec. 7, 1922, 3.

28. *Western American*, Nov. 30, 1922, 4, 6; *Oreg.*, Oct. 21, 1922, 16; *Tel.*, Oct. 21, 1922, 1; *Western American*, Sept. 7, 1923, 4; Oct. 12, 1923, 2. Stewart Holbrook wrote in 1937, with no evidence, that the Klan "Black Patrol" reportedly also drove four box cars of Wobblies out of the city during a 1923 loggers' strike; see *Oregonian*, Apr. 18, 1937, magazine section, 12.

29. *Western American*, Sept. 28, 1923, 1; Oct. 12, 1923, 3–4.

30. *Western American*, Nov. 30, 1922, 2, 4; Sept. 14, 1923, 4; Dec. 7, 1922, 5.

31. *Western American*, Dec. 7, 1922, 2, 8. Distrust of direct democracy was hardly the sole possession of the Klan in 1922. The *Oregonian* continued to complain that "in Oregon we have a close approach to a pure democracy" and that "there is a clear need for a brake upon use of the initiative." See *Oreg.*, Sept. 11, 1922, 8 and Sept. 2, 1922, 8. Opponents of the School Bill, in an advertisement "To Oregon Mothers," also declared that Hamilton had indeed been right to warn about unrestrained majorities and asked, "Is the majority rule then to transcend a mother's right to direct the education of her children?" See *Tel.*, Nov. 3, 1922, 1.

32. Coben, *Rebellion against Victorianism*, 140–41.

CHAPTER TWENTY
The Producer's Call and the Portland Housewives' Council: The Tenuous Survival of Petit Bourgeois Radicalism

1. For stories of populist declension, see Catherine McNicol Stock, *Rural Radicals: Righteous Rage in the American Grain* (Ithaca, 1996); and Kazin, *Populist Persuasion*. For an effective rebuttal of this narrative, see Mary Summers, "From the Heartland to Seattle: The Family Farm Movement of the 1980s and the Legacy of Agrarian State Building," in Stock and Johnston, *Countryside*, 304–25.

2. *PC*, Jan. 4, 1922, 1; Mar. 15, 1922, 1; May 3, 1922, 2; Apr. 12, 1922, 1.

3. For Cridge, see *PC*, Jan. 18, 1922; Feb. 22, 1922, 3; Mar. 1, 1922, 2; Mar. 8, 1922, 4; Mar. 29, 1922, 3; and his bland obituary, Apr. 12, 1922, 3. For Barzee, see *PC*, Jan. 18, 1922, 4; Feb. 22, 1922, 4; Mar. 1, 1922, 2 (quotation); June 28, 1922, 3;

July 19, 1922, 3; Sept. 6, 1922, 3; and Oct. 18, 1922, 5. For compulsory vaccination, spanking, and the death penalty, see *PC*, Nov. 15, 1922, 4 and July 13, 1922, 1.

4. On the Klan, see *PC*, Mar. 1, 1922, 2; Apr. 19, 1922, 3; May 17, 1922, 3; June 28, 1922, 2; Aug. 23, 1922, 1 (quotation); on the School Bill see *PC*, Oct. 25, 1922, 4; Nov. 1, 1922, 1.

5. *PC*, Nov. 1, 1922, 4; Aug. 30, 1922, 1; June 7, 1922, 1; July 19, 1922, 1.

6. *PC*, July 19, 1922, 1; June 7, 1922, 2; June 21, 1922, 2; Oct. 25, 1922, 4; June 14 1922, 2; Nov. 1, 1922, 4; Aug. 30, 1922, 1; May 3, 1922, 2; Oct. 18, 1922, 4; Sept. 6, 1922, 2.

7. *PC*, May 24, 1922, 1. H. D. Wagnon, old-time single taxer, was one of the prominent leaders of the recall; see *News*, June 17, 1922, 10. On the recall, see *Oreg.*, May 10, 1922, 10; May 18, 1922, 21; July 30, 1922, 11; Oct. 24, 1922, 16; Nov. 14, 1922, 1; *Tel.*, May 11, 1922, 1; Nov. 9, 1922, 4; *News*, Feb. 24, 1922, 1; May 18, 1922, 12; *OV*, May 20, 1922, 281; Nov. 4, 1922, 155; Rothwell, "The Klan in Oregon," 125, 130–31. On Robert Duncan, one of the most cantankerous anticorporate gadflies in Portland, see David A. Horowitz, "The Crusade against Chain Stores: Portland's Independent Merchants, 1928–1935," *OHQ* 89 (Winter 1988): 340–68.

8. *Jour.*, Aug. 14, 1919, 1; Oct. 1, 1919, 10; Oct. 15, 1919, 12; *Oreg.*, Apr. 14, 1920, 9; Apr. 16, 1920, 1; Apr. 18, 1920, I, 1; Dec. 1, 1920, 8; July 6, 1921, 1; July 7, 1921, 13; *OV*, Oct. 2, 1920, 16.

9. *News*, Feb. 24, 1922, 1; July 1, 1922, 2; *Oreg.*, July 1, 1922, 4; *PC*, Nov. 29, 1922, 2; *Oreg.*, Nov. 5, 1922, I, 12; *PC*, Oct. 11, 1922, 7; *Oreg.*, Nov. 8, 1922, 1; Apr. 28, 1923, 11. The *Oregon Labor Press* stated that the Housewives' Council betrayed the unions on this issue; see *OLP*, Dec. 22, 1922, 1. True or not, the issue of carfare reductions at the very least caused a split within the organization between the wives of PRL&P workers and others; see *Jour.*, Dec. 13, 1922, 2; *Oreg.*, Jan 11, 1923, 1.

10. Emerson P. Schmidt, "The Movement for Public Ownership of Power in Oregon," *Journal of Land and Public Utility Economics* 7 (Feb. 1931): 53; *Oreg.*, Sept. 3, 1924, 5; Oct. 4, 1924, 7; Oct. 9, 1924, 5; June 24, 1925, 6; Sept. 23, 1925, 21; Sam A. Kozer, *Biennial Report of the Secretary of State* (Salem, 1926), 124; *Oreg.*, Oct. 5, 1926, 2; Oct. 8, 1926, 2; Oct. 10, 1926, 1; Oct. 15, 1926, 11; *News*, Oct. 29, 1926, 1; *OV*, Oct. 30, 1926, 250. For the text of the measure, with arguments, see 1926 *VP*, 92–99.

The Housewives' Council's main ally in the fight for public utilities was Dan Kellaher, "than whom," according to the *Oregon Voter*, "there is no advocate of state or municipal ownership of public utilities more persistent, visionary, denunciatory and recurring." Kellaher, who had served as one of Harry Lane's few allies on the city council from 1905 to 1909 and as head of the Progressive Republicans in Portland, was a prominent East Side grocer about whom the *Voter* also said when he ran successfully for city commission in 1917 (replacing George Baker), "It would be hard to find in Portland any prominent public man more unfit for responsible public office, judged by his past performance and vitriolic utterances." *OV*, Oct. 9, 1926, 54; June 2, 1917, 318; Warren Marion Blankenship, "Progressives and the Progressive Party in Oregon, 1906–1916," Ph.D. diss., University of Oregon, 1966, 133, 153–54.

11. *Oreg.*, Feb., 14, 1933, 14; Feb. 18, 1933, 2; Jan. 29, 1931, 17.

12. Roberts, "Ku-Kluxing of Oregon," 491.

13. Brian Greenberg, *Worker and Community: Response to Industrialization in a Nine-*

teenth-Century American City, Albany, New York, 1850–1884 (Albany, 1985), esp. 89–101; Mary Ann Clawson, *Constructing Brotherhood: Class, Gender, and Fraternalism* (Princeton, 1989). Blumin, *Emergence of the Middle Class* is merely the most insistent and important book to make the middle-class "classlessness" argument. Clawson, despite her acknowledgment of the complexity of fraternalism, repeats—as does Blumin—this myth by way of Anthony Giddens; see 256. A recent recapitulation of the ahistorical thesis of middle-class classlessness is C. Dallett Hemphill, *Bowing to Necessities: A History of Manners in America, 1620–1860* (New York, 1999). Brian Roberts, in *American Alchemy: The California Gold Rush and Middle-Class Culture* (Chapel Hill, 2000), offers a related argument stressing the duplicitous middle-class self-denial of its class privilege. A self-conscious, but ultimately ineffective, attempt to historicize the issue is Robert Seguin, *Around Quitting Time: Work and Middle-Class Fantasy in American Fiction* (Durham, N.C., 2001).

14. The 1922 School Bill campaign grew out of a resolution advocating compulsory public education passed at the 1920 meeting of the Masonic Grand Lodge. Intriguingly, in terms of class bridging, one of those who submitted the resolution was William Galvani. Galvani, a civil engineer, had in the nineteenth century been a prominent member of the Knights of Labor, leader of the Spokane, Washington Trades Council, and an organizer for and a member of the People's Party national committee from Oregon. By 1921, however, the *Oregonian* mentioned him as a possible business candidate in that year's contentious school board election. See Donald Lewis Zelman, "Oregon's Compulsory Education Bill of 1922," M.A. thesis, University of Oregon, 1964, 67 n. 35; Schwantes, *Radical Heritage*, 119–20; Harrington, "Populist Movement," 33; *Oreg.*, Mar. 20, 1921, I, 12. On the role of the Masons in the Oregon School Bill campaign, see Lynn Dumenil, *Freemasonry and American Culture, 1880–1930* (Princeton, 1984), 143–47.

15. For the legal course of the School Bill, see M. Paul Holsinger, "The Oregon School Bill Controversy, 1922–1925," *Pacific Historical Review* 37 (Aug. 1968): 327–41; Lloyd P. Jorgenson, "The Oregon School Law of 1922: Passage and Sequel," *Catholic Historical Review* 54 (Oct. 1968): 455–66; and, especially, William G. Ross, *Forging New Freedoms: Nativism, Education, and the Constitution, 1917–1927* (Lincoln, 1994), 148–73. On Oregon politics during this period, see James D. Ziegler, "Epilogue to Progressivism: Oregon, 1920–1924," M.A. thesis, University of Oregon, 1958.

PART VI
Conclusion: Populism, Capitalism, and the Politics of the Twentieth-Century American Middle Class

1. *Tel.*, Nov. 14, 1922, 6.
2. *Tel.*, Nov. 14, 1992, 1. Robert Westbrook, noting John Dewey's use of similar class language, remarks that "in retrospect, Dewey's call for a broad coalition of farmers, labor, and the lower middle class seems no less realistic than the Marxists' advocacy of working-class revolt" (*John Dewey*, 468). Multnomah County gave La Follette 28 percent of the vote in the 1924 presidential election, the seventh highest urban percentage (after such industrial cities as Milwaukee, Cleveland, Pittsburgh, and Toledo). See Thelen, *Robert M. La Follette*, 191.

CHAPTER TWENTY-ONE
The Lower Middle Class in the American Century

1. Margo Anderson, "The Language of Class in Twentieth-Century America," *Social Science History* 12 (Winter 1988): 354–55.

2. Anderson, "Language of Class," 348 and passim.

3. Anderson, "Language of Class," 367.

4. Michael Kazin, "A People Not a Class: Rethinking the Political Language of the Modern US Labor Movement," in *Reshaping the US Left: Popular Struggles in the 1980s*, ed. Mike Davis and Michael Sprinker (New York, 1988), 262, 260. Despite their historically racist inflections, Kazin sees the potential of building a universal movement for justice and dignity out of such language and ideas.

5. For more systematic evidence of the strength of a "Middle American" class identity that blurs the collar line, see Richard P. Coleman and Lee Rainwater, with Kent A. McClelland, *Social Standing in America: New Dimensions of Class* (New York, 1978), 163.

6. Eli Chinoy, *Automobile Workers and the American Dream* (Garden City, N.Y., 1955), 86. Among historians, Walkowitz's *Working with Class* is a rare exception to the failure to pay attention to the relationship between working class and middle class. Walkowitz draws on some of the same sociological theory that I do, but he draws conclusions considerably different from mine about the promise of middle-class political identity. In turn, Olivier Zunz neglects this strain of thinking in his study of social scientific theories about the middle class in *Why the American Century?* (Chicago, 1998).

7. Bennett M. Berger, *Working-Class Suburb: A Study of Auto Workers in Suburbia* (Berkeley, 1960).

8. Berger, *Working-Class Suburb*, 84, 85–86, 89. The work of Herbert J. Gans also stresses the distinctiveness of lower-middle-class politics and culture; see Gans, *The Levittowners: Ways of Life and Politics in a New Suburban Community*, with a new introduction by the author (New York, 1982 [1967] and Gans, *Middle American Individualism: The Future of Liberal Democracy* (New York, 1988). During the 1970s the most intellectually compelling statements of the significance of the lower middle class came in the works of Richard Hamilton, which I discuss earlier in the book. For another brief but perceptive treatment of the issue of the relationship between the working class and the lower middle class, see Lillian Breslow Rubin, *Worlds of Pain: Life in the Working-Class Family* (New York, 1976), 8–9. The first historian to offer a substantive treatment of the postwar "alliances and tensions between white-collar and blue-collar workers" who made up the American middle class is Meg Jacobs, "Inflation: 'The Permanent Dilemma' of the American Middle Class," in *Social Contracts under Stress: The Middle Classes of America, Europe, and Japan at the Turn of the Century*, ed. Olivier Zunz, Leonard Schoppa, and Nobuhiro Hiwatari (New York, 2002), 39.

9. David Halle, *America's Working Man: Work, Home, and Politics among Blue-Collar Property Owners* (Chicago, 1984), 204, 218–19, 203.

10. Halle, *America's Working Man*, 243, 222, 299, 194, 231.

11. Halle, *America's Working Man*, 300, 302, 197–98, 243.

12. Robert Zussman, *Mechanics of the Middle Class: Work and Politics among American Engineers* (Berkeley, 1985), 1, 3, 198–99, 193, 205.

13. Zussman, *Mechanics*, 233, 215–16. In many ways, Zussman's "working middle class" could qualify as a "lower middle class," although he neglects to use that term. Certainly some of his engineers had an awareness of the term *lower middle class* and at least one placed himself in that category (*Mechanics*, 202–3). For another insistence that we pay attention to a suburban "working middle class" distinct from "the professional and clearly upper middle class," see Lyons, *Class of '66*, 243, 218.

14. Jonathan Rieder, *Canarsie: The Jews and Italians of Brooklyn against Liberalism* (Cambridge, Mass., 1985), 36–37, 96, 46–47. For a sample of the range of "middling" terms that Rieder uses to describe his subjects, see especially 1–9.

15. Rieder, *Canarsie*, 98.

16. Rieder, *Canarsie*, 99–100, 117–18.

17. Rieder, *Canarsie*, 118–19, 262.

18. George Steinmetz and Erik Olin Wright, "The Fall and Rise of the Petty Bourgeoisie: Changing Patterns of Self-Employment in the Postwar United States," *American Journal of Sociology* 94 (Mar. 1989): 984, 982, 978, 1007. For a bibliographical survey of the debate over the fate of the "middle class" as a whole, see Katherine S. Newman, *Falling from Grace: The Experience of Downward Mobility in the American Middle Class* (New York, 1988), 255–56; for a sympathetic ethnography that documents the persistence of small business and that also includes important policy suggestions for strengthening the petite bourgeoisie, see Tom Shachtman, *Around the Block: The Business of a Neighborhood* (New York, 1997).

19. Steinmetz and Wright, "Fall and Rise," 974–75. For an excellent ethnography of one very important but also very marginal petit bourgeois, see Douglas Harper, *Working Knowledge: Skill and Community in a Small Shop* (Chicago, 1987). Harper makes it clear that, at least in the far north of New York, nonpecuniary values still provide much of the motivation for small business. My argument differs considerably from Olivier Zunz, who discounts the survival of the petite bourgeoisie and instead argues, in the pluralist/consensus tradition, for the great peaceful expansion of the twentieth-century American middle class within modernizing corporate bureaucratic structures ("Class," 195).

20. The best analysis of the problematic historical use of declension remains Thomas Bender, *Community and Social Change in America* (Baltimore, 1976).

CHAPTER TWENTY-TWO
The Fate of Populism: Moral Economy and the Resurgence of Middle-Class Politics

1. Brinkley, *Voices of Protest*; Brinkley, *The End of Reform: New Deal Liberalism in Recession and War* (New York, 1995); and Nelson Lichtenstein, *The Most Dangerous Man in Detroit: Walter Reuther and the Fate of American Labor* (New York, 1995) are excellent starting points for this story. For the most compelling statement of petit bourgeois radicalism during the depression, see Herbert Agar and Allen Tate, eds., *Who Owns America? A New Declaration of Independence* (Boston, 1936).

2. Cohen, *Making a New Deal*, 315; also 209, 253, 286; *Fortune*, Feb. 1940, 134.

3. Michael Walzer, *Spheres of Justice: A Defense of Pluralism and Equality* (New York, 1983), 108–10, 161; Krouse and McPherson, "Logic of Liberal Equality," 134; Riley, "Justice under Capitalism," 150; Krouse and McPherson, "Logic of Liberal Equality," 133. See also Richard Krouse and Michael McPherson, "Capitalism, 'Property-Owning

Democracy,' and the Welfare State," in *Democracy and the Welfare State*, ed. Amy Gut-mann (Princeton, 1988), 79–105. Riley argues instead that the proper label is "pure capitalism" (126). See also D. W. Haslett, *Capitalism with Morality* (Oxford, 1994) and Fred Block's ideas about reforming the system of financing enterprises, while leaving private property and wage labor in place, to produce a "Capitalism without Class Power" where there would be "little operative distinction between capital hiring labor or labor hiring capital." Fred Block, "Capitalism without Class Power," *Politics and Society* 29 (Sept. 1992): 296. Other political theorists, for example Robert Dahl, argue that a genuine democracy must have "a wide diffusion of economic resources among citizens," an ideal that arises from Jeffersonian republicanism. Yet in seeking such an economy these theorists unfortunately dismiss the actually existing petite bourgeoisie, instead focusing solely on the creation of worker-governed enterprises. See Robert A. Dahl, *A Preface to Economic Democracy* (Berkeley, 1985), 108. The same can be said of Jeff Gates, *Democracy at Risk: Rescuing Main Street from Wall Street: A Populist Vision for the Twenty-First Century* (Cambridge, Mass., 2000) and Gates, *The Ownership Solution: Toward a Shared Capitalism for the Twenty-First Century* (Reading, Mass., 1998). David C. Korten, *The Post-corporate World: Life after Capitalism* (San Francisco, 1999), esp. 173–82, integrates small firms into a broader postcapitalist vision. Finally, Wendell Berry offers a lyrical, but simultaneously quite materialist, defense of the cultural, communitarian, and ecological benefits of proprietorship, especially in *Unsettling of America*.

Those more sympathetic to the welfare state, as opposed to populism, should not, however, give up on the middle class. Sociologist Peter Baldwin has made it clear that the triumph of the most well developed European welfare states, "supposedly the classic example of change from the bottom up, was in fact equally a victory for the middle classes" and that "In the long run, the unfortunate have gained most from those welfare states securely anchored in the interests and affections of the bour-geoisie." Peter Baldwin, *Politics of Social Solidarity: Class Bases of the European Welfare State, 1875–1975* (New York, 1990), 292, 298. Gøsta Esping-Andersen also demon-strates the importance of middle-class participation to the success of welfare states in *Politics against Markets: The Social Democratic Road to Power* (Princeton, 1985); for the nurturing of advanced forms of social democracy in New York City's non-Fordist business structure, see Joshua B. Freeman, *Working-Class New York: Life and Labor since World War II* (New York, 2000).

4. Francis X. Sutton, Seymour E. Harris, Carl Kaysen, and James Tobin, *The Ameri-can Business Creed* (Cambridge, Mass., 1956), 68; Charles F. Sabel and Jonathan Zeitlin, "Historical Alternatives to Mass Production: Politics, Markets, and Technology in Nineteenth-Century Industrialization," *Past and Present* 108 (Aug. 1985): 133–76; Michael J. Piore and Charles F. Sabel, *The Second Industrial Divide: Possibilities for Prosperity* (New York, 1984); Charles F. Sabel and Jonathan Zeitlin, eds., *Worlds of Possibilities: Flexibility and Mass Production in Western Industrialization* (Cambridge, 1997), esp. part 3; Charles Perrow, "Small Firm Networks," in *Explorations in Eco-nomic Sociology*, ed. Richard Swedberg (New York, 1993), 377–402; Michel Albert, *Capitalism against Capitalism*, trans. Paul Haviland (London, 1993). See also David Marquand, *The New Reckoning: Capitalism, States, and Citizens* (London, 1997). A dis-senting position on the liberating potential of the transition from "Fordism to flexible accumulation" is David Harvey, *The Condition of Postmodernity: An Enquiry into the Origins of Cultural Change* (Cambridge, Mass., 1989).

Jim Scott, in defending the economic viability of small enterprise, reminds us—in the best Jacksonian fashion—that "a great many of the economic obstacles faced by the petty bourgeoisie have nothing to do with their inefficiency per se but stem instead from the capacity of enormous firms (public or private) to gain protective legislation which gives them monopoly positions, tax advantages, subsidized credit, state-funded contracts, price breaks and so forth which small firms do not enjoy. The advantage of large enterprises is largely political not economic" ("Socialism and Small Property," 191).

5. Ellis, *American Political Cultures*, 42; Herbert McClosky and John Zaller, *The American Ethos: Public Attitudes toward Capitalism and Democracy* (Cambridge, Mass., 1984), 118, 118, 116–17, 102. This ranking made "big business the least trusted of the twenty-four groups about which the public was questioned" (134).

6. Alan Wolfe, *One Nation, after All: What Middle-Class Americans Really Think about God, Country, Family, Racism, Welfare, Immigration, Homosexuality, Work, the Right, the Left, and Each Other* (New York, 1998), 235, 236, 241, 247, 246, 237. For a dissent that emphasizes middle-class attachment to the values of capitalism, see Kathryn Marie Dudley, *Debt and Dispossession: Farm Loss in America's Heartland* (Chicago, 2000).

7. For an eloquent meditation on margins, see Berry, *Unsettling of America*, 170–233. No one has expressed more profoundly the meanings of proprietorship than Berry has in his many writings; Thomas Jefferson would be the one possible exception. For an appreciation of the growing middle-class questioning of capitalism, see Michael Pollan, "Land of the Free Market: How Sprawl Could Radicalize the Middle Class," *New York Times Magazine*, July 11, 1999, 11–12.

8. Horowitz, *Beyond Left and Right*, 153; Kazin, *Populist Persuasion*, 135; Horowitz, *Beyond Left and Right*, 142.

9. Philip Crass, *The Wallace Factor* (New York, 1976), 101; George C. Wallace, *Stand Up for America* (Garden City, N.Y., 1976), 122; George C. Wallace, *"Hear Me Out"* (Anderson, 1968), 106; Stephan Lesher, *George Wallace: American Populist* (Reading, Mass., 1994). See also Kazin, *Populist Persuasion*, especially 221, 234–35; and Dan T. Carter, *The Politics of Rage: George Wallace, the Origins of the New Conservatism, and the Transformation of American Politics* (New York, 1995).

10. *Larry King Live*, CNN, Nov. 9, 1994; *CNN News*, Feb. 19, 1996, 8:31 A.M.; *Larry King Live*, CNN, Mar. 14, 1996; *The Late Edition*, CNN, Feb. 25, 1996; Norman Mailer, "Searching for Deliverance," *Esquire*, Aug. 1996.

11. E. J. Dionne Jr., *Why Americans Hate Politics* (New York, 1991), 298; Kazin, *Populist Persuasion*; Stock, *Rural Radicals*; Thomas Byrne Edsall with Mary D. Edsall, *Chain Reaction: The Impact of Race, Rights, and Taxes on American Politics*, 2d ed. (New York, 1992); Kevin Phillips, especially *Boiling Point*; Dionne, *They Only Look Dead: Why Progressives Will Dominate the Next Political Era* (New York, 1996), especially 66–90.

12. *Los Angeles Times*, July 17, 1992, A10.

13. *Los Angeles Times*, July 17, 1992, A10; *Boston Globe*, Dec. 16, 1994, 1. Clinton's speech upon entering the race emphasized many of these same themes; indeed, he used the term *middle class* a dozen times. See *New York Times*, Oct. 4, 1991, A10; *Boston Globe*, Feb. 18, 1993, 1. Stanley B. Greenberg, *Middle Class Dreams: The Politics and Power of the New American Majority* (New York, 1995), 181–214 traces Clinton's political path toward becoming a defender of the middle class. Nelson Lichtenstein,

"What Happened to the Working Class?" *New York Times*, Sept. 7, 1992, I, 19, emphasizes the conservative effects of Clinton's middle-class language; in turn William Safire, "Middle-Class War," *New York Times*, Dec. 22, 1994, A19, decries the populist resentment and class conflict inherent in Clinton's appeals to the middle.

14. *New York Times*, Oct. 4, 2000, 30; *Washington Post*, Nov. 3, 2000, A20. Joe Lieberman extended this line of thinking in the vice presidential debate, speaking of coming from "a working class family" and assuring the nation of the Democrats' commitment to "hard-working middle class families." At the Democratic convention, Lieberman credited his father with rising from the night shift to ownership of a package store. Debate 2000 Video Search Archive, Oct. 5, 2000, www.cspan.org; *New York Times*, Aug. 17, 2000, A26.

For appropriate skepticism about Gore as a populist, see George Packer, "'I Will Fight for You'; Gore's Rhetoric Is about 100 Years Out of Date," *Washington Post*, Oct. 29, 2000, B01; and Jonathan Chait, "Mouth Off," *New Republic*, Aug. 21, 2000. Gore's main rival in the Democratic primary, Bill Bradley, devoted a chapter of his memoir to the economic problems of the middle class; see Bill Bradley, *Time Present, Time Past: A Memoir* (New York, 1996), 394–415.

15. *Christian Science Monitor*, Aug. 28, 2000, 1; "Real Plans for Real People: Blueprint for the Middle Class," www.georgewbush.com; *New York Times*, Oct. 28, 2000, A10; Sept. 19, 2000, A21; David Corn, "Bush's Tax Flim-Flam," *Nation*, Dec. 27, 1999. In comparison, the 1994 Contract with America contained almost no mention of the middle class; see Ed Gillespie and Bob Schellhas, eds., *Contract with America: The Bold Plan by Rep. Newt Gingrich, Rep. Dick Armey, and the House Republicans to Change the Nation* (New York, 1994).

16. Ted Halstead and Michael Lind, *The Radical Center: The Future of American Politics* (New York, 2001); Joe Klein, "Stalking the Radical Middle," *Newsweek*, Sept. 25, 1995, 32–36. Still the best treatment of this issue is Donald I. Warren, *The Radical Center: Middle Americans and the Politics of Alienation* (Notre Dame, 1976).

17. *Boston Herald*, Nov. 7, 2000, 6; "Statement of Ralph Nader, Announcing his Candidacy for the Green Party's Nomination for President," in *The Ralph Nader Reader* (New York, 2000), 5; Ralph Nader, "In the Public Interest," June 12, 2000, http://votenader.org/PublicInterest/pi-society_wealthdistribution.html; "Statement of Ralph Nader," 11.

18. For the best recent study of the ideological malleability of current populist politics, see Trevor Harrison, *Of Passionate Intensity: Right-Wing Populism and the Reform Party of Canada* (Toronto, 1995).

19. *Washington Post*, July 31, 1992, A8. For a statement of legitimate suspicion about populism, see Cornel West, "Populism: A Black Socialist Critique," in Boyte and Riessman, *The New Populism*, 207–12.

I do not mean to underestimate the difficulty in forging a multiracial populist coalition. For example, Thomas J. Sugrue provides powerful evidence for the intractability of populist racism in *Origins of the Urban Crisis*, esp. 209–29. For a complex study of how affirmative action and other liberal race-based policies "encouraged people who hovered between the economic middle and the bottom to conceive of themselves as the nation's have-nots or left-outs in a scheme of social engineering and income redistribution," see Samuel G. Freedman, *The Inheritance: How Three Families and the American Political Majority Moved from Left to Right* (New York, 1998 [1996]),

288. Even a forthright defender of middle-class values and politics like Stanley Green-berg argues that his Macomb County, Michigan, swing voters "expressed a profound distaste for black Americans, a sentiment that pervaded almost everything they thought about government and politics." Indeed, "not being black was what consti-tuted being middle class" (*Middle Class Dreams*, 39).

For a more hopeful view of racism as by no means the sole defining force of middle-class politics during and after World War II, see Murray, "Rethinking Middle-Class Populism." In turn, a vivid description of African American political use of a self-consciously "middle-class message" is James Traub, "Floyd Flake's Middle Amer-ica," *New York Times Magazine*, Oct. 19, 1997, 60–65, 102–6.

20. Theda Skocpol and Stanley B. Greenberg, "A Politics for Our Time," in *The New American Majority: Toward a Popular Progressive Politics*, ed. Skocpol and Green-berg (New Haven, 1997), 4–6; Skocpol, "Partnership with American Families," 124; and Greenberg, "Popularizing Progressive Politics," 282–83, both in Skocpol and Greenberg, *New American Majority*. Greenberg was a chief architect of Al Gore's popu-list rhetoric; for his defense against Democratic Leadership Council criticism, see *Washington Post*, Dec. 16, 2000, A20. For an extension of Skocpol's policy ideas that unfortunately does not contain a sustained reflection on the issue of the middle class, see *The Missing Middle: Working Families and the Future of American Social Policy* (New York, 2000).

21. Michael Zweig, *The Working Class Majority: America's Best Kept Secret* (Ithaca, 2000). Another example of the standard leftist attempt to argue that the middle class is "a genuine class with interests *in opposition to the working class*," see Reeve Vanne-man and Lynn Weber Cannon, *The American Perception of Class* (Philadelphia, 1987), 55.

22. Ruy Teixeira and Joel Rogers, *America's Forgotten Majority: Why the White Work-ing Class Still Matters* (New York, 2000), 16, 77, 157; *Milwaukee Journal Sentinel*, Oct. 10, 2000, 1A. Despite his greater adherence to Marxist orthodoxy, Zweig handles the issue of class ambiguity much better (34–37). Ruy Teixeira does, without explanation, switch from the "working class" of his book to "working middle class" in his "Gore's Tenuous Bond with Workers," *American Prospect*, Nov. 20, 2000, 15. For a refreshing proposal to "define progressive politics—clearly, bluntly and without compromise—as being about the permanent enlargement of the middle class," see Richard Parker, "Centrism, Populist Style," *Nation*, Oct. 7, 1996, 20.

23. S. M. Miller and Karen Marie Ferroggiaro, "Class Dismissed?" *American Pros-pect*, Spring 1995, 102.

24. Bradley, *Time Present*, 74 (emphasis added); Zweig, *Working Class Majority*, 74 (emphasis added). For a recognition of challenges to, as well as the promise of, mid-dle-class/working-class political alliances, see Fred Rose, *Coalitions across the Class Divide: Lessons from the Labor, Peace, and Environmental Movements* (Ithaca, 2000). More chastened in perspective is David Croteau, *Politics and the Class Divide: Working People and the Middle-Class Left* (Philadelphia, 1995).

25. One argument about middle-class selfishness as the controlling theme of our current politics is Nicholas Lemann, "The New American Consensus: Government of, by, and for the Comfortable," *New York Times Magazine*, Nov. 1, 1998.

INDEX

Page numbers appearing in italics refer to photographs or maps.

POLITICS AND SOCIETY IN TWENTIETH-CENTURY AMERICA

Morning in America: How Ronald Reagan Invented the 1980s by Gil Troy

Defending America: Military Culture and the Cold War Court-Martial by Elizabeth Lutes Hillman

Phyllis Schlafly and Grassroots Conservatism: A Woman's Crusade by Donald T. Critchlow

White Flight: Atlanta and the Making of Modern Conservatism by Kevin M. Kruse

The Silent Majority: Suburban Politics in the Sunbelt South by Matthew D. Lassiter

Troubling the Waters: Black-Jewish Relations in the American Century by Cheryl Lynn Greenberg